SELLING Y...   ...ES?

Warwick and Warwick have an expanding requirement for coin an... b...
British and worldwide and for coins and notes of individual value. Our cust...mer b...is
increasing dramatically and we need an ever larger supply of quality material
to keep pace with demand. The market has never been stronger and if you
are considering the sale of your collection, now is the time to act.

FREE VALUATIONS
We will provide a free, professional and without obligation
valuation of your collection. Either we will make you a fair,
binding private treaty offer, or we will recommend inclusion
of your property in our next specialist public auction.

FREE TRANSPORTATION
We can arrange insured transportation of your collection
to our Warwick offices completely free of charge. If you
decline our offer, we ask you to cover the return
carriage costs only.

FREE VISITS
Visits by our valuers are possible anywhere in the country
or abroad, usually within 48 hours, in order to value
larger collections. Please telephone for details.

VALUATION DAYS
We are staging a series of valuation days and will be visiting
all areas of England, Scotland, Wales and Ireland during
the coming months. Please visit our website or
telephone for further details.

EXCELLENT PRICES
Because of the strength of our customer base
we are in a position to offer prices that we
feel sure will exceed your expectations.

ACT NOW
Telephone or email Richard Beale today
with details of your property.

THE

COIN
Yearbook

2018

Edited by
John W. Mussell, FRGS
and the Editorial Team of COIN NEWS

ISBN 978-1-908828-37-8

Published by
TOKEN PUBLISHING LIMITED
40 Southernhay East, Exeter, Devon EX1 1PE
Telephone: 01404 46972
email: info@tokenpublishing.com. Website: www.tokenpublishing.com

Printed in Great Britain by Latimer Trend & Company Ltd., Plymouth

CONTENTS

FOREWORD

WELCOME to the 2018 edition of the COIN YEARBOOK, Britain's best selling price guide and collector's handbook for the numismatic hobby (that's coin collecting!). This is the 25th COIN YEARBOOK that we at Token Publishing Ltd have produced and some of you will be very familiar with the publication whilst others will be brand new to the whole thing and will be picking up the book for the first time. Many of you will have bought the book because you have started collecting Royal Mint coins—maybe you collect the "round pound" having suddenly realised it wouldn't be around for much longer so you thought you'd try and collect every one; maybe you're a Beatrix Potter fan and have been trying to save the Peter Rabbit and Jemima Puddleduck 50 pence pieces or perhaps you have been scouring your change for that elusive Kew Gardens 50p, the "drowning swimmer" Olympic 50p or the "dateless" 20p hoping to make a little profit (there's a modern 2p rarity out there too, it's worth hundreds of pounds—have you got one in your pocket . . . ?). Whatever your reason for coming in to coin collecting—welcome, we hope you have lots of fun. Of course, many of you won't think of yourself as one of us "coin collectors" at all. We are aware that we don't have a very "trendy" reputation and that many of you new to the hobby won't consider yourself one of our number. But I have news for you—if you've ever tried to find a Euro coin from each country of Europe whilst on holiday, or collected the States Quarters whilst in the US or saved our own £2 coins, ostensibly as a way to save but really because you like the designs, well whether you accept it or not you're one of us now! You don't have to be a crusty academic type, poring over a tray of ancient coins, magnifier in white gloved hand, to be a coin collector—all you need to do is collect coins!

There will also be those of you who have picked up the COIN YEARBOOK because you have inherited coins, you aren't the collector (yet) but maybe a relative was and now you need to know what you have—if this is the case there are a two things that you should initially look for when appraising a collection: date and condition (there are die varieties, errors, etc., too, but right now let's stick with the basics!). Condition or grade is the most important thing for a coin collector—you always want to have the best condition coin you can and even minor marks can affect the value of a coin quite considerably. The grade of the coin is all important and as you go through the book you will see a number of columns for each denomination, each with a different price associated with it . You will notice that the EF (Extremely Fine) or Unc (Uncirculated) coins are valued considerably higher than those that are simply F (Fine), so if you are trying to value a collection, or indeed looking to buy, you need to take that into account. You also need to know that in the UK at least grading is subjective, we don't use grading companies or "slab" coins like they do in the USA (a third party grades coins then put them in a plastic "slab" to forever keep them at that grade), so what you may think is EF someone else may not, so always err on the side of caution, that way you won't be disappointed. A full explanation of grading is found on page 108. The date of a coin is also hugely important. In some years only very few coins were minted (that denomination might not have been needed that year) and so they are rarer than coins from other years. The 1905 shilling for example is highly prized over the 1904 or 1906 and if you had a 1932 or 1934 penny no one would really be interested, but if you have a 1933 one—well in that case there would be plenty of people prepared to give you in excess of £50,000 for it! The mintage numbers of coins (also included in this book) relate directly to their rarity, and that's the reason the Kew Gardens 50p is so eagerly sought after today—most years will see 50p mintage in the millions but there were just over 200,000 Kew Gardens 50 pence pieces ever made, so they are much rarer than the other designs—it's that simple! This will explain the different prices within the book.

When or if you come to sell the coins you have (and we hope that you actually become collectors yourselves when you realise how interesting it can be), please remember that the prices listed are what you would expect to pay a dealer for a coin, not what he will pay you for it. Coin dealers are people too (honestly they are) and they need to make a living just like you do, so they need a profit on their transactions. How much of a profit will depend on the dealer and it is up to you to negotiate. If you decide to go down the auction route you will have to pay commission on the hammer price which in turn may be lower than the prices quoted here because there will also be a premium the buyer must pay. For example if a coin is quoted in the YEARBOOK as being worth £1,000 and you put it in to auction it may only sell for £800—that's because the buyer needs to pay (generally) 20% on top of the hammer price (£160) and then VAT on that premium (20% again, this time of £160 = £32) making the buyer's final bill £992, roughly the price quoted here. You however, would receive £800 (the hammer or sale price) less the seller's premium which can itself be as much as 20%. You need to be aware of all of these factors if you are selling.

Of course, the value of any coin is only what someone is prepared to pay for it and whilst precious metal coins (particularly sovereigns, half sovereigns and Britannia bullion coins) will have an intrinsic value based on the spot price of gold or silver on any given day, others will fetch what they do purely because of how much a collector is prepared to pay. This price is fairly fluid as markets go up and down all the time—but this is where the YEARBOOK comes in, we look at dealers' lists and websites, as well as auction results (both on-line and "live") in order to take get an overall picture of what coin is worth what. And as we are involved full time in the coin world (we publish COIN NEWS magazine every month) but aren't coin dealers ourselves so aren't influenced by what we might have in stock, you know you are getting an independent but trustworthy view of the market. Of course, we cannot check every price for every coin that ever comes on the market and we do rely on certain experts and specialists in their field to check and double check things for us, and we would particularly like to thank Chris Rudd and Elizabeth Cottam (Celtic), Mike Vosper (Roman), Stephen Mitchell of Studio Coins (Hammered), Roy Norbury of West Essex Coin Investments (Milled) , Nick Swabey (Maundy), David Fletcher (Modern), David Stuart (Scottish) Del Parker (Irish) and Charles Riley (Commemorative Medals). In addition we would like to place on record our grateful thanks to all those, particularly the major auction houses, who have allowed us to use their illustrations.

If you have any queries regarding this publication or coin collecting in general we are always available to help and should you require any accessories or publications on numismatics we stock a large number which can be seen on our website www. tokenpublishing.com. If you would like a free sample copy of our magazine COIN NEWS, just ask and we would be happy to send a copy with your compliments.

Finall, be aware of the volatility of the precious metals market which can sometimes have a marked effect on the prices of gold or silver coins—and remember when buying: if something seems too good to be true it usually is, so "buyer beware" and only purchase from bona fide sources.

CHARD

32 - 36 Harrowside
Blackpool FY4 1RJ
Tel: 01253 343081
Email: info@chards.co.uk
www.chards.co.uk
Open: Mon to Fri 9am - 5pm
First Saturday of each month

COINS · MEDALLIONS · BARS · HAMMERED · MILLED · BRITISH · FOREIGN · ANCIENT · MODERN · MEDALS

As one of the UK's leading coin and bullion dealers, we offer a wide selection of coins for sale.

Inform, Educate, Inspire

WE BUY COINS - High Grade Coins Wanted

No matter which coins you have for sale, we will always make you an offer. We are particularly interested in high grade numismatic material, including early sovereigns, British hammered and milled, Roman, Greek and Ancient coins.

No Minimum or Maximum Price or Quantity

Whether you have one coin or thousands, we will make you an offer. We pride ourselves in being fair and competitive with our prices - and that price is guaranteed - no waiting for auctions to end.

Immediate Payment

Payment is usually effected the same day, either by cheque, cash or bank transfer. No commission, no fees, no delay.

We Sell Coins

We have an increasing selection of coins from the world's leading mints and refineries. We sell the latest bullion and commemorative coins, we also have an exceptional range of coins going back to ancient times.

COINS · MEDALLIONS · BARS · HAMMERED · MILLED · BRITISH · FOREIGN · ANCIENT · MODERN · MEDALS

Decimal siblings:
the birth of the round pound and the 20p

As we wave goodbye to the round pound with the introduction of the new 12-sided £1 PHILIP McLOUGHLIN looks back to the 1980s when new denominations of a 20 pence coin and a £1 coin were introduced . . .

THE round pound was introduced in 1983 and lasted 34 years. It was a late addition to Britain's first decimal design series but eventually became the linchpin of Matthew Dent's so called jigsaw series. Its initial development was inextricably linked to that of the 20p piece, whose issue preceded it by a year. Let us take a look back at the early days of these two decimal siblings.

Britain went decimal in 1971 and the process ran very smoothly. However, inflation soared during the 1970s, and by the early 1980s, the need for a pound coin was clear. In 1981, an internal Royal Mint memo spelled out the reasons: the pound note was not suitable for frequent handling or for machine vending. The vending machine industry and London Transport had lobbied the Mint for a pound coin, which London Underground also thought would reduce ticket office queues. By 1981 the pound note had less purchasing power than the 10 shilling note did in 1969, when it was replaced by the 50p coin. And relative to their value, Britain's coins were significantly larger and heavier than those of other Western countries, partly because the 5p and 10p had retained the size of the shilling and two shilling coins they replaced, to ease the transition to decimalisation. Besides, more 10p coins were now being used, and the introduction of a 20p coin would bridge the gap between the 10p and the 50p, reducing both the number of coins used and the overall weight of the coinage.

On January 27, 1981, Geoffrey Howe, Chancellor of the Exchequer, announced that the Conservative government would introduce a 20p coin and a pound coin within the next three years. The 20p would be a seven-sided cupro-nickel coin, 22mm in diameter, to be issued in 1982. Additionally, a pound coin would be introduced in 1983: yellow in colour, like the old three pence, and of the approximate diameter of the gold

Christopher Ironside's designs for the 20 pence coin.

Christopher Ironside's designs for the pound coin.

sovereign, but considerably thicker and with a distinctive security edge. Initially it would circulate alongside the pound note, which the Bank of England planned to phase out over an extended period.

At the time, the pound note had an average life of nine months in circulation. The proposed pound coin would cost twice as much to produce as the note but was justified by its predicted lifetime of 40 years. The 20p and pound coin were developed in tandem so that they would both fit within the existing coinage system. Once the need for such coins had been accepted, the next priority was to determine their physical specifications. In 1971 the Decimal Currency Board, envisaging the future need for a 20p coin, had prescribed a round coin of 22mm. The Royal Mint felt that this would create confusion with the penny, whose diameter is 20.3mm. Ideally, coins of similar shape and colour should have a minimum gap of 3mm between their diameters in order to aid recognition. Plans were already afoot to reduce the size of the 5p and 10p in the near future, so choices were constrained. Coins of higher denominations could neither afford to be too small, relative to their value, nor too large, because of the need to keep the coinage light. The Royal Mint's solution was to make the 20p heptagonal, like the 50p, but with a broad outer rim, in effect giving it a countersunk surface. This latter feature distinguished it clearly from other coins and was particularly helpful to the blind.

The Royal Mint had already produced a round nickel-brass pound coin for Guernsey, which was issued in 1981. It was 22mm in diameter, with a thickness of 2.5mm and weighing 7.9g. The Mint appears to have used it as a template for the eventual UK pound coin. Despite their common planned diameter of 22mm, the different shape, colour and thickness of the 20p and the pound coin would make them readily distinguishable. However, the vending machine manufacturers explained that their machines needed a minimum gap of 1mm between coin sizes, so the Mint altered the planned sizes to 21.4mm for the 20p and 22.5mm for the pound. Additionally, their planned weights, at 4.5g for the 20p and 9g for the pound coin, meant that two 20p coins would be equal in weight to a pound coin. This could cause difficulties for banks, and vending machines would be vulnerable to fraud. The Mint accordingly altered the weights of the 20p and pound coin to 5g and 9.5g respectively. Humans also needed to be able to distinguish coins easily, both when mixed with other coins and in isolation. In early 1981, the Royal Mint commissioned Nottingham University's psychology department to research which options would work best. Psychology partly concerns itself with human cognition: how humans apprehend the world through their senses. The university's research involved using trial coins in tests with volunteers. The results showed that the pound coin needed to be thicker to distinguish it from similarly sized coins, such as the large 5p of the day, and also so that the blind could identify it in isolation. The vending machine manufacturers complained that their machines were unable to handle such a thick coin, but eventually they agreed to improve their technology to handle it.

Recently released documents show that the Conservative government was already considering the delicate issue of design as early as January 1981. In language worthy of the TV programme *Yes, Minister*, a Treasury official wrote to Nigel Lawson, Financial Secretary to the Treasury:

"Certain Scottish and Northern Irish banks have powers to issue their own bank notes and some nationalistic elements may see the introduction of a £1 coin as effectively replacing their own £1 notes. It has been suggested that there might be political advantage in issuing regional variants of the £1 coin and perhaps also the 20p. This would only marginally increase the initial cost of producing the coins. The design of the coinage is in the first instance a matter for the Royal Mint Advisory Committee but I have no reason to believe they would not be receptive to our suggestions."

When asked for their reaction, the Secretaries of State for Scotland, Wales and Northern Ireland were all duly enthusiastic. This solution satisfied both the Conservatives, as fervent supporters of the Union, and the proud citizens ("nationalistic" or not) of Britain's four nations. Shillings with separate English and Scottish designs had been minted annually from 1937 to 1966, which provided something of a precedent, and the Royal Mint Advisory Committee accepted the suggestion without demur.

The Royal Mint eventually decided on a UK theme for the 1983 pound coin, while a series of designs representing the four nations would be issued separately from 1984 to 1987. Competitions were held, with entries by prestigious designers such as Christopher Ironside. William Gardner's crowned rose of England was eventually chosen for the 20p. He had previously designed coins for Cyprus and the Falkland Islands. Eric Sewell, a former Chief Engraver of the Royal Mint, won the competition for the 1983 pound with his design of the Royal Arms. Leslie Durbin, a silversmith, provided the national floral emblems for the 1984 to 1987 pound coin series.

Meanwhile, the Currency Act 1982 came into effect on February 2, 1982, and it stated: *"The denominations of money in the currency of the United Kingdom shall be the pound sterling and the penny or new penny, being one hundredth part of a pound sterling."* The coinage could now legally omit the word "NEW" from its legends. The first 20p coin was duly issued on June 9, 1982, without the word "NEW", and the reverse designs of the 5p and 50p were heavily amended to accommodate the altered legends. Previously the 1973 EEC commemorative 50p had been the only decimal circulation coin to omit "NEW", due to a legal oversight, but it was retrospectively justified, with dubious logic, as merely a design detail.

Since the 20p filled a need and did not replace a cherished predecessor, it was quickly accepted by the public. Not so the pound coin, which was issued on April 21, 1983. In late 1983, the Prime Minister, Mrs Thatcher, even stated in the House of Commons that it was unpopular and would not catch on. Evidently unaware that the pound note was due to be withdrawn, she later backtracked. However, those who did like the coin often compared it affectionately to France's chunky nickel-brass 10 francs coin, which was slightly larger at 26mm but roughly equivalent to a pound in value. The pound note was last issued at the end of 1984, but long before its demonetisation on March 11, 1988, the public had become used to its replacement. The round pound was instantly recognisable and performed its function perfectly. Its disadvantage was its weight, particularly if you received four pound coins in change from a five pound note, and many years were to pass before the introduction of the two pound coin in 1998.

The first UK decimal pound coin carried the Latin edge inscription, "DECUS ET TUTAMEN". This translated as "An ornament and a safeguard", referring to the inscription itself, which was intended as a safeguard against counterfeiting. Though every round pound carried an edge inscription, forgeries gradually became common and were even eagerly documented by some collectors, and by 2014 the Royal Mint estimated that 3 per cent of round pounds were fake. A replacement became inevitable, and an ultra-secure 12-sided pound coin was duly issued on March 28, 2017. Though now obsolete, the round pound had added variety to a rather staid coinage, and its annual change of design helped to create today's army of change-checkers and coin collectors, who will remember it fondly. Meanwhile its sibling, the 20p, remains one of Britain's most popular and regularly used coins, and it will probably survive in circulation for several decades to come.

References:
The National Archives (TNA), Royal Mint documents:
  MINT 35/DF/Z: "UK coinage: Working Group—Minutes and Papers ", 1982 86.
  MINT 35/FG/Z: "Development of UK coinage: £1 and 20p", 1982–86.
This information is licensed under the terms of the Open Government Licence (http://www.nationalarchives.gov.uk/doc/open-government-licence/version/3).

Acknowledgments:
Sketches by Christopher Ironside are © Trustees of the British Museum.

This article first appeared in the May 2017 edition of COIN NEWS
COIN NEWS
is available monthly from your local newsagent or by subscription.
Alternatively you can access the digital version on your favoured device

For full details go to www.tokenpublishing.com

PUBLIC AUCTIONS
IN THE NORTH OF ENGLAND
Coins, Medals & Banknotes

MUSEUM
archive

Edward VIII model by Madge Kitchener

The original design for the twelve-sided threepence by the artist Madge Kitchener, intended to be issued during the reign of Edward VIII, carried a delicate depiction of the thrift plant, or sea pink as it is also known. It was later changed to a more angular version of the plant by the time the coin actually entered circulation under George VI and some have thought it a shame that the natural lines of Miss Kitchener's initial idea did not make it through to final approval.

The plaster model, pictured here, actually includes the word THRIFT and also indicates the early intention that the coin should be scalloped and not twelve-sided. There are scalloped-edge trial pieces of the threepence bearing a portrait of George V and there are also trial pieces showing the original more natural looking thrift design but no trial coins were made of this version of the design bearing the name of the plant, perhaps because it was thought an unnecessary point of detail. What remains is this elegant model of what could have been a much more decorative coin.

Tools for the sovereign of 1817

In 2009 tools from roughly 200 years ago were employed to create new dies for the sovereign, five-sovereign piece and double-sovereign in an effort to return as closely as possible to the St George and the dragon created Benedetto Pistrucci. For the half-sovereign the St George design was not used until the 1890s and so tools from that time were enlisted to the same end. The result was a distinct improvement, reviving the classic following many years of adaptation and minor re-engraving.

But in reverting to early tools it was not actually to the original design from 1817 in which St George is surrounded by the garter that reference was made but rather to the more familiar design in which the central composition fills the entire field. So that when a design was being considered to mark the 200th anniversary in 2017 of the modern sovereign it was with some justification that the 1817 design was chosen as a wholly appropriate solution. This particular version was dropped from the gold coinage from the end of George III's reign and so to create the coins for 2017 tools of the time from the collection of the Royal Mint Museum were employed to ensure the details of the revised version would stand comparison with the famous original.

Edge lettered sovereign of 1824

To enhance the security of guineas milling was added from the 1660s and when the sovereign was re-introduced from 1817 it was no surprise to see the coin bearing a milled edge. Larger gold and silver coins over this same period found their edges decorated with raised lettering but this never filtered down to the standard gold coin, despite its still being a fairly high value item, so the existence of an extremely rare edge-lettered sovereign of 1824 is something of a mystery.

Towards the end of George III's reign there was a revival of interest in edge lettering, with crowns, double-sovereigns and five-sovereign pieces all carrying beautifully executed examples of this feature. The 1824 sovereign in question has the inscription DECUS ET TUTAMEN ANNO REGNI QUINTO cut into the edge and the Royal Mint Museum still retains the related tooling. It would have made sense to enhance the security of the sovereign in this way but by the early 1820s the coin was being made in very large numbers and the practicality of further complicating the production process must have stood against the adoption of edge-lettered sovereigns.

Bull Head half-crown

In February 1817, 200 years ago to the month, a new silver coinage was released to a grateful British public and at the same time severely worn silver coins, some of which had been in circulation for 100 years, were finally withdrawn. Half-crowns, shillings and sixpences were issued, and the sight of horse-drawn waggons transporting tens of thousands of the new coins was greeted with jubilation as they arrived in towns the length and breadth of the country. The whole undertaking was a great achievement but the sense of satisfaction was clouded by the critical reception meted out in particular to the effigy of George III on the half-crown.

It had been copied by Thomas Wyon from an original prepared by Benedetto Pistrucci and has since become known as the Bull Head portrait on account of its bulky proportions. The Master of the Mint, William Wellesley Pole, had himself been critical of the way Wyon had copied the work and in November 1816 was asking for corrections to be made to the portrait. He was so concerned about an adverse reaction from commentators in London that he gave instructions for half-crowns struck from Wyon's dies to be sent to the most distant parts of the country. The proof specimen illustrated here from the Royal Mint Museum collection shows the effigy in all its uncompromising glory and, rightly or wrongly, the portrait was soon replaced by a more conventional likeness.

Early one pound coin

The new 12-sided one pound coin will start to be issued into circulation from March 2017. In a number of respects it is a ground-breaking coin, particularly in relation to the technology that underpins its security features and yet in other ways, such as its shape, it draws directly and deliberately from the history of the British coinage, in this instance the much-loved 12-sided threepence. Other elements of the new coin, such as its design, are also traditional but how the denomination appears is a little different from previously issued one pound coins.

Eric Sewell was the designer of the first one pound coin which entered circulation in 1983. He was a respected and fondly regarded Chief Engraver at the Royal Mint who died only a few months ago after a long and happy retirement. One of his early designs for the original pound coin, as shown here, was a depiction of the Royal Arms above which he arranged the words ONE POUND and below which he placed the symbol and the numeral £1. It is one of several such experimental pieces, probably struck in 1982, which survive in the Royal Mint Museum as evidence of how the coin evolved. At the time the Royal Mint Advisory Committee did not care for expressing the denomination as £1 but all these years later tastes have shifted and now on the new one pound coin, for the first time, as well as having the value written out as ONE POUND on the reverse it also appears as £1 on the obverse. Moreover, this element has been enlisted as one of the coin's many security features by being rendered as a latent image, similar to a hologram, which alters from a £ to a 1 depending on how the coin catches the light.

25

Newton's Cabinet

Isaac Newton, one of the most celebrated scientists the world has ever seen, spent the last 30 years of his life running the Royal Mint, first as Warden and then as Master. Accounts of his time at the Mint, including chasing down counterfeiters, altering the value of the guinea and generally raising the Mint's reputation for making coins to a high standard, have been published over the years. The physical record, too, is to be seen in the coins and medals made during the early 18th century but there are other items that survive which add colour to the story, one of the largest being the imposing walnut cabinet pictured here.

It has been spoken of within the Mint as Newton's cabinet for very many years and, while we do not have a purchase receipt, it is without question a Queen Anne cabinet and there are records which firmly make the association with Newton dating from the second half of the 19th century. From its early years in the Tower of London it was moved across the road to the Mint's new home on Tower Hill and there, in the late 1960s while the Deputy Master's office was being used as a film set in *The Charge of the Light Brigade*, it made a fleeting appearance alongside Sir John Gielgud. It then moved on to the Mint's offices in Victoria where it supposedly served as a drinks' cabinet and now, still relatively unscathed, it occupies pride of place in the Royal Mint Museum. It is an impressive artefact of the Mint's most famous son.

Restoration medal of Britannia

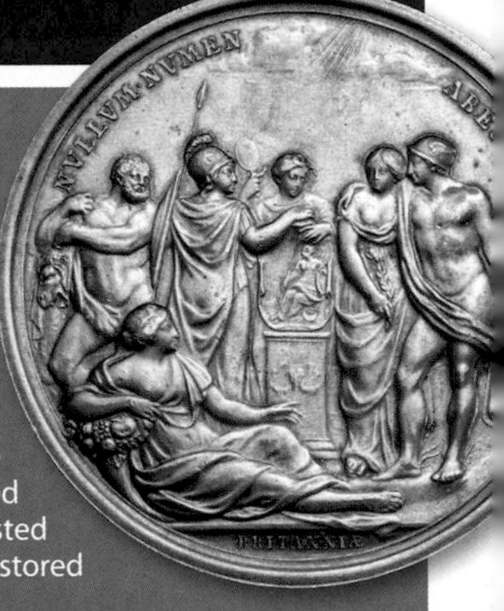

The 17th-century medal illustrated here is a very recent acquisition for the Royal Mint Museum. Designed by John Roettiers, it shows a small figure of Britannia carved into a stone tablet or scroll held up by Minerva in the company of other classical deities, such as Peace and Mercury. It celebrates the restoration of Charles II to the throne in 1660 and the portrait of Charles on the obverse, with short cropped hair and wearing the robes of a Roman emperor, anchors the classical association. It is one of a number of medals produced during the early part of his reign on which Britannia is enlisted to draw attention to the lineage and sense of stability the restored monarchy was seeking to project.

For those familiar with the appearance of Britannia on pattern coins of the mid 1660s and on the later regular issues of copper farthings and halfpennies from 1672, the medal raises an interesting question since the Britannia on the medal bears a strong resemblance to the image on the coinage: she faces left, with both legs visible, holding a spear and resting on a union shield. There are differences and the medal is not dated but it does, perhaps, raise the possibility that a draft of John Roettiers' coinage Britannia might have had its first outing on a medal celebrating the restoration.

The Royal Mint ®

Secure Storage

Keeping your valuables protected

Royal Mint purchases can be delivered direct to your Secure Storage deposit box

Our state-of-the-art Secure Storage facility is located on site at The Royal Mint. We offer both short and long term storage solutions, providing the perfect place to store your valuables including jewellery, documents and collections.

Call: 0800 03 22 150
Email: securestorage@royalmint.com
Website: royalmint.com/securestorage

MONARCHS of England

Here we list the Kings and Queens from Anglo-Saxon times to the present, with the dates of their rule. Before Eadgar became the King of all England the country had been divided up into small kingdoms, each with their own ruler.

ANGLO-SAXON KINGS

The Anglo-Saxon monarchs ruled over the various kingdoms which existed in England following the withdrawal of the Romans in the 5th century AD. The most prominent kingdoms in the land were Kent, Sussex, Wessex, Mercia and Northumbria. Each kingdom produced its own coinage but in 973 Eadgar introduced a new coinage that became the standard for the whole of the country.

Eadgar (959–975)
Edward the Martyr (975–978)
Aethelred II (978–1016)
Cnut (1016–1035)
Harold I (1035–1040)
Harthacanut (1035–1042)
Edward the Confessor (1042–1066)
Harold II (1066)

NORMAN KINGS

The Normans came to Britain from their native France following the establishment of a kingdom in Sicily and southern Italy. An expedition led by the powerful Duke William of Normandy culminated in the battle of Hastings in 1066 where he defeated Harold II and was proclaimed King of All England. Their influence spread from these new centres to the Crusader States in the Near East and to Scotland and Wales in Great Britain, and to Ireland. Today their influence can be seen in their typical Romanesque style of architecture.

William I (1066–1087)
William II (1087–1100)
Henry I (1100–1135)
Stephen (1135–1154)

PLANTAGENETS

The Plantagenet kings of England were descended from the first House of Anjou who were established as rulers of England through the Treaty of Wallingford, which passed over the claims of Eustace and William, Stephen of Blois's sons, in favour of Henry of Anjou, son of the Empress Matilda and Geoffrey V, Count of Anjou.

Henry II (1154–1189)
Richard I (1189–1199)
John (1199–1216)
Henry III (1216–1272)
Edward I (1272–1307)
Edward II (1307–1327)
Edward III (1327–1377)
Richard II (1377–1399)

HOUSE OF LANCASTER

The House of Lancaster, a branch of the English royal House of Plantagenet, was one of the opposing factions involved in the Wars of the Roses, the civil war which dominated England and Wales during the 15th century. Lancaster provided England with three Kings

Henry IV (1399–1413)
Henry V (1413–1422)
Henry VI (1422–1461) and again 1470

HOUSE OF YORK

The House of York was the other branch of the House of Plantagenet involved in the disastrous Wars of the Roses. Edward IV was descended from Edmund of Langley, 1st Duke of York, the fourth surviving son of Edward III.

Edward IV (1461–1483 and again 1471–83)
Richard III (1483–1485)

TUDORS

The House of Tudor was an English royal dynasty that lasted 118 years, from 1485 to 1603. The family descended from the Welsh courtier Owen Tudor (Tewdwr). Following the defeat of Richard III at Bosworth, the battle that ended the Wars of the Roses, Henry Tudor, 2nd Earl of Richmond, took the throne as Henry VII.

Henry VII (1485–1509)
Henry VIII (1509–1547)
Edward VI (1547–1553)
Mary (1553–1558)
Philip & Mary (1554–1558)
Elizabeth I (1558–1603)

STUARTS

The House of Stuart ruled Scotland for 336 years, between 1371 and 1707. Elizabeth I of England's closest heir was James VI of Scotland via her grandfather Henry VII of England, who was founder of the Tudor dynasty. On Elizabeth's death, James Stuart ascended the thrones of England and Ireland and inherited the English claims to the French throne. The Stuarts styled themselves "Kings and Queens of Great Britain", although there was no parliamentary union until the reign of Queen Anne, the last monarch of the House of Stuart.

James I (1603–1625)
Charles I (1625–1649)
The Commonwealth (1653–1658)
Charles II (1660–1685)
James II (1685–1688)
William III & Mary (1688–1694)
William III (1694–1702)
Anne (1702–1714)

HOUSE OF HANOVER

The House of Hanover was a Germanic royal dynasty which ruled the Duchy of Brunswick-Lüneburg and the Kingdom of Hanover. George Ludwig ascended to the throne of the Kingdom of Great Britain and Ireland through the female line from Princess Elizabeth, sister of Charles I.

George I (1714–1727)
George II (1727–1760)
George III (1760–1820)
George IV (1820–1830)
William IV (1830–1837)
Victoria (1837–1901)

HOUSES OF SAXE-COBURG-GOTHA AND WINDSOR

The name Saxe-Coburg-Gotha was inherited by Edward VII from his father Prince Albert, the second son of the Duke of Saxe-Coburg-Gotha and husband of Victoria. During World War I the name was changed to Windsor to avoid the Germanic connotatiion.

Edward VII (1901–1910)
George V (1910–1936)
Edward VIII (1936)
George VI (1936–1952)
Elizabeth II (1952–)

DATES *on coins*

The vast majority of modern coins bear the date prominently on one side. In most cases dates are expressed in modified Arabic numerals according to the Christian calendar and present no problem in identification. There have been a few notable exceptions to this general rule, however. Morocco, for example, has used European numerals to express dates according to the Moslem calendar, so that a coin dated 1321 actually signifies 1903. Dates are almost invariably written from left to right—even in Arabic script which writes words from right to left. An exception, however, occurred in the Philippines quarto of 1822 where the date appeared as 2281, and the "2"s back to front for good measure.

	ARABIC-TURKISH	CHINESE, JAPANESE KOREAN, ANNAMESE (ORDINARY)	CHINESE, JAPANESE KOREAN, ANNAMESE (OFFICIAL)	INDIAN	SIAMESE	BURMESE
1		一	壹			
2		二	貳			
3		三	叄			
4		四	肆			
5		五	伍			
6		六	陸			
7		七	柒			
8		八	捌			
9		九	玖			
0		・				
10		十	拾			
100		百				
1000		千				

Dates in Roman numerals have been used since 1234 when this practice was adopted by the Danish town of Roskilde. Such Roman numerals were used sporadically throughout the Middle Ages and in later centuries and survive fitfully to this day. This was the system used in England for the first dated coins, the gold half-sovereigns of Edward VI struck at Durham House in 1548 (MDXLVIII). This continued till 1550 (MDL) but thereafter Arabic numerals were used, beginning with the half-crown of 1551. Notable exceptions of more recent times include the Gothic coinage of Queen Victoria (1847–87).

The first coin with the date in European numerals was a plappart of St Gallen, Switzerland dated 1424, but this was an isolated case. In 1477 Maria of Burgundy issued a guldiner which bore a date on the reverse, in the form of two pairs of digits flanking the crown at the top. The numerals in this instance were true Gothic, an interesting transition between true Arabic numerals and the modified Arabic figures now used in Europe. The Tyrolese guldengroschen of 1484–6 were the first coins to be regularly dated in European numerals and thereafter this custom spread rapidly.

For the numismatist, the problem arises when coins bear a date in the numerals of a different alphabet or computed according to a different era. Opposite is a table showing the basic numerals used in different scripts. The various eras which may be found in coin dates are as listed and explained opposite.

Hijra

The era used on Moslem coins dates from the flight of Mohammed from Mecca to Medina on July 15, 622 and is often expressed as digits followed by AH (Anno Hegirae). Moslems employ a lunar calendar of twelve months comprising 354 11/30 days. Tipu Sultan of Mysore in 1201 AH (the fifth year of his reign) introduced a new era dating from the birth of Mohammed in AD 570 and using a luni-solar system. Tipu also adopted the Hindu cycle of sixty years (the Tamil Brihaspate Cycle), but changed this two or three years later, from Hijra to Muludi.

Afghan coins used the lunar calendar until 1920 and during 1929–31, but at other times have used the solar calendar. Thus the Democratic Republic began issuing its coins in SH 1358 (1979).

To convert an AH date to the Christian calendar you must translate the Arabic into European numerals. Taking an Arabic coin dated 1320, for example, first deduct 3% (to convert from the Moslem lunar year to our solar year). This gives 39.6 which, rounded up to the nearest whole number, is 40. Deduct 40 from 1320 (1280), then add 622. The answer is 1902.

There have been a few notable exceptions. Thus the Khanian era of Ilkhan Ghazan Mahmud began on 1st Rajab 701 AH (1301). This era used a solar calendar, but was shortlived, being confined to coins of Mahmud and his nephew Abu Said down to year 34 (1333).

The era of Tarikh Ilahi was adopted by the Mughal emperor Akbar in the thirteenth year of his reign (922 AH). This era dated from his accession on 5th Rabi al-Sani 963 AH (February 19, 1556). The calendar had solar months and days but no weeks, so each day of the month had a different name. This system was used by Akbar, Jahangir and Shah Jahan, often with a Hijra date as well.

Saphar

The era of the Caesars began on January 1, 38 BC and dated from the conquest of Spain by Augustus. Its use on coinage, however, seems to have been confined to the marabotins of Alfonso VIII of Castile and was expressed in both Latin and Arabic.

Samvat

The era of Vikramaditya began in 57 BC and was a luni-solar system used in some Indian states. Coins may be found with both Samvat and Hijra dates. Conversion to the Christian date is simple; merely subtract 57 from the Samvat to arrive at the AD date.

Saka

This originated in the southwestern district of Northern India and began in AD 78. As it used the luni-solar system it converts easily by adding 78 to the Saka date.

Nepal

Nepalese coins have used four different date systems. All coins of the Malla kings were dated in Nepal Samvat (NS) era, year 1 beginning in 881. This system was also used briefly by the state of Cooch Behar. Until 1888 all coins of the Gurkha dynasty were dated in the Saka era (SE) which began in AD 78. After 1888 most copper coins were dated in the Vikram Samvat (VS) era from 57 BC. With the exception of some gold coins struck in 1890 and 1892, silver and gold coins only changed to the VS era in 1911, but now this system is used for all coins struck in Nepal. Finally, dates in the Christian era have appeared on some commemorative coins of recent years.

Ethiopian

This era dates from August AD 7, so that EE 1885 is AD 1892. Ethiopian dates are expressed in five digits using Amharic numerals. The first two are the digits of the centuries, the third is the character for 100, while the fourth and fifth are the digits representing the decade and year. On modern coins dates are rendered in Amharic numerals using the Christian era.

Thailand

Thai coins mainly use the Buddhist era (BE) which dates from 543 BC, but some coins have used dates from the Chula-Sakarat calendar (CS) which began in AD 638, while others use a Ratanakosind Sok (RS) date from the foundation of the Chakri dynasty in AD 1781.

Hebrew

The coins of Israel use the Jewish calendar dating from the beginning of the world (Adam and Eve in the Garden of Eden) in 3760 BC. Thus the year 1993 is rendered as 5753. The five millennia are assumed in dates, so that only the last three digits are expressed. 735 therefore equates with AD 1975. Dates are written in Hebrew letters, reading from right to left. The first two characters signify 400 and 300 respectively, totalling 700. The third letter denotes the decades (lamedh = 30) and the fourth letter, following the separation mark (") represents the final digit (heh = 5). The Jewish year runs from September or October in the Christian calendar.

Dates from the creation of the world

This system was also used in Russia under Ivan IV. The dating system Anno Mundi (AM) was established by the Council of Constantinople in AD 680 which determined that the birth of Christ had occurred in 5508 AM. Ivan's coins expressed the date as 7055 (1447).

Dynastic dates

The system of dating coinage according to regnal years is a feature of Chinese and Japanese coins. Chinese coins normally have an inscription stating that they are coins of such and such a reign period (not the emperor's name), and during the Southern Sung dynasty this was joined by the numeral of the year of the reign. This system was continued under the republic and survives in Taiwan to this day, although the coins of the Chinese Peoples Republic are dated in western numerals using the Christian calendar.

Early Japanese coins bore a reference to the era (the title assumed by each emperor on his accession) but, like Chinese coins, could not be dated accurately. From the beginning of the Meiji era (1867), however, coins have included a regnal number. The Showa era, beginning in 1926 with the accession of Hirohito, eventually ran to sixty-three (expressed in western numerals on some denominations, in Japanese ideograms on others) to denote 1988, although the rest of the inscription was in Japanese characters.

Dynastic dates were used on Korean milled coins introduced in 1888. These bore two characters at the top Kae Kuk (founding of the dynasty) followed by quantitative numerals. The system dated from the founding of the Yi dynasty in 1392. Curiously enough, some Korean banknotes have borne dates from the foundation of the first dynasty in 2333 BC.

Iran adopted a similar system in 1975, celebrating the 15th anniversary of the Pahlavi regime by harking back to the glories of Darius. The new calendar dated from the foundation of the Persian Empire 2535 years earlier, but was abolished only three years later when the Shah was overthrown.

Political eras

France adopted a republican calendar in 1793 when the monarchy was abolished. Coins were then inscribed L'AN (the year) followed by Roman numerals, but later Arabic numerals were substituted. This continued to the year 14 (1806) but in that year the Emperor Napoleon restored the Christian calendar. The French system was emulated by Haiti whose coins dated from the revolution of 1803. The date appeared as AN followed by a number until AN 31 (1834) on some coins; others had both the evolutionary year and the Christian date from 1828 until 1850 (AN 47). Coins with a date in the Christian calendar appeared only in 1807–9 and then from 1850 onwards.

Mussolini introduced the Fascist calendar to Italy, dating from the seizure of power in October 1922. This system was widely employed on documents and memorials, but was first used on silver 20 lire coins of 1927 and then only in addition to the Christian date and appearing discreetly as Roman numerals. Subsequently it was extended to gold 50 lire and 100 lire coins in 1931 and the subsidiary coinage in 1936, being last used in the year XXI (1943).

YORK Racecourse
Stamp & Coin Fair

WORLD & ANCIENT COIN AUCTIONS
OUTSTANDING PRICES REALIZED

South Africa: Republic
gold Proof Pattern 6 Pence
1897 PR63 Cameo NGC
Price Realized: $329,000

Great Britain: Victoria gold Proof
'Una and the Lion' 5 Pounds
1839 PR64 Deep Cameo PCGS
Price Realized: $258,500

Spain: Castille. Enrique I gold
Morab 1253 Safard (1215)
MS64 NGC
Price Realized: $99,875

Guatemala: Ferdinand VI
gold 8 Escudos 1747 G-J
MS61 NGC
Price Realized: $235,000

Canada: George V gold
Sovereign 1916-C MS66 PCGS
*From The Eric Beckman
Collection of Canadian Coins.*
Price Realized: $88,125

Mexico: Guadalajara.
Ferdinand VII gold 4 Escudos
1812 Ga-MR XF45 NGC
Price Realized: $111,625

China: Fengtien. Kuang Hsu
aluminum Specimen Pattern Dollar
CD (1897) SP61 PCGS
Price Realized: $89,625

Korea: Japanese
Protectorate - Yung
Hi gold 5 Won Year 2
(1908) MS66 PCGS
Price Realized: $111,625

Brazil: Joao V gold 6400 Reis
(Peça) 1732-B MS61 NGC
*From The Santa Catarina
Collection of Brazilian Gold Coins.*
Price Realized: $146,875

*Coins shown not actual size.

To consign to an upcoming auction, contact a Heritage Consignment Director today.
800-872-6467 ext. 1005, WorldCoins@HA.com

COIN TERMS
glossary

In this section we list all the terms commonly encountered in numismatics or in the production of coins.

Abbey Coins Medieval coins struck in the abbeys, convents and other great religious houses which were granted coinage rights. These coins were often used also by pilgrims journeying from one monastery to another.

Abschlag (German for "discount") A *restrike* from an original die.

Accolated Synonym for *conjoined* or *jugate* and signifying two or more profiles overlapping.

Acmonital Acronym from *Aciaio Monetario Italiano*, a stainless steel alloy used for Italian coins since 1939.

Adjustment Reduction of metal in a *flan* or *blank* to the specified weight prior to striking, accomplished by filing down the face. Such file marks often survived the coining process and are occasionally met with in coins, especially of the 18th century.

Ae Abbreviation for the Latin *Aes* (bronze), used for coins made of brass, bronze or other copper alloys.

Aes Grave (Latin for heavy bronze) Heavy circular coins first minted at Rome in 269 BC.

Aes Rude (Latin for rough bronze) Irregular lumps of bronze which gradually developed into ingots of uniform shape and were the precursors of coins in Rome.

Aes Signatum (Latin for signed bronze) Bronze ingots of regular size and weight, bearing marks of authority to guarantee their weight (289–269 BC).

Agonistic (Greek) Term for coins issued to commemorate, or pertaining to, sporting events.

Alliance Coinage struck by two or more states acting together and having common features of design or inscription.

Alloy Coinage metal composed of two or more metallic elements.

Altered Deliberately changed, usually unofficially, with the aim of increasing the numismatic value of a coin, medal or note. This applies particularly to dates, where a common date may be altered to a rare date by filing or re-engraving one of the digits.

Aluminium (American *Aluminum*) Silvery lightweight metal, developed commercially in the late 19th century for commemorative medals, but used for tokens and emergency money during the First World War and since 1940 widely used in subsidiary coinage.

Aluminium-bronze Alloy of aluminium and copper. Hard-wearing and gold-coloured, it is now widely used in tokens and subsidiary coinage.

The five franc French coin of 1940 was struck in aluminium-bronze for general circulation.

Amulet Coin or medal believed to have talismanic qualities, such as warding off disease and bad luck. Many Chinese and Korean pieces come into this category. See also *Touchpiece*.

Androcephalous Heraldic term for creatures with a human head.

Anepigraphic Coins or medals without a legend.

Annealing Process of heating and cooling applied to metal to relieve stresses and prepare it for striking into coins.

Annulet Small circle often used as an ornament or spacing device in coin inscriptions.

Antimony Brittle white metal, chemical symbol *Sb*, virtually impractical as a coinage metal but used for the Chinese 10 cents of Kweichow, 1931. Alloyed with tin, copper or lead, it produces the white metal popular as a medallic medium.

Antoniniani Silver coins minted in Imperial Rome. The name derives from the Emperor Caracalla (Marcus Aurelius Antoninus) in whose reign they were first struck. The silver content was progressively reduced and by the last issue (AD 295) they were reduced to *billon*.

Ar Abbreviation for Latin *Argentum* (silver), used for coins struck in this metal.

Assay Mark Mark applied to a medal struck in precious metal by an assayer or assay office as a guarantee of the fineness of the metal.

Assignat Type of paper money used in France 1789–96, representing the land assigned to the holders.

Attribution Identification of a coin by characteristics such as issuing authority, date or reign, mint, denomination, metal, and by a standard reference.

Au Abbreviation for *aurum* (Latin for gold), denoting coins of this metal.

AU Abbreviation for "About Uncirculated", often found in catalogues and dealers' lists to describe the condition of a numismatic piece.

Autodollar Name given to the silver yuan issued by Kweichow, 1928, and having a contemporary motor car as the obverse motif.

Auxiliary Payment Certificate Form of paper money intended for use by American military personnel stationed in overseas countries. See also *Baf* and *Scrip*.

Babel Note Nickname given to the paper money of the Russian Socialist Federated Soviet Republic (1919) because it bore the slogan "workers of the world unite" in seven languages, a reference to the biblical tower of Babel.

Baf Acronym from British Armed Forces, the popular name for the vouchers which could only be exchanged for goods in service canteens from 1945 onwards.

Bag Mark Minor scratch or abrasion on an otherwise uncirculated coin, caused by coins in mint bags knocking together.

Banknote Form of paper money issued by banks and usually promising to pay the bearer on demand in coin of the realm.

Barbarous Imitation of Greek or Roman coins by the Celtic and Germanic tribes who lived beyond the frontiers of the civilised world.

Base Non-precious metals or alloys.

Bath Metal Inferior bronze alloy, named after the English city where it was used for casting cannon. Used by William Wood of Bristol for Irish and American tokens and by Amos Topping for Manx coins of 1733/4.

Beading Ornamental border found on the raised rim of a coin.

Behalfszahlungsmittel German term for auxiliary payment certificates used in occupied Europe from 1939 to 1945.

Bell Metal Alloy of copper and tin normally used for casting bells, but employed for the subsidiary coinage of the French Revolutionary period.

Billon Silver alloy containing less than 50 per cent fine silver, usually mixed with copper. In Spain this alloy was known as *vellon*.

Bi-metallic Coins struck in two separate metals or alloys. Patterns for such coins exist from the 19th century but actual coins with a centre of one metal surrounded by a ring of another did not appear till 1982 (Italy, San Marino and Vatican), since then many countries, including Great Britain, have introduced bi-metallic coins. See also *Clad, Plugged* and *Sandwich*.

Bi-metallism Monetary system in which two metals are in simultaneous use and equally available as legal tender, implying a definite ratio between the two. A double standard of gold and silver, with a ratio of 16:1, existed till the mid-19th century.

Bingle American term for a trade token, more specifically the US government issue of tokens for the Matacuska, Alaska colonization project, 1935.

Birthday Coins Coins celebrating the birthday of a ruler originated in Roman Imperial times, notably the reigns of Maximianus (286–305) and Constantinus I (307–37). Birthday talers were issued by many German states, and among recent examples may be cited coins marking the 70th, 80th and 90th birthdays of Gustaf Adolf VI of Sweden, 80th and 90th birthday coins from Great Britan and the British Commonwealth for Her Majesty the Queen, as well as other members of our Royal Family..

Bit Term denoting fragments of large silver coins, cut up and circulating as fractional values. Spanish dollars were frequently broken up for circulation in the American colonies and the West indies. Long bits and short bits circulated at 15 and 10 cents respectively, but the term came to be equated with the Spanish real or eighth peso, hence the American colloquialism "two-bit" signifying a quarter dollar.

Black Money English term for the debased silver deniers minted in France which circulated freely in England until they were banned by government decree in 1351.

Blank Piece of metal, cut or punched out of a roller bar or strip, and prepared for striking to produce coins. Alternate terms are *flan* and *planchet*.

Blundered Inscription Legend in which the lettering is jumbled or meaningless, indicating the illiteracy of the tribes who copied Greek and Roman coins.

James V ducat or "Bonnet" piece. Minted in Edinburgh in 1540, the coin was worth 40 shillings. This ducat was the first Scottish gold coin to bear a portrait.

Bonnet Piece Scottish gold coin, minted in 1539–40. The name is derived from the obverse portraying King James V in a large, flat bonnet.

Bon Pour French for "good for", inscribed on Chamber of Commerce brass tokens issued in 1920–7 during a shortage of legal tender coinage.

Bouquet Sou Canadian copper token halfpenny of 1837 deriving its name from the nosegay of heraldic flowers on the obverse.

Box Coin Small container formed by *obverse* and *reverse* of two coins, hollowed out and screwed together.

Bracteate (Latin *bractea*, a thin piece of metal) Coins struck on blanks so thin that the image applied to one side appears in reverse on the other. First minted in Erfurt and Thuringia in the 12th century, and later produced elsewhere in Germany, Switzerland and Poland till the 14th century.

Brass Alloy of copper and zinc, widely used for subsidiary coinage. The term was also formerly used for bronze Roman coins, known numismatically as first, second or third brass.

Breeches Money Derisive term given by the Royalists to the coinage of the Commonwealth, 1651, because the conjoined elongated oval shields on the reverse resembled a pair of breeches.

Brockage Mis-struck coin with only one design, normal on one side and *incuse* on the other. This occurs when a coin previously struck adheres to the die and strikes the next blank to pass through the press.

Broken Bank-note Note issued by a bank which has failed, but this is often applied more generally to banknotes which have actually been demonetised.

Bronze Alloy of copper and tin, first used as a coinage metal by the Chinese c. 1000 BC. Often used synonymously with copper, though it should be noted that bronze only superseded copper as the constituent of the base metal British coins in 1860.

Bull Neck Popular term for the coins of King George III, 1816–17.

Bullet Money Pieces of silver, *globular* in shape, bearing various *countermarks* and used as coins in Siam (Thailand) in the 18th and 19th centuries.

Bullion Precious metal in bars, ingots, strip or scrap (i.e. broken jewellery mounts, watch-cases and plate), its weight reckoned solely by weight and fineness, before being converted into coin.

Bullion Coin A coin struck in platinum, gold or silver, whose value is determined solely by the prevailing market price for the metal as a commodity. Such coins do not generally have a nominal face value, but include in their inscriptions their weight and fineness. Good examples of recent times include the Krugerrand (South Africa), the Britannia (UK), the Maple Leaf (Canada), the Libertad (Mexico), the Nugget (Australia) and the Eagle (USA).

Bun Coinage British coins of 1860–94 showing Queen Victoria with her hair in a bun.

Bungtown Coppers Derisive term (from Anglo-American slang *bung*, to swindle or bribe) for halfpence of English or Irish origin, often counterfeit, which circulated in North America towards the end of the colonial period.

Carat (American *Karat*) Originally a unit of weight for precious stones, based on carob seeds (ceratia), it also denotes the fineness or purity of gold, being 1/24th part of the whole. Thus 9 carat gold is .375 fine and 22 carat, the English sovereign standard, is .916 fine. Abbreviated as ct or kt.

Cartwheel Popular term for the large and cumbersome penny and twopenny pieces of 1797 weighing one and two ounces, struck by Matthew Boulton at the Soho Mint, Birmingham.

Cased Set Set of coins in mint condition, housed in the official case issued by the mint. Formerly leather cases with blue plush or velvet lining were used, but nowadays many sets are encapsulated in plastic to facilitate handling.

Cash (from Portuguese *caixa*, Hindi *kasu*). Round piece of bronze or brass with a square hole in the centre, used as subsidiary coinage in China for almost 2000 years, till the early 12th century. In Chinese these pieces were known as *Ch'ien* or

Li and strung together in groups of 1000 were equivalent to a silver tael.

Cast Coins   Coins cast from molten metals in moulds. This technique, widespread in the case of early commemorative medals, has been used infrequently in coins, the vast majority of which are struck from *dies*. Examples include the Chinese cash and the Manx coins of 1709.

Check   A form of *token* given as a means of identification, or issued for small amounts of money or for services of a specific nature.

Cheque   (American *Check*)   A written order directing a bank to pay money.

Chop   (Hindi, to seal). Countermark, usually

Typical Chinese cash coins.

consisting of a single character, applied by Chinese merchants to precious metal coins and ingots as a guarantee of their weight and fineness. Coins may be found with a wide variety of chop marks and the presence of several different marks on the same coin enhances its interest and value. See also *Shroff mark*.

Christmas   Coins issued as Christmas gifts date from the Middle Ages when the Venetian Doges struck *Osselle* as presents for their courtiers. In modern times, however, the custom has developed only since the late 1970s and several countries having issued them since then.

Cistophori   (Greek for chest bearing) a generic term for the coins of Pergamum with an obverse motif of a chest showing a serpent crawling out of the half-opened lid. Cistophori became very popular all over Asia Minor in the 3rd and 2nd centuries BC and were struck also at mints in Ionia, Phrygia, Lydia and Mysia.

Clad Coins   Coins with a core of one alloy, covered with a layer or coating of another. US half dollars from 1965 to 1970, for example, had a core of 21 per cent silver and 79 per cent copper, bonded to outer layers of 80 per cent silver and 20 per cent copper. More recently, however, coins usually have a body in a cheap alloy, with only a thin cladding of a more expensive material, such as the British 1p and 2p coins of stainless steel with a copper cladding, introduced late in 1992.

Clash Marks   Mirror image traces found on a coin which has been struck from a pair of dies, themselves damaged by having been struck together without a blank between.

Clipped Coins   Precious metal coins from which small amounts have been removed by clipping the edges. It was to prevent this that *graining* and *edge inscriptions* were adopted.

Cob   Crude, irregularly shaped silver piece, often with little more than a vestige of die impressions, produced in the Spanish American mints in the 16th–18th centuries.

Coin   Piece of metal, marked with a device, issued by government authority and intended for use as money.

Collar   Retaining ring within which the *dies* for the *obverse* and *reverse* operate. When the *blank* is struck under high pressure between the dies the metal flows sideways and is formed by the collar, taking up the impression of *reeding* or *edge inscription* from it.

Commemorative   Coin, medal, token or paper note issued to celebrate a current event or the anniversary of a historic event or personality.

Communion Token   Token, cast in lead, but later struck in pewter, brass, bronze or white metal, issued to members of a congregation to permit them to partake of the annual communion service in the Calvinist and Presbyterian churches. John Calvin himself is said to have invented the communion token in 1561 but they were actually referred to in the minutes of the Scottish General Assembly in 1560. Later they were adopted by the Reformed churches in many parts of Europe. They survived in Scotland till the early years of this century. Each parish had its own tokens, often bearing the names or initials of individual ministers, with dates, symbols and biblical texts.

Conjoined   Term denoting overlapped profiles of two or more rulers (e.g. William and Mary).

Contact mark   Abrasion, dent or other imperfection caused by contact with other coins.

Contorniate   (from Italian *contorno*, edge). Late 4th and 5th century Roman bronze piece whose name alludes to the characteristic grooving on the edges.

Contribution Coins   Coins struck by Bamberg, Eichstatt, Fulda and other German cities in the 1790s during the First Coalition War against the French Republic. The name alludes to the fact that the bullion used to produce the coins necessary to pay troops was raised by contribution from the Church and the public.

Convention Money   Any system of coinage agreed by neighbouring countries for mutual acceptance and interchange. Examples include the Amphictyonic coins of ancient Greece, and the Austrian and Bavarian talers and gulden of 1753–1857 which were copied by other south German states and paved the way for the German Monetary union.

Copper Metallic element, chemical symbol *Cu*, widely used as a coinage medium for 2,500 years. Pure or almost pure copper was used for subsidiary coinage in many countries till the mid-19th century, but has since been superseded by copper alloys which are cheaper and more durable: *bronze* (copper and tin), *brass* (copper and zinc), *Bath metal* or *bell metal* (low-grade copper and tin), *aluminium-bronze* (copper and aluminium), *potin* (copper, tin, lead and silver) or *cupro-nickel* (copper and nickel). Copper is also alloyed with gold to give it its reddish hue, and is normally alloyed with silver in coinage metals. When the copper exceeds the silver content the alloy is known as *billon*.

Copperhead Popular term for a copper *token* about the size and weight of an American cent which circulated in the USA during the Civil War (1861–65) during a shortage of subsidiary coinage. Many different types were produced, often of a political or patriotic nature.

As the thin layer of silver wore off of his debased coinage, King Henry VIII's nose appeared to turn copper as the base metal came to the surface, hence the unflattering nickname of "Old Coppernose".

Coppernose Popular name for the debased silver shillings of Henry VIII. Many of them were struck in copper with little more than a silver wash which tended to wear off at the highest point of the obverse, the nose on the full-face portrait of the king

Counter A piece resembling a coin but intended for use on a medieval accountancy board or in gambling. See also *jeton*.

Counterfeit Imitation of a coin, token or banknote intended for circulation to deceive the public and defraud the state.

Countermark Punch mark applied to a coin some time after its original issue, either to alter its nominal value, or to authorise its circulation in some other country.

Cowrie Small shell (*Cypraea moneta*) circulating as a form of primitive currency from 1000 BC (China) to the present century (East and West Africa) and also used in the islands of the Indian and Pacific Oceans.

Crockard Debased silver imitation of English pennies produced in the Netherlands and imported into England in the late 13th century. Edward I tried to prevent their import then, in 1299, allowed them to pass current as halfpennies. As they contained more than a halfpennyworth of silver this encouraged their trading in to be melted down and they disappeared from circulation within a year. Sometimes known as *pollards*. See also *Lushbourne*.

Crown Gold Gold of 22 carat (.916) fineness, so called on account of its adoption in 1526 for the English gold crown. It has remained the British standard gold fineness ever since.

Cuirassed Monarch's bust or effigy shown wearing a breast plate of armour.

Cumberland Jack Popular name for a counter or medalet of sovereign size, struck unofficially in 1837 in brass. The figure of St George was replaced by the Duke of Cumberland on horseback with the inscription "To Hanover" a reference to the unpopular Duke of Cumberland, uncle of Queen Victoria, who succeeded to the Hanoverian throne since Victoria, as a female, was debarred by Salic law from inheritance.

Cupellation (Latin *cupella*, a little cup). Process by which gold and silver were separated from lead and other impurities in their ores. A cupel is a shallow cup of bone-ash or other absorbent material which, when hot, absorbs any molten material that wets its surface. Lead melts and oxidises with impurities into the cupel, whereas gold and silver remain on the cupel. Cupellation is also used in assaying the fineness of these precious metals.

Cupro-nickel Coinage alloy of 75 per cent copper and 25 per cent nickel, now widely used as a base metal substitute for silver. A small amount of zinc is added to the alloy in modern Russian coins.

Currency Coins, tokens, paper notes and other articles intended to pass current in general circulation as money.

Current Coins and paper money still in circulation.

Cut Money Coins cut into smaller pieces to provide correspondingly smaller denominations. The cross on many medieval coins assisted the division of silver pennies into halfpence and farthings. Spanish dollars were frequently divided into *bits* which themselves became units of currency in America and the West Indies.

Darlehnskassen (German for "state loan notes"). Paper money issued during the First World War in an abortive bid to fill the shortage of coinage in circulation. These low-denomination notes failed to meet demand and were superseded by local issues of small *Notgeld* in 1916.

Debasement The reduction in the precious metal content of the coinage, widely practised since time immemorial by governments for economic reasons. British coins, for example, were debased from sterling (.925 fine) silver to .500 in 1920 and from silver to cupro-nickel in 1947.

Decimalisation A currency system in which the principal unit is subdivided into ten, a hundred, or a thousand fractions. Russia was the first country to decimalise, in 1534 when the rouble of 100 kopeks was introduced, but it was not till 1792 that France adopted the franc of 100 centimes and 1793 when the USA introduced the dollar of 100 cents. Most European countries decimalised their currency in the 19th century. Britain toyed with the idea, introducing the florin or tenth of a pound in 1849 as the first step, but did not complete the process till 1971. The last countries to decimalise were Malta and Nigeria, in 1972 and 1973 respectively.

Demidiated Heraldic term to describe the junction of two armorial devices, in which only half of each is shown.

Demonetisation The withdrawal of coins or paper money from circulation and declaring them to be worthless.

Device Heraldic term for the pattern or emblem on coins or paper notes.

Die Hardened piece of metal bearing a mirror image of the device to be struck on one side of a coin or medal.

Die Proof An impression, usually pulled on soft carton or India paper, of an *intaglio* engraving of a banknote, usually taken during the progress of the engraving to check the detail. Banknote proofs of this nature usually consist of the portrait or some detail of the design, such as the border, rather than the complete motif.

Dodecagonal Twelve-sided, a term applied to the nickel-brass threepence of Great Britain, 1937–67.

Dump Any primitive coin struck on a very thick *flan*, but more specifically applied to the circular pieces cut from the centre of Spanish dollars, countermarked with the name of the colony, a crown and the value, and circulated in New South Wales at 15 pence in 1813. See *Holey Dollar*.

Duodecimal Currency system based on units of twelve, i.e. medieval money of account (12 denarii = 1 soldo) which survived in Britain as 12 pence to the shilling as late as 1971.

Ecclesiastical Coins Coins struck by a religious authority, such as an archbishop, bishop, abbot, prior or the canons of a religious order. Such coins were common in medieval times but survived as late as the early 19th century, the bishops of Breslau (1817) and Gurk (1823) being the last prelates to exercise coinage rights. Coins were always struck by authority of the Pope at Rome till 1870 but since 1929 coinage has been struck at the Italian state mint on behalf of the Vatican.

Edge Inscription Lettering on the edge of a coin or medal to prevent clipping. Alluding to this, the Latin motto *Decus et Tutamen* (an ornament and a safeguard) was applied to the edge of English milled coins in the reign of Charles II.

Edge Ornament An elaboration of the *graining* found on many milled coins to prevent clipping, taking the form of tiny leaves, florets, interlocking rings, pellets and zigzag patterns. In some cases the ornament appears between layers of more conventional reeding.

EF Abbreviation for Extremely Fine.

Effigy An image or representation of a person, normally the head of state, a historical personage, or an allegorical figure, usually on the *obverse* or "heads" side of a coin or medal.

Electrotype A reproduction of a coin or medal made by an electrolytic process.

Electrum Alloy of gold and silver, sometimes called white gold, used for minting the staters of Lydia, 7th century BC, and other early European coins.

Elongated Coin An oval *medalet* created by passing a coin, such as an American cent, between rollers under pressure with the effect of squeezing it out and impressing on it a souvenir or commemorative motif.

Emergency Money Any form of money used in times of economic and political upheaval, when traditional kinds of currency are not available. Examples include the comparatively crude silver coins issued by the Royalists during the *Civil War* (1642–49), *obsidional* money, issued in time of siege, from Tyre (1122) to Mafeking (1900), the *Notgeld* issued by many German towns (1916–23), *encased money*, *fractional currency, guerrilla notes, invasion, liberation* and *occupation money* from the two World Wars and minor campaigns. Among the more recent examples may be cited the use of sweets and cheques in Italy (1976–77) and the issue of coupons and vouchers in many of the countries of the former Soviet Union pending the introduction of their own coins and notes.

Enamelled Coins Coins decorated by enamelling the obverse and reverse motifs in contrasting colours was an art practised by many jewellers in Birmingham and Paris in the 19th century, and revived in Europe and America in the 1970s.

Encased Money Postage and revenue stamps

enclosed in small metal and mica-faced discs, circulated as small change in times of emergency. The practice was invented by John Gault, a Boston sewing-machine salesman, during the American Civil War (1862). The face of the stamp was visible through the transparent window, while the back of the disc was embossed with firms' advertisements. This practice was revived during and after the First World War when there was again a shortage of small coins. Encased stamps have also been recorded from France, Austria, Norway, Germany and Monaco. See also under *Stamp Money*.

Engrailing Technical term for the close serrations or vertical bars round the edge of a coin, applied as a security device.

Engraving The art of cutting lines or grooves in plates, blocks or dies. Numismatically this takes the form of engraving images into the face of the dies used in striking coins, a process which has now been almost completely superseded by *hubbing* and the use of *reducing machinery*. In the production of paper money, *intaglio* engraving is still commonly practised. In this process the engraver cuts the design into a steel die and the printing ink lies in the grooves. The paper is forced under great pressure into the grooves and picks up the ink, and this gives banknotes their characteristic ridged feeling to the touch. Nowadays many banknotes combine traditional intaglio engraving with multicolour lithography or photogravure to defeat the would-be counterfeiter.

Epigraphy The study of inscriptions, involving the classification and interpretation of coin legends, an invaluable adjunct to the study of a coin series, particularly the classical and medieval coins which, in the absence of dates and mintmarks, would otherwise be difficult to arrange in chronological sequence.

Erasion The removal of the title or effigy of a ruler from the coinage issued after his or her death. This process was practised in imperial Rome, and applied to the coins of Caligula, Nero and Geta, as part of the more general practice of *damnatio memoriae* (damnation of the memory) ordered by the Senate.

Error Mistakes on coins and paper money may be either caused at the design or engraving stage, or as a result of a fault in the production processes. In the first category come mis-spellings in legends causing, in extreme cases, *blundered inscriptions*, or anachronisms or inaccuracies in details of the design. In the second, the most glaring error is the mule caused by marrying the wrong dies. Faulty alignment of dies can cause obverse and reverse to be out of true. Although many coins are issued with obverse and reverse upside down in relation to each other, this can also occur as an error in coins where both sides should normally be facing the same way up. Other errors caused at the production stage include striking coins in the wrong metal or with the wrong *collar* thus creating a different edge from the normal.

The 1858 Sydney Mint "HALF SOVRREIGN" error graded gVF, sold for a record £16,813 at Noble's of Australia's July 2017 sale.

Essay (From the French *essai*, a trial piece). The term is applied to any piece struck for the purposes of examination, by parliamentary or financial bodies, prior to the authorisation of an issue of coins or paper money. The official nature of these items distinguishes them from *patterns*, which denote trial pieces often produced by mints or even private individuals bidding for coinage contracts.

Evasion Close copy or imitation of a coin, with sufficient deliberate differences in the design or inscription to avoid infringing counterfeit legislation. A good example is the imitation of Sumatran coins by European merchants, inscribed SULTANA instead of SUMATRA.

Exergue Lower segment of a coin or medal, usually divided from the rest of the *field* by a horizontal line, and often containing the date, value, ornament or identification symbols.

Exonumia Generic term for numismatic items not authorised by a government, e.g. *patterns*, *tokens*, *medalets* or *model coins*.

F Abbreviation for Fine.

Face The surface of a coin, medal or token, referred to as the *obverse* or the *reverse*. The corresponding faces of a paper note are more correctly termed *verso* and *recto*, but the coin terms are often used instead.

Facing Term for the portrait, usually on the obverse, which faces to the front instead of to the side (profile).

Fantasy Piece of metal purporting to be the coinage of a country which does not exist. Recent examples include the money of Atlantis and the Hutt River Province which declared its independence of Western Australia.

FDC Abbreviation for *Fleur de Coin*, a term denoting the finest possible condition of a coin.

Fiat Money Paper notes issued by a government but not redeemable in coin or bullion.

Field Flat part of the surface of a coin or medal, between the *legend*, the *effigy* and other raised parts of the design.

Fillet Heraldic term for the ribbon or headband on the effigy of a ruler or allegorical figure.

Find Term applied to an archaeological discovery of one or more coins. A large quantity of such material is described as a *hoard*.

Flan Alternative name for *blank* or *planchet*, the piece of metal struck between dies to produce a coin or medal.

Forgery An unauthorised copy or imitation, made with the intention of deceiving collectors. Forgeries intended to pass current for real coins or banknotes are more properly called *counterfeits*.

Fractional Currency Emergency issue of small-denomonation notes by the USA in 1863–65, following a shortage of coins caused by the Civil War. This issue superseded the *Postage Currency* notes, but bore the inscription "Receivable for all US stamps", alluding to the most popular medium of small change at that time. Denominations ranged from 3c to 50c.

Franklinium Cupro-nickel alloy developed by the Franklin Mint of Philadelphia and used for coins, medals and gaming tokens since 1967.

Freak An *error* or *variety* of a non-recurring type, usually caused accidentally during production.

Frosting Matt surface used for the high relief areas of many proof coins and medals, for greater contrast with the mirrored surface of the field.

Funeral Money Imitations of banknotes, used in China and Latin America in funeral ceremonies.

Geat (Git) Channel through which molten metal is ducted to the mould. Cast coins often show tiny protrusions known as geat marks.

Ghost Faint image of the design on one side of a coin visible on the other. Good examples were the British penny and halfpenny of George V, 1911–27, the ghosting being eliminated by the introduction of a smaller effigy in 1928.

Globular Coins struck on very thick *dumps* with convex faces. Examples include some Byzantine coins, and the *bullet money* of Siam (Thailand).

Godless (or *Graceless*) Epithet applied to any coin which omits the traditional reference to the deity, e.g. the British florin of 1849 which omitted D.G. (*Dei Gratia*, "by the Grace of God").

Gold Precious metal, chemical symbol and numismatic abbreviation *Au*, from the *Latin Aurum*, used as a coinage medium from the 7th century BC till the present day. The purity of gold is reckoned in *carats* or a decimal system. Thus British gold sovereigns are 22 carat or .916 fine. Medieval coins were 23.5 carat or .995 fine, and some modern bullion coins are virtually pure gold, denoted by the inscription .999. Canadian maple leaves are now struck in "four nines" gold and bear the inscription .9999.

Goodfor Popular name for token coins and *emergency money* made of paper or card, from the inscription "Good for" or its equivalent in other languages (e.g. French *Bon pour* or Dutch *Goed voor*) followed by a monetary value. They have been recorded from Europe, Africa and America during times of economic crises or shortage of more traditional coinage.

Gothic Crown Popular name for the silver crown issued by the United Kingdom (1847–53), so-called on account of its script (more properly Old English, rather than Gothic).

Grain The weight of a single grain of wheat was taken as the smallest unit of weight in England. The troy grain was 1/5760 of a pound, while the avoirdupois grain was 1/7000 pound, the former being used in the weighing of precious metals and thus employed by numismatists in weighing coins. A grain is 1/480 troy ounce or 0.066 gram in the metric system.

Graining Term sometimes used as a synonym for the *reeding* on the edge of milled coins.

Gripped Edge Pattern of indentations found on the majority of American cents of 1797, caused by the milling process. Coins of the same date with a plain edge are rather scarcer.

Guerrilla Money Money issued in areas under the control of guerrillas and partisans during wartime range from the *veld ponds* of the Boers (1900–2) to the notes issued by the Garibaldi Brigade in Italy and the anti-fascist notes of Tito's forces in Yugoslavia. The most prolific issues were those produced in Luzon, Mindanao and Negros Occidental by the Filipino resistance during the Japanese occupation (1942–5).

Guilloche French term signifying the intricate pattern of curved lines produced by the rose engine and used as a security feature in the production of banknote, cheques, stocks and share certificates.

Gun Money Emergency coinage of Ireland (1689 –91) minted from gunmetal, a type of bronze used in the casting of cannon. All denominations of James II, from the sixpence to the crown, normally struck in silver, were produced in this base metal.

Gutschein   German word for voucher or coupon, denoting the paper money used aboard ships of the Imperial Navy during the First World War. The last issue was made at Scapa Flow, 1918–19, during the internment of the High Seas Fleet.

Hammered   Term denoting coins produce by the traditional method of striking a *flan* laid on an anvil with a hammer. A characteristic of hammered coins is their uneven shape which tended to encourage *clipping*. This abuse was gradually eliminated by the introduction of the screw press in the 15th century and the mechanisation of coining processes in the course of the 16th and 17th centuries.

Hard Times Token   Copper piece the size of the large cent, issued in the USA, 1834–44, during a shortage of coins caused by the collapse of the Bank of the United States, the panic of 1837 and the economic crisis of 1839, the landmarks in the period known as the Hard Times. Banks suspended *specie* payments and the shortage of coinage was filled by tradesmen's tokens. Many of these were more in the nature of satirical *medalets* than circulating pieces.

Hat Piece   Alternative name for the *bonnet piece* of James VI of Scotland, 1591.

Hell Notes   Imitation paper money used in Chinese funeral ceremonies and buried with the dead to pay for services in the next world.

Hoard   Accumulation of coins concealed in times of economic or political upheaval and discovered, often centuries later. Under English common law, such hoards are subject to th law of *treasure trove* if they contain precious metal.

Hog Money   Popular name for the early coinage of Bermuda, issued about 1616. The coins were minted in brass with a silver wash and circulated at various values from twopence to a shilling. They derived their name from the hog depicted on the obverse, an allusion to the pigs introduced to the island in 1515 by Juan Bermudez.

Holed   Term denoting two different categories: (a) coins which have been pierced for suspension as a form of jewellery or talisman, and (b) coins which have a hole as part of their design. In the latter category come the Chinese *cash* with a square hole, and numerous issues of the 19th and 20th centuries from many countries, with the object of reducing weight and metal without sacrificing overall diameter.

Holey Dollar   Spanish silver peso of 8 reales with the centre removed. The resultant ring was counter-marked "New South Wales" and dated 1813, with "Five Shillings" on the reverse, and placed into circulation during a shortage of British coin. The centre, known as a *dump*, was circulated at 15 pence.

The must-have coin of the Australian series is the "holey-dollar". An example dated 1813 was sold by Morton & Eden in June 2017 for £94,400 (inc. B. P.).

Hub   Heavy circular piece of steel on which the *die* for a coin or medal is engraved. The process of cutting the die and transferring the master die, by means of intermediary *punches*, to the die from which the coins will be struck, is known as hubbing. Soft steel is used in the preliminary process, and after the design has been transferred, the hub is hardened by chemical action.

Hybrid   Alternative name for a *mule*.

Imitation Money   Also known as play money or toy money, it consists of coins and notes produced for games of chance (like Monopoly), children's toy shops and post offices, as tourist souvenirs, or for political satire (e.g. the shrinking pound or dollar). See also *funeral money*, *hell notes*, *model coins* and *skit notes*.

Imprint   Inscription on a paper note giving the name of the printer.

Incuse   Impression which cuts into the surface of a coin or medal, as opposed to the more usual raised relief. Many of the earliest coins, especially those with a device on one side only, bear an incuse impression often in a geometric pattern. An incuse impression appears on one side of the coins, reflecting the image on the other side. Few modern coins have had an incuse design, notable examples being the American half and quarter eagle gold coins of 1908–29 designed by Bela Pratt. Incuse inscriptions on a raised rim, however, are more common, and include the British *Cartwheel* coins of 1797 and the 20p coins since 1982.

Inflation Money   Coins produced as a result of inflation date back to Roman times when bronze minimi, little bigger than a pinhead, circulated as denarii. Nearer the present day inflation has had devastating effects on the coinge and banknotes of Germany (1921–3), Austria (1923), Poland (1923), Hungary (1945–6), Greece (1946) and many Latin American countries since the 1980s. Hungary holds the record for the highest value of any note ever issued — one thousand million adopengos, which is written as 20,000,000,000,000,000, 000,000,000,000,000 pengos.

Ingot Piece of precious metal, usually cast in a mould, and stamped with the weight and fineness. A convenient method of storing bullion, ingots have been used as currency in many countries, notably Russia and Japan.

Inlay Insertion into the surface of a coin or medal of another substance for decorative effect. e.g. Poland Amber Trade Routes 20zl (amber), Isle of Man Queen Mother centenery (pearl) and various coins incorporating rubies or diamonds.

Intaglio Form of *engraving* in which lines are cut into a steel die for the recess-printing of banknotes.

Intrinsic The net metallic value of a coin, as distinguished from the nominal or face value.

Iron Metal, chemical symbol *Fe* (from Latin *Ferrum*), used as a primitive form of currency from classical times onwards. Iron spits (obeliskoi) preceded the obol as the lowest unit of Greek coinage, a handful of six spits being worth a drachma (from *drassomai*, "I grasp"). Cast iron coins were issued in China as a substitute for copper *cash*. Many of the emergency token issues of Germany during the First World War were struck in iron. Iron coins were issued by Bulgaria in 1943. See also *Steel*.

Ithyphallic (Greek for "erect penis"). Term descriptive of coins of classical Greece showing a satyr.

Janiform Double profiles back to back, after the Roman god Janus.

Jeton from Dordrecht 1588: the Armada destroyed.

Jeton (From French *jeter*, to throw). Alternative term for *counter*, and used originally on the chequerboard employed by medieval accountants. Nuremberg was the most important centre for the production of medieval jetons, often issued in lengthy portrait series. In modern parlance the term is often synonymous with *token*, though more specifically confined to pieces used in vending equipment, parking meters, laundromats, telephones and urban transport systems in many European countries. Apart from security, removing the temptation of vandals to break into the receptacles, the main advantage of such pieces is that they can be retariffed as charges increase, without any alteration in their design or composition, a method that is far cheaper than altering costly equipment to take larger coins.

Jubilee Head The effigy of Queen Victoria by Joseph Boehm adopted for British coinage after the 1887 Golden Jubilee.

Jugate (From Latin *jugum*, a yoke). Alternative to *accolated* or *conjoined* to denote overlapping profiles of rulers.

Key Date Term describing the rarest in a long-running series of coins with the dates changed at annual intervals.

Kipperzeit German term meaning the time of clipped money, denoting the period during and after the Thirty Years War (1618–48) in which debased and clipped money was in circulation.

Klippe Rectangular or square pieces of metal bearing the impression of a coin. Coins of this type were first struck in Sweden in the 16th century and were subsequently produced in many of the German states. The idea has been revived in recent years as a medium for striking commemorative pieces.

Knife Money Cast bronze pieces, with an elongated blade and a ring at one end to facilitate stringing together in bunches, were used as currency in China from the 9th century BC until the 19th century.

Kreditivsedlar (Swedish for "credit notes"). The name given to the first issue of paper money made in the western world. Paper money of this type was the brainchild of Johan Palmstruch at Riga in 1652, but nine years elapsed before it was implemented by the Stockholm Bank. The notes were redeemable in copper *platmynt*.

Laureate Heraldic term for a laurel wreath, often framing a state emblem or shown, in the Roman fashion, as a crown on the ruler's forehead.

Leather Money Pieces of leather embossed with an official device have been used as money on various occasions, including the sieges of Faenza and Leiden and in the Isle of Man in the 15th and 16th centuries. Several towns in Austria and Germany produced leather tokens during and after the First World War.

Legal Tender Coins or paper money which are declared by law to be current money and which tradesmen and shopkeers are obliged to accept in payment for goods or services. (See *Money and the Law*).

Legend The inscription on a coin or medal.

Liberation Money Paper money prepared for use in parts of Europe and Asia, formerly under Axis occupation. Liberation notes were used in

France, Belgium and the Netherlands in 1944–5, while various different Japanese and Chinese notes were overprinted for use in Hong Kong when it was liberated in 1945. Indian notes overprinted for use in Burma were issued in 1945–6 when that country was freed from Japanese occupation.

Ligature (From Latin *ligatus*, bound together). Term denoting the linking of two letters in a *legend*, e.g. Æ and Œ.

Long Cross Coinage Type of coinage introduced by King Henry III in 1247, deriving its name from the reverse which bore a cross whose arms extended right to the edge to help safeguard the coins against *clipping*. This remained the style of the silver penny, its fractions and multiples, till the reign of Henry VII, and vestiges of the long cross theme is seen in the silver coins throughout the remaining years of the Tudor period.

Love Token A coin which has been altered by smoothing one or both surfaces and engraving initials, dates, scenes, symbols of affection and messages thereon.

Lushbourne English word for base pennies made of inferior silver, said to have emanated from Luxembourg, from which the name derived. These coins were first minted under John the Blind who adopted the curious spelling of his name EIWANES in the hope that illiterate English merchants might confuse it with EDWARDVS and thus be accepted as coin issued in the name of Edward III. Lushbournes were also minted by Robert of Bethune, William I of Namur and the bishops of Toul during the mid 14th century.

Lustre The sheen or bloom on the surface of an uncirculated coin resulting from the centrifugal flow of metal caused by striking.

Magnimat Trade name used by VDM (*Verein Deutscher Metallwerke*) for a high-security alloy containing copper, nickel and magnetised steel. First used for the 5 deutschemark coin of 1975, it has since been adopted for other high-value coins in Germany and other countries.

Manilla Copper, bronze or brass rings, sometimes shaped like horseshoes and sometimes open, with flattened terminals, used as currency in West Africa until recent years.

Matrix Secondary die for a coin or medal, produced from the master die by means of an intermediate punch. In this way dies can be duplicated from the original cut on the reducing machine.

Matt or Matte Finely granulated surface or overall satin finish to proof coins, a style which was briefly fashionable at the turn of the century.

The Edward VII proof set of 1902 is a notable example. In more recent years many issues produced by the Franklin Mint have been issued with this finish.

Maundy purses from the 2017 ceremony held at Leicester Cathedral. The red purses contains £5.50 in normal currency while the white purses contain Maundy coins.

Maundy Money Set of small silver coins, in denominations of 1, 2, 3 and 4 pence, distributed by the reigning British monarch to the poor and needy on Maundy Thursday. The custom dates back to the Middle Ages, but in its present form, of distributing pence to as many men and women as the years in the monarch's age, it dates from 1666. At first ordinary silver pennies and multiples were used but after they went out of everyday use distinctive silver coins were produced specifically for the purpose from the reign of George II (1727–60) onwards. For centuries the ceremony took place in Westminster Abbey but since 1955 other venues have been used in alternate years.

Medal (French *medaille*, Italian *medaglia*, from Latin *metallum*). A piece of metal bearing devices and legends commemorating an event or person, or given as an award. Military medals date from the 16th and 17th centuries, but were not generally awarded to all ranks till the 19th century. Commemora-tive medals can be traced back to Roman times, but in their present form they date from the Italian Renaissance when there was a fashion for large cast portrait medals.

Medalet A small medal, generally 25mm or less in diameter.

Medallion Synonym for medal, but usually confined to those with a diameter of 50mm or more.

Milling   Process denoting the mechanical production of coins, as opposed to the handmade technique implied in *hammering*. It alludes to the use of watermills to drive the machinery of the screw presses and blank rollers developed in the 16th century. As the even thickness and diameter of milled coins permitted a security edge, the term milling is popularly, though erroneously, used as a synonym for *graining* or *reeding*.

Mint   The place in which coins and medals are produced. Mint condition is a term sometimes used to denote pieces in an uncirculated state.

Mint Set   A set of coins or medals in the package or case issued by the mint. See also *year set*.

Mintmark   A device appearing on a coin to denote the place of minting. Athenian coins of classical times have been recorded with up to 40 different marks, denoting individual workshops. In the 4th century AD the Romans adopted this system to identify coins struck in provincial mints. This system was widely used in the Middle Ages and survives in France and Germany to this day. Initials and symbols are also used to identify mints, especially where the production of a coin is shared between several different mints. From 1351 onwards symbols were adopted in England to denote periods between trials of the *Pyx*, and thus assist the proper chronological sequence of coins, in an era prior to the adoption of dating. These mintmarks continued into the 17th century, but gradually died out as the use of dates became more widespread. See also *countermark* and *privy mark*.

Mionnet Scale   Scale of nineteen diameters covering all sizes of coins belonging to the classical period, devised by the French numismatist, Theodore-Edme Mionnet (1770–1842) during the compilation of his fifteen-volume catalogue of the numismatic collection in the Bibliotheque Nationale in Paris.

Mirror Finish — The highly polished surface of proof coins.

Mirror Finish   The highly polished surface of proof coins.

Misstrike   A coin or medal on which the impression has been struck off-centre.

Model Coin   Tiny pieces of metal, either reproducing the designs of existing coins (used as play money by children) or, more specifically, denoting patterns produced by Joseph Moore and Hyam Hyams in their attempts to promote an improved subsidiary coinage in 19th century Britain. These small coins were struck in bronze with a brass or silver centre and were designed to reduce the size of the existing cumbersome range of pence, halfpence and farthings.

Modified Effigy   Any coin in which the profile on the obverse has been subtly altered. Examples include minor changes in the Victorian Young Head and Old Head effigies and the George V profile by Sir Bertram Mackennal.

Money Order   Certificate for a specified amount of money, which may be transmitted by post and encashed at a money order office or post office. This system was pioneered by Britain and the United States in the early 19th century and is now virtually worldwide. The term is now confined to certificates above a certain value, the terms *postal order* and *postal note* being used for similar certificates covering small amounts.

Mule   Coin whose obverse is not matched with its official or regular reverse. Mules include the erroneous combination of dies from different reigns, but in recent years such hybrids have arisen in mints where coins for several countries are struck. Examples include the Coronation Anniversary crowns combining Ascension and Isle of Man dies and the 2 cent coins with Bahamas and New Zealand dies. *Restrikes* of rare American coins have been detected in which the dated die has been paired with the wrong reverse die, e.g. the 1860 restrike of the rare 1804 large cent.

Mute   An *anepigraphic* coin, identifiable only by the devices struck on it.

Nail Mark   Small indentation on ancient coins. The earliest coins of Asia Minor developed from the electrum *dumps* which merchants marked with a broken nail as their personal guarantee of value, the ancient counterpart of the *chop* marks used in China and Japan.

NCLT Coins   Abbreviation for "Non Circulating Legal Tender", a term devised by modern coin catalogues to denote coins which, though declared *legal tender*, are not intended for general circulation on account of their precious metal content or superior finish.

Nicked Coin   Coin bearing a tiny cut or nick in its edge. Silver coins were tested by this method, especially in the reign of Henry I (1100–35) when so many base silver pennies were in circulation. Eventually people refused to accept these nicked coins a problem which was only overcome when the state decreed that all coins should have a nick in them.

Nickel Metallic element, chemical symbol *Ni*, a hard white metal relatively resistant to tarnish, and extensively used as a cheap substitute for silver. It was first used for the American 5 cent coin in 1866, hence its popular name which has stuck ever since, although nowadays the higher denominations are minted in an alloy of copper and nickel. Although best known as a silver substitute, nickel was widely used in Jamaica (1869–1969) for halfpence and pennies and in British West Africa for the tiny 1/10th pennies (1908–57). Pure nickel was used for French francs and German marks, but usually it is alloyed with copper or zinc to produce *cupronickel* or nickel brass.

Notaphily Hybrid word from Latin *nota* (note) and Greek philos (love), coined about 1970 to denote the branch of numismatics devoted to the study of paper money.

Notgeld German word meaning emergency money, applied to the *tokens*, in metals, wood, leather and even ceramic materials, issued during the First World War when coinage disappeared from circulation. These tokens were soon superseded by low-denomination paper money issued by shops and businessmen in denominations from 10 to 50 pfennige and known as *kleine Notgeld* (small emergency money). These notes were prohibited in September 1922 but by that time some 50,000 varieties are thought to have been issued. Inflation raced out of control and the government permitted a second issue of local notes, known as *large Notgeld*, as the denominations were in thousands, and latterly millions, of marks. Some 3,600 types appeared in 1922 and over 60,000 in 1923. These ceased to circulate in 1924 when the currency was reformed.

Numismatics The study of coins, medals and other related fields, a term derived from the Latin *numisma* and Greek *nomisma* (money).

Obsidional Currency (From Latin *obsidium*, a siege). Term for *emergency money* produced by the defenders of besieged towns and cities. These usually took the form of pieces of silver plate, commandeered for the purpose, crudely marked with an official device and the value. Instances of such seige coinage have been recorded from the 12th to the 19th centuries.

Obverse The "heads" side of a coin or medal, generally bearing the effigy of the head of state or an allegorical figure.

Off Metal Term denoting a piece struck in a metal other than the officially authorisied or issued

alloy. This originally applied to *patterns* which were often struck in lead or copper instead of gold and silver as trial pieces or to test the dies; but in recent years it has applied to collectors' versions, e.g. proofs in platinum, gold or silver of coins normally issued in bronze or cupro-nickel.

Overdate One or more digits in a date altered by superimposing another figure. Alterations of this kind, by means of small hand punches, were made to dated dies so that they could be used in years other than that of the original manufacture. Coins with overdates invariably show traces of the original digit.

Overstrike Coin, token or medal produced by using a previously struck pieces as a flan. The Bank of England dollar of 1804 was overstruck on Spanish pieces of eight, and examples showing traces of the original coins are worth a good premium.

Paduan Name given to imitations of medals and bogus coins produced in Italy in the 16th century, and deriving from the city of Padua where forgeries of bronze sculpture were produced for the antique market.

Patina Oxidation forming on the surface of metallic objects. So far as coins and medals are concerned, this applies mainly to silver, brass, bronze and copper pieces which may acquire oxidation from the atmosphere, or spectacular patination from salts in the ground in which they have been buried. In extreme forms patina leads to verdigris and other forms of rust which corrode the surface, but in uncirculated coins it may be little more than a mellowing of the original *lustre*. Coins preserved in blue velvet presentation cases often acquire a subtle toning from the dyes in the material.

Pattern Piece resembling a coin or medal, prepared by the mint to the specifications or on the authorisation of the coin-issuing authority, but also applied to pieces produced by mints when tendering for coinage or medal contracts. Patterns may differ from the final coins as issued in the type of alloy used (*off metal*) but more often they differ in details of the design.

Pellet Raised circular ornament used as a spacing device between words and abbreviations in the *legend* of coins and medals. Groups of pellets were also used as ornaments in the angles of the cross on the reverse of English silver pennies.

Piece de Plaisir (French for "fancy piece"). Term given to coins struck in a superior precious metal, or to a superior finish, or on a much thicker flan than usual. See *off metal*, *piedfort* and *proof*.

Piedfort (Piefort) Piece struck with coinage dies on a *flan* of much more than normal thickness. This practice originated in France in the late

16th century and continues to the present day. In recent years it has been adopted by mints in Britain and other countries as a medium for collectors' pieces.

Pile   Lower die incorporating the obverse motif, used in striking coins and medals. See also *trussel*.

Planchet   French term used as an alternative for *blank* or *flan*.

Plaque or **Plaquette**   Terms sometimes used for medals struck on a square or rectangular flan.

Plaster   Cast taken from the original model for a coin or medal sculpted by an artist, and used in modern reducing machines in the manufacture of the master *die*.

Plated Coins   Coins stuck in base metal but given a wash of silver or some other precious metal. This expedient was adopted in inflationary times, from the Roman Republic (91 BC) till the Tudor period. American cents of 1943 were struck in steel with a zinc coating, and more recently *clad* coins have produced similar results.

Platinum   The noblest of all precious metals, platinum has a higher specific gravity than gold and a harder, brighter surface than silver. Until an industrial application was discovered in the mid-19th century, it was regarded as of little value, and was popular with counterfeiters as a cheap substitute for gold in their forgeries which, with a light gold wash, could be passed off as genuine. It was first used for circulating coins in Russia (the chief source of the metal since 1819) and 3, 6 and 12 rouble coins were mined at various times between 1828 and 1845. In recent years platinum has been a popular metal for limited-edition proof coins.

Platmynt   (Swedish for "plate money"). Large copper plates bearing royal cyphers and values from half to ten dalers produced in Sweden between 1643 and 1768. They represented laudable attempts by a country rich in copper to produce a coinage in terms of its silver value, but the net result was far too cumbersome to be practical. The weight of the daler plate, for example, ranged from 766 grams to 1.1kg, and special carts had to be devised to transport them!

Plugged Coins   Coins struck predominantly in one metal, but containing a small plug of another. This curious practice may be found in the farthings of Charles II (1684–85) and the halfpence or farthings of James II (1685–87), which were struck in tin, with a copper plug, to defeat forgers.

Porcelain Money   Tokens made of porcelain circulated in Thailand from the late 18th century till 1868. The Meissen pottery struck tokens in 1920–22 as a form of small *Notgeld*, using reddish-brown Bottger stoneware and white *bisque* porcelain. These ceramic tokens circulated in various towns of Saxony.

Postage Currency   Small paper notes in denominations of 5 (shown above), 10, 25 and 50 cents, issued by the US federal government in 1862–63, were thus inscribed and had reproductions of postage stamps engraved on them — five 5c stamps on the 25c and five 10c stamps on the 50c notes. The earliest issue even had perforations in the manner of stamps, but this unnecessary device was soon done away with. See also *stamp money*.

Postal Notes or Orders   Low-value notes intended for transmission by post and encashable at post offices. Introduced by Britain in 1883, they were an extension of the earlier *money order* system, and are now issued by virtually every country.

Potin   (French for pewter). Alloy of copper, tin, lead and silver used as a coinage metal by the Celtic tribes of eastern Gaul at the beginning of the Christian era.

Privy Mark   Secret mark incorporated in the design of a coin or medal to identify the minter, or even the particular die used. The term is also used more loosely to denote any small symbol or initials appearing on a coin other than a *mint mark*, and is sometimes applied to the symbols associated with the trial of the *Pyx* found on English coins.

Prize Coins   Coins of large size and value struck primarily as prizes in sporting contests. this principle dates from the late 5th century BC when Syracuse minted decadrachms as prizes in the Demareteian Games. The most notable example in modern times is the lengthy series of talers and five-franc coins issued by the Swiss cantons since 1842 as prizes in the annual shooting festivals, the last of which honoured the Lucerne contest of 1939.

Profile   A side view of the human face, widely used as a coinage effigy.

Proof   Originally a trial strike testing the *dies*, but now denoting a special collectors' version struck with dies that have been specially polished on *flans* with a mirror finish. Presses operating at a very slow speed, or multi-striking processes, are also used.

Propaganda Notes   Paper money containing a political slogan or a didactic element. During the Second World War forgeries of German and Japanese notes were produced by the Allies and additionally inscribed or overprinted with slogans such as "Co-Prosperity Sphere — What is it worth?" (a reference to the Japanese occupied areas of SE Asia). Forged dollars with anti-American propaganda were airdropped over Sicily by the Germans in 1943 and counterfeit pounds with Arabic propaganda over Egypt in 1942–43. Various anti-communist organisations liberated propaganda forgeries of paper money by balloon over Eastern Europe during the Cold War period.

Provenance Mark   Form of *privy mark* denoting the source of the metal used in coins. Examples include the plumes or roses on English coins denoting silver from Welsh or West of England mines, and the elephant or elephant and castle on gold coins denoting bullion imported by the African Company. Coins inscribed VIGO (1702–03) or LIMA (1745–46) denote bullion seized from the Spaniards by Anglo-Dutch privateers and Admiral Anson respectively. Other provenance marks on English coins include the letters EIC and SSC, denoting bullion imported by the East India Company or the South Sea Company.

Pseudo Coins   Derisory term coined in recent years to signify pieces of precious metal, often struck in *proof* versions only, aimed at the international investment market. Many of these pieces, though bearing a nominal face value, are not *legal tender* in the countries purporting to issue them and in many cases they go straight from the overseas mint where they are produced to coin dealers in America and western Europe, without ever appearing in the so-called country of origin. See also *NCLT coins*.

Punch or Puncheon   Intermediate *die* whereby working dies can be duplicated from the master die, prior to the striking of coins and medals.

Pyx   Box in which a specimen from every 15 pounds troy weight of gold and every 60 pounds of silver minted in England is kept for annual trial by weight and assay. Many of the *mintmarks* on English coins of the 14th–17th centuries were in use from one trial to the next and still exist today and can therefore be used to date them.

Reducing Machinery   Equipment designed on the pantographic principle for transferring the image from a *plaster* to a *hub* and reducing it to the size of the actual coin or medal. The image is transferred by means of a stylus operating rather like a gramophone needle, but working from the centre to the outer edge.

Reeding   Security edging on coins, consisting of close vertical ridges. As a rule, this appears all round the edge but some coins, e.g. New Zealand's 50c (1967) and the Isle of Man's £1 (1978) have segments of reeding alternating with a plain edge, to help blind and partially sighted persons to identify these coins.

Re-issue   A coin or note issued again after an extended lapse of time.

Relief   Raised parts of the *obverse* and *reverse* of coins and medals, the opposite of *incuse*.

Remainder   A note from a bank or issuing authority which has never been circulated, due to inflation, political changes or bank failure. Such notes, some-times in partial or unfinished state (e.g. missing serial numbers or signatures), are generally unloaded on to the numismatic market at a nominal sum and provide a good source of inexpensive material for the beginner.

Restrike   Coin, medal or token produced from *dies* subsequent to the original use.   Usually restrikes are made long after the original and can often be identified by marks caused by damage, pitting or corrosion of the dies after they were taken out of service.

Retrograde   Term describing inscriptions running from right to left, or with the letters in a mirror image, thought to arise from unskilled die-cutters failing to realise that inscriptions have to be engraved in negative form to achieve a positive impression. Retrograde inscriptions are common on ancient Greek coins, but also found on Roman and Byzantine coins.

Reverse   The side of a coin or medal regarded as of lesser importance; in colloquial parlance, the "tails" side.

Saltire   Heraldic term for a cross in the shape of an X.

Sandwich   Coin *blank* consisting of thin outer layers in one alloy bonded to a core in another. See *clad coins*.

Sceat   (Anglo-Saxon for "treasure", or German *Schatz*). Money of account in Kent early in the 7th century as the twelfth part of a shilling or Merovingian gold tremissis.   As a silver coin, it dates from about AD 680–700 and weighed about 20 grains, putting it on par with the Merovingian denier or penny.   Sceats spread to other parts of England in the 8th century but tended to decline in weight and value, but from about 760 it was gradually superseded by the silver penny minted under Offa and his successors.

Scissel The clippings of metal left after a *blank* has been cut. Occasionally one of these clippings accidentally adheres to the blank during the striking process, producing characteristic crescent-shaped flaws which are present on on the finished coin.

Scrip Paper money of restricted validity or circulation, e.g. *Bafs* and other military scrip used in canteens and post exchanges.

Scyphate (Greek *scypha*, a skiff or small boat). Byzantine coin with a concave *flan*.

Italy, Papal States. Sede Vacante. 1846

Sede Vacante (Latin for "Vacant See"). Coins struck at *ecclesiastical mints* between the death of a prelate and the election of his successor are often thus inscribed. This practice originated at Rome in the 13th century.

Seignorage or Seigneurage Royalty or percentage paid by persons bringing *bullion* to a mint for conversion into coin, but nowadays synonymous with the royalty paid by mints in respect of the precious metal versions of coins sold direct to collectors. It arises from the medieval right of the king to a small portion of the proceeds of a mint, and amounted to a tax on moneying. It has also been applied to the money accruing to the state when the coinage is re-issued in an alloy of lesser fineness, as, for example, the debased sovereigns of Henry VIII in 20 instead of 23 carat gold, the king's treasury collecting the difference.

Series Term applied to sets of medals of a thematic character, which first became fashionable in the early 18th century. Jean Dassier pioneered the medallic series in the 1720s with his set of 72 medals portraying the rulers of France till Louis XV. The idea was developed by J. Kirk, Sir Edward Thomason, J. Mudie and A. J. Stothard in Britain, and by Moritz Fuerst and Amedee Durand in Europe. The fashion died out in the 19th century, but has been revived in America and Europe since 1964.

Serrated Having a notched or toothed edge, rather like a cogwheel. Coins of this type, struck in *electrum*, an alloy of silver and gold, are known from Carthage in the 2nd century BC, and some silver denarii of Rome in the 2nd century AD also come into this category.

Sexagesimal System Monetary system in which the principal unit is divided into 60 parts. The oldest system in the Western world was based on the gold talent of 60 minae and the mina of 60 shekels. In medieval Europe 60 groschen were worth a fine mark; in England from 1551, the silver coinage was based on the crown of 60 pence, and in the south German states till 1873 the gulden was worth 60 kreuzers.

Shin Plasters Derisory term originally applied to the Continental currency notes issued during the American War of Independence, the fractional currency of the Civil War period and also the low-denomination notes of Canada between 1870 and 1935, but often applied indiscriminately to any other low-denomination, small-format notes.

Short Cross Coinage Term for the silver coinage introduced by Henry II in 1180 and minted till 1247 at which time it was replaced by the *Long Cross* type. The termination of the arms of the cross on the reverse well within the circumference encouraged the dishonest practice of *clipping*.

Shroff Mark A *countermark* applied by Indian bankers or merchants to attest the full weight and purity of coins. See also *chop*.

Siege Money See *Obsidional Currency*

Silver Precious metal, chemical symbol *Ag*, numismatic abbreviation *Ar*, from Latin *Argentum*, widely used as a coinage metal from the 6th century BC to the present day.

Sterling silver denotes an alloy of .925 fine silver with .075 copper. Fine silver alloys used over the past 2,500 years have ranged from .880 to .960 fine, but base silver has also been all too common. British coins from 1920 to 1946 were struck in .500 fine silver, while alloys of lesser fineness are known as *billon* or *vellon*. Silver alloyed with gold produces a metal called *electrum*, used for the earliest coinage of the western world, the staters of Lydia in the 7th century BC. Since 1970 silver as a medium for circulating coinage has almost virtually disappeared, yet the volume of silver coins for sale to collectors has risen considerably in recent years.

Skit Note Piece of paper masquerading as a banknote. It differs from a *counterfeit* in that its design parodies that of a genuine note, often for political, satirical or advertising reasons. Others were produced as April Fools' Day jokes or a form of Valentine (e.g. the Bank of Lovers). In recent years they have been produced as advertising gimmicks, or as coupons permitting a discount off the list price of goods.

Slug Popular name for the $50 gold pieces produced by private mints in California in the mid-19th century. The term is also applied nowadays to *tokens* intended for use in gaming machines.

Spade Guinea Name given to the guineas of George III issued between 1787 and 1799 because the shield on the reverse design resembled the shape of a spade. In Victorian times the spade guinea was extensively copied in brass for gaming counters.

Spade Money Cast bronze pieces resembling miniature spades and other agricultural implements, used as money and derived from the actual implements which had previously been used in barter. Often referred to as *Pu* or *Boo* money.

Specie Financial term denoting money in the form of precious metals (silver and gold), usually struck as coin, as opposed to money in the form of paper notes and bills of exchange. It occurs in the name of some European coins (e.g. *speciedaler, speciestaler* and *speciesducat*) to denote the use of fine silver or gold.

Specimen Generally used to denote a single piece, but more specifically applying to a coin in a special finish, less than *proof* in quality but superior to the general circulating version. It also denotes paper notes intended for circulation between banks or for press publicity and distinguished from the generally issued version by zero serial numbers, punch holes or a security endorsement.

Spintriae Metal tokens produced in Roman imperial times, with erotic motifs, thought to have been tickets of admission to brothels.

Spit Copper or iron rod used as a primitive form of currency in the Mediterranean area. The Greek word *belos* meant a spit, dart or bolt, and from this came the word *obolos* used for a coin worth a 6th of a drachma.

Stamp Money Both postage and revenue (fiscal) stamps have circulated as money during shortages of coins, from the American Civil War onwards. *Encased postage stamps* were used in the USA, 1861–62, before they were superseded by *Postage Currency* notes, but the same expedient was adopted by many countries during and immediately after the First World War. Stamps affixed to special cards have circulated

as money in Rhodesia (now Zimbabwe) in 1900, the French colonies and Turkey during the First World War, in Spain during the Civil War (1936–39) and the Philippines during the Second World War. Stamps printed on thick card, with an inscription on the reverse signifying their parity with silver coins, were issued in Russia (1917–18) and also in Armenia, the Crimea and the Ukraine (1918–20). During the Second World War Ceylon (now Sri Lanka) and several Indian states issued small money cards with contemporary stamps printed on them.

Steel Refined and tempered from *iron*, and used in chromed or stainless versions as a coinage metal in the 20th century. Zinc-coated steel cents were issued by the USA (1943) but in the form known as *acmonital* (nickel steel) it has been extensively used by Italy since 1939. Other alloys of nickel and steel have been used for coins of the Philippines (1944–45) and Roumania since 1963. Chrome steel was used by France for 5 centime coins in 1961–64. Copper-clad steel is now extensively used for subsidiary coins formerly struck in bronze.

Sterling Word of uncertain origin denoting money of a standard weight and fineness, and hence the more general meaning of recognised worth. The traditionally accepted derivation from the Easterlings, north German merchants who settled in London in the 13th century and produced silver pennies of uniform fineness, is unlikely as the term has been found in documents a century earlier. A more plausible explanation is from Old English *steorling* ("little coin with a star"), alluding to Viking pennies with this device, or even as a diminutive of *stater*. Sterling silver denotes silver of .925 fineness.

Stone Money Primitive currency in the form of large stone discs, used in West Africa in the pre-colonial period, and in the Pacific Island of Yap (now Micronesia) as recently as 1940.

Striation A pattern of alternate light and dark parallel marks or minute grooves on the surface of a coin or medal. In the latter case it is sometimes done for textural effect, but in coins it may result from faulty *annealing*. Deliberate ridging of the surface, however, was a distinctive feature of Japanese *koban* and *goryoban* coins of 1736–1862.

Styca Name given to the debased silver *sceats* of Northumbria in the 8th century.

Tael Chinese unit of weight corresponding to the European ounce and sometimes referred to as a liang. It was a measure of silver varying between 32 and 39 grams. In the 19th century it served as *money of account*, 100 British or Mexican trade dollars being worth 72 tael. The term has also been loosely applied to the Chinese silver yuan, although this was worth only .72 tael, or 7 mace and 2 candareens (10 candareens = 1 mace; 10 mace = 1 tael).

Anglo-Saxon thrymsa AD 650-675

Thrymsa Early Anglo-Saxon gold coin based on the Merovingian tremissis or third-solidus, current in Kent, London and York around AD 63–75.

Tical Unit of weight in Thailand, first appearing as coins in the form of crudely shaped *bullet money* current from the 14th till the late 19th centuries. When European-style coins were introduced in 1860 the word was retained as a denomination (32 solot = 16 atts = 8 peinung or sio = 4 songpy or sik = 2 fuang= 1 salung or quarter-tical. The currency was decimalised in 1909 (100 satangs = 1 tical), and the tical was superseded by the baht about 1950.

Tin Metallic element, chemical symbol *Sn* (from Latin *Stannum*). Because of its unstable nature and tendency to oxidise badly when exposed to the atmosphere, it is unsatisfactory as a coinage metal, but has been used on several occasions, notably in Malaya, Thailand and the East Indies. In was also used for British halfpence and farthings, 1672–92.

Token Any piece of money whose nominal value is greater than its intrinsic value is, strictly speaking, a token or promise. Thus most of the coins issued since 1964 can be regarded in this light, but numismatists reserve the term for a piece of limited validity and circulation, produced by tradesmen, chambers of commerce and other organisations during times of a shortage of government coinage. The term is also loosely applied to metal tickets of admission, such as *communion tokens*, or *jetons* and *counters* intended for games of chance. Tokens with a nominal value may be produced for security reasons to lessen the possibility of theft from milk bottles, vending machines, telephones, parking meters and transport facilities. Tokens exchangeable for goods have been issued by co-operative societies and used in prisons and internment camps in wartime. In addition to the traditional coinage alloys, tokens have been produced in ceramics, plastics, wood, stout card, leather and even rubber, in circular, square or polygonal shapes.

Tombac Type of brass alloy with a high copper content, used in coinage requiring a rich golden colour. It is, in fact, a modern version of the *aurichalcum* used by the Romans. It was used for the Canadian 5-cent coins of 1942–43, while 5- and 10-pfennig coins of Germany have a tombac cladding on a steel core.

Touchpiece Coin kept as a lucky charm, but more specifically the medieval gold angel of England which was worn round the neck as an antidote to scrofula, otherwise known as king's evil, from the belief that the reigning monarch possessed the power of healing by touch. The ceremony of touching for king's evil involved the suspension of an angel round the victim's neck, hence the prevalence of these coins pierced for suspension.

Trade Coins Coins widely used as a medium of international trade, often far beyond the boundaries of the country issuing them. The earliest examples were the Aiginetan turtles and Athenian tetrdrachms of the classical period. In the Middle Ages the English *sterling* was widely prized on account of its silver purity. Arab dinars and Italian florins were popular as gold coins in late-medieval times, while the British gold sovereign has been the preferred gold coin of modern times. The Maria Theresa silver thaler of Austria, with its date frozen at 1782, has been minted widely down to the present time for circulation in the Near and Middle East as a trade coin. Trade dollars were minted by Britain, the USA, the Netherlands and Japan to compete with the Spanish, and later the Mexican, peso or 8-reales coins as a trading medium in the Far East.

Transport Tokens Coin-like pieces of metal, plastic or card, issued by companies and corporations to employees and exchangeable for rides on municipal transport systems, date from the mid-19th century. In more recent times similar tokens have been used in many countries to activate turnstiles in buses, trams and rapid-transit railway systems.

Treasury Note Paper money worth 10 shillings or one pound, issued by the British Treasury on the outbreak of the First World War when *specie* payments were suspended, and continuing till 1928 when the Bank of England took over responsibility for note-issuing.

Treasure Trove Articles of precious metal concealed in times of economic or political upheaval and discovered years (often centuries) later are deemed by law to be treasure trove (from the French word *trouve*, found). For further details see *Money and the Law*.

Trial Plate Plate of the same metal as the current coinage against which the fineness and quality of the coins produced are compared and tested.

Troy Weight System of weights derived from the French town of Troyes whose standard pound was adopted in England in 1526. It continued in Britain till 1879 when it was abolished, with the exception of the troy ounce and its decimal parts and multiples, which were retained for gold, silver, platinum and precious stones. The troy ounce of 480 grains is used for weighing coins.

Truncation Stylised cut at the base of a coinage effigy, sometimes containing a die number, engraver's initials or *mintmark*.

Trussel Reverse die in *hammered* coinage, the opposite of the *pile*.

Type Principal motif on a coin or medal, enabling numismatists to identify the issue.

Type Set A set of coins comprising one of each coin in a particular series, regardless of the actual date of issue.

Uncirculated Term used in grading coins to denote specimens in perfect condition, with original mint lustre. In recent years the term "Brilliant Uncirculated" has been adopted (abbreviated as BUnc or BU) both to indicate the condition of a coin, and, by The Royal Mint, to indicate the standard to which some coins are minted, being a standard between Circulation and Proof.

Uniface Coin with a device on one side only.

Vecture Term (mainly used in the US) for a *transport token*.

Veiled or "Old" head effigy

Veiled Head The effigy of Queen Victoria by Thomas Brock adopted for British coinage after 1893 — often referred to as the "Old Head" coinage.

Veld Pond (Dutch for "field pound"). Gold coin struck by the Boer guerrillas at Pilgrims Rest in 1902, in imitation of the British sovereign.

VF Standard abbreviation for Very Fine, used to describe the state of a coin or medal.

VG Abbreviation for Very Good, used to describe the state of a coin or medal, however, it is not a standard grade of a coin in the grading scale.

Vignette Strictly speaking the pictorial element of a paper note shading off into the surrounding unprinted paper rather than having a clearly defined border or frame; but nowadays applied generally to the picture portion of a banknote, as opposed to the portrait, armorial or numeral elements.

Vis-à-Vis (French for "face to face"). Term describing coins with double portraits of rulers, their profiles or busts facing each other. A good example is the English coinage of Philip and Mary, 1554–58.

Wampum Barter currency of the North American Indians, composed of shells of *Venus mercenaria* strung together to form belts or "fathoms" worth 5 shillings. Wampum were tariffed variously from three to six to the English penny in the American colonies till 1704.

Wire Money Primitive currency of the Maldive Islands in the form of lengths of silver wire known as lari, from which the modern currency unit *laree* is derived. The term was also applied to English coins of the 18th century in which the numerals of value were exceptionally thin, resembling wire. Many Russian coins of the 17th/18th century were also made from pieces of wire cut from strips which were then roughly flattened, often in an oval shape. These blanks were then struck with round dies which often meant that parts of the wording and design was missed off.

Wooden Coins Thin pieces of wood used as tokens are known from many parts of China and Africa, and as small *Notgeld* from Austria and Germany during World War I. Wooden nickels is the name given to tokens of a commemorative nature, widely popular in the USA since 1930.

Young Head Profile of Queen Victoria sculpted by William Wyon for the Guildhall Medal of 1837 and subsequently utilised for British coins struck from 1837 to 1860 (copper) and 1887 (silver and gold).

Zinc Metallic element, chemical symbol *Zn*, widely used, with copper, as a constituent of brass. Alloyed with copper to form *tombac*, it was used for Canadian 5-cent coins (1942–43) and, coated on steel, it was used for American cents (1943). Zinc was used for *emergency coinage* in Austria, Belgium, Luxembourg and Germany (1915–18) and in Germany and German-occupied countries during World War II. Since then alloys of copper, nickel and zinc have been used for coinage in Eastern Europe.

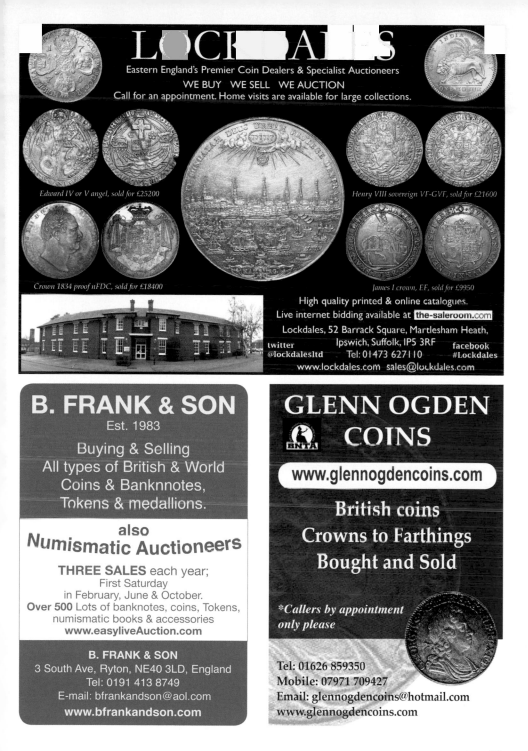
63

MINTMARKS *of the world*

The following is a list of the initials and symbols denoting mints. In many cases, notably the Royal Mint, no mintmark was used on either British coins or those struck on behalf of other countries. Conversely many countries have only used one mintmark, that of one or other of the leading private mints.

It should be noted that the mintmarks of the main private mints have been recorded on the coins of the following countries:

H (Heaton, later the Birmingham Mint): Australia, Bolivia, British Honduras, British North Borneo, British West Africa, Bulgaria, Canada, Ceylon, Chile, Colombia, Costa Rica, Cyprus, Dominican Republic, East Africa, Ecuador, Egypt, El Salvador, Finland, French Indochina, Great Britain, Greece, Guatemala, Guernsey, Haiti, Hong Kong, Iran, Israel, Italy, Jamaica, Jersey, Liberia, Malaya and British Borneo, Mauritius, Mombasa, Mozambique, Newfoundland, Nicaragua, Poland, Roumania, Sarawak, Serbia, Siam, Straits Settlements, Uruguay and Venezuela.

FM (Franklin Mint, Philadelphia): Bahamas, Belize, British Virgin Islands, Cayman Islands, Cook Islands, Guyana, Jamaica, Liberia, Malaysia, Malta, Panama, Papua New Guinea, Philippines, Solomon Islands, Trinidad and Tobago.

PM (Pobjoy Mint, Sutton, Surrey): Ascension, Bosnia, Cook Islands, Gibraltar, Isle of Man, Liberia, Macau, Niue, Philippines, St Helena, Senegal, Seychelles, Tonga and Tristan da Cunha.

ALBANIA

L	London
R	Rome
V	Valona

ARGENTINA

BA	Buenos Aires
Bs	Buenos Aires
B.AS	Buenos Aires
JPP	Jose Policarpo Patino
M	Mendoza
PNP	Pedro Nolasco Pizarro
PP	Pedro Nolasco Pizarro
PTS	Potosi
R	Rioja
RA	Rioja
SE	Santiago del Estero
SoEo	Santiago del Estero
TN	Tucuman

AUSTRALIA

A	Perth
D	Denver
H	Heaton (1912–16)
I	Bombay (1942–43)
I	Calcutta (1916–18)
M	Melbourne
P	Perth
PL	Royal Mint, London
S	Sydney
S	San Francisco (1942–43)
Dot before and after PENNY and I on obverse	Bombay (1942–43)
Dot before and after HALFPENNY and I on obverse	Bombay (1942–43)
Dot before and after PENNY	Bombay (1942–43)
Dot after HALFPENNY	Perth
Dot before SHILLING	Perth (1946)
Dot above scroll on reverse	Sydney (1920)
Dot below scroll on reverse	Melbourne (1919–20)
Dot between designer's initials KG	Perth (1940–41)
Dot after AUSTRALIA	Perth (1952–53)

AUSTRIA

A	Vienna (1765–1872)
AH–AG	Carlsburg, Transylvania (1765–76)
AH–GS	Carlsburg (1776–80)
A–S	Hall, Tyrol (1765–74)
AS–IE	Vienna (1745)
AW	Vienna (1764, 1768)
B	Kremnitz (1765–1857)
B–L	Nagybanya (1765–71)
B–V	Nagybanya (1772–80)
C	Carlsburg (1762–64)
C	Prague (1766–1855)
C–A	Carlsburg (1746–66)
C–A	Vienna (1774–80)
CG–AK	Graz (1767–72)
CG–AR	Graz (1767)
C–K	Vienna (1765–73)
CM	Kremnitz (1779)
CVG–AK	Graz (1767–72)
CVG–AR	Graz (1767)
D	Graz (1765–72), Salzburg (1800–09)
E	Carlsburg (1765–1867)
EC–SK	Vienna (1766)
EvM–D	Kremnitz (1765–74)
EvS–AS	Prague (1765–73)
EvS–IK	Prague (1774–80)
F	Hall (1765–1807)
FH	Hall
G	Graz (1761–63)
G	Gunzburg (1764–79)
G	Nagybanya (1766–1851)
G–K	Graz (1767–72)
G–R	Graz (1746–67)
GTK	Vienna (1761)
H	Hall (1760–80)
H	Gunzburg (1765–1805)
H–A	Hall (1746–65)
H–G	Carlsburg (1765–77)
H–S	Carlsburg (1777–80)
IB–FL	Nagybanya (1765–71)
IB–IV	Nagybanya (1772–80)
IC–FA	Vienna (1774–80)
IC–IA	Vienna (1780)
IC–SK	Vienna (1765–73)
I–K	Graz (1765-67)
I–K	Vienna (1767)
IZV	Vienna (1763–65)
K	Kremnitz (1760–63)
K–B	Kremnitz (1619–1765)
K–D	Kremnitz (1765)
K–M	Kremnitz (1763–65)
M	Milan (1780–1859)
N	Nagybanya (1780)
N–B	Nagybanya (1630–1777, 1849)
O	Oravicza (1783–1816)
P	Prague (1760–63)
P–R	Prague (1746–67)
PS–IK	Prague (1774–80)
S	Hall (1765–80), Schmollnitz (1763–1816)
S–C	Gunzburg (1765–74)
SC–G	Gunzburg (1765)
S–F	Gunzburg (1775–80)
S–G	Gunzburg (1764–65)
S–IE	Vienna (1745)
SK–PD	Kremnitz (1774–80)
TS	Gunzburg (1762–88)
V	Venice (1805–66)
VC–S	Hall (1774–80)
VS–K	Prague (1774–80)
VS–S	Prague (1765–73)
W	Vienna (1748–63)
W–I	Vienna (1746–71)

BAHAMAS

FM	Franklin Mint
JP	John Pinches

BELGIUM

A	Vienna
B	Kremnitz
C	Prague
E	Carlsburg
F	Hall
G	Nagybanya
H	Gunzburg
hand	Antwerp
lion	Bruges

BELIZE (British Honduras)

FM	Franklin Mint
H	Heaton (1912–16)

BOLIVIA

H	Heaton (1892–1953)
P, PTR, PTS	Potosi

BRAZIL

A	Berlin (1913)
B	Bahia (1714–1831)
C	Cuiaba (1823–33)
G	Goias (1823–33)
M	Minas Gerais (1823–28)
P	Pernambuco
R	Rio de Janeiro (1703–1834)
RS	Rio de Janeiro (1869)
SP	Sao Paulo (1825–32)

BRITISH NORTH BORNEO (Sabah)

H	Heaton (1882–1941)

BRITISH WEST AFRICA

G	JR Gaunt, Birmingham
H	Heaton, Birmingham (1911–57)
K	King's Norton
KN	King's Norton
SA	Pretoria

BULGARIA

A	Berlin
BP	Budapest
Heaton	Heaton, Birmingham (1881–1923)
KB	Kormoczbanya
cornucopia	Paris
thunderbolt	Poissy

CANADA

C	Ottawa
H	Heaton (1871–1907)
maple leaf	Ottawa (on coins struck after the year inscribed on them)

CENTRAL AMERICAN REPUBLIC

CR	San Jose (Costa Rica)
G	Guatemala
NG	Guatemala
T	Tegucigalpa (Honduras)

CEYLON

H	Heaton (1912)

CHILE

A	Agustin de Infante y Prado (1768–72)
AJ	The above and Jose Maria de Bobadilla (1800–01)
D	Domingo Eizaguirre
DA	Domingo Eizaguirre and Agustin de Infante (1772–99)
BFF	Francisco Rodriguez Brochero
FJJF	Brochero and Jose Maria de Bobadilla (1803–17)
H	Heaton (1851)
J	Jose Larraneta (1749–67)
So	Santiago
VA	Val Distra

COLOMBIA

A	Paris
B	Bogota
BA	Bogota
B,B	Bogota
H	Heaton (1912)
M	Medellin
NR	Nuevo Reino
NoRo	Nuevo Reino
P	Popayan
PN, Pn	Popayan
SM	Santa Marta

COSTA RICA

CR	San Jose (1825–1947)
HBM	Heaton (1889–93)
S	San Domingo
SD	San Domingo

COURLAND

ICS	Justin Carl Schroder
IFS	Johan Friedrich Schmickert

CYPRUS

H	Heaton (1881–2)

DENMARK

FF	Altona
KM	Copenhagen Altona (1842)
crown	Copenhagen
heart	Copenhagen

orb	Altona (1839–48)

Other letters are the initials of mintmasters and moneyers

DOMINICAN REPUBLIC

HH	Heaton (1888–1919)

EAST AFRICA

A	Ackroyd & Best, Morley
H	Heaton (1910–64)
I	Bombay
K	Kynoch (IMI)
KN	King's Norton
SA	Pretoria

ECUADOR

BIRMᴹH	Heaton (1915)
BIRMING-HAM	Heaton (1899–1900, 1928)
D	Denver
H	Heaton (1890, 1909, 1924–5)
HEATON BIRMING-HAM	Heaton (1872–95)
HF	Le Locle
LIMA	Lima
Mo	Mexico
PHILA	Philadelphia
QUITO	Quito
SANTIAGO	Santiago de Chile

EGYPT

H	Heaton (1904–37)

EL SALVADOR

CAM	Central American Mint, San Salvador
H	Heaton (1889–1913)
Mo	Mexico
S	San Francisco

FIJI

S	San Francisco

FINLAND

H	Heaton (1921)
heart	Copenhagen (1922). Since then coins have been struck at Helsinki without a mintmark.

Initials of mintmasters:

S	August Soldan (1864–85)
L	Johan Lihr (1885–1912)
S	Isaac Sundell (1915–47)
L	V. U. Liuhto (1948)
H	Uolevi Helle (1948–58)
S	Allan Soiniemi (1958–75)
SH	Soiniemi & Heikki Halvaoja (1967–71)
K	Timo Koivuranta (1977, 1979)
KN	Koivuranta and Antti Neuvonen (1978)
KT	Koivuranta and Erja Tielinen (1982)
KM	Koivuranta and Pertti Makinen (1983)
N	Reino Nevalainen (1983)

FRANCE

A	Paris (1768)
AA	Metz (1775–98)
B	Rouen (1786–1857)
B	Beaumont le Roger (1943–58)
BB	Strasbourg (1743–1870)
C	Castelsarrasin (1914, 1942–46)
CC	Genoa (1805)
CL	Genoa (1813–14)
D	Lyons (1771–1857)
G	Geneva (1796–1805)
H	La Rochelle (1770–1837)
L	Limoges (1766–1837)
K	Bordeaux (1759–1878)
L	Bayonne (1761–1837)
M	Toulouse (1766–1837)
MA	Marseilles (1787–1857)
N	Montpellier (1766–93)
O	Riom
P	Dijon
Q	Perpignan (1777–1837)
R	Royal Mint, London (1815)
R	Orleans (1780–92)
T	Nantes (1739–1835)
U	Turin (1814)
V	Troyes
W	Lille (1759–1857)
X	Amiens (1740)
&	Aix en Provence (1775)
9	Rennes
cow	Pau (1746–93)
flag	Utrecht (1811–14)
crowned R	Rome (1811–14)
thunderbolt	Poissy (1922-24)
star	Madrid (1916)

In addition, French coins include symbols denoting the privy marks of Engravers General (Chief Engravers since 1880) and Mint Directors.

GERMANY

The first name gives the location of the mint, and the second the name of the country or state issuing the coins.

A	Amberg, Bavaria (1763–94)
A	Berlin (1850)
A	Clausthal, Hannover (1832–49)
AE	Breslau, Silesia (1743–51)
AGP	Cleve, Rhineland (1742–43)
AK	Dusseldorf, Julich-Berg (1749–66)
ALS	Berlin (1749)
B	Bayreuth, Franconia (1796–1804)
B	Breslau, Silesia (1750–1826)
B	Brunswick, Brunswick (1850–60)
B	Brunswick, Westphalia (1809–13)
B	Dresden, Saxony (1861–72)
B	Hannover, Brunswick (1860–71)
B	Hannover, East Friesland (1823–25)
B	Hannover, Hannover (1821–66)
B	Hannover, Germany (1866-78)
B	Regensburg, Regensburg (1809)
B	Vienna, Germany (1938–45)

BH	Frankfurt (1808)
B–H	Regensburg, Rhenish Confederation (1802–12)
C	Cassel, Westphalia (1810–13)
C	Clausthal, Brunswick
C	Clausthal, Westphalia (1810–11)
C	Dresden, Saxony (1779–1804)
C	Frankfurt, Germany (1866–79)
CHI	Berlin (1749–63)
CLS	Dusseldorf, Julich-Berg (1767–70)
D	Aurich, East Friesland (1750–1806)
D	Dusseldorf, Rhineland (1816–48)
D	Munich, Germany (1872)
E	Dresden, Germany (1872–87)
E	Koenigberg, East Prussia (1750–98)
E	Muldenhutte, Germany (1887–1953)
EC	Leipzig, Saxony (1753–63)
EGN	Berlin (1725–49)
F	Dresden, Saxony (1845–58)
F	Magdeburg, Lower Saxony (1740–1806)
F	Cassel, Hesse-Cassel (1803–07)
F	Stuttgart, Germany (1872)
FW	Dresden, Saxony (1734–63)
G	Dresden, Saxony (1833–44, 1850–54)
G	Glatz, Silesia (1807–09)
G	Karlsruhe, Germany (1872)
G	Stettin, Pomerania (1750–1806)
GK	Cleve (1740–55)
GN	Bamberg, Bamberg
H	Darmstadt, Germany (1872–82)
H	Dresden, Saxony (1804–12)
HK	Rostock, Rostock (1862–64)
I	Hamburg, Germany (1872)
IDB	Dresden, Prussian occupation (1756–59)
IEC	Dresden, Saxony (1779–1804)
IF	Leipzig, Saxony (1763–65)
IGG	Leipzig, Saxony (1716–34, 1813–32)
J	Hamburg, Germany (1873)
J	Paris, Westphalia (1808–09)
L	Leipzig, Saxony (1761–62)
MC	Brunswick, Brunswick (1813–14, 1820)
PM	Dusseldorf, Julich-Berg (1771–83)
PR	Dusseldorf, Julich-Berg (1783–1804)
S	Dresden, Saxony (1813–32)
S	Hannover, Hannover (1839–44)
S	Schwabach, Franconia (1792–94)
SGH	Dresden, Saxony (1804–12)
ST	Strickling, Blomberg (1820–40)

GREAT BRITAIN

A	Ashby (1645)
B	Nicolas Briot (1631–39)
B	Bridgnorth (1646)
B	Bristol (1696)
Br	Bristol (1643–45)
C	Chester (1696)
CARL	Carlisle (1644–45)
CC	Corfe Castle (1644)
CHST	Chester (1644)
CR	Chester (1644)
E	Southwark (1547–49)

E	Exeter (1696)
E	Edinburgh (1707–13)
E*	Edinburgh (1707–09)
H	Heaton, Birmingham (1874–1919)
HC	Hartlebury Castle (1646)
K	London (1547–49)
KN	King's Norton
N	Norwich (1696)
OX	Oxford (1644–45)
OXON	Oxford (1644)
PC	Pontefract (1648–49)
SC	Scarborough (1644–45)
SOHO	Birmingham (1797–1806)
T	Canterbury (1549)
TC	Bristol (1549)
WS	Bristol (1547–49)
Y	Southwark (1551)
boar	Shrewsbury (1643–44)
book	Aberystwyth (1638–42)
bow	Durham House (1548–49)
castle	Exeter (1644–45)
crown	Aberystwyth Furnace (1648–49)
plume	Shrewsbury (1642)
plume	Oxford (1642–46)
plume	Bristol (1643–46)

Other symbols and marks on the hammered coins of Great Britain are usually referred to as Initial Marks. Complete listings of these marks appear in a number of specialist publications.

GREECE

A	Paris
B	Vienna
BB	Strasbourg
H	Heaton (1921)
K	Bordeaux
KN	King's Norton
owl	Aegina (1828–32)
owl	Athens (1838–55)
thunderbolt	Poissy

GUATEMALA

CG	Guatemala City (1733–76)
G	Guatemala City (1776)
H	Heaton (1894–1901)
NG	Nueva Guatemala (1777)

GUERNSEY

H	Heaton (1855–1949)

HAITI

A	Paris
HEATON	Heaton (1863)

HONDURAS

A	Paris (1869–71)
T	Tegucigalpa (1825–62)

HONG KONG

H	Heaton (1872–1971)
KN	King's Norton

HUNGARY

A	Vienna
B	Kremnitz
BP	Budapest
CA	Vienna
G	Nagybanya
GN	Nagybanya
GYF	Carlsburg
HA	Hall
K	Kremnitz
KB	Kremnitz
NB	Nagybanya
S	Schmollnitz
WI	Vienna

INDIA

B	Bombay (1835-1947)	
C	Calcutta (1835-1947)	
I	Bombay (1918)	
L	Lahore (1943-45)	
M	Madras (1869)	
P	Pretoria (1943-44)	
diamond	Bombay	
dot in diamond		Hyderabad
split diamond		Hyderabad
star	Hyderabad	

IRAN

H	Heaton (1928–29)

IRAQ

I	Bombay

ISRAEL

H	Heaton (1951–52)
star of David	Jerusalem

ITALY AND STATES

B	Bologna
B/I	Birmingham (1893–4)
FIRENZE	Florence
H	Heaton (1866–67)
KB	Berlin
M	Milan
N	Naples
OM	Strasbourg
R	Rome
T	Turin
V	Venice
ZV	Venice
anchor	Genoa
eagle head	Turin

JAMAICA

C	Ottawa
FM	Franklin Mint
H	Heaton (1882–1916)

JERSEY

H	Heaton (1877)

KENYA
C/M	Calcutta
H	Heaton (1911–64)

LIBERIA
B	Berne
FM	Franklin Mint
H	Heaton (1896–1906)
PM	Pobjoy Mint

LIECHTENSTEIN
A	Vienna
B	Berne
M	Munich

LUXEMBOURG
A	Paris
H	Gunzburg
anchor	Paris
angel	Brussels
caduceus	Utrecht
double eagle	Brussels
sword	Utrecht

MALAYSIA
B	Bombay
FM	Franklin Mint
H	Heaton (1955–61)
I	Calcutta (1941)
I	Bombay (1945)
KN	King's Norton
W	James Watt, Birmingham

MAURITIUS
H	Heaton (1877–90)
SA	Pretoria

MEXICO
A, As	Alamos
C, CN	Culiacan
CA, CH	Chihuahua
Ce	Real del Catorce
D, Do	Durango
Eo	Tlalpam
GA	Guadalajara
GC	Guadelupe y Calvo
Go	Guanajuato
Ho	Hermosillo
M, Mo	Mexico City
Mo	Morelos
MX	Mexico City
O, OA, OKA	Oaxaca
Pi	San Luis Potosi
SLPi	San Luis Potosi
TC	Tierra Caliente
Z, Zs	Zacatecas

MONACO
A	Paris
M	Monte Carlo
clasped hands	Cabanis
thunderbolt	Poissy

MOZAMBIQUE
H	Heaton (1894)
R	Rio

NETHERLANDS AND COLONIES
Austrian Netherlands (1700-93)
H	Amsterdam
S	Utrecht
W	Vienna
hand	Antwerp
head	Brussels
lion	Bruges

Kingdom of the Netherlands
B	Brussels (1821–30)
D	Denver (1943–45)
P	Philadelphia (1941–45)
S	Utrecht (1816–36)
S	San Francisco (1944–45)
Sa	Surabaya
caduceus	Utrecht

NICARAGUA
H	Heaton (1880–1916)
NR	Leon de Nicaragua

NORWAY
hammers	Kongsberg

PANAMA
CHI	Valcambi
FM	Franklin Mint

PERU
AREQ, AREQUIPA	Arequipa
AYACUCHO	Ayacucho
CUZCO, Co	Cuzco
L, LM, LR	Lima
LIMAE	Lima
PASCO	Pasco
Paz, Po	Pasco
P	Lima (1568-70)
P	Philadelphia
S	San Francisco

PHILIPPINES
BSP	Bangko Sentral Pilipinas
D	Denver (1944–45)
FM	Franklin Mint
M, MA	Manila
PM	Pobjoy Mint
S	San Francisco (1903–47)
5 point star	Manila

POLAND
AP	Warsaw (1772–74)
CI	Cracow (1765–68)
EB	Warsaw (1774–92)
EC	Leipzig (1758–63)
FF	Stuttgart (1916–17)
FH	Warsaw (1815–27)
FS	Warsaw (1765–68)
FWoF	Dresden (1734–64)
G	Cracow (1765–72)

H	Heaton (1924)
IB	Warsaw (1811–27)
IGS	Dresden (1716–34)
IP	Warsaw (1834–43)
IS	Warsaw (1768–74)
JGG	Leipzig (1750–53)
JS	Warsaw (1810–11)
KG	Warsaw (1829–34)
MV, MW	Warsaw
arrow	Warsaw (1925–39)
Dot after	
date	Royal Mint (1925)
8 torches	Paris (1924)

ROUMANIA

B	Bucharest (1879–85)
C	Bucharest (1886)
H	Heaton (1867–1930)
HUGUENIN	Le Locle
J	Hamburg
KN	King's Norton
V	Vienna
W	Watt, Birmingham
thunderbolt	Poissy

RUSSIA

AM	Annensk (1762–96)
BM	Warsaw (1825–55)
bM	St Petersburg (1796)
C–M	Sestroretsk (1762–96)
CM	Souzan (1825–55)
E–M	Ekaterinburg (1762–1810)
KM	Kolpina (1810)
K–M	Kolyvan (1762–1810)
MM, M–M	Moscow (1730–96)
MMD	Moscow (1730–96)
MW	Warsaw (1842–54)
NM	Izhorsk (1811–21)
SP	St Petersburg (1798–1800)
SPB	St Petersburg (1724–1915)
SPM	St Petersburg (1825–55)
T–M	Feodosia (1762–96)

SAN MARINO

M	Milan
R	Rome

SIAM

(Thailand)	H Heaton (1898)

SOUTH AFRICA

SA	Pretoria

SPAIN

B	Burgos
B, BA	Barcelona
Bo	Bilbao
C	Catalonia
C	Cuenca
C	Reus
CA	Zaragoza
G	Granada
GNA	Gerona
LD	Lerida

J, JA	Jubia
M, MD	Madrid
P	Palma de Majorca
PpP, PL, PA	Pamplona
S, S/L	Seville
Sr	Santander
T, To, Tole	Toledo
TOR:SA	Tortosa
V, VA, VAL	Valencia
crowned C	Cadiz
crowned M	Madrid
aqueduct	Segovia
crowned shield	Tarragona
pomegranate	Granada
quartered shield	Palma
scallop	Coruna
stars:	
3 points	Segovia
4 points	Jubia
5 points	Manila
6 points	Madrid
7 points	Seville (1833)
8 points	Barcelona (1838)
wavy lines	Valladolid

SURINAM

P	Philadelphia
S	Sydney
caduceus	Utrecht

SWITZERLAND

A	Paris
AB	Strasbourg
B	Berne
B	Brussels (1874)
BA	Basle
BB	Strasbourg
S	Solothurn

URUGUAY

H	Heaton (1869)

UNITED STATES OF AMERICA

C	Charlotte, North Carolina
Cc	Carson City, Nevada
D	Dahlonega, Georgia (1838–61)
D	Denver, Colorado (1906)
O	New Orleans
P	Philadelphia
S	San Francisco
W	West Point

VENEZUELA

A	Paris
H	Heaton (1852)
HEATON	Heaton (1852–63)

YUGOSLAVIA (including former Serbia)

A	Paris
H	Heaton (1883–84)
KOBHNUA, A.D.	Kovnica
V	Vienna
thunderbolt	Poissy

COIN *inscriptions*

This alphabetical listing is confined to inscriptions found on coins, mainly in the form of mottoes or of a commemorative nature. Names of rulers are, for the most part, excluded. Where the inscription is in a language other than English a translation is given, followed by the name of the issuing country or authority in parentheses.

A Deo et Caesare   From God and the Emperor (Frankfurt).

A Domino Factum est Istud et est Mirabile in Oculis Nostris   This is the Lord's doing and it is marvellous in our eyes (England, Mary).

A Solo Iehova Sapientia   From God alone comes true wisdom (Wittgenstein).

Ab Inimicis Meis Libera Me Deus   Free me from enemies (Burgundy).

Ad Legem Conventionis   According to the law of the Convention (Furstenberg).

Ad Normam Conventionis   According to the standard of the Convention (Prussia).

Ad Palmam Pressa Lecturo Roourgo   Proceed to the palm I rise more joyfully (Wittgenstein).

Ad Usam Luxemburgi CC Vallati   For the use of the besieged Luxembourgers (Luxembourg siege coins).

Adiuva Nos Deus Salutaris Noster   Help us, O God, our Saviour (Lorraine).

Adventus Optimi Principis   The coming of the noblest prince (Papacy).

Acs Usibus Aptius Auro   Bronze in its uses is more suitable than gold (Brazil).

Aeternum Meditans Decus   An ornament intended for all time (Alencon).

Aliis Inserviendo Consumor   I spend my life devoted to others (Brunswick-Wolfenbuttel).

Alles Mit Bedacht   All with reflection (Brunswick).

Amor Populi Praesidium Regis   The love of the people is the king's protection (England, Charles I).

Ang Fra Dom Hib & Aquit   (King) of England and France, Lord of Ireland and Aquitaine (England, Edward III).

Anno Regni Primo   In the first year of the reign (Britain, edge inscription on crowns).

Apres les Tenebres la Lumiere   After the shadows, the light (Geneva).

Archangelus Michael   Archangel Michael (Italy, Grimoald IV).

Ardua ad Gloriam Via   Struggles are the way to glory (Waldeck).

Arte Mea Bis Iustus Moneta Lud Iust   By my art I am twice the just coin of King Louis (France, 1641).

Aspera Oblectant   Wild places delight (Nassau-Weilburg).

Aspice Pisas Sup Omnes Specio   Behold the coin of Pisa, superior to all (Pisa).

Audiatur Altera Pars   Let the other part be heard (Stavelot).

Auf Gott Trawe Ich   In God I trust (Brunswick).

Ausen Gefaesen der Kirchen und Burger   From the vessels of the Church and citizens (Frankfurt siege, 1796).

Auspicio Regis et Senatus Angliae   By authority of the king and parliament of England (East India Company).

Auxilio fortissimo Dei   With the strongest help of God (Mecklenburg).

Auxilium de Sanctio   Aid from the sanctuary (Papacy).

Auxilium Meum a Dno Qui Fecit Celum e Terram   My help comes from God who made heaven and earth (Portugal).

Beata Tranquillatis   Blessed tranquillity (Rome, Licinius II).

Beatus Qui Speravit in dom   Blessed is he who has hoped in the Lord (Mansfeld).

Benedic Haereditati Tuae   Blessings on your inheritance (Savoy).

Benedicta Sit Sancta Trinitas   Blessed be the Holy Trinity (Albon).

Benedictio Domini Divites Facit   The blessing of the Lord makes the rich (Teschen).

Benedictus Qui Venit in Nomine Domini   Blessed is he who comes in the name of the Lord (Flanders).

Beschaw das Ziel Sage Nicht Viel   Consider the matter but say little (Quedlinburg).

Besser Land und Lud Verloren als ein Falscher Aid Geschworn   Better to lose land and wealth than swear a false oath (Hesse).

Bey Gott ist Rath und That   With God is counsel and deed (Mansfeld).

Britanniarum Regina   Queen of the Britains (Britain, Victoria).

Britt Omn Rex   King of all the Britains (i.e. Britain and the overseas dominions) (Britain, 1902–52).

Cal et Car Com de Fugger in Zin et Norn Sen & Adm Fam   Cajetan and Carl, Counts of Fugger in Zinnenberg and Nordendorf, Lords and Administrators of the Family (Empire, Fugger).

Candide et Constanter   Sincerely and steadfastly (Hesse-Cassel).

Candide sed Provide   Clearly but cautiously (Osterwitz).

Candore et Amore   With sincerity and love (Fulda).

Candore et Constantia   With sincerity and constancy (Bavaria).

Capit Cath Ecclesia Monasteriensis   Chapter of the Cathedral Church of Munster (Munster).

Capit Eccle Metropolit Colon   Chapter of the Metropolitan Church of Cologne (Cologne).

Capitulum Regnans Sede Vacante   Chapter governing, the See being vacant (Eichstadt).

Carola Magna Ducissa Feliciter Regnante   Grand Duchess Charlotte, happily reigning (Luxembourg).

Carolus a Carolo   Charles (I) to Charles (II) (England).

Cedunt Prementi Fata   The fates yield to him who presses (Ploen, Hese-Cassel).

Charitate et Candore   With charity and sincerity (East Frisia).

Charta Magna Bavariae   The Great Charter of Bavaria (Bavaria).

Christo Auspice Regno   I reign under the auspices of Christ (England, Charles I).

Christus Spes Una Salutis   Christ is our one hope of salvation (Cleve).

Chur Mainz   Electoral Principality of Mainz (Mainz).

Circumeundo Servat et Ornat   It serves and decorates by going around (Sweden).

Civibus Quorum Pietas Coniuratione Die III Mai MDCCXCI Obrutam et Deletam Libertate Polona Tueri Conabatur Respublica Resurgens   To the citizens whose piety the resurgent commonwealth tried to protect Poland overturned and deprived of liberty by the conspiracy of the third day of May 1791 (Poland).

Civitas Lucemborgiensis Millesimum Ovans Expletannum   Completing the celebration of a thousand years of the city of Luxembourg (Luxembourg).

Civium Industria Floret Civitas   By the industry of its people the state flourishes (Festival of Britain crown, 1951).

Cluniaco Cenobio Petrus et Paulus   Peter and Paul from the Abbey of Cluny (Cluny).

Comes Provincie Fili Regis Francie   Court of Provence and son of the King of France (Provence).

Communitas et Senatus Bonon   City and senate of Bologna (Bologna).

Concordia Fratrum   The harmony of the brothers (Iever).

Concordia Patriae Nutrix   Peace, the nurse of the fatherland (Waldeck).

Concordia Res Parvae Crescunt   Little things increase through harmony (Batavian Republic).

Concordia Res Parvae Crescunt, Discordia Dilabuntur   By harmony little things increase, by discord they fall apart (Lowenstein-Wertheim-Virneburg).

Concordia Stabili   With lasting peace (Hildesheim).

Confidens Dno Non Movetur   He who trusts in God is unmoved (Spanish Netherlands).

Confidentia in Deo et Vigilantia   Trust in God and vigilance (Prussian Asiatic Company).

Confoederato Helvetica   Swiss Confederation (Switzerland)

Conjuncto Felix   Fortunate in his connections (Solms).

Conservator Urbis Suae   Saviour of his city (Rome, 4th century).

Consilio et Aequitate   With deliberation and justice (Fulda).

Consilio et Virtutis   With deliberation and valour (Hesse-Cassel).

Constanter et Sincere   Steadfastly and sincerely (Lautern).

Crescite et Multiplicamini   Increase and multiply (Maryland).

Cristiana Religio   Christian religion (Germany, 11th century).

Crux Benedicat   May the cross bless you (Oldenburg).

Cuius Cruore Sanati Sumus   By His sacrifice are we healed (Reggio).

Cultores Sui Deus Protegit   God protects His followers (England, Charles I).

Cum Deo et Die (Jure)   With God and the day (Wurttemberg).

Cum Deo et Jure   With God and the law (Wurttemberg).

Cum Deo et Labore   With God and work (Wittgenstein).

Cum His Qui Orderant Pacem Eram Pacificus   With those who order peace I was peaceful (Zug).

Curie Bonthon to so Doulo   Protect his servant, o Lord (Byzantine Empire).

Custos Regni Deus   God is the guardian of the kingdom (Naples and Sicily).

Da Gloriam Deo et Eius Genitrici Marie   Give glory to God and His mother Mary (Wurttemberg).

Da Mihi Virtutem Contra Hostes Tuos   Give me valour against mine enemies (Netherlands, Charles V).

Dat Wort is Fleis Gworden   The word is made flesh (Muster).

Date Caesaris Caesari et Quae Sunt Dei Deo   Render unto Caesar the things that are Caesar's and unto God the things that are God's (Stralsund).

De Oficina . . .   From the mint of . . . (France, medieval).

Decreto Reipublicae Nexu Confoederationis Iunctae Die V Xbris MDCCXCII Stanislao Augusto Regnante   By decree of the state in conjunction with the joint federation on the fifth day of December 1792, Stanislaus Augustus ruling (Poland).

Decus et Tutamen   An ornament and a safeguard (Britain, pound).

Deducet Nos Mirabiliter Dextera Tua   Thy right hand will guide us miraculously (Savoy).

Denarium Terrae Mariae   Penny of Maryland (Maryland).

Deo Conservatori Pacis   To God, preserver of peace (Brandenburg-Ansbach).

Deo OM Auspice Suaviter et Fortiter sed Luste nec Sibi sed Suis   Under the auspices of God, greatest and best, pleasantly and bravely but justly, not for himself but for his people (Speyer).

Deo Patriae et Subditio   For God, fatherland and neighbourhood (Mainz).

Der Recht Glaubt In Ewig Lebt   Who believes In right will live in eternity (Linange-Westerburg).

Der Rhein ist Deutschlands Strom Nicht Deutschlands Grenze   The Rhine is Germany's River not Germany's Frontier.

Deum Solum Adorabis   You will venerate God alone (Hesse).

Deus Constituit Regna   God establishes kingdoms (Nijmegen).

Deus Dat Qui Vult   God gives to him who wishes (Hanau-Munzenberg).

Deus et Dominus   God and Lord (Rome, 3rd century).

Deus in Adiutorium Meum Intende   God stretch out in my assistance (France).

Deus Providebit   God will provide (Lowenstein-Wertheim-Virneburg).

Deus Refugium Meum   God is my refuge (Cleve).

Deus Solatium Meum   God is my comfort (Sweden).

Dextera Domini Exaltavit Me   The right hand of God has raised me up (Modena, Spain).

Dextra Dei Exalta Me   The right hand of God exalts me (Denmark).

Dieu et Mon Droit   God and my right (Britain, George IV).

Dilexit Dns Andream   The Lord delights in St Andrew (Holstein).

Dilexit Dominus Decorem Iustitiae   The Lord is pleased with the beauty of justice (Unterwalden).

Dirige Deus Gressus Meos   O God, direct my steps (Tuscany, Britain, Una £5).

Discerne Causam Meam   Distinguish my cause (Savoy).

Divina Benedictiae et Caesarea Iustitia   Sacrifice of blessings and imperial justice (Coblenz).

Dn Ihs Chs Rex Regnantium   Lord Jesus Christ, King of Kings (Rome, Justinian II).

Dns Ptetor Ms Z Lib'ator Ms   The Lord is my protector and liberator (Scotland, David II).

Dominabitur Gentium et Ipse   He himself will also be lord of the nations (Austrian Netherlands).

Domine Conserva Nos in Pace   O Lord preserve us in peace (Basle, Mulhausen).

Domine Elegisti Lilium Tibi   O Lord Thou hast chosen the lily for Thyself (France, Louis XIV).

Domine ne in Furore Tuo Arguas Me   O Lord rebuke me not in Thine anger (England, Edward III).

Domine Probasti Me et Congnovisti Me   O Lord Thou hast tested me and recognised me (Mantua).

Domini est Regnum   The Kingdom is the Lord's (Austrian Netherlands).

Dominus Deus Omnipotens Rex   Lord God, almighty King (Viking coins).

Dominus Mihi Adiutor   The Lord is my helper (Spanish Netherlands).

Dominus Providebit   The Lord will provide (Berne).

Dominus Spes Populi Sui   The Lord is the hope of his people (Lucerne).

Donum Dei ex Fodinis Vilmariens   A gift of God from the Vilmar mines (Coblenz).

Duce Deo Fide et Justicia   By faith and justice lead us to God (Ragusa).

Dum Praemor Amplior   I increase while I die prematurely (Savoy).

Dum Spiro Spero   While I live, I hope (Pontefract siege coins).

Dum Totum Compleat Orbem   Until it fills the world (France, Henri II).

Dura Pati Virtus   Valour endures hardships (Saxe-Lauenburg).

Durae Necessitatis   Through force of necessity (Bommel siege, 1599).

Durum Telum Necessitas   Hardship is a weapon of necessity (Minden).

Dux et Gubernatores Reip Genu   Duke and governors of the republic of Genoa (Genoa).

E Pluribus Unum   One out of more (USA).

Eccl S. Barbarae Patronae Fodin Kuttenbergensium Duo Flor Arg Puri   The church of St Barbara, patron of the Kuttensberg mines, two florins of pure silver (Hungary).

Een en Ondelbaer Sterk   One and indivisible (Batavian Republic).

Eendracht Mag Macht   Unity makes strength (Belgium, South African Republic).

Einigkeit Recht und Freiheit   Union, right and freedom (Germany).

Electorus Saxoniae Administrator   Elector and administrator of Saxony (Saxony).

Elimosina   Alms (France, Pepin).

Ep Fris & Ratisb Ad Prum Pp Coad Aug   Bishop of Freising and Regensburg, administrator of Pruem, prince-provost, co-adjutant bishop of Augsburg (Trier).

Equa Libertas Deo Gratia Frat Pax in Virtute Tua et in Domino Confido   I believe in equal liberty by the grace of God, brotherly love in Thy valour and in the Lord (Burgundy).

Equitas Iudicia Tua Dom   Equity and Thy judgments O Lord (Gelderland).

Espoir Me Conforte   Hope comforts me (Mansfeld).

Espreuve Faicto Par Lexpres Commandement du Roy   Proof made by the express commandment of the King (France, piedforts).

Et in Minimis Integer   Faithful even in the smallest things (Olmutz).

Ex Auro Argentes Resurgit   From gold it arises, silver again (Sicily).

Ex Auro Sinico   From Chinese gold (Denmark).

Ex Flammis Orior   I arise from the flames (Hohenlohe-Neuenstein-Ohringen).

Ex Fodinis Bipontio Seelbergensibus   From the Seelberg mines of Zweibrucken (Pfalz-Birkenfeld).

Ex Metallo Novo   From new metal (Spain).

Ex Uno Omnis Nostra Salus   From one is all our salvation (Eichstadt, Mulhouse).

Ex Vasis Argent Cleri Mogunt Pro Aris et Focis   From the silver vessels of the clergy of Mainz for altars and for hearths (Mainz).

Ex Visceribus Fodinse Bieber   From the bowels of the Bieber mine (Hanau-Munzenberg).

Exaltabitur in Gloria   He shall be exalted in glory (England, quarter nobles).

Exemplum Probati Numismatis   An example of a proof coin (France, Louis XIII piedforts).

Exemtae Eccle Passau Episc et SRI Princ   Prince Bishop of the freed church of Passau, prince of the Holy Roman Empire (Passau).

Expectate Veni   Come, o expected one (Roman Britain, Carausius).

Extremum Subidium Campen   Kampen under extreme siege (Kampen, 1578).

Exurgat Deus et Dissipentur Inimici Eius   Let God arise and let His enemies be scattered (England, James I).

Faciam Eos in Gentem Unam   I will make them one nation (England, unites and laurels).

Faith and Truth I will Bear unto You   (UK £5, 1993).

Fata Consiliis Potiora   The fates are more powerful than councils (Hesse-Cassel).

Fata Viam Invenient   The fates will find a way (Gelderland).

Fecit Potentiam in Brachio Suo   He put power in your forearm (Lorraine).

Fecunditas   Fertility (Naples and Sicily).

Fel Temp Reparatio   The restoration of lucky times (Rome, AD 348).

Felicitas Perpetua   Everlasting good fortune (Rome, Constantius II).

Felix coniunctio   Happy Union (Brandenburg-Ansbach).

Fiat Misericordia Tua Dne   Let Thy mercy be O Lord (Gelderland).

Fiat Voluntas Domini Perpetuo   Let the goodwill of the Lord last for ever (Fulda).

Fidei Defensor   Defender of the Faith (Britain).

Fidelitate et Fortitudine   With fidelity and fortitude (Batthanyi).

Fideliter et Constanter   Faithfully and steadfastly (Saxe-Coburg-Gotha).

Fidem Servando Patriam Tuendo   By keeping faith and protecting the fatherland (Savoy).

Filius Augustorum   Son of emperors (Rome, 4th century).

Fisci Iudaici Calumnia Sublata   The false accusation of the Jewish tax lifted (Rome, Nerva).

Florent Concordia Regna   Through harmony kingdoms flourish (England, Charles I and II).

Fortitudo et Laus Mea Dominu   Fortitude and my praise in the Lord (Sardinia).

Free Trade to Africa by Act of Parliment *(Sic)* (Gold Coast).

Friedt Ernehrt Unfriedt Verzehrt   Peace nourishes, unrest wastes (Brunswick).

Fulgent Sic Littora Rheni   Thus shine the banks of the Rhine (Mannheim).

Fundator Pacis   Founder of peace (Rome, Severus).

Gaudium Populi Romani   The joy of the Roman people (Rome, 4th century).

Gen C Mar VI Dim Col USC & RAMAI Cons & S Conf M   General field marshal, colonel of the only dragoon regiment, present privy councillor of both their sacred imperial and royal apostolic majesties, and state conference minister (Batthanyi).

Gerecht und Beharrlich   Just and steadfast (Bavaria).

Germ Hun Boh Rex AAD Loth Ven Sal   King of Germany, Hungary and Bohemia, Archduke of Austria, Duke of Lorraine, Venice and Salzburg (Austria).

Germ Jero Rex Loth Bar Mag Het Dux   King of Germany, Jerusalem, Lorraine and Bar, Grand Duke of Tuscany (Austrian Netherlands).

Germania Voti Compos   Germany sharing the vows (Brandenburg-Ansbach).

Gloria ex Amore Patriae   Glory from love of country (Denmark).

Gloria in Excelsis Deo   Glory to God in the highest (France, Sweden).

Gloria Novi Saeculi   The glory of a new century (Rome, Gratian).

God With Us   (England, Commonwealth).

Godt Met Ons   God with us (Oudewater).

Gottes Freundt der Pfaffen Feindt   God's friend, the Pope's enemy (Brunswick, Christian).

Gratia Dei Sum Id Quod Sum   By the grace of God, I am what I am (Navarre).

Gratia Di Rex   By the grace of God, king (France, 8th century).

Gratitudo Concivibus Exemplum Posteritati   Gratitude to fellow Citizens, an example to posterity (Poland).

Gud och Folket   God and the people (Sweden).

Hac Nitimur Hanc Tuemur   With this we strive, this we shall defend (Batavian Republic).

Hac Sub Tutela   Under this protection (Eichstadt).

Haec Sunt Munera Minerae S Antony Eremitae   These are the rewards of the mine of St Antony the hermit (Hildesheim).

Hanc Deus Dedit   God has given this (Pontefract siege coins).

Hanc Tuemur Hac Nitimur   This we defend, by this we strive (Batavian Republic).

Has Nisi Periturus Mihi Adimat Nemo   Let no one remove these (Letters) from me under penalty of death (Commonwealth, edge inscription).

Henricus Rosas Regna Jacobus   Henry (united) the roses, James the kingdoms (England and Scotland, James VI and I).

Herculeo Vincta Nodo   Bound by a Herculean fetter (Savoy).

Herr Nach Deinem Willen   O Lord Thy will be done (Palatinate, Erbach).

Herre Gott Verleich Uns Gnade   Lord God grant us grace (Brunswick).

Hic Est Qui Multum Orat Pro Populo   Here is he who prays a lot for the people (Paderborn).

Hir Steid te Biscop   Here is represented the bishop (Gittelde).

His Ventis Vela Levantur   By these winds the sails are raised up (Hesse-Cassel).

Hispaniarum Infans   Infante of Spain and its dominions (Spain).

Hispaniarum et Ind Rex   King of Spain and the Indies (Spain).

Hispaniarum Rex   King of Spain (Spain).

Hoc Signo Victor Eris   With this sign you will be victor (Rome, Vetranio).

Honeste et Decenter   Honestly and decently (Nassau-Idstein).

Honi Soit Qui Mal y Pense   Evil to him who evil thinks (Britain, George III).

Honni Soit Qui Mal y Pense   (Hesse-Cassel).

Hospitalis et S Sepul Hierusal   Hospital and Holy Sepulchre of Jerusalem (Malta).

Hun Boh Gal Rex AA Lo Wi et in Fr Dux   King of Hungary, Bohemia and Galicia, Archduke of Austria, Dalmatia, Lodomeria, Wurzburg and Duke in Franconia (Austria).

Hung Boh Lomb et Ven Gal Lod III Rex Aa   King of Hungary, Bohemia, Lombardo-Venezia, Galicia, Lodomeria, Illyria, Archduke (Austria).

Ich Dien   I serve (Aberystwyth 2d, UK 2p).

Ich Getrawe Got in Aller Noth   I trust in God in all my needs (Hesse-Marburg).

Ich Habe Nur Ein Vaterland und das Heisst Deutschland   I have only one fatherland and that is called Germany (Germany).

Ielithes Penniae   Penny of Gittelde (Gittelde, 11th century).

Iesus Autem Transiens Per Medium Illorum Ibat   But Jesus, passing through the midst of them, went His way (England, Scotland, Anglo-Gallic).

Iesus Rex Noster et Deus Noster   Jesus is our king and our God (Florence).

Ihs Xs Rex Regnantium   Jesus Christ, King of Kings (Byzantine Empire).

Ihsus Xristus Basileu Baslie   Jesus Christ, King of Kings (Byzantine Empire).

Imago Sanch Regis Illustris Castelle Legionis e Toleto   The image of Sancho the illustrious king of Castile, Leon and Toledo.

In Casus Per Vigil Omnes   In all seasons through vigil (Wertheim).

In Deo Meo Transgrediar Murum   In my God I shall pass through walls (Teschen).

In Deo Spes Mea   In God is my hope (Gelderland).

In Domino Fiducia Nostra   In the Lord is our trust (Iever).

In Equitate Tua Vivificasti Me   In thy equity Thou hast vivified me (Gelderland).

In God We Trust   (USA).

In Hoc Signo Vinces   In this sign shalt thou conquer (Portugal).

In Honore Sci Mavrici Marti   In honour of the martyr St Maurice (St Maurice, 8th century).

In Manibus Domini sortes Meae   In the hands of the Lord are my fates (Mainz siege, 1688–9).

In Memor Vindicatae Libere ac Relig   In memory of the establishment of freedom and religion (Sweden).

In Memoriam Conjunctionis Utriusque Burgraviatus Norice   In memory of the union of both burgraviates in peace (Brandenburg-Ansbach).

In Memorian Connub Feliciaes Inter Princ Her Frider Carol et Dub Sax August Louis Frider Rodas D 28 Nov 1780 Celebrati   In memory of the most happy marriage between the hereditary prince Friedrich Karl and the Duchess of Saxony Augusta Louisa Frederika, celebrated on 28 Nov 1780 (Schwarzburg-Rudolstadt).

In Memorian Felicisssimi Matrimonii   In memory of the most happy marriage (Wied).

In Memoriam Pacis Teschinensis   Commemorating the Treaty of Teschen (Brandenburg-Ansbach).

In Nomine Domini Amen   In the name of the Lord amen (Zaltbommel).

In Omnem Terram Sonus Eorum   In to all the land their shall go sound (Chateau Renault, Papal States).

In Silencio et Spe Fortitudo Mea   In silence and hope is my fortitude (Brandenburg-Kustrin).

In Spe et Silentio Fortitudo Mea   In hope and silence is my fortitude (Vianen).

In Te Domine Confido   In you O Lord I place my trust (Hesse).

In Te Domine Speravi   In You, O Lord, I have hoped (Gurk).

In Terra Pax   Peace in the land (Papacy).

In Via Virtuti Nulla Via   There is no way for virtue on the way. (Veldenz).

Ind Imp, Indiae Imperator, Imperatrix   Emperor (Empress) of India (Britain).

India Tibi Cessit   India has yielded to thee (Portuguese India).

Infestus Infestis   Hostile to the troublesome (Savoy).

Inimicos Eius Induam Confusione   As for his enemies, I shall clothe them in shame (Sardinia, England, Edward VI).

Insignia Capituli Brixensis   The badge of the chapter of Brixen (Brixen).

Isti Sunt Patres Tui Verique Pastores   These are your fathers and true shepherds (Papacy).

Iudicium Melius Posteritatis Erit   Posterity's judgment will be better (Paderborn).

Iure et Tempore   By right and time (Groningen).

Iusques a Sa Plenitude   As far as your plenitude (France, Henri II).

Iuste et Constanter   Justly and constantly (Paderborn).

Iustirt   Adjusted (Hesse-Cassel).

Iustitia et Concordia   Justice and harmony (Zurich).

Iustitia et Mansuetudine   By justice and mildness (Bavaria, Cologne).

Iustitia Regnorum Fundamentum   Justice is the foundation of kingdoms (Austria).

Iustitia Thronum Firmat   Justice strengthens the throne (England, Charles I).

Iustus Non Derelinquitur   The just person is not deserted (Brandenburg-Calenberg).

Iustus Ut Palma Florebit   The just will flourish like the palm (Portugal).

L Mun Planco Rauracorum Illustratori Vetustis-simo   To L Municius Plancus the most ancient and celebrated of the Rauraci (Basle).

Landgr in Cleggov Com in Sulz Dux Crum   Landgrave of Klettgau, count of Sulz, duke of Krumlau (Schwarzburg-Sondershausen).

Latina Emeri Munita   Latin money of Merida (Suevi).

Lege et Fide   By law and faith (Austria).

Lex Tua Veritas   Thy law is the truth (Tuscany).

Liberta Eguaglianza   Freedom and equality (Venice).

Libertad en la Ley   Freedom within the law (Mexico).

Libertas Carior Auro   Freedom is dearer than gold (St Gall).

Libertas Vita Carior   Freedom is dearer than life (Kulenberg).

Libertas Xpo Firmata   Freedom strengthened by Christ (Genoa).

Liberte, Egalite, Fraternite   Liberty, equality, fraternity (France).

Lucerna Pedibus Meis Verbum Est   Thy word is a lamp unto mine feet (England, Edward VI).

Lumen ad Revelationem Gentium   Light to enlighten the nations (Papacy).

L'Union Fait la Force   The union makes strength (Belgium).

Macula Non Est in Te   There is no sin in Thee (Essen).

Magnus ab Integro Saeculorum Nascitur Ordo   The great order of the centuries is born anew (Bavaria).

Mandavit Dominus Palatie hanc Monetam Fiert   The lord of the Palatine ordained this coin to be made (Balath).

Manibus Ne Laedar Avaris   Lest I be injured by greedy hands (Sweden).

Mar Bran Sac Rom Imp Arcam et Elec Sup Dux Siles   Margrave of Brandenburg, archchamberlain of the Holy Roman Empire and elector, senior duke of Silesia (Prussia).

Maria Mater Domini Xpi   Mary mother of Christ the Lord (Teutonic Knights).

Maria Unxit Pedes Xpisti   Mary washes the feet of Christ (France, Rene d'Anjou).

Mater Castrorum   Mother of fortresses (Rome, Marcus Aurelius).

Matrimonio Conjuncti   Joined wedlock (Austria).

Me Coniunctio Servat Dum Scinditur Frangor   The relationship serves me while I am being torn to pieces (Lowenstein-Wertheim).

Mediolani Dux   Duke of Milan (Milan).

Mediolani et Man   Duke of Mantua and Milan (Milan).

Memor Ero Tui Iustina Virgo   I shall remember you, o maiden Justina (Venice).

Merces Laborum   Wages of work (Wurzburg).

Mirabilia Fecit   He wrought marvels (Viking coinage).

Misericordia Di Rex   King by the mercy of God (France, Louis II).

Mo Arg Ord Foe Belg D Gel & CZ   Silver coin of the order of the Belgian Federation, duchy of Guelder-land, county of Zutphen (Guelderland).

Moneta Abbatis   Coin of the abbey (German ecclesiastical coins, 13th–14th centuries).

Moneta Argentiae Ord Foed Belgii Holl   Silver coin of the federated union of Belgium and Holland (Batavian Republic).

Mo No Arg Con Foe Belg Pro Hol   New silver coin of the Belgian Federation, province of Holland (Holland).

Mo No Arg Pro Confoe Belg Trai Holl   New silver coin of the confederated Belgian provinces, Utrecht and Holland (Batavian Republic).

Mon Lib Reip Bremens   Coin of the free state of Bremen (Bremen).

Mon Nova Arg Duc Curl Ad Norma Tal Alb   New silver coin of the duchy of Courland, according to the standard of the Albert thaler (Courland).

Mon Nov Castri Imp   New coin of the Imperial free city of . . . (Friedberg).

Moneta Bipont   Coin of Zweibrucken (Pfalz-Birkenfeld-Zweibrucken).

Monet Capit Cathedr Fuld Sede Vacante   Coin of the cathedral chapter of Fulda, the see being vacant (Fulda).

Moneta in Obsidione Tornacensi Cusa   Coin struck during the siege of Tournai (Tournai, 1709).

Moneta Livosesthonica   Coin of Livonia (Estonia).

Moneta Nov Arg Regis Daniae   New silver coin of the king of Denmark (Denmark).

Moneta Nova Ad Norman Conventionis   New coin according to the Convention standard (Orsini-Rosenberg).

Moneta Nova Domini Imperatoris   New coin of the lord emperor (Brunswick, 13th century).

Moneta Nova Lubecensis   New coin of Lubeck.

Moneta Nova Reipublicae Halae Suevicae   New coin of the republic of Hall in Swabia.

Moneta Reipublicae Ratisbonensis   Coin of the republic of Regensburg.

Nach Alt Reichs Schrot und Korn   According to the old empire's grits and grain (Hesse).

Nach dem Conventions Fusse   According to the Convention's basis (German Conventionsthalers).

Nach dem Frankf Schlus   According to the Frankfurt standard (Solms).

Nach dem Schlus der V Staend   According to the standard of the union (Hesse).

Navigare Necesse Est   It is necessary to navigate (Germany).

Nec Aspera Terrent   Nor do difficulties terrify (Brunswick).

Nec Cito Nec Temere   Neither hastily nor rashly (Cambrai).

Nec Numina Desunt   Nor is the divine will absent (Savoy).

Nec Temere Nec Timide   Neither rashly nor timidly (Danzig, Lippe).

Necessitas Legem Non Habet   Necessity has no law (Magdeburg).

Nemo Me Impune Lacessit   No one touches me with impunity (UK, Scottish pound edge inscription).

Nihil Restat Reliqui   No relic remains (Ypres).

Nil Ultra Aras   Nothing beyond the rocks (Franque-mont).

No Nobis Dne Sed Noi Tuo Da Gloriam   Not to us, o Lord but to Thy name be glory given (France, Francis I).

Nobilissimum Dom Ac Com in Lipp & St   Most noble lord and count in Lippe and Sternberg (Schaumburg-Lippe).

Nomen Domini Turris Fortissima   The name of the Lord is the strongest tower (Frankfurt).

Non Aes Sed Fides   Not bronze but trust (Malta).

Non Est Mortale Quod Opto   What I desire is not mortal. (Mecklenburg).

Non Mihi Sed Populo   Not to me but to the people (Bavaria).

Non Relinquam Vos Orphanos   I shall not leave you as orphans (Papacy).

Non Surrexit Major   None greater has arisen (Genoa, Malta).

Nullum Simulatum Diuturnum Tandem   Nothing that is feigned lasts long (Wittgenstein).

Nummorum Famulus   The servant of the coinage (England, tin halfpence and farthings).

Nunquam Retrorsum   Never backwards (Brunswick-Wolfenbuttel).

O Crux Ave Spes Unica   Hail, o Cross, our only hope (England half-angels, France, Rene d'Anjou).

O Maria Ora Pro Me   O Mary pray for me (Bavaria).

Ob Cives Servatos   On account of the rescued citizens (Rome, Augustus).

Oculi Domini Super Iustos   The eyes of the Lord look down on the just (Neuchatel).

Omnia Auxiliante Maria   Mary helping everything (Schwyz).

Omnia Cum Deo   Everything with God (Reuss-Greiz).

Omnia cum Deo et Nihil Sine Eo   Everthing with God and nothing without Him (Erbach).

Omnis Potestas a Deo Est   All power comes from God (Sweden).

Opp & Carn Dux Comm Rittb SCM Cons Int & Compi Mareschal   Duke of Troppau and Carniola, count of Rietberg, privy councillor of his sacred imperial majesty, field marshal (Liechtenstein).

Opp & Carn . . . Aur Velleris Eques   Duke of Troppau . . . knight of the Golden Fleece (Liechtenstein).

Opportune   Conveniently (Savoy).

Optimus Princeps   Best prince (Rome, Trajan).

Opulentia Salerno   Wealthy Salerno (Siculo-Norman kingdom).

Pace et Iustitia   With peace and justice (Spanish Netherlands).

Pacator Orbis   Pacifier of the world (Rome, Aurelian).

Palma Sub Pondere Crescit   The palm grows under its weight (Waldeck).

Pater Noster   Our Father (Flanders, 14th century).

Pater Patriae   Farther of his country (Rome, Caligula).

Patria Si Dreptul Meu   The country and my right (Roumania).

Patrimon Henr Frid Sorte Divisum   The heritage of Heinrich Friedrich divided by lot (Hohenlohe-Langenberg).

Patrimonia Beati Petri   The inheritance of the blessed Peter (Papacy).

Patrona Franconiae   Patron Franconia (Wurzburg).

Pax Aeterna   Eternal peace (Rome, Marcus Aurelius).

Pax et Abundantia   Peace and plenty (Burgundy, Gelderland).

Pax Missa Per Orbem   Peace sent throughout the world (England, Anne).

Pax Petrus   Peace Peter (Trier, 10th century).

Pax Praevalet Armis   May peace prevail by force of arms (Mainz).

Pax Quaeritur Bello   Peace is sought by war (Commonwealth, Cromwell).

Pecunia Totum Circumit Orbem   Money goes round the whole world (Brazil).

Per Aspera Ad Astra   Through difficulties to the stars (Mecklenburg-Schwerin).

Per Angusta ad Augusta   Through precarious times to the majestic (Solms-Roedelheim, a pun on the name of the ruler Johan August).

Per Crucem Tuam Salva Nos Christe Redemptor   By Thy cross save us, O Christ our Redeemer (England, angels).

Per Crucem Tuam Salva Nos Xpe Redemt   By Thy cross save us, O Christ our Redeemer (Portugal, 15th century).

Perdam Babillonis Nomen   May the name of Babylon perish (Naples).

Perennitati Iustissimi Regis   For the duration of the most just king (France, Louis XIII).

Perennitati Principis Galliae Restitutionis   For the duration of the restoration of the prince of the Gauls (France, Henri IV).

Perfer et Obdura Bruxella   Carry on and stick it out, Brussels (Brussels siege, 1579–80).

Perpetuus in Nemet Vivar   Hereditary count in Nemt-Ujvar (Batthanyi).

Pietate et Constantia   By piety and constancy (Fulda).

Pietate et Iustitia   By piety and justice (Denmark).

Plebei Urbanae Frumento Constituto   Free distribu-tion of grain to the urban working-class established (Rome, Nerva).

Pleidio Wyf Im Gwlad   True am I to my country (UK, Welsh pound edge inscription).

Plus Ultra   Beyond (the Pillars of Hercules) (Spanish America).

Point du Couronne sans Peine   Point of the crown without penalty (Coburg).

Pons Civit Castellana   The bridge of the town of Castellana (Papacy).

Populus et Senatus Bonon   The people and senate of Bologna (Bologna).

Post Mortem Patris Pro Filio   For the son after his father's death (Pontefract siege coins).

Post Tenebras Lux   After darkness light (Geneva).

Post Tenebras Spero Lucem   After darkness I hope for light (Geneva).

Posui Deum Adiutorem Meum   I have made God my helper (England, Ireland, 1351–1603).

Praesidium et Decus   Protection and ornament (Bologna).

Prima Sedes Galliarum   First see of the Gauls (Lyon).

Primitiae Fodin Kuttenb ab Aerari Iterum Susceptarum   First results dug from the Kuttenberg mines in a renewed undertaking (Austria).

Princps Iuventutis   Prince of youth (Roman Empire).

Pro Defensione Urbis et Patriae   For the defence of city and country (France, Louis XIV).

Pro Deo et Patria   For God and the fatherland (Fulda).

Pro Deo et Populo   For God and the people (Bavaria).

Pro Ecclesia et Pro Patria   For the church and the fatherland (Constance).

Pro Fausio PP Reitur VS   For happy returns of the princes of the Two Sicilies (Naples and Sicily).

Pro Lege et Grege   For law and the flock (Fulda).

Pro maximo Dei Gloria et Bono Publico   For the greatest glory of God and the good of the people (Wurttemberg).

Pro Patria   For the fatherland (Wurzburg).

Propitio Deo Secura Ago   With God's favour I lead a secure life. (Saxe-Lauenburg).

Protector Literis Literae Nummis Corona et Salus   A protection to the letters (on the face of the coin), the letters (on the edge) are a garland and a safeguard to the coinage (Commonwealth, Cromwell broad).

Protege Virgo Pisas   Protect Pisa, O Virgin (Pisa).

Provide et Constanter   Wisely and firmly (Wurttem-berg).

Providentia et Pactis   Through foresight and pacts (Brandenburg-Ansbach).

Providentia Optimi Principis   With the foresight of the best prince (Naples and Sicily).

Proxima Fisica Finis   Nearest to natural end (Orciano).

Proxima Soli   Nearest to the sun (Modena).

Pulcra Virtutis Imago   The beautiful image of virtue (Genoa).

Pupillum et Viduam Suscipiat   May he support the orphan and the widow (Savoy).

Quae Deus Conjunxit Nemo Separet   What God hath joined let no man put asunder (England, James I).

Quem Quadragesies et Semel Patriae Natum Esse Gratulamur   Whom we congratulate for the forty-first time for being born for the fatherland (Lippe-Detmold).

Qui Dat Pauperi Non Indigebit   Who gives to the poor will never be in need (Munster).

Quid Non Cogit Necessitas   To what does Necessity not drive. (Ypres).

Quin Matrimonii Lustrum Celebrant   They celebrate their silver wedding (Austria, 1879).

Quocunque Gesseris (Jeceris) Stabit   Whichever way you throw it it will stand (Isle of Man).

Quod Deus Vult Hoc Semper Fit   What God wishes always occurs. (Saxe-Weimar).

Reconduntur non Retonduntur   They are laid up in store, not thundered back (Savoy).

Recta Tueri   Defend the right (Austria).

Recte Constanter et Fortiter   Rightly, constantly and bravely (Bavaria).

Recte Faciendo Neminem Timeas   May you fear no one in doing right. (Solms-Laubach).

Rector Orbis   Ruler of the world (Rome, Didius Julianus).

Rectus et Immotus   Right and immovable (Hesse).

Redde Cuique Quod Suum Est   Render to each that which is his own (England, Henry VIII).

Redeunt antiqui Gaudia Moris   There return the joys of ancient custom (Regensburg).

Reg Pr Pol et Lith Saxon Dux   Royal prince of Poland and Lithuania and duke of Saxony (Trier).

Regia Boruss Societas Asiat Embdae   Royal Prussian Asiatic Society of Emden (Prussia).

Regier Mich Her Nach Deinen Wort   Govern me here according to Thy word (Palatinate).

Regnans Capitulum Ecclesiae Cathedralis Ratisbonensis Sede Vacante   Administering the chapter of the cathedral church at Regensburg, the see being vacant (Regensburg).

Regni Utr Sic et Hier   Of the kingdom of the Two Sicilies and of Jerusalem (Naples and Sicily).

Religio Protestantium Leges Angliae Libertas Parliamenti   The religion of the Protestants, the laws of England and the freedom of Parliament (England, Royalists, 1642).

Relinquo Vos Liberos ab Utroque Homine   I leave you as children of each man (San Marino).

Restauracao da Independencia   Restoration of inde-pendence (Portugal, 1990).

Restitutor Exercitus   Restorer of the army (Rome, Aurelian).

Restitutor Galliarum   Restorer of the Gauls (Rome, Gallienus).

Restitutor Generis Humani   Restorer of mankind (Rome, Valerian).

Restitutor Libertatis   Restorer of freedom (Rome, Constantine).

Restitutor Orbis   Restorer of the world (Rome, Valerian).

Restitutor Orientis   Restorer of the east (Rome).

Restitutor Saeculi   Restorer of the century (Rome, Valerian).

Restitutor Urbis   Restorer of the city (Rome, Severus).

Rosa Americana Utile Dulci   The American rose, useful and sweet (American colonies).

Rosa Sine Spina   A rose without a thorn (England, Tudor coins).

Rutilans Rosa Sine Spina   A dazzling rose without a thorn (England, Tudor gold coins).

S Annae Fundgruben Ausb Tha in N Oe   Mining thaler of the St Anne mine in Lower Austria (Austria).

S Ap S Leg Nat Germ Primas   Legate of the Holy Apostolic See, born Primate of Germany (Salzburg).

S Carolus Magnus Fundator   Charlemagne founder (Munster).

S. Gertrudis Virgo Prudens Niviella   St Gertrude the wise virgin of Nivelles (Nivelles).

Sl Aul Reg Her & P Ge H Post Mag   General hereditary postmaster, supreme of the imperial court of the hereditary kingdom and provinces (Paar).

S. Ian Bapt F. Zachari   St John the Baptist, son of Zachary (Florence).

S. Kilianus Cum Sociis Francorum Apostoli   St Kilian and his companions, apostles to the Franks (Wurzburg).

S. Lambertus Patronus Leodiensis   St Lambert, patron of Liege (Liege).

Sac Nupt Celeb Berol   For the holy matrimony celebrated at Berlin (Brandenburg-Ansbach).

Sac Rom Imp   Holy Roman Empire (German states).

Sac Rom Imp Provisor Iterum   Administrator of the Holy Roman Empire for the second time (Saxony).

Salus Generis Humani   Safety of mankind (Rome, Vindex).

Salus Patriae   Safety of the fatherland (Italy).

Salus Populi   The safety of the people (Spain).

Salus Provinciarum   Safety of the provinces (Rome, Postumus).

Salus Publica Salus Mea   Public safety is my safety (Sweden).

Salus Reipublicae   The safety of the republic (Rome, Theodosius II).

Salus Reipublicae Suprema Lex   The safety of the republic is the supreme law (Poland).

Salvam Fac Rempublicam Tuam   Make your state safe (San Marino).

Sanctus Iohannes Innoce   St John the harmless (Gandersheim).

Sans Changer   Without changing (Isle of Man).

Sans Eclat   Without pomp (Bouchain siege, 1711).

Sapiente Diffidentia   Wise distrust (Teschen).

Scutum Fidei Proteget Eum / Eam   The shield of faith shall protect him / her (England, Edward VI and Elizabeth I).

Secundum Voluntatem Tuam Domine   Your favourable will o Lord (Hesse).

Securitati Publicae   For the public safety (Brandenburg-Ansbach).

Sede Vacante   The see being vacant (Papal states, Vatican and ecclesiastical coinage).

Sena Vetus Alpha et W Principum et Finis   Old Siena alpha and omega, the beginning and the end (Siena).

Senatus Populus QR   Senate and people of Rome (Rome, 1188).

Si Deus Nobiscum Quis Contra Nos   If God is with us who can oppose us (Hesse).

Si Deus Pro Nobis Quis Contra Nos   If God is for us who can oppose us (Roemhild).

Sieh Deine Seeligkeit Steht Fest Ins Vaters Liebe   Behold thy salvation stands surely in thy Father's love (Gotha).

Signis Receptis   When the standards had been recovered (Rome, Augustus).

Signum Crucis   The sign of the cross (Groningen).

Sincere et Constanter   Truthfully and steadfastly (Hesse-Darmstadt).

Sit Nomen Domini Benedictum   Blessed be the name of the Lord (Burgundy, Strasbourg).

St T X Adiuto Reg Iste Domba   Let it be to you, o Christ, the assistant to the king of Dombes (Dombes).

Sit Tibi Xpe Dat q'tu Regis Iste Ducat   May this duchy which Thou rulest be given to Thee, O Christ (Venice, ducat).

Sit Unio Haec Perennis   May this union last for ever (Hohenlohe-Langenberg).

Sola Bona Quae Honesta   The only good things are those which are honest (Brunswick).

Sola Facta Deum Sequor   Through deeds alone I strive to follow God (Milan).

Soli Deo Honor et Gloria   To God alone be honour and glory (Nassau).

Soli Reduci   To him, the only one restored (Naples and Sicily).

Solius Virtutis Flos Perpetuus   The flower of Virtue alone is perpetual (Strasbourg).

Spes Confisa Deo Nunquam Confusa Recedit   Hope entrusted in God never retreats in a disorderly fashion (Lippe).

Spes Nr Deus   God is our hope (Oudenarde siege, 1582).

Spes Rei Publicae   The hope of the republic (Rome, Valens).

Strena ex Argyrocopeo Vallis S Christoph   A New Year's gift from the silver-bearing valley of St Christopher (Wurttemberg, 1625).

Sub His Secura Spes Clupeus Omnibus in Te Sperantibus   Under these hope is safe, a shield for all who reside hope in Thee (Bavaria).

Sub Pondere   Under weight (Fulda).

Sub Protectione Caesarea   Under imperial protection (Soragna).

Sub Tuum Praesidium Confug   We flee to Thy protection (Salzburg).

Sub Umbra Alarum Tuarum   Under the shadow of Thy wings (Iever, Scotland, James V).

Subditorum Salus Felicitas Summa   The safety of the subjects is the highest happiness (Lubeck).

Sufficit Mihi Gratia Tua Domine   Sufficient to me is Thy grace, o Lord (Ploen).

Supra Firmam Petram   Upon a firm rock (Papacy).

Susceptor Noster Deus   God is our defence (Tuscany).

Sydera Favent Industriae   The stars favour industry (Furstenberg).

Sylvarum Culturae Praemium   Prize for the culture of the forest (Brandenburg-Ansbach).

Tali Dicata Signo Mens Fluctuari Nequit   Consecrated by such a sign the mind cannot waver (England, Henry VIII George noble).

Tandem Bona Caus Triumphat   A good cause eventually triumphs (Dillenburg).

Tandem Fortuna Obstetrice   With good luck ultimately as the midwife (Wittgenstein).

Te Stante Virebo   With you at my side I shall be strong (Moravia).

Tene Mensuram et Respice Finem   Hold the measure and look to the end (Burgundy).

Tert Ducat Secular   Tercentenary of the duchy (Wurttemberg).

Thu Recht Schev Niemand   Go with right and fear no one (Saxe-Lauenburg).

Tibi Laus et Gloria   To Thee be praise and glory (Venice).

Timor Domini Fons Vitae   The fear of the Lord is a fountain of life (England, Edward VI shillings).

Tout Avec Dieu   Everything with God (Brunswick, 1626).

Traiectum ad Mosam   The crossing of the Maas (Maastricht).

Transvolat Nubila Virtus   Marriageable virtue soon flies past (Grueyeres).

Travail, Famille, Patrie   Work, family, country (Vichy France).

Triumphator Gent Barb   Victor over the barbarian people (Byzantine Empire, Arcadius).

Tueatur Unita Deus   May God guard these united (Kingdoms) (England, James I; Britain, 1847).

Turck Blegert Wien   Vienna besieged by the Turks (Vienna, 1531).

Tut Mar Gab Pr Vid de Lobk Nat Pr Sab Car et Aug Pr de Lobk   Regency of Maria Gabriela, widow of the prince of Lobkowitz, born princess of Savoy-Carignan, and August prince of Lobkowitz (Lobkowitz).

Tutela Italiae   The guardianship of Italy (Rome, Nerva).

Ubi Vult Spirat   He breathes where he will (Papacy).

Ubique Pax   Peace everywhere (Rome, Gallienus).

Union et Force   Union and strength (France).

Urbe Obsessa   The city under siege (Maastricht).

Urbem Virgo Tuam Serva   Protects thy city o virgin (Mary) (Strasbourg).

USC & RAM Cons Int Gen C Mar & Nob Praet H Turmae Capit   Privy councillor of both their holy imperial and royal apostolic majesties, general field marshal and captain of the noble praetorian Hungarian squadrons (Eszterhazy).

Veni Luumen Cordium   Come light of hearts (Vatican).

Veni Sancte Spiritus   Come Holy Ghost (Vatican).

Verbum Domini Manet in Aeternum   The word of the Lord abides forever (Hesse-Darmstadt, Veldenz).

Veritas Lex Tua   The truth is your law (Salzburg).

Veritas Temporis Filia   Truth is the daughter of time (England and Ireland, Mary Tudor).

Veritate et Labore   By truth and work (Wittgenstein).

Veritate et Iustitia By truth and justice (German states).
Victoria Principum The victory of princes (Ostrogoths).
Videant Pauperes et Laetentur Let the poor see and rejoice (Tuscany).
Virgo Maria Protege Civitatem Savonae Virgin Mary Protect the city of Savona (Savona).
Viribus Unitis With united strength (Austria).
Virtute et Fidelitate By virtue and faithfulness (Hesse-Cassel).
Virtute et Prudentia With virtue and prudence (Auersperg).
Virtute Viam Dimetiar I shall mark the way with valour (Waldeck).
Virtutis Gloria Merces Glory is the reward of valour (Holstein-Gottorp).
Vis Unita Concordia Fratrum Fortior United power is the stronger harmony of brothers (Mansfeld).
Visitavit Nos Oriens ex Alto He has visited us arising on high (Luneburg).
Vivit Post Funera He lives after death (Bremen).

Vota Optata Romae Fel Vows taken for the luck of Rome (Rome, Maxentius).
Vox de Throno A voice from the throne (Papacy).
Was Got Beschert Bleibet Unerwert What God hath endowed leave undisturbed
Wider macht und List Mein Fels Gott Ist Against might and trickery God is my rock (Hesse-Cassel).
Xpc Vincit Xpc Regnat Christ conquers, Christ reigns (Scotland, Spain).
Xpc Vivet Xpc Regnat Xpc Impat Christ lives, Christ reigns, Christ commands (Cambrai).
Xpe Resurescit Christ lives again (Venice).
Xpistiana Religio Christian religion (Carolingian Empire).
Xps Ihs Elegit me Regem Populo Jesus Christ chose me as king to the people (Norway).
Zelator Fidei Usque ad Montem An upholder of the faith through and through (Portugal).
Zum Besten des Vaterlands To the best of the fatherland (Bamberg).

ABBREVIATIONS COMMONLY USED TO DENOTE METALLIC COMPOSITION	
Cu	Copper
Cu/Steel	Copper plated Steel
Ag/Cu	Silver plated copper
Ae	Bronze
Cu-Ni	Cupro-Nickel
Ni-Ag	Nickel Silver (note-does not contain silver)
Brass/Cu-Ni	Brass outer, Cupro-Nickel inner
Ni-Brass	Nickel-Brass
Ag	Silver
Au/Ag	Gold plated silver
Au	Gold
Pl	Platinum

CARE *of coins*

There is no point in going to a great deal of trouble and expense in selecting the best coins you can afford, only to let them deteriorate in value by neglect and mishandling. Unless you give some thought to the proper care of your coins, your collection is unlikely to make a profit for you if and when you come to sell it. Housing your coins is the biggest problem of all, so it is important to give a lot of attention to this.

Storage

The ideal, but admittedly the most expensive, method is the coin cabinet, constructed of air-dried mahogany, walnut or rosewood *(never oak, cedar or any highly resinous timber likely to cause chemical tarnish)*. These cabinets have banks of shallow drawers containing trays made of the same wood, with half-drilled holes of various sizes to accommodate the different denominations of coins. Such cabinets are handsome pieces of furniture but, being largely handmade, tend to be rather expensive. Occasionally good specimens can be picked up in secondhand furniture shops, or at the dispersal of house contents by auction, but the best bet is still to purchase a new cabinet, tailored to your own requirements. These collectors cabinets are hand-made using certified solid mahogany, as specified by leading museums, as mahogany does not contain any chemicals or resins that could result in the discolouration of the collection inside the cabinet. The polish used on the outside of the cabinets is based on natural oils and hand applied then finished with bees wax. The trays are left as untreated mahogany so as not to introduce any harmful contaminants. The coin trays are available as single thickness or double thickness for holding thicker coins, capsules or artifacts.

Peter Nichols Cabinets (telephone 0115 9224149, www.coincabinets.com) was established in 1967 and is now run by Geoff Skinner, Shirley Watts and Ben Skinner-Watts. Based in Nottingham, the family run business provides specialist and bespoke display and storage systems to suit every need from standard cabinets for the average collector all the way up to the massive 40-tray specials supplied to the British Museum. There are other makers of quality wooden coin cabinets such as **Rob Davis** of Ticknall, Derbyshire, who also provide a first-class bespoke product as well as a standard off-the-shelf range. All of these manufacturers use materials from sustainable sources and their products are exquisite examples of the cabinet maker's craft.

An excellent storage option is provided by a number of firms who manufacture coin trays in durable, felt-lined, man-made materials with shallow compartments to suit the various sizes of coins. Most of these trays interlock so that they build up into a cabinet of the desired size, and there are also versions designed as carrying cases, which are ideal for transporting coins.

The Mascle Classic from Peter Nichols Cabinets —the ideal "entry-level" coin cabinet for collectors and just one of an extensive range of hand-made pieces.

The popular and extensive **Lighthouse** range is available from The Duncannon Partnership, 4 Beaufort Road, Reigate, RH2 9DJ (telephone 01737 244222, www.duncannon.co.uk) or Token Publishing Ltd (telephone 01404 46972, www.tokenpublishing.com). This range includes a wide variety of cases and albums for the general collector in basic or de luxe styles as required, as well as printed albums for the specialist. Their cases, including the popular aluminium range, are manufactured to the highest standards, lined with blue plush which displays any coin to its best advantage. The red-lined single trays come in deep or standard size and make an ideal cabinet when stacked together or housed in their attractive aluminium case, which is available separately.

Adding on to the stacking Lindner range is easy.

The trays themselves come with a variety of compartments for every size of coin. Their complete range can be viewed on-line.

The extensive **Lindner** range is supplied in the UK by Prinz Publications of 3A Hayle Industrial Park, Hayle, Cornwall TR27 5JR (telephone 01736 751914, www.prinz.co.uk) or from Token Publishing Ltd (telephone 01404 46972, www.tokenpublishing.com). Well-known for their wide range of philatelic and numismatic accessories, but these include a full array of coin boxes, capsules, carrying cases and trays. The basic Lindner coin box is, in fact, a shallow tray available in a standard version or a smoked glass version. These trays have a crystal clear frame, red felt inserts and holes for various diameters of coins and medals. A novel feature of these trays is the rounded insert which facilitates the removal of coins from their spaces with the minimum of handling. These boxes are designed in such a manner that they interlock and can be built up into banks of trays, each fitted with a draw-handle and sliding in and out easily. Various types of chemically inert plastic capsules and envelopes have been designed for use in combination with plain shallow trays, without holes drilled. Lindner also manufacture a range of luxury cases lined in velvet and Atlas silk with padded covers and gold embossing on the spines, producing a most tasteful and elegant appearance.

Safe Albums of 16 Falcon Business Park, 38 Ivanhoe Road, Finchampstead, Berkshire RG40 4QQ (telephone 0118 932 8976, www.safealbums.co.uk) are the UK agents for the German Stapel-Element, a drawer-stacking system with clear plasticiser-free trays that fit into standard bookshelves. The sliding coin compartments, lined with blue velvet, can be angled for display to best advantage. Stackable drawers can be built up to any height desired. A wide range of drawer sizes is available, with compartments suitable for the smallest coins right up to four-compartment trays designed for very large artefacts such as card-cases or cigarette cases. The Mobel-Element cabinet is a superb specialised cabinet constructed of the finest timber with a steel frame and steel grip bars which can be securely locked.

There are also various other storage systems, such as the simple cardboard or plastic box which is made specifically to hold coins stored in see-through envelopes of chemically-inert plastic of various sizes, or white acid-free envelopes, usually 50mm square.

An alternative to these is the card coin holder which has a window made of inert cellophane-type see-through material. The card is folded over with the coin inside and is then stapled or stuck together with its own self-adhesive lining. The cards are a standard 50mm square with windows of various sizes from 15 to 39mm and fit neatly into the storage box or album page.

Coin Albums

When coin collecting became a popular hobby in the 1960s, several firms marketed ranges of coin albums. They had clear plastic sleeves divided into tiny compartments of various sizes and had the merit of being cheap and taking up little room on a bookshelf.

They had several drawbacks, however, not the least being the tendency of the pages to sag with the weight of the coins, or even, in extreme cases, to pull away from the pegs or rings holding them on to the spine. They required very careful handling as the coins could easily fall out of the top row as the pages were turned. The more expensive albums had little flaps that folded over the top of the coin to overcome this problem.

Arguably the worst aspect of these albums was the use of polyvinyl chloride (PVC) in the construction of the sleeves. Collectors soon discovered to their horror that this reacted chemically with their coins, especially those made of silver and many fine collections were ruined as a result.

Fortunately the lesson has been learned and the coin albums now on the market are quite safe. Lighthouse and Lindner offer a wide range of albums designed to house coins, medals or banknotes. The old problem about sagging pages is overcome by the use of a multi-ring binding welded to a very stout spine, while the sleeves contain neither Styrol nor PVC and will not affect any metals at all. In addition to pages with pockets of uniform size, the Karat range of albums operates on a slide principle which enables the user to insert vertical strips of different sizes on the same page, so that the coins of one country or series, or perhaps a thematic display of coins from different countries, can be displayed side by side.

Safe Albums offer a wide range of albums in the Coinholder System and Coin-Combi ranges. These, too, offer the choice of fixed pages with uniform-sized pockets, or interchangeable sliding inserts for different sizes side by side.

The "slab"

In the United States in the past few decades one of the preferred methods for keeping coins in pristine condition is the use of "slabs"—these tough plastic rectangles cannot be easily broken into, meaning that the coin inside remains in exactly the same condition as when it was placed in there. This has led to the rise of professional grading and encapsulation companies who not only "slab" your coin but also grade it and guarantee that grade. This allows coins to be bought and sold with both vendor and purchaser knowing exactly what the grade is, thus taking out the subjectivity of dealer or collector—an issue that can mean a huge difference in the value of the coin. Slabbing in this way is essentially a tool to help a coin maintain a grade and thus more easily guarantee its value, however, many collectors prefer it as a method of protecting their coins as it allows them to be stored or transported easily with no fear of damage.

The biggest companies in the United States for the encapsulation of coins are **PCGS** (Professional Coin Grading Service) and **NGC** (Numismatic Gauaranty Corporation). They have been in business for some years and in America the "slabbed" coin is a common sight. It is less common in the UK, with many collectors still unsure about the benefits of the "slab", but undoubtedly with the US companies opening offices and grading centres throughout the world more and more collectors are using the service and the "slab" is becoming accepted everywhere. However, anyone wishing to photograph a coin undoubtedly has a problem, as

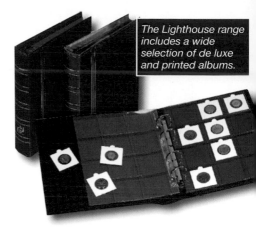

The Lighthouse range includes a wide selection of de luxe and printed albums.

can be seen in many auction catalogues offering such items. The tell-tale grips that hold the coin obscure part of the edge of the coin.

Token Publishing Ltd stock a varied range of coin accessories from magnifying glasses to coin albums. To find out more, log onto www.tokenpublishing.com or call 01404 446972 for an up-to-date illustrated, colour catalogue.

CLEANING *coins*

This is like matrimony—it should not be embarked on lightly. Indeed, the advice given by the magazine *Punch* in regard to marriage is equally sound in this case—don't do it! It is far better to have a dirty coin than an irretrievably damaged one. Every dealer has horror stories of handling coins that previous owners have cleaned, to their detriment. Probably the worst example was a display of coins found by a metal detectorist who "improved" his finds by abrading them in the kind of rotary drum used by lapidarists to polish gemstones. If you really must remove the dirt and grease from coins, it is advisable to practise on coins of little value.

Warm water containing a mild household detergent or washing-up liquid will work wonders in removing surface dirt and grease from most coins, but silver is best washed in a weak solution of ammonia and warm water—one part ammonia to ten parts water. Gold coins can be cleaned with diluted citric acid, such as lemon juice. Copper or bronze coins present more of a problem, but patches of verdigris can usually be removed by careful washing in a 20 per cent solution of sodium sesquicarbonate. Wartime coins made of tin, zinc, iron or steel can be cleaned in a 5 per cent solution of caustic soda containing some aluminium or zinc foil or filings, but they must be rinsed afterwards in clean water and carefully dried. Cotton buds are ideal for gently prising dirt out of coin legends and crevices in the designs. Soft brushes (with animal bristles—*never* nylon or other artificial bristles) designed for cleaning silver are most suitable for gently cleaning coins.

Coins recovered from the soil or the sea bed present special problems, due to chemical reaction between the metals and the salts in the earth or sea water. In such cases, the best advice is to take them to the nearest museum and let the professional experts decide on what can or should be done.

There are a number of proprietary coin-cleaning kits and materials on the market suitable for gold, silver, copper and other metals but all of these should be used with caution and always read the instructions that come with them. When using any type of chemical cleaner rubber gloves should be worn and care taken to avoid breathing fumes or getting splashes of liquid in your eyes or on your skin. Obviously, the whole business of cleaning is a matter that should not be entered into without the utmost care and forethought.

POLISHING: A WARNING

If cleaning should only be approached with the greatest trepidation, polishing is definitely OUT! Beginners sometimes fall into the appalling error of thinking that a smart rub with metal polish might improve the appearance of their coins. Short of actually punching a hole through it, there can hardly be a more destructive act. Polishing a coin may improve its superficial appearance for a few days, but such abrasive action will destroy the patina and reduce the fineness of the high points of the surface.

Even if a coin is only polished once, it will never be quite the same again, and an expert can tell this a mile off.

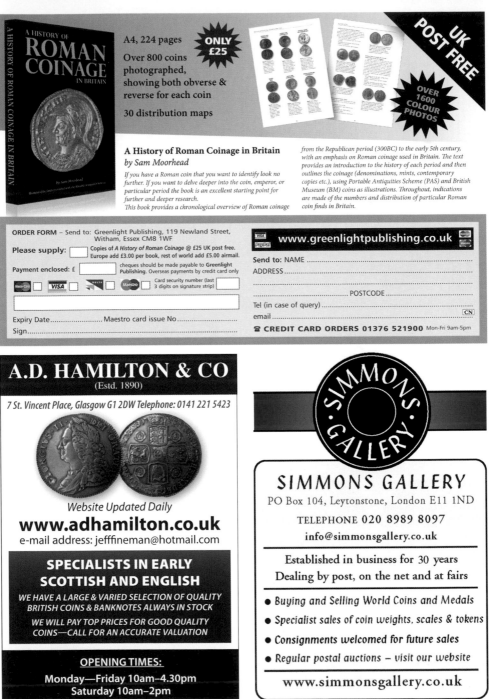

DISPELLING
some numismatic myths...

In this enlightening article MARK T. RAY of Collectors World, Nottingham shares some personal observations on running a collector's shop

Having been a dealer for 25+ years and a lifelong collector, one comes across the same niggling questions and misconceptions that annoy or frustrate, and mount up over the years, and perhaps I now need to redress the balance from my somewhat blinkered view of non collectors and the uninitiated. What am I trying to say? That a large section of the general public cannot understand the mentality of a collector, and those that do have some collecting interest fall into the same traps over and over again.

I have a retail shop and as most people's first port of call for advice (after the internet of course), I find myself imparting the same information again and again in response to a few simple questions, and having to correct many common misconceptions. So here are a few of my experiences, some of which you may have come across yourselves as you became interested in coins.

Firstly, not all crowns are £5 coins. Although modern UK £5 coins will always state a value of Five Pounds, prior to 1990 crowns were available at banks at their face value of 25 pence (five shillings pre-decimal). Confusion was inevitable as these earlier crown-size coins do not state a value and as it was all such a long time ago. One of the reasons the banks have stopped exchanging commemorative coins such as these is the easy confusion for bank staff and possible financial loss to the banks when

Two memorial crowns: Churchill (1965) and Princess Diana (1997). Both are crowns but the former was issued at 25p (5 shillings) whilst the other was issued at £5.

presented with a selection of crowns for cashing.

Secondly, a coin is not automatically valuable because you've had it a long time. . . . Considering the crowns again, it's hard for a layman to believe the Churchill crown he has kept for 50 years is still only worth 25p when they look the same as £5 crowns that cost £5 face value at least. Commemoratives like these were issued to be kept as souvenirs and mementos, not for spending or as investments. Issued in large numbers in base metal and always kept, they will be around in quantity without ever increasing in value, sorry to disappoint you! Age is not the important factor —take Roman coins for example, possibly a stray find dug up in the garden by Grandad. Yes it's a nice piece of history but surprisingly worth little as an average Constantine family AE3/4 in poor condition is not that unusual a find in mainland Britain—ask any seasoned metal detectorist" there are a lot of "grots" out there!

Thirdly, most collections we see are actually just accumulations. Over the years, a family's "shrapnel"—odd coins and unused holiday change—migrate together in a drawer, or a jar, added to almost without thought, until an event such as moving house or clearing out a relative's possessions means that we stumble across this long-forgotten treasure trove of goodies that might just be worth a fortune. These accumulations, put together by accident rather than design are what as a dealer we see every working day—very few lots brought to us have been purchased with the idea of forming a serious collection. Buying these mixed lots and sorting them makes us something of a metals dealer—scrapping bronze pennies by the ton (yes, literally), worn silver to the smelters, and repatriating foreign currency—with only the odd item being worthy of salvaging, placing in a coin packet with a price tag, and sitting in a tray awaiting the right collector.

Don't get me wrong, there are serious collections out there, lovingly put together with time, effort and money, and it is always a pleasure to see them. They have often been accumulated over a long period without specific regard to their future value or investment potential—and so much the better for that.

Next: Condition, condition, condition . . . An expert's view of condition is always going to be different to the layman's. What looks to be perfect on first sight rarely stands up to scrutiny. The conversation goes something like this: "Is it in perfect condition?" I ask. "Yes," comes the reply "I

> " . . . The conversation goes something like this: "Is it in perfect condition?" I ask. "Yes," comes the reply "I can see the head and read the lettering." I'm sorry but if it's been in the ground for years and years it's not likely to still be in collectable condition. And you didn't mention the hole! . . . "

can see the head and read the lettering." I'm sorry but if it's been in the ground for years and years it's not likely to still be in collectable condition. And you didn't mention the hole! Condition is all important. I would rather have a common coin in outstanding condition that a rare coin in poor condition.

Catalogues don't always help, sometimes only giving values in top grades rather than in all the grades that they turn up in. Modern coins priced only in "Unc" do not tell the average reader that they are only worth face value in circulated condition. Other coins that people regularly ask about are pennies with a letter H (for Heaton Mint) next to the date, and Victorian bun pennies (worn flat of course)—so many people put them to one side in the late 1960s when they were avidly collected, that they are no longer of any value. Then there are—let's be polite—less erudite callers, who expect me to value their coin when all they can tell me is that it's got a head on one

side and date on the other. They don't understand the meaning of the word denomination let alone how to describe it in detail. It's like me expecting a car dealer to value my car when all I tell him is that it's blue and goes well! Fortunately they are usually asking about the same few items — if it's 1977, it's a jubilee crown; 1797 will be a worn penny, Napoleon will be a French 10c of Napoleon III, etc., but almost always worth less than the cost of the telephone call. No wonder it is sometimes difficult to be polite and calm to everyone, especially when every other call starts "I've looked on the internet. . .", or "I've found this rare £2 coin . . .". AAARGH!

Of course there are rare and valuable coins, such as the recent chance find of a Queen Anne Vigo Five Guineas, detected hoards and salvaged treasure, but the reality is that the few coins the average person comes across are unlikely to be the exception to the rule that most coins were made in large quantities, with plenty surviving in circulated condition, with more than enough around to satisfy current collector demand.

I apologise for sounding somewhat negative, I like nothing more than making someone's day by telling them that they have a valuable coin. The old couple or young family who come in with a few odd coins saying they don't know what they are, and I can say they are sovereigns each worth £200 plus makes everyone smile. And it happens; surprisingly often I'm pleased to say.

Sometimes with collectors' items it is all hype and rumours circulate until taken as fact. The latest band-wagon merry-go-round was for the new polymer £5 note. All sorts of serial numbers were suddenly fetching hundreds if not thousands of pounds, most of which was not true of course, but it didn't stop the phones ringing constantly with eager sellers of standard notes. Having to explain why a note was or wasn't worth a premium became a real chore. What was noticeable was that I didn't have a single call from anyone wanting to buy said notes. Another gripe: all those items when sold online described as rare. It's the most overused word in the collector's vocabulary. But people believe it. Identical items listed online for sale one states rare and the other doesn't—which will fetch more? You tell me!

As for the internet (I could go on for hours), it is a brilliant help to the collector, but without a bit of background knowledge it is very easy to be misled and misinformed by the overwhelming amount of available information and conflicting detail. Usually the inaccurate attribution or valuation comes from not comparing like with like—yes, there is a version of your coin worth £1,000 but yours is only worth 10p because it's not the proof version, or it's a different date, or it's a different coin altogether! Your local coin dealer generally has years of experience to call on and has likely seen this before on many occasions so can offer a genuine appraisal without you having to understand all the subtle differences that can affect a coins value. It is true that you can almost always find a similar item for sale on an online auction site such as eBay, but even excepting the above reasons for misidentification it is very easy to take a buy-it-now price for a true value. Look at the sold prices not the hoped for and often unrealistic prices being asked. In short, take everything you read on the internet with a pinch of salt!

Next the old adage that there are no new collectors, no youngsters taking up the hobby, just the old generation gradually dying off. Well no, of course this is not true. There are always new collectors. When I was young decimalisation was the reason we all started collecting, then it was through metal detecting or BBC's "Time Team" that people gained an interest in history and coins. Then the silver and gold booms of the 1980s and again more recently, created new collectors. These days it is the marketing companies' direct selling, and the internet, that makes buying a simple sit-at-home and collect experience. And now the vast array of commemorative circulating designs that one can find in your pocket—over 100 different, with the 29 Olympic 50p designs responsible for literally thousands of new collectors, some of whom will without doubt progress to be serious numismatists of the future. Collecting this way has become fun and inexpensive again for the first time since pre-decimal coins were in standard circulation.

Collecting coins and notes has a bright future, helped partly by the Royal Mint who now actively pursue collectors with new editions and special versions in proof, silver and gold to augment the circulating currency, and ensure that no selling opportunity is missed. Of course, now every time someone finds a commemorative in their change that they have not seen before they believe it must be worth a small fortune and have to ring their local dealer—who unsurprisingly already has more than enough of them.

On the subject of new issues, it has to be said that the marketing companies are excellent at what they do, offering well produced items for the connoisseur or armchair-collector, but the second-hand value of the items is almost without exception going to be just a fraction of the initial cost, despite any claims that they are investments. Enjoy them for what they are, but do not expect to realise more than their intrinsic or face value when the time comes to sell, let alone get a return on your outlay. Remember that the issuer of a "Limited Edition" coin is not going to limit it to 500 if he knows he can sell 5,000. On the other hand, a limited edition of 50,000 for example may not be fully subscribed, and even less sought after once initial interest has waned. Beware the more unscrupulous advertisers who try to hide the issuing authority of a coin—a £5 coin for a fiver sounds a bargain but if it turns out it was issued under the authority of TDC for example—the tiny islands of Tristan Da Cunha in the South Atlantic —it's hardly a cashable item and any hint of face value is rather tenuous

Another worrying aspect of collecting that seems to be increasing year on year is the advent of modern copies of coins. In my shop I keep an album of copy coins—those intended to deceive the public in circulation, and others intended to deceive collectors. When I have to tell someone that their coin is a forgery it is so much easier when I can show them another exact copy labelled as such and priced at just a pound or two. However, nowadays, unofficial mints have sprung up, particularly in China, and have become adept at producing quality forgeries of all sorts of coins, usually in base metal and available over the internet at a fraction of the normal cost. If you want a cheap copy of an Edward VIII sovereign, a Krugerrand, a Gothic crown, or even a 1933 penny, they are all out there, sold as copies but clearly intending to deceive and not marked in any way to differentiate them from the real thing. Now you can have a collection of all your favourite rare coins for just a small outlay! Not buying a copy by mistake is all a matter of experience—if you have never handled a sovereign before how are you going to know that the one you are being offered is indeed right or not? The answer as always is to do some homework first. Check the design, check the weight, check the seller, buy the book, ask a professional dealer, and if the price seems too good to be true, then it most surely is a warning signal to stay well away and stick to what you know.

In recent years the quality of intrinsically valuable coins containing gold and silver has improved with 24ct purity .999 gold and .999 silver bullion coins being offered by leading countries in various forms. Whether as US Eagles, Australian Kookaburras, Chinese Pandas or UK Britannias, one ounce coins have proved very popular and often a good investment. Customers ask what they should invest in, and expect me to guarantee a return. I can advise you to buy what you like, what appeals, and to learn about them, but I cannot forecast the future price of gold. . .

I am, of course, preaching to the converted here. You have a sufficient interest to buy this book, you want to learn about the coins and notes

you collect, and as such you have risen above the majority of the general public who may have had their interest temporarily piqued by a chance find long forgotten or a coin found in today's pocket change and the immediate thought that you can become rich from it. You understand the importance of condition, the difference between Fine and Unc; that most coins are not rare, and that the chances are that you have the common variety not the unique one pictured online. You may have a collection to feel proud of, which should be shown to and shared with friends and family, and which after years of careful acquisition still brings you hours of pleasure and hopefully will show a return at the end of the day. Collecting coins and notes is a great hobby, good luck with your collection—seek out your local dealer, a collectors fair or favourite website and add something to it today!

....

Another view . . .

"It's that Mr. Veldshooen trying to get away with this useless foreign rubbish—a krugerrand or something—for that lovely bit of stilton!"

CELTIC *coinage of Britain*

Pritanic coins were the first coins made in Britain. They were issued for a century and a half before the Roman invasion, and possibly a little later in some areas. They were minted by the rulers of thirteen tribal groups or administrative authorities situated on the southeast of a line from the Humber to the Severn. In this short article Pritanic specialist CHRIS RUDD introduces this increasingly popular series.

Most folk call them British Celtic or Celtic coins of Britain. But I'll begin by letting you into a little known secret: most folk may be wrong. You see, there is no ancient textual evidence—none whatsoever—that anyone in iron age Britain called themselves a Celt. Neither is there a hint—not a whisper—that anyone else in the ancient world ever referred to the Brits as Celts. The Greeks didn't, the Gauls didn't, the Romans didn't. The correct name for iron age Britons is Pritani—well formed people or people of the forms. How do we know? Because a sailor from Marseilles said so.

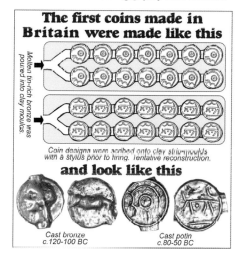

The first coins made in Britain were made like this

Molten tin-rich bronze was poured into clay moulds

Coin designs were scribed onto clay strip-moulds with a stylus prior to firing. Tentative reconstruction.

and look like this

Cast bronze
c. 120–100 BC

Cast potin
c. 80–50 BC

Many Gaulish coins were imported to Britain, like this silver stater of the Coriosolites (ABC 70), typical of many in the huge Jersey hoard found in June 2012, containing an estimated 50,000 coins.

Around 330 BC an explorer, Pytheas of Marseilles, sailed to Britain in search of tin. His visit indicates early trade links with southern Gaul and that the Britons were called Pritani. Marseilles inspired Britain's first homemade coinage: potin coins cast in clay strip-moulds, with Apollo on one side and a bull on the other, plus MA for Massalia (Marseilles). Made in Kent c. 120–100 BC, these cast potins circulated alongside gold coins imported from Gaul. During the Gallic Wars (58–51 BC) many other Gaulish coins—gold, silver and bronze—came to Britain, some brought by refugees, others by British mercenaries, others by trade.

The most famous Gallic migrant was Commios "friend", a former ally of Caesar, who became king of the Regini and Atrebates in the south of England c. 50–25 BC. Commios was the first British ruler to place his name on coins. His three sons—Tincomarus (great in peace), Eppillus (little horse) and Verica (the high one), made the Commian dynasty one of the wealthiest and most powerful in Britain. Most of their coins adopted Roman imagery and archaeology indicates that they imported Roman luxury goods, especially Italian wine. Many coins of Verica show grapes, vine leaves and wine cups.

The main rivals of the Regini and Atrebates were the Catuvellauni of Hertfordshire. Their first known ruler was probably Cassivellaunos "bronze commander", leader of the British coalition against Caesar in 54 BC. Many of Britain's earliest gold coins were probably struck to fund resistance to Caesar and then to pay tribute to him. Cassivellaunos may have organised this war money. Addedomaros "great in chariots" (c. 45–25 BC) was the first ruler north of the Thames to inscribe his coins, perhaps copying Commios.

Thirteen possible tribal groups which were producing coins by c.50-40 BC (Cantiaci much earlier). By c.30 BC the Belgae, East Wiltshire and Berkshire group had apparently stopped minting independently.

Gold stater of Commios (ABC 1022) the first British king to place his name on coins. There are two hidden faces on the obverse.

Verica silver minim with wine cup (ABC 1331) and Verica gold stater with vine leaf (ABC 1193)—evidence of Britain's thirst for fine Italian wine and Roman silverware.

Catuvellaunian expansion continued under Tasciovanos "killer of badgers" whose coins became increasingly Roman in style. His son Cunobelinus "hound of Belenus"—Shakespeare's *Cymbeline*) was the most potent tribal king in Atlantic Europe. Suetonius called him "king of the Britons". During his thirty-year reign (c. AD 8–41) Cunobelinus may have minted well over a million gold staters, most of them displaying a corn ear and CAMV— short for *Camulodunon* (Colchester). When his brother Epaticcus "leader of horsemen" and his son Caratacus "the beloved"—both clad as Hercules on their silver coins—crossed the Thames and attacked the Atrebates, Verica fled to Claudius who invaded Britain in AD 43. The minting of tribal coins ceased shortly afterwards.

Other tribes that issued coins included the Cantiaci of Kent, the Belgae of Hampshire, the Durotriges of Dorset, the Dobunni of the West Midlands, the Trinovantes of Essex, the Iceni of East Anglia and the Corieltavi of Lincolnshire. However, only a minority of people in the British Isles used coins regularly—the moneyed minority in southeast England. Cornwall, Devon, Wales, northern England, Scotland and Ireland remained coinless. Which is why ancient British coins are relatively rare. For example, whereas Greek coins were minted for about 600 years, Roman for about 800 years and Gaulish for about 250 years, ancient British coins were produced for little more than 150 years, and often in much smaller runs.

700 600 500 400 300 200 100 BC-AD 100 200 300 400 500 600

GREEK

ROMAN

GAULISH

BRITISH

Ancient British coins weren't minted for as long as Greek, Roman or Gaulish coins were. That's one of the reasons they are so scarce.

This century and a half of Pritanic (not Celtic) coin production generated a remarkable flowering of insular creativity and insular technology, unmatched by any other northern European nation of the period. Though initially influenced by Gallic minting techniques and Gallic iconography, ancient British coinage rapidly developed its own denominational systems, its own gold standards and its own highly distinctive coin designs — often inspired by Roman prototypes, but invariably modified to suit local needs. Between c. 110 BC and c. AD 45 around a thousand different coin types were minted in Britain. Many if not most of these thousand types displayed what might loosely be described as "religious" imagery. Not surprising, really, when one recalls that Caesar says that Druidism originated in Britain. Moreover, Tasciovanos struck coins in no fewer than five different denominations, whereas most Gaulish rulers issued no more than two or three.

The history of late iron age Britain, particularly the century prior to the Claudian conquest, has largely been rewritten with the help of ancient British coins. Most of the recent advances in our knowledge of this period have been due to amateur metal detecting. As a direct result of coin finds made by metal detectorists since the 1970s four new coin-issuing groups and maybe ten new rulers, previously unknown or unrecognised, have been identified. Not bad for barely forty years of unfunded, unofficial fieldwork.

Unlike Gaul, most of the British Isles was virtually coinless throughout the late iron age (and later). Coin production was confined to south-east Britain. That's why, overall, ancient British coins are much rarer than Gaulish coins.

What is it about ancient British coins that is making them increasingly popular with collectors all over the world? Having been involved with them for many years (I excavated my first in 1952) I'll tell you why they appeal to me.

I love the *primal antiquity* of Pritanic coins. They were the first coins made in Britain over two thousand years ago. When you see the flamboyant freedom of their designs you realise that they are the most boisterously British coins ever minted, unlike the unsmiling Roman, Anglo-Saxon and Norman series that marched soberly in their dancing footsteps.

I love the *anarchic regality* of Pritanic coins. Like the rumbustious tribal kings that issued them, their personality is wild, strong and highly irregular. These coins were made by the first British rulers known by name to us — unruly, quarrelsome, beer-swilling, tribal warlords such as Cassivellaunos who fought Julius Caesar in 54 BC and Caratacus, the British resistance leader who opposed Claudius in AD 43.

I love the *imaginative imagery* you find on Pritanic coins: all the different gods and goddesses, armed warriors, chariot wheels, hidden faces, decapitated heads, suns, moons, stars, thunderbolts, floral motifs, magic signs and phallic symbols. Plus an amazing menagerie of wild animals, birds and mythical beasts.

I love the *myths, mystery and mysticism* behind Pritanic coins. Look closely at this late iron age money of Albion and you'll catch glimpses

Ancient British denominations

There was no national currency in pre-Roman Britain and little consistency from region to region. Different tribes issued different mixtures of low, medium and high value coins. Here are the most common denominations used by the ancient Brits. The names are ours, not theirs. We've no idea what they called their coins, shown here actual size.

GOLD STATERS
Can also be silver, billon or bronze

Norfolk Wolf, ABC 1393

GOLD QUARTER STATERS
Can also be silver or billon

Irstead Smiler, ABC 1480

SILVER UNITS

Norfolk God, ABC 1567

SILVER HALF UNITS

Aunt Cost Half, ABC 1953

SILVER MINIMS

Verica Sphinx, ABC 1340

BRONZE UNITS

Cunobelinus Centaur, ABC 2957

BRONZE HALF UNITS

Tasciovanos Goat, ABC 2709

CAST POTIN UNITS

Nipples, ABC 174

of long-lost legends and ancient pagan rituals such as head-hunting, bull sacrificing and shape-shifting. You'll marvel at the plethora of occult signs and arcane symbols and you may even feel the secret power of the Druids.

I love the *palpitating unpredictability* of Pritanic coins. Even after sixty years of heart-racing intimacy they are constantly and delightfully surprising me. Attributions, names and dates are always being revised. Not long ago the Coritani were renamed Corieltavi and Tincommios was rechristened Tincomarus. Almost every month exciting new types and new variants keep leaping out of the ground, thanks to metal detectorists. For example, on September 4, 2010 the late

Bronze units of Cunobelinus, son of Tasciovanos,showing a bull being sacrificed (ABC 2972) and a man—perhaps a Druid priest?—carrying a severed human head (ABC 2987).

Danny Baldock discovered the first recorded coin of Anarevitos, a Kentish ruler previously unknown to history.

I love the *uncommon scarcity* of Pritanic coins. Ask any metdet how many so-called Celtic coins he or she has found and you'll immediately realise that they are rarer than Roman coins—at least a thousand times rarer on average—for the reasons stated above.

Finally I love the *galloping good value* of this horsey money (some Pritanic horses have three tails, some breathe fire, others have a human torso). Their greater rarity doesn't mean they are

Silver unit of freedom-fighter Caratacus (ABC 1376) who defied the Roman invaders for eight years until he was betrayed by Cartimandua, queen of the Brigantes.

costlier than other ancient coins. In fact, they are often cheaper because demand determines price and because there are far fewer collectors of ancient British coins than there are, say, of Greek or Roman coins. For example, a very fine British gold stater typically costs less than half the price—sometimes even a third the price of a Roman aureus or English gold noble of comparable quality and rarity. But the disparity is gradually diminishing as more and more canny collectors are appreciating the untamed beauty and undervalued scarcity of Pritanic coins.

Coin Yearbook provides a great guide to current prices of commoner Pritanic types, but because new types keep turning up and because big hoards are sometimes found (causing values to fluctuate temporarily) you'd be well advised to also keep an eye on dealers' catalogues and prices realised at auction. If you're buying in Britain, buy from people who are members of the BNTA (British Numismatic Trade Association). If you're buying overseas, check that your suppliers

A unique gold stater of Anarevitos, a previously unknown ruler of the Cantiaci, probably a son of Eppillus, king of Calleva (Silchester). Sold by Elizabeth Cottam of Chris Rudd for £21,000, a record price for an ancient British coin (Coin News, December 2010).

belong to the IAPN (International Association of Professional Numismatists). And, if you're a beginner, beware of dodgy traders on the internet, or you could end up with a fistful of fakes and no refund.

I'd also counsel you to spend a day at the British Museum. Its collection of almost 7,000 ancient British coins is the most comprehensive, publicly accessible collection of its kind in the world. As their curator, Ian Leins, says: "They're public coins . . . your coins, and they're here for you to see. So come and see them. We'll be pleased to show them to you". Access to the collection is free for everyone. But you'll need to make an appointment before you go, and take some photo ID and proof of address. Email: coins@thebritishmuseum.ac.uk or telephone: 020 7323 8607.

Before you buy coins—any coins of any period—it always pays to read about them first. As an old adman I'm not shy about blowing my own trumpet. The best little introduction to Pritanic coins is *Britain's First Coins* by Chris Rudd (expected late 2012) and the most comprehensive catalogue of the series is *Ancient British Coins* also by Chris Rudd (2010), known in the trade as ABC. If you have even half the fun I've had with ancient British coins (and am still having)—I can promise you that you'll be a very happy person indeed. Never bored, and never with a complete collection.

COLLECTING *ancient coins*

Ancient coins differ from most other series which are collected in Britain in that every piece has spent the major part of the last two thousand years in the ground. As JOHN CUMMINGS, dealer in ancient coins and antiquities explains here, the effect that burial has had on the surface of the coin determines more than anything else the value of a particular piece. With more modern coins, the only things which affect price are rarity and grade. There may be a premium for coins exhibiting particularly fine tone, or with outstanding pedigrees, but an 1887 crown in "extremely fine" condition has virtually the same value as every other piece with the same grade and of the same date. With ancient coins the story is very different.

A large number of different criteria affect the price of an ancient coin. Factors affecting prices can be broken down into several categories:

Condition

The most important factor by far in determining price. Ancient coins were struck by hand and can exhibit striking faults. Value suffers if the coin is struck with the designs off-centre, is weakly struck, or if the flan is irregular in shape. Many of the Celtic tribes issued coins of varying fineness and those made from low quality gold or silver are worth less than similar specimens where the metal quality is better. Conversely, coins on exceptional flans, particularly well struck, or with fine patinas command a premium.

Many ancient coins have suffered during their stay in the ground. It must be borne in mind that the prices given in the price guide are for uncorroded, undamaged examples. A Roman denarius should be graded using the same criteria as those used for grading modern coins. The surfaces must be good, and the coin intact. The fact that the coin is 2,000 years old is irrelevant as far as grading is concerned. Coins which are not perfectly preserved are certainly not without value, however, the value for a given grade decreases with the degree of fault.

Rarity

As with all other series, rare coins usually command higher prices than common ones. A unique variety of a small fourth century Roman bronze coin, even in perfect condition, can be worth much less than a more worn and common piece from an earlier part of the empire. In the Celtic series, there is an almost infinite variety of minor types and a unique variety of an uninscribed type will rarely outbid an inscribed issue of a known king.

Historical and local significance

Types which have historical or local interest can command a price far above their scarcity value. Denarii of the emperor Tiberius are believed to have been referred to in the New Testament and command a far higher price than a less interesting piece of similar rarity. Similarly, pieces which have British reverse types such as the "VICT BRIT" reverse of the third century AD are more expensive than their scarcity would indicate. The 12 Caesars remain ever popular especially in the American market and this affects prices throughout the world. In the Celtic series, coins of Cunobelin or Boudicca are far more popular than pieces which have no historical interest but which may be far scarcer.

Reverse types

All Roman emperors who survived for a reasonable time issued coins with many different reverse types. The most common of these usually show various Roman gods. When a coin has an unusual reverse it always enhances the value. Particularly popular are architectural scenes, animals, references to Judaism, and legionary types.

Artistic merit

The Roman coinage is blessed with a large number of bust varieties and these can have a startling effect on price. For example, a common coin with the bust facing left instead of right can be worth several times the price of a normal specimen. Like many of the emperors, the coinage of Hadrian has a large number of bust varieties, some of which are extremely artistic and these, too, can command a premium.

The coinage used in Britain from the time of the invasion in AD 43 was the same as that introduced throughout the Empire by the emperor Augustus around 20 BC. The simple divisions of 2 asses equal to one dupondius, 2 dupondii equal to 1 sestertius, 4 sestertii equal to one denarius and 25 denarii equal to one aureus continued in use until the reformation of the coinage by Caracalla in AD 214.

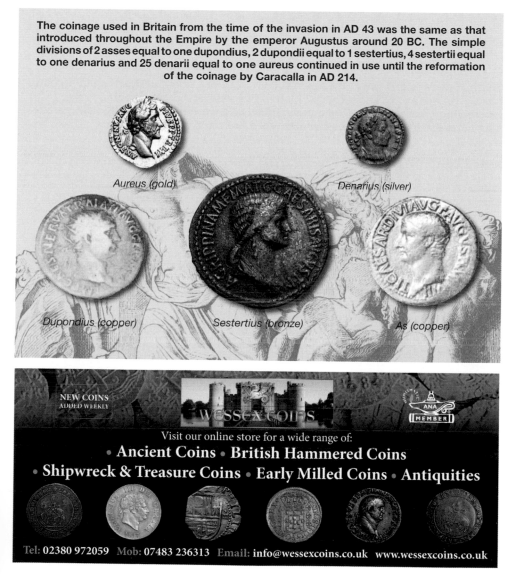

Aureus (gold)

Denarius (silver)

Dupondius (copper)

Sestertius (bronze)

As (copper)

HAMMERED *coinage*

The hammered currency of medieval Britain is among some of the most interesting coinage in the world. The turbulent history of these islands is reflected in the fascinating changes in size, design, fineness and workmanship, culminating in the many strange examples that emanated from the strife of the Civil War.

The Norman Conquest of England in 1066 and succeeding years had far-reaching effects on all aspects of life. Surprisingly, however, it had little impact on the coinage. William the Conqueror was anxious to emphasise the continuity of his reign, so far as the ordinary people were concerned, and therefore he retained the fabric, size and general design pattern of the silver penny. Almost 70 mints were in operation during this reign, but by the middle of the 12th century the number was reduced to 55 and under Henry II (1154–89) it fell to 30 and latterly to only eleven. By the early 14th century the production of coins had been centralised on London and Canterbury, together with the ecclesiastical mints at York and Canterbury. The silver penny was the principal denomination throughout the Norman period, pieces cut along the lines of the cross on the reverse continuing to serve as halfpence and farthings.

Eight types of penny were struck under William I and five under his son William Rufus, both profiles (left and right) and facing portraits being used in both reigns allied to crosses of various types. Fifteen types were minted under Henry I (1100–35), portraiture having now degenerated to crude caricature, the lines engraved on the coinage dies being built up by means of various punches. Halfpence modelled on the same pattern were also struck, but very sparingly and are very rare.

On Henry's death the succession was contested by his daughter Matilda and his nephew Stephen of Blois. Civil war broke out in 1138 and continued till 1153. Stephen controlled London and its mint, but Matilda and her supporters occupied the West Country and struck their own coins at Bristol. Several of the powerful barons struck their own coins, and there were distinct regional variants of the regal coinage. Of particular interest are the coins

Silver pennies of, from left to right, William I, William Rufus, Henry I and Stephen.

struck from obverse dies with Stephen's portrait erased or defaced, believed to date from 1148 when the usurper was under papal interdict.

Peace was restored in 1153 when it was agreed that Matilda's son Henry should succeed Stephen. On the latter's death the following year, Henry II ascended the throne. Coins of Stephen's last type continued to be minted till 1158, but Henry then took the opportunity to overhaul the coinage which had become irregular and sub-standard during the civil war. The new "Cross Crosslet" coins, usually known as the Tealby coinage (from the hoard of over 5,000 pennies found at Tealby, Lincolnshire in 1807), were produced at 30 mints, but when the recoinage was completed this number was reduced to a dozen. The design of Henry's coins remained virtually the same throughout more than two decades, apart from minor variants. Then, in 1180, a new type, known as the Short Cross coinage, was introduced. This was a vast improvement over the poorly struck Cross Crosslet coins and continued without alteration, not only to the end of the reign of Henry II in 1189, but throughout the reigns of his sons Richard (1189–99) and John (1199–1216) and the first half of the reign of his grandson Henry III (1216–46). Throughout that 66 year period, however, there were minor variations in portraits and lettering which enable numismatists to attribute the HENRICUS coins to specific reigns and periods.

"Tealby" type penny (top), and "Short Cross" penny of Henry II.

The style and workmanship of the Short Cross coinage deteriorated in the reign of Henry III. By the 1220s coin production was confined to the regal mints at London and Canterbury, the sole exception being the ecclesiastical mint maintained by the Abbot of Bury St Edmunds.

Halfpence and farthings were briefly struck in 1221–30, though halfpence are now extremely rare and so far only a solitary farthing has been discovered.

By the middle of this reign the coinage was in a deplorable state, being poorly struck, badly worn and often ruthlessly clipped. In 1247 Henry ordered a new coinage and in this the arms of the cross on the reverse were extended to the rim as a safeguard against clipping. This established a pattern of facing portrait and long cross on obverse and reverse respectively that was to continue till the beginning of the 16th century. Several provincial mints were re-activated to assist with the recoinage but they were all closed down again by 1250, only the regal mints at London and Canterbury and the ecclesiastical mints at Durham and Bury St Edmunds remaining active.

"Long Cross" pennies of Henry III (top), and Edward I.

In 1257 Henry tentatively introduced a gold penny (worth 20 silver pence and twice the weight of a silver penny). The coin was undervalued and soon disappeared from circulation.

The Long Cross coinage of Henry III continued under Edward I till 1279 when the king introduced a new coinage in his own name. The penny continued the style of its predecessors, though much better designed and executed; but new denominations were now added. Henceforward halfpence and farthings became a regular issue and, at the same time, a fourpenny coin known as the groat (from French *gros*) was briefly introduced (minting ceased in 1282 and was not revived till 1351). Due to the centralisation of coin production the name of the moneyer was now generally dropped, although it lingered on a few years at Bury St Edmunds. The provincial mints were again revived in 1299–1302 to recoin the lightweight foreign imitations of pennies which had flooded in from the Continent.

The coinage of Edward II (1307–27) differed only in minor respects from that of his father, and a similar pattern prevailed in the first years of Edward III. In 1335 halfpence and farthings below the sterling fineness were struck. More importantly, further attempts were made to introduce gold coins. In 1344 the florin or double

Pre-Treaty Noble of Edward III which contained reference to France in the legend.

leopard of six shillings was introduced, along with its half and quarter. This coinage was not successful and was soon replaced by a heavier series based on the noble of 80 pence (6s. 8d.), half a mark or one third of a pound. The noble originally weighed 138.5 grains but it was successively reduced to 120 grains, at which weight it continued from 1351. During this reign the protracted conflict with France known as the Hundred Years' War erupted. Edward III, through his mother, claimed the French throne and inscribed this title on his coins. By the Treaty of Bretigny (1361) Edward temporarily gave up his claim and the reference to France

Noble of Edward IV, issued before he was forced to abandon the throne of England.

was dropped from the coins, but when war was renewed in 1369 the title was resumed, and remained on many English coins until the end of the 18th century. The silver coinage followed the pattern of the previous reign, but in 1351 the groat was re-introduced and with it came the twopence or half-groat. Another innovation was the use of mintmarks at the beginning of the inscriptions. Seven types of cross and one crown were employed from 1334 onwards and their sequence enables numismatists to date coins fairly accurately.

The full range of gold (noble, half-noble and quarter-noble) and silver (groat, half-groat, penny, halfpenny and farthing) continued under Richard II (1377–99). Little attempt was made to alter the facing portrait on the silver coins, by now little more than a stylised caricature anyway.

Noble of Henry IV which was reduced in weight due to the shortage of gold.

Under Henry IV (1399–1413) the pattern of previous reigns prevailed, but in 1412 the weights of the coinage were reduced due to a shortage of bullion. The noble was reduced to 108 grains and its sub-divisions lightened proportionately. The penny was reduced by 3 grains, and its multiples and sub-divisions correspondingly reduced. One interesting change was the reduction of the fleur de lis of France from four to three in the heraldic shield on the reverse of the noble; this change corresponded with the alteration in the arms used in France itself. The Calais mint, opened by Edward III in 1363, was closed in 1411. There was no change in the designs used for the coins of Henry V (1413–22) but greater use was now made of mintmarks to distinguish the various periods of production. Coins were by now produced mainly at London, although the episcopal mints at Durham and York were permitted to strike pennies.

The supply of gold dwindled early in the reign of Henry VI and few nobles were struck after 1426. The Calais mint was re-opened in 1424 and struck a large amount of gold before closing finally in 1440. A regal mint briefly operated at York in 1423–24. Mintmarks were now much more widely used and tended to correspond more closely to the annual trials of the Pyx. The series of civil upheavals known as the Wars of the Roses erupted in this period.

In 1461 Henry VI was deposed by the Yorkist Earl of March after he defeated the Lancastrians at Mortimer's Cross. The Yorkists advanced on London where the victor was crowned Edward IV. At first he continued the gold series of his predecessor, issuing nobles and quarter-nobles, but in 1464 the weight of the penny was reduced to 12 grains and the value of the noble was raised to 100 pence (8s. 4d.).The ryal or rose-

Groat of Richard III (1483–85).

noble of 120 grains, together with its half and quarter, was introduced in 1465 and tariffed at ten shillings or half a pound. The need for a coin worth a third of a pound, however, led to the issue of the angel of 80 grains, worth 6s. 8d., but this was initially unsuccessful and very few examples are now extant. The angel derived its name from the figure of the Archangel Michael on the obverse; a cross surmounting a shield appeared on the reverse.

In 1470 Edward was forced to flee to Holland and Henry VI was briefly restored. During this brief period (to April 1471) the ryal was discontinued but a substantial issue of angels and half-angels was made both at London and Bristol. Silver coins were struck at York as well as London and Bristol, the issues of the provincial mints being identified by the initials B or E (Eboracum, Latin for York). Edward defeated the Lancastrians at Tewkesbury and deposed the luckless Henry once more. In his

second reign Edward struck only angels and half-angels as well as silver from the groat to halfpenny. In addition to the three existing mints, silver coins were struck at Canterbury, Durham and the archiepiscopal mint at York. Mintmarks were now much more frequent and varied. Coins with a mark of a halved sun and rose are usually assigned to the reign of Edward IV, but they were probably also struck in the nominal reign of Edward V, the twelve-year-old prince held in the Tower of London under the protection of his uncle Richard, Duke of Gloucester. Coins with this mark on the reverse had an obverse mark of a boar's head, Richard's personal emblem. The brief reign of Richard III (1483–5) came to an end with his defeat at Bosworth and the relatively scarce coins of this period followed the pattern of the previous reigns, distinguished by the sequence of mint marks and the inscription RICAD or RICARD.

In the early years of Henry VII's reign the coinage likewise followed the previous patterns, but in 1489 the first of several radical changes was effected, with the introduction of the gold sovereign of 20 shillings showing a full-length portrait of the monarch seated on an elaborate throne. For reverse, this coin depicted a Tudor rose surmounted by a heraldic shield. A similar reverse appeared on the ryal of 10 shillings, but the angel and angelet retained previous motifs. The silver coins at first adhered to the medieval pattern, with the stylised facing portrait and long cross, but at the beginning of the 16th century a large silver coin, the testoon or shilling of 12 pence, was introduced and adopted a realistic profile of the king, allied to a reverse showing a cross surmounted by the royal arms. The same design was also used for the later issue of groat and half groat.

First coinage Angel of Henry VIII which retained the traditional 23.5 carat fineness.

105

This established a pattern which was to continue till the reign of Charles I. In the reign of Henry VIII, however, the coinage was subject to considerable debasement. This led to the eventual introduction of 22 carat (.916 fine) gold for the crown while the traditional 23 1/2 carat gold was retained for the angel and ryal. This dual system continued until the angel was discontinued at the outset of the Civil War in 1642; latterly it had been associated with the ceremony of touching for "King's Evil" or scrofula, a ritual used by the early Stuart monarchs to bolster their belief in the divine right of kings.

Under the Tudors and Stuarts the range and complexity of the gold coinage increased, but it was not until the reign of Edward VI that the silver series was expanded. In 1551 he introduced the silver crown of five shillings, the first English coin to bear a clear date on the obverse. Under Mary dates were extended to the shilling and sixpence.

The mixture of dated and undated coins continued under Elizabeth I, a reign remarkable for the range of denominations—nine gold and

The magnificent second coinage Rose-Ryal of James I (1603–25).

eight silver. The latter included the sixpence, threepence, threehalfpence and threefarthings, distinguished by the rose which appeared behind the Queen's head.

The coinage of James I was even more complex, reflecting the king's attempts to unite his dominions. The first issue bore the legend ANG: SCO (England and Scotland), but from 1604 this was altered to MAG: BRIT (Great Britain). This period witnessed new denominations, such as the rose-ryal and spur-ryal, the unite, the Britain crown and the thistle crown, and finally the laurel of 20 shillings and its sub-divisions.

In the reign of Elizabeth experiments began with milled coinage under Eloi Mestrell. These continued sporadically in the 17th century, culminating in the beautiful coins struck by Nicholas Briot (1631–39). A branch mint was established at Aberystwyth in 1637 to refine and coin silver from the Welsh mines. Relations between King and Parliament deteriorated in the reign of Charles I and led to the Civil War (1642). Parliament controlled London but continued to strike coins in the King's name. The Royalists struck coins, both in pre-war and new types, at Shrewsbury, Oxford, Bristol, Worcester, Exeter, Chester, Hereford and other Royalist strongholds, while curious siege pieces were pressed into service at Newark, Pontefract and Scarborough.

After the execution of Charles I in 1649 the Commonwealth was proclaimed and gold and silver coins were now inscribed in English instead of Latin. Patterns portraying Cromwell and a crowned shield restored Latin in 1656. Plans for milled coinage were already being considered before the Restoration of the monarchy in 1660. Hammered coinage appeared initially, resuming the style of coins under Charles I, but in 1662 the hand-hammering of coins was abandoned in favour of coins struck on the mill and screw press. The hammered coins of 1660–62 were undated and bore a crown mintmark, the last vestiges of medievalism in British coinage.

Images courtesy of Spink.

COIN *grading*

Condition is the secret to the value of virtually anything, whether it be antiques, jewellery, horses or second-hand cars—and coins are certainly no exception. When collecting coins it is vital to understand the recognised standard British system of grading, i.e. accurately assessing a coin's condition or state of wear. Grading is an art which can only be learned by experience and so often it remains one person's opinion against another's, therefore it is important for the beginner or inexperienced collector to seek assistance from a reputable dealer or knowledgeable numismatist when making major purchases.

The standard grades as used in the Price Guide are as follows:	
UNC	**Uncirculated** A coin that has never been in circulation, although it may show signs of contact with other coins during the minting process.
EF	**Extremely Fine** A coin in this grade may appear uncirculated to the naked eye but on closer examination will show signs of minor friction on the highest surface.
VF	**Very Fine** A coin that has had very little use, but shows signs of wear on the high surfaces.
F	**Fine** A coin that has been in circulation and shows general signs of wear, but with all legends and date clearly visible.
Other grades used in the normal grading system are:	
BU	**Brilliant Uncirculated** As the name implies, a coin retaining its mint lustre.
Fair	A coin extensively worn but still quite recognisable and legends readable.
Poor	A coin very worn and only just recognisable.
Other abbreviations used in the Price Guide are:	
Obv	**Obverse**
Rev	**Reverse**
Other abbreviations, mintmarks, etc. can be identified under the appropriate section of this Yearbook.	

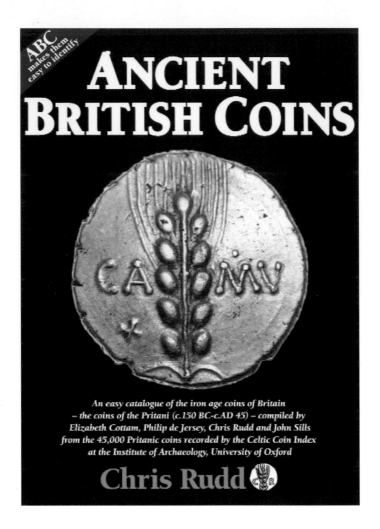

A SIMPLIFIED PRICE GUIDE TO

ANCIENT COINS
USED IN BRITAIN

PART 1 *Ancient British*

The prices given in this section are those that you would expect to pay from a reputable dealer and not the prices at which you could expect to sell coins.

The list below, which has been generously provided by Celtic coin dealer Elizabeth Cottam of Chris Rudd, contains most of the commonly available types: a fully comprehensive guide is beyond the scope of this book. Prices are for coins with good surfaces which are not weakly struck or struck from worn dies. Examples which are struck from worn or damaged dies can be worth considerably less. Particularly attractive examples of bronze Celtic coins command a very high premium. Where a price is given for an issue of which there are many varieties, the price is for the most common type. The illustrations are representative examples only and are not shown actual size.

UNINSCRIBED COINAGE

	F	VF	EF
GOLD STATERS			
Broad Flan	£700	£1775	£5750
Gallic War Uniface	£225	£300	£675
Remic types	£250	£400	£800
Wonersh types	£250	£450	£1900
Chute	£200	£300	£675
Cheriton	£250	£450	£975
Iceni (various types)	£300	£500	£1350
Norfolk "wolf" type			
fine gold	£250	£475	£1350
brassy gold	£175	£300	£695
very debased	£120	£200	£475
Corieltavi (various types)	£200	£400	£875
Dobunni	£250	£500	£1350
Whaddon Chase types	£275	£475	£1300
GOLD QUARTER STATERS			
Gallic Imported Types	£80	£175	£395
Kent types	£200	£300	£550
Southern types	£125	£200	£375
Iceni	£150	£250	£450
Corieltavi	£125	£200	£475
Dobunni	£175	£300	£575
East Wiltshire	£300	£500	£1,000
Durotriges	£120	£225	£395
North Thames types	£220	£300	£550
SILVER COINAGE			
Armorican billion staters	£95	£175	£450
Kent Types	£150	£300	£675
South Thames types	£120	£175	£375

Cheriton Smiler gold stater

Cranborne Chase silver stater

111

	F	VF	EF
Iceni ('crescent' types).........................	£35	£85	£185
Iceni ('Norfolk God' types)....................	£60	£100	£295
Corieltavi..	£50	£110	£225
Dobunni..	£85	£125	£295
Durotriges full stater			
fine silver...	£80	£175	£350
base silver..	£30	£55	£175
Durotriges quarter silver	£25	£35	£95

(Note—most examples are for base coins as better quality items are appreciably higher)

	F	VF	EF
North Thames types.............................	£110	£195	£375

Hengistbury cast bronze

POTIN COINAGE

	F	VF	EF
Kent	£25	£50	£135

BRONZE COINAGE

	F	VF	EF
Durotriges debased stater....................	£30	£75	£125
Durotriges cast bronze	£65	£125	£225
North Thames types. Various issues from:	£45	£110	£450

INSCRIBED CELTIC COINAGE

CANTIACI

	F	VF	EF
Dubnovellaunos			
stater...	£320	£600	£1500
silver unit...	£135	£220	£575
bronze unit	£65	£175	£395
Vosenos			
stater...	£1100	£2500	£5200
quarter stater	£295	£585	£1250
silver unit...	£140	£300	£675
Sam			
stater (unique)...................................	—	—	—
silver unit...	£185	£350	£800
bronze unit	£110	£275	£550
Eppillus			
stater...	£1100	£2000	£4575
quarter stater	£150	£265	£575
silver unit...	£75	£145	£395
bronze unit	£65	£125	£495
bronze minim	£85	£175	£300
Anarevitos			
stater (unique)			—
Touto			
silver unit...	£200	£450	£875
Verica...			
silver unit...	£200	£350	£695
bronze unit	£165	£300	£635
Sego			
stater...	£525	£1000	£3250
quarter stater	£220	£500	£1275
silver unit...	£150	£350	£675
silver minim......................................	£80	£200	£425
bronze unit	£80	£165	£495
Amminus			
silver unit...	£175	£325	£695
silver minim......................................	£110	£215	£475
bronze unit	£85	£175	£535
Solidus			
silver unit...	£535	£1100	£2350
silver minim......................................	£535	£1100	£1575

Vosenos gold quarter stater

Verica gold stater

	F	VF	EF
REGINI & ATREBATES			
Commios			
stater	£595	£1575	£3000
silver unit	£80	£160	£345
silver minim	£65	£125	£295
Tincomarus			
stater	£465	£895	£2250
quarter stater	£150	£250	£475
silver unit	£75	£145	£300
silver minim	£65	£125	£200
Eppillus			
quarter stater	£160	£245	£575
silver unit	£80	£165	£345
Verica			
stater	£275	£575	£1300
quarter stater	£155	£275	£435
silver unit	£55	£160	£275
silver minim	£50	£120	£245
Epaticcus			
stater	£1000	£2000	£4250
silver unit	£50	£100	£275
silver minim	£55	£120	£295
Caratacus			
silver unit	£175	£320	£475
silver minim	£110	£220	£345
VECTUARII			
Crab			
silver unit	£165	£325	£695
silver minim	£120	£295	£435
ICENI			
Cani Duro			
silver unit	£115	£275	£575
Antedios			
stater	£425	£1000	£2500
silver unit	£40	£65	£195
silver half unit	£45	£100	£150
Ecen			
stater	£425	£1200	£2575
silver unit	£45	£85	£195
silver half unit	£50	£100	£175
Saenu			
silver unit	£65	£125	£300
Aesu			
silver unit	£65	£125	£300
Ale Scavo			
silver unit	£275	£500	£1275
Esuprasto			
silver unit	£425	£1000	£2000
CORIELTAVI			
Cat			
silver unit	£400	£1100	£2200
silver half unit (unique)			—
VEPO			
stater	£450	£1000	£2600
silver unit	£85	£150	£350
Esuprasu			
stater	£350	£675	£1375
silver unit	£175	£325	£575

Tincomarus gold stater

Ale Scavo silver unit

Vep CorF gold stater

	F	VF	EF
Aunt Cost			
stater	£275	£575	£1395
silver unit	£90	£195	£350
silver half unit	£90	£175	£325
Lat Ison			
stater	£1000	£2100	£4300
silver unit	£175	£425	£1175
silver half unit	£160	£300	£575
Dumnocoveros Tigirseno			
stater	£850	£2000	£3750
silver unit	£100	£195	£595
silver half unit	£100	£210	£625
Volisios Dumnocoveros			
stater	£350	£675	£1350
silver unit	£100	£185	£500
silver half unit	£100	£195	£495
Volisios Cartivellaunos			
stater	£1000	£2000	£4100
silver half unit	£300	£675	£1200
Volisios Dumnovellaunos			
stater	£320	£765	£1675
silver half unit	£150	£325	£675

Catti gold stater

DOBUNNI

Bodvoc			
stater	£1000	£2250	£3250
quarter stater (unique)			—
silver unit	£200	£500	£895
Corio			
stater	£275	£560	£1550
quarter stater	£200	£350	£675
Comux			
stater	£285	£560	£1550
Catti			
stater	£285	£565	£1600
Inamn			
plated stater (unique)			—
silver unit (unique)			—
Anted			
stater	£350	£700	£1600
silver unit	£60	£125	£325
Eisu			
stater	£450	£750	£1600
silver unit	£75	£125	£335

Dumno Tigir Seno gold stater

TRINOVANTES

Dubnovellaunos			
stater	£275	£475	£1350
quarter stater	£175	£350	£650
silver unit	£75	£150	£375
silver half unit	£100	£200	£475
bronze unit	£65	£140	£295

CATUVELLAUNI

Addedomaros			
stater	£300	£450	£1300
quarter stater	£300	£550	£675
silver unit	£100	£200	£420
silver half unit	£100	£200	£475
bronze unit	£35	£95	£295

Addedomaros gold stater

	F	VF	EF
Tasciovanos			
stater..	£250	£475	£1650
quarter stater	£165	£250	£500
silver unit..	£85	£175	£395
bronze unit..	£60	£135	£275
bronze half unit	£60	£135	£295
Andoco			
stater..	£350	£575	£1695
quarter stater	£200	£420	£775
silver unit..	£155	£400	£775
bronze unit..	£85	£225	£365
Dias			
silver unit..	£100	£200	£425
bronze unit..	£50	£150	£425
Rues			
bronze unit..	£50	£150	£425
Cat			
plated silver unit (unique).................			—

Tasciovanos gold stater

CATUVELLAUNI & TRINOVANTES

Cunobelinus			
stater..	£250	£450	£1650
quarter stater	£150	£250	£495
silver unit..	£85	£175	£495
bronze unit..	£60	£145	£395
bronze half	£60	£145	£285
Trocc			
bronze unit..	£50	£150	£550
Agr			
quarter stater	£125	£275	£895
silver unit..	£100	£200	£525
bronze unit (only two)........................		(too rare to price)	
Dubn			
quarter stater (only three).................		(too rare to price)	

Cunobelinus gold stater

Illustrations by courtesy of Chris Rudd

Gold staters from the Queensland collection including a Wonersh (ABC 527), Tincomarus Alton (ABC 1052), Norfolk Wolf (ABC 1393), Andoco (ABC 2715) and Cunobelinus Biga (ABC 2771) to be sold at auction by Chris Rudd, November 19, 2017.

ANCIENT COINS USED IN BRITAIN

PART II *Roman Britain*

The list below has been generously provided by coin dealer Mike Vosper. These prices are for the most common types unless otherwise noted. In most cases, especially with large bronze coins, the price for coins in extremely fine condition will be <u>much</u> higher than the price for the same coin in very fine condition as early bronze coins are seldom found in hoards and perfect, undamaged examples are rarely available.

The illustrations provided are a representative guide to assist with identification only.

REPUBLICAN COINAGE 280–41 BC

	FROM F	VF	EF
Republican			
Quadrigatus (or Didrachm) (Janus/Quadriga)	£135	£450	£2000
Victoriatus (Jupiter/Victory)	£35	£100	£500
+Denarius (Roma/Biga)	£20	£75	£450
+Denarius (other types)	£30	£90	£525
Denarius (Gallic warrior—L.Hostilius			
Saserna)..	£400	£1100	£6925
Quinarius	£25	£80	£495
Cast Aes Grave, As	£400	£1100	—
Struck As/Semis/Litra	£60	£205	—
Struck Triens/Quadrands	£50	£150	—

Gnaeus Pompey Junior

IMPERATORIAL COINAGE 49–27 BC

Pompey the Great			
Denarius (Hd. of Pompilius/Prow)	£150	£450	£2600
Scipio			
Denarius (Jupiter/Elephant..............	£100	£295	£1650
Cato Uticensis			
Quinarius (Bacchus/Victory)	£45	£125	£675
Gnaeus Pompey Junior			
Denarius (Roma/Hispania)	£110	£325	£1700
Sextus Pompey			
Denarius (his bust)	£275	£750	£4500
Denarius (other types).....................	£190	£565	£3250
As...	£160	£565	—
Julius Caesar			
Aureus	£1200	£3300	£23,000
Denarius ("elephant" type)	£150	£475	£2500
Denarius (Ceasar portrait)	£450	£1400	£7500
Denarius (heads of godesses)..........	£115	£375	£1850

Julius Caesar

	FROM F	VF	EF
Brutus			
Denarius (his portrait/EID MAR)........	£25,000	£70,000	£350,000
Denarius (others)..............................	£150	£450	£2700
Cassius			
Denarius......................................	£125	£400	£1900
Ahenobarbus			
Denarius	£450	£1225	£6100
Mark Antony			
Denarius ("Galley" type)	£75	£265	£1800
Denarius (with portrait)	£100	£375	£2150
Denarius (other types)	£70	£295	£2000
Mark Antony & Lepidus			
AR quinarius	£75	£185	£1050
Mark Antony & Octavian			
AR denarius	£175	£595	£2825
Quninarius	£55	£165	£950
Mark Antony & Lucius Antony			
AR denarius	£345	£850	£4250
Mark Antony & Octavia			
AR Cistophorus	£225	£650	£3250
Cleopatra VII & Mark Antony			
AR denarius	£1400	£4200	£35,000
Fulvia			
AR quinarius	£125	£350	£2100
Octavian (later known as Augustus)			
Gold Aureus	£1200	£4000	£25,000
Denarius	£125	£350	£2300
Quinarius (ASIA RECEPTA)	£50	£125	£850
Octavian & Divos Julius Caesar			
AE sestertius	£275	£1500	—

Brutus

Mark Antony & Octavian

IMPERIAL COINAGE—Julio-Claudian Dynasty 27BC–AD 69

Augustus			
Gold Aureus (Caius & Lucius Caesar)	£1200	£3200	£17000
AR Cistophorus................................	£200	£650	£3300
Denarius (Caius & Lucius Caesar)	£60	£175	£925
Denarius (other types)	£65	£215	£1250
AR quinarius	£50	£150	£875
Sestertius (large SC)	£135	£395	£1900
Dupondius or as (large SC)..............	£55	£160	£800
Quadrans	£20	£70	£275
Divus Augustus (struck under Tiberius)			
As	£70	£200	£1250
Augustus & Agrippa			
Dupondius (Crocodile rev)	£70	£210	£1250
Livia			
Sestertius or Dupondius	£200	£595	£4200
Gaius Caesar			
AR denarius	£375	£1350	£4000
Tiberius			
Aureus (Tribute penny)	£1000	£2850	£11,000
Denarius (Tribute penny)	£85	£230	£1100
Sestertius	£195	£595	£3300
Dupondius	£165	£550	£2800
As	£75	£230	£1100
Drusus			
Sestertius...	£275	£900	£4550
As (Large S C)................................	£75	£200	£1300
Caligula			
Denarius (rev. portrait)	£450	£1300	£6800
Sestertius (PIETAS & Temple)	£300	£1800	£8600
As (VESTA)..	£95	£275	£1500

Augustus

Tiberius

	FROM F	VF	EF
Agrippa (struck under Caligula)			
As......................................	£65	£170	£1100
Germanicus (struck under Caligula or Claudius)			
As (Large S C)	£65	£195	£1100
Agrippina Senior (struck under Caligula)			
Sestertius (Carpentum)...................	£500	£1450	£9150
Nero & Drusus (struck under Caligula)			
Dupondius (On horseback, galloping)	£185	£650	£3800
Claudius			
Aureus ("DE BRITANN" type)	£1650	£5000	£35,000
Denarius as above	£400	£1700	£9200
Didrachm as above	£375	£1100	£6150
Denarius other types	£375	£950	£6100
Sestertius	£165	£500	£3800
Dupondius	£60	£225	£1550
As	£45	£140	£1050
Quadrans	£20	£50	£300
Irregular British Sestertius................	£30	£85	£505
Irregular British As	£20	£75	£390
Claudius & Agrippina Junior or Nero			
Denarius	£450	£1350	£7300
Nero Cludius Drusus (struck under Claudius)			
Sestertius	£250	£850	£6100
Antonia (struck under Claudius)			
Dupondius	£150	£450	£2900
Britannicus			
Sestertius	£6500	£28000	—
Nero			
Aureus	£1000	£3200	£17000
Denarius	£95	£260	£1850
Sestertius	£135	£575	£4000
Sestertius (Port of Ostia)	£1800	£6000	£60000
Dupondius	£85	£270	£1600
As	£50	£165	£1300
Semis..	£45	£125	£675
Quadrans	£20	£75	£350
Civil War			
Denarius	£190	£550	£3100
Galba			
Denarius	£110	£360	£2150
Sestertius	£170	£495	£3100
Dupondius	£180	£500	£2800
As	£110	£350	£2000
Otho			
Denarius	£195	£585	£3600
Vitellius			
Denarius	£100	£275	£1800
Sestertius	£1000	£2800	£19000
Dupondius	£350	£950	£5700
As	£195	£500	£3100

IMPERIAL COINAGE—Flavian Dynasty AD 69–96

	FROM F	VF	EF
Vespasian			
Aureus	£850	£2500	£13900
Denarius	£30	£100	£525
Denarius (IVDAEA)	£80	£200	£1300
Sestertius	£195	£595	£4600
Dupondius	£70	£210	£1550
As	£55	£200	£1300
Titus			
Aureus	£900	£2650	£15000
Denarius as Caesar	£40	£115	£800
Denarius as Augustus	£45	£130	£1000

Caligula

Agrippina Senior

Claudius

Nero

Galba

Vespasian

	FROM F	VF	EF
Sestertius	£135	£450	£3550
Dupondius	£50	£185	£1300
As	£45	£160	£1300
As (IVDAEA CAPTA)	£170	£500	£3000

Julia Titi

| Denarious | £190 | £580 | £3100 |

Domitian

Aureus	£950	£2400	£13100
Cistophorus	£125	£400	£2100
Denarius as Caesar	£35	£90	£480
Denarius as Augustus	£25	£80	£410
Sestertius	£95	£340	£1800
Dupondius	£35	£120	£1250
As	£35	£110	£790
Ae Semis	£30	£90	£525
Ae Quadrands	£25	£75	£350

Domitia

| Cistophorus | £235 | £695 | £3650 |

Titus

Domitian

IMPERIAL COINAGE—Adoptive Emperors AD 96–138

Nerva

Aureus	£1850	£5600	£33000
Denarius	£50	£120	£800
Sestertius	£140	£500	£3300
Sestertius (Palm-tree)	£500	£1600	£1100
Dupondius	£70	£225	£1250
As	£65	£160	£1100

Trajan

Aureus	£950	£2400	£13000
Denarius	£25	£60	£450
Denarius (Trajan's Column)	£40	£130	£805
Sestertius	£65	£225	£1550
Sestertius (Dacian rev.)	£75	£250	£1650
Dupondius or as	£35	£100	£650
Ae Quadrands	£25	£65	£415

Plotina, Marciana or Matidia

| Denarius | £425 | £1300 | £4300 |

Hadrian

Aureus	£950	£2600	£15000
Cistophourus	£120	£500	£2000
Denarius (Provinces)	£45	£140	£850
Denarius other types	£25	£80	£550
Sestertius	£75	£230	£1500
Sestertius (RETITVTORI province types)	£135	£420	£2800
Sestertius (Britannia std)	£3000	£10000	—
Dupondius or As	£35	£120	£690
As (Britannia std)	£210	£650	—
Ae Semiis or Quadrands	£30	£100	£500
Eygpt, Alexandrian Billon Tetradrachm	£30	£95	£520

Sabina

Denarius	£30	£85	£525
Sestertius	£115	£365	£2300
As or Dupondius	£70	£195	£1200

Aelius Ceasar

Denarius	£70	£200	£1250
Sestertius	£145	£500	£2825
As or Dupondius	£65	£100	£1300

Nerva

Trajan

Hadrian

	FROM F	VF	EF

IMPERIAL COINAGE — The Antonines AD 138–193

Antoninus Pius

Aureus	£750	£2000	£10500
Denarius	£20	£50	£270
Sestertius Britannia seated	£500	£1400	£12500
Sestertius other types	£40	£150	£970
As - Britannia rev.	£65	£200	£1500
Dupondius or As other types	£25	£95	£425

Antoninus Pius & Marcus Aurelius

Denarius (bust each side)	£30	£110	£575

Diva Faustina Senior

Denarius	£20	£45	£325
Sestertius	£45	£145	£820
As or Dupondius	£25	£80	£475

Marcus Aurelius

Aureus	£850	£2400	£13300
Denarius as Caesar	£22	£65	£400
Denarius as Augustus	£20	£50	£330
Sestertius	£45	£170	£110
As or Dupondius	£25	£75	£475

Faustina Junior

Denarius	£20	£60	£415
Sestertius	£40	£175	£1250
As or Dupondius	£28	£85	£525

Lucius Verus

Denarius	£25	£90	£475
Sestertius	£45	£200	£1250
As or Dupondius	£30	£100	£600

Lucilla

Denarius	£20	£66	£400
Sestertius	£65	£180	£1250
As or Dupondius	£30	£95	£600

Commodus

Aureus	£1050	£2950	£16000
Denarius as Caesar	£20	£75	£500
Denarius as Augustus	£18	£50	£400
Sestertius	£45	£160	£1200
Sestertius (VICT BRIT)	£150	£500	£3300
As or Dupondius	£25	£85	£525

Crispina

Denarius	£25	£80	£475
Sestertius	£70	£225	£1400
As or Dupondius	£35	£115	£700

IMPERIAL COINAGE — The Severan Dynasty AD 193–235

Pertinax

Denarius	£225	£645	£4000
Sestertius	£500	£1750	£13000

Didius Julianus

Denarius	£395	£1250	£7700
Sestertius or Dupondius	£325	£1000	£8150

Manlia Scantilla or Didia Clara

Denarius	£395	£1250	£8750

Pescennius Niger

Denarius	£270	£750	£4950

Clodius Albinus

Denarius as Caesar	£45	£130	£700
Denarius as Augustus	£85	£290	£1525
Sestertius	£275	£800	£5395
As	£85	£250	£1420

Antoninus Pius

Marcus Aurelius

Faustina Junior

Lucius Verus

Commodus

	FROM F	VF	EF
Septimius Severus			
Aureus	£900	£2500	£13875
Aureus (VICT BRIT)	£1200	£3500	£22500
+Denarius (Mint of Rome)	£15	£50	£255
+Denarius (Mints of Emesa & Laodicea)	£20	£45	£285
Denarius (LEG XIIII)	£30	£85	£530
Denarius (VICT BRIT)	£25	£100	£490
Sestertius other types	£75	£240	£1700
Sestertius (VICT BRIT)......................	£350	£1000	£7250
Dupondius or as	£50	£160	£1200
Dupondius or As (VICT BRIT)	£125	£365	£2250
Julia Domna			
Denarius	£15	£40	£275
Sestertius	£75	£230	£1600
As or Dupondius	£50	£160	£1000
Caracalla			
Aureus (VICT BRIT)	£1350	£3500	£23000
Denarius as Caesar	£15	£45	£300
Denarius as Augustus	£15	£40	£300
Denarius (VICT BRIT)	£30	£95	£525
Antoninianus	£25	£75	£475
Sestertius	£100	£295	£1800
Sestertius (VICT BRIT)......................	£300	£860	£6850
Dupondius or As	£50	£165	£980
Dupondius or As (VICT BRIT)	£100	£300	£1800
Plautilla			
Denarius	£25	£75	£500
Geta			
Denarius as Caesar	£15	£45	£325
Denarius as Augustus	£25	£70	£500
Denarius (VICT BRIT)	£30	£95	£625
Sestertius	£125	£350	£2100
Sestertius (VICT BRIT)......................	£250	£770	£4800
Dupondius or as	£75	£230	£1500
As (VICT BRIT)	£120	£340	£2300
Macrinus			
Antoninianus	£90	£275	£1700
Denarius	£40	£125	£800
Sestertius	£175	£400	£3300
Diadumenian			
Denarius	£75	£195	£1100
Dupondius or As	£135	£395	£2600
Elagabalus			
Aureus	£1200	£3500	£18000
Antoninianus	£20	£65	£475
Denarius	£15	£35	£275
Sestertius	£100	£320	£1900
Dupondius or As	£60	£175	£1100
Julia Paula			
Denarius	£30	£110	£625
Aquilla Severa			
Denarius	£55	£185	£1275
Julia Soaemias			
Denarius	£30	£75	£500
Dupondius or As	£65	£225	£1400
Julia Maesa			
Denarius	£15	£45	£300
Sestertius	£80	£250	£1800
Severus Alexander			
Aureus	£900	£2400	£14000
Denarius as Caesar	£65	£200	£1300
Denarius as Augustus	£15	£35	£300
Sestertius	£35	£100	£615
Dupondius or As	£25	£95	£525

Septimus Severus

Julia Domna

Geta

Macrinus

Elagabalus

Julia Maesa

	FROM F	VF	EF
Orbiana			
Denarius	£60	£195	£1275
As	£90	£325	£1900
Julia Mamaea			
Denarius	£15	£45	£300
Sestertius	£35	£110	£630

IMPERIAL COINAGE—Military Anarchy AD 235–270

	FROM F	VF	EF
Maximinus I			
Denarius	£15	£75	£310
Sestertius, Dupondius or As	£35	£125	£715
Diva Paula			
Denarius	£150	£460	£2600
Maximus Caesar			
Denarius	£70	£200	£1300
Sestertius	£65	£165	£1300
Gordian I & II, Africanus			
Denarius	£550	£1500	£6600
Sestertius......................................	£550	£1750	£9100
Balbinus & Pupienus			
Antoninanus	£90	£250	£1430
Denarius	£80	£260	£1600
Gordian III			
Antoninianus	£10	£25	£190
Denarius	£15	£35	£230
Sestertius or As	£25	£85	£510
Tranquillina			
Common Colonial	£30	£110	£620
Philip I			
Antoninianus "Animal"			
Lion, stag, antelope, wolf & twins ...	£20	£60	£400
Other Antoninianus	£10	£25	£175
Sestertius, Dupondius or As	£25	£80	£510
Otacilla Severa			
Antoninaus	£10	£25	£195
Antoninianus "Hipo"	£25	£80	£515
Sestertius	£25	£85	£500
Philip II			
Antoninianus	£10	£22	£185
Antoninianus "Goat"	£20	£65	£400
Sestertius, Dupondius or As	£30	£85	£510
Pacatian			
Antoninianus....................................	£1500	£4850	—
Trajan Decius			
Antoninianus	£10	£30	£155
Antoninianus (DIVI series Augustus, Trajan etc)	£40	£125	£700
Double Sestertius	£260	£950	£4625
Sestertius, Dupondius or As	£25	£85	£515
Herennius Etruscilla			
Antoninaus	£10	£35	£195
Sestertius, Dupondius or As	£30	£110	£705
Herennius Etruscus			
Antoninianus	£16	£55	£365
Sestertius, Dupondius or As	£55	£185	£1300
Hostilian			
Antoninianus as Caesar	£30	£110	£600
Antoninianus as Augustus	£70	£220	£1275
Trebonianus Gallus			
Antoninianus	£10	£30	£175
Sestertius or As	£30	£110	£580
Volusian			
Antoninianus....................................	£10	£35	£275
Sestertius..	£30	£110	£1100

Orbiana

Julia Mamaea

Diva Paula

Gordian III

Trajan Decius

Hostilian

	FROM F	VF	EF
Aemilian			
Antoninianus	£45	£140	£800
Valerian I			
Antoninianus	£10	£25	£200
Sestertius & As................................	£45	£150	£920
Diva Mariniana			
Antoninianus	£35	£125	£700
Gallienus			
Silver Antoninianus	£10	£30	£160
AE Antoninianus	£5	£20	£150
Ae Antoninianus (Military bust)	£10	£25	£200
AE Antoninianus (Legionary)	£70	£220	—
Ae Sestertius	£40	£140	£1100
Ae Denarius	£45	£125	£800
Saloninus			
Ae Antoninianus	£5	£20	£175
Valerian II			
Billon Antoninianus	£10	£35	£225
Saloninus			
Antoninianus	£15	£45	£295
Macrianus & Quietus			
Billon Antoninianus	£45	£135	£775
Regalianus or Dryantilla			
Billon Antoninianus	£1850	£7200	—
Postumus			
Silver Antoninianus	£10	£22	£195
Ae Antoninianus	£5	£20	£125
Radiated sestertius.............................	£45	£175	£1275
Laelianus			
Ae Antoninianus	£250	£750	£3300
Marius			
Ae Antoninianus	£40	£125	£700
Victorinus			
Ae Antoninianus	£5	£20	£150
Tetricus I & II			
Ae Antoninianus	£5	£20	£150
Claudius II Gothicus			
Ae Antoninianus	£5	£20	£175
Egypt, Alexandrian Billon tetradrachm	£5	£25	£175
DIVO Ae Antoninianus	£5	£25	£195
Quintillus			
Ae Antoninianus	£10	£30	£215

Postumus

Aurelian

Severina

IMPERIAL COINAGE—The Illyrian Emperors—AD 270–285

	FROM F	VF	EF
Aurelian			
Ae Antoninianus	£5	£40	£175
Ae Denarius	£20	£65	£425
Vabalathus & Aurelian			
Ae Antoninianus (bust both sides) ...	£20	£65	£410
Vabalathus			
Ae Antoninianus	£350	£950	—
Severina			
Ae Antoninianus	£15	£50	£270
Ae As...	£35	£100	£620
Zenobia			
Eygpt, Alexandrian Billon Tetradrachm	£700	£2500	—
Tacitus			
Ae Antoninianus	£15	£30	£220
Florian			
Ae Antoninianus	£25	£85	£500
Probus			
Gold Aureus	£1150	£3200	£17000
Ae Antoninianus	£10	£20	£195

Tacitus

Florian

	FROM F	VF	EF
Antoninianus (military or imp. Busts RIC G or H)	£10	£35	£210
Antoninianus			
(Other military or imp NOT BUSTS G or H)	£20	£65	£400
Antoninianus (VICTOR GERM rev.) ..	£10	£50	£200
Egypt, Alexandrian Billon tetradrachm	£5	£15	£105
Carus			
Ae Antoninianus	£15	£40	£255
Numerian			
Ae Antoninianus	£15	£40	£230
Carinus			
Ae Antoninianus	£10	£60	£225
Magna Urbica			
Ae Antoninianus	£95	£250	£1555
Julian of Pannonia			
Ae Antoninianus	£600	£2500	-

Carinus

IMPERIAL COINAGE—The Tetrarchy AD 285–307

Diocletian			
Gold Aureus	£1000	£2750	£15000
AR Argenteus	£90	£275	£1300
Ae Antoninianus & Radiates	£10	£25	£195
Ae Follis (London Mint)	£15	£45	£295
As above with LON mint mark	£100	£300	£1700
Ae Follis (other mints)	£10	£30	£175
Ae Follis (Imperial bust)....................	£25	£75	£410
Maximianus			
AR Argenteus	£90	£275	£1300
Ae Follis (London mint)	£15	£40	£265
Ae Follis (other mints)	£10	£30	£175
Ae Follis (MONETA rev.)	£10	£35	£205
Carausius			
Aureus	£8000	£25500	—
Denarius	£400	£1100	£6600
Ae Antoninianus (PAX).....................	£25	£85	£500
As above but full silvering	£35	£116	£700
Legionary Antoninianus	£70	£200	£1700
Expectate Veni Antoninianus	£100	£300	—
In the name of Diocletian or Maximian	£35	£120	£775
Allectus			
Aureus	£11000	£32000	—
Ae Antoninianus	£25	£90	£630
As above but full silvering	£45	£145	£935
Quinarius	£25	£90	£675
Constantius I			
AR Argenteus	£95	£285	£1375
Ae Follis (London Mint)	£15	£45	£295
Ae Follis (other mints)	£8	£30	£175
Ae Follis (SALVS rev.)......................	£15	£50	£280
Ae 4 (Lion or Eagle)	£10	£30	£185
Galerius			
Ae Follis (London mint)	£15	£35	£225
Ae Follis (other mints)	£10	£25	£150
Galeria Valeria			
Ae Follis	£30	£80	£450
Severus II			
Ae Follis (London mint)	£35	£100	£600
Ae Follis (other mints)	£30	£85	£450
Ae Radiate	£15	£50	£250
Ae Denarius	£25	£85	£500
Maximinus II			
Ae Follis (London mint)	£15	£40	£275
Ae Follis (other mints)	£5	£20	£125
Ae Radiate	£10	£30	£175

Diocletian

Maximianus

Carausius

Severus II

Maximinus II

	FROM F	VF	EF
Maxentius			
Ae Follis	£10	£30	£200
Romulus			
Ae Follis	£40	£135	£1400
Licinius I			
Billon Argenteus	£45	£150	£815
Ae Follis (London mint)	£10	£25	£150
Ae Follis (other mints)	£10	£20	£125
AE3	£5	£15	£115
Licinius II			
AE3	£10	£25	£150
Alexander or Martinian			
AE	£1500	£4200	—

Licinius II

IMPERIAL COINAGE—Family of Constantine AD 307–350

	FROM F	VF	EF
Constantine I			
Billon Argenteus	£50	£160	£900
Ae Follis (London mint)	£10	£25	£175
As above—helmeted bust	£15	£45	£275
Ae Follis (other mints) as Caesar ...	£15	£50	£300
Ae Follis (other mints) as Augustus	£5	£15	£110
AE3	£5	£15	£110
AE3 (London mint)	£10	£25	£175
AE3 (SARMATIA rev)	£10	£35	£210
Urbs Roma / Wolf & twins AE3/4..........	£5	£20	£125
Constantinopolis AE3/4	£5	£15	£115
Fausta & Helena			
AE3 (London mint)	£50	£155	£800
AE3 (other mints)	£14	£55	£285
Theodora			
AE4	£10	£25	£185
Crispus			
AE3 (London mint)	£10	£30	£185
AE3	£10	£20	£120
Delmatius			
AE3/4	£15	£40	£225
Hanniballianus Rex			
AE4	£75	£225	£1200
Constantine II			
AE3 (London mint)	£10	£25	£185
AE3	£5	£25	£125
AE3/4	£5	£10	£100
Constans			
AE2 (centenionalis)	£10	£30	£185
AE3 (half centenionalis)	£5	£20	£160
AE4	£5	£15	£100
Constantius II			
Gold Solidus	£300	£750	£4000
Siliqua	£25	£85	£500
AE2 (or centenionalis)	£10	£25	£210
AE3 (or half centenionalis)	£5	£15	£120
AE3 (London mint)..........................	£15	£45	£250
AE3...	£5	£10	£75

Constantine I

Constantine II

Magnentius

IMPERIAL COINAGE—Late period to the collapse of the Empire AD 350 to end

	FROM F	VF	EF
Magnentius			
Gold Solidus..................................	£800	£2200	£12,500
Silver Siliqua	£250	£790	£3900
Double centenionalis	£45	£185	£1250
Centenionalis	£15	£50	£310
Decentius			
Double centenionalis......................	£70	£225	£1500
Centenionalis	£20	£60	£350
Vetranio			
AE2 (centenionalis)	£40	£125	£700
AE3 (half centenionalis)	£30	£100	£565

Vetranio

	FROM F	VF	EF
Nepotian			
AE2 (centenionalis)	£1950	£6500	—
Constantius Gallus			
AE2 (centenionalis)	£15	£35	£200
AE3 (half centenionalis)	£5	£25	£95
Julian II			
Siliqua	£28	£85	£500
AE1	£40	£125	£715
AE3 (helmeted bust)	£10	£28	£175
Anonymous, Serapis + Jupiter AE3	£195	£550	—
Jovian			
AE1	£65	£215	£1200
AE3	£15	£50	£200
Valentinian I			
Sold Solidus	£200	£525	£2300
Silver Milliarense...........................	£165	£550	£3000
Siliqua	£25	£90	£500
AE3	£5	£15	£100
Valens			
Gold Solidus	£200	£500	£2250
Silver Milliarense...........................	£190	£600	£3300
Siliqua	£25	£85	£500
AE3	£5	£15	£95
Procopius			
AE3	£45	£140	£775
Gratian			
Silver Milliarense...........................	£165	£520	£2250
Siliqua	£25	£80	£500
AE3	£5	£25	£100
AE4	£6	£20	£85
Valentinian II			
Solidus	£220	£550	£2550
Siliqua	£25	£85	£490
AE2	£10	£28	£175
AE4	£2	£10	£80
Theodosius I			
Solidus	£225	£550	£2550
Siliqua	£30	£100	£575
AE2	£10	£40	£200
AE3	£8	£30	£200
Aelia Flaccilla			
AE2	£30	£110	£595
AE4	£15	£50	£300
Magnus Maximus			
Solidus (AVGOB)	£4800	£13000	—
Solidus	£800	£2300	£13500
Siliqua	£40	£125	£775
Siliqua (AVGPS)	£730	£2200	—
AE2	£20	£65	£375
Flavius Victor			
Silver Sliqua	£140	£450	£2250
AE4	£30	£75	£405
Eugenius			
Silver Siliqua	£150	£475	£2300
Arcadius			
Gold Solidus..................................	£200	£500	£2230
Silver Siliqua..................................	£25	£100	£500
Silver Half-siliqua	£150	£450	£2350
AE2	£10	£40	£195
AE4	£2	£13	£75

Julian II

Jovian

Valentinian I

Valens

Theodosius I

Arcadius

	FROM F	VF	EF
Eudoxia			
AE3	£25	£70	£415
Honorius			
Gold Solidus	£200	£475	£2150
Silver Siliqua	£30	£95	£515
AE4	£5	£15	£100
Constantine III			
Silver Siliqua	£145	£475	£2350
Theodosius II			
Gold Solidus	£200	£475	£2150
Johannes			
AE4	£115	£450	—
Valentinian III			
Gold Soldius...................................	£200	£495	£2150
AE4	£25	£80	£410

Honorius

Theodosius II

Ae = bronze; AE 1, 2, 3, 4 = bronze coins in descending order of size.

Coin illustrations by courtesy of Classical Numismatic Group/ Seaby Coins and Mike Vosper.

The Seaton Down Hoard of 22,888 Roman coins is the third largest coin hard discovered in Britain. Found by a metal detectorist in East Devon, the hoard is now one of the highlights at the Royal Albert Memorial Museum in Exeter. TV presenter, Alice Roberts, examines some of the Roman finds at the launch of the collection in the summer of 2017.

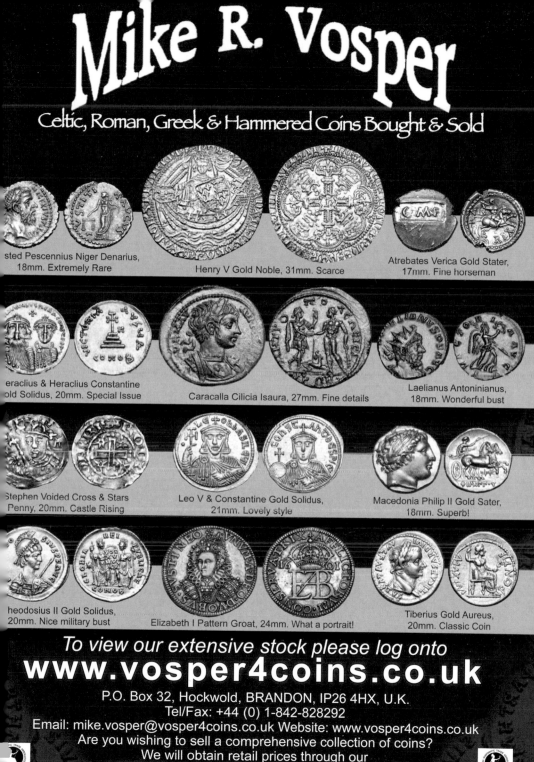

A SIMPLIFIED PRICE GUIDE TO

ENGLISH HAMMERED COINS

PART I

780–1485

INTRODUCTION

We have taken our starting point for English hammered coin prices back to the middle Anglo-Saxon period. This time sees the country divided into separate kingdoms, the Viking divided areas and numismatically the introduction of the silver "penny" as the standard unit of currency (as well as a few struck halfpennies). This is a complicated time in our history and that is reflected numismatically. We have therefore listed only the commonest or most frequently found pieces or rulers within their kingdoms. For many later rulers the price is for the more common non-portait issue.

PRICING

The prices given in the following pages are intended to be used as a "Pocket book guide" to the values of the *most common* coins within any denomination of any one reign. The price quoted is what a collector may expect to pay for such a piece in the condition indicated. For more detailed information we recommend the reader to one of the many specialist publications.

GRADING

The prices quoted are generally for three different grades of condition: Fine (F), Very Fine (VF) and Extromely Fine (EF). A "Fine" coin is assumed to be a fairly worn, circulated, piece but with all or most of the main features and lettering still clear. "Very Fine" is a middle grade with a small amount of wear and most details fairly clear. For this edition we have included the prices for coins in Extremely Fine condition where appropriate, although very few hammered coins actually turn up in this grade (i.e. nearly mint state with hardly any wear). In some instances the prices quoted are theoretically based and are only included to provide a guide. It is important to note that on all hammered coins the very nature of striking, i.e. individually, by hand, means hammered coinage is rarely a straight grade and when listed by a dealer the overall condition will often be qualified by terms such as: *weak in parts, struck off-centre, cracked or chipped flan, double struck*, etc. When applicable the price should be adjusted accordingly.

HISTORY

Below the heading for each monarch we have given a few historical notes as and when they apply to significant changes in the coinage.

KINGS OF KENT

	F	VF	
CUTHRED (798–807)	£800	£3500	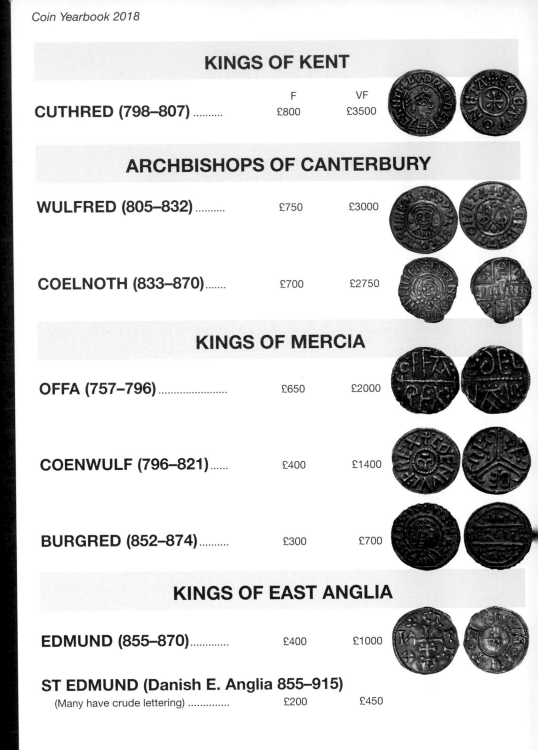

ARCHBISHOPS OF CANTERBURY

WULFRED (805–832)	£750	£3000
COELNOTH (833–870)	£700	£2750

KINGS OF MERCIA

OFFA (757–796)	£650	£2000
COENWULF (796–821)	£400	£1400
BURGRED (852–874)	£300	£700

KINGS OF EAST ANGLIA

EDMUND (855–870)	£400	£1000
ST EDMUND (Danish E. Anglia 855–915) (Many have crude lettering)	£200	£450

VIKING ISSUES OF YORK

	F	VF
CNUT (READS CV N•NET•TI)	£175	£400
ST PETER COINAGE (905–915)	£350	£1000

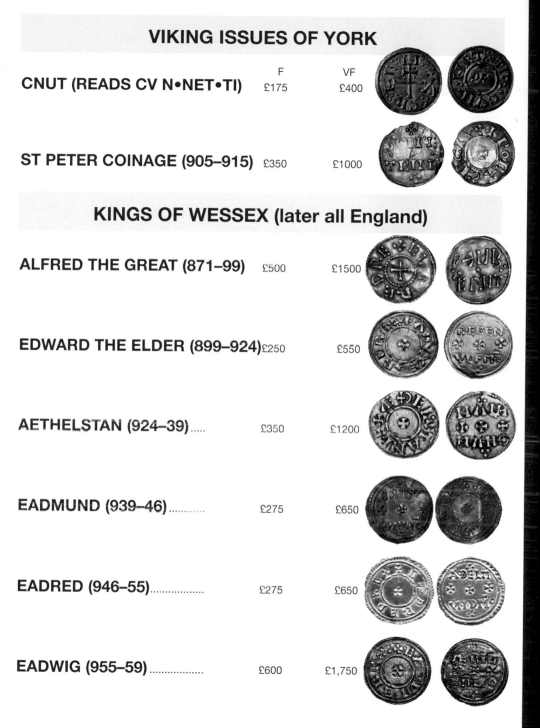

KINGS OF WESSEX (later all England)

	F	VF
ALFRED THE GREAT (871–99)	£500	£1500
EDWARD THE ELDER (899–924)	£250	£550
AETHELSTAN (924–39)	£350	£1200
EADMUND (939–46)	£275	£650
EADRED (946–55)	£275	£650
EADWIG (955–59)	£600	£1,750

EDGAR (First King of All England)
(959–975)

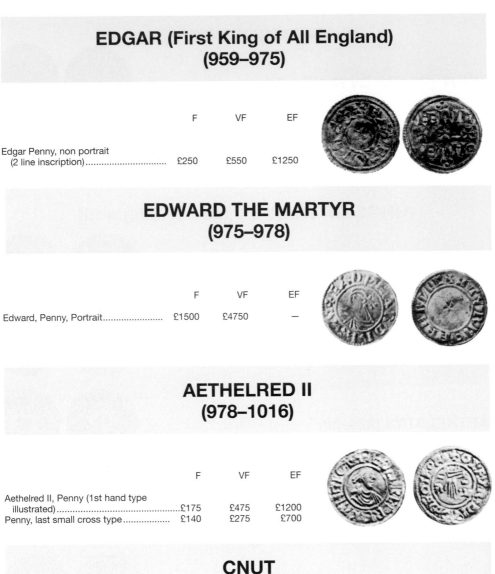

	F	VF	EF
Edgar Penny, non portrait (2 line inscription)	£250	£550	£1250

EDWARD THE MARTYR
(975–978)

	F	VF	EF
Edward, Penny, Portrait	£1500	£4750	—

AETHELRED II
(978–1016)

	F	VF	EF
Aethelred II, Penny (1st hand type illustrated)	£175	£475	£1200
Penny, last small cross type	£140	£275	£700

CNUT
(1016–1035)

	F	VF	EF
Cnut, Penny (Quatrefoil type illustrated)	£140	£250	£600
Penny (short cross type)	£120	£225	£550

HAROLD I
(1035–40)

	F	VF	EF
Harold I, Penny (long cross type Illustrated)..£375		£850	£2200

HARTHACANUTE
(1035–42)

	F	VF	EF
Harthacanute, Penny, English Mint (in his own name)	£1250	£4500	—
Harthacanute Penny (king's name given as "CNUT")..............................	£600	£1800	—
Harthacanute, Penny, Danish type........	£300	£675	—

Danish type

EDWARD THE CONFESSOR
(1042–66)

	F	VF	EF
Edward the Confessor, Penny (helmet type illustrated)...	£165	£350	£1000
Edward the Confessor, Penny, facing bust type £125		£300	£700

HAROLD II
(1066)

	F	VF	EF
Harold II, Penny...................................	£1500	£3500	—

Coin Yearbook 2018

WILLIAM I
(1066–87)

The Norman Conquest had very little immediate effect on the coinage of England. The Anglo-Saxon standard of minting silver pennies was very high and the practice of the moneyer putting his name and mint town on the reverse continued as before, except with William's portrait of course. It is worth noting here that non-realistic, stylised portraits were used until the reign of Henry VII.
There are eight major types of pennies of which the last, the PAXS type, is by far the commonest.

	F	VF	EF
William I, Penny (PAXS type illustrated)	£275	£525	£1250

WILLIAM II
(1087–1100)

Very little change from his father's reign except that five new types were issued, most of which were much more crudely designed than previous, all are scarce.

	F	VF	EF
William II, Penny (cross in quatrefoil type illustrated)	£850	£2250	—

HENRY I
(1100–35)

There are fifteen different types of penny for this reign of which the last two are the most common. Most issues are of a very poor standard both in workmanship and metal, the prices reflect a poor quality of issue.

	F	VF	EF
Henry I, Penny (type XIV illustrated)	£200	£450	—
Halfpenny	£2000	£6000	—

STEPHEN
(1135–54)

This is historically a very complicated time for the coinage, mainly due to civil war and a consequential lack of central control in the country which resulted in very poor quality and deliberately damaged pieces. Coins were struck not only in the name of Stephen and his main rival claimant Matilda but also by their supporters. The commonest issue is the "Watford" type; so named, as are many issues, after the area in which a hoard was found.

	F	VF	EF
Stephen, Penny ("Watford" type illustrated)	£250	£750	—

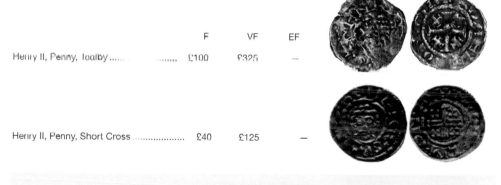

HENRY II
(1154–89)

There were two distinct issues struck during this reign. The first, Cross and Crosslets or "Tealby" coinage (named after Tealby in Lincolnshire), continued to be very poorly made and lasted 20 years. However, in 1180 the new and superior "Short Cross" issue commenced, being issued from only twelve major towns.

	F	VF	EF
Henry II, Penny, Tealby	£100	£325	—
Henry II, Penny, Short Cross	£40	£125	—

RICHARD I
(1189–1199)

There were no major changes during this reign, in fact pennies continued to be struck with his father Henry's name throughout the reign. The coins struck under Richard tend to be rather crude in style.

	F	VF	EF
Richard I, Penny	£60	£200	—

JOHN
(1199–1216)

As with his brother before him, there were no major changes during the reign of King John, and pennies with his father's name were struck throughout the reign, although they tended to be somewhat neater in style than those struck during the reign of Richard I.

	F	VF	EF
John, Penny.....................................	£50	£125	£275

HENRY III
(1216–72)

The coinage during Henry III's reign continued as before with the short cross issue. However, in 1247 a new long cross design was introduced to prevent clipping. This design was to last in one form or another for many centuries. Late in the reign saw a brief appearance of the 1st English gold coin.

	F	VF	EF
Henry III, Penny, Short Cross	£25	£75	£240
Henry III, Penny, Long Cross..................	£20	£50	£150

EDWARD I
(1272–1307)

After a few years of issuing similar pieces to his father, in 1279 Edward I ordered a major re-coinage. This consisted of well-made pennies, halfpennies and farthings in relatively large quantities, and for a brief period a groat (four pence) was produced. These were often mounted and gilded, price is for an undamaged piece.The pennies are amongst the most common of all hammered coins.

	F	VF	EF
Edward I (and Edward II)			
Groat (often damaged) see below ...	£3750	£9250	—
Penny..	£20	£45	—
Halfpenny...	£20	£55	—
Farthing..	£20	£45	—

Groat often damaged by contemporary gilding and/or mounting (price is for undamaged pieces)

Edward I penny

EDWARD II
(1307–1327)

	F	VF	EF
Edward II, long cross Pennies, Halfpennies and Farthings (very similar to Edward I)	£25	£60	—

EDWARD III
(1327–77)

This was a long reign which saw major changes in the coinage, the most significant being the introduction of a gold coinage (based on the Noble, valued at 6s 8d, and its fractions) and a regular issue of a large silver groat (and half groat). The provincial mints were limited to a few episcopal cities but coins of English type were also struck in the newly-acquired Calais Mint.

	F	VF	EF
Gold			
Noble	£850	£2500	£5000
Half Noble	£525	£1500	£3500
Quarter Noble	£300	£625	£1250
Silver			
Groat	£45	£150	£750
Half Groat	£25	£90	£375
Penny	£20	£80	£300
Half Penny	£20	£80	£250
Farthing	£30	£100	£300

Gold Noble

RICHARD II
(1377–1399)

The denominations continued during this reign much as before. However, coins are quite rare mainly due to the lack of bullion gold and silver going into the mints, mainly because of an inbalance with European weights and fineness.

	F	VF	EF
Gold			
Noble	£1200	£3600	—
Half Noble	£1250	£4400	—
Quarter Noble	£400	£1100	—
Silver			
Groat	£550	£2000	—
Half Groat	£250	£850	—
Penny	£65	£300	—
Half Penny	£30	£100	—
Farthing	£125	£450	—

Gold Noble

HENRY IV
(1399–1413)

Because of the continuing problems with the scarcity of gold and silver the coinage was reduced in weight in 1412, towards the end of the reign. All coins of this reign are quite scarce.

	F	VF
Gold		
Noble, Light coinage...................	£2000	£7000
Half Noble, Light coinage	£2000	£7000
Quarter Noble, Light coinage	£700	£2200
Silver		
Groat, Light coinage	£2750	£8000
Half Groat, Heavy coinage..........	£800	£2500
Penny..	£500	£1350
Half Penny	£300	£800
Farthing..	£750	£2250

Noble

HENRY V
(1413–22)

Monetary reform introduced towards the end of his father's reign in 1412 improved the supply of bullion and hence coins of Henry V are far more common. All of the main denominations continued as before.

	F	VF	EF
Gold			
Noble £1000	£3250	£6000	
Half Noble £850	£2750	—	
Quarter Noble £350	£775	£1600	
Silver			
Groat, class "C" £175	£550	—	
Half Groat..............................£125	£350	—	
Penny.......................................£30	£140	—	
Half Penny..............................£25	£85	—	
Farthing...............................£3258	£800	—	

Groat

HENRY VI
(1422–61 and again 1470–71)

Although there were no new denominations except for the Angel & Halfangel during the 2nd reign during these reigns (see Edward IV below), Henry's first reign saw eleven different issues, each for a few years and distinguished by privy marks, i.e. annulets, pinecones, mascles, leaves etc.

HENRY VI *continued*

	F	VF	EF
Gold			
First reign—			
Noble, Annulet issue	£875	£2750	£5250
Half Noble, Annulet issue	£700	£2000	£4250
Quarter Noble, Annulet issue	£335	£725	£1400
2nd reign—			
Angel	£1850	£5250	—
Half Angel	£4750	£13750	—
Silver			
Groat, Annulet issue	£50	£135	£350
Half Groat, Annulet issue	£30	£100	£300
Penny	£25	£80	£350
Half Penny, Annulet issue	£20	£60	£185
Farthing, Annulet issue	£100	£300	—

Noble

EDWARD IV
(1461–70 and again 1471–83)

The significant changes during these reigns were the replacement of the noble by the rose ryal (and revalued at 10 shillings) and the continuation of the angel at the old noble value. We also start to see mint-marks or initial marks appearing, usually at the top of the coin, they were used to denote the period of issue for dating purposes and often lasted for two to three years e.g. rose, lis, crown etc. Groats were issued at London, Bristol, Coventry, Norwich and York.

	F	VF	EF
Gold			
Ryal	£850	£2500	£4250
Half Ryal	£750	£2100	£3500
Quarter Ryal	£425	£1150	£2000
Angel, 2nd reign	£850	£2250	£3750
Half Angel, 2nd reign	£750	£2200	—
"Flemish" copy of Ryal	£750	£2250	—
Silver			
Groat	£45	£120	£450
Half Groat	£40	£130	£400
Penny	£20	£120	£350
Half Penny	£20	£80	—
Farthing, Heavy coinage	£225	£800	—

Angel

RICHARD III
(1483–85)

The close of the Yorkist Plantagenet and Medieval period come together at this time. There are no new significant numismatic changes but most silver coins of Richard whilst not really rare, continue to be very popular and priced quite high. The smaller denominations are usually poor condition.

	F	VF	EF
Gold			
Angel	£5500	£17500	—
Half Angel	£7500	£25000	—
Silver			
Groat	£850	£2300	—
Half Groat	£1500	£4350	—
Penny	£450	£1200	—
Half Penny	£400	£1150	—
Farthing	£1650	£4750	—

Groat

141

PART II

Among the more significant features of the post-Renaissance period as it affected coinage is the introduction of realistic portraiture during the reign of Henry VII. We also have a much wider and varied number of new and revised denominations, for example eleven different gold denominations of Henry VIII and the same number of silver for Elizabeth I. Here we only mention the introduction or changes in the main denominations, giving a value for all of them, once again listing the commonest type.

HENRY VII
(1485–1509)

The gold sovereign of 20 shillings makes its first appearance in 1489 as does the testoon (later shilling) in about 1500. The silver penny was re-designed to a rather crude likeness of the sovereign, enthroned.

	F	VF	EF
Gold			
Sovereign	£27500	£90,000	—
Ryal	£35000	£135,000	—
Angel	£725	£2000	—
Half Angel	£675	£1800	—
Silver			
Testoon 1/-	£18000	£40,000	—
Groat, facing bust	£65	£190	£650
Half Groat	£30	£100	£325
Penny, sovereign type	£30	£90	£300
Half Penny	£20	£75	—
Farthing	£450	£1400	—

Profile Groat

HENRY VIII
(1509–47)

After a long initial period of very little change in the coinage, in 1526 there were many, with an attempt to bring the gold/silver ratio in line with the continental currencies. Some gold coins only lasted a short time and are very rare. The crown (in gold) makes its first appearance. Towards the end of the reign we see large issues of debased silver coins (with a high copper content) bearing the well-known facing portrait of the ageing King. These tend to turn up in poor condition and include the shilling in greater numbers. Similar posthumous issues were minted during early reign of Edward VI.

Gold			
Sovereign, 3rd coinage	£6000	£22000	—
Half Sovereign	£900	£3000	—
Angel	£750	£2000	£3250
Half Angel	£700	£1800	£2750
Quarter Angel	£775	£2250	—
George Noble	£10000	£35000	—
Half George Noble	£10000	£35000	—
Crown of the rose	£7250	£26500	—
Crown of the double rose	£725	£2250	—
Half Crown of the double rose	£550	£1500	—
Silver			
Testoon 1/-	£850	£4500	—
Groat, 2nd coinage	£80	£240	£1100
Half Groat, 2nd coinage	£50	£160	£600
Penny	£35	£100	£425
Half Penny	£25	£75	—
Farthing	£300	£850	—

Gold Sovereign

EDWARD VI
(1547–53)

Some of the coins struck in the first few years of this short reign could really be called Henry VIII posthumous issues as there is continuity in both name and style from his father's last issue. However, overlapping this period are portrait issues of the boy King, particularly shillings (usually poor quality coins). This period also sees the first dated English coin (shown in Roman numerals) MDXLIX (1549). In 1551 however, a new coinage was introduced with a restored silver quality from the Crown (dated 1551) down to the new sixpence and threepence.

	F	VF	EF
Gold			
Sovereign (30s)	£7000	£25000	—
Half Sovereign	£1750	£6500	—
Crown	£2000	£6750	—
Half Crown	£1650	£5500	—
Angel	£14000	£40000	—
Half Angel	—	£45000	—
Sovereign (20s)	£5500	£17000	—
Silver			
Crown	£900	£2750	—
Half Crown	£650	£1800	—
Shilling	£125	£400	—
Sixpence	£130	£450	—
Groat	£750	£4000	—
Threepence	£225	£1150	—
Half Groat	£350	£1250	—
Penny	£50	£215	—
Half Penny	£200	£825	—
Farthing	£1250	£4250	—

Crowned bust half sovereign

MARY
(1553–54)

The early coins of Mary's sole reign are limited and continue to use some of the same denominations as Edward, except that the gold ryal was reintroduced.

	F	VF
Gold		
Sovereign (30s)	£8000	£26000
Ryal	£35000	—
Angel	£2300	£7250
Half Angel	£5500	£15000
Silver		
Groat	£170	£550
Half Groat	£700	£2350
Penny	£600	£2150

Groat

PHILIP & MARY
(1554–58)

After a very short reign alone, Mary married Philip of Spain and they technically ruled jointly (although not for very long in practise) until her death. After her marriage we see both her and Philip on the shillings and sixpences with both full Spanish and then English titles alone.

	F	VF
Gold		
Angel	£6500	£22000
Half Angel	£14000	—
Silver		
Shilling	£475	£2150
Sixpence	£450	£1750
Groat	£190	£600
Half Groat	£475	£1750
Penny	£60	£210

Shilling

ELIZABETH I
(1558–1603)

As might be expected with a long reign there are a number of significant changes in the coinage which include several new denominations—so many in silver that every value from the shilling downwards was marked and dated to distinguish them. Early on we have old base Edward VI shillings countermarked to a new reduced value (not priced here). Also due to a lack of small change and the expense of making a miniscule farthing we have a new threehalfpence and threefarthings. Finally we see the beginnings of a milled (machine produced) coinage for a brief period from 1561–71.

	F	VF	EF
Gold			
Sovereign (30s)	£6750	£18000	—
Ryal (15s)	£25000	£80000	—
Angel	£1100	£3200	—
Half Angel	£1000	£3000	—
Quarter Angel	£900	£2800	—
Pound (20s)	£3000	£10000	—
Half Pound	£1600	£4750	—
Crown	£1200	£3500	—
Half Crown	£1150	£3400	—
Silver			
Crown (mm l)	£1600	£5000	—
Half Crown (mm l)	£1100	£2550	—
Shilling	£100	£450	£1500
Sixpence	£50	£200	£850
Groat	£65	£275	£775
Threepence	£40	£175	£475
Half Groat	£25	£90	£275
Threehalfpence	£45	£175	—
Penny	£20	£70	£225
Threefarthings	£70	£225	—
Half Penny	£25	£90	£150

Shilling

JAMES I
(1603–25)

Although the size of the gold coinage remains much the same as Elizabeth's reign, the name and weight or value of the denominations have several changes, i.e. Pound = Sovereign = Unite = Laurel. A new four shilling gold coin (thistle crown) was introduced. A number of the silver coins now have their value in Roman numerals on the coin. Relatively few angels were made from this period onwards and they are usually found pierced.

	F	VF	EF
Gold			
Sovereign (20s)	£2750	£12500	—
Unite	£675	£1700	£3750
Double crown/half unite	£450	£1175	£2750
Crown	£300	£675	£1750
Thistle Crown	£325	£735	£1850
Half Crown	£240	£500	—
Rose Ryal (30s)	£3250	£12000	—
Spur Ryal (15s)	£7750	£30000	—
Angel (pierced)	£725	£2150	—
Half Angel (Unpierced)	£3500	£12500	—
Laurel	£650	£1700	£3750
Half Laurel	£450	£1400	£3200
Quarter Laurel	£275	£700	£1700
Silver			
Crown	£750	£2000	—
Half Crown	£325	£800	—
Shilling	£70	£275	—
Sixpence	£60	£225	—
Half Groat	£20	£60	£140
Penny	£20	£50	£130
Half Penny	£10	£40	£100

Gold Unite, second bust

Silver Halfcrown

CHARLES I
(1625–49)

This reign is probably the most difficult to simplify as there are so many different issues and whole books have been produced on this period alone. From the beginning of the King's reign and throughout the Civil War, a number of mints operated for varying lengths of time, producing both regular and irregular issues. The Tower mint was taken over by Parliament in 1642 but before this a small quantity of milled coinage was produced alongside the regular hammered issues. The Court then moved to Oxford from where, for the next three years, large quantities of gold and silver were struck (including rare triple unites and large silver pounds). The most prolific of the provincial mints were those situated at Aberystwyth, York, Oxford, Shrewsbury, Bristol, Exeter, Truro, Chester and Worcester as well as some smaller mints mainly situated in the West Country. Among the more interesting coins of the period are the pieces struck on unusually-shaped flans at Newark and Pontefract whilst those towns were under siege. As many of the coins struck during the Civil War were crudely struck on hastily gathered bullion and plate, they provide a fascinating area of study. The prices indicated below are the minimum for the commonest examples of each denomination irrespective of town of origin.

Triple unite

	F	VF	EF
Gold			
Triple Unite (£3) (Oxford)	£15000	£40000	—
Unite	£700	£1800	—
Double crown/Half unite	£475	£1350	—
Crown	£300	£650	—
Angel (pierced)	£800	£2600	—
Angel (unpierced)	£2750	£8500	—
Silver			
Pound (20 shillings—Oxford)	£3000	£9000	—
Half Pound (Shrewsbury)	£1350	£3750	—
Crown (Truro, Exeter)	£450	£1350	—
Half Crown	£50	£220	—
Shilling	£40	£160	£900
Sixpence	£35	£140	£800
Groat (Aberystwyth)	£60	£180	£550
Threepence (Aberystwyth)	£50	£170	£475
Half Groat	£20	£60	£175
Penny	£20	£55	£150
Half Penny	£15	£25	£60

Above: Newark siege shilling.

Oxford Halfcrown

THE COMMONWEALTH
(1649–60)

After the execution of Charles I, Parliament changed the design of the coinage. They are simple non- portrait pieces with an English legend.

	F	VF	EF
Gold			
Unite	£2250	£5250	—
Double crown/Half unite	£1600	£4400	—
Crown	£1300	£3650	—
Silver			
Crown	£1150	£2750	£7000
Half Crown	£325	£825	£3500
Shilling	£250	£625	£2350
Sixpence	£235	£575	£1750
Half Groat	£40	£120	£350
Penny	£40	£120	£350
Halfpenny	£30	£75	£175

Crown

CHARLES II
(1660–85)

Although milled coins had been produced for Oliver Cromwell in 1656–58, after the Restoration of the monarchy hammered coins continued to be produced until 1663, when the machinery was ready to manufacture large quantities of good milled pieces.

	F	VF	EF
Gold			
Unite (2nd issue)	£1800	£5000	—
Double crown/Half unite	£1450	£4400	—
Crown (2nd issue)	£1700	£5250	—
Silver			
Half Crown (3rd issue)	£250	£850	—
Shilling (3rd issue)	£150	£600	—
Sixpence (3rd issue)	£125	£475	—
Fourpence (3rd issue)	£40	£130	£275
Threepence (3rd issue)	£35	£120	£225
Twopence (3rd issue)	£20	£60	£160
Penny (3rd issue)	£30	£75	£175

Halfcrown

A COMPREHENSIVE PRICE GUIDE
TO THE COINS OF

THE
UNITED KINGDOM
1656–2017

including

*England, Scotland,
Isle of Man,
Guernsey, Jersey, Alderney,
also Ireland*

When referring to this price guide one must bear a number of important points in mind. The points listed here have been taken into consideration during the preparation of this guide and we hope that the prices given will provide a true reflection of the market at the time of going to press. Nevertheless, the publishers can accept no liability for the accuracy of the prices quoted.

1. "As struck" examples with flaws will be worth less than the indicated price.
2. Any coin which is particularly outstanding, with an attractive natural toning or in superb state will command a much *higher* price than that shown.
3. These prices refer strictly to the British market, and do not reflect outside opinions.
4. Some prices given for coins not seen in recent years are estimates based on a knowledge of the market.
5. In the case of coins of high rarity, prices are not generally given.
6. In the listing, "−" indicates, where applicable, one of the following:
    a. Metal or bullion value only
    b. Not usually found in this grade
    c. Not collected in this condition
7. Proof coins are listed in FDC under the UNC column.
8. All prices are quoted in £ sterling, exclusive of VAT (where applicable).

FIFTY SHILLINGS

	F	VF	EF

OLIVER CROMWELL (1656–58)

	F	VF	EF
1656..	£18,000	£45,000	£130,000

Opinions differ as to whether the portrait coinage of Oliver Cromwell was ever meant for circulation but for the sake of completeness it has been decided to include it in this Yearbook. The fifty shillings gold coin is unique as it was only struck during Cromwell's time using the same dies that were used for the broad or 20 shillings coin but with a weight of approximately 2.5 times that of the broad.

FIVE GUINEAS

CHARLES II (1660–85)

1668 First bust	£3000	£7000	£22000
1668 — Elephant below bust	£2750	£6000	£22000
1669 —	£2750	£6775	—
1669 — Elephant..................................	£3300	£7000	—
1670 —	£2750	£7000	£22000
1670 Proof..	—	—	£135000
1671 —	£3000	£7000	£24000
1672 —	£2750	£7000	£22000
1673 —	£2750	£7000	£22000
1674 —	£3500	£7500	£25000
1675 —	£3000	£7000	£24000
1675 — Elephant..................................	£3200	£8000	—
1675 — Elephant & Castle below bust...	£3750	£8000	£30000
1676 —	£3000	£6500	£22000
1676 — Elephant & Castle	£3000	£7500	£25000
1677 —	£3200	£7000	£24500
1677/5 — Elephant..............................	£3500	£8000	£27500
1677 — Elephant & Castle	£3200	£7000	£24000
1678/7 — 8 over 7................................	£2700	£7000	£22000
1678/7 — Elephant & Castle	£3250	£7500	£24000
1678/7 Second Bust.............................	£3000	£7000	£22000
1679 —	£2700	£7000	£22000
1680 —	£2750	£7000	£22000
1680 — Elephant & Castle	£3250	£7000	£24000
1681 —	£3000	£6750	£24000
1681 — Elephant & Castle	£3000	£7000	£24000
1682 —	£2700	£6500	£22000
1682 — Elephant & Castle	£2750	£7000	£22500
1683 —	£3000	£7000	£24000
1683 — Elephant & Castle	£3000	£7500	£25000
1684 —	£2600	£6500	£22000
1684 — Elephant & Castle	£2750	£7000	£22500

Charles II

JAMES II (1685–88)

1686...	£3500	£8000	£28000
1687...	£3250	£8000	£25000
1687 Elephant & Castle........................	£3300	£7750	£25000
1688	£3300	£7500	£24000
1688 Elephant & Castle........................	£3500	£8000	£26500

	F	VF	EF

WILLIAM AND MARY (1688–94)

	F	VF	EF
1691	£2750	£6750	£20000
1691 Elephant & Castle	£2800	£6750	£20000
1692	£2900	£6500	£20000
1692 Elephant & Castle	£3000	£6500	£21000
1693	£2800	£6500	£20000
1693 Elephant & Castle	£2800	£6750	£21000
1694	£2800	£6500	£20000
1694 Elephant & Castle	£2800	£6500	£21000

WILLIAM III (1694–1702)

	F	VF	EF
1699 First bust	£3000	£8000	£26000
1699 — Elephant & Castle	£3250	£8500	£27500
1700 —	£3000	£8000	£26500
1701 Second bust "fine work"	£3250	£8000	£25000

(1701 "fine work"—beware recent forgeries)

ANNE (1702–14)

Pre-Union with Scotland

	F	VF	EF
1703 VIGO below bust	£40000	£90000	£275000
1705	£4750	£12000	£40000
1706	£4500	£11000	£37500

Post-Union (different shields)

	F	VF	EF
1706	£3200	£7000	£24000
1709 Narrow shields	£3500	£7000	£24000
1711 Broader shields	£3500	£7500	£25000
1713 —	£3500	£7000	£23500
1714 —	£3700	£7750	£26000
1714/3	£3750	£7750	£27000

William & Mary

GEORGE I (1714–27)

	F	VF	EF
1716	£4000	£10000	£32000
1717	£4000	£10500	£30000
1720	£4100	£9000	£30000
1726	£3700	£9500	£28000

GEORGE II (1727–60)

	F	VF	EF
1729 Young head	£2750	£6200	£21000
1729 — E.I.C. below head	£2700	£6000	£18500
1731 —	£3250	£7000	£25000
1735 —	£2800	£7200	£25000
1738 —	£2750	£6000	£22000
1741	£2650	£6000	£21000
1741/38 41 over 38	£2750	£6200	£22000
1746 Old head, LIMA	£2750	£6000	£21000
1748 —	£2750	£6000	£20000
1753 —	£2750	£6250	£20000

GEORGE III (1760–1820)

	F	VF	EF
1770 Patterns	—	—	£250000
1773	—	—	£225000
1777	—	—	£200000

Anne

TWO GUINEAS

	F	VF	EF

CHARLES II (1660–85)

	F	VF	EF
1664 First bust	£1800	£4250	£11000
1664 — Elephant	£1700	£3800	£9500
1665 —		Extremely rare	
1669 —		Extremely rare	
1671 —	£2200	£5500	£16000
1673 First bust		Extremely rare	
1675 Second bust	£1800	£4000	£10000
1676 —	£1650	£4000	£10000
1676 — Elephant & Castle	£1700	£4000	£10000
1677 —	£1700	£3750	£9000
1677 — Elephant & Castle		Extremely rare	
1678/7 —	£1600	£3500	£9500
1678 — Elephant		Extremely rare	
1678 — Elephant & Castle	£1800	£4000	£10000
1679 —	£1700	£4000	£9500
1680 —	£1800	£4500	£12000
1681 —	£1700	£3500	£9000
1682 — Elephant & Castle	£1750	£3750	£11000
1683 —	£1700	£3700	£9500
1683 — Elephant & Castle	£1800	£4500	£12000
1684 —	£1700	£4000	£9750
1684 — Elephant & Castle	£1850	£4500	£12000

Charles II

JAMES II (1685–88)

	F	VF	EF
1687	£2200	£4750	£15000
1688/7	£2400	£5500	£15000

WILLIAM AND MARY (1688–94)

	F	VF	EF
1691 Elephant & Castle		Extremely rare	
1693	£1800	£4500	£12000
1693 Elephant & Castle	£2000	£4750	£15000
1694 — 4 over 3	£1750	£4500	£12000
1694/3 Elephant & Castle	£1700	£4500	£12500

James II

WILLIAM III (1694–1702)

	F	VF	EF
1701 "fine work"	£2000	£4500	£14000

ANNE (1702–14)

	F	VF	EF
1709 Post Union	£1600	£3500	£10000
1711	£1550	£3500	£9750
1713	£1500	£3300	£9000
1714/3	£1600	£3750	£11000

GEORGE I (1714–27)

	F	VF	EF
1717	£1400	£2750	£8000
1720	£1400	£2750	£8200
1720/17	£1500	£3000	£8250
1726	£1350	£2750	£7500

Anne

	F	VF	EF

GEORGE II (1727–60)

	F	VF	EF
1733 Proof only FDC		Extremely Rare	
1734 Young head 4 over 3	£1700	£4200	—
1735 —	£1100	£2250	£7000
1738 —	£900	£1700	£3600
1739 —	£900	£1700	£3600
1739 Intermediate head	£900	£1700	£3300
1740 —	£900	£1700	£3500
1748 Old head	£950	£1850	£4500
1753 —	£1000	£1900	£5400

GEORGE III (1760–1820)

	F	VF	EF
1768 Patterns only	—	Extremely Rare	
1773 Patterns only	—	Extremely Rare	
1777 Patterns only	—	Extremely Rare	

George II

GUINEAS

CHARLES II (1660–85)

	F	VF	EF
1663 First bust	£3000	£10000	£37500
1663 — Elephant below	£2500	£8000	—
1664 Second bust	£3000	£8500	
1664 — Elephant	£3600	£10000	£35000
1664 Third bust	£900	£3000	£12000
1664 — Elephant	£1500	£4600	£15000
1665 —	£900	£3000	£11000
1665 — Elephant	£1500	£5000	£17500
1666 —	£850	£3000	£11000
1667 —	£850	£3000	£11000
1668 —	£850	£3000	£11000
1668 — Elephant		Extremely rare	
1669 —	£850	£2850	£10000
1670 —	£850	£2500	£11000
1671 —	£850	£2500	£11000
1672 —	£850	£3000	£11000
1672 Fourth bust	£800	£2200	£6750
1673 Third bust	£900	£3000	£12000
1673 Fourth bust	£700	£2000	£7000
1674 —	£700	£2000	£7000
1674 — Elephant & Castle		Extremely rare	
1675 —	£700	£2200	£7000
1675 — CRAOLVS Error		Extremely rare	
1675 — Elephant & Castle	£850	£2500	£10000
1676 —	£700	£2200	£7000
1676 — Elephant & Castle	£800	£2500	£9500
1677 —	£675	£2100	£7000
1677/5 — Elephant 7 over 5		Extremely rare	
1677 — Elephant & Castle	£800	£2200	£9000
1678 —	£750	£2000	£7000
1678 — Elephant		Extremely rare	
1678 — Elephant & Castle	£800	£2500	£10000

Charles II, third bust

Charles II, fourth bust, elephant & castle below

	F	VF	EF
1679 —	£750	£2000	£7000
1679 — Elephant & Castle	£800	£2500	£10500
1680 —	£700	£1900	£7000
1680 — Elephant & Castle	£800	£2500	£10000
1681 —	£750	£2100	£7000
1681 — Elephant & Castle	£750	£2500	£9000
1682 —	£700	£2000	£7000
1682 — Elephant & Castle	£850	£2800	£10000
1683 —	£700	£2200	£7250
1683 — Elephant & Castle	£800	£2500	£10000
1684 —	£700	£2200	£7000
1684 — Elephant & Castle	£850	£2600	£11000

James II, first bust, elephant & castle below

JAMES II (1685–1688)

	F	VF	EF
1685 First bust	£700	£2500	£9000
1685 — Elephant & Castle	£800	£2600	£9500
1686 —	£800	£2600	£9000
1686 — Elephant & Castle		Extremely rare	
1686 Second bust	£700	£2300	£7500
1686 — Elephant & Castle	£800	£2500	£9500
1687 —	£700	£2300	£7500
1687 —Elephant & Castle	£800	£2500	£9500
1688 —	£700	£2400	£7500
1688 — Elephant & Castle	£800	£2500	£8750

James II, second bust

WILLIAM AND MARY (1688–94)

	F	VF	EF
1689...	£650	£2000	£8000
1689 Elephant & Castle	£650	£2200	£8000
1690...	£700	£2200	£8000
1690 GVLIFLMVS..............................	£800	£2200	£8000
1690 Elephant & Castle	£800	£2400	£8800
1691...	£650	£2200	£7500
1691 Elephant & Castle	£700	£2200	£7500
1692...	£650	£2000	£7500
1692 Elephant	£900	£3000	£9750
1692 Elephant & Castle	£700	£2500	£8250
1693...	£650	£2000	£7500
1693 Elephant		Extremely rare	
1693 Elephant & Castle		Extremely rare	
1694...	£700	£2000	£7000
1694/3	£700	£2000	£7000
1694 Elephant & Castle	£700	£2200	£7000
1694/3 Elephant & Castle...................	£750	£2400	£7500

WILLIAM III (1694–1702)

	F	VF	EF
1695 First bust	£600	£2000	£6250
1695 — Elephant & Castle	£1000	£3000	£12000
1696 —	£600	£2000	£7000
1696 — Elephant & Castle		Extremely rare	
1697 —	£650	£2000	£6500
1697 Second bust	£600	£2000	£7500
1697 — Elephant & Castle	£1400	£4500	—
1698 —	£600	£1900	£6000
1698 — Elephant & Castle	£600	£2000	£6000
1699 —	£600	£1900	£6500
1699 — Elephant & Castle		Extremely rare	
1700 —	£600	£1800	£6000
1700 — Elephant & Castle	£1200	£4500	—
1701 —	£600	£1800	£5500
1701 — Elephant & Castle		Extremely rare	
1701 Third bust "fine work".............................	£1100	£3500	£12000

William III, second bust

	Г	VГ	EF

ANNE (1702–1714)

	Г	VF	EF
1702 (Pre-Union) First bust	£1000	£3250	£11000
1703 — VIGO below	£15000	£35000	£90000
1705 —	£1100	£3000	£10000
1706 —	£1100	£3000	£10000
1707 —	£1100	£3000	£10000
1707 — (Post-Union)	£725	£2500	£8500
1707 — Elephant & Castle	£800	£3000	£10000
1707 Second bust	£625	£2200	£7500
1708 First bust	£675	£2500	£8500
1708 Second bust	£600	£1950	£6500
1708 — Elephant & Castle	£800	£3000	£10000
1709 —	£600	£1800	£6000
1709 — Elephant & Castle	£800	£2800	£8500
1710 Third bust	£625	£1500	£4600
1711 —	£625	£1500	£4600
1712 —	£600	£1500	£4500
1713 —	£550	£1400	£4200
1714 —	£550	£1400	£4200
1714 GRΛTIΛ	£700	£1700	£4000

Anne, second bust

GEORGE I (1714–27)

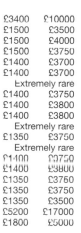

	Г	VF	EF
1714 First bust (Prince Elector)	£1350	£3400	£10000
1715 Second bust	£600	£1500	£3500
1715 Third bust	£500	£1500	£4000
1716 —	£525	£1500	£3750
1716 Fourth bust	£525	£1400	£3700
1717 —	£525	£1400	£3700
1718 —			Extremely rare
1719 —	£500	£1400	£3750
1720 —	£500	£1400	£3800
1721 —	£500	£1400	£3800
1721 — Elephant & Castle			Extremely rare
1722 —	£500	£1350	£3750
1722 — Elephant & Castle			Extremely rare
1723 —	£525	£1400	£3750
1723 Fifth bust	£525	£1400	£3800
1724 —	£525	£1350	£3750
1725 —	£525	£1350	£3750
1726 —	£500	£1350	£3500
1726 — Elephant & Castle	£1750	£5200	£17000
1727 —	£600	£1800	£5000

George I, third bust

GEORGE II (1727–60)

	Г	VF	EF
1727 First young head, early large shield	£900	£2600	£8000
1727 — Larger lettering, early small shield	£800	£2500	£8000
1728 — —	£900	£2800	£8500
1729 2nd young head E.I.C. below	£1100	£3500	£11000
1729 — Proof			Very Rare
1730 —	£625	£1500	£5000
1731 —	£550	£1600	£4500
1731 — E.I.C. below	£900	£2750	£8000
1732 —	£700	£2500	£7500
1732 — E.I.C. below	£800	£2500	£8000
1732 — Larger lettering obverse	£650	£1600	£4600
1732 — — E.I.C. below	£900	£1800	£8000
1733 — —	£550	£1400	£3500
1734 — —	£550	£1400	£3500
1735 — —	£550	£1400	£3500
1736 — —	£550	£1500	£3250
1737 — —	£550	£1500	£3250

George II, 1759, old head, larger lettering

	F	VF	EF
1738 — —	£550	£1400	£3500
1739 Intermediate head	£500	£1100	£3000
1739 — E.I.C. below....................................	£1100	£2900	£9000
1740 —	£550	£1400	£5000
1741/39 —	£800	£2400	£6250
1743 —	£800	£2400	£6250
1745 — Larger lettering obv. Older bust	£500	£1350	£4500
1745 — LIMA below....................................	£1500	£4500	£12000
1746 — (GEORGIVS) Larger lettering obv.	£500	£1500	£3800
1747 Old head, large lettering	£400	£1100	£3200
1748 —	£400	£1100	£3300
1749 —	£450	£1200	£3500
1750 —	£400	£1100	£3600
1751 — small lettering.................................	£400	£1100	£3500
1753 —	£400	£1100	£3500
1755 —	£400	£1100	£3300
1756 —	£400	£1100	£3400
1758 —	£400	£1100	£3400
1759 —	£400	£1100	£3300
1760 —	£400	£1100	£3000

George III first head

GEORGE III (1760–1820)

1761 First head.................................	£1900	£5000	£9500
1763 Second head	£1500	£4000	£9000
1764 —	£1300	£3700	£8500
1765 Third head	£450	£800	£1850
1766 —	£450	£800	£1850
1767 —	£500	£850	£2200
1768 —	£450	£800	£2000
1769 —	£450	£800	£2100
1770 —	£1000	£2000	£5000
1771 —	£450	£600	£1400
1772 —	£450	£600	£1400
1773 —	£450	£650	£1600
1774 Fourth head	£400	£600	£1100
1775 —	£425	£650	£1050
1776 —	£425	£675	£1100
1777 —	£425	£600	£1100
1778 —	£650	£1000	£2750
1779 —	£450	£725	£1250
1781 —	£400	£600	£1200
1782 —	£400	£600	£1200
1783 —	£375	£625	£1200
1784 —	£375	£625	£1200
1785 —	£375	£625	£1200
1786 —	£450	£700	£1250
1787 Fifth head, "Spade" reverse	£400	£575	£1050
1788 —	£400	£575	£1050
1789 —	£400	£575	£1100
1790 —	£425	£650	£1200
1791 —	£400	£600	£1100
1792 —	£400	£600	£1100
1793 —	£400	£600	£1150
1794 —	£400	£600	£1100
1795 —	£400	£600	£1100
1796 —	£400	£600	£1100
1797 —	£400	£600	£1100
1798 —	£400	£600	£1100
1799 —	£475	£800	£1600
1813 Sixth head, "Military" reverse	£900	£2000	£4500

(Beware of counterfeits of this series—many dangerous copies exist)

Fourth head

Fifth head, Spade reverse

Sixth "Military" head

HALF GUINEAS

	F	VF	EF
CHARLES II (1660–85)			
1669 First bust	£375	£1250	£4000
1670 —	£375	£1250	£3500
1671 —	£475	£1400	£5000
1672 —	£400	£1150	£4250
1672 Second bust	£400	£1000	£3750
1673 —	£450	£1350	£4250
1674 —	£500	£1600	£4400
1675 —	£500	£1650	£4400
1676 —	£400	£1150	£3750
1676 — Elephant & Castle	£725	£3000	—
1677 —	£375	£1150	£3500
1677 — Elephant & Castle	£600	£2000	—
1678 —	£400	£1250	£3650
1678 — Elephant & Castle	£500	£1650	£5500
1679 —	£400	£1250	£3500
1680 —	£400	£2000	—
1680 — Elephant & Castle	£600	£2000	£5750
1681 —	£400	£1600	—
1682 —	£400	£1350	£3750
1682 — Elephant & Castle	£600	£2000	—
1683 —	£375	£1150	£3750
1683 — Elephant & Castle	Extremely rare		
1684 —	£350	£1000	£3750
1684 — Elephant & Castle	£600	£2000	£6000

Charles II, first bust

	F	VF	EF
JAMES II (1685–88)			
1686	£500	£1150	£4000
1686 Elephant & Castle	£850	£3750	£7000
1687	£500	£1500	£4250
1688	£500	£1500	£4250

	F	VF	EF
WILLIAM AND MARY (1688–94)			
1689 First busts	£500	£1850	£4250
1690 Second busts	£500	£2000	£4300
1691 —	£500	£1850	£4250
1691 — Elephant & Castle	£500	£1750	£4400
1692 —	£450	£1600	£3500
1692 — Elephant	Extremely rare		
1692 — Elephant & Castle	£450	£1600	£4000
1693 —	Extremely rare		
1694 —	£450	£1600	£4000

William & Mary, first busts

	F	VF	EF
WILLIAM III (1694–1702)			
1695	£350	£850	£3250
1695 Elephant & Castle	£600	£1500	£4550
1696 —	£400	£1000	£3500
1697 Larger Harp rev.	£500	£1500	£4500
1698	£500	£1250	£4150
1698 Elephant & Castle	£600	£1500	£3500
1699	Extremely rare		
1700	£325	£850	£3250
1701	£300	£800	£3200

William III, elephant & castle below bust

	F	VF	EF

ANNE (1702–14)

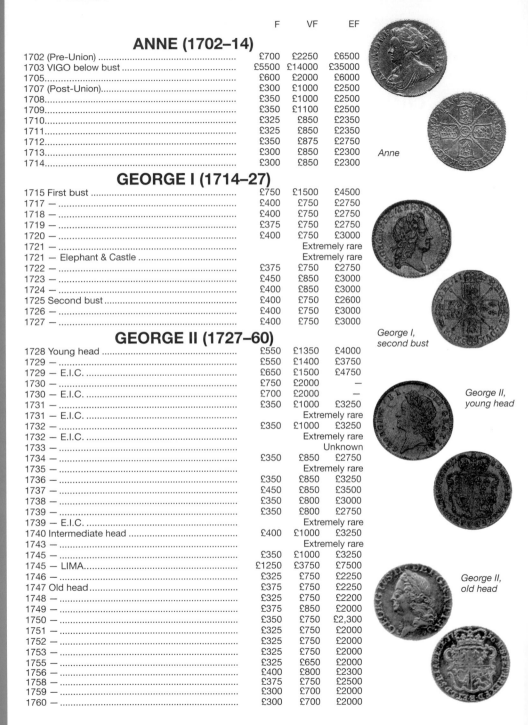

	F	VF	EF
1702 (Pre-Union)	£700	£2250	£6500
1703 VIGO below bust	£5500	£14000	£35000
1705	£600	£2000	£6000
1707 (Post-Union)	£300	£1000	£2500
1708	£350	£1000	£2500
1709	£350	£1100	£2500
1710	£325	£850	£2350
1711	£325	£850	£2350
1712	£350	£875	£2750
1713	£300	£850	£2300
1714	£300	£850	£2300

Anne

GEORGE I (1714–27)

	F	VF	EF
1715 First bust	£750	£1500	£4500
1717 —	£400	£750	£2750
1718 —	£400	£750	£2750
1719 —	£375	£750	£2750
1720 —	£400	£750	£3000
1721 —		Extremely rare	
1721 — Elephant & Castle		Extremely rare	
1722 —	£375	£750	£2750
1723 —	£450	£850	£3000
1724 —	£400	£850	£3000
1725 Second bust	£400	£750	£2600
1726 —	£400	£750	£3000
1727 —	£400	£750	£3000

George I, second bust

GEORGE II (1727–60)

	F	VF	EF
1728 Young head	£550	£1350	£4000
1729 —	£550	£1400	£3750
1729 — E.I.C.	£650	£1500	£4750
1730 —	£750	£2000	—
1730 — E.I.C.	£700	£2000	—
1731 —	£350	£1000	£3250
1731 — E.I.C.		Extremely rare	
1732 —	£350	£1000	£3250
1732 — E.I.C.		Extremely rare	
1733 —		Unknown	
1734 —	£350	£850	£2750
1735 —		Extremely rare	
1736 —	£350	£850	£3250
1737 —	£450	£850	£3500
1738 —	£350	£800	£3000
1739 —	£350	£800	£2750
1739 — E.I.C.		Extremely rare	
1740 Intermediate head	£400	£1000	£3250
1743 —		Extremely rare	
1745 —	£350	£1000	£3250
1745 — LIMA	£1250	£3750	£7500
1746 —	£325	£750	£2250
1747 Old head	£375	£750	£2250
1748 —	£325	£750	£2200
1749 —	£375	£850	£2000
1750 —	£350	£750	£2,300
1751 —	£325	£750	£2000
1752 —	£325	£750	£2000
1753 —	£325	£750	£2000
1755 —	£325	£650	£2000
1756 —	£400	£800	£2300
1758 —	£375	£750	£2500
1759 —	£300	£700	£2000
1760 —	£300	£700	£2000

George II, young head

George II, old head

GEORGE III (1760–1820)

	F	VF	EF
1762 First head	£700	£1900	£4500
1763 —	£750	£2250	£4000
1764 Second head	£275	£525	£1100
1765 —	£500	£1225	£3250
1766 —	£275	£500	£1350
1768 —	£275	£550	£1350
1769 —	£325	£550	£1500
1772 —		Extremely rare	
1773 —	£325	£600	£1600
1774 —	£350	£700	£1900
1774 Third head		Extremely rare	
1775 —	£1000	£2500	£6500
1775 Fourth head	£225	£350	£600
1775 — Proof		Extremely rare	
1776 —	£250	£500	£1250
1777 —	£250	£450	£900
1778 —	£250	£450	£900
1779 —	£250	£450	£1000
1781 —	£250	£450	£1050
1783 —	£500	£1800	—
1784 —	£225	£375	£850
1785 —	£225	£375	£750
1786 —	£225	£375	£750
1787 Fifth head, "Spade" rev.	£225	£375	£750
1788 —	£225	£375	£750
1789 —	£225	£375	£750
1790 —	£225	£375	£675
1791 —	£225	£375	£675
1792 —	£1200	£3500	—
1793 —	£225	£450	£750
1794 —	£225	£450	£750
1795 —	£225	£500	£850
1796 —	£225	£450	£750
1797 —	£225	£450	£750
1798 —	£225	£450	£750
1800 —	£325	£900	£2250
1801 Sixth head, Shield in Garter rev.	£225	£325	£600
1802 —	£225	£325	£600
1803 —	£225	£325	£600
1804 Seventh head	£225	£325	£600
1805		Extremely rare	
1806 —	£225	£375	£700
1808 —	£225	£375	£700
1809 —	£225	£375	£700
1810 —	£225	£400	£700
1811 —	£325	£600	£1400
1813 —	£325	£600	£1000

George III, second head

George III, fifth head, "spade" reverse

THIRD GUINEAS

GEORGE III (1760–1820)

DATE	F	VF	EF
1797 First head, date in legend	£150	£250	£525
1798 — —	£150	£250	£525
1799 — —	£150	£275	£525
1800 — —	£150	£250	£525
1801 Date under crown	£150	£250	£525
1802 —	£150	£250	£525
1803 —	£150	£250	£525
1804 Second head	£140	£225	£550
1806 —	£140	£250	£525
1808 —	£140	£300	£525
1809 —	£140	£300	£525
1810 —	£140	£300	£525
1811 —	£500	£1300	£2600
1813 —	£300	£550	£1100

George III, date in legend

George III, date under crown

QUARTER GUINEAS

GEORGE I (1714–27)
	F	VF	EF
1718	£150	£275	£650

GEORGE III (1760–1820)
	F	VF	EF
1762	£225	£425	£750

George I

FIVE POUNDS

DATE	Mintage	F	VF	EF	UNC

GEORGE III (1760–1820)
| 1820 (pattern only) | — | | | | Extremely rare |

GEORGE IV (1820–30)
| 1826 proof only | — | — | — | | £26,500 |

VICTORIA (1837–1901)
| 1839 Proof Only (Una & The Lion) Many Varieties FDC £60,000 upwards |
1887	53,844	£1400	£1900	£2500	£3300
1887 Proof	797	—	—	—	£5000
1887 S on ground on rev. (Sydney Mint)				Excessively rare
1893	20,405	£1800	£2500	£4000	£5500
1893 Proof	773	—	—	—	£7000

EDWARD VII (1902–10)
| 1902 | 34,910 | £1500 | £2000 | £2600 | £3500 |
| 1902 Matt proof | 8,066 | — | — | — | £3000 |

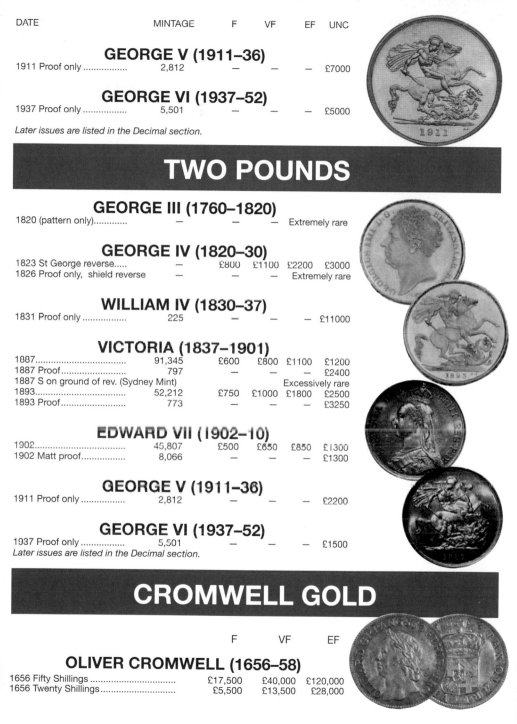

DATE	MINTAGE	F	VF	EF	UNC

GEORGE V (1911–36)
1911 Proof only 2,812   —   —   —   £7000

GEORGE VI (1937–52)
1937 Proof only 5,501   —   —   —   £5000

Later issues are listed in the Decimal section.

TWO POUNDS

GEORGE III (1760–1820)
1820 (pattern only).............   —   —   —   Extremely rare

GEORGE IV (1820–30)
1823 St George reverse.....   —   £800   £1100   £2200   £3000
1826 Proof only, shield reverse   —   —   —   Extremely rare

WILLIAM IV (1830–37)
1831 Proof only 225   —   —   —   £11000

VICTORIA (1837–1901)
1887................................... 91,345   £600   £800   £1100   £1200
1887 Proof........................ 797   —   —   —   £2400
1887 S on ground of rev. (Sydney Mint)   Excessively rare
1893................................... 52,212   £750   £1000   £1800   £2500
1893 Proof........................ 773   —   —   —   £3250

EDWARD VII (1902–10)
1902................................... 45,807   £500   £650   £850   £1300
1902 Matt proof................. 8,066   —   —   —   £1300

GEORGE V (1911–36)
1911 Proof only 2,812   —   —   —   £2200

GEORGE VI (1937–52)
1937 Proof only 5,501   —   —   —   £1500
Later issues are listed in the Decimal section.

CROMWELL GOLD

	F	VF	EF

OLIVER CROMWELL (1656–58)
1656 Fifty Shillings £17,500   £40,000   £120,000
1656 Twenty Shillings............................ £5,500   £13,500   £28,000

SOVEREIGNS

DATE	MINTAGE	F	VF	EF	UNC
GEORGE III (1760–1820)					
1817..	3,235,239	£500	£850	£2000	£4000
1818..	2,347,230	£600	£1000	£4500	£8000
1819..	3,574		Exceedingly rare		
1820..	931,994	£500	£775	£1750	£3400
GEORGE IV (1820–30)					
1821 First bust, St George reverse	9,405,114	£450	£750	£1800	£2750
1821 — Proof	incl. above	—	—	—	£6500
1822 —	5,356,787	£450	£750	£2000	£3000
1823 —	616,770	£1000	£2750	£7800	—
1824 —	3,767,904	£500	£900	£2250	£3500
1825 —	4,200,343	£700	£2000	£6000	£8500
1825 Second bust, shield reverse	incl. above	£425	£700	£1750	£2500
1826 —	5,724,046	£425	£700	£1500	£2500
1826 — Proof	—	—	—	—	£5500
1827 —	2,266,629	£475	£750	£1750	£3200
1828 —	386,182	£6000	£15000	£30000	—
1829 —	2,444,652	£475	£800	£2500	£3500
1830 —	2,387,881	£475	£800	£2500	£3500
WILLIAM IV (1830–37)					
1831..	598,547	£600	£1000	£3250	£4750
1831 Proof, plain edge	—	—	—	—	£10,000
1832..	3,737,065	£500	£900	£2500	£3750
1833..	1,225,269	£500	£900	£2500	£3750
1835..	723,441	£500	£900	£2500	£3750
1836..	1,714,349	£500	£900	£2000	£3750
1837..	1,172,984	£525	£950	£2000	£4000

George III

George IV, shield reverse

Note—from the Victoria reign onwards, the prices of coins in lower grade will be subject to the bullion price of gold.

VICTORIA (1837–1901)

Many of the gold coins struck at the colonial mints found their way into circulation in Britain, for the sake of completeness these coins are listed here. These can easily be identified by a tiny initial letter for the appropriate mint which can be found below the base of the reverse shield or, in the case of the St George reverse, below the bust on the obverse of the Young Head issues, or on the "ground" below the horse's hoof on the later issues.

YOUNG HEAD ISSUES

Shield reverse
(Note—Shield back sovereigns in Fine/VF condition, common dates, are normally traded as bullion + a percentage)

1838	2,718,694	£700	£1200	£3750	£5500
1839	503,695	£1000	£2750	£4000	£6500
1839 Proof, plain edge	—	—	—	—	£7000
1841..	124,054	£4750	£9500	£20000	—
1842	4,865,375	£300	£400	£1000	£1750
1843..	5,981,968	£300	£400	£1000	£1750
1843 "Narrow shield" variety......	incl. above	£5000	£10000	—	—
1843 Roman I in date not 1841 ...	—	£750	£1500	—	—
1844	3,000,445	£300	£400	£1000	£1500
1845	3,800,845	£300	£400	£1000	£1500
1846	3,802,947	£300	£400	£1000	£1500

William IV

DATE	MINTAGE	F	VF	EF	UNC
1847	4,667,126	£275	£325	£1000	£1500
1848	2,246,701	£275	£325	£1000	£1500
1849	1,755,399	£275	£325	£1000	£1500
1850	1,402,039	£275	£325	£1000	£1500
1851	4,013,624	£275	£325	£750	£1500
1852	8,053,435	£275	£325	£850	£1500
1853	10,597,993	£275	£325	£750	£1500
1853 Proof	—	—	—	—	£18000
1854 Incuse WW	3,589,611	£275	£325	£750	£1500
1854 Surface raised WW	3,589,611	£275	£325	£750	£1800
1855	4,806,160	£275	£325	£750	£1500
1856	8,448,482	£275	£325	£750	£1500
1857	4,495,748	£275	£325	£750	£1500
1858	803,234	£275	£325	£750	£1500
1859	1,547,603	£275	£325	£750	£1500
1859 "Ansell" (additional line on lower part of hair ribbon)	—	£750	£1700	£8500	—
1860	2,555,958	£230	£250	£650	£1250
1861	7,624,736	£230	£250	£600	£1250
1862	7,836,413	£230	£250	£650	£1250
1863	5,921,669	£230	£250	£600	£1250
1863 Die No 827 on Truncation...				Extremely rare	
1863 with Die number below shield	incl. above	£230	£250	£600	£1100
1864 —	8,656,352	£230	£250	£650	£1100
1865 —	1,450,238	£230	£250	£650	£1100
1866 —	4,047,288	£230	£250	£600	£1100
1868 —	1,653,384	£230	£250	£550	£1100
1869 —	6,441,322	£230	£250	£550	£1000
1870 —	2,189,960	£230	£250	£550	£1100
1871 —	8,767,250	£230	£250	£500	£1100
1872 —	8,767,250	£230	£250	£500	£1000
1872 no Die number	incl. above	£230	£250	£500	£1000
1873 with Die number	2,368,215	£230	£250	£600	£1000
1874 —	520,713	£2000	£4000	£12,000	—

M below reverse shield (Melbourne Mint)

1872	748,180	£230	£250	£500	£1250
1873	—			Extremely rare	
1874	1,373,298	£230	£250	£350	£1250
1879				Extremely rare	
1880	3,053,454	£700	£1650	£3000	£50000
1881	2,325,303	£230	£250	£350	£1500
1882	2,465,781	£230	£250	£350	£1000
1883	2,050,450	£230	£250	£600	£3000
1884	2,942,630	£230	£250	£350	£900
1885	2,967,143	£230	£250	£350	£900
1886	2,902,131	£1800	£4000	£6500	£8000
1887	1,916,424	£600	£1350	£3500	£5000

S below reverse shield (Sydney Mint)

1871	2,814,000	£230	£250	£320	£1300
1872	1,815,000	£230	£250	£320	£1600
1873	1,478,000	£230	£250	£320	£1300
1875	2,122,000	£230	£250	£320	£1300
1877	1,590,000	£230	£250	£320	£1300
1878	1,259,000	£230	£250	£400	£1400
1879	1,366,000	£230	£250	£350	£1300
1880	1,459,000	£230	£250	£320	£1500
1881	1,360,000	£230	£250	£350	£1500
1882	1,298,000	£230	£250	£320	£1300
1883	1,108,000	£230	£250	£320	£1100
1884	1,595,000	£230	£250	£320	£1100
1885	1,486,000	£230	£250	£300	£1100
1886	1,667,000	£230	£250	£300	£1100
1887	1,000,000	£230	£250	£320	£1500

The mint initial appears below the shield, i.e. "S" indicates that the coin was struck at the Sydney Mint

IMPORTANT NOTE: The prices quoted in this guide are set at August 2017 with the price of 22ct gold at £1000 per ounce and silver £13 per ounce—market fluctuations can have a marked effect on the values of modern precious metal coins.

DATE	MINTAGE	F	VF	EF	UNC
St George & Dragon reverse					
1871	incl. above	£200	£220	£300	£500
1872	incl. above	£200	£220	£300	£500
1873	incl. above	£200	£220	£350	£500
1874	incl. above	£200	£220	£300	£500
1876	3,318,866	£200	£220	£300	£500
1878	1,091,275	£200	£220	£320	£500
1879	20,013	£550	£1500	£12,000	—
1880	3,650,080	£200	£220	£325	£500
1884	1,769,635	£200	£220	£300	£500
1885	717,723	£200	£220	£350	£500
M below bust on obverse (Melbourne Mint)					
1872	incl. above	£250	£500	£1150	£4000
1873	752,199	£200	£220	£350	£500
1874	incl. above	£200	£220	£350	£500
1875	incl. above	£200	£220	£300	£500
1876	2,124,445	£200	£220	£350	£550
1877	1,487,316	£200	£220	£300	£500
1878	2,171,457	£200	£220	£275	£500
1879	2,740,594	£200	£220	£275	£500
1880	incl. above	£200	£220	£300	£500
1881	incl. above	£200	£220	£300	£500
1882	incl. above	£200	£220	£300	£500
1883	incl. above	£200	£220	£300	£500
1884	incl. above	£200	£220	£275	£500
1885	incl. above	£200	£220	£275	£500
1886	incl. above	£200	£220	£275	£500
1887	incl. above	£200	£220	£275	£500
S below bust on obverse (Sydney Mint)					
1871	2,814,000	£200	£220	£350	£500
1872	incl. above	£200	£220	£300	£700
1873	incl. above	£200	£220	£300	£500
1874	1,899,000	£200	£220	£300	£500
1875	inc above	£200	£220	£300	£500
1876	1,613,000	£200	£220	£350	£500
1877	—			Unknown	
1879	incl. above	£200	£220	£350	£500
1880	incl. above	£200	£220	£350	£500
1881	incl. above	£200	£220	£350	£500
1882	incl. above	£200	£220	£300	£550
1883	incl. above	£200	£220	£300	£500
1884	incl. above	£200	£220	£300	£500
1885	incl. above	£200	£220	£300	£500
1886	incl. above	£200	£220	£300	£500
1887	incl. above	£200	£220	£300	£500
JUBILEE HEAD ISSUES					
1887	1,111,280	£200	£220	£300	£350
1887 Proof	797	—	—	—	£2750
1888	2,717,424	£200	£220	£350	£500
1889	7,257,455	£200	£220	£325	£500
1890	6,529.887	£200	£220	£325	£500
1891	6,329,476	£200	£500	£2000	£5500
1892	7,104,720	£200	£220	£300	£500
M on ground on reverse (Melbourne Mint)					
1887	940,000	£200	£220	£375	£500
1888	2,830,612	£200	£220	£300	£450
1889	2,732,590	£200	£220	£325	£450
1890	2,473,537	£200	£220	£325	£450
1891	2,749,592	£200	£220	£325	£450
1892	3,488,750	£200	£220	£325	£450
1893	1,649,352	£200	£220	£325	£450

"M" below the horse's hoof above the date indicates that the coin was struck at the Melbourne Mint

Jubilee head type

DATE	MINTAGE	F	VF	EF	UNC

S on ground on reverse (Sydney Mint)

DATE	MINTAGE	F	VF	EF	UNC
1887	1,002,000	£250	£400	£1500	£2500
1888	2,187,000	£230	£240	£325	£500
1889	3,262,000	£230	£240	£325	£500
1890	2,808,000	£230	£240	£325	£500
1891	2,596,000	£230	£240	£325	£500
1892	2,837,000	£230	£240	£325	£500
1893	1,498,000	£230	£240	£325	£500

OLD HEAD ISSUES

DATE	MINTAGE	F	VF	EF	UNC
1893	6,898,260	£230	£240	£325	£500
1893 Proof	773	—	—	—	£2400
1894	3,782,611	£230	£240	£300	£400
1895	2,285,317	£230	£240	£300	£400
1896	3,334,065	£230	£240	£300	£400
1898	4,361,347	£230	£240	£300	£400
1899	7,515,978	£230	£240	£300	£400
1900	10,846,741	£230	£240	£300	£400
1901	1,578,948	£230	£240	£300	£400

M on ground on reverse (Melbourne Mint)

DATE	MINTAGE	F	VF	EF	UNC
1893	1,914,000	£230	£240	£300	£350
1894	4,166,874	£230	£240	£300	£350
1895	4,165,869	£230	£240	£300	£350
1896	4,456,932	£230	£240	£300	£350
1897	5,130,565	£230	£240	£300	£350
1898	5,509,138	£230	£240	£300	£350
1899	5,579,157	£230	£240	£300	£350
1900	4,305,904	£230	£240	£300	£350
1901	3,987,701	£230	£240	£300	£350

P on ground on reverse (Perth Mint)

DATE	MINTAGE	F	VF	EF	UNC
1899	690,992	£250	£275	£500	£2500
1900	1,886,089	£230	£240	£300	£350
1901	2,889,333	£230	£240	£300	£350

S on ground on reverse (Sydney Mint)

DATE	MINTAGE	F	VF	EF	UNC
1893	1,346,000	£240	£250	£300	£450
1894	3,067,000	£230	£240	£300	£350
1895	2,758,000	£230	£240	£300	£350
1896	2,544,000	£230	£240	£350	£500
1897	2,532,000	£230	£240	£300	£350
1898	2,548,000	£230	£240	£300	£350
1899	3,259,000	£230	£240	£300	£350
1900	3,586,000	£230	£240	£300	£350
1901	3,012,000	£230	£240	£300	£350

Old head type

EDWARD VII (1902–10)

DATE	MINTAGE	F	VF	EF	UNC
1902	4,737,796	£230	£240	£320	£350
1902 Matt proof	15,123	—	—	—	£625
1903	8,888,627	£230	£240	£300	£350
1904	10,041,369	£230	£240	£300	£350
1905	5,910,403	£230	£240	£300	£350
1906	10,466,981	£230	£240	£300	£350
1907	18,458,663	£230	£240	£300	£350
1908	11,729,006	£230	£240	£300	£350
1909	12,157,099	£230	£240	£300	£350
1910	22,379,624	£230	£240	£300	£350

C on ground on reverse (Ottawa Mint)

DATE	MINTAGE	F	VF	EF	UNC
1908 Satin finish Proof only	633			Extremely rare	
1909	16,300	£240	£275	£500	£750
1910	28,020	£240	£275	£500	£675

DATE	MINTAGE	F	VF	EF	UNC
M on ground on reverse (Melbourne Mint)					
1902	4,267,157	£230	£240	£300	£350
1903	3,521,780	£230	£240	£300	£350
1904	3,743,897	£230	£240	£300	£350
1905	3,633,838	£230	£240	£300	£350
1906	3,657,853	£230	£240	£300	£350
1907	3,332,691	£230	£240	£300	£350
1908	3,080,148	£230	£240	£300	£350
1909	3,029,538	£230	£240	£300	£350
1910	3,054,547	£230	£240	£300	£350
P on ground on reverse (Perth Mint)					
1902	3,289,122	£230	£240	£300	£350
1903	4,674,783	£230	£240	£300	£350
1904	4,506,756	£230	£240	£300	£350
1905	4,876,193	£230	£240	£300	£350
1906	4,829,817	£230	£240	£300	£350
1907	4,972,289	£230	£240	£300	£350
1908	4,875,617	£230	£240	£300	£350
1909	4,524,241	£230	£240	£300	£350
1910	4,690,625	£230	£240	£300	£350
S on ground on reverse (Sydney Mint)					
1902	2,813,000	£230	£240	£300	£280
1902 Proof	incl. above			Extremely rare	
1903	2,806,000	£230	£240	£300	£350
1904	2,986,000	£230	£240	£300	£350
1905	2,778,000	£230	£240	£300	£350
1906	2,792,000	£230	£240	£300	£350
1907	2,539,000	£230	£240	£300	£350
1908	2,017,000	£230	£240	£320	£375
1909	2,057,000	£230	£240	£320	£375
1910	2,135,000	£230	£240	£320	£375

GEORGE V (1911–36)

(Extra care should be exercised when purchasing as good quality forgeries exist of virtually all dates and mintmarks)

DATE	MINTAGE	F	VF	EF	UNC
1911	30,044,105	£230	£240	£300	£350
1911 Proof	3,764	—	—	—	£900
1912	30,317,921	£230	£240	£300	£350
1913	24,539,672	£230	£240	£300	£350
1914	11,501,117	£230	£240	£300	£350
1915	20,295,280	£230	£240	£300	£350
1916	1,554,120	£230	£240	£500	£750
1917	1,014,714	£1500	£5000	£17000	—
1925	4,406,431	£230	£240	£300	£350
C on ground on reverse (Ottawa Mint)					
1911	256,946	£230	£240	£500	£750
1913	3,715	£285	£375	£1750	—
1914	14,891	£230	£240	£1500	—
1916	6,111			Extremely rare	
1917	58,845	£230	£240	£600	£850
1918	106,516	£230	£240	£500	£650
1919	135,889	£230	£240	£500	£650
I on ground on reverse (Bombay Mint)					
1918	1,295,372	£230	£240	£320	—
M on ground on reverse (Melbourne Mint)					
1911	2,851,451	£230	£240	£300	£350
1912	2,469,257	£230	£240	£300	£350
1913	2,323,180	£230	£240	£300	£350
1914	2,012,029	£230	£240	£300	£350
1915	1,637,839	£230	£240	£320	£375
1916	1,273,643	£230	£240	£320	£375
1917	934,469	£230	£240	£500	£750
1918	4,969,493	£230	£240	£300	£350
1919	514,257	£230	£240	£350	£425

DATE	MINTAGE	F	VF	EF	UNC
1920	530,266	£1350	£2500	£4000	£6500
1921	240,121	£4000	£7000	£10000	£24000
1922	608,306	£4000	£7000	£10000	£23000
1923	510,870	£230	£240	£270	£300
1924	278,140	£230	£240	£270	£300
1925	3,311,622	£230	£240	£270	£300
1926	211,107	£230	£240	£270	£300
1928	413,208	£500	£900	£1500	£3000
1929	436,719	£900	£1500	£2500	£4750
1930	77,547	£230	£240	£270	£300
1931	57,779	£230	£240	£400	£700

P on ground on reverse (Perth Mint)

DATE	MINTAGE	F	VF	EF	UNC
1911	4,373,165	£230	£240	£270	£300
1912	4,278,144	£230	£240	£270	£300
1913	4,635,287	£230	£240	£270	£300
1914	4,815,996	£230	£240	£270	£300
1915	4,373,596	£230	£240	£270	£300
1916	4,096,771	£230	£240	£270	£300
1917	4,110,286	£230	£240	£270	£300
1918	3,812,884	£230	£240	£270	£300
1919	2,995,216	£230	£240	£270	£300
1920	2,421,196	£230	£240	£270	£300
1921	2,134,360	£230	£240	£270	£300
1922	2,298,884	£230	£240	£270	£300
1923	2,124,154	£230	£240	£270	£300
1924	1,464,416	£230	£240	£270	£300
1925	1,837,901	£230	£240	£400	£600
1926	1,313,578	£500	£900	£1500	£3200
1927	1,383,544	£230	£240	£270	£500
1928	1,333,417	£230	£240	£270	£375
1929	1,606,625	£230	£240	£270	£375
1930	1,915,352	£230	£240	£270	£375
1931	1,173,568	£230	£240	£270	£375

S on ground on reverse (Sydney Mint)

DATE	MINTAGE	F	VF	EF	UNC
1911	2,519,000	£230	£240	£270	£300
1912	2,227,000	£230	£240	£270	£300
1913	2,240,000	£230	£240	£270	£300
1914	1,774,000	£230	£240	£270	£300
1915	1,346,000	£230	£240	£270	£300
1916	1,242,000	£230	£240	£270	£300
1917	1,666,000	£230	£240	£270	£300
1918	3,716,000	£230	£240	£270	£300
1919	1,835,000	£230	£240	£270	£300

DATE	MINTAGE	F	VF	EF	UNC
1920..	—			Excessively rare	
1921..	839,000	£600	£900	£1750	£2750
1922..	578,000			Extremely rare	
1923..	416,000			Extremely rare	
1924..	394,000	£600	£1100	£1500	£2750
1925..	5,632,000	£185	£200	£320	£400
1926..	1,031,050			Extremely rare	

SA on ground on reverse (Pretoria Mint)

1923	719	£800	£1850	£3500	£7000
1923 Proof..................................	655			Extremely rare	
1924..	3,184	—	£3000	£5000	—
1925..	6,086,264	£230	£240	£300	£350
1926..	11,107,611	£230	£240	£300	£350
1927..	16,379,704	£230	£240	£300	£350
1928..	18,235,057	£230	£240	£300	£350
1929	12,024,107	£230	£240	£300	£350
1930..	10,027,756	£230	£240	£300	£350
1931..	8,511,792	£230	£240	£300	£350
1932..	1,066,680	£230	£240	£320	£375

GEORGE VI (1937–52)

1937 Proof only	5,501	—	—	£3750	£5000

ELIZABETH II (1952–)

Pre Decimal Issues

1957..	2,072,000	£230	£240	£350	£350
1958..	8,700,140	£230	£240	£300	£350
1959..	1,358,228	£230	£240	£300	£350
1962..	3,000,000	£230	£240	£300	£350
1963..	7,400,000	£230	£240	£300	£350
1964..	3,000,000	£230	£240	£300	£350
1965..	3,800,000	£230	£240	£300	£350
1966..	7,050,000	£230	£240	£300	£350
1967..	5,000,000	£230	£240	£300	£350
1968..	4,203,000	£230	£240	£300	£350

Later issues are included in the Decimal section.

HALF SOVEREIGNS

GEORGE III (1760–1820)

1817..	2,080,197	£200	£370	£1000	£1500
1818..	1,030,286	£220	£400	£1000	£1500
1820..	35,043	£220	£400	£800	£1200

GEORGE IV (1820–30)

1821 First bust, ornate shield reverse	231,288	£600	£1600	£3750	£5000
1821 — Proof	unrecorded	—	—	—	£6250
1823 First bust, Plain shield rev.................................	224,280	£200	£280	£1000	£1500
1824 —	591,538	£200	£280	£850	£1250
1825 —	761,150	£200	£280	£750	£1000
1826 bare head, shield with full legend reverse............	344,830	£200	£320	£1000	£1500
1826 — Proof	unrecorded	—	—	—	£2800
1827 —	492,014	£200	£340	£1000	£1500
1828 —	1,224,754	£200	£350	£800	£1200

WILLIAM IV (1830–37)

DATE	MINTAGE	F	VF	EF	UNC
1831 Proof only	unrecorded	—	—	—	£6000
1834	133,899	£275	£550	£1500	£2000
1835	772,554	£225	£550	£1000	£1500
1836	146,865	£200	£400	£1250	£1600
1836 obverse from 6d die	incl. above	£1600	£3500	£7000	—
1837	160,207	£220	£475	£1250	£1500

VICTORIA (1837–1901)

YOUNG HEAD ISSUES

Shield reverse

	MINTAGE	F	VF	EF	UNC
1838	273,341	£130	£190	£1000	£1500
1839 Proof only	1,230	—	—	—	£6500
1841	508,835	£140	£225	£1250	£20000
1842	2,223,352	£130	£200	£1000	£1500
1843	1,251,762	£130	£200	£1000	£1500
1844	1,127,007	£130	£200	£850	£1000
1845	887,526	£300	£600	£3000	£4500
1846	1,063,928	£140	£180	£850	£1000
1847	982,636	£140	£180	£750	£900
1848	410,595	£140	£180	£850	£1000
1849	845,112	£140	£180	£750	£900
1850	179,595	£180	£500	£2500	£3000
1851	773,573	£140	£200	£700	£850
1852	1,377,671	£140	£200	£700	£850
1853	2,708,796	£140	£200	£700	£850
1853 Proof	unrecorded	—	—	—	£8500
1855	1,120,362	£140	£180	£700	£850
1856	2,391,909	£140	£180	£700	£850
1857	728,223	£140	£180	£700	£850
1858	855,578	£140	£180	£700	£850
1859	2,203,813	£140	£180	£700	£850
1860	1,131,500	£140	£180	£700	£850
1861	1,130,867	£140	£180	£700	£850
1862	unrecorded	£750	£2000	£10000	—
1863	1,571,574	£140	£180	£700	£800
1863 with Die number	incl. above	£140	£180	£800	£850
1864 —	1,758,490	£140	£180	£650	£850
1865 —	1,834,750	£140	£180	£650	£850
1866 —	2,058,776	£140	£180	£650	£850
1867 —	992,795	£140	£180	£650	£850
1869 —	1,861,764	£140	£180	£650	£850
1870 —	1,159,544	£140	£180	£650	£800
1871 —	2,062,970	£140	£180	£650	£850
1872 —	3,248,627	£140	£180	£650	£850
1873 —	1,927,050	£140	£180	£650	£850
1874 —	1,884,432	£140	£180	£650	£850
1875 —	516,240	£140	£180	£650	£850
1876 —	2,785,187	£140	£180	£650	£850
1877 —	2,197,482	£140	£180	£650	£850
1878 —	2,081,941	£140	£180	£650	£850
1879 —	35,201	£140	£180	£650	£850
1880 —	1,009,049	£140	£180	£650	£850
1880 no Die number	incl. above	£140	£180	£750	£1000
1883 —	2,870,457	£140	£180	£600	£750
1884 —	1,113,756	£140	£180	£650	£850
1885 —	4,468,871	£140	£180	£600	£850

M below shield (Melbourne Mint)

	MINTAGE	F	VF	EF	UNC
1873	165,034	£120	£200	£1000	—
1877	80,016	£120	£250	£2000	—
1881	42,009	£120	£300	£2000	—
1882	107,522	£120	£195	£600	—
1884	48,009	£120	£195	£1750	—
1885	11,003	£120	£300	£3750	—

Date	Mintage	F	VF	EF	UNC
1886..	38,008	£120	£250	£6000	—
1887..	64,013	£120	£400	£8000	£10,000

S below shield (Sydney Mint)

Date	Mintage	F	VF	EF	UNC
1871	180,000 (?)	£120	£180	£750	—
1872..	356,000	£120	£180	£750	—
1875..	unrecorded	£120	£180	£750	—
1879..	94,000	£120	£180	£650	—
1880..	80,000	£120	£200	£850	—
1881..	62,000	£120	£250	£1000	—
1882..	52,000		Extremely rare		
1883..	220,000	£120	£180	£900	—
1886..	82,000	£120	£150	£600	—
1887..	134,000	£125	£200	£2000	£8000

JUBILEE HEAD ISSUES

Date	Mintage	F	VF	EF	UNC
1887..	871,770	£120	£130	£250	£350
1887 Proof.................................	797	£120	£130	—	£1850
1890..	2.266,023	£120	£130	£500	£750
1891..	1,079,286	£120	£130	£300	£475
1892..	13,680,486	£120	£130	£300	£475
1893..	4,426,625	£120	£130	£300	£475

M below shield (Melbourne Mint)

Date	Mintage	F	VF	EF	UNC
1887	incl. above	£120	£130	£400	£600
1893..	110,024	£120	£130	£450	£750

S below shield (Sydney Mint)

Date	Mintage	F	VF	EF	UNC
1887	incl. above	£120	£130	£300	£500
1889..	64,000	£120	£250	£12500	—
1891..	154,000	£120	£150	£1000	—

OLD HEAD ISSUES

Date	Mintage	F	VF	EF	UNC
1893..	incl. above	£120	£130	£185	£250
1893 Proof.................................	773	—	—	—	£1200
1894..	3,794,591	£120	£130	£185	£250
1895..	2,869,183	£120	£130	£185	£250
1896..	2,946,605	£120	£130	£185	£250
1897..	3,568,156	£120	£130	£185	£250
1898..	2,868,527	£120	£130	£185	£250
1899..	3,361,881	£120	£130	£185	£250
1900..	4,307,372	£120	£130	£185	£250
1901..	2,037,664	£120	£130	£185	£250

M on ground on reverse (Melbourne Mint)

Date	Mintage	F	VF	EF	UNC
1893	unrecorded		Extremely rare		
1896..	218,946	£120	£150	£450	—
1899..	97,221	£120	£150	£550	—
1900..	112,920	£120	£150	£600	—

P on ground on reverse (Perth Mint)

Date	Mintage	F	VF	EF	UNC
1900	119,376	£120	£300	£550	—

S on ground on reverse (Sydney Mint)

Date	Mintage	F	VF	EF	UNC
1893	250,000	£120	£150	£600	—
1897..	unrecorded	£120	£150	£500	—
1900..	260,00	£120	£150	£400	—

EDWARD VII (1902–10)

Date	Mintage	F	VF	EF	UNC
1902..	4,244,457	£120	£125	£200	£150
1902 Matt proof..........................	15,123	—	—	—	£500
1903..	2,522,057	£120	£125	£175	£225
1904..	1,717,440	£120	£125	£175	£225
1905..	3,023,993	£120	£125	£175	£225
1906..	4,245,437	£120	£125	£175	£225
1907..	4,233,421	£120	£125	£225	£250
1908..	3,996,992	£120	£125	£250	£250
1909..	4,010,715	£120	£125	£275	£350
1910..	5,023,881	£120	£125	£150	£200

DATE		Г	VF	EF	UNC
M on ground on reverse (Melbourne Mint)					
1906	82,042	£115	£150	£750	£850
1907	405,034	£115	£120	£250	£325
1908	incl. above	£115	£120	£250	£350
1909	186,094	£115	£120	£600	£756
P on ground on reverse (Perth Mint)					
1904	60,030	£115	£150	£1000	—
1908	24,668	£115	£150	£950	—
1909	44,022	£115	£120	£500	—
S on ground on reverse (Sydney Mint)					
1902	84,000	£115	£125	£200	£325
1902 Proof				Extremely rare	
1903	231,000	£100	£120	£250	£325
1906	308,000	£115	£125	£200	£300
1908	538,000	£115	£120	£150	£300
1910	474,000	£115	£120	£150	£300

GEORGE V (1911–36)

		Г	VF	EF	UNC
1911	6,104,106	£115	£120	£150	£175
1911 Proof	3,764	—	—	—	£575
1912	6,224,316	£115	£120	£150	£175
1913	6,094,290	£115	£120	£150	£175
1914	7,251,124	£115	£120	£150	£175
1915	2,042,747	£115	£120	£150	£175
M on ground on reverse (Melbourne Mint)					
1915	125,664	£115	£120	£150	£175
P on ground on reverse (Perth Mint)					
1911	130,373	£115	£120	£250	£325
1915	136,219	£115	£120	£250	£325
1918	unrecorded	£175	£500	£1750	£3000
1919	56,786				Rare
1920	53,208				Rare
S on ground on reverse (Sydney Mint)					
1911	252,000	£115	£120	£150	£175
1912	278,000	£115	£120	£150	£175
1914	322,000	£115	£120	£150	£175
1915	892,000	£115	£120	£150	£175
1916	448,000	£115	£120	£150	£175
SA on ground on reverse (Pretoria Mint)					
1923 Proof only	655	—	—	—	£1150
1925	946,615	£115	£120	£160	£175
1926	806,540	£115	£120	£150	£175

GEORGE VI (1937–52)

		Г	VF	EF	UNC
1937 Proof only	5,501	—	—	—	£650

Later issues are included in the Decimal section.

173

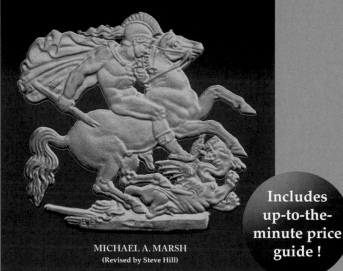

CROWNS

DATE	F	VF	EF	UNC

OLIVER CROMWELL

	F	VF	EF	UNC
1658 8 over 7 (always)	£1900	£3500	£6750	—
1658 Dutch Copy		Extremely rare		
1658 Patterns. In Various Metals		Extremely rare		

CHARLES II (1660–85)

	F	VF	EF	UNC
1662 First bust, rose (2 varieties)	£250	£800	£5000	—
1662 — no rose (2 varieties)	£250	£800	£5000	—
1663 —	£250	£800	£4750	—
1664 Second bust	£200	£800	£4250	—
1665 —	£1500	£4000	—	—
1666 —	£300	£1000	£5000	—
1666 — error RE.X for REX		Extremely rare		
1666 — Elephant below bust	£750	£2750	£15000	—
1667 —	£160	£500	£3000	—
1668/7 — 8 over 7	£170	£550	—	—
1668 —	£170	£550	£3500	—
1669/8 — 9 over 8	£350	£800	—	—
1669 —	£300	£1000	£4750	—
1670/69 — 70 over 69	£200	£1000	—	—
1670 —	£175	£600	£3600	—
1671	£170	£600	£3200	—
1671 Third bust	£170	£600	£3200	—
1672 —	£170	£500	£3200	—
1673 —	£170	£500	£3200	—
1674 —		Extremely rare		
1675 —	£700	£2200	—	—
1675/3 —	£700	£2200	—	—
1676 —	£175	£550	£3200	—
1677 —	£190	£600	£3250	—
1677/6 — 7 over 6	£200	£900	—	—
1677/7 —	£200	£900	—	—
1678/7 — 8 over 7	£275	£900	—	—
1679 —	£180	£600	£3200	—
1679 Fourth bust	£180	£600	£3200	—
1680 Third bust	£180	£800	£3500	—
1680/79 — 80 over 79	£200	£800	—	—
1680 Fourth bust	£100	£750	£4000	—
1680/79 — 80 over 79	£200	£1000	—	—
1681 —	£180	£600	£3800	—
1681 — Elephant & Castle below bust	£3200	£11000	—	—
1682/1 —	£180	£700	£3400	—
1682 — edge error QVRRTO for QVARTO	£400	—	—	—
1683 —	£400	£1000	£4000	—
1684 —	£400	£1300	—	—

JAMES II (1685–88)

	F	VF	EF	UNC
1686 First bust	£325	£1000	£5000	—
1686 — No stops on obv	£400	£1500	—	—
1687 Second bust	£300	£700	£3500	—
1688/7 — 8 over 7	£320	£850	—	—
1688 —	£280	£800	£3500	—

WILLIAM AND MARY (1688–94)

	F	VF	EF	UNC
1691	£750	£1700	£5000	—
1692	£750	£1700	£4850	—
1692 2 over upside down 2	£750	£1700	£4850	—

DATE	F	VF	EF	UNC

WILLIAM III (1694–1702)

	F	VF	EF	UNC
1695 First bust	£100	£300	£1900	—
1696 —	£90	£275	£1750	—
1696 — no stops on obv.	£225	£400	—	—
1996 — no stops obv./rev.	£250	£400	—	—
1696 — GEI for DEI	£750	£1800	—	—
1696 Second bust				Unique
1696 Third bust	£90	£275	£1800	—
1697 —	£1500	£5000	£20000	—
1700 Third bust variety edge year DUODECIMO	£140	£550	£1800	—
1700 — edge year DUODECIMO TERTIO..	£140	£550	£1800	—

ANNE (1702–14)

	F	VF	EF	UNC
1703 First bust, VIGO.................................	£350	£1000	£4000	—
1705 — Plumes in angles on rev.	£500	£1500	£6250	—
1706 — Roses & Plumes in angles on rev...	£160	£600	£2200	—
1707 — —	£160	£600	£2200	—
1707 Second bust, E below	£160	£500	£2100	—
1707 — Plain	£160	£500	£2100	—
1708 — E below	£160	£500	£2100	—
1708/7 — 8 over 7	£160	£800	—	—
1708 — Plain	£160	£650	£2100	—
1708 — — error BR for BRI.......................			Extremely rare	
1708 — Plumes in angles on rev.	£180	£700	£2500	—
1713 Third bust, Roses & Plumes in angles on rev..	£180	£700	£2600	—

GEORGE I (1714–27)

	F	VF	EF	UNC
1716..	£650	£1700	£6000	—
1718 8 over 6..	£650	£1700	£5250	—
1720 20 over 18..	£650	£1700	£5250	—
1723 SSC in angles on rev. (South Sea Co.)	£650	£1700	£5250	—
1726	£650	£1700	£5750	—

GEORGE II (1727–60)

	F	VF	EF	UNC
1732 Young head, Plain, Proof		—	£12,500	—
1732 — Roses & Plumes in angles on rev ..	£325	£700	£2750	—
1734 — —	£325	£700	£2750	—
1735 — —	£325	£700	£2750	—
1736 — —	£325	£700	£2750	—
1739 — Roses in angles on rev..................	£325	£600	£2750	—
1741 — —	£325	£600	£2600	—
1743 Old head, Roses in angles on rev.......	£225	£600	£2250	—
1746 — — LIMA below bust	£225	£600	£2250	—
1746 — Plain, Proof	—	—	£8000	—
1750 — —	£450	£1200	£3750	—
1751 — —	£550	£1600	£4200	—

GEORGE III (1760–1820)

	F	VF	EF	UNC
Dollar with oval counterstamp....................	£175	£650	£1000	—
Dollar with octagonal counterstamp	£200	£600	£850	—
1804 Bank of England Dollar, Britannia rev.	£120	£275	£550	—
1818 LVIII..	£40	£100	£300	£800
1818 LIX	£40	£100	£300	£800
1819 LIX	£40	£100	£300	£800
1819 LIX 9 over 8	£45	£150	£425	—
1819 LIX no stops on edge	£60	£150	£400	£1000
1819 LX	£40	£100	£325	£900
1820 LX	£35	£100	£300	£800
1820 LX 20 over 19	£35	£200	£500	—

DATE	MINTAGE	F	VF	EF	UNC

GEORGE IV (1820–30)

1821 First bust, St George rev.

SECUNDO on edge 437,976		£40	£180	£700	£1500
1821 — — Proof........................Incl. above		£40	£180	—	£5500
1821 — — Proof TERTIO (error edge)Incl above		£40	£180	—	£5000
1822 — — SECUNDO................... 124,929		£40	£180	£700	£1500
1822 — — TERTIO.....................Incl above		£40	£180	£700	£1500
1823 — — Proof only				Extremely rare	
1826 Second bust, shield rev, SEPTIMO					
Proof only..		—	—	£2400	£9000

WILLIAM IV (1830–37)

				UNC
1831 Proof only W.W. on truncation............		—	—	£15000
1831 Proof only W. WYON on truncation....		—	—	£17500
1834 Proof only		—	—	—£30000

VICTORIA (1837–1901)

YOUNG HEAD ISSUES

1839 Proof only	—	—	—	—	£14000
1844 Star stops on edge............	94,248	£50	£260	£1200	£3000
1844 Cinquefoil stops on edge ...	incl. above	£50	£260	£1200	£3000
1845 Star stops on edge............	159,192	£50	£260	£1200	£3000
1845 Cinquefoil stops on edge ...	incl. above	£50	£260	£1200	£3000
1847..	140,976	£65	£300	£1400	£4200

GOTHIC HEAD ISSUES (Proof only)

1847 mdcccxlvii UNDECIMO on edge	8,000	£800	£1500	£2350	£3750
1847 — Plain edge......................	—	—	—	—	£4750
1853 mdccccliii SEPTIMO on edge	460	—	—	—	£10000
1853 — Plain edge......................	—	—	—	—	£15000

JUBILEE HEAD ISSUES

1887	173,581	£20	£30	£60	£160
1887 Proof..................................	1,084	—	—	—	£1200
1888 Narrow date	131,899	£20	£35	£90	£250
1888 Wide date..........................	incl above	£25	£60	£300	—
1889..	1,807,224	£20	£30	£60	£150
1890..	997,862	£20	£30	£70	£240
1891..	556,394	£20	£30	£70	£240
1892..	451,334	£20	£30	£80	£260

OLD HEAD ISSUES (Regnal date on edge in Roman numerals)

1893 LVI....................................	497,845	£20	£45	£150	£375
1893 LVII...................................	incl. above	£20	£45	£200	£425
1893 Proof.................................	1,312	—	—	—	£1400
1894 LVII...................................	144,906	£20	£45	£175	£400
1894 LVIII..................................	incl. above	£20	£45	£175	£400
1895 LVIII	252,862	£20	£45	£175	£400
1895 LIX	incl. above	£20	£45	£175	£400
1896 LIX	317,599	£20	£45	£175	£450
1896 LX	incl. above	£20	£45	£175	£400
1897 LX	262,118	£20	£45	£175	£400
1897 LXI	incl. above	£20	£45	£175	£450
1898 LXI	166,150	£20	£45	£175	£500
1898 LXII	incl. above	£20	£45	£175	£400
1899 LXII	166,300	£20	£45	£175	£400
1899 LXIII..................................	incl. above	£20	£45	£175	£400
1900 LXIII..................................	353,356	£20	£45	£175	£400
1900 LXIV	incl. above	£20	£45	£175	£400

Victoria, Jubilee head

DATE	MINTAGE	F	VF	EF	UNC

EDWARD VII (1901–10)

DATE	MINTAGE	F	VF	EF	UNC
1902	256,020	£70	£130	£200	£290
1902 "Matt Proof"	15,123	—	—	—	£300

GEORGE V (1910–36)

DATE	MINTAGE	F	VF	EF	UNC
1927 Proof only	15,030	—	£100	£170	£350
1928	9,034	£110	£160	£300	£500
1929	4,994	£110	£160	£300	£500
1930	4,847	£110	£160	£300	£525
1931	4,056	£110	£160	£300	£500
1932	2,395	£200	£400	£800	£1250
1933	7,132	£110	£160	£300	£525
1934	932	£800	£1600	£3500	£5500
1935 Jubilee issue. Incuse edge inscription	714,769	£15	£20	£30	£45
1935 — — error edge inscription	incl. above	—	—	—	£1500
1935 — Specimen in box	incl. above	—	—	—	£60
1935 — Proof	incl. above	—	—	—	£200
1935 — Proof. Raised edge inscription	2,500	—	—	£275	£550
1935 — — fine lettering	incl. above	—	—	—	£1000
1935 — — error edge inscription	incl. above	—	—	—	£1500
1935 — Gold proof	30	—	—	Extremely rare	
1936	2,473	£180	£350	£600	£1000

GEORGE VI (1936–52)

DATE	MINTAGE	F	VF	EF	UNC
1937 Coronation	418,699	£18	£24	£38	£55
1937 Proof	26,402	—	—	—	£65
1951 Festival of Britain, Proof-like	1,983,540	—	—	£4	£7

ELIZABETH II (1952–   )

Pre-Decimal issues (Five Shillings)

DATE	MINTAGE	F	VF	EF	UNC
1953	5,962,621	—	—	£3	£6
1953 Proof	40,000	—	—	—	£25
1960	1,024,038	—	—	£3	£6
1960 Polished dies	70,000	—	—	—	£9
1965 Churchill	19,640,000	—	—	—	£1

Later issues are listed in the Decimal section.

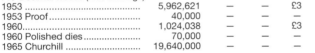

DOUBLE FLORINS

VICTORIA (1837–1901)

DATE	MINTAGE	F	VF	EF	UNC
1887 Roman I	483,347	£15	£30	£50	£115
1887 Roman I Proof	incl. above	—	—	—	£600
1887 Arabic 1	incl. above	£15	£30	£50	£115
1887 Arabic 1 Proof	incl. above	—	—	—	£550
1888	243,340	£15	£40	£80	£150
1888 Second I in VICTORIA an inverted 1	incl. above	£25	£50	£100	£375
1889	1,185,111	£18	£30	£45	£140
1889 inverted 1	incl. above	£25	£50	£100	£400
1890	782,146	£15	£40	£60	£130

Patterns were also produced in 1911, 1914 and 1950 and are all extremely rare.

HALFCROWNS

DATE	MINTAGE	F	VF	EF	UNC

OLIVER CROMWELL

1656				Extremely rare	
1658		£1350	£2500	£5000	—
1658 Proof in Gold				Extremely rare	

CHARLES II (1660–1685)

1663 First bust		£170	£600	£3500	—
1663 — no stops on obv.		£200	£800	—	—
1664 Second bust		£250	£1200	£5000	—
1666 Third bust		£900	—	—	—
1666 — Elephant		£800	£3300	—	—
1667/4 — 7 over 4				Extremely rare	
1668/4 — 8 over 4		£300	£1500	—	—
1669 —		£400	£1600	—	—
1669/4 — 9 over 4		£250	£900	—	—
1670 —		£125	£500	£2500	—
1670 — MRG for MAG		£300	£1000	—	—
1671 —		£150	£500	£2500	—
1671/0 — 1 over 0		£160	£600	£3000	—
1672 — Third bust				Extremely rare	
1672 Fourth bust		£150	£500	£2750	—
1673 —		£150	£500	£2500	—
1673 — Plumes both sides				Extremely rare	
1673 — Plume below bust		£6500	£18,000	—	—
1674 —		£150	£700	—	—
1675 —		£145	£400	£2000	—
1676 —		£145	£400	£2000	—
1676 — inverted 1 in date		£145	£400	£2000	—
1677 —		£145	£400	£1800	—
1678 —		£200	£800	—	—
1679 — GRATTA error				Extremely rare	
1679 —		£150	£420	£1800	—
1680 —		£175	£750	—	—
1681/0 — 1 over 0		£250	—	—	—
1681 —		£160	£550	£2450	—
1681 — Elephant & Castle		£3500	£10000	—	—
1682 —		£150	£500	£3000	—
1683 —		£150	£500	£2750	—
1683 — Plume below bust				Extremely rare	
1684/3 — 4 over 3		£325	£900	£4200	—

JAMES II (1685–1688)

1685 First bust		£220	£650	£3200	—
1686 —		£220	£650	£3500	—
1686/5 — 6 over 5		£220	£700	—	—
1686 — V over S		£225	£750	—	—
1687 —		£220	£675	£3300	—
1687/6 — 7 over 6		£300	£850	—	—
1687 Second bust		£200	£600	£3200	—
1688 —		£200	£600	£3000	—

WILLIAM AND MARY (1688–1694)

1689 First busts; first shield		£100	£350	£1600	—
1689 — — no pearls in crown		£100	£350	£1600	—
1689 — — FRA for FR		£160	£600	£2000	—
1689 — — No stop on obv		£100	£500	£1850	—
1689 — Second shield		£100	£350	£1600	—
1689 — — no pearls in crown		£100	£350	£1600	—
1690 — —		£160	£700	£2600	—
1690 — — error GRETIA for GRATIA		£550	£1600	£5250	—
1691 Second busts		£150	£450	£2200	—
1692 —		£150	£450	£2200	—

DATE	MINTAGE	F	VF	EF	UNC
1693 —		£170	£475	£2200	—
1693 — 3 over inverted 3		£180	£650	£2750	—

WILLIAM III (1694–1702)

	F	VF	EF	UNC
1696 First bust, large shields, early harp	£70	£240	£900	—
1696 — — — B (Bristol) below bust	£70	£240	£1000	—
1696 — — — C (Chester)	£80	£325	£1100	—
1696 — — — E (Exeter)	£100	£400	£1300	—
1696 — — — N (Norwich)	£90	£400	£1300	—
1696 — — — y (York)	£80	£350	£1500	—
1696 — — — — Scottish arms at date............			Extremely rare	
1696 — — ordinary harp	£80	£275	£1400	—
1696 — — — C..	£110	£500	£1200	—
1696 — — — E..	£100	£500	£1200	—
1696 — — — N...	£150	£600	£2250	—
1696 — Small shields, ordinary harp	£70	£250	£1000	—
1696 — — — B..	£90	£300	£1100	—
1696 — — — C..	£90	£300	£1300	—
1696 — — — E..	£100	£450	£2000	—
1696 — — — N...	£110	£450	£1500	—
1696 — — — y..	£100	£500	£1600	—
1696 Second bust			Only one known	
1697 First bust, large shields, ordinary harp	£75	£300	£1150	—
1697 — — — GRR for GRA			Extremely rare	
1697 — — — B..	£80	£300	£1250	—
1697 — — — C..	£80	£350	£1300	—
1697 — — — E..	£90	£350	£1300	—
1697 — — — N...	£100	£350	£1300	—
1697 — — — y..	£90	£350	£1350	—
1698 — —	£100	£350	£1350	—
1698/7 — — 8 over 7			Extremely rare	
1699 — —	£150	£475	£1950	—
1699 — — Scottish arms at date.....................			Extremely rare	
1700 — —	£140	£400	£1750	—
1701 — —	£145	£450	£1800	—
1701 — — No stops on rev..............................	£160	£625	—	—
1701 — — Elephant & Castle below .... Fair £2200				
1701 — — Plumes in angles on rev.	£230	£650	£3000	—

ANNE (1702–1714)

	F	VF	EF	UNC
1703 Plain (pre-Union)......................................	£600	£2300	—	—
1703 VIGO below bust	£100	£340	£1100	—
1704 Plumes in angles on rev..........................	£150	£500	£1600	—
1705 —	£120	£500	£1800	—
1706 Roses & Plumes in angles on rev.	£90	£350	£1500	—
1707 —	£80	£300	£1100	—
1707 Plain (post-Union)....................................	£80	£200	£900	—
1707 E below bust..	£80	£200	£900	—
1707 — SEPTIMO edge			Extremely rare	
1708 Plain...	£80	£250	£1000	—
1708 E below bust..	£80	£250	£1000	—
1708 Plumes in angles on rev..........................	£90	£275	£1100	—
1709 Plain...	£75	£275	£900	—
1709 E below bust..	£220	£900	—	—
1710 Roses & Plumes in angles on rev.	£80	£325	£1000	—
1712 —	£80	£325	£1000	—
1713 Plain...	£80	£325	£1000	—
1713 Roses & Plumes in angles on rev.	£80	£325	£1000	—
1714 —	£80	£325	£1000	—
1714/3 4 over 3	£125	£500	—	—

GEORGE I (1714–1727)

	F	VF	EF	UNC
1715 Roses & Plumes in angles on rev.	£475	£950	£3200	—
1715 Plain edge...			Extremely rare	
1717 —	£475	£950	£3200	—
1720 —	£450	£950	£3200	—
1720/17 20 over 17	£425	£850	£3000	—
1723 SSC in angles on rev.	£425	£850	£2800	—
1726 Small Roses & Plumes in angles on rev.. .	£4500	£13,000	—	—

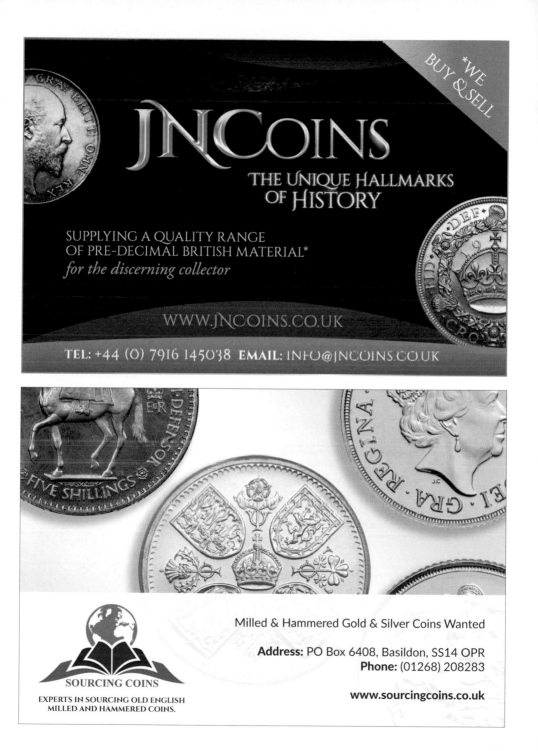

DATE	MINTAGE	F	VF	EF	UNC

GEORGE II (1727–1760)

DATE	MINTAGE	F	VF	EF	UNC
1731 Young head, Plain, proof only..................	—	—	£6500	—	
1731 — Roses & Plumes in angles on rev.........	£160	£400	£1600	—	
1732 — —	£160	£400	£1600	—	
1734 — —	£160	£400	£1650	—	
1735 — —	£160	£400	£1650	—	
1736 — —	£160	£400	£1650	—	
1739 — Roses in angles on rev.	£150	£400	£1500	—	
1741/39 — — 41 over 30	£160	£550	—	—	
1741 — —	£150	£400	£1500	—	
1743 Old head, Roses in angles on rev.	£85	£225	£1000	—	
1745 — —	£85	£225	£1000	—	
1745 — LIMA below bust................................	£70	£175	£650	—	
1746 — —	£70	£175	£650	—	
1746/5 — — 6 over 5	£80	£220	£800	—	
1746 — Plain, Proof	—	—	£3500	—	
1750 — —	£225	£550	£1900	—	
1751 — —	£250	£750	£2100	—	

GEORGE III (1760–1820)

DATE	MINTAGE	F	VF	EF	UNC
1816 "Bull head"	—	£25	£80	£250	£500
1817 —	8,092,656	£25	£80	£250	£500
1817 "Small head"........................	incl. above	£25	£80	£250	£500
1818 —	2,905,056	£25	£80	£250	£500
1819/8 — 9 over 8........................	incl. above			Extremely rare	
1819 —	4,790,016	£25	£80	£250	£525
1820 —	2,396,592	£50	£140	£500	£1000

GEORGE IV (1820–30)

DATE	MINTAGE	F	VF	EF	UNC
1820 First bust, first reverse........	incl. above	£30	£80	£300	£600
1821 — —	1,435,104	£30	£80	£300	£600
1821 — — Proof...........................	incl. above	—	—	—	£2700
1823 — —	2,003,760	£1000	£3200	—	—
1823 — Second reverse..............	incl. above	£30	£80	£300	£600
1824 — —	465,696	£30	£90	£275	£650
1824 Second bust, third reverse .	incl. above			Extremely rare	
1825 — —	2,258,784	£30	£80	£200	£450
1826 — —	2,189,088	£30	£80	£200	£450
1826 — — Proof...........................	incl. above	—	—	—	£1600
1828 — —	49,890	£80	£200	£600	£1500
1829 — —	508,464	£60	£150	£450	£900

WILLIAM IV (1830–37)

DATE	MINTAGE	F	VF	EF	UNC
1831..	—			Extremely rare	
1831 Proof (W.W. in script & block)	—	—	—	—	£2200
1834 W.W. in block......................	993,168	£30	£80	£300	£700
1834 W.W. in script......................	incl. above	£30	£80	£300	£700
1835..	281,952	£35	£90	£300	£750
1836..	1,588,752	£30	£70	£300	£675
1836/5 6 over 5	incl. above	£60	£125	£600	—
1837..	150,526	£45	£160	£600	£1200

VICTORIA (1837–1901)

YOUNG HEAD ISSUES

DATE	MINTAGE	F	VF	EF	UNC
1839 (two varieties)	—	£1200	£3750	£9000	—
1839 Proof...................................	—	—	—	—	£5000
1840..	386,496	£60	£200	£700	£1800
1841..	42,768	£900	£2000	£4000	£7500
1842..	486,288	£55	£150	£700	£1500
1843..	454,608	£140	£450	£1100	£3200
1844..	1,999,008	£45	£110	£550	£1500
1845..	2,231,856	£45	£110	£550	£1500
1846..	1,539,668	£55	£140	£600	£1500
1848 Plain 8................................	367,488	£150	£450	£1400	£3750
1848/6	incl. above	£120	£300	£800	£2800
1849..	261,360	£70	£160	£600	£1600
1849 Small date	incl. above	£90	£220	£850	£1900
1850..	484,613	£70	£200	£600	£2000
1853 Proof only	—	—	—	—	£6000

DATE	MINTAGE	F	VF	EF	UNC
1874	2,188,599	£25	£70	£260	£600
1875	1,113,483	£25	£70	£260	£550
1876	633,221	£30	£80	£280	£650
1876/5 6 over 5	incl. above	£35	£80	£280	£650
1876/6 6 over 6	incl. above	£75	£150	£450	—
1877	447,059	£25	£70	£250	£550
1878	1,466,323	£25	£70	£250	£550
1879	901,356	£35	£80	£280	£650
1880	1,346,350	£25	£70	£250	£500
1881	2,301,495	£25	£70	£250	£475
1882	808,227	£30	£70	£250	£500
1883	2,982,779	£25	£70	£250	£450
1884	1,569,175	£25	£70	£250	£450
1885	1,628,438	£25	£70	£250	£440
1886	891,767	£25	£70	£250	£440
1887	1,438,046	£25	£65	£260	£450
JUBILEE HEAD ISSUES					
1887	incl. above	£8	£14	£30	£75
1887 Proof	1,084	—	—	—	£400
1888	1,428,787	£12	£25	£50	£180
1889	4,811,954	£10	£20	£50	£160
1890	3,228,111	£12	£22	£70	£180
1891	2,284,632	£12	£22	£70	£180
1892	1,710,946	£12	£22	£75	£200
OLD HEAD ISSUES					
1893	1,792,600	£12	£25	£60	£110
1893 Proof	1,312	—	—	—	£600
1894	1,524,960	£15	£35	£90	£250
1895	1,772,662	£12	£30	£70	£190
1896	2,148,505	£12	£22	£65	£190
1897	1,678,643	£12	£22	£65	£175
1898	1,870,055	£12	£22	£65	£175
1899	2,865,872	£12	£22	£65	£175
1900	4,479,128	£12	£22	£65	£175
1901	1,516,570	£12	£22	£65	£175

DATE	MINTAGE	F	VF	EF	UNC

EDWARD VII (1901–10)

DATE	MINTAGE	F	VF	EF	UNC
1902	1,316,008	£12	£30	£80	£170
1902 "Matt Proof"	15,123	—	—	—	£250
1903	274,840	£175	£550	£2200	£4500
1904	709,652	£60	£225	£500	£1500
1905	166,008	£500	£1400	£5000	£9000
1906	2,886,206	£12	£50	£200	£900
1907	3,693,930	£12	£50	£200	£900
1908	1,758,889	£20	£80	£400	£1300
1909	3,051,592	£12	£60	£340	£800
1910	2,557,685	£12	£45	£130	£475

GEORGE V (1910–36)

First issue

DATE	MINTAGE	F	VF	EF	UNC
1911	2,914,573	£12	£30	£75	£200
1911 Proof	6,007	—	—	—	£260
1912	4,700,789	£10	£22	£50	£185
1913	4,090,169	£10	£24	£75	£200
1914	18,333,003	£7	£12	£40	£70
1915	32,433,066	£7	£12	£35	£65
1916	29,530,020	£7	£12	£35	£65
1917	11,172,052	£8	£15	£45	£100
1918	29,079,592	£7	£12	£35	£70
1919	10,266,737	£7	£15	£45	£100

Second issue—debased silver

DATE	MINTAGE	F	VF	EF	UNC
1920	17,982,077	£4	£8	£22	£70
1921	23,677,889	£4	£8	£30	£65
1922	16,396,724	£5	£9	£24	£70
1923	26,308,526	£6	£8	£20	£45
1924	5,866,294	£15	£35	£90	£220
1925	1,413,461	£30	£75	£300	£900
1926	4,473,516	£10	£25	£45	£175

Third issue — Modified effigy

DATE	MINTAGE	F	VF	EF	UNC
1926	incl. above	£6	£14	£40	£100
1927	6,837,872	£6	£12	£35	£75

Fourth issue—New shield reverse

DATE	MINTAGE	F	VF	EF	UNC
1927 Proof	15,000	—	—	—	£100
1928	18,762,727	£5	£8	£20	£35
1929	17,632,636	£5	£8	£20	£35
1930	809,051	£15	£60	£325	£900
1931	11,264,468	£5	£8	£20	£35
1932	4,793,643	£6	£10	£25	£90
1933	10,311,494	£5	£8	£20	£40
1934	2,422,399	£7	£12	£65	£185
1935	7,022,216	£5	£8	£18	£25
1936	7,039,423	£5	£8	£18	£20

George V, fourth issue, new shield reverse

GEORGE VI (1936–52)

DATE	MINTAGE	F	VF	EF	UNC
1937	9,106,440	—	£6	£9	£14
1937 Proof	26,402	—	—	—	£20
1938	6,426,478	£5	£6	£15	£25
1939	15,478,635	£5	£6	£9	£10
1940	17,948,439	£5	£6	£9	£10
1941	15,773,984	£5	£6	£9	£10
1942	31,220,090	£5	£6	£9	£10
1943	15,462,875	£5	£6	£9	£10
1944	15,255,165	£5	£6	£9	£10
1945	19,849,242	£5	£6	£9	£10
1946	22,724,873	£5	£6	£9	£10

Cupro-nickel

DATE	MINTAGE	F	VF	EF	UNC
1947	21,911,484	—	£1	£2	£4
1948	71,164,703	—	£1	£2	£4
1949	28,272,512	—	£1	£2	£6
1950	28,335,500	—	£1	£2	£6
1950 Proof	17,513	—	—	—	£35
1951	9,003,520	—	£1	£2	£6
1951 Proof	20,000	—	—	—	£10
1952			Only one known		

ELIZABETH II (1952–)

DATE	MINTAGE	F	VF	EF	UNC
1953	4,333,214	—	—	£1	£3
1953 Proof	40,000	—	—	—	£8
1954	11,614,953	—	£1	£6	£40
1955	23,628,726	—	—	£1	£6
1956	33,934,909	—	—	£1	£6
1957	34,200,563	—	—	£1	£6
1958	15,745,668	—	£1	£6	£28
1959	9,028,844	—	£1	£9	£32
1960	19,929,191	—	—	£1	£2
1961	25,887,897	—	—	—	£2
1961 Polished dies	incl. above	—	—	£1	£2
1962	24,013,312	—	—	—	£1
1963	17,625,200	—	—	—	£1
1964	5,973,600	—	—	—	£1
1965	9,778,440	—	—	—	£1
1966	13,375,200	—	—	—	£1
1967	33,058,400	—	—	—	£1
1970 Proof	—	—	—	—	£8

FLORINS

VICTORIA (1837–1901)

YOUNG (CROWNED) HEAD ISSUES
"Godless" type (without D.G.–"Dei Gratia")

1848 "Godless" Pattern only plain edge	—			Very rare	
1848 "Godless" Pattern only milled edge	—			Extremely rare	
1849	413,820	£25	£60	£200	£400

(Beware of recent forgeries)

"Gothic" type i.e. date in Roman numerals in obverse legend
"brit." in legend. No die no.

1851 mdcccli Proof	1,540			Extremely rare	
1852 mdccclii	1,014,552	£25	£60	£220	£600
1853 mdcccliii	3,919,950	£25	£60	£220	£600
1853 — Proof	incl. above			—	£3750
1854 mdcccliv	550,413	£500	£1500	—	—
1855 mdccclv	831,017	£30	£70	£250	£625
1856 mdccclvi	2,201,760	£30	£70	£250	£625
1857 mdccclvii	1,671,120	£30	£60	£250	£650
1858 mdccclviii	2,239,380	£30	£60	£250	£625
1859 mdccclix	2,568,060	£30	£60	£250	£650
1860 mdccclx	1,475,100	£35	£85	£275	£800
1862 mdccclxii	594,000	£250	£650	£1200	£3500
1863 mdccclxiii	938,520	£900	£1800	£3500	£7000

"brit" in legend. Die no. below bust

1864 mdccclxiv	1,861,200	£30	£60	£250	£600
1864 Gothic Piedfort flan	incl. above			Extremely rare	
1865 mdccclxv	1,580,044	£35	£70	£275	£650
1866 mdccclxvi	914,760	£35	£70	£275	£600
1867 mdccclxvii	423,720	£45	£110	£400	£850
1867 — only 42 arcs in border	incl. above			Extremely rare	

"britt" in legend. Die no. below bust

1868 mdccclxviii	896,940	£30	£75	£320	£700
1869 mdccclxix	297,000	£30	£80	£350	£850
1870 mdccclxx	1,080,648	£28	£60	£250	£550
1871 mdccclxxi	3,425,605	£28	£60	£280	£500
1872 mdccclxxii	7,199,690	£28	£60	£225	£475
1873 mdccclxxiii	5,921,839	£28	£60	£240	£475
1874 mdccclxxiv	1,642,630	£28	£60	£240	£475
1874 — iv over iii in date	incl. above	£30	£70	£300	£650
1875 mdccclxxv	1,117,030	£28	£60	£220	£525
1876 mdccclxxvi	580,034	£40	£110	£425	£850
1877 mdccclxxvii	682,292	£28	£60	£220	£500
1877 — 48 arcs in border no W.W.	incl. above	£28	£60	£220	£500
1877 — 42 arcs	incl. above	£28	£60	£220	£500
1877 — no die number	incl. above			Extremely rare	
1878 mdccclxxviii with die number	1,786,680	£28	£60	£220	£475

"Gothic" florin

DATE	MINTAGE	F	VF	EF	UNC
1879 mdccclxxix no die no	1,512,247			Extremely rare	
1879 — 48 arcs in border	incl. above	£28	£60	£220	£475
1879 — no die number	incl. above			Extremely rare	
1879 — 38 arcs, no W.W..	incl. above	£28	£60	£220	£475
1880 mdccclxxx Younger portrait	—			Extremely rare	
1880 — 34 arcs, Older portrait ...	2,167,170	£28	£60	£200	£450
1881 mdccclxxxi — —	2,570,337	£25	£55	£200	£450
1881 — xxГi broken puncheon...	incl. above	£35	£70	£200	£500
1883 mdccclxxxiii — —	3,555,667	£25	£60	£200	£440
1884 mdccclxxxiv — —	1,447,379	£25	£55	£200	£440
1885 mdccclxxxv — —	1,758,210	£25	£55	£200	£440
1886 mdccclxxxvi — —	591,773	£25	£55	£200	£440
1887 mdccclxxxvii — —	1,776,903	£50	£120	£300	£675
1887 — 46 arcs......................	incl. above	£50	£120	£350	£725
JUBILEE HEAD ISSUES					
1887	incl. above	£7	£16	£30	£60
1887 Proof	1,084	—	—	—	£330
1888	1,547,540	£7	£15	£45	£120
1889	2,973,561	£8	£18	£50	£140
1890....................................	1,684,737	£10	£25	£80	£260
1891....................................	836,438	£20	£60	£200	£550
1892....................................	283,401	£30	£100	£325	£850
VICTORIA—OLD HEAD ISSUES					
1893....................................	1,666,103	£8	£16	£40	£90
1893 Proof	1,312	—	—	—	£400
1894	1,952,842	£10	£25	£70	£240
1895	2,182,968	£10	£28	£70	£200
1896	2,944,416	£8	£24	£60	£180
1897	1,699,921	£8	£24	£60	£170
1898	3,061,343	£8	£24	£60	£170
1899	3,966,953	£8	£24	£60	£170
1900	5,528,630	£8	£24	£60	£170
1901	2,648,870	£8	£24	£60	£170

EDWARD VII (1901–10)

1902....................................	2,189,575	£10	£22	£60	£115
1902 "Matt Proof"......................	15,123	—	—	—	£170
1903....................................	1,995,298	£10	£35	£120	£550
1904....................................	2,769,932	£12	£40	£150	£500
1905....................................	1,187,596	£65	£175	£600	£1600
1906....................................	6,910,128	£10	£35	£130	£525
1907....................................	5,947,895	£11	£35	£130	£525
1908....................................	3,280,010	£20	£55	£350	£900
1909....................................	3,482,829	£15	£50	£240	£700
1910....................................	5,650,713	£14	£35	£100	£320

GEORGE V (1910–36)

First issue

1911	5,951,284	£7	£12	£40	£90
1911 Proof	6,007	—	—	—	£180
1912	8,571,731	£7	£15	£35	£130
1913	4,545,278	£10	£25	£50	£180
1914	21,252,701	£7	£18	£28	£60
1915	12,367,939	£7	£18	£26	£60
1916	21,064,337	£7	£18	£25	£60
1917	11,181,617	£7	£22	£35	£90
1918	29,211,792	£7	£18	£28	£80
1919	9,469,292	£9	£20	£40	£95

Second issue — debased silver

1920....................................	15,387,833	£4	£12	£40	£85
1921....................................	34,863,895	£4	£12	£40	£65
1922....................................	23,861,044	£4	£12	£40	£65
1923....................................	21,546,533	£4	£10	£30	£60
1924....................................	4,582,372	£12	£35	£95	£250
1925....................................	1,404,136	£30	£75	£300	£800
1926....................................	5,125,410	£8	£22	£50	£150

Fourth issue — new reverse

1927 Proof only........................	101,497	—	—	—	£110
1928....................................	11,087,186	£4	£7	£15	£40

DATE	MINTAGE	F	VF	EF	UNC
1929	16,397,279	£4	£7	£16	£35
1930	5,753,568	£4	£7	£20	£50
1931	6,556,331	£4	£7	£18	£35
1932	717,041	£14	£35	£225	£600
1933	8,685,303	£4	£7	£18	£40
1935	7,540,546	£4	£7	£14	£30
1936	9,897,448	£4	£7	£14	£30

GEORGE VI (1936–52)

1937	13,006,781	£4	£5	£7	£12
1937 Proof	26,402	—	—	—	£20
1938	7,909,388	£6	£8	£15	£30
1939	20,850,607	£4	£5	£8	£10
1940	18,700,338	£4	£5	£7	£12
1941	24,451,079	£4	£5	£7	£9
1942	39,895,243	£4	£5	£7	£9
1943	26,711,987	£4	£5	£7	£9
1944	27,560,005	£4	£5	£7	£9
1945	25,858,049	£4	£5	£7	£9
1946	22,300,254	£4	£5	£7	£9
Cupro-nickel					
1947	22,910,085	—	—	£1	£3
1948	67,553,636	—	—	£1	£3
1949	28,614,939	—	—	£1	£5
1950	24,357,490	—	—	£2	£7
1950 Proof	17,513	—	—	£1	£9
1951	27,411,747	—	—	£2	£8
1951 Proof	20,000	—	—	—	£9

ELIZABETH II (1952–)

1953	11,958,710	—	—	—	£2
1953 Proof	40,000	—	—	—	£6
1954	13,085,422	—	—	£6	£40
1955	25,887,253	—	—	£1	£3
1956	47,824,500	—	—	£1	£3
1957	33,071,282	—	—	£4	£25
1958	9,564,580	—	—	£3	£30
1959	14,080,319	—	—	£4	£30
1960	13,831,782	—	—	£1	£4
1961	37,735,315	—	—	£1	£2
1962	36,147,903	—	—	£1	£2
1963	26,471,000	—	—	£1	£2
1964	16,539,000	—	—	£1	£2
1965	48,163,000	—	—	—	£1.50
1966	83,999,000	—	—	—	£1.50
1967	39,718,000	—	—	—	£1.50
1970 Proof	—	—	—	—	£10

SHILLINGS

OLIVER CROMWELL

1658	£900	£2000	£4000	—
1658 Dutch Copy		Extremely rare		

CHARLES II (1660–85)

1663 First bust	£125	£500	£1500	—
1663 — GARTIA error		Extremely rare		
1663 — Irish & Scottish shields transposed	£270	£800	—	—
1666 — Elephant below bust	£500	£1500	£6000	—
1666 "Guinea" head, elephant	£1800	£4500	—	—
1666 Second bust		Extremely rare		
1668 —	£120	£400	£1400	—
1668/3 — 8 over 3	£150	£500	—	—
1668 Second bust	£120	£450	£1400	—
1669/6 First bust variety		Extremely rare		
1669		Extremely rare		

DATE	F	VF	EF	UNC
1669 Second bust			Extremely rare	
1670 —	£150	£500	£1800	—
1671 —	£150	£500	£1800	—
1671 — Plume below, plume in centre rev.	£425	£1000	£4200	—
1672 —	£150	£550	£1800	—
1673 —	£150	£550	£1800	—
1673 — Plume below, plume in centre rev.	£450	£1200	£5000	—
1673/2 — 3 over 2	£175	£600	—	—
1674/3 — 4 over 3	£150	£550	—	—
1674 —	£150	£550	£2000	—
1674 — Plume below bust, plume in centre rev.	£375	£1200	£4500	—
1674 — Plume rev. only	£700	£2000	£4750	—
1674 Third bust	£450	£1600	—	—
1675 Second bust	£200	£800	—	—
1675/4 — 5 over 4	£220	£850	—	—
1675 — Plume below bust, plume in centre rev.	£400	£1100	£5000	—
1675 Third bust	£350	£1300	—	—
1675/3 — 5 over 3	£300	£1100	—	—
1676 Second bust	£125	£450	£1800	—
1676/5 — 6 over 5	£160	£550	—	—
1676 — Plume below bust, plume in centre rev.	£425	£1500	£5000	—
1677 —	£130	£500	£2000	—
1677 — Plume below bust	£1000	£2500	£8000	—
1678 —	£140	£500	£1850	—
1678/7 — 8 over 7	£160	£700	—	—
1679 —	£140	£500	£2200	—
1679 — Plume below bust, plume in centre rev.	£400	£1100	£5000	—
1679 — Plume below bust	£700	£2500	£6000	—
1679 — 9 over 7	£160	£600	—	—
1680 —			Extremely rare	
1680 — Plume below bust, plume in centre rev.	£1000	£2750	£6250	—
1680/79 — — 80 over 79	£850	£2500	—	—
1681 —	£300	£850	£3000	—
1681 — 1 over 0	£375	£900	£3250	—
1681/0 Elephant & Castle below bust	£3000	£9000	—	—
1682/1 — 2 over 1	£1000	£3300	—	—
1683 —			Extremely rare	
1683 Fourth (Larger) bust	£220	£700	£2300	—
1684 —	£220	£700	£2300	—

JAMES II (1685–88)

	F	VF	EF	UNC
1685	£200	£500	£2000	—
1685 Plume in centre rev. rev			Extremely rare	
1685 No stops on rev.	£220	£650	—	—
1686	£220	£550	£2300	—
1686/5 6 over 5	£225	£600	£2250	—
1687	£200	£600	£2200	—
1687/6 7 over 6	£200	£550	£2300	—
1688	£200	£600	£2400	—
1688/7 last 8 over 7	£220	£550	£2250	—

WILLIAM & MARY (1688–94)

	F	VF	EF	UNC
1692	£180	£500	£2250	—
1692 inverted 1	£210	£550	£2300	—
1693	£180	£500	£2250	—

WILLIAM III (1694–1702)

Provincially produced shillings carry privy marks or initials below the bust:
B: Bristol. C: Chester. E: Exeter. N: Norwich. Y or y: York.

	F	VF	EF	UNC
1695 First bust	£40	£120	£600	—
1696 —	£40	£100	£450	—
1696 — no stops on rev.	£60	£140	£750	—
1696 — MAB for MAG			Extremely rare	
1696 — 1669 error			Extremely rare	
1696 — 1669 various GVLELMVS errors			Extremely rare	
1696 — B below bust	£60	£150	£850	—
1696 — C	£55	£150	£850	—
1696 — E	£60	£160	£900	—

DATE	F	VF	EF	UNC
1696 — N	£55	£150	£800	—
1696 — y	£55	£150	£800	—
1696 — Y	£55	£150	£800	—
1696 Second bust		Only one known		
1696 Third bust C below	£160	£400	£1500	—
1696 — Y		Extremely rare		
1697 First bust	£50	£110	£400	—
1697 — GRI for GRA error		Extremely rare		
1697 — Scottish & Irish shields transposed		Extremely rare		
1697 — Irish arms at date		Extremely rare		
1697 — no stops on rev	£60	£180	£700	—
1697 — GVLELMVS error		Extremely rare		
1697 — B	£60	£150	£850	—
1697 — C	£60	£150	£850	—
1697 — E	£60	£150	£850	—
1697 — N	£60	£150	£800	—
1697 — — no stops on obv		Extremely rare		
1697 — y	£60	£150	£775	—
1697 — — arms of France & Ireland transposed		Extremely rare		
1697 — Y	£50	£150	£650	—
1697 Third bust	£50	£125	£550	—
1697 — B	£60	£150	£650	—
1697 — C	£60	£150	£750	—
1697 — — Fr.a error	£150	£500	—	—
1697 — — no stops on obv	£90	£300	—	—
1697 — — arms of Scotland at date		Extremely rare		
1697 — E	£60	£150	£750	—
1697 — N	£60	£150	£850	—
1697 — y	£60	£150	£800	—
1697 Third bust variety	£60	£140	£575	—
1697 — B	£60	£150	£900	—
1697 — C	£120	£650	—	—
1698 —	£80	£250	£1000	—
1698 — Plumes in angles of rev.	£200	£500	£2000	—
1698 Fourth bust "Flaming hair"	£150	£500	£2000	—
1699 —	£110	£400	£1400	—
1699 Fifth bust	£100	£300	£1100	—
1699 — Plumes in angles on rev.	£150	£450	£1800	—
1699 — Roses in angles on rev	£160	£500	£1800	—
1700 —	£70	£140	£600	—
1700 — Small round oo in date	£70	£140	£600	—
1700 — no stop after DEI		Extremely rare		
1700 — Plume below bust	£2500	£9500	—	—
1701 —	£80	£250	£900	—
1701 — Plumes in angles on rev.	£160	£600	£1800	—

ANNE (1702–14)

	F	VF	EF	UNC
1702 First bust (pre-Union with Scotland)	£80	£300	£700	—
1702 — Plumes in angles on rev.	£90	£275	£800	—
1702 — VIGO below bust	£70	£220	£650	—
1702 — — colon before ANNA		Extremely rare		
1703 Second bust, VIGO below	£65	£180	£700	—
1704 — Plain	£500	£1800	—	—
1704 — Plumes in angles on rev.	£80	£200	£800	—
1705 — Plain	£75	£200	£700	—
1705 — Plumes in angles on rev.	£70	£200	£750	—
1705 — Roses & Plumes in angles on rev.	£70	£200	£700	—
1707 — —	£60	£180	£650	—
1707 Second bust (post-Union) E below bust	£50	£140	£550	—
1707 — E* below bust	£70	£200	£750	—
1707 Third bust, Plain	£35	£100	£450	—
1707 — Plumes in angles on rev.	£50	£160	£750	—
1707 — E below bust	£40	£90	£500	—
1707 "Edinburgh" bust, E* below		Extremely rare		
1708 Second bust, E below	£50	£100	£450	—
1708 — E* below bust	£55	£165	£700	—
1708/7 — — 8 over 7		Extremely rare		

William III First bust

Anne, VIGO below bust

DATE	MINTAGE	F	VF	EF	UNC
1708 — Roses & Plumes in angles on rev.........		£80	£275	£650	—
1708 Third bust, Plain		£40	£120	£425	—
1708 — Plumes in angles on rev.		£70	£200	£600	—
1708 Third bust, E below bust		£60	£175	£650	—
1708/7 — — 8 over 7		£200	£450	—	—
1708 — Roses & Plumes in angles on rev.........		£70	£180	£600	—
1708 "Edinburgh" bust, E* below.....................		£60	£170	£550	—
1709 Third bust, Plain		£50	£150	£500	—
1709 "Edinburgh" bust, E* below.....................		£50	£170	£650	—
1709 — E no star (filled in die?)......................		£70	£160	£550	—
1710 Third bust, Roses & Plumes in angles......		£60	£140	£650	—
1710 Fourth bust, Roses & Plumes in angles ...		£60	£150	£650	—
1711 Third bust, Plain		£70	£160	£450	—
1711 Fourth bust, Plain		£30	£75	£250	—
1712 — Roses & Plumes in angles on rev.........		£60	£120	£425	—
1713 — —		£60	£120	£400	—
1713/2 — 3 over 2..		£70	£220	—	—
1714 — —		£60	£100	£340	—
1714/3 —				Extremely rare	

GEORGE I (1714–27)

1715 First bust, Roses & Plumes in angles on rev.		£80	£200	£900	—
1716 — —		£150	£500	£2000	—
1717 — —		£90	£300	£1350	—
1718 — —		£70	£225	£800	—
1719 — —		£120	£400	£2000	—
1720 — —		£70	£175	£450	—
1720/18 — —		£150	£500	£1450	—
1720 — Plain		£40	£100	£450	—
1721 — Roses & Plumes in angles on rev.........		£100	£350	£1600	—
1721/0 — — 1 over 0		£70	£220	£900	—
1721 — Plain		£120	£450	£1400	—
1721/19 — — 21 over 19		£125	£400	—	—
1721/18 21 over 18 error, Plumes & Roses.......		£500	£1800	—	—
1722 — Roses & Plumes in angles on rev.........		£80	£220	£1000	—
1723 — —		£90	£240	£1000	—
1723 — SSC rev., Arms of France at date		£100	£275	£750	—
1723 — SSC in angles on rev		£35	£110	£275	—
1723 Second bust, SSC in angles on rev.		£50	£170	£550	—
1723 — Roses & Plumes in angles		£90	£240	£1000	—
1723 — WCC (Welsh Copper Co) below bust ..		£700	£1800	£6000	—
1724 — Roses & Plumes in angles on rev.........		£80	£200	£750	—
1724 — WCC below bust..................................		£700	£1800	£6000	—
1725 — Roses & Plumes in angles on rev.........		£80	£200	£1000	—
1725 — — no stops on obv...............................		£90	£225	£1100	—
1725 — WCC below bust..................................		£750	£2000	£6500	—
1726 — — Roses & Plumes		£650	£1750	£6500	—
1726 — WCC below bust..................................		£750	£2000	£6500	—
1727 — —				Extremely rare	
1727 — — no stops on obv...............................				Extremely rare	

GEORGE II (1727–60)

*George II
Young head*

1727 Young head, Plumes in angles on rev......		£75	£300	£950	—
1727 — Roses & Plumes in angles on rev.........		£60	£180	£650	—
1728 — —		£65	£180	£650	—
1728 — Plain		£75	£220	£700	—
1729 — Roses & Plumes in angles on rev.........		£60	£200	£700	—
1731 — —		£70	£200	£700	—
1731 — Plumes in angles on rev.		£100	£400	£1250	—
1732 — Roses & Plumes in angles on rev.........		£65	£200	£750	—
1734 — —		£65	£200	£700	—
1735 — —		£65	£200	£700	—
1736 — —		£65	£200	£700	—
1736/5 — — 6 over 5		£70	£200	£800	—
1737 — —		£65	£200	£650	—
1739 — Roses in angles on rev.		£50	£160	£450	—
1739/7 — — 9 over 7				Extremely rare	
1741 — —		£50	£160	£450	—
1741/39 — — 41 over 39				Extremely rare	
1743 Old head, Roses in angles on rev............		£30	£80	£325	—
1745 — —		£30	£80	£325	—

DATE	MINTAGE	F	VF	EF	UNC
1745 — — LIMA below bust		£35	£90	£325	—
1745/3 — — — 5 over 3........................		£60	£175	£400	—
1746 — —		£50	£175	£650	—
1746/5 — — — 6 over 5........................		£100	£300	—	—
1746 — Plain, Proof		—	—	£3500	—
1747 — Roses in angles on rev.		£45	£100	£400	—
1750 — Plain		£40	£140	£400	—
1750/6 — — 0 over 6		£60	£150	£500	—
1751 — —		£125	£500	£1500	—
1758 — —		£20	£50	£140	—

George II Old head

GEORGE III (1760–1820)

1763 "Northumberland" bust		£450	£800	£1600	—
(Beware recent counterfeits)					
1787 rev. no semée of hearts in 4th shield........		£20	£35	£100	—
1787 — No stop over head		£25	£40	£120	—
1787 — No stop at date		£45	£75	£150	—
1787 — No stops on obv		£100	£250	£850	—
1787 rev. with semée of hearts in shield		£35	£65	£125	—
1798 "Dorrien Magens" bust........................		—	—	—	£27,500

NEW COINAGE—shield in garter reverse

1816........................	—	£12	£25	£75	£150
1817........................	3,031,360	£12	£35	£85	£175
1817 GEOE for GEOR	incl. above	£120	£250	£625	—
1818........................	1,342,440	£25	£45	£150	£400
1819........................	7,595,280	£15	£35	£100	£200
1819/8 9 over 8	incl. above	£20	£50	£150	
1820........................	7,975,440	£12	£25	£100	£200

GEORGE IV (1820–30)

1821 First bust, first reverse	2,463,120	£15	£40	£150	£475
1821 — — Proof........................	incl. above	—	—	—	£1400
1823 — Second reverse..............	693,000	£50	£90	£250	£600
1824 — —	4,158,000	£12	£40	£150	£400
1825 — —	2,459,160	£20	£50	£150	£550
1825/3 — — 5 over 3	incl. above			Extremely rare	
1825 Second bust, third reverse .	incl. above	£10	£25	£60	£200
1825 — — Roman I................	incl. above			Extremely rare	
1826 — —	6,351,840	£10	£25	£80	£200
1826 — — Proof........................	incl. above	—	—	—	£675
1827 — —	574,200	£30	£70	£200	£475
1829 — —	879,120	£20	£60	£175	£425

WILLIAM IV (1830–37)

1831 Proof only		—	—	—	£1350
1834........................	3,223,440	£15	£35	£170	£400
1835........................	1,449,360	£15	£35	£170	£400
1836........................	3,567,960	£15	£35	£170	£400
1837........................	478,160	£20	£60	£200	£550

VICTORIA (1837–1901)

YOUNG HEAD ISSUES
First head

1838 WW on truncation..............	1,956,240	£20	£50	£200	£450
1839 —	5,666,760	£20	£50	£200	£450

Second head

1839 WW on truncation, Proof only	incl. above	—	—	—	£1400
1839 no WW........................	incl. above	£20	£50	£180	£450
1840	1,639,440	£20	£50	£180	£450
1841	875,160	£22	£50	£180	£450
1842	2,094,840	£20	£45	£170	£475
1843	1,465,200	£20	£50	£180	£475
1844	4,466,880	£15	£40	£150	£400
1845	4,082,760	£15	£40	£150	£400
1846	4,031,280	£15	£40	£150	£400
1848 last 8 of date over 6..........	1,041,480	£80	£160	£600	£1300

DATE	MINTAGE	F	VF	EF	UNC
1849	845,480	£28	£70	£220	£650
1850	685,080	£800	£1500	£3000	£6500
1850/49	incl. above	£800	£1500	£4500	—
1851	470,071	£45	£110	£400	£900
1852	1,306,574	£15	£35	£125	£400
1853	4,256,188	£15	£35	£125	£400
1853 Proof.................................	incl. above	—	—	—	£1600
1854	552,414	£200	£550	£1200	£3200
1854/1 4 over 1	incl. above	£200	£900	—	—
1855	1,368,400	£12	£30	£110	£300
1856	3,168,000	£12	£30	£110	£300
1857	2,562,120	£12	£30	£110	£300
1857 error F:G with inverted G ...	incl. above	£200	£600	—	—
1858	3,108,600	£12	£30	£110	£300
1859	4,561,920	£12	£30	£110	£300
1860	1,671,120	£12	£30	£110	£350
1861	1,382,040	£14	£40	£150	£500
1862	954,360	£60	£160	£450	£1350
1863	859,320	£125	£375	£850	£1800
1863/1 3 over 1	incl. above			Extremely rare	

Die no. added above date up to 1879

DATE	MINTAGE	F	VF	EF	UNC
1864	4,518,360	£10	£30	£110	£250
1865	5,619,240	£10	£30	£110	£250
1866	4,984,600	£10	£30	£110	£250
1866 error BBITANNIAR	incl. above	£80	£250	£800	—
1867	2,166,120	£10	£35	£110	£275

Third head—with die no

DATE	MINTAGE	F	VF	EF	UNC
1867	incl. above	£100	£450	—	—
1868	3,330,360	£12	£40	£110	£275
1869	736,560	£18	£50	£120	£350
1870	1,467,471	£14	£40	£100	£275
1871	4,910,010	£12	£40	£100	£250
1872	8,897,781	£12	£40	£100	£250
1873	6,489,598	£12	£40	£100	£250
1874	5,503,747	£14	£40	£100	£250
1875	4,353,983	£12	£40	£100	£250
1876	1,057,487	£14	£45	£110	£425
1877	2,989,703	£12	£40	£100	£275
1878	3,127,131	£12	£40	£100	£275
1879	3,611,507	£20	£60	£200	£550

Fourth head—no die no

DATE	MINTAGE	F	VF	EF	UNC
1879 no Die no.	incl. above	£10	£28	£75	£190
1880	4,842,786	£10	£28	£75	£190
1881	5,255,332	£10	£28	£75	£190
1882	1,611,786	£25	£80	£200	£550
1883	7,281,450	£10	£28	£65	£180
1884	3,923,993	£10	£28	£65	£180
1885	3,336,526	£10	£28	£65	£180
1886	2,086,819	£10	£28	£65	£180
1887	4,034,133	£10	£28	£65	£180

JUBILEE HEAD ISSUES

DATE	MINTAGE	F	VF	EF	UNC
1887	incl. above	£4	£8	£15	£40
1887 Proof.................................	1,084	—	—	—	£300
1888..	4,526,856	£6	£10	£25	£70
1889..	7,039,628	£35	£90	£300	—
1889 Large bust (until 1892)........	incl. above	£6	£12	£45	£80
1890..	8,794,042	£6	£12	£45	£80
1891..	5,665,348	£6	£12	£45	£85
1892..	4,591,622	£6	£12	£45	£110

OLD HEAD ISSUES

DATE	MINTAGE	F	VF	EF	UNC
1893..	7,039,074	£5	£10	£30	£65
1893 small lettering	incl. above	£5	£10	£30	£65
1893 Proof.................................	1,312	—	—	—	£240
1894..	5,953,152	£9	£25	£60	£160
1895..	8,880,651	£9	£25	£55	£150
1896..	9,264,551	£7	£15	£40	£80
1897..	6,270,364	£7	£12	£40	£75
1898..	9,768,703	£7	£12	£40	£70
1899..	10,965,382	£7	£12	£40	£70
1900..	10,937,590	£7	£12	£40	£75
1901..	3,426,294	£7	£12	£40	£70

Victoria Jubilee head

Victoria Old or Veiled head

DATE	MINTAGE	F	VF	EF	UNC

EDWARD VII (1901–10)

DATE	MINTAGE	F	VF	EF	UNC
1902	7,809,481	£5	£15	£45	£80
1902 Proof matt	13,123	—	—	—	£110
1903	2,061,823	£10	£35	£140	£475
1904	2,040,161	£8	£35	£130	£460
1905	488,390	£110	£300	£1100	£3500
1906	10,791,025	£5	£12	£40	£120
1907	14,083,418	£5	£12	£40	£130
1908	3,806,969	£10	£25	£150	£500
1909	5,664,982	£9	£22	£110	£400
1910	26,547,236	£5	£10	£45	£100

GEORGE V (1910–36)

First issue

DATE	MINTAGE	F	VF	EF	UNC
1911	20,065,901	£5	£9	£22	£55
1911 Proof	6,007	—	—	—	£140
1912	15,594,009	£6	£11	£25	£80
1913	9,011,509	£7	£20	£50	£150
1914	23,415,843	£4	£7	£25	£55
1915	39,279,024	£4	£7	£25	£55
1916	35,862,015	£4	£7	£25	£55
1917	22,202,608	£4	£7	£25	£60
1918	34,915,934	£4	£7	£25	£55
1919	10,823,824	£5	£8	£30	£65

Second Issue — debased silver

DATE	MINTAGE	F	VF	EF	UNC
1920	22,825,142	£2	£4	£20	£45
1921	22,648,763	£2	£4	£20	£45
1922	27,215,738	£2	£4	£20	£45
1923	14,575,243	£2	£4	£20	£45
1924	9,250,095	£7	£15	£50	£150
1925	5,418,764	£6	£10	£40	£110
1926	22,516,453	£3	£8	£30	£110

George V First obverse

Third issue — Modified bust

DATE	MINTAGE	F	VF	EF	UNC
1926	incl. above	£2	£4	£25	£55
1927 —	9,247,344	£2	£4	£25	£55

Fourth issue — large lion and crown on rev., date in legend

DATE	MINTAGE	F	VF	EF	UNC
1927	incl. above	£2	£4	£20	£40
1927 Proof	15,000	—	—	—	£60
1928	18,136,778	£2	£4	£15	£40
1929	19,343,006	£2	£4	£15	£40
1930	3,172,092	£2	£4	£20	£50
1931	6,993,926	£2	£4	£15	£40
1932	12,168,101	£2	£4	£15	£45
1933	11,511,624	£2	£4	£15	£35
1934	6,138,463	£2	£4	£18	£50
1935	9,183,462	—	£4	£10	£22
1936	11,910,613	—	£4	£9	£20

GEORGE VI (1936–52)

George V Second obverse

E = England rev. (lion standing on large crown). S = Scotland rev. (lion seated on small crown holding sword and mace)

DATE	MINTAGE	F	VF	EF	UNC
1937 E	8,359,122	—	£2	£4	£6
1937 E Proof	26,402	—	—	—	£20
1937 S	6,748,875	—	£2	£4	£6
1937 S Proof	26,402	—	—	—	£20
1938 E	4,833,436	—	£3	£10	£20
1938 S	4,797,852	—	£3	£10	£20
1939 E	11,052,677	—	£2	£4	£6
1939 S	10,263,892	—	£2	£4	£6
1940 E	11,099,126	—	—	£4	£7
1940 S	9,913,089	—	—	£4	£7

DATE	MINTAGE	F	VF	EF	UNC
1941 E	11,391,883	—	—	£4	£6
1941 S	8,086,030	—	—	£4	£5
1942 E	17,453,643	—	—	£4	£5
1942 S	13,676,759	—	—	£4	£5
1943 E	11,404,213	—	—	£4	£6
1943 S	9,824,214	—	—	£4	£5
1944 E	11,586,751	—	—	£4	£5
1944 S	10,990,167	—	—	£4	£5
1945 E	15,143,404	—	—	£4	£6
1945 S	15,106,270	—	—	£4	£5
1946 E	16,663,797	—	—	£4	£5
1946 S	16,381,501	—	—	£4	£5
Cupro-nickel					
1947 E	12,120,611	—	—	—	£2
1947 S	12,283,223	—	—	—	£2
1948 E	45,576,923	—	—	—	£2
1948 S	45,351,937	—	—	—	£2
1949 E	19,328,405	—	—	—	£5
1949 S	21,243,074	—	—	—	£5
1950 E	19,243,872	—	—	—	£5
1950 E Proof	17,513	—	—	—	£20
1950 S	14,299,601	—	—	—	£5
1950 S Proof	17,513	—	—	—	£20
1951 E	9,956,930	—	—	—	£5
1951 E Proof	20,000	—	—	—	£20
1951 S	10,961,174	—	—	—	£6
1951 S Proof	20,000	—	—	—	£20

English reverse

Scottish reverse

ELIZABETH II (1952–)

E = England rev. (shield with three lions). S = Scotland rev. (shield with one lion).

DATE	MINTAGE	F	VF	EF	UNC
1953 E	41,942,894	—	—	—	£1
1953 E Proof	40,000	—	—	—	£4
1953 S	20,663,528	—	—	—	£1
1953 S Proof	40,000	—	—	—	£4
1954 E	30,262,032	—	—	—	£2
1954 S	26,771,735	—	—	—	£2
1955 E	45,259,908	—	—	—	£2
1955 S	27,950,906	—	—	—	£2
1956 E	44,907,008	—	—	—	£10
1956 S	42,853,639	—	—	—	£10
1957 E	42,774,217	—	—	—	£1
1957 S	17,959,988	—	—	—	£10
1958 E	14,392,305	—	—	—	£10
1958 S	40,822,557	—	—	—	£1
1959 E	19,442,778	—	—	—	£1
1959 S	1,012,988	£1	£3	£10	£45
1960 E	27,027,914	—	—	—	£1
1960 S	14,376,932	—	—	—	£1
1961 E	39,816,907	—	—	—	£1
1961 S	2,762,558	—	—	—	£3
1962 E	36,704,379	—	—	—	£1
1962 S	17,475,310	—	—	—	£1
1963 E	49,433,607	—	—	—	£1
1963 S	32,300,000	—	—	—	£1
1964 E	8,590,900	—	—	—	£1
1964 S	5,239,100	—	—	—	£1
1965 E	9,216,000	—	—	—	£1
1965 S	2,774,000	—	—	—	£2
1966 E	15,002,000	—	—	—	£1
1966 S	15,604,000	—	—	—	£1
1970 E Proof	—				£10
1970 S Proof	—				£10

English reverse

Scottish reverse

SIXPENCES

DATE	F	VF	EF	UNC

OLIVER CROMWELL

1658 Patterns by Thos. Simon & Tanner
Four varieties .... Extremely rare

CHARLES II (1660–85)

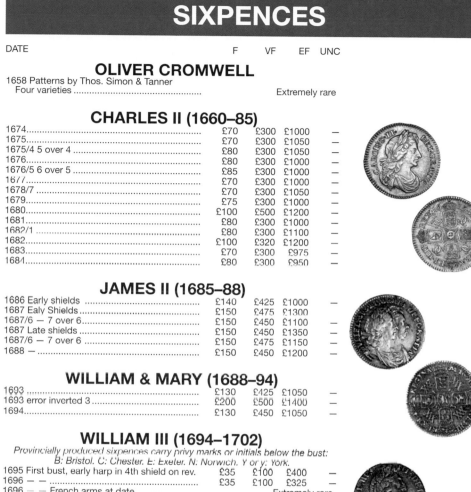

DATE	F	VF	EF	UNC
1674...	£70	£300	£1000	—
1675...	£70	£300	£1050	—
1675/4 5 over 4	£80	£300	£1050	—
1676...	£80	£300	£1000	—
1676/5 6 over 5	£85	£300	£1000	—
1677	£70	£300	£1000	—
1678/7	£70	£300	£1050	—
1679...	£75	£300	£1000	—
1680...	£100	£500	£1200	—
1681...	£80	£300	£1000	—
1682/1	£80	£300	£1100	—
1682...	£100	£320	£1200	—
1683...	£70	£300	£975	—
1684...	£80	£300	£950	—

JAMES II (1685–88)

DATE	F	VF	EF	UNC
1686 Early shields	£140	£425	£1000	—
1687 Ealy Shields	£150	£475	£1300	
1687/6 — 7 over 6..	£150	£450	£1100	—
1687 Late shields	£150	£450	£1350	—
1687/6 — 7 over 6	£150	£475	£1150	—
1688 —	£150	£450	£1200	—

WILLIAM & MARY (1688–94)

DATE	F	VF	EF	UNC
1693	£130	£425	£1050	—
1693 error inverted 3	£200	£500	£1400	—
1694...	£130	£450	£1050	—

WILLIAM III (1694–1702)

Provincially produced sixpences carry privy marks or initials below the bust:
B: Bristol. C: Chester. E: Exeter. N: Norwich. Y or y: York.

DATE	F	VF	EF	UNC
1695 First bust, early harp in 4th shield on rev.	£35	£100	£400	—
1696 — —	£35	£100	£325	—
1696 — — French arms at date		Extremely rare		
1696 — — Scottish arms at date		Extremely rare		
1696 — — DFI for DEI....................................		Extremely rare		
1696 — — No stops on obv.	£50	£140	£500	—
1696 — — B	£40	£100	£425	—
1696 — — — B over E		Extremely rare		
1696 — — C	£40	£100	£450	—
1696 — — E...	£50	£110	£450	—
1696 — — N...	£45	£100	£450	—
1696 — — y...	£40	£110	£550	—
1696 — — Y...	£50	£200	£550	—
1696 — Later harp	£50	£175	£400	—
1696 — — B	£70	£225	£600	—
1696 — — — no stops on obv........................	£80	£275	£550	—
1696 — — C..	£80	£350	£850	—
1696 — — N..	£70	£325	—	—
1696 Second bust...	£300	£800	£2200	—
1697 First bust, later harp	£30	£75	£300	—
1697 — — Arms of France & Ireland transposed		Extremely rare		

DATE	MINTAGE	F	VF	EF	UNC
1697 — — B		£50	£110	£450	—
1697 — — C		£70	£200	£500	—
1697 — — — Irish shield at date			Extremely rare		
1697 — — E		£70	£200	£500	—
1697 — — — error GVLIEMVS			Extremely rare		
1697 — — y		£60	£125	£475	—
1697 — — — Irish shield at date			Extremely rare		
1697 Second bust		£200	£500	£1600	—
1697 Third bust		£30	£75	£300	—
1697 — error GVLIEIMVS			Extremely rare		
1697 — B		£50	£110	£450	—
1697 — — IRA for FRA			Extremely rare		
1697 — C		£75	£220	£525	—
1697 — E		£75	£200	£550	—
1697 — Y		£60	£200	£525	—
1698 —		£60	£190	£500	—
1698 — Plumes in angles on rev.		£80	£220	£750	—
1699 —		£90	£250	£800	—
1699 — Plumes in angles on rev.		£70	£250	£800	—
1699 — Roses in angles on rev.		£70	£250	£800	—
1699 — — error GⱯLIELMVS			Extremely rare		
1700 —		£45	£110	£400	—
1700 — Plume below bust		£2000	—	—	—
1701 —		£65	£160	£525	—

ANNE (1702–14)

DATE	MINTAGE	F	VF	EF	UNC
1703 VIGO below bust Before Union with Scotland		£40	£130	£425	—
1705 Plain		£60	£170	£500	—
1705 Plumes in angles on rev.		£45	£150	£475	—
1705 Roses & Plumes in angles on rev.		£60	£150	£475	—
1707 Roses & Plumes in angles on rev.		£50	£150	£425	—
1707 (Post-Union), Plain		£40	£85	£340	—
1707 E (Edinburgh) below bust		£40	£85	£320	—
1707 Plumes in angles on rev.		£45	£120	£330	—
1708 Plain		£45	£100	£400	—
1708 E below bust		£50	£100	£350	—
1708 E* below bust		£60	£140	£400	—
1708 "Edinburgh" bust E* below		£50	£140	£400	—
1708 Plumes in angles on rev.		£55	£150	£475	—
1710 Roses & Plumes in angles on rev.		£35	£110	£450	—
1711 Plain		£25	£70	£250	—

GEORGE I (1714–27)

DATE	MINTAGE	F	VF	EF	UNC
1717 Roses & Plumes in angles on rev.		£90	£300	£800	—
1717 Plain edge			Extremely rare		
1720 —		£90	£300	£700	—
1723 SSC in angles on rev.		£30	£70	£200	—
1723 Larger lettering		£30	£70	£200	—
1726 Small Roses & Plumes in angles on rev.		£80	£225	£650	—

GEORGE II (1727–60)

DATE	MINTAGE	F	VF	EF	UNC
1728 Young head, Plain		£70	£240	£525	—
1728 — Proof		—	—	£3500	—
1728 — Plumes in angles on rev.		£40	£140	£400	—
1728 — Roses & Plumes in angles on rev.		£35	£125	£350	—
1731 — —		£40	£140	£375	—
1732 — —		£35	£130	£360	—
1734 — —		£40	£140	£375	—
1735 — —		£35	£140	£375	—
1735/4 5 over 4		£45	£150	£425	—
1736 — —		£45	£150	£400	—
1739 — Roses in angles on rev.		£30	£100	£325	—
1741 —		£30	£100	£300	—
1743 Old head, Roses in angles on rev.		£25	£75	£250	—
1745 — —		£25	£75	£250	—

DATE	MINTAGE	F	VF	EF	UNC
1745 — — 5 over 3		£30	£85	£275	—
1745 — Plain, LIMA below bust		£30	£80	£275	—
1746 — —		£30	£80	£275	—
1746 — Proof..		—	—	£1750	—
1750 — —		£30	£120	£325	—
1751 — —		£35	£150	£350	—
1757 — —		£18	£35	£95	—
1758 — —		£18	£35	£95	—

GEORGE III (1760–1820)

1787 rev. no semée of hearts on 4th shield		£15	£35	£80	£110
1787 rev. with semée of hearts.........................		£15	£35	£80	£110

NEW COINAGE

1816	—	£7	£15	£40	£100
1817	10,921,680	£7	£15	£40	£100
1818...	4,284,720	£10	£25	£80	£175
1819...	4,712,400	£8	£15	£40	£90
1819 very small 8 in date.............	incl. above	£12	£22	£60	£140
1820...	1,488,960	£8	£15	£50	£120

GEORGE IV (1820–30)

1821 First bust, first reverse	863,280	£12	£30	£120	£350
1821 error BBRITANNIAR............		£100	£300	£950	—
1821 — — Proof............................	incl. above	—	—	—	£1000
1824 — Second (garter) reverse..	633,000	£10	£30	£100	£325
1825 —	483,120	£12	£30	£100	£300
1826 — —	689,040	£40	£100	£250	£550
1826 Second bust, third (lion on crown) reverse	incl. above	£10	£30	£100	£220
1826 — — Proof............................	incl. above	—	—	—	£600
1827 — —	166,320	£40	£100	£300	£675
1828 — —	15,840	£20	£50	£150	£325
1829 — —	403,290	£15	£45	£125	£350

WILLIAM IV (1830–37)

1831...	1,340,195	£15	£40	£125	£300
1831 Proof, milled edge	incl. above	—	—	—	£700
1834...	5,892,480	£15	£40	£125	£300
1835...	1,552,320	£15	£40	£125	£300
1836...	1,987,920	£15	£45	£150	£350
1837...	506,880	£20	£45	£220	£500

VICTORIA (1837–1901)

YOUNG HEAD ISSUES
First head

1838...	1,607,760	£15	£40	£130	£350
1839	3,310,560	£15	£40	£130	£350
1839 Proof....................................	incl. above	—	—	—	£1200
1840...	2,098,800	£15	£40	£130	£350
1841...	1,386,000	£18	£45	£140	£400
1842...	601,920	£15	£40	£130	£350
1843...	3,160,080	£15	£40	£130	£350
1844...	3,975,840	£15	£30	£140	£350
1844 Large 44 in date..................	incl. above	£18	£40	£130	£400
1845...	3,714,480	£15	£35	£90	£350
1846...	4,226,880	£15	£35	£90	£350
1848...	586,080	£50	£110	£340	£475
1848/6 final 8 over 6....................	incl. above	£50	£120	£400	—
1850...	498,960	£12	£35	£100	£380
1850/3 0 over 3	incl. above	£18	£40	£110	£400
1851...	2,288,107	£10	£30	£100	£375
1852...	904,586	£10	£30	£150	£370
1853...	3,837,930	£10	£30	£150	£370

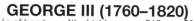

DATE	MINTAGE	F	VF	EF	UNC
1853 Proof..................................	incl above	—	—	—	£1100
1854..	840,116	£175	£500	£1000	£2750
1855..	1,129,684	£10	£30	£120	£250
1855/3 last 5 over 3....................	incl. above	£15	£45	£140	£300
1856..	2,779,920	£10	£40	£120	£300
1857..	2,233,440	£10	£40	£120	£280
1858..	1,932,480	£10	£40	£120	£280
1859..	4,688,640	£10	£40	£120	£280
1859/8 9 over 8	incl. above	£12	£40	£120	£400
1860..	1,100,880	£10	£35	£120	£325
1862..	990,000	£100	£200	£600	£1700
1863..	491,040	£70	£150	£475	£1250
Die no. added above date from 1864 to 1879					
1864..	4,253,040	£10	£25	£110	£250
1865..	1,631,520	£10	£25	£100	£250
1866..	4,140,080	£10	£25	£100	£250
1866 no Die no.	incl. above			Extremely Rare	
Second head					
1867..	1,362,240	£10	£30	£120	£300
1868..	1,069,200	£10	£30	£110	£270
1869..	388,080	£10	£30	£110	£280
1870..	479,613	£10	£30	£110	£270
1871..	3,662,684	£8	£30	£75	£200
1871 no Die no.	incl. above	£8	£30	£75	£220
1872..	3,382,048	£8	£30	£75	£200
1873..	4,594,733	£8	£30	£75	£200
1874..	4,225,726	£8	£30	£75	£240
1875..	3,256,545	£8	£30	£75	£220
1876..	841,435	£8	£30	£75	£220
1877..	4,066,486	£8	£30	£75	£220
1877 no Die no	incl. above	£8	£30	£75	£220
1878..	2,624,525	£8	£30	£75	£230
1878 Dritanniar Error	incl. above	£125	£300	£1000	—
1879	3,326,313	£8	£25	£80	£220
1879 no Die no	incl. above	£8	£25	£80	£220
1880 no Die no	3,892,501	£8	£25	£75	£220
Third head					
1880	incl above	£8	£20	£80	£175
1881..	6,239,447	£8	£20	£80	£175
1882..	759,809	£15	£50	£150	£450
1883..	4,986,558	£8	£20	£70	£150
1884..	3,422,565	£8	£20	£70	£150
1885..	4,652,771	£8	£20	£70	£150
1886..	2,728,249	£8	£20	£70	£140
1887..	3,675,607	£8	£20	£70	£150
JUBILEE HEAD ISSUES					
1887 Shield reverse	incl. above	£6	£10	£15	£30
1887 — Proof	incl. above	—	—	—	£190
1887 Six Pence in wreath reverse	incl. above	£6	£8	£18	£35
1888 —	4,197,698	£8	£12	£35	£60
1889 —	8,738,928	£8	£12	£35	£70
1890 —	9,386,955	£8	£12	£35	£70
1891 —	7,022,734	£8	£12	£35	£70
1892 —	6,245,746	£8	£12	£35	£80
1893 —	7,350,619	£750	£1400	£4000	—
OLD HEAD ISSUES					
1893..	incl. above	£7	£12	£22	£50
1893 Proof..................................	1,312	—	—	—	£200
1894..	3,467,704	£8	£18	£50	£130
1895	7,024,631	£8	£18	£45	£110
1896..	6,651,699	£7	£15	£35	£65
1897..	5,031,498	£7	£15	£35	£65
1898..	5,914,100	£7	£15	£35	£65
1899..	7,996,80	£7	£15	£35	£55
1900..	8,984,354	£7	£15	£35	£55
1901..	5,108,757	£7	£15	£35	£55

Jubilee head, shield reverse

Jubilee head, wreath reverse

DATE	MINTAGE	F	VF	EF	UNC

EDWARD VII (1901–10)

DATE	MINTAGE	F	VF	EF	UNC
1902	6,367,378	£5	£10	£30	£60
1902 "Matt Proof"	15,123	—	—	—	£120
1903	5,410,096	£7	£20	£50	£170
1904	4,487,098	£15	£50	£175	£500
1905	4,235,556	£8	£20	£70	£220
1906	7,641,146	£7	£12	£40	£110
1907	8,733,673	£7	£12	£45	£120
1908	6,739,491	£10	£30	£110	£350
1909	6,584,017	£8	£18	£50	£175
1910	12,490,724	£5	£8	£25	£50

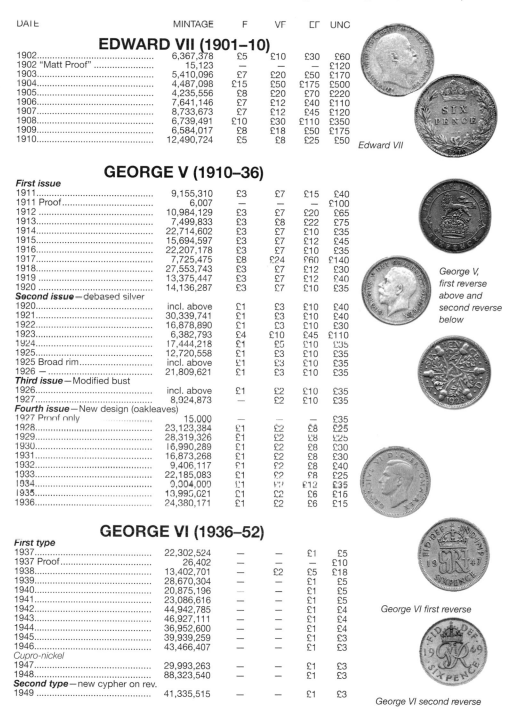

Edward VII

GEORGE V (1910–36)

First issue

DATE	MINTAGE	F	VF	EF	UNC
1911	9,155,310	£3	£7	£15	£40
1911 Proof	6,007	—	—	—	£100
1912	10,984,129	£3	£7	£20	£65
1913	7,499,833	£3	£8	£22	£75
1914	22,714,602	£3	£7	£10	£35
1915	15,694,597	£3	£7	£12	£45
1916	22,207,178	£3	£7	£10	£35
1917	7,725,475	£8	£24	£60	£140
1918	27,553,743	£3	£7	£12	£30
1919	13,375,447	£3	£7	£12	£40
1920	14,136,287	£3	£7	£10	£35

Second issue — debased silver

DATE	MINTAGE	F	VF	EF	UNC
1920	incl. above	£1	£3	£10	£40
1921	30,339,741	£1	£3	£10	£40
1922	16,878,890	£1	£3	£10	£30
1923	6,382,793	£4	£10	£45	£110
1924	17,444,218	£1	£5	£10	£35
1925	12,720,558	£1	£3	£10	£35
1925 Broad rim	incl. above	£1	£3	£10	£35
1926 —	21,809,621	£1	£3	£10	£35

Third issue — Modified bust

DATE	MINTAGE	F	VF	EF	UNC
1926	incl. above	£1	£2	£10	£35
1927	8,924,873	—	£2	£10	£35

Fourth issue — New design (oakleaves)

DATE	MINTAGE	F	VF	EF	UNC
1927 Proof only	15,000	—	—	—	£35
1928	23,123,384	£1	£2	£8	£25
1929	28,319,326	£1	£2	£8	£25
1930	16,990,289	£1	£2	£8	£30
1931	16,873,268	£1	£2	£8	£30
1932	9,406,117	£1	£2	£8	£40
1933	22,185,083	£1	£2	£8	£25
1934	9,304,000	£1	£2	£12	£35
1935	13,995,621	£1	£2	£6	£16
1936	24,380,171	£1	£2	£6	£15

George V, first reverse above and second reverse below

GEORGE VI (1936–52)

First type

DATE	MINTAGE	F	VF	EF	UNC
1937	22,302,524	—	—	£1	£5
1937 Proof	26,402	—	—	—	£10
1938	13,402,701	—	£2	£5	£18
1939	28,670,304	—	—	£1	£5
1940	20,875,196	—	—	£1	£5
1941	23,086,616	—	—	£1	£5
1942	44,942,785	—	—	£1	£4
1943	46,927,111	—	—	£1	£4
1944	36,952,600	—	—	£1	£4
1945	39,939,259	—	—	£1	£3
1946	43,466,407	—	—	£1	£3

Cupro-nickel

DATE	MINTAGE	F	VF	EF	UNC
1947	29,993,263	—	—	£1	£3
1948	88,323,540	—	—	£1	£3

Second type — new cypher on rev.

DATE	MINTAGE	F	VF	EF	UNC
1949	41,335,515	—	—	£1	£3

George VI first reverse

George VI second reverse

DATE	MINTAGE	F	VF	EF	UNC
1950	32,741,955	—	—	£1	£3
1950 Proof	17,513	—	—	—	£7
1951	40,399,491	—	—	£1	£3
1951 Proof	20,000	—	—	—	£7
1952	1,013,477	£6	£20	£45	£120

ELIZABETH II (1952–   )

1953	70,323,876	—	—	—	£2
1953 Proof	40,000	—	—	—	£4
1954	105,241,150	—	—	—	£3
1955	109,929,554	—	—	—	£1
1956	109,841,555	—	—	—	£1
1957	105,654,290	—	—	—	£1
1958	123,518,527	—	—	—	£3
1959	93,089,441	—	—	—	£1
1960	103,283,346	—	—	—	£3
1961	115,052,017	—	—	—	£3
1962	166,483,637	—	—	—	25p
1963	120,056,000	—	—	—	25p
1964	152,336,000	—	—	—	25p
1965	129,644,000	—	—	—	25p
1966	175,676,000	—	—	—	25p
1967	240,788,000	—	—	—	25p
1970 Proof	—				£8

GROATS OR FOURPENCES

DATE	MINTAGE	F	VF	EF	UNC

The earlier fourpences are included in the Maundy oddments section as they are generally considered to have been issued for the Maundy ceremony.

WILLIAM IV (1831–37)

1836	—	£8	£18	£40	£90
1837	962,280	£8	£18	£40	£95

VICTORIA (1838–1901)

1837	Extremely Rare Proofs or Patterns only				
1838	2,150,280	£7	£15	£40	£90
1838 over last 8 on its side		£10	£20	£60	£120
1839	1,461,240	£7	£16	£50	£100
1839 Proof	incl. above				Rare
1840	1,496,880	£7	£15	£50	£100
1840 Small 0 in date	incl. above	£7	£15	£50	£100
1841	344,520	£7	£15	£50	£100
1842/1 2 over 1	incl. above	£7	£15	£50	£100
1842	724,680	£7	£15	£45	£100
1843	1,817640	£8	£16	£50	£120
1843 4 over 5	incl. above	£7	£15	£50	£120
1844	855,360	£7	£15	£50	£110
1845	914,760	£7	£15	£50	£110
1846	1,366,200	£7	£15	£50	£100
1847 7 over 6	225,720	£15	£35	£125	—
1848	712,800	£7	£15	£50	£90
1848/6 8 over 6	incl. above	£30	£110	—	—
1848/7 8 over 7	incl. above	£8	£20	£60	£110
1849	380,160	£7	£15	£50	£100
1849/8 9 over 8	incl. above	£8	£20	£70	£135
1851	594,000	£35	£80	£250	£425
1852	31,300	£55	£130	£400	—
1853	11,880	£80	£170	£550	—
1853 Proof Milled Rim	incl. above	—	—	—	£1000
1853 Plain edge Proof			Extremely rare		
1854	1,096,613	£7	£15	£40	£90
1855	646,041	£7	£15	£40	£90
1857 Proofs only			Extremely rare		
1862 Proofs only			Extremely rare		
1888 Jubilee Head	—	£12	£22	£50	£110

THREEPENCES

DATE	MINTAGE	F	VF	EF	UNC

The earlier threepences are included in the Maundy oddments section.

WILLIAM IV (1830–37)

(issued for use in the West Indies)

DATE	MINTAGE	F	VF	EF	UNC
1834		£10	£20	£80	£200
1835		£10	£20	£80	£200
1836		£10	£20	£80	£200
1837		£10	£25	£100	£230

VICTORIA (1837–1901)

DATE	MINTAGE	F	VF	EF	UNC
1838 BRITANNIAB error			Extremely rare		
1838	—	£10	£25	£80	£220
1839	—	£10	£25	£80	£220
1840	—	£10	£25	£80	£220
1841	—	£10	£25	£70	£225
1842	—	£10	£25	£70	£220
1843	—	£10	£25	£60	£190
1843/34 43 over 34	—	£10	£25	£90	£240
1844	—	£12	£25	£80	£210
1845	1,319,208	£12	£25	£70	£200
1846	52,008	£15	£35	£150	£375
1847	4,488		Extremely rare		
1848	incl. above		Extremely rare		
1849	131,208	£12	£25	£80	£230
1850	954,888	£12	£25	£60	£190
1851	479,065	£12	£30	£70	£220
1851 5 over 8	incl. above	£25	£50	£220	—
1852	4,488		Extremely rare		
1853	36,168	£50	£120	£275	£650
1854	1,467,246	£8	£25	£60	£195
1855	383,350	£12	£26	£60	£195
1856	1,013,760	£10	£25	£60	£190
1857	1,758,240	£10	£25	£70	£200
1858	1,441,440	£10	£25	£60	£195
1858 BRITANNIAB error	incl. above		Extremely rare		
1858/6 final 8 over 6	incl. above	£10	£30	£125	
1858/5 final 8 over 5	incl. above	£10	£30	£125	—
1859	3,579,840	£8	£20	£50	£170
1860	3,405,600	£10	£25	£60	£180
1861	3,001,700	£10	£20	£60	£170
1862	1,156,320	£10	£25	£60	£170
1863	950,400	£30	£70	£125	£300
1864	1,330,560	£7	£22	£50	£160
1865	1,742,400	£7	£22	£50	£160
1866	1,900,800	£7	£22	£50	£160
1867	712,800	£7	£22	£50	£160
1868	1,457,280	£7	£22	£50	£160
1868 RRITANNIAR error	incl. above		Extremely rare		
1869	—	£80	£130	£250	£475
1870	1,283,218	£5	£16	£45	£100
1871	999,633	£5	£16	£40	£100
1872	1,293,271	£5	£16	£40	£100
1873	4,055,550	£5	£16	£40	£100
1874	4,427,031	£5	£16	£40	£100
1875	3,306,500	£5	£16	£40	£100
1876	1,834,389	£5	£16	£40	£100
1877	2,622,393	£5	£16	£40	£100
1878	2,419,975	£5	£16	£40	£120
1879	3,140,265	£5	£16	£40	£100
1880	1,610,069	£5	£16	£40	£90
1881	3,248,265	£5	£16	£40	£90
1882	472,965	£8	£25	£70	£190
1883	4,369,971	£5	£10	£30	£65

Victoria first type

DATE	MINTAGE	F	VF	EF	UNC
1884	3,322,424	£5	£12	£30	£65
1885	5,183,653	£5	£12	£30	£65
1886	6,152,669	£5	£12	£30	£60
1887	2,780,761	£5	£12	£30	£65
JUBILEE HEAD ISSUES					
1887	incl. above	£2	£4	£12	£25
1887 Proof	incl. above	—	—	—	£140
1888	518,199	£2	£5	£20	£40
1889	4,587,010	£2	£5	£20	£45
1890	4,465,834	£2	£5	£20	£45
1891	6,323,027	£2	£5	£20	£45
1892	2,578,226	£2	£5	£20	£45
1893	3,067,243	£10	£40	£125	£300
OLD HEAD ISSUES					
1893	incl. above	£2	£4	£15	£30
1893 Proof	incl. above	—	—	—	£100
1894	1,608,603	£3	£6	£25	£60
1895	4,788,609	£2	£5	£22	£50
1896	4,598,442	£2	£5	£18	£35
1897	4,541,294	£2	£5	£18	£35
1898	4,567,177	£2	£5	£18	£35
1899	6,246,281	£2	£5	£18	£35
1900	10,644,480	£2	£5	£18	£35
1901	6,098,400	£2	£5	£14	£30

*Victoria
Jubilee head*

*Victoria
Old or Veiled
head*

EDWARD VII (1901–10)

	MINTAGE	F	VF	EF	UNC
1902	8,268,480	£2	£2	£7	£15
1902 "Matt Proof"	incl. above	—	—	—	£40
1903	5,227,200	£2	£4	£20	£50
1904	3,627,360	£3	£10	£45	£100
1905	3,548,160	£2	£4	£25	£60
1906	3,152,160	£3	£8	£28	£70
1907	4,831,200	£2	£4	£20	£50
1908	8,157,600	£2	£3	£20	£50
1909	4,055,040	£2	£4	£20	£50
1910	4,563,380	£2	£4	£18	£35

GEORGE V (1910–36)

First issue

	MINTAGE	F	VF	EF	UNC
1911	5,841,084	—	—	£3	£10
1911 Proof	incl. above	—	—	—	£60
1912	8,932,825	—	—	£3	£12
1913	7,143,242	—	—	£3	£12
1914	6,733,584	—	—	£3	£12
1915	5,450,617	—	—	£3	£15
1916	18,555,201	—	—	£3	£10
1917	21,662,490	—	—	£3	£10
1918	20,630,909	—	—	£3	£10
1919	16,845,687	—	—	£3	£10
1920	16,703,597	—	—	£3	£10
Second issue—debased silver					
1920	incl. above	—	—	£3	£12
1921	8,749,301	—	—	£3	£12
1922	7,979,998	—	—	£3	£40
1925	3,731,859	—	—	£5	£25
1926	4,107,910	—	—	£7	£30
Third issue—Modified bust					
1926	incl. above	—	—	£8	£22
Fourth issue—new design (oakleaves)					
1927 Proof only	15,022	—	—	—	£110
1928	1,302,106	£4	£10	£30	£65
1930	1,319,412	£2	£4	£10	£40
1931	6,251,936	—	—	£2	£7
1932	5,887,325	—	—	£2	£7
1933	5,578,541	—	—	£2	£7
1934	7,405,954	—	—	£2	£7
1935	7,027,654	—	—	£2	£7
1936	3,328,670	—	—	£2	£7

*George V
second issue*

*George V,
fourth issue
oak leaves
design reverse*

GEORGE VI (1936–52)

DATE	MINTAGE	F	VF	EF	UNC
Silver					
1937	8,148,156	—	—	£1	£4
1937 Proof	26,402	—	—	—	£15
1938	6,402,473	—	—	£1	£4
1939	1,355,860	—	—	£4	£15
1940	7,914,401	—	—	£1	£3
1941	7,979,411	—	—	£1	£3
1942	4,144,051	£2	£5	£12	£35
1943	1,397,220	£2	£5	£12	£35
1944	2,005,553	£7	£15	£40	£90
1945				Only one known	
Nickel brass					
1937	45,707,957	—	—	£1	£4
1937 Proof	26,402	—	—	—	£10
1938	14,532,332	—	—	£1	£18
1939	5,603,021	—	—	£3	£40
1940	12,636,018	—	—	£3	£30
1941	60,239,489	—	—	£1	£8
1942	103,214,400	—	—	£1	£8
1943	101,702,400	—	—	£1	£8
1944	69,760,000	—	—	£1	£8
1945	33,942,466	—	—	£3	£20
1946	620,734	£6	£25	£220	£750
1948	4,230,400	—	—	£7	£50
1949	464,000	£5	£25	£250	£800
1950	1,600,000	—	£2	£20	£110
1950 Proof	17,513	—	—	—	£15
1951	1,184,000	—	£2	£25	£110
1951 Proof	20,000	—	—	—	£20
1952	25,494,400	—	—	—	£10

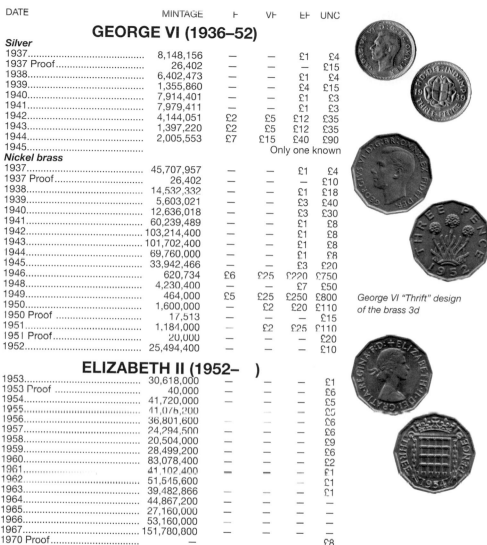

George VI "Thrift" design of the brass 3d

ELIZABETH II (1952–)

DATE	MINTAGE	F	VF	EF	UNC
1953	30,618,000	—	—	—	£1
1953 Proof	40,000	—	—	—	£6
1954	41,720,000	—	—	—	£5
1955	41,075,200	—	—	—	£5
1956	36,801,600	—	—	—	£6
1957	24,294,500	—	—	—	£6
1958	20,504,000	—	—	—	£9
1959	28,499,200	—	—	—	£6
1960	83,078,400	—	—	—	£2
1961	41,102,400	—	—	—	£1
1962	51,545,600	—	—	—	£1
1963	39,482,866	—	—	—	£1
1964	44,867,200	—	—	—	—
1965	27,160,000	—	—	—	—
1966	53,160,000	—	—	—	—
1967	151,780,800	—	—	—	—
1970 Proof	—				£8

TWO PENCES

GEORGE III (1760–1820)

1797 "Cartwheel"	722,972	£30	£75	£400	£1000
1797 Copper Proofs			Many types from £500+		

VICTORIA (1837–1901)

For use in the Colonies

1838	£4	£10	£18	£40
1848	£4	£12	£20	£45

Earlier issues of the small silver two pences are listed in the Maundy section.

THREE-HALFPENCES

DATE	F	VF	EF	UNC

WILLIAM IV (1830–37)

For use in the Colonies

	F	VF	EF	UNC
1834	£6	£16	£35	£80
1835	£10	£25	£75	£200
1835 over 4	£6	£16	£40	£90
1836	£8	£18	£45	£100
1837	£15	£35	£110	£300

VICTORIA (1837–1901)

For use in the Colonies

	F	VF	EF	UNC
1838	£6	£15	£35	£75
1839	£6	£15	£35	£75
1840	£8	£20	£60	£140
1841	£6	£15	£35	£80
1842	£6	£18	£40	£90
1843	£6	£15	£30	£70
1860	£10	£25	£75	£170
1862	£15	£35	£90	£200

PENNIES

DATE	MINTAGE	F	VF	EF	UNC

The earlier small silver pennies are included in the Maundy oddments section.

GEORGE III (1760–1820)

	MINTAGE	F	VF	EF	UNC
1797 "Cartwheel", 10 laurel leaves	43,969,204	£25	£60	£300	£1000

Numerous proofs in different metals are known for this issue—all are rare.

	MINTAGE	F	VF	EF	UNC
1797 — 11 laurel leaves	incl. above	£25	£60	£300	£1000
1806 Fourth issue	19,355,480	£7	£18	£75	£300
1807	11,290,168	£7	£18	£75	£300
1808	—				Unique

GEORGE IV (1820–30)

	MINTAGE	F	VF	EF	UNC
1825	1,075,200	£12	£45	£250	£625
1826 (varieties)	5,913,600	£12	£45	£250	£625
1826 Proof	—	—	—	—	£900
1827	1,451,520	£250	£900	£3500	—

WILLIAM IV (1830–37)

	MINTAGE	F	VF	EF	UNC
1831 (varieties)	806,400	£25	£70	£425	£1100
1831 Proof	—	—	—	—	£1000
1834	322,560	£30	£70	£400	£1250
1837	174,720	£65	£200	£800	£3000

VICTORIA (1837–1901)

YOUNG HEAD ISSUES
Copper

	MINTAGE	F	VF	EF	UNC
1839 Proof	unrecorded	—	—	—	£2500
1841	913,920	£10	£50	£300	£800
1841 No colon after REG	incl. above	£8	£20	£175	£550
1843	483,840	£90	£350	£2000	£5000
1844	215,040	£12	£25	£175	£550
1845	322,560	£15	£35	£220	£750
1846	483,840	£15	£25	£200	£725
1846 FID: DEF colon spaced	incl. above	£15	£25	£200	£725
1846 FID:DEF colon close	incl. above	£16	£28	£210	£750
1847	430,080	£12	£25	£180	£575
1848	161,280	£10	£25	£160	£525

George III "Cartwheel" penny

Note: Mintage figures for the Soho Mint strikings are from the on-line thesis, "Matthew Boulton and the Soho Mint—Copper to Customer", by Sue Tungate, Birmingham University, October 2011 (information supplied by Dennis Onions)

DATE	MINTAGE		F	VF	EF	UNC
1848/7 final 8 over 7	incl. above	£8	£20	£150	£475	
1848/6 final 8 over 6	incl. above	£20	£120	£525	—	
1849	268,800	£225	£600	£2400	—	
1851	268,800	£15	£45	£200	£800	
1853	1,021,440	£7	£15	£100	£200	
1853 Proof	—	—	—	—	£2500	
1854	6,720,000	£8	£20	£100	£200	
1854/3 4 over 3	incl. above	£14	£45	£180	—	
1855	5,273,856	£8	£20	£100	£250	
1856	1,212,288	£110	£250	£700	£2800	
1857 Plain trident	752,640	£7	£18	£80	£280	
1857 Ornamental trident	incl. above	£6	£18	£70	£280	
1858/7 final 8 over 7	incl. above	£7	£18	£80	£300	
1858/6 final 8 over 6	—	£40	£120	£500	—	
1858/3 final 8 over 3	incl. above	£25	£90	£400	—	
1858	1,599,040	£7	£16	£100	£280	
1859	1,075,200	£8	£25	£150	£375	
1860/59	32,256	£800	£1800	£3750	£7000	

Bronze

Prices of bronze Victoria Young "bun" head pennies are for the common types. There are many known varieties which are listed in detail in other more specialised publications. Prices for coins in mint with full lustre will be considerably higher.

Victoria copper penny

	MINTAGE		F	VF	EF	UNC
1860 Beaded border	5,053,440	£25	£50	£180	£750	
1860 Toothed border	incl. above	£6	£20	£60	£350	
1860 — Piedfort flan	—		Extremely rare			
1861	36,449,280	£5	£12	£50	£300	
1862	50,534,400	£5	£12	£50	£280	
1862 8 over 6	incl. above		Extremely rare			
1863	28,002,720	£5	£12	£45	£275	
1863 Die no below date	incl. above		Extremely rare			
1864 Plain 4	3,440,640	£25	£140	£600	£3000	
1864 Crosslet 4	incl. above	£30	£150	£600	£3200	
1865	8,601,600	£7	£16	£55	£370	
1865/3 5 over 3	incl. above	£20	£125	£500	—	
1866	9,999,360	£6	£20	£80	£500	
1867	5,483,520	£7	£20	£95	£800	
1868	1,182,720	£15	£70	£200	£1900	
1869	2,580,480	£130	£450	£1800	£5750	
1870	5,695,022	£12	£40	£150	£750	
1871	1,290,318	£35	£130	£475	£2200	
1872	8,494,572	£6	£20	£60	£280	
1873	8,101,000	£0	£20	£60	£280	
1874	5,621,865	£7	£20	£60	£280	
1874 H	6,666,240	£7	£22	£65	£290	
1874 Later (older) bust	incl. above	£14	£35	£90	£460	

Victoria Young or "Bun" head bronze penny

DATE	MINTAGE	F	VF	EF	UNC
1875	10,691,040	£7	£22	£75	£325
1875 H	752,640	£35	£120	£800	£2500
1876 H	11,074,560	£5	£12	£60	£275
1877	9,624,747	£5	£14	£60	£275
1878	2,764,470	£5	£14	£60	£275
1879	7,666,476	£4	£15	£55	£275
1880	3,000,831	£4	£15	£55	£300
1881	2,302,362	£5	£15	£55	£275
1881 H	3,763,200	£5	£15	£55	£275
1882 H	7,526,400	£5	£15	£55	£275
1882 no H	—		Extremely Rare		
1883	6,237,438	£5	£15	£55	£250
1884	11,702,802	£5	£15	£55	£250
1885	7,145,862	£5	£15	£55	£250
1886	6,087,759	£5	£15	£55	£250
1887	5,315,085	£5	£15	£55	£250
1888	5,125,020	£5	£15	£60	£275
1889	12,559,737	£5	£15	£50	£325
1890	15,330,840	£5	£15	£50	£200
1891	17,885,961	£5	£12	£50	£200
1892	10,501,671	£7	£18	£80	£275
1893	8,161,737	£5	£12	£55	£240
1894	3,883,452	£10	£40	£150	£475

OLD HEAD ISSUES

1895 Trident 2mm from P(ENNY)	5,395,830	£20	£90	£300	£800
1895 Trident 1mm from P	incl. above	—	£2	£18	£75
1896	24,147,156	—	£2	£18	£65
1897	20,756,620	—	£2	£15	£60
1897 Raised dot after One (O·NE)		£140	£250	£850	—
1898	14,296,836	—	£3	£18	£60
1899	26,441,069	—	£3	£16	£55
1900	31,778,109	—	£3	£16	£45
1901	22,205,568	—	£3	£10	£30

EDWARD VII (1901–10)

1902	26,976,768	—	£1	£8	£30
1902 "Low tide" to sea line	incl. above	£4	£15	£60	£200
1903	21,415,296	—	£3	£15	£85
1904	12,913,152	—	£4	£25	£190
1905	17,783,808	—	£3	£15	£80
1906	37,989,504	—	£3	£15	£70
1907	47,322,240	—	£3	£15	£70
1908	31,506,048	—	£3	£18	£125
1909	19,617,024	—	£3	£20	£150
1910	29,549,184	—	£3	£15	£60

GEORGE V (1910–36)

1911	23,079,168	—	£3	£12	£65
1912	48,306,048	—	£3	£12	£60
1912 H	16,800,000	—	£4	£40	£230
1913	65,497,812	—	£3	£15	£75
1914	50,820,997	—	£3	£18	£75
1915	47,310,807	—	£3	£20	£85
1916	86,411,165	—	£3	£15	£65
1917	107,905,436	—	£3	£15	£60
1918	84,227,372	—	£3	£12	£55
1918 H	3,660,800	£1	£15	£100	£500
1918 KN	incl. above	£8	£80	£550	£2200
1919	113,761,090	—	£2	£15	£55
1919 H	5,209,600	£1	£15	£200	£700
1919 KN	incl. above	£15	£110	£750	£3000
1920	124,693,485	—	£2	£12	£30
1921	129,717,693	—	£2	£12	£40
1922	16,346,711	—	£3	£25	£150
1922 with reverse of 1927		£1000	£2500	—	—
1926	4,498,519	—	£6	£25	£150
1926 Modified effigy	incl above	£25	£150	£800	£2500
1927	60,989,561	—	£2	£10	£40

DATE	MINTAGE	F	VF	EF	UNC
1928	50,178,00	—	£2	£10	£35
1929	49,132,800	—	£2	£10	£40
1930	29,097,600	—	£2	£20	£70
1931	19,843,200	—	£2	£10	£50
1932	8,277,600	—	£2	£15	£100
1933			Only 7 examples known		
1934	13,965,600	—	£2	£25	£100
1935	56,070,000	—	—	£2	£14
1936	154,296,000	—	—	£2	£12

GEORGE VI (1936–52)

1937	88,896,000	—	—	—	£4
1937 Proof	26,402	—	—	—	£14
1938	121,560,000	—	—	—	£6
1939	55,560,000	—	—	—	£15
1940	42,284,400	—	—	£8	£25
1944 Mint Dark	42,600,000	—	—	—	£8
1945 Mint Dark	79,531,200	—	—	—	£8
1946 Mint Dark	66,855,600	—	—	—	£8
1947	52,220,400	—	—	—	£5
1948	63,961,200	—	—	—	£5
1949	14,324,400	—	—	—	£8
1950	240,000	£7	£15	£30	£50
1950 Proof	17,513	—	—	—	£25
1951	120,000	£20	£26	£50	£75
1951 Proof	20,000	—	—	—	£40

ELIZABETH II (1952–)

1953	1,308,400	—	—	£1	£4
1953 Proof	40,000	—	—	—	£8
1954			Only one known		
1961	48,313,400	—	—	—	£2
1962	143,308,600	—	—	—	50p
1963	125,235,600	—	—	—	50p
1964	153,294,000	—	—	—	50p
1965	121,310,400	—	—	—	50p
1966	165,739,200	—	—	—	50p
1967	654,564,000	—	—	—	—
1970 Proof	—				£8

Later issues are included in the Decimal section.

HALFPENNIES

CHARLES II (1660–85)

1672	£70	£300	£1300	—
1672 CRAOLVS error			Extremely rare	
1673	£70	£300	£1300	—
1673 CRAOLVS error			Extremely rare	
1673 No rev. stop	£100	£600	—	—
1673 No stops on obv.			Extremely rare	
1675	£60	£500	£1500	—
1675 No stops on obv.	£80	£550	—	—
1675/3 5 over 3	£175	£625	—	—

JAMES II (1685–88)

1685 (tin)	£250	£750	£4000	—
1686 (tin)	£280	£750	£4200	—
1687 (tin)	£320	£800	£4000	—

WILLIAM & MARY (1688–94)

Tin

1689 Small draped busts, edge dated			Extremely rare	
1690 Large cuirassed busts, edge dated	£200	£750	£3400	—
1691 — date on edge and in exergue	£180	£700	£3200	—
1692 — —	£200	£750	£3200	—

*Copper halfpenny
of William & Mary*

DATE	F	VF	EF	UNC

Copper

1694 Large cuirassed busts, date in exergue	£80	£300	£1200	—
1694 — — GVLIEMVS error		Extremely rare		
1694 — — MΛRIΛ error		Extremely rare		
1694 — — No stops on rev.		Extremely rare		

WILLIAM III (1694–1702)

1695 First issue (date in exergue)...................	£50	£200	£1100	—
1695 — No stop after BRITANNIA on rev.		Extremely rare		
1696 —	£40	£180	£1000	—
1696 — TERTVS error		Extremely rare		
1697 —	£45	£170	£1000	—
1697 — No stop after TERTIVS on obv.	£50	£300	—	—
1698 —	£50	£200	£1000	—
1698 Second issue (date in legend)	£50	£180	—	—
1698 — No stop after date...............................	£50	£180	—	—
1699 —	£55	£210	£1100	—
1699 — No stop after date...............................	£225	—	—	—
1699 Third issue (date in exergue) (Britannia with right hand on knee)..	£40	£175	£900	—
1699 — No stop after date...............................		Extremely rare		
1699 — BRITΛNNIΛ error	£200	—	—	—
1699 — TERTVS error		Extremely rare		
1699 — No stop on rev....................................		Extremely rare		
1699 — No stops on obv.................................	£90	£375	—	—
1700 —	£45	£190	£950	—
1700 — No stops on obv.................................	£100	£350	—	—
1700 — No stops after GVLIELMUS	£100	£350	—	—
1700 — BRITVANNIA error...............................		Extremely rare		
1700 — GVIELMS error	£100	£350	—	—
1700 — GVLIEEMVS error...............................	£100	£350	—	—
1701 —	£40	£175	£900	—
1701 — BRITΛNNIΛ error	£80	£300	—	—
1701 — No stops on obv..................................		Extremely rare		
1701 — inverted As for Vs...............................	£80	£320	—	—

William III first issue

GEORGE I (1714–27)

1717 "Dump" issue	£45	£250	£800	
1718 —	£35	£225	£775	—
1719 "Dump" issue. Patterns.........................				Rare
1719 Second issue..	£40	£200	£800	—
1720 —	£35	£160	£600	—
1721 —	£35	£150	£600	—
1721 — Stop after date...................................	£45	£150	—	—
1722 —	£35	£140	£650	—
1722 — inverted A for V on obv.		Extremely rare		
1723 —	£35	£150	£625	—
1723 — No stop on rev....................................	£110	£500	—	—
1724 —	£35	£150	£625	—

GEORGE II (1727–60)

1729 Young head	£28	£90	£400	—
1729 — No stop on rev....................................	£28	£80	£400	—
1730 —	£22	£90	£400	—
1730 — GEOGIVS error..................................	£70	£225	£650	—
1730 — Stop after date...................................	£28	£120	£425	—
1730 — No stop after REX on obv.	£32	£150	£450	—
1731 —	£22	£110	£400	—
1731 — No rev. stop.......................................	£26	£125	£425	—
1732 —	£22	£100	£400	—
1732 — No rev. stop.......................................	£26	£125	£450	—
1733 —	£22	£90	£400	—
1734/3 — 4 over 3..	£35	£210	—	—
1734 — No stop on obv.	£35	£210	—	—

George I "Dump" type

DATE	MINTAGE	F	VF	EF	UNC
1735 —		£22	£80	£400	—
1736 —		£22	£80	£400	—
1737 —		£22	£85	£420	—
1738 —		£22	£80	£350	—
1739 —		£20	£70	£350	—
1740 Old head		£17	£70	£320	—
1742 —		£17	£70	£320	—
1742/0 — 2 over 0		£25	£150	£450	—
1743 —		£17	£70	£320	—
1744 —		£17	£70	£330	—
1745 —		£17	£70	£340	—
1746 —		£17	£70	£320	—
1747 —		£17	£70	£320	—
1748 —		£17	£70	£330	—
1749 —		£17	£70	£330	—
1750 —		£17	£70	£330	—
1751 —		£17	£70	£330	—
1752 —		£17	£70	£330	—
1753 —		£17	£70	£330	—
1754 —		£17	£70	£330	—

George II "Old" head

GEORGE III (1760–1820)

First type—Royal Mint

DATE	MINTAGE	F	VF	EF	UNC
1770		£18	£50	£300	—
1770 No stop on rev.		£25	£65	£350	—
1771		£12	£50	£280	—
1771 No stop on rev.		£20	£65	£300	—
1772 Error GEORIVS		£80	£240	£700	—
1772		£12	£50	£225	—
1772 No stop on rev.		£20	£65	£280	—
1773		£10	£45	£280	—
1773 No stop after REX		£30	£80	£400	—
1773 No stop on rev.		£20	£70	£300	—
1774		£12	£40	£220	—
1775		£12	£40	£220	—

Second type—Soho Mint

DATE	MINTAGE	F	VF	EF	UNC
1799	42,481,118	£5	£12	£55	£120

Third type

DATE	MINTAGE	F	VF	EF	UNC
1806	87,993,526	£5	£11	£60	£110
1807	41,394,384	£5	£11	£60	£110

George III second type

GEORGE IV (1820–30)

DATE	MINTAGE	F	VF	EF	UNC
1825	215,040	£12	£45	£190	£380
1826 (varieties)	9,031,630	£12	£45	£190	£380
1826 Proof	—	—	—	—	£550
1827	5,376,000	£12	£45	£160	£340

WILLIAM IV (1830–37)

DATE	MINTAGE	F	VF	EF	UNC
1831	806,400	£12	£30	£130	£325
1831 Proof	—	—	—	—	£500
1834	537,600	£12	£30	£130	£325
1837	349,440	£12	£30	£130	£325

VICTORIA (1837–1901)

Copper

DATE	MINTAGE	F	VF	EF	UNC
1838	456,960	£8	£18	£80	£320
1839 Proof	268,800	—	—	—	£500
1841	1,075,200	£6	£16	£60	£220
1843	967,680	£35	£55	£200	£750
1844	1,075,200	£12	£40	£180	£375

William IV

DATE	MINTAGE	F	VF	EF	UNC
1845	1,075,200	£200	£450	£1800	—
1846	860,160	£12	£25	£85	£250
1847	725,640	£12	£22	£85	£250
1848	322,560	£12	£22	£80	£250
1848/7 final 8 OVER 7	incl. above	£14	£35	£100	£275
1851	215,040	£7	£18	£75	£250
1852	637,056	£10	£22	£80	£250
1853	1,559,040	£5	£10	£40	£120
1853/2 3 over 2	incl. above	£15	£30	£60	£240
1853 Proof	—	—	—	—	£775
1854	12,354,048	£5	£9	£40	£130
1855	1,455,837	£5	£9	£40	£130
1856	1,942,080	£10	£24	£80	£300
1857	1,820,720	£6	£18	£50	£140
1858	2,472,960	£5	£12	£50	£130
1858/7 final 8 over 7	incl. above	£5	£12	£50	£130
1858/6 final 8 over 6	incl. above	£5	£12	£50	£130
1859	1,290,240	£7	£22	£70	£230
1859/8 9 over 8	incl. above	£8	£25	£70	£275
1860	unrecorded	£1400	£3500	£7000	£12000

Bronze

	MINTAGE	F	VF	EF	UNC
1860 Beaded border	6,630,400	£3	£10	£50	£190
1860 Toothed border		£4	£12	£60	£270
1861	54,118,400	£4	£10	£40	£185
1862 Die letter A, B or C to left of lighthouse				Extremely rare	
1862	61,107,200	£3	£9	£40	£160
1863	15,948,800	£3	£9	£75	£160
1864	537,600	£3	£10	£45	£175
1865	8,064,000	£4	£18	£75	£300
1865/3 5 over 3	incl. above	£50	£120	£450	—
1866	2,508,800	£5	£15	£70	£240
1867	2,508,800	£5	£15	£60	£220
1868	3,046,400	£5	£15	£70	£260
1869	3,225,600	£30	£100	£250	£1500
1870	4,350,739	£5	£15	£60	£250
1871	1,075,280	£75	£100	£500	£1500
1872	4,659,410	£4	£10	£50	£180
1873	3,404,880	£4	£10	£50	£200
1874	1,347,655	£6	£25	£110	£300
1874 H	5,017,600	£3	£10	£60	£230
1875	5,430,815	£3	£8	£60	£200
1875 H	1,254,400	£5	£12	£60	£200
1876 H	5,809,600	£4	£10	£60	£230
1877	5,209,505	£3	£10	£60	£180
1878	1,425,535	£6	£20	£100	£350
1878 Wide date		£100	£200	£550	—
1879	3,582,545	£3	£10	£40	£200
1880	2,423,465	£4	£12	£60	£210
1881	2,007,515	£4	£12	£50	£180
1881 H	1,792,000	£3	£10	£50	£200
1882 H	4,480,000	£3	£10	£50	£220
1883	3,000,725	£3	£12	£60	£225
1884	6,989,580	£3	£10	£45	£160
1885	8,600,574	£3	£10	£45	£160
1886	8,586,155	£3	£10	£45	£160
1887	10,701,305	£3	£10	£45	£160
1888	6,814,670	£3	£10	£45	£160
1889	7,748,234	£3	£10	£45	£160
1889/8 9 over 8	incl. above	£30	£60	£250	—
1890	11,254,235	£3	£10	£40	£120
1891	13,192,260	£3	£10	£35	£120
1892	2,478,335	£3	£10	£45	£140

Victoria copper halfpenny

Victoria bronze halfpenny

DATE	MINTAGE	F	VF	EF	UNC
1893	7,229,344	£3	£10	£35	£130
1894	1,767,635	£5	£12	£70	£275

OLD HEAD ISSUES

1895	3,032,154	£2	£7	£20	£65
1896	9,142,500	£1	£4	£10	£45
1897	8,690,315	£1	£4	£10	£45
1898	8,595,180	£1	£5	£12	£55
1899	12,108,001	£1	£4	£10	£45
1900	13,805,190	£1	£4	£10	£35
1901	11,127,360	£1	£3	£8	£25

EDWARD VII (1901–10)

1902	13,672,960	£2	£4	£8	£30
1902 "Low tide"	incl. above	£22	£90	£180	£450
1903	11,450,880	£2	£5	£20	£60
1904	8,131,200	£2	£6	£25	£80
1905	10,124,800	£2	£5	£20	£55
1906	16,849,280	£2	£5	£25	£70
1907	16,849,280	£2	£5	£20	£70
1908	16,620,800	£2	£5	£20	£70
1909	8,279,040	£2	£5	£20	£70
1910	10,769,920	£2	£5	£20	£50

GEORGE V (1910–36)

1911	12,570,880	£1	£4	£15	£40
1912	21,185,920	£1	£3	£15	£35
1913	17,476,480	£1	£3	£15	£40
1914	20,289,111	£1	£3	£15	£40
1915	21,563,040	£2	£3	£20	£55
1916	39,386,143	£1	£2	£15	£40
1917	38,245,436	£1	£2	£15	£35
1918	22,321,072	£1	£2	£15	£35
1919	28,104,001	£1	£2	£15	£35
1920	35,146,793	£1	£2	£15	£40
1921	28,027,293	£1	£2	£15	£40
1922	10,734,964	£1	£4	£25	£45
1923	12,266,282	£1	£2	£15	£35
1924	13,971,038	£1	£2	£15	£30
1925	12,216,123	—	£2	£15	£30
1925 Modified effigy	incl. above	£4	£10	£50	£90
1926	6,172,306	—	£2	£10	£40
1927	15,589,622	—	£2	£10	£40
1928	20,935,200	—	£2	£8	£35
1929	25,680,000	—	£2	£8	£35
1930	12,532,800	—	£2	£8	£35
1931	16,137,600	—	£2	£8	£35
1932	14,448,000	—	£2	£8	£35
1933	10,560,000	—	£2	£8	£35
1934	7,704,000	—	£2	£12	£45
1935	12,180,000	—	£1	£6	£20
1936	23,008,800	—	£1	£5	£15

GEORGE VI (1936–52)

1937	24,504,000	—	—	£1	£5
1937 Proof	26,402	—	—	—	£18
1938	40,320,000	—	—	£1	£6
1939	28,924,800	—	—	£1	£5
1940	32,162,400	—	—	£2	£10

DATE	MINTAGE	F	VF	EF	UNC
1941	45,120,000	—	—	£1	£8
1942	71,908,800	—	—	£1	£5
1943	76,200,000	—	—	£1	£5
1944	81,840,000	—	—	£1	£5
1945	57,000,000	—	—	£1	£5
1946	22,725,600	—	—	£1	£6
1947	21,266,400	—	—	£1	£6
1948	26,947,200	—	—	£1	£4
1949	24,744,000	—	—	£1	£4
1950	24,153,600	—	—	£1	£5
1950 Proof	17,513	—	—	—	£18
1951	14,868,000	—	—	£1	£6
1951 Proof	20,000	—	—	—	£18
1952	33,784,000	—	—	£1	£4

ELIZABETH II (1952–)

1953	8,926,366	—	—	—	£1
1953 Proof	40,000	—	—	—	£4
1954	19,375,000	—	—	—	£3
1955	18,799,200	—	—	—	£3
1956	21,799,200	—	—	—	£3
1957	43,684,800	—	—	—	£1
1957 Calm sea	incl. above	—	—	£10	£30
1958	62,318,400	—	—	—	£1
1959	79,176,000	—	—	—	£1
1960	41,340,000	—	—	—	£1
1962	41,779,200	—	—	—	£1
1963	45,036,000	—	—	—	20p
1964	78,583,200	—	—	—	20p
1965	98,083,200	—	—	—	20p
1966	95,289,600	—	—	—	20p
1967	146,491,200	—	—	—	10p
1970 Proof	—				£5

Later issues are included in the Decimal section.

FARTHINGS

DATE		F	VF	EF	UNC

OLIVER CROMWELL

Undated (copper) Draped bust, shield rev. Variations — Extremely rare

CHARLES II (1660–85)

Copper

	F	VF	EF	UNC
1672	£40	£225	£775	—
1673	£45	£240	£800	—
1673 CAROLA for CAROLO error	£125	£500	—	—
1673 No stops on obv.			Extremely rare	
1673 No stop on rev.			Extremely rare	
1674	£50	£250	£850	—
1675	£45	£220	£800	—
1675 No stop after CAROLVS			Extremely rare	
1679	£55	£275	£950	—
1679 No stop on rev.	£65	£320	—	—

Tin

	F	VF	EF	UNC
1684 with date on edge	£250	£825	—	—
1685 —			Extremely rare	

Charles II copper issue

DATE	F	VF	EF	UNC

JAMES II (1685–88)

1684 (tin) Cuirassed bust			Extremely rare	
1685 (tin) —	£180	£625	£2250	—
1686 (tin) —	£190	£625	£2250	—
1687 (tin) —			Extremely rare	
1687 (tin) Draped bust	£230	£850	—	—

WILLIAM & MARY (1688–94)

1689 (tin) Small draped busts	£300	£700	—	—
1689 (tin) — with edge date 1690			Extremely rare	
1690 (tin) Large cuirassed busts	£170	£650	£2750	—
1690 (tin) — with edge date 1689			Extremely rare	
1691 (tin) —	£175	£650	—	—
1692 (tin) —	£185	£650	£2750	—
1694 (copper) —	£70	£260	£950	—
1694 No stop after MARIΛ			Extremely rare	
1694 No stop on obv.			Extremely rare	
1694 No stop on rev.			Extremely rare	
1694 Unbarred As in BRITANNIA			Extremely rare	

WILLIAM III (1694–1702)

1695 First issue (date in exergue)	£45	£250	£825	—
1695 — GVLIELMV error			Extremely rare	
1696 —	£45	£225	£850	—
1697 —	£45	£225	£850	—
1697 — GVLIELMS error			Extremely rare	
1698	£220	£750		
1698 Second issue (date in legend)	£50	£250	£850	—
1699 First issue	£40	£200	£825	—
1699 Second issue	£40	£200	£825	—
1699 — No stop after date	£50	£300	—	—
1700 First issue	£35	£150	£700	—
1700 — error RRITANNIA			Extremely rare	

Queen Anne

ANNE (1702–14)

1714	£425	£675	£1500	—

GEORGE I (1714–27)

1717 First small "Dump" issue	£200	£600	£1200	—
1718 1 Known				—
1719 Second issue	£30	£140	£475	—
1719 — No stop on rev.	£70	£350	—	—
1719 — No stops on obv.	£70	£300	—	—
1720 —	£30	£140	£550	—
1721 —	£25	£140	£550	—
1721/0 — Last 1 over 0	£40	£160	—	—
1722 —	£35	£125	£500	—
1723 —	£35	£125	£525	—
1723 — R over sideways R in REX			Extremely rare	
1724 —	£35	£140	£525	—

George I, first "Dump" type

GEORGE II (1727–60)

1730 Young head	£15	£60	£340	—
1731 —	£15	£60	£340	—
1732 —	£15	£75	£400	—
1733 —	£15	£70	£400	—
1734 —	£15	£65	£400	—
1734 — No stop on obv.	£30	£110	£450	—

George I second type

DATE	MINTAGE	F	VF	EF	UNC
1735 —		£15	£60	£370	—
1735 — 3 over 5............................		£24	£110	£450	—
1736 —		£14	£60	£350	—
1737 —		£14	£60	£330	—
1739 —		£14	£60	£330	—
1741 Old Head..............................		£14	£50	£320	—
1744 —		£14	£50	£320	—
1746 —		£14	£50	£300	—
1746 — V over LL in GEORGIVS.....................				Extremely rare	
1749 —		£16	£65	£320	—
1750 —		£15	£55	£285	—
1754 —		£10	£30	£200	—
1754 — 4 over 0............................		£28	£120	£350	—

George II Young head

GEORGE III (1760–1820)

	MINTAGE	F	VF	EF	UNC
1771 First (London) issue		£20	£65	£275	—
1773 —		£12	£40	£200	—
1773 — No stop on rev....................		£20	£60	£240	—
1773 — No stop after REX		£25	£75	£250	—
1774 —		£12	£40	£200	—
1775 —		£12	£40	£200	—
1797 Second (Soho Mint) issue				Patterns only	
1799 Third (Soho Mint) issue............	4,225,428	£2	£8	£40	£100
1806 Fourth (Soho Mint) issue	4,833,768	£2	£8	£40	£100
1807 —	1,075,200	£2	£8	£40	£100

George III, third (Soho Mint) issue

GEORGE IV (1820–30)

	MINTAGE	F	VF	EF	UNC
1821 First bust (laureate, draped), first reverse (date in exergue)...	2,688,000	£3	£10	£60	£120
1822 —	5,924,350	£3	£10	£60	£120
1823 —	2,365,440	£4	£10	£60	£120
1823 I for 1 in date	incl. above	£20	£70	£300	£600
1825 —	4,300.800	£4	£10	£60	£130
1826 —	6,666,240	£4	£10	£60	£120
1826 Second bust (couped, date below), second reverse (ornament in exergue)..............	incl. above	£4	£10	£60	£120
1826 — Proof	—	—	—	—	£425
1827 —	2,365,440	£4	£12	£60	£145
1828 —	2,365,440	£4	£12	£60	£145
1829 —	1,505,280	£4	£12	£60	£145
1830 —	2,365,440	£4	£12	£60	£145

George III, fourth (Soho Mint) issue

WILLIAM IV (1830–37)

	MINTAGE	F	VF	EF	UNC
1831...	2,688,000	£5	£12	£45	£135
1831 Proof....................................	—	—	—	—	£440
1834...	1,935,360	£5	£12	£50	£130
1835...	1.720.320	£5	£12	£50	£130
1836...	1,290.240	£5	£12	£55	£130
1837...	3.010,560	£5	£12	£55	£165

VICTORIA (1837–1901)
FIRST YOUNG HEAD (COPPER) ISSUES

	MINTAGE	F	VF	EF	UNC
1838...	591,360	£5	£15	£45	£175
1839...	4,300,800	£5	£15	£45	£175
1839 Proof....................................	—	—	—	—	£500
1840...	3,010,560	£4	£15	£40	£160
1841...	1,720,320	£4	£15	£40	£175
1841 Proof....................................				Extremely rare	
1842...	1,290,240	£10	£35	£100	£350
1843...	4,085,760	£5	£14	£40	£180

William IV

DATE	MINTAGE	F	VF	EF	UNC
1843 I for 1 in date		£90	£425	£900	—
1844..	430,080	£80	£220	£800	£2200
1845..	3,225,600	£6	£10	£40	£150
1846..	2,580,480	£7	£20	£55	£200
1847..	3,879,720	£5	£12	£50	£160
1848..	1,290,240	£5	£12	£50	£150
1849..	645,120	£50	£100	£350	£900
1850..	430,080	£5	£10	£40	£140
1851..	1,935,360	£8	£20	£80	£250
1851 D over sideways D in DEI ...	incl. above	£80	£110	£450	—
1852..	822,528	£10	£20	£70	£220
1853..	1,028,628	£4	£7	£30	£65
1853 Proof................................	—	—	—	—	£900
1854..	6,504,960	£4	£10	£35	£70
1855..	3,440,640	£4	£10	£35	£70
1856..	1,771,392	£10	£25	£75	£260
1856 R over E in VICTORIA.........	incl. above	£20	£50	£250	—
1857..	1,075,200	£4	£10	£35	£80
1858..	1,720,320	£4	£10	£35	£80
1859..	1,290,240	£12	£25	£80	£340
1860..	unrecorded	£1500	£3750	£6750	—

Victoria Young Head first (copper) issue

SECOND YOUNG OR "BUN" HEAD (BRONZE) ISSUES

DATE	MINTAGE	F	VF	EF	UNC
1860 Toothed border...................	2,867,200	£2	£5	£40	£110
1860 Beaded border	incl. above	£3	£7	£40	£120
1860 Toothed/Beaded border mule	incl. above			Extremely rare	
1861..	8,601,600	£2	£5	£35	£110
1862..	14,336,000	£1	£5	£35	£110
1862 Large 8 in date..................	incl. above			Extremely rare	
1863..	1,433,600	£40	£75	£300	£675
1864..	2,508,800	£1	£5	£30	£100
1865..	4,659,200	£1	£5	£30	£90
1865 5 over 2.............................	incl. above	£10	£20	£70	—
1866..	3,584,000	£1	£5	£25	£100
1867..	5,017,600	£1	£5	£25	£100
1868..	4,851,210	£1	£5	£25	£100
1869..	3,225,600	£2	£10	£45	£160
1872..	2,150,400	£1	£5	£25	£90
1873..	3,225,620	£1	£5	£25	£85
1874 H..	3,584,000	£1	£5	£25	£110
1874 H both Gs over sideways G	incl. above	£150	£350	£1000	—
1875..	712,700	£1	£17	£40	£130
1875 H..	6,092,800	£1	£5	£20	£80
1876 H..	1,175,200	£4	£15	£60	£175
1878..	4,008,540	£1	£4	£20	£75
1879..	3,977,180	£1	£4	£20	£75
1880..	1,842,710	£1	£4	£20	£75
1881..	3,494,670	£1	£4	£20	£75
1881 H..	1,792,000	£1	£4	£20	£75
1882 H..	1,792,000	£1	£5	£22	£80
1883..	1,128,680	£5	£18	£60	£150
1884..	5,782,000	£1	£4	£20	£40
1885..	5,442,308	£1	£4	£20	£40
1886..	7,707,790	£1	£4	£20	£40
1887..	1,340,800	£1	£4	£20	£40
1888..	1,887,250	£1	£4	£20	£40
1890..	2,133,070	£1	£4	£20	£40
1891..	4,959,690	£1	£4	£20	£40
1892..	887,240	£3	£14	£55	£150
1893..	3,904,320	£1	£4	£20	£40
1894..	2,396,770	£1	£4	£20	£40
1895..	2,852,852	£10	£28	£90	£240

Victoria Young Head second (bronze) issue

215

DATE	MINTAGE	F	VF	EF	UNC
OLD HEAD ISSUES					
1895 Bright finish	incl. above	£1	£2	£16	£35
1896 —	3,668,610	£1	£2	£16	£25
1897 —	4,579,800	£1	£2	£16	£25
1897 Dark finish	incl. above	£1	£2	£16	£25
1898 —	4,010,080	£1	£2	£16	£25
1899 —	3,864,616	£1	£2	£16	£25
1900 —	5,969,317	£1	£2	£16	£25
1901 —	8,016,460	£1	£2	£10	£20

*Victoria
Old head*

EDWARD VII (1901–10)

1902....................................	5,125,120	50p	£1	£10	£15
1903....................................	5,331,200	50p	£1	£12	£20
1904....................................	3,628,800	£2	£5	£20	£45
1905....................................	4,076,800	£1	£2	£12	£30
1906....................................	5,340,160	50p	£1	£12	£25
1907....................................	4,399,360	50p	£1	£10	£20
1908....................................	4,264,960	50p	£1	£10	£20
1909....................................	8,852,480	50p	£1	£10	£20
1910....................................	2,298,400	£4	£9	£28	£70

GEORGE V (1910–36)

1911....................................	5,196,800	50p	£1	£6	£14
1912....................................	7,669,760	50p	£1	£8	£14
1913....................................	4,184,320	50p	£1	£6	£14
1914....................................	6,126,988	50p	£1	£5	£14
1915....................................	7,129,255	50p	£1	£5	£16
1916....................................	10,993,325	50p	£1	£5	£14
1917....................................	21,434,844	25p	50p	£4	£10
1918....................................	19,362,818	25p	50p	£4	£10
1919....................................	15,089,425	25p	50p	£4	£10
1920....................................	11,480,536	25p	50p	£4	£8
1921....................................	9,469,097	25p	50p	£4	£8
1922....................................	9,956,983	25p	50p	£4	£8
1923....................................	8,034,457	25p	50p	£4	£8
1924....................................	8,733,414	25p	50p	£4	£8
1925....................................	12,634,697	25p	50p	£4	£8
1926 Modified effigy....................	9,792,397	25p	50p	£4	£8
1927	7,868,355	25p	50p	£4	£8
1928	11,625,600	25p	50p	£4	£8
1929	8,419,200	25p	50p	£4	£8
1930	4,195,200	25p	50p	£4	£8
1931	6,595,200	25p	50p	£4	£8
1932	9,292,800	25p	50p	£4	£8
1933	4,560,000	25p	50p	£4	£8
1934	3,052,800	25p	50p	£4	£8
1935	2,227,200	£1	£3	£10	£25
1936	9,734,400	25p	50p	£3	£6

GEORGE VI (1936–52)

1937....................................	8,131,200	—	—	50p	£1
1937 Proof..............................	26,402	—	—	—	£8
1938....................................	7,449,600	—	—	£1	£6
1939....................................	31,440,000	—	—	50p	£1
1940....................................	18,360,000	—	—	50p	£1
1941....................................	27,312,000	—	—	50p	£1
1942....................................	28,857,600	—	—	50p	£1
1943....................................	33,345,600	—	—	50p	£1
1944....................................	25,137,600	—	—	50p	£1
1945....................................	23,736,000	—	—	50p	£1

DATE	MINTAGE	F	VF	EF	UNC
1946	24,364,800	—	—	50p	£1
1947	14,745,600	—	—	50p	£1
1948	16,622,400	—	—	50p	£1
1949	8,424,000	—	—	50p	£1
1950	10,324,800	—	—	50p	£1
1950 Proof	17,513	—	—	50p	£8
1951	14,016,000	—	—	50p	£1
1951 Proof	20,000	—	—	50p	£8
1952	5,251,200	—	—	50p	£1

ELIZABETH II (1952–)

1953	6,131,037	—	—	—	£1
1953 Proof	40,000	—	—	—	£7
1954	6,566,400	—	—	—	£2
1955	5,779,200	—	—	—	£2
1956	1,996,800	—	£1	£2	£6

HALF FARTHINGS

DATE	MINTAGE	F	VF	EF	UNC

GEORGE IV (1820–30)

1828 (two different obverses) (Issued for Ceylon)	7,680,000	£10	£20	£50	£160
1830 (large or small date) (issued for Coylon)	8,766,320	£10	£20	£50	£150

WILLIAM IV (1830–37)

1837 (issued for Ceylon)	1,935,360	£20	£55	£140	£250

VICTORIA (1837–1901)

1839	2,042,880	£5	£10	£30	£85
1842	unrecorded	£4	£8	£25	£85
1843	3,440,640	£3	£6	£20	£50
1844	6,451,200	£3	£6	£15	£50
1844 E over N in REGINA	incl. above	£10	£45	£100	—
1847	3,010,560	£6	£12	£35	£90
1851	unrecorded	£6	£12	£35	£120
1851 5 over 0	unrecorded	£8	£20	£60	£160
1852	989,184	£6	£12	£40	£125
1853	955,224	£6	£15	£50	£140
1853 Proof	incl. above	—	—	—	£550
1854	677,376	£9	£30	£80	£195
1856	913,920	£9	£30	£80	£195
1868 Proof	unrecorded				£1000

THIRD FARTHINGS

DATE	MINTAGE	F	VF	EF	UNC

GEORGE IV (1820–30)

DATE	MINTAGE	F	VF	EF	UNC
1827 (issued for Malta)	unrecorded	£8	£20	£50	£125

WILLIAM IV (1830–37)

DATE	MINTAGE	F	VF	EF	UNC
1835 (issued for Malta)	unrecorded	£8	£20	£50	£150

VICTORIA (1837–1901)

DATE	MINTAGE	F	VF	EF	UNC
1844 (issued for Malta)	1,301,040	£12	£28	£85	£200
1844 RE for REG	incl. above	£30	£60	£250	—
1866	576,000	£6	£15	£35	£70
1868	144,000	£6	£15	£35	£65
1876	162,000	£6	£15	£35	£85
1878	288,000	£6	£15	£35	£70
1881	144,000	£6	£15	£35	£75
1884	144,000	£6	£15	£35	£75
1885	288,000	£6	£15	£35	£75

EDWARD VII (1902–10)

DATE	MINTAGE	F	VF	EF	UNC
1902 (issued for Malta)	288,000	£5	£10	£25	£45

GEORGE V (1911–36)

DATE	MINTAGE	F	VF	EF	UNC
1913 (issued for Malta)	288,000	£5	£10	£25	£45

QUARTER FARTHINGS

DATE	MINTAGE	F	VF	EF	UNC

VICTORIA (1837–1901)

DATE	MINTAGE	F	VF	EF	UNC
1839 (issued for Ceylon)	3,840,000	£40	£70	£125	£250
1851 (issued for Ceylon)	2,215,680	£40	£70	£125	£250
1852 (issued for Ceylon)	incl. above	£40	£70	£125	£260
1853 (issued for Ceylon)	incl. above	£40	£70	£125	£250
1853 Proof	—	—	—	—	£1000

EMERGENCY ISSUES

DATE	F	VF	EF	UNC

GEORGE III (1760–1820)

To alleviate the shortage of circulating coinage during the Napoleonic Wars the Bank of England firstly authorised the countermarking of other countries' coins, enabling them to pass as English currency. The coins, countermarked with punches depicting the head of George III, were mostly Spanish American 8 reales of Charles III. Although this had limited success it was later decided to completely overstrike the coins with a new English design on both sides— specimens that still show traces of the original host coin's date are avidly sought after by collectors. This overstriking continued for a number of years although all the known coins are dated 1804. Finally, in 1811 the Bank of England issued silver tokens which continued up to 1816 when a completely new regal coinage was introduced.

DOLLAR
Oval countermark of George III

	F	VF	EF	UNC
On "Pillar" type 8 reales	£175	£650	£1000	—
*On "Portrait" type.............	£200	£350	£800	—

Octagonal countermark of George III

	F	VF	EF	UNC
On "Portrait" type..............	£200	£600	£850	—

HALF DOLLAR
Oval countermark of George III

	F	VF	EF	UNC
On "Portrait" type 4 reales	£200	£400	£900	—

FIVE SHILLINGS OR ONE DOLLAR
These coins were overstruck on Spanish-American coins

	F	VF	EF	UNC
1804..................................	£120	£275	£550	—

   With details of original coin still visible add from 10%

BANK OF ENGLAND TOKENS

THREE SHILLINGS

	F	VF	EF	UNC
1811 Draped bust..............	£35	£60	£200	—
1812 —	£35	£60	£220	—
1812 Laureate bust	£35	£60	£150	—
1813 —	£35	£60	£150	—
1814 —	£35	£60	£150	—
1815 —	£35	£60	£150	—
1816 —	£200	£400	£1250	—

ONE SHILLING AND SIXPENCE

	F	VF	EF	UNC
1811 Draped bust..............	£20	£45	£100	£175
1812 —	£20	£45	£100	£175
1812 Laureate bust	£20	£45	£100	£175
1812 Proof in platinum				Unique
1813 —	£20	£40	£75	£175
1813 Proof in platinum				Unique
1814 —	£20	£35	£75	£160
1815 —	£20	£35	£75	£160
1816 —	£20	£35	£75	£160

NINEPENCE

1812 Pattern (three types)			from £2000	

MAUNDY SETS

DATE	F	VF	EF	UNC

DATE	F	VF	EF	UNC

Sets in contemporary dated boxes are usually worth a higher premium. For example approximately £30 can be added to sets from Victoria to George VI in contemporary undated boxes and above £40 for dated boxes.

CHARLES II (1660–85)

	F	VF	EF	UNC
Undated	£240	£370	£800	—
1670	£225	£370	£750	—
1671	£245	£400	£850	—
1672	£215	£350	£735	—
1673	£215	£330	£720	—
1674	£225	£340	£735	—
1675	£210	£325	£715	—
1676	£230	£365	£755	—
1677	£195	£310	£690	—
1678	£270	£460	£850	—
1679	£225	£360	£750	—
1680	£225	£345	£730	—
1681	£240	£355	£750	—
1682	£230	£360	£715	—
1683	£230	£360	£725	—
1684	£250	£415	£775	—

JAMES II (1685–88)

	F	VF	EF	UNC
1686	£230	£375	£725	—
1687	£230	£370	£750	—
1688	£240	£400	£775	—

WILLIAM & MARY (1688–94)

	F	VF	EF	UNC
1689	£855	£1250	£2000	—
1691	£715	£915	£1750	—
1692	£710	£925	£1800	—
1693	£625	£1000	£1900	—
1694	£485	£735	£1300	—

WILLIAM III (1694–1702)

	F	VF	EF	UNC
1698	£245	£480	£900	—
1699	£540	£725	£1650	—
1700	£265	£490	£925	—
1701	£245	£440	£875	—

ANNE (1702–14)

	F	VF	EF	UNC
1703	£225	£440	£750	—
1705	£245	£450	£775	—
1706	£200	£375	£675	—
1708	£600	£900	£1900	—
1709	£250	£475	£850	—
1710	£265	£460	£825	—
1713	£240	£435	£725	—

GEORGE I (1714–27)

	F	VF	EF	UNC
1723	£250	£450	£750	—
1727	£225	£435	£715	—

GEORGE II (1727–60)

	F	VF	EF	UNC
1729	£195	£325	£675	—
1731	£195	£335	£675	—
1732	£190	£320	£650	—
1735	£190	£320	£650	—
1737	£190	£325	£640	—
1739	£190	£320	£625	—
1740	£175	£300	£585	—
1743	£300	£445	£875	—
1746	£170	£300	£565	—
1760	£185	£325	£595	—

GEORGE III (1760–1820)

	F	VF	EF	UNC
1763	£170	£290	£480	—
1763 Proof	—			£15000
1766	£215	£325	£550	—
1772	£185	£300	£525	—
1780	£225	£350	£600	—
1784	£190	£320	£500	—
1786	£195	£310	£515	—
1792 Wire	£260	£450	£625	£810
1795	£115	£200	£325	£405
1800	£115	£200	£300	£395
New Coinage				
1817	£135	£210	£290	£425
1818	£135	£205	£280	£415
1820	£140	£220	£285	£420

GEORGE IV (1820–30)

	F	VF	EF	UNC
1822	—	£160	£245	£415
1823	—	£155	£255	£400
1824	—	£160	£260	£405
1825	—	£150	£250	£380
1826	—	£145	£245	£380
1827	—	£145	£255	£385
1828	—	£150	£250	£400
1828 Proof	—			£3650
1829	—	£150	£250	£385
1830	—	£150	£240	£375

WILLIAM IV (1830–37)

	F	VF	EF	UNC
1831	—	£170	£280	£450
1831 Proof	—	—		£2000
1831 Proof Gold	—	—		£37000
1832	—	£195	£300	£450
1833	—	£170	£275	£410
1834	—	£175	£280	£410
1835	—	£160	£265	£400
1836	—	£175	£285	£425
1837	—	£190	£300	£445

VICTORIA (1837–1901)

YOUNG HEAD ISSUES

DATE	MINTAGE	EF	UNC
1838	4,158	£240	£425
1838 Proof	unrecorded		£3200
1838 Proof Gold			£37000
1839	4,125	£285	£525
1839 Proof	unrecorded	£650	£1800
1840	4,125	£300	£445
1841	2,574	£395	£650
1842	4,125	£395	£600
1843	4,158	£260	£410
1844	4,158	£345	£550
1845	4,158	£225	£400
1846	4,158	£550	£875
1847	4,158	£575	£925
1848	4,158	£525	£875
1849	4,158	£365	£535
1850	4,158	£250	£415
1851	4,158	£295	£445
1852	4,158	£600	£900
1853	4,158	£625	£1000
1853 Proof	unrecorded		£1850
1854	4,158	£260	£420
1855	4,158	£300	£500
1856	4,158	£235	£375
1857	4,158	£265	£425
1858	4,158	£240	£375
1859	4,158	£215	£325
1860	4,158	£240	£375
1861	4,158	£205	£375
1862	4,158	£245	£390
1863	4,158	£260	£445
1864	4,158	£240	£345
1865	4,150	£240	£350
1866	4,158	£225	£340
1867	4,158	£220	£345
1867 Proof	unrecorded	—	£2800
1868	4,158	£200	£315
1869	4,158	£240	£405
1870	4,158	£100	£290
1871	4,488	£185	£280
1871 Proof	unrecorded	—	£2550
1872	4,328	£180	£280
1873	4,162	£180	£270
1874	4,488	£185	£275
1875	4,154	£180	£265
1876	4,488	£190	£270
1877	4,488	£180	£255
1878	4,488	£185	£255
1878 Proof	unrecorded	—	£2500
1879	4,488	£190	£245
1879 Proof	unrecorded	—	£2850
1880	4,488	£185	£240
1881	4,488	£180	£240
1881 Proof	unrecorded	—	£2350
1882	4,146	£215	£285
1882 Proof	unrecorded	—	£2550
1883	4,488	£160	£225
1884	4,488	£160	£225
1885	4,488	£160	£225
1886	4,488	£165	£225
1887	4,488	£180	£255

JUBILEE HEAD ISSUES

DATE	MINTAGE	EF	UNC
1888	4,488	£160	£230
1888 Proof	unrecorded	—	£2100
1889	4,488	£155	£240
1890	4,488	£160	£230
1891	4,488	£160	£230
1892	4,488	£170	£245

OLD HEAD ISSUES

DATE	MINTAGE	EF	UNC
1893	8,976	£100	£185
1894	8,976	£130	£200
1895	8,976	£115	£190
1896	8,976	£115	£195
1897	8,976	£115	£185
1898	8,976	£115	£190
1899	8,976	£115	£190
1900	8,976	£100	£180
1901	8,976	£100	£180

EDWARD VII (1902–110)

DATE	MINTAGE	EF	UNC
1902	8,976	£95	£175
1902 Matt proof	15,123	—	£200
1903	8,976	£100	£180
1904	8,976	£110	£185
1905	8,976	£110	£190
1906	8,800	£100	£180
1907	8,760	£100	£185
1908	8,769	£90	£180
1909	1,983	£165	£275
1910	1,440	£190	£300

GEORGE V (1911–136)

DATE	MINTAGE	EF	UNC
1911	1,786	£150	£240
1911 Proof	6,007	—	£275
1912	1,246	£160	£250
1913	1,228	£155	£250
1914	982	£185	£275
1915	1,293	£165	£265
1916	1,128	£160	£250
1917	1,237	£160	£250
1918	1,375	£165	£255
1919	1,258	£160	£250
1920	1,399	£160	£250
1921	1,306	£160	£255
1922	1,373	£165	£200
1923	1,430	£165	£260
1924	1,515	£165	£260
1925	1,438	£150	£245
1926	1,504	£150	£245
1927	1,647	£155	£255
1928	1,642	£155	£250
1929	1,761	£160	£255
1930	1,724	£150	£240
1931	1,759	£150	£240
1932	1,835	£145	£245
1933	1,872	£140	£240
1934	1,887	£140	£240
1935	1,928	£155	£255
1936	1,323	£200	£300

GEORGE VI (1936–52)

DATE	MINTAGE	EF	UNC
1937	1,325	£140	£200
1937 Proof	20,900	£140	£200
1938	1,275	£170	£255
1939	1,234	£175	£260
1940	1,277	£170	£255
1941	1,253	£180	£260
1942	1,231	£170	£255
1943	1,239	£175	£260
1944	1,259	£170	£255

DATE	MINTAGE	EF	UNC
1945	1,355	£170	£255
1946	1,365	£175	£255
1947	1,375	£180	£275
1948	1,385	£180	£280
1949	1,395	£185	£280
1950	1,405	£185	£285
1951	1,468	£190	£290
1952	1,012	£200	£305
1952 Proof (copper)			£11000

ELIZABETH II (1952–   )

DATE AND PLACE OF ISSUE	MINTAGE	UNC
1953 St. Paul's Cathedral	1,025	—£1025
1953 Proof in gold	unrecorded	Ex. rare
1953 Proof Matt		Very rare
1954 Westminster Abbey	1,020	— £200
1955 Southwark Cathedral	1,036	— £200
1955 Proof Matt		—£3250
1956 Westminster Abbey	1,088	— £205
1957 St. Albans Cathedral	1,094	— £205
1958 Westminster Abbey	1,100	— £205
1959 St. George's Chapel, Windsor	1,106	— £205
1960 Westminster Abbey	1,112	— £205
1961 Rochester Cathedral	1,118	— £205
1962 Westminster Abbey	1,125	— £205
1963 Chelmsford Cathedral	1,131	— £205
1964 Westminster Abbey	1,137	— £205
1965 Canterbury Cathedral	1,143	— £205
1966 Westminster Abbey	1,206	— £205
1967 Durham Cathedral	986	— £220
1968 Westminster Abbey	964	— £225
1969 Selby Cathedral	1,002	— £220
1970 Westminster Abbey	980	— £220
1971 Tewkesbury Abbey	1,018	£215
1972 York Minster	1,026	£220
1973 Westminster Abbey	1,004	£215
1974 Salisbury Cathedral	1,042	£215
1975 Peterborough Cathedral	1,050	£215
1976 Hereford Cathedral	1,158	£220
1977 Westminster Abbey	1,138	£225
1978 Carlisle Cathedral	1,178	£215

DATE AND PLACE OF ISSUE	MINTAGE	UNC
1979 Winchester Cathedral	1,188	£215
1980 Worcester Cathedral	1,198	£215
1981 Westminster Abbey	1,178	£215
1982 St David's Cathedral	1,218	£220
1983 Exeter Cathedral	1,228	£215
1984 Southwell Minster	1,238	£215
1985 Ripon Cathedral	1,248	£215
1986 Chichester Cathedral	1,378	£225
1987 Ely Cathedral	1,390	£225
1988 Lichfield Cathedral	1,402	£220
1989 Birmingham Cathedral	1,353	£220
1990 Newcastle Cathedral	1,523	£220
1991 Westminster Abbey	1,384	£220
1992 Chester Cathedral	1,424	£225
1993 Wells Cathedral	1,440	£225
1994 Truro Cathedral	1,433	£225
1995 Coventry Cathedral	1,466	£225
1996 Norwich Cathedral	1,629	£230
1997 Birmingham Cathedral	1,786	£230
1998 Portsmouth Cathedral	1,654	£230
1999 Bristol Cathedral	1,676	£230
2000 Lincoln Cathedral	1,686	£220
2000 Silver Proof	13,180	£195
2001 Westminster Abbey	1,132	£250
2002 Canterbury Cathedral	1,681	£215
2002 Gold Proof	2,002	£2250
2003 Gloucester Cathedral	1,608	£235
2004 Liverpool Cathedral	1,613	£240
2005 Wakefield Cathedral	1,685	£240
2006 Guildford Cathedral	1,937	£240
2006 Silver Proof	6,394	£195
2007 Manchester Cathedral	1,822	£275
2008 St Patrick's Cathedral (Armagh)	1,833	£750
2009 St. Edmundsbury Cathedral	1,602	£675
2010 Derby Cathedral	1,617	£600
2011 Westminster Abbey	1,734	£550
2012 York Minster	1,633	£600
2013 Christ Church Cathedral Oxford	1,627	£600
2014 Blackburn Cathedral	1,693	£625
2015 Sheffield Cathedral	1,721	£625
2016 St. George's Chapel, Windsor	1,940	£650
2017 Leicester Cathedral		£700

Despite the decimalisation of the coinage in 1971, in keeping with ancient tradition the Royal Maundy sets are still made up of four silver coins (4p, 3p, 2p and 1p). The designs for the reverse of the coins are a crowned numeral in a wreath of oak leaves—basically the same design that has been used for Maundy coins since Charles II.

MAUNDY ODDMENTS
SINGLE COINS

DATE	F	VF	EF

FOUR PENCE
CHARLES II (1660–85)

	F	VF	EF
Undated	£70	£115	£185
1670	£70	£120	£220
1671	£80	£160	£275
1672/1	£65	£105	£175
1673	£75	£110	£180
1674	£70	£105	£170
1674 7 over 6	£75	£130	£205
1675	£60	£100	£165
1675/4	£70	£115	£190
1676	£65	£100	£185
1676 7 over 6	£80	£120	£200
1677	£55	£95	£165
1678	£55	£95	£160
1678 8 over 7	£65	£115	£175
1679	£55	£85	£150
1680	£60	£95	£170
1681	£55	£100	£180
1682	£60	£90	£180
1682/1	£65	£95	£190
1683	£60	£90	£180
1684	£70	£110	£200
1684 4 over 3	£85	£120	£225

JAMES II (1685–88)

	F	VF	EF
1686	£65	£110	£200
1686 Date over crown	£75	£125	£215
1687	£60	£100	£180
1687 7 over 6	£75	£115	£190
1688	£80	£120	£210
1688 1 over 8	£90	£135	£225

WILLIAM & MARY (1688–94)

	F	VF	EF
1689	£60	£110	£175
1689 GV below bust	£70	£120	£190
1689 GVLFFI MVS	£135	£225	£325
1690	£60	£115	£210
1690 6 over 5	£90	£130	£230
1691	£80	£130	£225
1691 1 over 0	£90	£150	£230
1692	£120	£170	£275
1692 Maria	£200	£245	£350
1692 2 over 1	£130	£160	£260
1693	£110	£215	£350
1693 3 over 2	£125	£225	£375
1694	£80	£135	£225

WILLIAM III (1694–1702)

	F	VF	EF
1698	£80	£135	£215
1699	£70	£120	£210
1700	£90	£150	£240
1701	£85	£135	£225
1702	£80	£130	£225

ANNE (1702–14)

	F	VF	EF
1703	£75	£125	£210
1704	£60	£105	£185
1705	£110	£195	£275

It is nowadays considered that the early small denomination silver coins 4d–1d were originally struck for the Maundy ceremony although undoubtedly many subsequently circulated as small change—therefore they are listed here under "Maundy silver single coins".

Charles II

William & Mary

Queen Anne

DATE	F	VF	EF	UNC
1706	£70	£115	£175	—
1708	£75	£120	£205	—
1709	£80	£120	£205	—
1710	£60	£100	£165	—
1713	£70	£120	£190	—

GEORGE I (1714–27)

	F	VF	EF	UNC
1717	£65	£110	£180	—
1721	£65	£110	£185	—
1723	£85	£135	£205	—
1727	£80	£125	£200	—

George I

GEORGE II (1727–60)

	F	VF	EF	UNC
1729	£75	£115	£170	—
1731	£60	£105	£160	—
1732	£65	£110	£160	—
1735	£55	£95	£150	—
1737	£70	£115	£170	—
1739	£55	£100	£155	—
1740	£50	£95	£140	—
1743	£130	£180	£300	—
1743 3 over 0	£140	£210	£315	
1746	£55	£85	£135	—
1760	£65	£115	£160	—

George II

GEORGE III (1760–1820)

	F	VF	EF	UNC
1763 Young head	£50	£95	£135	—
1763 Proof	—	—	Extremely rare	
1765	£450	£680	£1175	—
1766	£65	£100	£140	—
1770	£155	£230	£360	—
1772	£80	£130	£190	—
1776	£65	£120	£170	—
1780	£50	£95	£135	—
1784	£50	£95	£130	—
1786	£65	£120	£170	—
1792 Older head, Thin 4	£90	£155	£220	£325
1795	—	£55	£100	£140
1800	—	£50	£90	£125
1817 New coinage	—	£50	£80	£130
1818	—	£50	£80	£125
1820	—	£50	£80	£130

George III

GEORGE IV (1820–30)

	F	VF	EF	UNC
1822	—	—	£75	£140
1823	—	—	£70	£130
1824	—	—	£70	£135
1826	—	—	£65	£120
1827	—	—	£70	£130
1828	—	—	£65	£120
1829	—	—	£60	£115
1830	—	—	£60	£115

George IV

WILLIAM IV (1830–37)

	F	VF	EF	UNC
1831–37	—	—	£70	£145
1831 Proof	—	—	£300	£500

VICTORIA (1837–1901)

	F	VF	EF	UNC
1838 Proof	—	—	—	£825
1839 Proof	—	—	—	£575
1853 Proof	—	—	—	£550
1838–87 (Young Head)	—	—	£40	£65
1841	—	—	£50	£75
1888–92 (Jubilee Head)	—	—	£35	£60
1893–1901 (Old Head)	—	—	£30	£50

Victoria

DATE	F	VF	EF	UNC
EDWARD VII (1901–10)				
1902–08	—	—	£30	£50
1909 & 1910	—	—	£60	£90
1902 Proof	—	—	£35	£55
GEORGE V (1910–36)				
1911–36	—	—	£50	£65
1911 Proof	—	—	£55	£75
GEORGE VI (1936–52)				
1937–52	—	—	£55	£75
1937 Proof	—	—	£40	£60
ELIZABETH II (1952–)				
1953	—	—	£200	£250
1954–85	—	—	£45	£75
1986–2007	—	—	£60	£85
2002 in Gold Proof	—	—	£500	£750
2008	—	—	—	£190
2009	—	—	—	£180
2010	—	—	—	£160
2011	—	—	—	£145
2012	—	—	—	£160
2013	—	—	—	£165
2014	—	—	—	£160
2015	—	—	—	£160
2016	—	—	—	£170
2017	—	—	—	£180

Elizabeth II

THREEPENCE

CHARLES II (1660–85)

	F	VF	EF	UNC
Undated	£65	£105	£195	—
1670	£75	£120	£185	—
1671	£65	£120	£175	—
1671 GRVTIA	£75	£135	£240	—
1672	£80	£130	£195	—
1673	£60	£95	£160	—
1674	£70	£110	£175	—
1675	£70	£110	£180	—
1676	£70	£115	£210	—
1676 ERA for FRA	£90	£135	£225	—
1677	£65	£90	£165	—
1678	£50	£80	£135	—
1679	£50	£80	£135	—
1679 O/A in CAROLVS	£105	£140	£250	—
1680	£60	£100	£175	—
1681	£70	£110	£190	—
1682	£60	£100	£170	—
1683	£60	£105	£170	—
1684	£60	£105	£175	—
1684/3	£70	£110	£180	—

Charles II

JAMES II (1685–88)

	F	VF	EF	UNC
1685	£65	£105	£190	—
1685 Struck on fourpence flan	£130	£185	£290	—
1686	£65	£95	£175	—
1687	£60	£90	£170	—
1687 7 over 6	£65	£95	£175	—
1688	£65	£120	£195	—
1688 8 over 7	£70	£130	£215	—

James II

WILLIAM & MARY (1688–94)

	F	VF	EF	UNC
1689	£55	£100	£190	—
1689 No stop on reverse	£65	£115	£200	—
1689 LMV over MVS (obverse)	£100	£145	£240	—
1690	£75	£120	£195	—

William & Mary

DATE	F	VF	EF	UNC
1690 6 over 5...........................	£85	£135	£210	—
1691 First bust	£390	£590	£850	—
1691 Second bust	£250	£400	£550	—
1692....................................	£100	£155	£265	—
1692 G below bust	£90	£165	£270	—
1692 GV below bust	£90	£150	£270	—
1692 GVL below bust	£90	£155	£275	—
1693....................................	£130	£205	£300	—
1693 3 over 2.........................	£135	£225	£310	—
1694....................................	£80	£115	£200	—
1694 MARIΛ	£130	£170	£265	—

WILLIAM III (1694–1702)

1698....................................	£75	£125	£210	—
1699....................................	£60	£110	£180	—
1700....................................	£70	£135	£210	—
1701....................................	£70	£125	£195	—
1701 GBA instead of GRA......	£85	£150	£215	—

William III

ANNE (1702–14)

1703....................................	£70	£100	£195	—
1703 7 of date above crown...	£80	£130	£210	—
1704....................................	£60	£90	£160	—
1705....................................	£80	£130	£200	—
1706....................................	£65	£100	£170	—
1707....................................	£55	£100	£155	—
1708....................................	£60	£115	£180	—
1709....................................	£65	£135	£195	—
1710....................................	£50	£95	£145	—
1713....................................	£65	£125	£180	—

GEORGE I (1714–27)

Queen Anne

1717....................................	£60	£100	£160	—
1721....................................	£60	£100	£165	—
1723....................................	£75	£125	£200	—
1727....................................	£70	£120	£195	—

GEORGE II (1727–60)

1729....................................	£55	£95	£145	—
1731....................................	£55	£95	£150	—
1731 Small lettering...............	£70	£115	£170	—
1732....................................	£55	£95	£145	—
1732 Stop over head..............	£65	£110	£165	—
1735....................................	£70	£110	£175	—
1737....................................	£55	£95	£165	—
1739....................................	£65	£100	£175	—
1740 Small and large lettering	£55	£90	£145	—
1743 Small and large lettering	£65	£90	£155	—
1743 Stop over head..............	£65	£95	£160	—
1746....................................	£45	£80	£140	—
1746 6 over 3.........................	£50	£85	£150	—
1760....................................	£60	£90	£155	—

George I

GEORGE III (1760–1820)

1762....................................	£30	£50	£70	—
1763....................................	£30	£50	£75	—
1763 Proof............................	—	—	Extremely rare	
1765....................................	£350	£500	£800	—
1766....................................	£70	£110	£180	—
1770....................................	£70	£110	£190	—
1772....................................	£55	£85	£120	—
1780....................................	£55	£85	£120	—
1784....................................	£80	£115	£190	—
1786....................................	£80	£110	£180	—
1792....................................	£95	£135	£215	£325
1795....................................	—	£40	£80	£120

George II

DATE	F	VF	EF	UNC
1800	—	£45	£85	£130
1817	—	£50	£90	£155
1818	—	£50	£90	£155
1820	—	£45	£90	£155

GEORGE IV (1820–30)

1822	—	—	£85	£165
1823	—	—	£75	£155
1824	—	—	£75	£160
1825–30	—	—	£75	£155

WILLIAM IV (1830–37)

1831 Proof	—	—	£350	£650
1831–1832	—	—	£125	£250
1833–1836	—	—	£80	£170
1837	—	—	£105	£190

VICTORIA (1837–1901)

1838	—	—	£115	£225
1838 Proof	—	—	—	£1750
1839	—	—	£215	£400
1839 Proof	—	—	—	£625
1840	—	—	£160	£275
1841	—	—	£300	£525
1842	—	—	£275	£450
1843	—	—	£125	£225
1844	—	—	£200	£350
1845	—	—	£85	£165
1846	—	—	£400	£700
1847	—	—	£425	£800
1848	—	—	£375	£750
1849	—	—	£215	£385
1850	—	—	£115	£225
1851	—	—	£160	£300
1852	—	—	£450	£775
1853	—	—	£475	£825
1853 Proof	—	—	—	£900
1864	—	—	£155	£275
1855	—	—	£170	£355
1856	—	—	£100	£220
1857	—	—	£150	£275
1858	—	—	£120	£225
1859	—	—	£100	£195
1860	—	—	£135	£240
1861	—	—	£130	£235
1862	—	—	£135	£255
1863	—	—	£175	£300
1864	—	—	£125	£235
1865	—	—	£130	£250
1866	—	—	£120	£240
1867	—	—	£125	£235
1868	—	—	£115	£215
1869	—	—	£155	£275
1870	—	—	£105	£195
1871	—	—	£100	£185
1872	—	—	£95	£180
1873	—	—	£90	£170
1874	—	—	£90	£175
1875	—	—	£85	£165
1876	—	—	£85	£165
1877	—	—	£80	£160
1878	—	—	£85	£165
1879	—	—	£85	£160
1880	—	—	£80	£150
1881	—	—	£80	£150
1882	—	—	£130	£225
1883	—	—	£75	£145

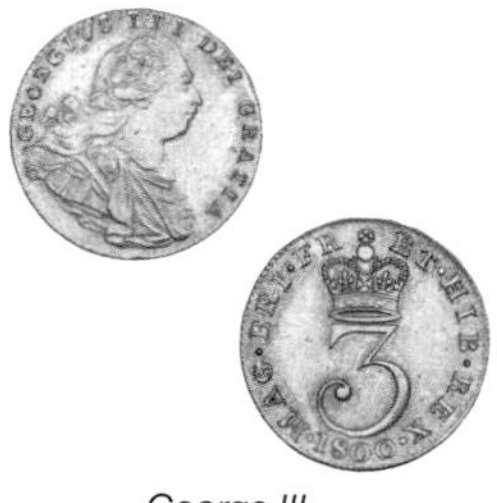

George III

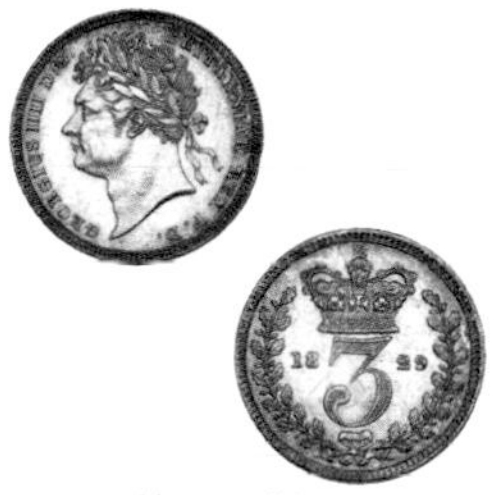

George IV

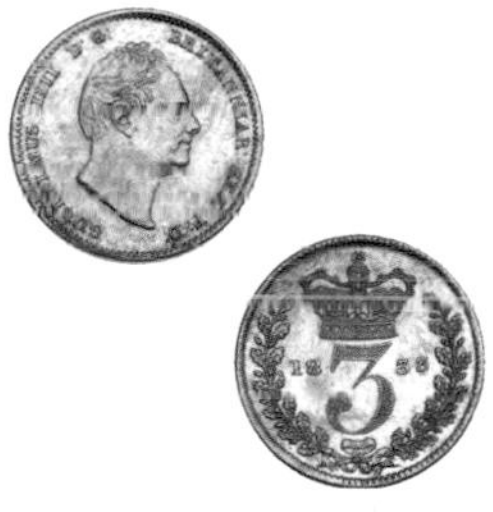

William IV

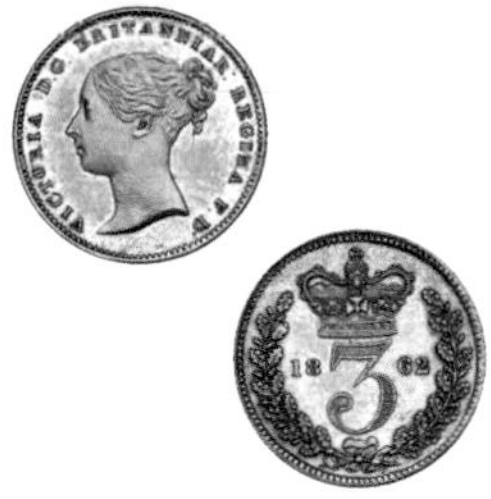

Victoria

DATE	F	VF	EF	UNC
1884	—	—	£75	£145
1885	—	—	£70	£130
1886	—	—	£70	£125
1887	—	—	£80	£170
1888–1892 (Jubilee Head)	—	—	£50	£110
1893–1901 (Old Head)	—	—	£40	£65

EDWARD VII (1901–10)

	F	VF	EF	UNC
1902	—	—	£30	£50
1902 Proof	—	—	—	£55
1903	—	—	£40	£85
1904	—	—	£55	£105
1905	—	—	£55	£95
1906	—	—	£45	£90
1907	—	—	£45	£90
1908	—	—	£40	£80
1909	—	—	£70	£120
1910	—	—	£80	£150

Edward VII

GEORGE V (1910–36)

	F	VF	EF	UNC
1911–34	—	—	£55	£85
1911 Proof	—	—	—	£95
1935	—	—	£65	£100
1936	—	—	£75	£135

GEORGE VI (1936–52)

	F	VF	EF	UNC
1937–52	—	—	£55	£100
1937 Proof	—	—	—	£70

Elizabeth

ELIZABETH II (1952–   )

	F	VF	EF	UNC
1953	—	—	£180	£295
1954–85	—	—	£45	£80
1986–2007	—	—	£55	£85
2002 In gold (proof)	—	—	—	£615
2008	—	—	—	£170
2009	—	—	—	£160
2010	—	—	—	£150
2011	—	—	—	£130
2012	—	—	—	£140
2013	—	—	—	£140
2014	—	—	—	£150
2015	—	—	—	£145
2016	—	—	—	£150
2017	—	—	—	£160

George V

TWOPENCE

CHARLES II (1660–85)

	F	VF	EF	UNC
Undated	£55	£90	£155	—
1668	£65	£90	£160	—
1670	£50	£80	£150	—
1671	£50	£85	£150	—
1672	£50	£85	£150	—
1672/1	£65	£100	£160	—
1673	£50	£85	£155	—
1674	£55	£90	£150	—
1675	£50	£90	£140	—
1676	£55	£95	£155	—
1677	£45	£85	£135	—
1678	£35	£75	£130	—
1679	£40	£70	£125	—
1680	£50	£85	£135	—
1681	£55	£80	£135	—
1682	£65	£90	£165	—
1682/1 ERA for FRA	£75	£110	£210	—
1683	£60	£100	£160	—
1684	£55	£95	£155	—

Charles II

James II

DATE	F	VF	EF	UNC

JAMES II (1685–88)

DATE	F	VF	EF	UNC
1686	£60	£95	£160	—
1686 reads IACOBVS	£75	£120	£215	—
1687	£65	£95	£165	—
1687 ERA for FRA	£75	£130	£215	—
1688	£50	£85	£150	—
1688/7	£65	£90	£170	—

WILLIAM & MARY (1688–94)

DATE	F	VF	EF	UNC
1689	£60	£100	£175	—
1691	£55	£85	£140	—
1692	£75	£130	£200	—
1693	£65	£110	£185	—
1693 GV below bust	£75	£115	£185	—
1693/2	£65	£100	£170	—
1694	£50	£85	£140	—
1694 MARLA error	£80	£130	£250	—
1694 HI for HIB	£75	£120	£210	—
1694 GVLI under bust	£60	£100	£185	—
1694 GVL under bust	£55	£95	£185	—

William & Mary

WILLIAM III (1694–1702)

DATE	F	VF	EF	UNC
1698	£60	£115	£175	—
1699	£50	£90	£145	—
1700	£65	£115	£185	—
1701	£65	£110	£170	—

ANNE (1702–14)

DATE	F	VF	EF	UNC
1703	£65	£100	£180	—
1704	£50	£80	£135	—
1704 No stops on obverse	£00	£90	£170	—
1705	£60	£100	£160	—
1706	£80	£120	£195	—
1707	£50	£85	£150	—
1708	£70	£100	£175	—
1709	£85	£135	£225	—
1710	£45	£80	£115	—
1713	£70	£110	£195	—

William III

GEORGE I (1714–27)

DATE	F	VF	EF	UNC
1717	£45	£80	£130	—
1721	£50	£85	£125	—
1723	£65	£95	£160	—
1726	£50	£80	£135	—
1727	£60	£85	£150	—

Queen Anne

GEORGE II (1727–60)

DATE	F	VF	EF	UNC
1729	£40	£80	£120	—
1731	£40	£80	£125	—
1732	£40	£80	£115	—
1735	£45	£75	£110	—
1737	£40	£80	£115	—
1739	£45	£80	£120	—
1740	£40	£70	£115	—
1743	£35	£65	£105	—
1743/0	£45	£80	£115	—
1746	£35	£70	£95	—
1756	£35	£65	£95	—
1759	£35	£70	£95	—
1760	£50	£75	£100	—

George II

GEORGE III (1760–1820)

DATE	F	VF	EF	UNC
1763	£40	£70	£95	—
1763 Proof			Extremely rare	
1765	£345	£500	£700	—

DATE	F	VF	EF	UNC
1766..............................	£45	£75	£95	—
1772..............................	£35	£70	£90	—
1780..............................	£35	£70	£90	—
1784..............................	£40	£70	£90	—
1786..............................	£50	£80	£95	—
1792..............................	—	£80	£125	£190
1795..............................	—	£30	£60	£85
1800..............................	—	£30	£70	£85
1817..............................	—	£35	£70	£90
1818..............................	—	£35	£70	£90
1820..............................	—	£45	£80	£100

George III

GEORGE IV (1820–30)

1822–30..............................	—	—	£40	£70
1825 TRITANNIAR	—	—	£60	£115

WILLIAM IV (1830–37)

1831–37..............................	—	—	£45	£80
1831 Proof..............................	—	—	£125	£275

VICTORIA (1837–1901)

1838–87 (Young Head)	—	—	£30	£60
1859 BEITANNIAR	—	—	£75	£135
1861 6 over 1.........................	—	—	£40	£80
1888–92 (Jubilee Head).........	—	—	£30	£60
1893–1901 (Old Head.............	—	—	£25	£50
1838 Proof..............................	—	—	—	£475
1839 Proof..............................	—	—	—	£300
1853 Proof..............................	—	—	—	£325

George IV

EDWARD VII (1901–10)

1902–08..............................	—	—	£25	£35
1909..............................	—	—	£45	£80
1910..............................	—	—	£50	£90
1902 Proof..............................	—	—	£30	£50

William IV

GEORGE V (1910–36)

1911–34..............................	—	—	£35	£65
1911 Proof..............................	—	—	£40	£70
1935..............................	—	—	£40	£65
1936..............................	—	—	£50	£75

GEORGE VI (1936–52)

1937–47..............................	—	—	£40	£60
1948–52..............................	—	—	£45	£70
1937 Proof..............................	—	—	£35	£60

Victoria

ELIZABETH II (1952–)

1953..............................	—	—	£140	£225
1954–85..............................	—	—	£40	£65
1986–2007..............................	—	—	£40	£70
2002 Gold Proof	—	—	—	£450
2008..............................	—	—	—	£125
2009..............................	—	—	—	£115
2010..............................	—	—	—	£110
2011..............................	—	—	—	£85
2012..............................	—	—	—	£100
2013..............................	—	—	—	£110
2014..............................	—	—	—	£110
2015..............................	—	—	—	£115
2016..............................	—	—	—	£135
2017..............................	—	—	—	£160

Elizabeth

DATE	F	VF	EF	UNC

PENNY
CHARLES II (1660–85)

DATE	F	VF	EF	UNC
Undated	£70	£110	£200	—
1670	£65	£110	£175	—
1671	£65	£110	£170	—
1672/1	£70	£110	£175	—
1673	£65	£110	£170	—
1674	£70	£110	£175	—
1674 Gratia (error)	£100	£160	£250	—
1675	£65	£115	£170	—
1675 Gratia (error)	£100	£165	£260	—
1676	£80	£120	£185	—
1676 Gratia (error)	£110	£170	£275	—
1677	£60	£100	£165	—
1677 Gratia (error)	£95	£135	£230	—
1678	£150	£265	£380	—
1678 Gratia (error)	£180	£280	£400	—
1679	£85	£125	£210	—
1680	£80	£115	£200	—
1681	£110	£155	£230	—
1682	£75	£125	£195	—
1682 ERA for FRA	£90	£150	£245	—
1683	£85	£115	£195	—
1683/1	£85	£150	£225	—
1684	£150	£240	£300	—
1684/3	£160	£250	£315	—

Charles II

JAMES II (1685–88)

DATE	F	VF	EF	UNC
1685	£65	£100	£165	—
1686	£80	£110	£175	—
1687	£80	£120	£180	—
1687/8	£85	£130	£190	—
1688	£65	£90	£165	—
1688/7	£70	£105	£185	—

James II

WILLIAM & MARY (1688–94)

DATE	F	VF	EF	UNC
1689	£450	£675	£950	
1689 MΛRIΛ	£470	£685	£950	
1689 GVIELMVS (Error)	£450	£700	£975	—
1690	£75	£145	£230	—
1691	£75	£150	£225	—
1692	£240	£340	£550	—
1692/1	£250	£355	£570	—
1693	£95	£160	£265	—
1694	£75	£130	£230	—
1694 HI for HIB	£110	£170	£275	—
1694 No stops on obverse	£90	£150	£240	—

William & Mary

WILLIAM III (1694–1702)

DATE	F	VF	EF	UNC
1698	£85	£135	£200	—
1698 HI. BREX (Error)	£100	£165	£270	—
1699	£290	£425	£650	—
1700	£95	£150	£225	—
1701	£85	£130	£205	—

William III

ANNE (1702–14)

DATE	F	VF	EF	UNC
1703	£75	£125	£195	—
1705	£65	£110	£180	—
1706	£70	£95	£165	—
1708	£475	£600	£850	—
1709	£60	£95	£150	—
1710	£135	£200	£325	—
1713/0	£85	£120	£180	—

Anne

DATE	F	VF	EF	UNC

GEORGE I (1714–27)

DATE	F	VF	EF	UNC
1716	£45	£90	£115	—
1718	£45	£90	£115	—
1720	£50	£95	£125	—
1720 HIPEX (Error)	£75	£115	£205	—
1723	£70	£120	£175	—
1725	£50	£85	£130	—
1726	£50	£85	£125	—
1727	£60	£115	£165	—

George I

GEORGE II (1727–60)

DATE	F	VF	EF	UNC
1729	£40	£85	£120	—
1731	£45	£85	£125	—
1732	£50	£80	£120	—
1735	£40	£70	£100	—
1737	£40	£70	£105	—
1739	£40	£70	£100	—
1740	£40	£65	£100	—
1743	£35	£70	£95	—
1746	£45	£80	£115	—
1746/3	£50	£80	£120	—
1750	£30	£55	£85	—
1752	£30	£55	£85	—
1753	£30	£55	£85	—
1754	£30	£55	£85	—
1755	£30	£55	£85	—
1756	£30	£55	£80	—
1757	£30	£55	£80	—
1757 No colon after Gratia	£45	£80	£100	—
1758	£30	£60	£85	—
1759	£35	£60	£80	—
1760	£40	£75	£95	—

George III

GEORGE III (1760–1820)

DATE	F	VF	EF	UNC
1763	£45	£70	£100	—
1763 Proof	—	—	Extremely rare	
1766	£40	£70	£90	—
1772	£40	£70	£85	—
1780	£85	£135	£190	—
1781	£35	£60	£85	—
1784	£45	£65	£90	—
1786	£35	£60	£90	—
1792	£35	£60	£90	£125
1795	—	£25	£50	£70
1800	—	£25	£50	£70
1817	—	£25	£50	£70
1818	—	£25	£50	£70
1820	—	£30	£55	£75

George IV

GEORGE IV (1820–30)

DATE	F	VF	EF	UNC
1822–30	—	—	£35	£60

WILLIAM IV (1830–37)

DATE	F	VF	EF	UNC
1831–37	—	—	£45	£70
1831 Proof	—	—	£150	£250

William IV

VICTORIA (1837–1901)

DATE	F	VF	EF	UNC
1838–87 (Young Head)	—	—	£30	£55
1888–92 (Jubilee Head)	—	—	£30	£50
1893–1901 (Old Head)	—	—	£25	£40
1838 Proof	—	—	—	£265
1839 Proof	—	—	—	£175
1853 Proof	—	—	—	£215

Victoria

DATE	F	VF	EF	UNC

EDWARD VII (1901–10)

	F	VF	EF	UNC
1902–08	—	—	£20	£35
1909	—	—	£40	£75
1910	—	—	£50	£90
1902 Proof	—	—	£25	£40

Edward VII

GEORGE V (1910–36)

	F	VF	EF	UNC
1911–14	—	—	£45	£80
1915	—	—	£50	£85
1916–19	—	—	£45	£80
1920	—	—	£45	£80
1921–28	—	—	£45	£75
1929	—	—	£45	£80
1930–34	—	—	£40	£75
1935	—	—	£45	£80
1936	—	—	£55	£85
1911 Proof	—	—	£45	£80

George V

GEORGE VI (1936–52)

	F	VF	EF	UNC
1937–40	—	—	£50	£80
1941	—	—	£55	£90
1942–47	—	—	£50	£85
1948–52	—	—	£60	£95
1937 Proof	—	—	£45	£80

ELIZABETH II (1952–)

	F	VF	EF	UNC
1953	—	—	£285	£400
1965–85	—	—	£45	£80
1986–2007	—	—	£45	£85
2002 Proof in gold	—	—	—	£485
2008	—	—	—	£145
2009	—	—	—	£140
2010	—	—	—	£120
2011	—	—	—	£105
2012	—	—	—	£120
2013	—	—	—	£125
2014	—	—	—	£120
2015	—	—	—	£110
2016	—	—	—	£135
2017	—	—	—	£145

Elizabeth II

DECIMAL COINAGE

Since the introduction of the Decimal system in the UK, many coins have been issued for circulation purposes in vast quantities. In addition, from 1982 sets of coins to non-proof standard, and including examples of each denomination found in circulation, have been issued each year. For 1982 and 1983 they were to "circulation" standard and described as "Uncirculated". Individual coins from these sets are annotated "Unc" on the lists that follow. From 1984 to the present day they were described as "Brilliant Uncirculated" (BU on the lists), and from around 1986 these coins are generally distinguishable from coins intended for circulation. They were from then produced by the Proof Coin Division of the Royal Mint (rather than by the Coin Production Room which produces circulation-standard coins). For completeness however, we have included the annotations Unc and BU back to 1982, the start year for these sets.

It is emphasised that the abbreviations Unc and BU in the left-hand columns adjacent to the date refer to an advertising description or to an engineering production standard, not the preservation condition or grade of the coin concerned. Where no such annotation appears adjacent to the date, the coin is circulation-standard for issue as such.

We have included the "mintage" figures for circulation coins down to Half Penny. The figure given for the 1997 Two Pounds, is considerably less than the actual quantity struck, because many were scrapped before issue due to failing an electrical conductivity test. Where a coin is available in uncirculated grade at, or just above, face value no price has been quoted.

Base metal Proof issues of circulation coinage (£2 or £1 to one or half penny) of the decimal series were only issued, as with Unc or BU, as part of Year Sets, but many of these sets have been broken down into individual coins, hence the appearance of the latter on the market.

The lists do not attempt to give details of die varieties, except where there was an obvious intention to change the appearance of a coin, e.g. 1992 20p.

2008 saw new reverses and modified obverses for all circulation denominations from the One Pound to the One Penny. All seven denominations were put into circulation dated 2008, all with both the old and the new reverses.

The circulation standard mintage figures have mainly been kindly supplied by courtesy of the Head of Historical Services and the Department of UK Circulation Coin Sales, both at the Royal Mint.

KILO COINS
(gold and silver)

The UK's first-ever Kilo coins were struck to commemorate the 2012 Olympic Games in 0.999 fine gold and 0.999 fine silver. These and subsequent issues are listed in detail below, and all were struck to proof standard and to similar metallic standards.

DATE	FACE VALUE	AUTHORISED ISSUE QTY.	NO. ISSUED	PRICE
2012 Olympic Gold;				
obverse: 1998 Ian Rank-Broadley's Royal Portrait				
reverse: Sir Anthony Caro's "Individual Endeavour" £1,000		60	20	£100,000
2012 Olympic Silver;				
obverse: 1998 Rank-Broadley Royal Portrait				
reverse: Tom Phillip's "Team Endeavour"... £500		2,912	910	£3,000
2012 Diamond Jubilee Gold;				
obverse: Queen in Garter Robes (Rank-Broadley)				
reverse: Royal Arms (Buckingham Palace Gates) £1,000		21	21	£60,000
2012 Diamond Jubilee Silver;				
obverse: Queen in Garter Robes (Rank-Broadley)				
reverse: Royal Arms (Buckingham Palace Gates) £500		1,250	206	£2,600
2013 Coronation Anniversary Gold;				
obverse: 1998 Rank-Broadley Royal Portrait				
reverse: John Bergdahl's Coronation Regalia £1,000		27	13	£50,000
2013 Coronation Anniversary Silver;				
obverse: 1998 Rank-Broadley Royal Portrait				
reverse: John Bergdahl's Coronation Regalia £500		400	301	£2,600
2013 Royal Christening Gold;				
obverse: 1998 Rank-Broadley Royal Portrait				
reverse: John Bergdahl's Lily Font £1,000		22	19	£48,000
2013 Royal Christening Silver;				
obverse: 1998 Rank-Broadley Royal Portrait				
reverse: John Bergdahl's Lily Font £500		500	194	£2,600
2014 First World War Outbreak Gold;				
obverse: 1998 Rank-Broadley Royal Portrait				
reverse: Sandle's Hostile Environment.. £1,000		25	—	£45,000
2014 First World War Outbreak Silver;				
obverse: 1998 Rank-Broadley Royal Portrait				
reverse: Sandle's Hostile Environment... £500		430	—	£2,000
2015 50th Anniversary of Death of Sir Winston Churchill Gold;				
obverse: 1998 Rank-Broadley Royal Portrait				
reverse: Millner's image of Churchill.. £1,000		15	—	£45,000
2015 50th Anniversary of Death of Sir Winston Churchill Silver;				
obverse: 1998 Rank-Broadley Royal Portrait				
reverse: Milner's image of Churchill £500		170	—	£2,000
2015 The Longest Reign Gold;				
obverse: Butler Royal Portrait				
reverse: Stephen Taylor Queen's Portraits £1,000		15	—	£42,500
2016 The Longest Reign Silver;				
obverse: Butler Royal Portrait				
reverse: Stephen Taylor Queen's Portraits £500		320	—	£2,000
2016 Year of the Monkey Gold;				
obverse: Clark Royal Portrait				
reverse: Wuon-Gean Ho's Rhesus monkey £1,000		8	—	£42,500
2016 Year of the Monkey Silver;				
obverse: Butler Royal Portrait				
everse: Wuon-Gean Ho's Rhesus monkey....................................... £500		88	—	£2,000

DATE	FACE VALUE	AUTHORISED ISSUE QTY.	NO. ISSUED	PRICE
2016 Queen's 90th Birthday Gold; obverse: Clark Royal Portrait reverse: Christopher Hobbs Floral design	£1,000	25	—	—
2016 Queen's 90th Birthday Silver; obverse: Clark Royal Portrait reverse: Christopher Hobbs Floral design	£500	450	—	£2,000
2017 The Queen's Sapphire Jubilee Silver; obverse: Clark Royal Portrait reverse: Gregory Cameron's design of Crowned Coat of Arms	£500	300	—	£2,050
2017 Lunar Year of the Rooster Gold; obverse: Clark Royal Portrait reverse: Wuon-Gean Ho's Rooster	£1000	8	—	£2,050
2017 Lunar Year of the Rooster Silver; obverse: Clark Royal Portrait reverse: Wuon-Gean Ho's Rooster	£500	68	—	£2,050

See also under "The Queen's Beasts" series

2012 Olympic Silver

2013 Royal Christening Gold

2012 Diamond Jubilee Gold

2014 First World War Outbreak Gold

2017 The Year of the Rooster

2017 The Queen's Sapphire Jubilee

Illustrations on this page are not shown to scale.

FIVE-OUNCE COINS
(gold and silver, including Britannia Coins)

Also appearing for the first time in 2012 were Five-Ounce coins, minted in the same metals and standards as the Kilo Coins. Included here also are Five-Ounce Britannia coins, both gold and silver proofs, which appeared first in 2013. It should be noted that the reverses of these coins, in common with other denominations of Britannias, have a different design from those minted to BU ("bullion") standard.

DATE	FACE VALUE	AUTHORISED ISSUE QTY.	NO ISSUED	PRICE
2012 Olympic Gold; obverse: 1998 Rank-Broadley Royal Portrait reverse: Pegasus (C. Le Brun) £10		500	193	£11,500
2012 Olympic Silver; obverse: 1998 Rank-Broadley Royal Portrait reverse: Pegasus (C. Le Brun) £10		7,500	5,056	£525
2012 Diamond Jubilee Gold; obverse: Queen in Garter Robes (Rank-Broadley) reverse: Queen seated (facing)...........................£10		250	140	£9,500
2012 Diamond Jubilee Silver; obverse: Queen in Garter Robes (Rank-Broadley) reverse: Queen seated (facing)...........................£10		1,952	1,933	£450
2013 Coronation Anniversary Gold; obverse: 1998 Rank-Broadley Royal Portrait reverse: Regalia in Westminster Abbey (J. Olliffe) £10		129	74	£9,500
2013 Coronation Anniversary Silver; obverse: 1998 Rank-Broadley Royal Portrait reverse: Regalia in Westminster Abbey (J. Olliffe) £10		1,953	1,604	£450
2013 Britannia Gold; obverse: 1998 Rank-Broadley Royal Portrait reverse: Britannia seated with owl (R. Hunt)..............................£500		125	61	£8,200

DATE	FACE VALUE	AUTHORISED ISSUE QTY.	NO ISSUED	PRICE
2013 Britannia Silver; obverse: 1998 Rank-Broadley Royal Portrait reverse: Britannia seated with owl (R. Hunt)..................£10 £450		4,655	4,054	—
2013 Royal Christening Gold; obverse: 1998 Rank-Broadley Royal Portrait reverse: Bergdahl's Lily Font £10 £8,200		150	48	—
2013 Royal Christening Silver; obverse: 1998 Rank-Broadley Royal Portrait reverse: Bergdahl's Lily Font £10 £450		1,660	912	—
2014 Britannia Gold; obverse: 1998 Rank-Broadley Royal Portrait reverse: Clark's portrayal of Britannia £500		75	—	£7,500
2014 Britannia Silver; obverse: 1998 Rank-Broadley Royal Portrait reverse: Clark's portrayal of Britannia £10		1,350	—	£395
2014 First World War Outbreak Gold; obverse: 1998 Rank-Broadley Royal Portrait reverse: Bergdahl's Britannia.......................£10		110	—	£7,500
2014 First World War Outbreak Silver; obverse: 1998 Rank-Broadley Royal Portrait reverse: Bergdahl's Britannia.......................£10		1,300	—	£395
2015 Year of the Sheep Gold; obverse: 1998 Rank-Broadley Royal Portrait reverse: Wuon-Gean Ho's Swaledale Sheep £500		38	—	£7,500
2015 Year of the Sheep Silver; obverse: 1998 Rank-Broadley Royal Portrait reverse: Wuon-Gean Ho's Swaledale Sheep £10		1,088	—	£395
2015 Britannia Gold; obverse: Clark Royal Portrait reverse: Dufort's Britannia.............................£500		50	—	£7,500
2015 Britannia Silver; obverse: Clark Royal Portrait reverse: Dufort's Britannia.............................£10		1,150	—	£395
2015 50th Anniversary of Death of Sir Winston Churchill Gold; obverse: Clark Royal Portrait reverse: Millner's image of Churchill..........................£10		60	—	£7,500
2015 50th Anniversary of Death of Sir Winston Churchill Silver; obverse: Clark Royal Portrait reverse: Millner's image of Churchill..........................£10		500	—	£395
2015 First World War Gold; obverse: Clark Royal Portrait reverse: James Butler Devastation of War £500		50	—	£6,050
2015 First World War Silver; obverse: Clark Royal Portrait reverse: James Butler Devastation of War £10		500	—	£395
2015 The Longest Reign Gold; obverse: Butler Royal Portrait reverse: Stephen Taylor Queen's Portrait..................£500		180	—	£6,950
2015 The Longest Reign Silver; obverse: Butler Royal Portrait reverse: Stephen Taylor Queen's Portrait..................£10		1,500	—	£395
2016 Year of the Monkey Gold; obverse: Clark Royal Portrait reverse: Wuon-Gean Ho's Rhesus monkey £500		38	—	£7,500
2016 Year of the Monkey Silver; obverse: Butler Royal Portrait reverse: Wuon-Gean Ho's Rhesus monkey £10		588	—	£395

DATE	FACE VALUE	AUTH ISSUE QTY.	ISSUE PRICE
2016 Queen's 90th Birthday Gold; obverse: Clark Royal Portrait reverse: Christopher Hobbs Floral design........................ £500		170	£7,500
2016 Queen's 90th Birthday Silver; obverse: Clark Royal Portrait reverse: Christopher Hobbs Floral design......................... £10		1,750	£395
2016 Britannia Gold; obverse: Clark Royal Portrait; reverse: Suzie Zamit Britannia.. £500		75	£7,500
2016 Britannia Silver; obverse: Clark Royal Portrait; reverse: Suzie Zamit Britannia.. £10		800	£395
2016 Shakespeare Gold; obverse: Clark Royal Portrait; reverse: Tom Phillips Shakespeare Portrait £500		—	—
2016 Shakespeare Silver; obverse: Clark Royal Portrait; reverse: Tom Phillips Shakespeare Portrait £10		750	£395
2017 The Queen's Sapphire Jubilee Gold; obverse: Clark Royal Portrait reverse: Gregory Cameron's design of Crowned Coat of Arms— ... £500		110	£8,250
2017 The Queen's Sapphire Jubilee Silver; obverse: Clark Royal Portrait reverse: Gregory Cameron's design of Crowned Coat of Arms— £10		1,500	£415
2017 Britannia Gold; obverse: Clark Royal Portrait reverse: Modern interpretation of Britannia by Louis Tamlyn £500		125	£8,250
2017 Britannia Silver; obverse: Clark Royal Portrait reverse: Modern interpretation of Britannia by Louis Tamlyn £10		1,500	£415
2017 The 100th Anniversary of the First World War Gold; obverse: Clark Royal Portrait reverse: Soldier design by sculptor Philip Jackson............................ £10		50	£8,250
2017 The 100th Anniversary of the First World War Silver; obverse: Clark Royal Portrait reverse: Soldier design by sculptor Philip Jackson............................ £10		450	£415
2017 Lunar Year of the Rooster Gold; obverse: Clark Royal Portrait reverse: Wuon-Gean Ho's Rooster.. £500		38	£8,250

5 ounce silver coin shown actual size (65mm)

5 ounce gold coin shown actual size (50mm)

FIVE POUNDS (Sovereign series)

This series is all minted in gold, and, except where stated, have the Pistrucci St George and Dragon reverse. BU coins up to 2001 bear a U in a circle. From 2009 the initials B.P. in the exergue are replaced by PISTRUCCI in small letters on the left. From 2014 the denomination is called the "Five-Sovereign" piece by the Royal Mint in their marketing publications.

DATE	Mintage	UNC
1980 Proof	10,000	£1100
1981 Proof	5,400	£1100
1982 Proof	2,500	£1100
1984 BU	15,104	£1100
1984 Proof	8,000	£1250
1985 New portrait BU	13,626	£1100
1985 — Proof	6,130	£1100
1986 BU	7,723	£1100
1987 Uncouped portrait BU	5,694	£1100
1988 BU	3,315	£1100
1989 500th Anniversary of the Sovereign. Enthroned portrayal obverse and Crowned shield reverse BU	2,937	£1400
1989 — Proof	5,000	£1500
1990 Reverts to couped portrait BU	1,226	£1100
1990 Proof	1,721	£1100
1991 BU	976	£1100
1991 Proof	1,336	£1100
1992 BU	797	£1100
1992 Proof	1,165	£1100
1993 BU	906	£1100
1993 Proof	1,078	£1100
1994 BU	1,000	£1100
1994 Proof	918	£1100
1995 BU	1,000	£1100
1995 Proof	1,250	£1100
1996 BU	901	£1100
1996 Proof	742	£1200
1997 BU	802	£1100
1997 Proof	860	£1100
1998 New portrait BU	825	£1150
1998 Proof	789	£1250
1999 BU	991	£1100
1999 Proof	1,000	£1250
2000 ("Bullion")	10,000	£1100
2000 BU	994	£1150
2000 Proof	3,000	£1250
2001 BU	1,000	£1100
2001 Proof	3,500	£1250
2002 Shield rev. ("Bullion")	—	£1100
2002 BU	—	£1150
2002 Proof	3,000	£1250
2003 BU	812	£1100
2003 Proof	—	£1250
2004 BU	1,000	£1100
2004 Proof	—	£1250
2005 Noad's heraldic St George and Dragon BU	936	£1250
2005 — Proof	—	£1400
2006 BU	731	£1100
2006 Proof	—	£1250
2007 BU	768	£1100
2007 Proof	—	£1250
2008 BU	750	£1100
2008 Proof	—	£1250
2009 BU	1,000	£1100
2009 Proof	—	£1250
2010 BU	1,000	£1100
2010 Proof	—	£1150

NOTE: The prices quoted in this guide are set at August 2017 with the price of gold at £1000 per ounce and silver £13 per ounce—market fluctuations will have a marked effect on the values of modern precious metal coins.

Pistrucci's famous rendering of St George and the Dragon which appears on all except special commemorative five pound coins.

The obverse of the 1989 500th Anniversary of the origional Sovereign coin portray HM the Queen enthroned.

DATE	Mintage	UNC
2011 BU	657	£1100
2011 Proof	—	£1150
2012 Day's St George and Dragon BU	496	£1250
2012 — Proof	—	£1450
2013 BU	262	£1100
2013 Proof..	—	£1250
2014 BU	—	£1100
2014 Proof..	—	£1250
2015 Proof..	—	£1500
2015 New Portrait BU	—	£1450
2015 — Proof	—	£1550
2016 BU	—	£1100
2016 Butler Portrait Proof.....................................	—	£1450
2017 200th Anniversary of the Sovereign	—	£1500

2017 200th Anniversary reverse design as the original issue.

FIVE POUNDS (Crown series)

This series commenced in 1990 when the "Crown" was declared legal tender at £5, instead of 25p as all previous issues continued to be. Mintage is in cupro-nickel unless otherwise stated. BU includes those in individual presentation folders, and those in sets sold with stamp covers and/or banknotes.

DATE	Mintage	UNC
1990 Queen Mother's 90th Birthday.	2,761,431	£8
1990 — BU	48,477	£10
1990 — Silver Proof	56,800	£40
1990 — Gold Proof..	2,500	£1400
1993 Coronation 40th Anniversary	1,834,655	£8
1993 — BU	—	£10
1993 — Proof	—	£15
1993 — Silver Proof	58,877	£45
1993 — Gold Proof..	2,500	£1400
1996 HM the Queen's 70th Birthday	2,396,100	£8
1996 — BU	—	£10
1996 — Proof	—	£15
1996 — Silver Proof	39,336	£45
1996 — Gold Proof..	2,127	£1400
1997 Royal Golden Wedding	1,733,000	£8
1997 — BU	—	£10
1997 — — with £5 note..	5,000	£75
1997 — Proof	—	£20
1997 — Silver Proof	33,689	£45
1997 — Gold Proof..	2,750	£1400
1998 Prince of Wales 50th Birthday	1,407,300	£9
1998 — BU	—	£12
1998 — Proof	—	£20
1998 — Silver Proof	13,379	£50
1998 — Gold Proof..	—	£1400
1999 Princess of Wales Memorial.	1,600,000	£10
1999 — BU	—	£14
1999 — Proof	—	£20
1999 — Silver Proof	49,545	£60
1999 — Gold Proof..	7,500	£3000
1999 Millennium	3,796,300	£8
1999 — BU	—	£12
1999 — Proof	—	£20
1999 — Silver Proof	49,057	£45
1999 — Gold Proof..	2,500	£1450
2000 —	3,147,092*	£12
2000 — BU	—	£20
2000 — — with special Millennium Dome mintmark	—	£30
2000 — Proof	—	£25
2000 — Silver Proof with gold highlight...................	14,255	£50
2000 — Gold Proof..	2,500	£1400

DATE	Mintage	UNC
2000 Queen Mother's 100th Birthday	—	£8
2000 — BU	—	£12
2000 — Silver Proof	31,316	£45
2000 — — — Piedfort	14,850	£60
2000 — Gold Proof	3,000	£1400
2001 Victorian Era	851,491	£10
2001 — BU	—	£12
2001 — Proof	—	£20
2001 — Silver Proof	19,216	£50
2001 — — with frosted relief	596	£150
2001 — Gold Proof	3,000	£1400
2001 — — with frosted relief	733	£1500
2002 Golden Jubilee	3,469,243	£9
2002 — BU	—	£12
2002 — Proof	—	£20
2002 — Silver Proof	54,012	£45
2002 — Gold Proof	5,502	£1400
2002 Queen Mother Memorial .... *incl. above**		£9
2002 — BU	—	£12
2002 — Silver Proof	16,117	£45
2002 — Gold Proof	3,000	£1400
2003 Coronation Jubilee	1,307,147	£10
2003 — BU	100,481	£13
2003 — Proof	—	£20
2003 — Silver Proof	28,758	£45
2003 — Gold Proof	1,896	£1400
2004 Entente Cordiale Centenary	1,205,594	£10
2004 — Proof Reverse Frosting	6,065	£15
2004 — Silver Proof	11,295	£50
2004 — — — Piedfort	2,500	£125
2004 — Gold Proof	926	£1400
2004 — Platinum Proof Piedfort	501	£4000
2005 Trafalgar Bicentenary	1,075 516	£12
2005 — BU	—	£14
2005 — Proof	—	£25
2005 — Silver Proof	21,448	£50
2005 — — Piedfort	2,818	£75
2005 Gold Proof	1,805	£1400
2005 Bicentenary of the Death of Nelson .... *incl. above**		£12
2005 — BU	—	£14
2005 — Proof	—	£25
2005 — Silver Proof	12,852	£50
2005 — — Piedfort	2,818	£75
2005 — Gold Proof	1,760	£1150
2005 — Platinum Proof Piedfort	200	£4000
2006 Queen's 80th Birthday	52,267	£10
2006 — BU	—	£14
2006 — Proof	—	£20
2006 — Silver Proof	20,790	£50
2006 — — — Piedfort, selective gold plating on reverse	5,000	£75
2006 — Gold Proof	2,750	£1400
2006 — Platinum Proof Piedfort	250	£4000
2007 Queen's Diamond Wedding	30,561	£10
2007 — BU	—	£15
2007 — Proof	—	£20
2007 — Silver Proof	15,186	£50
2007 — — Piedfort	2,000	£80
2007 — Gold Proof	2,380	£1400
2007 — Platinum Proof Piedfort	250	£4000
2008 Prince of Wales 60th Birthday	14,088	£12
2008 — BU	54,746	£15
2008 — Proof	—	£20
2008 — Silver Proof	6,264	£55
2008 — — Piedfort	1,088	£90
2008 — Gold Proof	867	£1400
2008 Elizabeth I 450th Anniversary of Accession	20,047	£12
2008 — BU	26,700	£15
2008 — Proof	—	£20
2008 — Silver Proof	9,216	£50

DATE	Mintage	UNC
2008 — — — Piedfort	1,602	£90
2008 — Gold Proof	1,500	£1400
2008 — Platinum Proof Piedfort	125	£4000
2009 500th Anniversary of Henry VIII accession	30,000	£12
2009 — BU	69,119	£15
2009 — Proof	—	£25
2009 — Silver Proof	10,419	£50
2009 — — — Piedfort	3,580	£90
2009 — Gold Proof	1,130	£1400
2009 — Platinum Proof Piedfort	100	£4250
2009 Olympic Countdown (3 years) BU	184,921	£12
2009 — Silver Proof	26,645	£55
2009 — — — Piedfort	4,874	£90
2009 — Gold Proof	1,860	£1250
2009 Olympic Celebration of Britain "The Mind" series (incl. green logo):		
Stonehenge Silver Proof	—	£60
Palace of Westminster/Big Ben Silver Proof	—	£60
— Cu Ni Proof	—	£20
Angel of the North Silver Proof	—	£60
Flying Scotsman Silver Proof	—	£60
Globe Theatre Silver Proof	—	£60
Sir Isaac Newton Silver Proof	—	£60
2010 350th Anniversary of the Restoration of the Monarchy	15,000	£12
2010 — BU	30,247	£15
2010 — Proof	—	£25
2010 — Silver Proof	6,518	£50
2010 — — — Piedfort	4,435	£100
2010 — Gold Proof	1,182	£1400
2010 — Platinum Proof Piedfort	—	£4000
2010 Olympic Countdown (2 years) BU	153,080	£12
2010 — Silver Proof	20,159	£55
2010 — — — Piedfort	2,197	£150
2010 — Gold Proof	1,562	£1250
2010 Olympic Celebration of Britain, "The Body" series (incl. red logo):		
Coastline of Britain (Rhossili Bay) Silver Proof	—	£65
Giants Causeway Silver Proof	—	£65
River Thames Silver Proof	—	£65
British Fauna (Barn Owl) Silver Proof	—	£65
British Flora (Oak Leaves and Acorn) Silver Proof	—	£65
Weather Vane Silver Proof	—	£65
2010 Olympic Celebration of Britain "The Spirit" series (incl. blue logo):		
Churchill Silver Proof	—	£75
— CuNi Proof	—	£20
Spirit of London (Kind Hearts etc.) Silver Proof	—	£75
— CuNi Proof	—	£20
Humour Silver Proof	—	£75
Unity (Floral emblems of Britain) Silver Proof	—	£75
Music Silver Proof	—	£75
Anti-slavery Silver Proof	—	£75
2011 90th Birthday of the Duke of Edinburgh BU	18,730	£12
2011 — Silver Proof	4,599	£75
2011 — — — Piedfort	2,659	£115
2011 — Gold Proof	636	£1400
2011 — Platinum Proof Piedfort	—	£6000
2011 Royal Wedding of Prince William and Catherine Middleton BU	250,000	£15
2011 — Silver Proof	26,069	£60
2011 — Gold-plated Silver Proof	7,451	£80
2011 — Silver Proof Piedfort	2,991	£95
2011 — Gold Proof	2,066	£1400
2011 — Platinum Proof Piedfort	—	£5500
2011 Olympic Countdown (1 year) BU	163,235	£12
2011 — Silver Proof	25,877	£55
2011 — — — Piedfort	4,000	£100
2011 — Gold Proof	1,300	£1250
2012 Diamond Jubilee BU	484,775	£15
2012 — Proof	16,370	£25

DATE	Mintage	UNC
2012 — Silver Proof	—	£65
2012 — Gold-plated silver proof	12,112	£85
2012 — Silver Piedfort Proof	3,187	£100
2012 — Gold proof	1,025	£1250
2012 — Platinum Piedfort Proof	20	£5500
2012 Olympic Countdown (Games Time) BU	52,261	£13
2012 — Silver Proof	12,670	£65
2012 — Silver Piedfort Proof	2,324	£120
2012 — Gold proof	1,007	£1450
2012 Official Olympic BU	315,983	£15
2012 — Silver Proof	20,810	£70
2012 — Gold Plated Silver Proof	2,180	£90
2012 — Silver Piedfort Proof	5,946	£125
2012 — Gold proof	1,045	£1450
2012 Official Paralympic BU	—	£15
2012 — Silver Proof	—	£70
2012 — Silver Piedfort Proof	—	£125
2012 — Gold proof	—	£1750
2013 60th Anniversary of the Queen's Coronation BU	57,262	£15
2013 — Proof	—	£35
2013 — Silver Proof	4,050	£80
2013 — Silver Piedfort Proof	2,626	£125
2013 — Gold-plated silver proof	2,547	£100
2013 — Gold proof	418	£1750
2013 — Platinum Piedfort Proof	106	£6000
2013 Queen's Portraits, 4 coins each with one of the four portraits, paired with James Butler's Royal Arms. Issued only as sets of 4 in precious metals (see under Proof and Specimen Set section)	—	£300
2013 Royal Birth of Prince George (St George & Dragon), Silver Proof	7,460	£100
2013 Christening of Prince George BU	56,014	£15
2013 — Silver Proof	7,264	£80
2013 — — Piedfort	2,251	£160
2013 — Gold Proof	486	£1750
2013 — Platinum Proof Piedfort	38	£6000
2014 300th Anniversary of the death of Queen Anne BU	—	£15
2014 — Proof	—	£35
2014 — Silver Proof	—	£80
2014 — — Piedfort	—	£100
2014 — Gold-plated Silver Proof	—	£100
2014 — Gold Proof	—	£1800
2014 First Birthday of Prince George Silver Proof	—	£80
2014 100th Anniversary of the First World War, issued only as set of 6 coins (see under Proof and Specimen Sets)	—	—
2014 Portrait of Britain, issued only as set of 4 coins, with trichromatic colour-printing (see under Proof and Specimen Sets section)	—	—
2015 50th Anniversary of death of Sir Winston Churchill BU	—	£15
2015 — Silver Proof	—	£80
2015 — — Piedfort	—	£160
2015 — Gold Proof	—	£1800
2015 — Platinum Proof Piedfort	65	£5000
2015 200th Anniversary of the Battle of Waterloo, BU	—	£15
2015 — Silver Proof	—	£80
2015 — — Piedfort	—	£160
2015 — Gold Proof	100	£1650
2015 First World War 100th Anniversary, continued, issued only as set of 6 coins	—	—
New Portrait		
2015 2nd Birthday of Prince George, Silver Proof —	£80	
2015 Birth of Princess Charlotte, BU	—	£15
2015 — Silver Proof	—	£80
2015 — Gold Proof	500	£1800
2015 Christening of Princess Charlotte, Silver Proof	—	£80
2015 The Longest Reign, BU	—	£15
2015 — Silver Proof	—	£80
2015 — — Piedfort	—	£160

DATE	Mintage	UNC
2015 — Gold Proof..	—	£1650
2015 — Platinum Proof Piedfort................................	—	£5000
2016 Queen's 90th Birthday, BU...............................	—	£15
2016 — Proof	—	£25
2016 — Silver Proof	—	£80
2016 — — Piedfort..	—	£160
2016 — Gold Proof..	—	£1800
2016 — Platinum Proof Piedfort................................	—	£4500
2016 Portrait of Britain, issued only as set of 4 coins, with trichromatic colour-printing (see under Proof and Specimen Sets section)	2,016	£350
2016 First World War Centenary, continued, issued only as a set of 6 Silver Proof coins..	1,916	£450
2016 Battle of the Somme, Silver Proof	4,000	£85
2017 Portrait of Britain, issued only as set of 4 coins, with trichromatic colour-printing (see under Proof and Specimen Sets section)	1,500	£350
2017 1000th Anniversary of the Coronation of King Canute, BU	—	£15
2017 — Proof	—	£30
2017 — Silver Proof	1,500	£85
2017 — — Piedfort..	1,500	£175
2017 — Gold Proof..	284	£1945
2017 Prince Philip Celebrating a Life of Service, BU ...	—	£15
2017 — Proof	—	£30
2017 — Silver Proof	3,000	£85
2017 — — Piedfort..	—	£175
2017 — Gold Proof..	300	£1945
2017 First World War Centenary, continued, issued only as set of 6 Silver Proof coins..	1,917	£500
2017 House of Windsor Centenary, BU	—	£15
2017 — Proof	—	£30
2017 — Silver Proof	13,000	£85
2017 — — Piedfort..	5,500	£175
2017 — Gold Proof..	884	£1935
2017 Her Majesty's Sapphire Jubilee, BU...................	—	£15
2017 — Proof	—	£30
2017 — Silver Proof	8,600	£85
2017 — — Piedfort..	3,000	£155

2017 Portrait of Britain, issued only as set of 4 coins, with trichromatic colour-printing.

DOUBLE SOVEREIGN

As with the Sovereign series Five Pound coins, those listed under this heading bear the Pistrucci St George and Dragon reverse, except where otherwise stated, and are minted in gold. They are, and always have been, legal tender at £2, and have a diameter indentical to that of the base metal Two Pound coins listed further below under a different heading. The denomination does not appear on Double Sovereigns. Most were originally issued as part of Royal Mint sets.

DATE	Mintage	UNC
1980 Proof	10,000	£550
1982 Proof	2,500	£550
1983 Proof	12,500	£550
1985 New Portrait Proof	5,849	£550
1987 Proof	14,301	£550
1988 Proof	12,743	£550
1989 500th Anniversary of the Sovereign. Enthroned portrayal obverse and Crowned shield reverse Proof	2,000	£850
1990 Proof	4,374	£550
1991 Proof	3,108	£550
1992 Proof	2,608	£550
1993 Proof	2,155	£550
1996 Proof	3,167	£550
1998 New Portrait Proof	4,500	£550
2000 Proof	2,250	£550
2002 Shield reverse Proof	8,000	£550
2003 Proof	2,250	£550
2004 Proof	2,500	£550
2005 Noad's heraldic St George and Dragon reverse Proof	—	£650
2006 Proof	—	£550
2007 Proof	—	£550
2008 Proof	—	£550
2009 Proof	—	£550
2010 Proof	2,750	£550
2011 Proof	2,950	£550
2012 Day's styllsed St George and Dragon reverse, BU	60	£600
2012 — Proof	1,945	£750
2013 BU	—	£650
2013 Proof	1,895	£650
2014 BU	1,300	£550
2014 Proof	—	£650
2015 Proof	1,100	£650
2015 New Portrait by Jody Clark Proof	1,100	£750
2016 Butler Portrait Proof	925	£750
2017 200th Anniv. of the Sovereign design as 1817 issue	1,200	£850

Standard reverse

Reverse by Timothy Noad.

Reverse by Paul Day

ABBREVIATIONS COMMONLY USED TO DENOTE METALLIC COMPOSITION

Cu	Copper
Cu/Steel	Copper plated steel
Ag/Cu	Silver plated copper
Ae	Bronze
Cu-Ni	Cupro-nickel
Ni-Ag	Nickel silver (note—does not contain silver)
Brass/Cu-Ni	Brass outer, cupro-nickel inner
Ni-Brass	Nickel-brass
Ag	Silver
Au/Ag	Gold plated silver
Au	Gold
Pl	Platinum

TWO POUNDS

This series commenced in 1986 with nickel-brass commemorative coins, with their associated base metal and precious metal BU and proof coins. From 1997 (actually issued in 1998) a thinner bi-metal version commenced with a reverse theme of the advance of technology, and from this date the coin was specifically intended to circulate. This is true also for the parallel issues of anniversary and commemorative Two Pound issues in 1999 and onwards. All have their BU and proof versions, as listed below.

In the case of Gold Proofs, a few have Certificates of Authenticity and/or green boxes of issue describing the coin as a Double Sovereign. All Gold Proofs since 1997 are of bi-metallic gold except for 2001 (red gold with the inner circle coated in yellow gold) and 2002 (Technology issue, uncoated red gold).

A new definitive design was introduced during 2015 incorporating the Jody Clark portrait and Britannia by Antony Dufort

NOTE: The counterfeiting of circulation £2 coins has been around for several years but 2015 saw several proof-like base metal designs. Five types are known at present: 2011 (Mary Rose) and 2015 (all four designs).

DATE	Mintage	UNC
1986 Commonwealth Games......................................	8,212,184	£4
1986 — BU..	—	£8
1986 — Proof...	59,779	£15
1986 — Silver BU..	—	£25
1986 — — Proof..	—	£35
1986 — Gold Proof..	—	£525
1989 Tercentenary of Bill of Rights.	4,392,825	£8
1989 — BU (issued in folder with Claim of Right)	—	£25
1989 — BU folder..	—	£8
1989 — Proof...	—	£15
1989 — Silver Proof	—	£35
1989 — — — Piedfort..	—	£50
1989 Tercentenary of Claim of Right (issued in Scotland)	381,400	£15
1989 — BU (see above)..	—	£15
1989 — Proof...	—	£25
1989 — Silver Proof	—	£35
1989 — — — Piedfort..	—	£50
1994 Tercentenary of the Bank of England	1,443,116	£5
1994 — BU...	—	£8
1994 — Proof...	—	£12
1994 — Silver Proof	27,957	£35
1994 — — — Piedfort..	9,569	£60
1994 — Gold Proof..	—	£550
1994 — — — with Double Sovereign obverse (no denomination)	—	£900
1995 50th Anniversary of End of WWII.	4,394,566	£5
1995 — BU...	—	£8
1995 — Proof...	—	£12
1995 — Silver Proof	35,751	£35
1995 — — — Piedfort..	—	£60
1995 — Gold Proof..	—	£525
1995 50th Anniversary of The United Nations.............	1,668,575	£6
1995 — BU...	—	£9
1995 — Proof...	—	£12
1995 — Silver Proof	—	£40
1995 — — — Piedfort..	—	£60
1995 — Gold Proof..	—	£525
1996 European Football Championships.	5,195,350	£6
1996 — BU	—	£8
1996 — Proof...	—	£10
1996 — Silver Proof	25,163	£40
1996 — — — Piedfort..	7,634	£60
1996 — Gold Proof..	—	£525
1997 First Bi-metallic issue	13,734,625	£4
1997 BU	—	£8
1997 Proof	—	£12
1997 Silver Proof..	29,910	£35
1997 — — Piedfort..	16,000	£60
1997 Gold Proof (red (outer) and yellow (inner) 22ct)..	—	£525

DATE	Mintage	UNC
1998 **New Portrait by Ian Rank-Broadley**	—	£3
1998 BU	91,110,375	£8
1998 Proof	—	£12
1998 Silver Proof	19,978	£35
1998 — — Piedfort	7,646	£60
1999	33,719,000	£3
1999 Rugby World Cup	4,933,000	£6
1999 — BU	—	£10
1999 — Silver Proof (gold plated ring)	9,665	£45
1999 — — — Piedfort (Hologram)	10,000	£85
1999 — Gold Proof	—	£525
2000	25,770,000	£3
2000 BU	—	£6
2000 Proof	—	£10
2000 Silver Proof	—	£40
2001	34,984,750	£3
2001 BU	—	£4
2001 Proof	—	£10
2001 Marconi	4,558,000	£4
2001 — BU	—	£8
2001 — Proof	—	£10
2001 — Silver Proof (gold plated ring)	11,488	£40
2001 — — Reverse Frosting (issued in set with Canada $5)	—	£65
2001 — — — Piedfort	6,759	£60
2001 — Gold Proof	—	£525
2002	13,024,750	£3
2002 BU	—	£6
2002 Proof	—	£10
2002 Gold Proof (red 22ct)	—	£525
2002 Commonwealth Games, Scotland	771,750	£8
2002 — Wales	558,500	£8
2002 — Northern Ireland	485,500	£8
2002 — England	650,500	£8
2002 — BU (issued in set of 4)	—	£50
2002 — Proof (issued in set of 4)	—	£75
2002 — Silver Proof (issued in set of 4)	—	£150
2002 — — — Piedfort (painted) (issued in set of 4)	—	£275
2002 — Gold Proof (issued in set of 4)	—	£2300
2003	17,531,250	£4
2003 BU	—	£8
2003 Proof	—	£12
2003 DNA Double Helix	4,299,000	£4
2003 — BU	41,568	£8
2003 — Proof	—	£10
2003 — Silver Proof (Gold plated ring)	11,204	£40
2003 — — — Piedfort	8,728	£60
2003 — Gold Proof	3,237	£525
2004	11,981,500	£3
2004 BU	—	£6
2004 Proof	—	£12
2004 Trevithick Steam Locomotive	5,004,500	£4
2004 — BU	56,871	£8
2004 — Proof	—	£10
2004 — Silver BU	1,923	£25
2004 — — Proof (Gold-plated ring)	10,233	£45
2004 — — — Piedfort	5,303	£60
2004 — Gold Proof	1,500	£525
2005	3,837,250	£3
2005 BU	—	£6
2005 Proof	—	£8
2005 Gunpowder Plot	5,140,500	£4
2005 — BU	—	£8
2005 — Proof	—	£10
2005 — Silver Proof	4,394	£40
2005 — — — Piedfort	4,585	£65
2005 — Gold Proof	914	£525

DATE	Mintage	UNC
2005 End of World War II....................................	10,191,000	£4
2005 — BU..	—	£8
2005 — Silver Proof	21,734	£40
2005 — — — Piedfort..	4,798	£65
2005 — Gold Proof..	2,924	£525
2006	16,715,000	£3
2006 Proof	—	£6
2006 Brunel, The Man (Portrait)	7,928,250	£4
2006 — BU..	—	£6
2006 — Proof	—	£10
2006 — Silver Proof	7,251	£40
2006 — — — Piedfort..	3,199	£65
2006 —Gold Proof..	1,071	£525
2006 Brunel, His Achievements (Paddington Station)	7,452,250	£4
2006 — BU..	—	£6
2006 — Proof	—	£10
2006 — Silver Proof	5,375	£40
2006 — — — Piedfort..	3,018	£65
2006 —Gold Proof..	746	£525
2007	10,270,000	£3
2007 Proof	—	£8
2007 Tercentenary of the Act of Union......................	7,545,000	£4
2007 BU	—	£6
2007 — Proof	—	£8
2007 — Silver Proof	8,310	£45
2007 — — — Piedfort..	4,000	£65
2007 — Gold Proof..	750	£525
2007 Bicentenary of the Abolition of the Slave Trade .	8,445,000	£4
2007 — BU..	—	£6
2007 — Proof	—	£10
2007 — Silver Proof	7,095	£45
2007 — — — Piedfort..	3,990	£65
2007 — Gold Proof..	1,000	£500
2008...	15,346,000	£3
2008 BU	—	£6
2008 Proof	—	£12
2008 Centenary of 4th Olympiad, London	910,000	£4
2008 — BU..	—	£6
2008 — Proof	—	£12
2008 — Silver Proof	6,841	£45
2008 — — — Piedfort..	1,619	£70
2008 — Gold Proof..	1,908	£500
2008 Olympic Games Handover Ceremony................	853,000	£4
2008 — BU..	47,765	£7
2008 — Silver Proof	30,000	£45
2008 — — — Piedfort..	3,000	£75
2008 — Gold Proof..	3,250	£500
2009	8,775,000	£3
2009 BU	—	£4
2009 Proof	—	£10
2009 Silver Proof...	—	£45
2009 250th Anniversary of birth of Robert Burns........	3,253,000	£3
2009 — BU..	120,223	£8
2009 — Proof	—	£12
2009 — Silver Proof	9,188	£45
2009 — — — Piedfort..	3,500	£70
2009 — Gold Proof..	1,000	£500
2009 200th Anniversary of birth of Charles Darwin.....	3,903,000	£3
2009 — BU..	119,713	£8
2009 — Proof	—	£12
2009 — Silver Proof	9,357	£45
2009 — — — Piedfort..	3,282	£70
2009 Gold Proof	1,000	£500
2010...	6,890,000	£3
2010 BU	—	£8
2010 Proof..	—	£12

DATE	Mintage	UNC
2010 Silver Proof	—	£40
2010 Florence Nightingale 150 Years of Nursing	6,175,000	£4
2010 — BU	73,160	£10
2010 — Proof	—	£12
2010 — Silver Proof	5,117	£45
2010 — — Piedfort	2,770	£70
2010 — Gold Proof	472	£500
2011	24,375,000	£4
2011 BU	—	£5
2011 Proof	—	£12
2011 Silver Proof	—	£35
2011 500th Anniversary of the Mary Rose	1,040,000	£6
2011 — BU	53,013	£9
2011 — Proof	—	£12
2011 — Silver Proof	6,618	£45
2011 — — Piedfort	2,680	£75
2011 — Gold Proof	692	£500
2011 400th Anniversary of the King James Bible	975,000	£6
2011 — BU	56,268	£9
2011 — Proof	—	£15
2011 — Silver Proof	4,494	£45
2011 — — Piedfort	2,394	£75
2011 — Gold Proof	355	£500
2012	3,900,000	£3
2012 BU	—	£6
2012 Proof	—	£12
2012 Silver Proof	—	£30
2012 Gold Proof	—	£550
2012 200th Anniversary of birth of Charles Dickens	8,190,000	£4
2012 — BU	15,035	£9
2012 — Proof	—	£12
2012 — Silver Proof	2,631	£45
2012 — — Piedfort	1,279	£75
2012 — Gold Proof	202	£500
2012 Olympic Handover to Rio	845,000	£8
2012 — BU	28,356	£15
2012 — Silver Proof	3,781	£50
2012 — — Piedfort	2,000	£100
2012 — Gold Proof	771	£500
2013	15,000,280	£3
2013 BU	—	£6
2013 Proof	—	£12
2013 Silver Proof	—	£65
2013 Gold Proof	—	£550
2013 150th Anniversary of the London Underground, Roundel design	1,560,000	£6
2013 — BU	11,647	£12
2013 — Proof	—	£18
2013 — Silver Proof	3,389	£50
2013 — — Piedfort	162	£100
2013 — Gold Proof	132	£550
2013 150th Anniversary of the London Underground, Train design	1,690,000	£6
2013 — BU	11,647	£12
2013 — Proof	—	£18
2013 — Silver Proof	4,246	£50
2013 — — Piedfort	186	£100
2013 — Gold Proof	140	£550
2013 350th Anniversary of the Guinea	2,990,000	£5
2013 — BU	10,340	£10
2013 — Proof	—	£15
2013 — Silver Proof	1,640	£50
2013 — — Piedfort	969	£100
2013 — Gold Proof	284	£600
2014	18,200,000	£5
2014 BU	—	£10

DATE	Mintage	UNC
2014 Proof..	—	£25
2014 Silver Proof..	—	£55
2014 100th Anniversary of First World War Outbreak.	5,720,000	£4
2014 — BU...	—	£10
2014 — Proof	—	£20
2014 — Silver Proof	—	£50
2014 — — — Piedfort..	—	£100
2014 — Gold Proof...	—	£750
2014 500th Anniversary of Trinity House.....................	3,705,000	£4
2014 — BU...	—	£10
2014 — Proof	—	£20
2014 — Silver Proof	—	£50
2014 — — — Piedfort..	—	£100
2014 — Gold Proof...	—	£750
2015	35,360,058	£3
2015 BU	—	£10
2015 Proof..	—	£20
2015 Silver Proof..	—	£50
2015 Gold Proof	—	£750
2015 Anniversary of First World War — Royal Navy	650,000	£6
2015 — BU...	—	£10
2015 — Proof	—	£20
2015 — Silver Proof	—	£50
2015 — — — Piedfort..	—	£100
2015 — Gold Proof...	—	£750
2015 800th Anniversary of Magna Carta......................	1,495,000	£5
2015 — BU...	—	£10
2015 — Proof	—	£20
2015 — Silver Proof	—	£50
2015 — — — Piedfort..	—	£100
2015 — Gold Proof...	—	£695
New Portrait by Jody Clark		
2015 — Silver Proof	—	£50
2015 — — — Piedfort..	—	£100
2015 — Gold Proof...	—	£695
2015 Britannia	650,000	£6
2015 — BU...	—	£10
2015 — Proof	—	£20
2015 — Silver Proof	—	£50
2015 — Gold Proof...	—	£750
2015 — Platinum Proof	—	£900
2016...	2,925,000	£3
2016 BU	—	£10
2016 Proof..	—	£20
2016 Silver Proof..	—	£50
2016 400th Anniversary, Shakespeare"s death, Comedies	4,355,000	£3
2016 — — BU...	—	£10
2016 — — Proof...	—	£20
2016 — — Silver Proof..	—	£50
2016 — — — — Piedfort...	—	£125
2016 — — Gold Proof...	—	£750
2016 — Tragedies	5,695,000	£3
2016 — — BU	—	£10
2016 — — Proof...	—	£20
2016 — — Silver Proof	—	£50
2016 — — — — Piedfort...	—	£125
2016 — — Gold Proof...	—	£750
2016 — Histories..	4,615,000	£3
2016 — — BU	—	£10
2016 — — Proof...	—	£20
2016 — — Silver Proof	—	£50
2016 — — — — Piedfort...	—	£125
2016 — — Gold Proof...	—	£750

DATE	Mintage	UNC
2016 350th Anniversary of Great Fire of London	5,135,000	£3
2016 — BU..	—	£10
2016 — Proof...	—	£20
2016 — Silver Proof	—	£50
2016 — — — Piedfort...	—	£125
2016 — Gold Proof..	800	£750
2016 Anniversary of First World War—Army	9,550,000	£3
2016 — BU..	—	£10
2016 — Proof...	—	£20
2016 — Silver Proof	—	£50
2016 — — — Piedfort...	—	£125
2016 — Gold Proof..	—	£750
2017 Anniversary of First World War—Aviation...........	—	£3
2017 — BU..	—	£10
2017 — Proof...	—	£20
2017 — Silver Proof	7,000	£75
2017 — — — Piedfort...	3,500	£125
20177 — Gold Proof..	634	£750
2017 Jane Austen..	—	£3
2017 — BU..	—	£10
2017 — Proof...	—	£20
2017 — Silver Proof	8,000	£75
201/ — — — Piedfort...	4,000	£125
2017 — Gold Proof..	884	£850

Note: The silver editions are silver centres with silver outers plated with gold. The gold issues are 22ct yellow gold centres with 22ct red gold outers.

As well as a new £2 coin to mark the 200th anniversary of the death of Jane Austen, a new £10 was also issued in 2017. Bank of England Chief Cashier Victoria Cleland with the Lord Mayor, Chancellor David McLean, the 818th Mayor of Winchester and the newly unveiled £10 Jane Austen note.

SOVEREIGN

All are minted in gold, bear the Pistrucci St George and Dragon reverse except where stated, and are legal tender at one pound. From 2009 there is no streamer behind St George's Helmet in the Pistrucci design.

DATE	Mintage	UNC
1974	5,002,566	£300
1976	4,150,000	£300
1976 Brilliant Proof	—	£10,000
1978	6,550,000	£300
1979	9,100,000	£280
1979 Proof	50,000	£300
1980	5,100,000	£280
1980 Proof	91,200	£350
1981	5,000,000	£280
1981 Proof	32,960	£350
1982	2,950,000	£300
1982 Proof	22,500	£350
1983 Proof	21,250	£350
1984 Proof	19,975	£350
1985 **New portrait** Proof	17,242	£400
1986 Proof	17,579	£350
1987 Proof	22,479	£350
1988 Proof	18,862	£350
1989 500th Anniversary of the Sovereign—details as Five Pounds (Sov. Series). Proof	23,471	£1000
1990 Proof	8,425	£400
1991 Proof	7,201	£400
1992 Proof	6,854	£400
1993 Proof	6,090	£400
1994 Proof	7,165	£405
1995 Proof	9,500	£400
1996 Proof	9,110	£400
1997 Proof	9,177	£400
1998 **New Portrait** Proof	11,349	£450
1999 Proof	11,903	£400
2000 (first Unc issue since 1982)	129,069	£350
2000 Proof	12,159	£450
2001	49,462	£300
2001 Proof	10,000	£450
2002 Golden Jubile Shield Rev. ("bullion")	74,263	£350
2002 Proof	20,500	£550
2003 ("bullion")	43,208	£350
2003 Proof	12,433	£450
2004 ("bullion")	30,688	£300
2004 Proof	10,175	£400
2005 Noad heraldic St George and Dragon	75,542	£450
2005 — Proof	12,500	£550
2006 ("bullion")	—	£350
2006 Proof	9,195	£450

Standard reverse

500th Anniversary reverse

Golden Jubilee Shield reverse

Noad modern reverse

IMPORTANT NOTE:

The prices quoted in this guide are set at August 2017 with the price of gold at £1000 per ounce and silver £13 per ounce—market fluctuations can have a marked effect on the values of modern precious metal coins.

DATE	Mintage	UNC
2007 ("bullion")	75,000	£350
2007 Proof	8,199	£450
2008 ("bullion")	35,000	£350
2008 Proof..	12,500	£450
2009 ("bullion")	75,000	£350
2009 Proof..	9,770	£400
2010 ("bullion")	243,986	£300
2010 Proof..	8,828	£450
2011 ("bullion")	250,000	£300
2011 Proof..	15,000	£300
2012 Day's St George and Dragon BU "bullion".........	250,000	£400
2012 — Proof	5,501	£750
2013 BU "bullion"...	2,695	£300
2013 Proof..	8,243	£450

Day's stylised reverse.

DATE	Mintage	UNC
2013 With "I" mintmark, minted by MMTC-PAMP, Haryana, India, under Licence from, and the supervision of, the Royal Mint......	—	£375
2014 BU "bullion"..	15,000	£300
2014 Proof..	9,725	£450
2014 BU "bullion" with "I" mintmark	—	£375
2015 BU "bullion"..	10,000	£350
2015 Proof..	9,800	£450
2015 **New Portrait** by Jody Clark BU.......................	10,000	£325
2015— Proof	8,800	£450
2016 BU "bullion"..	1,500	£300
2016 90th Birthday Butler portrait Proof	9,675	£500
2017 200th Anniversary of the Sovereign. Original 1817 "garter" design. Proof-like	1,817	—
2017 — Piedfort	3,750	—
2017 — With 200 Privy mark...................................	—	—

200th Anniversary reverse

HALF SOVEREIGN

Legal Tender at 50 pence, otherwise the notes for the Sovereign apply. From 2009 the exergue in the Pistrucci design is larger in area, and the initials B.P. are absent. From 2011, however, the initials were restored.

Standard reverse

DATE	Mintage	UNC
1980 Proof only	86,700	£200
1982	2,500,000	£150
1982 Proof..	21,590	£200
1983 Proof	19,710	£200
1984 Proof	19,505	£200
1985 New portrait Proof	15,800	£200
1986 Proof	17,075	£200
1987 Proof	20,687	£200
1988 Proof	18,266	£200
1989 500th Anniversary of the Sovereign—details as Five Pounds (Sov. Series) Proof............................	21,824	£500
1990 Proof	7,889	£250
1991 Proof	6,076	£250
1992 Proof	5,915	£235
1993 Proof	4,651	£235
1994 Proof	7,167	£235
1995 Proof	7,500	£235
1996 New Portrait Proof	7,340	£250
1997 Proof	9,177	£235
1998 Proof	7,496	£235
1999 Proof	9,403	£235
2000...	146,822	£135
2000 Proof	9,708	£200
2001	98,763	£150
2001 Proof	7,500	£200

500th Anniversary reverse

Noad Heraldic reverse

DATE	Mintage	UNC
2002 Golden Jubilee Shield reverse ("bullion")	61,347	£175
2002 Proof	—	£200
2003 ("bullion")	47,805	£150
2003 Proof	—	£200
2004 ("bullion")	32,479	£135
2004 Proof	—	£200
2005 Noad heraldic St George and Dragon	—	£250
2005 — Proof	—	£285
2006 ("bullion")	—	£135
2006 Proof	—	£200
2006 ("bullion")	—	£135
2007 Proof	—	£200
2008 ("bullion")	—	£135
2008 Proof	—	£200
2009 ("bullion")	—	£135
2009 Proof	—	£200
2010 ("bullion")	16,485	£135
2010 Proof	—	£200
2011 ("bullion")	—	£135
2011 Proof	—	£200
2012 Diamond Jubilee "bullion" or BU	—	£200
2012 — Proof	—	£250
2013 BU "bullion"	—	£135
2013 Proof	—	£250
2014 BU "bullion"	—	£150
2014 Proof	—	£250
2014 BU "bullion" with "I" mintmark	—	£200
2015 BU "bullion"	—	£135
2015 Proof	—	£250
2015 New portrait Proof	—	£250
2016 BU "bullion"	—	£135
2016 90th Birthday Butler portrait Proof	—	£250
2017 200th Anniversary of the Sovereign. Original 1817 "garter" design. Proof-like	1,817	—
2017 — With 200 Privy mark	—	—

Golden Jubilee Shield reverse

Diamond Jubilee reverse.

200th Anniversary reverse

QUARTER SOVEREIGN

Minted in 22ct Gold, this new denomination was introduced in 2009, and follows on from two different patterns of 1853.

DATE	Mintage	UNC
2009 ("bullion")	50,000	£100
2009 Proof	13,495	£125
2010 ("bullion")	250,000	£100
2010 Proof	6,007	£125
2011 ("bullion")	50,000	£100
2011 Proof	7,764	£125
2012 Diamond Jubilee "bullion"	250,000	£150
2012 — Proof	7,579	£200
2013 ("bullion")	—	£100
2013 Proof	1,729	£100
2014 ("bullion")	—	£100
2014 Proof	1,696	£125
2015 ("bullion")	4,600	£100
2015 Jody Clark bust Proof	—	£125
2016 Butler Portrait Proof	4,575	£175
2017 200th Anniversary Proof	5,100	£175

ONE POUND

Introduced into circulation in 1983 to replace the £1 note, all are minted in nickel-brass unless otherwise stated. The reverse changed yearly until 2008, and until 2008 the Royal Arms was the "definitive" version. 2008 also saw the introduction of the Matthew Dent Uncrowned Shield of the Royal Arms, a new "definitive", and this reverse appeared in 2008 and every year since then. A Capital Cities Series of two coins each year for two years commenced in 2010. From 2013 a further 4-coin series over two years was issued, portraying two floral emblems associated with each of the four countries making up the United Kingdom. Collectors and others should be aware of the many different counterfeit £1 coin versions in circulation, a high proportion of which do not have matching obverses and reverses although many do.

A 12-sided bi-metallic coin replaced the round £1 coin in 2017 which incorporates several security features to help defeat the counterfeiters.

1983, 1993, 1998, 2003
EDGE: *DECUS ET TUTAMEN*

DATE	Mintage	UNC
1983 Royal Arms	443,053,510	£3
1983 — BU	1,134,000	£5
1983 — Proof	107,800	£8
1983 — Silver Proof	50,000	£32
1983 — — — Piedfort	10,000	£85
1984 Scottish Thistle	146,256,501	£3
1984 — BU	199,430	£6
1984 — Proof	106,520	£8
1984 — Silver Proof	44,855	£35
1984 — — — Piedfort	15,000	£50
1985 *New portrait.* Welsh Leek	228,430,749	£3
1985 — BU	213,679	£5
1985 — Proof	102,015	£6
1985 — Silver Proof	50,000	£35
1985 — — — Piedfort	15,000	£50
1986 Northern Ireland Flax	10,409,501	£3
1986 — BU	—	£6
1986 — Proof	—	£7
1986 — Silver Proof	37,958	£35
1986 — — — Piedfort	15,000	£50
1987 English Oak	39,298,502	£3
1987 — BU	—	£5
1987 — Proof	—	£8
1987 — Silver Proof	50,000	£35
1987 — — — Piedfort	15,000	£50
1988 Crowned Shield Of The Royal Arms	7,118,825	£4
1988 — BU	—	£6
1988 — Proof	—	£8
1988 — Silver Proof	50,000	£35
1988 — — — Piedfort	10,000	£60
1989 Scottish Thistle	70,580,501	£4
1989 — BU	—	£6
1989 — Proof	—	£9
1989 — Silver Proof	22,275	£35
1989 — — — Piedfort	10,000	£50
1990 Welsh Leek	—	£4
1990 — BU	97,269,302	£6
1990 — Proof	—	£7
1990 — Silver Proof	23,277	£35
1991 Northern Ireland Flax	38,443,575	£3
1991 — BU	—	£6
1991 — Proof	—	£9
1991 — Silver Proof	22,922	£35
1992 English Oak	36,320,487	£2
1992 — BU	—	£6
1992 — Proof	—	£7
1992 — Silver Proof	13,065	£35
1993 Royal Arms	114,744,500	£3
1993 — BU	—	£6

1984, 1989
NEMO ME IMPUNE LACESSIT

1985, 1990
PLEIDIOL WYF I'M GWLAD

1986, 1991
DECUS ET TUTAMEN

1987, 1992
DECUS ET TUTAMEN

DATE	Mintage	UNC
1993 — Proof	—	£7
1993 — Silver Proof	16,526	£35
1993 — — Piedfort	12,500	£55
1994 Scottish Lion	29,752,525	£4
1994 — BU	—	£6
1994 — Proof	—	£8
1994 — Silver Proof	25,000	£35
1994 — — Piedfort	11,722	£55
1995 Welsh Dragon	34,503,501	£3
1995 — BU	—	£6
1995 — — (Welsh)	—	£7
1995 — Proof	—	£10
1995 — Silver Proof	27,445	£35
1995 — — Piedfort	8,458	£65
1996 Northern Ireland Celtic Cross	89,886,000	£4
1996 — BU	—	£6
1996 — Proof	—	£7
1996 — Silver Proof	25,000	£35
1996 — — Piedfort	10,000	£55
1997 English Lions	57,117,450	£4
1997 — BU	—	£6
1997 — Proof	—	£7
1997 — Silver Proof	20,137	£35
1997 — — Piedfort	10,000	£55
1998 **New portrait.** Royal Arms. BU	—	£12
1998 — Proof	—	£15
1998 — Silver Proof	13,863	£35
1998 — — Piedfort	7,894	£50
1999 Scottish Lion. BU	—	£12
1999 — Proof	—	£15
1999 — Silver Proof	16,328	£35
1999 — — — Reverse Frosting	—	£45
1999 — — — Piedfort	9,975	£60
2000 Welsh Dragon	109,496,500	£3
2000 — BU	—	£6
2000 — Proof	—	£8
2000 — Silver Proof	15,913	£35
2000 — — Reverse Frosting	—	£45
2000 — — Piedfort	9,994	£55
2001 Northern Ireland Celtic Cross	63,968,065	£3
2001 — BU	58,093,731	£6
2001 — Proof	—	£8
2001 — Silver Proof	11,697	£35
2001 — — Reverse Frosting	—	£45
2001 — — Piedfort	8,464	£50
2002 English Lions	77,818,000	£3
2002 — BU	—	£5
2002 — Proof	—	£8
2002 — Silver Proof	17,693	£35
2002 — — Reverse Frosting	—	£45
2002 — — Piedfort	6,599	£50
2002 — Gold Proof	—	£425
2003 Royal Arms	61,596,500	£4
2003 — BU	23,760	£6
2003 — Proof	—	£10
2003 — Silver Proof	15,830	£35
2003 — — Piedfort	9,871	£50
2004 Forth Railway Bridge	39,162,000	£4
2004 — BU	24,014	£6
2004 — Proof	—	£10
2004 — Silver Proof	11,470	£35
2004 — — Piedfort	7,013	£50
2004 — Gold Proof	—	£425
2005 Menai Bridge	99,429,500	£4
2005 — BU	—	£6
2005 — Proof	—	£10
2005 — Silver Proof	8,371	£35

1988
DECUS ET TUTAMEN

1994, 1999
NEMO ME IMPUNE LACESSIT

1995, 2000
PLEIDIOL WYF I'M GWLAD

1996, 2001
DECUS ET TUTAMEN

1997, 2002
DECUS ET TUTAMEN

2004
PATTERNED EDGE

DATE	Mintage	UNC
2005 — — — Piedfort	6,007	£50
2005 — Gold Proof	—	£425
2006 Egyptian Arch	38,938,000	£4
2006 — BU	—	£6
2006 — Proof	—	£10
2006 — Silver Proof	14,765	£35
2006 — — Piedfort	5,129	£50
2006 — Gold Proof	—	£425
2007 Gateshead Millennium Bridge	26,180,160	£4
2007 — BU	—	£6
2007 — Proof	—	£10
2007 — Silver Proof	10,110	£40
2007 — — — Piedfort	5,739	£50
2007 — Gold Proof	—	£425
2008 Royal Arms	3,910,000	£4
2008 — BU	18,336	£6
2008 — Proof	—	£8
2008 — Silver Proof	8,441	£35
2008 — Gold Proof	674	£425
2008 — Platinum Proof	—	£500
2008 A series of 14 different reverses, the 25th Anniversary of the modern £1 coin, Silver Proof with selected gold highlighting on the reverses. the latter being all those used since 1983, the coins being with appropriate edge lettering	—	£400
2008 The same as above, Gold Proof (the 2008 Royal Arms being already listed above)	150	£5800
2008 **New Rev.,** Shield of the Royal Arms, no border beads on Obv	29,518,000	£3
2008 BU	—	£5
2008 Proof	—	£6
2008 Silver Proof	5,000	£35
2008 Silver Proof Piedfort	2,456	£55
2008 Gold Proof	860	£450
2008 Platinum Proof	—	£575
2009	7,820,000	£4
2009 BU	130,644	£5
2009 Proof	—	£6
2009 Silver Proof	8,508	£35
2009 Gold Proof	540	£595
2010	38,505,000	£4
2010 BU	—	£5
2010 Proof	—	£6
2010 Silver BU	—	£30
2010 — Proof	—	£40
2010 City Series (London)	2,635,000	£4
2010 — BU	66,313	£5
2010 — Proof	—	£6
2010 — Silver Proof	7,693	£40
2010 — — — Piedfort	3,682	£55
2010 — Gold Proof	950	£450
2010 City Series (Belfast)	6,205,000	£3
2010 — BU	64,461	£5
2010 — Proof	—	£6
2010 — Silver Proof	5,805	£40
2010 — — — Piedfort	3,503	£55
2010 — Gold Proof	585	£500
2011	25,415,000	£2
2011 BU	—	£3
2011 Proof	—	£8
2011 Silver BU (in 21st and 18th Birthday cards)	—	£45
2011 — Proof	—	£55
2011 City Series (Cardiff)	1,615,000	£4

2005
PATTERNED EDGE

2006
PATTERNED EDGE

2007
PATTERNED EDGE

2008 (proof sets—silver and gold)
DECUS ET TUTAMEN

2008, 2009, 2010, 2011
DECUS ET TUTAMEN

2011
Y DDRAIG GOCH DDYRY CYCHWYN

DATE	Mintage	UNC
2011 — BU	47,933	£5
2011 — Proof	—	£7
2011 — Silver Proof	5,553	£40
2011 — — — Piedfort	1,615	£60
2011 — Gold Proof	524	£500
2011 City Series (Edinburgh)	935,000	£4
2011 — BU	47,896	£5
2011 — Proof	—	£8
2011 — Silver Proof	4,973	£45
2011 — — — Piedfort	2,696	£60
2011 — Gold Proof	499	£500
2012	35,700,030	£3
2012 BU	—	£5
2012 Proof	—	£8
2012 Silver BU (in Silver Baby Gift)	—	£75
2012 Silver Proof	—	£50
2012 — with selective gold plating	—	£35
2012 Gold Proof	—	£450
2013	13,090,500	£3
2013 BU	—	£6
2013 Proof	—	£8
2013 Silver BU	—	£60
2013 Silver Proof	—	£45
2013 Gold Proof	—	£450
2013 Floral Series (England)	5,270,000	£3
2013 — BU	6112	£6
2013 — Proof	—	£10
2013 — Silver Proof	3,334	£45
2013 — — — Piedfort	1,071	£60
2013 — Gold Proof	284	£500
2013 Floral Series (Wales)	5,270,000	£3
2013 — BU	6112	£6
2013 — Proof	—	£10
2013 — Silver Proof	3,094	£45
2013 — — — Piedfort	860	£60
2013 — Gold Proof	274	£500
2013 Royal Coat of Arms (Sewell), Gold Proof	—	£500
2013 Crowned Royal Arms (Gorringe), Gold Proof	—	£500

(The above two coins are part of a set of three, along with the 2013 gold proof, with definitive reverse with Uncrowned Royal Arms (Dent)).

DATE	Mintage	UNC
2014	79,305,200	£3
2014 BU	—	£6
2014 Proof	—	£10
2014 Silver BU	—	£50
2014 Silver Proof	—	£55
2014 Floral Series (Scotland)	5,185,000	£3
2014 — BU	—	£6
2014 — Proof	—	£10
2014 — Silver Proof	—	£45
2014 — — — Piedfort	—	£60
2014 — Gold Proof	—	£850
2014 Floral Series (Northern Ireland)	5,780,000	£3
2014 — BU	—	£6
2014 — Proof	—	£10
2014 — Silver Proof	—	£45
2014 — — — Piedfort	—	£60
2014 — Gold Proof	—	£850
2015	29,580,000	£3
2015 BU	—	£6
2015 Proof	—	£10
2015 Silver Proof	—	£50
2015 Gold Proof	—	£450
2015 Platinum Proof	—	—

2011
NISI DOMINUS FRUSTRA

2013 Wales £1 Floral gold proof.

Most £1 coins are also available in precious metals

2014 Scotland £1 Floral gold proof.

2015

261

DATE	Mintage	UNC
2015 *New Portrait* BU............................	62,495,640	£3
2015 Proof...	—	£10
2015 Silver Proof....................................	—	£50
2015 Gold Proof.....................................	—	£450
2015 Platinum Proof...............................	—	£650
2015 Heraldic Royal Arms.......................	—	£3
2015 — BU..	—	£6
2015 — Silver Proof	—	£50
2015 — — Piedfort................................	—	£100
2015 — Gold Proof................................	—	£450
2016 BU	—	£4
2016 Proof...	—	£8
2016 Silver Proof	—	£45
2016 The Last Round Pound		
2016 — BU..	—	—
2016 — Proof...	—	—
2016 — Silver Proof	—	—
2016 — — Piedfort................................	—	—
2016 — Gold Proof................................	—	—
2016 **12-sided coin Nations of the Crown design**		
2016 BU	—	—
2017..	—	—
2017 BU	—	—
2017 Silver Proof...................................	26,000	—
2017 Silver Proof Piedfort	4,500	
2017 Gold Proof.....................................	2,951	
2017 Platinum Proof...............................	250	

2016 The last round pound

12-sided issue with Jody Clark portrait obverse and reverse by 15-year-old David Pearce

FIFTY PENCE

Introduced as legal tender for 10 shillings to replace the banknote of that value prior to decimalisation, coins of the original size are no longer legal tender. Unless otherwise stated, i.e. for commemoratives, the reverse design is of Britannia. The reverse legend of NEW PENCE became FIFTY PENCE from 1982.

The description of "Unc" has been used against some 50 pence pieces dated 2009 and 2011 (for Olympic and Paralympic sports) to distinguish them from coins minted to circulation standard and BU standard, being a standard between the latter two. The uncirculated standard coins have a more even rim than the circulation standard examples, particularly observable on the obverse.

Since the surge of interest in collecting 50p coins prices have increased. The following values are for uncirculated coins. Any found in change will of course have been circulated and will not command such a high premium but the rarer ones will still be worth more than face value.

DATE	Mintage	UNC
1969..	188,400,000	£6
1970..	19,461,500	£5
1971 Proof...	—	£8
1972 Proof...	—	£7
1973 Accession to EEC	89,775,000	£3
1973 — Proof	—	£5
1973 — Silver Proof Piedfort....................	About 24	£3000
1974 Proof...	—	£7
1975 Proof	—	£8
1976..	43,746,500	£5
1976 Proof...	—	£7
1977..	49,536,000	£5
1977 Proof	—	£6
1978..	72,005,000	£5
1978 Proof	—	£6

Accession to the EEC 1973.

DATE	Mintage	UNC
1979	58,680,000	£5
1979 Proof	—	£6
1980	89,086,000	£5
1980 Proof	—	£6
1981	74,002,000	£6
1981 Proof	—	£8
1982	51,312,000	£5
1982 Unc	—	£6
1982 Proof	—	£8
1983	62,824,000	£5
1983 Unc	—	£6
1983 Proof	—	£8
1984 BU	—	£6
1984 Proof	—	£8
1985 *New portrait*	682,103	£3
1985 BU	—	£5
1985 Proof	—	£6
1986 BU	—	£5
1986 Proof	—	£12
1987 BU	—	£4
1987 Proof	—	£12
1988 BU	—	£4
1988 Proof	—	£12
1989 BU	—	£4
1989 Proof	—	£12
1990 BU	—	£4
1990 Proof	—	£12
1991 BU	—	£5
1991 Proof	—	£12
1992 BU	—	£7
1992 Proof	—	£12
1992 Presidency of EC Council and EC accession 20th anniversary (includes 1993 date)	109,000	£18
1992 — BU	—	£18
1992 — Proof	—	£20
1992 — Silver Proof	26,890	£40
1992 — — — Piedfort	10,993	£55
1992 — Gold Proof	—	£500
1993 BU	—	£5
1993 Proof	—	£12
1994 50th Anniversary of the Normandy Landings	6,705,520	£3
1994 — BU (also in presentation folder)	—	£5
1994 — Proof	—	£12
1994 — Silver Proof	40,000	£35
1994 — — — Piedfort	10,000	£60
1994 — Gold Proof	—	£500
1995 BU	—	£8
1995 Proof	—	£12
1996 BU	—	£8
1996 Proof	—	£12
1996 Silver Proof	—	£25
1997 BU	—	£8
1997 Proof	—	£10
1997 Silver Proof	—	£25
1997 *New reduced size*	456,364,100	£4
1997 BU	—	£5
1997 Proof	—	£6
1997 Silver Proof	—	£25
1997 — — Piedfort	—	£35
1998 *New portrait*	64,306,500	£3
1998 BU	—	£5
1998 Proof	—	£8
1998 Presidency and 25th anniversary of EU entry	5,043,000	£4
1998 — BU	—	£5
1998 — Proof	—	£8
1998 — Silver Proof	8,859	£30
1998 — — — Piedfort	8,440	£45
1998 — Gold Proof	—	£450

Presidency of the EC Council 1992.

1994

1998 EU Presidency

1998 NHS

2000 Public Libraries

DATE	Mintage	UNC
1998 50th Anniversary of the National Health Service	5,001,000	£3
1998 — BU	—	£5
1998 — Silver Proof	9,032	£30
1998 — — — Piedfort	5,117	£45
1998 — Gold Proof	—	£450
1999	24,905,000	£2
1999 BU	—	£5
1999 Proof	—	£10
2000	27,915,500	£2
2000 BU	—	£5
2000 Proof	—	£7
2000 150th Anniversary of Public Libraries	11,263,000	£5
2000 — BU	—	£6
2000 — Proof	—	£9
2000 — Silver Proof	7,634	£30
2000 — — Piedfort	5,721	£45
2000 — Gold proof	—	£400
2001	84,998,500	£2
2001 BU	—	£5
2001 Proof	—	£7
2002	23,907,500	£2
2002 BU	—	£5
2002 Proof	—	£7
2002 Gold Proof	—	£375
2003	23,583,000	£2
2003 BU	—	£5
2003 Proof	—	£6
2003 Suffragette	3,124,030	£4
2003 — BU	9582	£6
2003 — Proof	—	£7
2003 — Silver Proof	6,267	£30
2003 — — — Piedfort	6,795	£45
2003 — Gold Proof	942	£350
2004	35,315,500	£1
2004 BU	—	£5
2004 Proof	—	£8
2004 Roger Bannister	9,032,500	£5
2004 — BU	10,371	£6
2004 — Proof	—	£8
2004 — Silver Proof	4,924	£30
2004 — — — Piedfort	4,054	£45
2004 — Gold Proof	644	£350
2005	25,363,500	£3
2005 BU	—	£6
2005 Proof	—	£8
2005 Samuel Johnson	17,649,000	£3
2005 — BU	—	£5
2005 — Proof	—	£8
2005 — Silver Proof	4,029	£30
2005 — — — Piedfort	3,808	£45
2005 — Gold Proof	—	£350
2006	24,567,000	£2
2006 Proof	—	£8
2006 Silver Proof	—	£30
2006 Victoria Cross, The Award	12,087,000	£3
2006 — BU	—	£5
2006 — Proof	—	£8
2006 — Silver Proof	6,310	£30
2006 — — — — Piedfort	3,532	£50
2006 — Gold Proof	866	£350
2006 Victoria Cross, Heroic Acts	10,000,500	£2
2006 — BU	—	£5
2006 — Proof	—	£8
2006 — Silver Proof	6,872	£30
2006 — — — Piedfort	3,415	£50
2006 — Gold Proof	804	£350
2007	11,200,000	£2
2007 BU	—	£6
2007 Proof	—	£8

2003 Suffragettes

2004 Roger Bannister

2005 Samuel Johnson

2006 Victoria Cross—the award

2007 Centenary of Scouting

2008 Shield design

DATE	Mintage	UNC
2007 Centenary of Scout Movement	7,710,750	£5
2007 — BU	—	£8
2007 — Proof	—	£12
2007 — Silver Proof	10,895	£30
2007 — — Piedfort	1,555	£65
2007 — Gold Proof	1,250	£400
2008	3,500,000	£2
2008 — BU	—	£5
2008 — Proof	—	£6
2008 — Silver Proof	—	£25
2008 — Gold Proof	—	£400
2008 — Platinum Proof	—	£1550
2008 **New Shield Rev.** Obv. rotated by approx. 26 degrees	22,747,000	£5
2008 BU	—	£6
2008 Proof	—	£8
2008 Silver Proof	—	£25
2008 Silver Proof Piedfort	—	£45
2008 Gold Proof	—	£400
2008 Platinum Proof	—	£1550
2009 BU	—	£4
2009 Proof	—	£6
2009 Silver Proof	—	£20
2009 250th Anniversary of Kew Gardens	210,000	£50
2009 — BU	128,364	£80
2009 — Proof	—	£100
2009 — Silver Proof	7,575	£135
2009 — — Piedfort	2,967	£150
2009 — Gold Proof	629	£500
2009 Olympic and Paralympic Sports (Track & Field Athletics) Unc (Blue Peter Pack)	—	£12
2009 16 different reverses from the past marking the 40th Anniversary of the 50p coln. Proof	1,039	£300
2009 — Silver Proof	1,163	£650
2009 — Gold Proof	70	£8000
2009 — — Piedfort	40	£20,950
2010 BU	—	£4
2010 Proof	—	£25
2010 Silver Proof	—	£35
2010 100 years of Girl Guiding UK	7,410,090	£2
2010 — BU	99,075	£7
2010 — Proof	—	£20
2010 — Silver Proof	5,271	£35
2010 — — Piedfort	2,879	£55
2010 — Gold Proof	355	£575
2011 BU	—	£2
2011 Proof	—	£8
2011 Silver Proof	—	£45
2011 50th Anniversary of the WWF	3,400,000	£2
2011 — BU	67,299	£5
2011 — Proof	—	£25

2009 Kew Gardens

2010 100 years of Guiding

2011 WWF Anniversary

2011 The rare Olympic Swimmer. For the rest of the Olympic series see overleaf and page 277.

DATE	Mintage	UNC
2011 — Silver Proof	24,870	£45
2011 — — Piedfort	2,244	£65
2011 — Gold Proof	243	£675
2011 Olympic & Paralympic Sports Issues:		
Aquatics Unc, head clear of lines	2,179,000	£2
— Head with lines BU (as illustrated)	—	£750
— Head clear of lines. BU	—	£4
— Silver BU	30,000	£25
Archery Unc	3,345,000	£2
— BU	—	£3
— Silver BU	30,000	£25
Athletics Unc	2,224,000	£2
— BU	—	£3
— Silver BU	30,000	£25
Badminton Unc	2,133,000	£2
— BU	—	£3
— Silver BU	30,000	£25
Basketball Unc	1,748,000	£2
— BU	—	£3
— Silver BU	30,000	£25
Boccia Unc	2,166,000	£2
— BU	—	£3
— Silver BU	30,000	£25
Boxing Unc	2,148,000	£2
— BU	—	£3
— Silver BU	30,000	£25
Canoeing Unc	2,166,000	£2
— BU	—	£3
— Silver BU	30,000	£25
Cycling Unc	2,090,000	£2
— BU	—	£3
— Silver BU	30,000	£25
Equestrian Unc	2,142,000	£2
— BU	—	£3
— Silver BU	30,000	£25
Fencing Unc	2,115,000	£2
— BU	—	£3
— Silver BU	30,000	£25
Football Unc	1,125,000	£10
— BU	—	£153
— Silver BU	30,000	£35
Goalball Unc	1,615,000	£8
— BU	—	£10
— Silver BU	30,000	£25
Gymnastics Unc	1,720,000	£1
— BU	—	£3
— Silver BU	30,000	£25
Handball Unc	1,676,000	£8
— BU	—	£10
— Silver BU	30,000	£30
Hockey Unc	1,773,000	£2
— BU	—	£3
— Silver BU	30,000	£25
Judo Unc	1,161,000	£10
— BU	—	£5
— Silver BU	30,000	£35
Modern Pentathlon Unc	1,689,000	£2
— BU	—	£3
— Silver BU	30,000	£25
Rowing Unc	1,717,000	£2
— BU	—	£3
— Silver BU	30,000	£25
Sailing Unc	1,749,000	£2
— BU	—	£3
— Silver BU	30,000	£25
Shooting Unc	1,656,000	£2
— BU	—	£3
— Silver BU	30,000	£25

DATE	Mintage	UNC
Table Tennis Unc	1,737,000	£2
— BU	—	£3
— Silver BU	30,000	£25
Taekwondo Unc	1,664,000	£2
— BU	—	£3
— Silver BU	30,000	£5
Tennis Unc	1,454,000	£8
— BU	—	£3
— Silver BU	30,000	£25
Triathlon Unc	1,163,000	£10
— BU	—	£15
— Silver BU	30,000	£30
Volleyball Unc	2,133,000	£2
— BU	—	£3
— Silver BU	30,000	£25
Weightlifting Unc	1,879,000	£2
— BU	—	£3
— Silver BU	30,000	£25
Wheelchair Rugby Unc	1,765,000	£2
— BU	—	£3
— Silver BU	30,000	£25
Wrestling Unc	1,129,000	£10
— BU	—	£5
— Silver BU	30,000	£35

For the remainder of the 29 coins in the 2011 Olympic and Paralympic series see page 277.

Note—Each of the artists of the 29 Olympic sports above was presented with a gold proof coin with their own design. The Track & Field Athletics design coin was dated 2009, the Cycling was dated 2010, and the remaining 2011. No other examples of these coins were issued.

	Mintage	UNC
2012	32,300,030	£2
2012 BU	—	£5
2012 Proof	—	£10
2012 Silver Proof with selective gold plating	—	£50
2012 Gold Proof	—	£500
2012 Gold Proof Piedfort. The 11 Olympic sports in which the United Kingdom Team GB achieved a Gold Medal was celebrated with an issue of 29 Piedfort coins for each sport, some in sets, some as individual coins (see under Proof and Specimen sets)	—	—
2013	10,301,000	£2
2013 BU	—	£5
2013 Proof	—	£10
2013 Silver Proof	—	£55
2013 Gold Proof	—	£450
2013 100th anniversary of birth of Christopher Ironside	7,000,000	£2
2013 — BU	4,403	£5
2013 — Proof	—	£12
2013 — Silver Proof	1,023	£45
2013 — — Piedfort	816	£90
2013 — Gold Proof	198	£450
2013 Centenary of the Birth of Benjamin Britten	5,300,000	£2
2013 — BU	—	£5
2013 — Silver Proof	717	£55
2013 — — Piedfort	515	£90
2013 — Gold Proof	70	£450
2014	49,001,000	£2
2014 BU	—	£5
2014 Proof	—	£12
2014 Silver Proof	—	£55
2014 XX Commonwealth Games	6,500,000	£2
2014 — BU	—	£5
2014 — Proof	—	£12
2014 — Silver Proof	—	£45
2014 — — Piedfort	—	£100
2014 — Gold Proof	—	£450
2015	20,101,000	£2
2015 BU	—	£5

2013 Christopher Ironside

2013 Benjamin Britten

2014 Commonwealth Games

DATE	Mintage	UNC
2015 Proof...	—	£10
2015 Silver Proof...................................	—	£30
2015 Gold Proof....................................	—	£350
2015 Platinum Proof..............................	—	—
2015 Battle of Britain 75th Anniversary BU................	5,900,000	£2
2015 — Proof	—	£12
2015 — Silver Proof	—	£30
2015 — — — Piedfort	—	£80
2015 — Gold Proof...............................	—	£350
2015 **New Portrait**.............................	—	£2
2015 BU	—	£5
2015 Proof..	—	£12
2015 Silver Proof.................................	—	£30
2015 Gold Proof..................................	—	£350
2015 Platinum Proof.............................	—	—
2016 BU	—	£4
2016 Proof..	—	£12
2016 Silver Proof.................................	—	£35

2015 Battle of Britain

2016 Battle of Hastings 950th Anniversary..................	6,100,000	£2
2016 — BU...	—	£5
2016 — Proof	—	£10
2016 — Silver Proof	—	£35
2016 — — — Piedfort	—	£150
2016 — Gold Proof...............................	—	£350
2016 Beatrix Potter 150th Anniversary.................	6,900,000	£2
2016 — BU...	—	£5
2016 — Proof	—	£10
2016 — Silver Proof	—	£35
2016 — — — Piedfort	2,500	£250
2016 — Gold Proof...............................	—	£400
2016 Beatrix Potter: Peter Rabbit	9,600,000	£4
2016 — BU...	—	£15
2016 — Silver Proof with coloured highlights	—	£50
2016 — — — Piedfort	—	£100
2016 Beatrix Potter: Jemima Puddle-Duck................	2,100,000	£3
2016 — BU...	—	£12
2016 — Silver Proof with coloured highlights	—	£75
2016 — — — Piedfort	—	£250
2016 Beatrix Potter: Mrs. Tiggy-Winkle	8,800,000	£3
2016 — BU...	—	£10
2016 — Silver Proof with coloured highlights	—	£50
2016 Beatrix Potter: Squirrel Nutkin..........................	5,000,000	£3
2016 — BU...	—	£10
2016 — Silver Proof with coloured highlights	—	£50
2016 Team GB for Olympics	6,400,000	£3
2016 — BU...	—	£10
2016 — Silver Proof	—	£25
2016 — — — Piedfort	—	£150
2016 — Gold Proof...............................	—	£400

2016 Beatrix Potter

2016 Peter Rabbit

2017 375th anniversary of Sir Isaac Newton's birth....	—	£2
2017 — BU...	—	£10
2017 — Proof	—	£15
2017 — Silver Proof	7,000	£50
2017 — — — Piedfort	4,500	£95
2017 — Gold Proof...............................	634	£760
2017 Beatrix Potter: Peter Rabbit	—	£4
2017 — BU...	—	£12
2017 — — Silver Proof with coloured highlights.........	40,000	£50
2017 Beatrix Potter: Mr. Jeremy Fisher......................	—	£4
2017 — BU...	—	£8
2017 — Silver Proof with coloured highlights	40,000	£50
2017 Beatrix Potter: Tom Kitten	—	£4
2017 — BU...	—	£8
2017 — Silver Proof with coloured highlights	40,000	£50
2017 Beatrix Potter: Benjamin Bunny	—	£4
2017 — BU...	—	£8
2017 — Silver Proof with coloured highlights	—	£50

2016 Team GB

2017 Isaac Newton

The four 2017 Beatric Potter 50p commemoratives

TWENTY-FIVE PENCE (CROWN)

This series is a continuation of the pre-decimal series, there having been four crowns to the pound. The coins below have a legal tender face value of 25p to this day, and are minted in cupro-nickel except where stated otherwise.

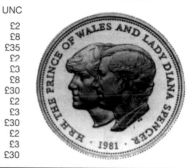

DATE	Mintage	UNC
1972 Royal Silver Wedding	7,452,100	£2
1972 — Proof	150,000	£8
1972 — Silver Proof	100,000	£35
1977 Silver Jubilee	37,061,160	£2
1977 — in Presentation folder	Incl. above	£3
1977 — Proof	193,000	£8
1977 — Silver Proof	377,000	£30
1980 Queen Mother 80th Birthday	9,306,000	£2
1980 — in Presentation folder	Incl. above	£3
1980 — Silver Proof	83,670	£30
1981 Royal Wedding	26,773,600	£2
1981 — in Presentation folder	Incl. above	£3
1981 — Silver Proof	218,140	£30

Could the enchanting series of coins depicting the lovable characters of author Beatrix Potter prove to be the most successful new coin issue the Royal Mint has ever done?

TWENTY PENCE

The series commenced in 1982, some 11 years after the introduction of decimal coinage. Its presence from introduction date meant that there was no requirement for ten pence circulation-standard coins until the latter's size was reduced in 1992. Its alloy is uniquely 84% copper and 16% nickel, unlike the 75/25 of the fifty pence.

DATE	Mintage	UNC
1982	740,815,000	£2
1982 Unc	—	£3
1982 Proof	—	£7
1982 Silver Proof Piedfort	—	£25
1983	158,463,000	£1
1983 Unc	—	£3
1983 Proof	—	£6
1984	65,350,000	£1
1984 BU	—	£3
1984 Proof	—	£6
1985 *New portrait*	74,273,699	£2
1985 BU	—	£4
1985 Proof	—	£6
1986 BU	—	£5
1986 Proof	—	£8
1987	137,450,000	£1
1987 BU	—	£3
1987 Proof	—	£5
1988	38,038,344	£1
1988 BU	—	£3
1988 Proof	—	£5
1989	132,013,890	£1
1989 BU	—	£3
1989 Proof	—	£5
1990	88,097,500	£1
1990 BU	—	£3
1990 Proof	—	£6
1991	35,901,250	£1
1991 BU	—	£3
1991 Proof	—	£6
1992	Est. approx. 1,500,000	£4
1992 BU	—	£5
1992 *Enhanced effigy*		
.... Est. approx. 29,705,000		£4
1992 — BU	—	£5
1992 — Proof	—	£8
1993	123,123,750	£1
1993 BU	—	£3
1993 Proof	—	£5
1994	67,131,250	£1
1994 BU	—	£3
1994 Proof	—	£5
1995	102,005,000	£1
1995 BU	—	£3
1995 Proof	—	£5
1996	83,163,750	£2
1996 BU	—	£3
1996 Proof	—	£5
1996 Silver Proof	—	£25
1997	89,518,750	£2
1997 BU	—	£3
1997 Proof	—	£5
1998 *New portrait*	76,965,000	£2
1998 BU	—	£4
1998 Proof	—	£5
1999	73,478,750	£2
1999 BU	—	£3
1999 Proof	—	£5
2000	136,428,750	£2
2000 BU	—	£3
2000 Proof	—	£5
2000 Silver Proof	—	£25
2001	148,122,500	£2
2001 BU	—	£3
2001 Proof	—	£5
2002	93,360,000	£2
2002 BU	—	£3
2002 Proof	—	£5
2002 Gold Proof	—	£225
2003	153,383,750	£2
2003 BU	—	£4
2003 Proof	—	£6
2004	120,212,500	£2
2004 BU	—	£4
2004 Proof	—	£6
2005	124,488,750	£2
2005 BU	—	£4
2005 Proof	—	£6
2006	114,800,000	£2
2006 BU	—	£6
2006 Proof	—	£7
2006 Silver Proof	—	£25
2007	117,075,000	£2
2007 BU	—	£4
2007 Proof	—	£6
2008	11,900,000	£2
2008 BU	—	£4
2008 Proof	—	£7
2008 Silver Proof	—	£25
2008 Gold Proof	—	£250
2008 Platinum Proof	—	£750
2008 *New Rev.,* date on Obv.	115,022,000	£2
2008 — paired with old Obv. (thus no date).. Est. approx. 120,000 (?) .		£50
2008 BU	—	£3
2008 Proof	—	£6
2008 Silver Proof	—	£25
2008 — — Piedfort	—	£30
2008 Gold Proof	—	£250
2008 Platinum Proof	—	£750
2009	121,625,300	£2
2009 BU	—	£5
2009 Proof	—	£7
2009 Silver Proof	—	£25
2010	112,875,500	£2
2010 BU	—	£5
2010 Proof	—	£7
2010 Silver Proof	—	£25
2011	191,625,000	£2
2011 BU	—	£5
2011 Proof	—	£8
2011 Silver Proof	—	£25
2012	69,650,030	£2
2012 BU	—	£5
2012 Proof	—	£8
2012 Silver Proof (issued in set with Victorian 4 Shilling piece)	—	£25
2012 — — with selective gold plating	—	£35
2012 Gold Proof	—	£300
2013	66,325,000	£2

DATE	Mintage	UNC	DATE	Mintage	UNC
2013 BU	—	£5	2015 New Portrait	131,250,000	£3
2013 Proof	—	£10	2015 — BU	—	£5
2013 Silver Proof	—	£20	2015 — Proof	—	£5
2013 Gold Proof	—	£300	2015 — Silver Proof	—	£30
2014	173,775,000	£2	2015 — Gold Proof	—	£300
2014 BU	—	£5	2015 — Platinum Proof	—	—
2014 Proof	—	£10	2016	161,000,000	£3
2014 Silver Proof	—	£25	2016 BU	—	£5
2015	63,175,000	£3	2016 Proof	—	£10
2015 BU	—	£5	2016 Silver Proof	—	£25
2015 Proof	—	£10	2017	161,000,000	£2
2015 Silver Proof	—	£25	2017 BU	—	£5
2015 Gold Proof	—	£350	2017 Proof	—	£10
2015 Platinum Proof	—	—	2017 Silver Proof	—	£25

TEN PENCE

The series commenced before decimalisation with the legend NEW PENCE, this changed to TEN PENCE from 1982. These "florin-sized" coins up to 1992 are no longer legal tender. Cupro-nickel was replaced by nickel-plated steel from 2011.

DATE	Mintage	UNC	DATE	Mintage	UNC
1968	336,143,250	£3	1989 Proof	—	£9
1969	314,008,000	£4	1990 BU	—	£6
1970	133,571,000	£3	1990 Proof	—	£9
1971	63,205,000	£3	1991 BU	—	£6
1971 Proof	—	£4	1991 Proof	—	£9
1972 Proof only	—	£5	1992 BU	—	£5
1973	152,174,000	£3	1992 Proof	—	£7
1973 Proof	—	£4	1992 Silver Proof	—	£12
1974	92,741,000	£3	1992 *Size reduced (24.5mm)*	1,413,455,170	£3
1974 Proof	—	£4	1992 BU	—	£4
1975	181,559,000	£3	1992 Proof	—	£5
1975 Proof	—	£4	1992 Silver Proof	—	£12
1976	228,220,000	£3	1992 — — Piedfort	—	£35
1976 Proof	—	£4	1993 BU	—	£2
1977	59,323,000	£6	1993 Proof	—	£7
1977 Proof	—	£8	1994 BU	—	£2
1978	—	£6	1994 Proof	—	£7
1979	115,457,000	£2	1995	43,259,000	£1
1979 Proof	—	£4	1995 BU	—	£5
1980	88,650,000	£3	1995 Proof	—	£7
1980 Proof	—	£4	1996	118,738,000	£2
1981	3,487,000	£8	1996 BU	—	£4
1981 Proof	—	£15	1996 Proof	—	£7
1982 BU	—	£4	1996 Silver Proof	—	£25
1982 Proof	—	£6	1997	99,196,000	£2
1983 BU	—	£3	1997 BU	—	£4
1983 Proof	—	£4	1997 Proof	—	£4
1984 BU	—	£4	1998 *New portrait* BU	—	£8
1984 Proof	—	£6	1998 Proof	—	£10
1985 *New portrait* BU	—	£5	1999 BU	—	£4
1985 Proof	—	£7	1999 Proof	—	£11
1986 BU	—	£4	2000	134,733,000	£1
1986 Proof	—	£6	2000 BU	—	£4
1987 BU	—	£4	2000 Proof	—	£7
1987 Proof	—	£7	2000 Silver Proof	—	£15
1988 BU	—	£5	2001	129,281,000	£1
1988 Proof	—	£7	2001 BU	—	£3
1989 BU	—	£6	2001 Proof	—	£4

DATE	Mintage	UNC	DATE	Mintage	UNC
2002	80,934,000	£2	2010 Proof	—	£7
2002 BU	—	£3	2010 Silver Proof	—	£25
2002 Proof	—	£5	2011 Nickel-plated steel	59,603,850	£1
2002 Gold Proof	—	£250	2011 — BU	—	£5
2003	88,118,000	£2	2011 — Proof	—	£10
2003 BU	—	£3	2011 Silver Proof	—	£25
2003 Proof	—	£5	2012	11,600,030	£1
2004	99,602,000	£1	2012 BU	—	£5
2004 BU	—	£3	2012 Proof	—	£10
2004 Proof	—	£5	2012 Silver proof with selective gold plating	—	£30
2005	69,604,000	£1	2012 Gold Proof	—	£250
2005 BU	—	£2	2013	320,200,750	£1
2005 Proof	—	£4	2013 BU	—	£5
2006	118,803,000	£1	2013 Proof	—	£10
2006 BU	—	£3	2013 Silver Proof	—	£25
2006 Proof	—	£7	2013 Gold Proof	—	£250
2006 Silver Proof	—	£25	2014	490,202,020	£1
2007	72,720,000	£1	2014 BU	—	£5
2007 BU	—	£4	2014 Proof	—	£12
2007 Proof	—	£7	2014 Silver Proof	—	£25
2008	9,720,000	£1	2015	119,000,000	£1
2008 BU	—	£4	2015 BU	—	£4
2008 Proof	—	£5	2015 Proof	—	£5
2008 Silver Proof	—	£25	2015 Silver Proof	—	£25
2008 Gold Proof	—	£250	2015 Gold Proof	—	£250
2008 Platinum Proof	—	£450	2015 Platinum Proof	—	—
2008 **New Rev.**, no border beads on Obv.	71,447,000	£1	2015 **New Portrait**	91,900,000	£1
2008 BU	—	£4	2015 — BU	—	£5
2008 Proof	—	£5	2015 — Proof	—	£6
2008 Silver Proof	—	£25	2015 — Silver Proof	—	£25
2008 — — Piedfort	—	£45	2015 — Gold Proof	—	£250
2008 Gold Proof	—	£250	2015 — Platinum Proof	—	—
2008 Platinum Proof	—	£450	2016	135,200,000	£1
2009	84,360,000	£1	2016 BU	—	£4
2009 BU	—	£3	2016 Proof	—	£6
2009 Proof	—	£5	2016 Silver Proof	—	£25
2009 Silver Proof	—	£25	2017	119,000,000	£1
2010	96,600,500	£1	2017 BU	—	£4
2010 BU	—	£5	2017 Proof	—	£5
			2017 Silver Proof	—	£25

SIX PENCE

This new denomination has been struck, dated 2016, as part of the Royal Mint's gifting range. They are of Sterling silver to BU standard, and of diameter 19.41mm. Being similar in size to the pre-decimal 6d (or latterly 2 1/2p) they have also been marketed as part of a 3-coin set along with two old sixpences (£50), the 2016 6p being £30 on its own.

FIVE PENCE

This series commenced simultaneously with the Ten Pence (qv). They were the same size and weight as their predecessor, the shilling, and such coins up to 1990 are no longer legal tender. As with the Ten Pence, cupro-nickel was replaced by nickel-plated steel from 2011.

DATE	Mintage	UNC	DATE	Mintage	UNC
1968	98,868,250	£3	1971	81,783,475	£3
1969	120,270,000	£3	1971 Proof	—	£3
1970	225,948,525	£3	1972 Proof	—	£7

DATE	Mintage	UNC
1973 Proof	—	£8
1974 Proof	—	£8
1975	141,539,000	£3
1975 Proof	—	£6
1976 Proof	—	£7
1977	24,308,000	£8
1977 Proof	—	£9
1978	61,094,000	£4
1978 Proof	—	£4
1979	155,456,000	£4
1979 Proof	—	£4
1980	220,566,000	£3
1980 Proof	—	£4
1981 Proof	—	£7
1982 BU	—	£7
1982 Proof	—	£9
1983 BU	—	£5
1983 Proof	—	£6
1984 BU	—	£4
1984 Proof	—	£6
1985 **New Portrait**. BU	—	£2
1985 Proof	—	£7
1986 BU	—	£2
1986 Proof	—	£7
1987	48,220,000	£1
1987 BU	—	£3
1987 Proof	—	£5
1988	120,744,610	£1
1988 BU	—	£3
1988 Proof		£5
1989	101,406,000	£1
1989 BU	—	£4
1989 Proof	—	£5
1990 BU	—	£2
1990 Proof	—	£5
1990 Silver Proof	—	£15
1990 **Size reduced (18mm)**	1,634,976,005	£2
1990 BU	—	£3
1990 Proof	—	£4
1990 Silver Proof	—	£20
1990 — — Piedfort	—	£25
1991	724,979,000	£1
1991 BU	—	£3
1991 Proof	—	£5
1992	453,173,500	£1
1992 BU	—	£3
1992 Proof	—	£7
1993 BU	—	£3
1993 Proof	—	£5
1994	93,602,000	£1
1994 BU	—	£5
1994 Proof	—	£7
1995	183,384,000	£1
1995 BU	—	£5
1995 Proof	—	£7
1996	302,902,000	£1
1996 BU	—	£4
1996 Proof	—	£7
1996 Silver proof	—	£25
1997	236,596,000	£1
1997 BU	—	£4
1997 Proof	—	£7

DATE	Mintage	UNC
1998 **New portrait**	217,376,000	£1
1998 BU	—	£4
1998 Proof	—	£7
1999	195,490,000	£1
1999 BU	—	£4
1999 Proof	—	£7
2000	388,512,000	£1
2000 BU	—	£4
2000 Proof	—	£7
2000 Silver Proof	—	£25
2001	337,930,000	£1
2001 BU	—	£3
2001 Proof	—	£5
2002	219,258,000	£1
2002 BU	—	£3
2002 Proof	—	£5
2002 Gold Proof	—	£150
2003	333,230,000	£1
2003 BU	—	£3
2003 Proof	—	£5
2004	271,810,000	£1
2004 BU	—	£3
2004 Proof	—	£5
2005	236,212,000	£1
2005 BU	—	£3
2005 Proof	—	£5
2006	317,697,000	£1
2006 BU	—	£3
2006 Proof	—	£7
2006 Silver Proof	—	£25
2007	246,720,000	£1
2007 BU	—	£5
2007 Proof	—	£7
2008	92,880,000	£1
2008 BU	—	£3
2008 Proof	—	£5
2008 Silver Proof	—	£20
2008 Gold Proof	—	£150
2008 Platinum Proof	—	£250
2008 **New Rev.,** no border beads on Obv	155,170,000	£1
2008 BU	—	£4
2008 Proof	—	£5
2008 Silver Proof	—	£15
2008 — — Piedfort	—	£35
2008 Gold Proof	—	£150
2008 Platinum Proof	—	£250
2009	132,960,300	£1
2009 BU	—	£6
2009 Proof	—	£7
2009 Silver Proof	—	£15
2010	296,245,500	£1
2010 BU	—	£4
2010 Proof	—	£5
2010 Silver Proof	—	£15
2011 Nickel-plated steel	50,400,000	£1
2011 — BU	—	£4
2011 — Proof	—	£6
2011 Silver Proof	—	£15
2012	339,802,350	£1
2012 BU	—	£5
2012 Proof	—	£8

2012 Silver Proof with selective gold plating.. —	£15
2012 Gold Proof .... —	£150
2013.................................... 318,800,750	£1
2013 BU .... —	£5
2013 Proof .... —	£8
2013 Silver Proof .... —	£25
2013 Gold Proof .... —	£225
2014.................................... 885,004,520	£1
2014 BU .... —	£5
2014 Proof .... —	£8
2014 Silver Proof .... —	£20
2015 **New Portrait**.................. 163,000,000	£1
2015 BU .... —	£3
2015 Proof .... —	£5
2015 Silver Proof .... —	£20
2015 Gold Proof .... —	£250

2015 Platinum Proof................................ —	—
2015 **New Portrait**.................. 536,600,000	£2
2015 — BU .... —	£4
2015 — Proof .... —	£6
2015 — Silver Proof .... —	£20
2015 — Gold Proof .... —	£250
2015 — Platinum Proof .... —	—
2016.................................... 308,200,000	£2
2016 BU .... —	£4
2016 Proof .... —	£6
2016 Silver Proof .... —	£20
2017..3—	—
2017 BU .... —	—
2017 Proof .... —	—
2017 Silver Proof .... —	£25
2017 Gold Proof .... —	£250

TWO PENCE

Dated from 1971, and legal tender from Decimal Day that year, early examples are found in the blue Specimen decimal set wallets of 1968. They were minted in bronze up to 1991, and mainly in copper-plated steel from 1992. However details of where this rule does not totally apply (1992, 1996, 1998–2000 and 2002, 2006, 2008 and 2009) are given below. As with other denominations, "NEW" was replaced by the quantity of pence in word from 1982.

DATE	Mintage	UNC	DATE	Mintage	UNC
1971........................... 1,454,856,250		£2	1987 Proof... —		£4
1971 Proof.. —		£3	1988................................... 419,889,000		£1
1972 Proof.. —		£5	1988 BU .... —		£2
1973 Proof.. —		£6	1988 Proof.. —		£4
1974 Proof.. —		£6	1989................................... 359,226,000		£1
1975.................Est. approx. 273,145,000		£2	1989 BU .... —		£2
1975 Proof.. —		£2	1989 Proof.. —		£4
1976.................Est. approx. 53,779,000		£2	1990................................... 204,499,700		£1
1976 Proof.. —		£2	1990 BU .... —		£2
1977 109,281,000		£2	1990 Proof.. —		£3
1977 Proof.. —		£2	1991..................................... 86,625,250		£1
1978.................................. 189,658,000		£3	1991 BU .... —		£2
1978 Proof.. —		£2	1991 Proof.. —		£5
1979.................................. 260,200,000		£2	1992 Copper plated steel 102,247,000		£1
1979 Proof........................... 408,527,000		£2	1992 Bronze BU .... —		£2
1980.. —		£1	1992 — Proof .... —		£5
1980 Proof.. —		£2	1993................................... 235,674,000		£1
1981.................................. 353,191,000		£4	1993 BU .... —		£2
1981 Proof.. —		£4	1993 Proof.. —		£3
1982 Legend changed to TWO PENCE .... —		£4	1994................................... 531,628,000		£1
1982 Proof.. —		£5	1994 BU .... —		£2
1983.. —		£2	1994 Proof.. —		£5
1983 Error NEW instead of TWO.................. —		£850	1995................................... 124,482,000		£1
1983 Proof.. —		£4	1995 BU .... —		£2
1984.. —		£2	1995 Proof.. —		£5
1984 Proof..		£4	1996................................... 296,278,000		£1
1985 ***New portrait*** 107,113,000		£2	1996 BU .... —		£2
1985 BU .... —		£2	1996 Proof.. —		£5
1985 Proof.. —		£4	1996 Silver Proof .... —		£25
1986.................................. 168,967,500		£1	1997................................... 496,116,000		£1
1986 BU .... —		£2	1997 BU .... —		£2
1986 Proof.. —		£4	1997 Proof.. —		£5
1987.................................. 218,100,750		£1	1998 ***New portrait*** ....Est. approx. 120,243,000		£1
1987 BU .... —		£2	1998 BU .... —		£2

DATE	Mintage	UNC	DATE	Mintage	UNC
1998 Proof	—	£4	2009	150,500,500	£2
1998 Bronze	Est. approx. 93,587,000	£1	2009 BU	—	£3
1999	353,816,000	£1	2009 Proof	—	£5
1999 Bronze BU	—	£2	2009 Silver Proof	—	£25
1999 — Proof	—	£4	2010	99,600,000	£2
2000	536,659,000	£1	2010 BU	—	£3
2000 BU	—	£3	2010 Proof	—	£6
2000 Proof	—	£5	2010 Silver Proof	—	£25
2000 Silver Proof	—	£22	2011	144,300,000	£2
2001	551,880,000	£1	2011 BU	—	£3
2001 BU	—	£2	2011 Proof	—	£6
2001 Proof	—	£4	2011 Silver Proof	—	£25
2002	168,556,000	£1	2012	67,800,000	£2
2002 BU	—	£3	2012 BU	—	£3
2002 Proof	—	£4	2012 Proof	—	£8
2002 Gold Proof	—	£275	2012 Silver Proof with selective gold plating	—	£45
2003	260,225,000	£1	2012 Gold Proof	—	£250
2003 BU	—	£2	2013	40,600,000	£2
2003 Proof	—	£4	2013 BU	—	£3
2004	356,396,000	£1	2013 Proof	—	£8
2004 BU	—	£2	2013 Silver Proof	—	£25
2004 Proof	—	£4	2013 Gold Proof	—	£250
2005	280,396,000	£1	2014	247,600,020	£2
2005 BU	—	£2	2014 BU	—	£3
2005 Proof	—	£3	2014 Proof	—	£8
2006	170,637,000	£1	2014 Silver Proof	—	£45
2006 BU	—	£3	2015 New Portrait	85,900,000	£2
2006 Proof	—	£4	2015 BU	—	£3
2006 Silver Proof	—	£15	2015 Proof	—	£5
2007	254,500,000	£2	2015 Silver Proof	—	£25
2007 BU	—	£3	2015 Gold Proof	—	£250
2007 Proof	—	£5	2015 Platinum Proof	—	—
2008	10,600,000	£2	2015 *New Portrait*	139,200,000	£2
2008 BU	—	£3	2015 — BU	—	£3
2008 Proof	—	£5	2015 — Proof	—	£5
2008 Silver Proof	—	£25	2015 — Silver Proof		£25
2008 Gold Proof		£275	2015 — Gold Proof		£250
2008 Platinum Proof		£450	2015 — Platinum Proof	—	—
2008 *New Rev.*,			2016	185,200,000	—
no border beads on Obv	241,679,000	£2	2016 BU	—	—
2008 — BU	—	£3	2016 Proof	—	—
2008 — Proof	—	£5	2016 Silver Proof		—
2008 — Silver Proof	—	£20	2017	—	—
2008 — Silver Proof Piedfort	—	£45	2017 BU	—	—
2008 — Gold Proof	—	£300	2017 Proof	—	—
2008 — Platinum Proof	—	£500	2017 Silver Proof	—	—

ONE PENNY

The history of this coin is very similar to that of the Two Pence coin (qv) except that all 1998 examples were of copper-plated steel.

DATE	Mintage	UNC	DATE	Mintage	UNC
1971	1,521,666,250	£1	1975	221,604,000	£2
1971 Proof	—	£2	1975 Proof	—	£4
1972 Proof	—	£5	1976	300,160,000	£2
1973	280,196,000	£2	1976 Proof	—	£3
1973 Proof	—	£5	1977	285,430,000	£2
1974	330,892,000	£2	1977 Proof	—	£3
1974 Proof	—	£3	1978	292,770,000	£3

DATE	Mintage	UNC
1978 Proof	—	£3
1979	459,000,000	£3
1979 Proof	—	£3
1980	416,304,000	£2
1980 Proof	—	£3
1981	301,800,000	£2
1981 Proof	—	£3
1982 Legend ONE PENNY	100,292,000	£1
1982 Unc	—	£2
1982 Proof	—	£3
1983	243,002,000	£1
1983 Unc	—	£2
1983 Proof	—	£4
1984	154,759,625	£1
1984 BU	—	£2
1984 Proof	—	£3
1985 New portrait	200,605,245	£1
1985 BU	—	£2
1985 Proof	—	£3
1986	369,989,130	£1
1986 BU	—	£2
1986 Proof	—	£3
1987	4999,946,000	£1
1987 BU	—	£2
1987 Proof	—	£3
1988	793,492,000	£1
1988 BU	—	£2
1988 Proof	—	£3
1989	658,142,000	£1
1989 BU	—	£2
1989 Proof	—	£3
1990	529,047,500	£2
1990 BU	—	£3
1990 Proof	—	£4
1991	206,457,000	£1
1991 BU	—	£2
1991 Proof	—	£4
1992 Copper-plated steel	253,867,000	£3
1992 Bronze BU	—	£6
1992 — Proof	—	£4
1993	602,590,000	£1
1993 BU	—	£2
1993 Proof	—	£5
1994	843,834,000	£1
1994 BU	—	£2
1994 Proof	—	£5
1995	303,314,000	£1
1995 BU	—	£3
1995 Proof	—	£5
1996	723,840,060	£1
1996 BU	—	£2
1996 Proof	—	£5
1996 Silver Proof	—	£28
1997	396,874,000	£1
1997 BU	—	£2
1997 Proof	—	£4
1998 New portrait	739,770,000	£1
1998 — BU	—	£3
1998 Proof	—	£4
1999	891,392,000	£2
1999 Bronze BU	—	£4
1999 Bronze Proof	—	£8
2000	1,060,420,000	£1
2000 BU	—	£2
2000 Proof	—	£2
2000 Silver Proof	—	£25
2001	928,698,000	£1

DATE	Mintage	UNC
2001 BU	—	£2
2001 Proof	—	£4
2002	601,446,000	£1
2002 BU	—	£2
2002 Proof	—	£4
2002 Gold Proof	—	£175
2003	539,436,000	£1
2003 BU	—	£2
2003 Proof	—	£3
2004	739,764,000	£1
2004 BU	—	£2
2004 Proof	—	£4
2005	536,318,000	£1
2005 BU	—	£2
2005 Proof	—	£3
2006	524,605,000	£1
2006 BU	—	£2
2006 Proof	—	£4
2006 Silver Proof	—	£15
2007	548,002,000	£1
2007 BU	—	£4
2007 Proof	—	£7
2008	180,600,000	£1
2008 BU	—	£3
2008 Proof	—	£5
2008 Silver Proof	—	£15
2008 Gold Proof	—	£150
2008 Platinum Proof	—	£200
2008 *New Rev,* no border beads	507,952,000	£1
2008 — BU	—	£2
2008 — Proof	—	£3
2008 — Silver Proof	—	£15
2008 — Silver Proof Piedfort	—	£25
2008 — Gold Proof	—	£150
2008 — Platinum Proof	—	£200
2009	556,412,800	£1
2009 BU	—	£3
2009 Proof	—	£4
2009 Silver BU, in "Lucky Baby Gift Pack"	—	£15
2009 — Proof	—	£15
2010	609,603,000	£1
2010 BU	—	£3
2010 Proof	—	£4
2010 Silver BU, in "Lucky Baby Gift Card"	9,701	£15
2010 — Proof	—	£15
2011	431,004,000	£1
2011 BU	—	£2
2011 Proof	—	£3
2011 Silver BU in "Lucky Baby Pack"	—	£18
2011 – Proof	—	£15
2012	227,201,000	£1
2012 BU	—	£2
2012 Proof	—	£4
2012 Silver BU (three different packagings)	—	£15
2012 Silver Proof with selective gold plating	—	£18
2012 Gold Proof	—	£175
2013	260,900,000	£1
2013 BU	—	£2
2013 Proof	—	£5
2013 Silver BU	—	£25
2013 — Proof	—	£30
2013 Gold Proof	—	£175
2014	464,801,520	£1
2014 BU	—	£2
2014 Proof	—	£5
2014 Silver BU	—	£20
2014 Silver Proof	—	£25

DATE	Mintage	UNC	DATE	Mintage	UNC
2015	154,600,000	£1	2015 — Platinum Proof	—	—
2015 BU	—	£2	2016	371,002,000	£1
2015 Proof	—	£5	2016 BU	—	£2
2015 Silver BU	—	£20	2016 Proof	—	£5
2015 — Proof	—	£25	2016 Silver BU	—	£20
2015 Gold Proof	—	£200	2016 Silver Proof	—	£25
2015 Platinum Proof	—	—	2017	—	£1
2015 *New Portrait*	418,201,016	£2	2017 BU	—	£2
2015 — BU	—	£3	2017 Proof	—	£5
2015 — Proof	—	£6	2017 Silver BU	—	£20
2015 — Silver Proof	—	£25	2017 Silver Proof	—	£25
2015 — Gold Proof	—	£200			

HALF PENNY

No longer legal tender, its history tracks that of the Two Pence and One Penny.

1971	1,394,188,250	£2	1979 Proof	—	£4
1971 Proof	—	£3	1980	202,788,000	£2
1972 Proof	—	£15	1980 Proof	—	£3
1973	365,680,000	£2	1981	46,748,000	£2
1973 Proof	—	£3	1981 Proof	—	£4
1974	365,448,000	£2	1982 Legend changed to		
1974 Proof	—	£3	HALF PENNY	190,752,000	50p
1975	197,600,000	£2	1982 Unc	—	£2
1975 Proof	—	£3	1982 Proof	—	£3
1976	412,172,000	£2	1983	7,600,000	50p
1976 Proof	—	£3	1983 Unc	—	£1
1977	66,368,000	£1	1983 Proof	—	£4
1977 Proof	—	£3	1984	40,000	£4
1978	59,532,000	£1	1984 BU	—	£5
1978 Proof	—	£4	1984 Proof	—	£6
1979	219,1322,000	£2			

For the other 9 coins in the 29-coin 2011 Olympic and Paralympic series see pages 257–259.

THE BRITANNIA SERIES

In addition to the large Britannia coin issues already listed, the series, which started in 1997, has grown to include many denominations and strikes in silver, gold and platinum. The coins are essentially bullion pieces and their values are usually related to the current price of precious metals, therefore no attempt has been made in this publication to give values for the series. To ascertain the value of a piece it is necessary to check with the prevailing price of precious metals. These issues are not listed in this publication for reasons of space but full information is available on the Royal Mint's website, www.royalmint.com. It is anticipated that the full list of issues will be included in this publication in due course.

SILVER

The silver Britannia series commenced in 1997, and, as with the Gold Britannia series, sets of the coins are listed in the "Proof and Specimen Sets" section. Coins contain one Troy ounce of fine silver (£2) alloyed to Britannia standard, i.e. 95.8 per cent fine silver, or fractions of one ounce as follows: half ounce (£1), quarter ounce (50 pence) and one tenth of an ounce (20 pence). Reverses change anually, all four coins of any particular date being of the same design. The reverses by Philip Nathan appear as follows:

1997 Chariot, 1998 Standing Britannia, 1999 Chariot, 2000 Standing Britannia, 2001 Una and the Lion, 2002 Standing Britannia, 2003 Britannia's Helmeted Head, 2004 Standing Britannia, 2005 Britannia Seated, 2006 Standing Britannia, 2009 Chariot.

The 2007 design is by Christopher Le Brun, and features a seated Britannia with Lion at her feet. The 2008 is by John Bergdahl, and features a standing Britannia facing left.

Two pounds Britannia coins to BU or "bullion" standard have been issued as individual coins for each year from 1998 onwards. 2010 features Suzie Zamit's Britannia with a portrait with a Corinthian style helmet.

The 2011 coins feature a seated Britannia and Union Flag, as described in the Britannia gold series above.

2012 saw the 15th anniversary of the Silver Series, but the reverse chosen was that of the Standing Britannia by Philip Nathan, which also marked the 25th Gold series. In addition, there is a 9-coin proof set of Half-Ounce silver coins dated 2012 featuring each of the Reverses used in the past, a 25th Anniversary collection. The story of the 2013 silver Britannia coins closely parallels that of the gold coins. The silver one-twentieth of an ounce has the logical face value of 10 pence.

The 2014 Silver Britannias closely follow the pattern of the three designs of 2014 Gold. This included the introduction of the silver one-fortieth of an ounce, with a face value of 5 pence. The Nathan Britannia has crenellated borders on both the obverse and the reverse, while the Year of the Horse has plain borders on both. Examples exist, however, of both One ounce silver bullion coins having the Other's obverse, thus producing two error coins, or "mules". 2014 also saw the SS *Gairsoppa* Quarter-ounce silver Britannia bullion coin with the edge inscription SS GAIRSOPPA. These coins have the Nathan Britannia reverse, and are struck from metal recovered from the vessel which was sunk by enemy action in 1941.

Both 2013 and 2014 one-ounce BU bullion Nathan Britannia coins exist with snakes or horses (respectively) on a plain edge. These were the result of a contract between the Royal Mint and the bullion dealers A-mark of Santa Monica, California, and commemorate Chinese Lunar years. In 2015 Designer Jody Clark scored a first when his portrayal of Britannia was used on the £50 coin which also carried his new portrait of the Queen.

GOLD

In 1987 the gold Britannia £100 coin was introduced. It contained one Troy ounce of fine gold, alloyed to 22 carat, and this has continued to the present day. At the same time, and also continuing, gold coins of face value £50, £25 and £10 appeared, containing a half ounce, quarter ounce and one tenth of an ounce of fine gold respectively. From 1987 to 1989 the alloy was of copper (Red Gold), whereas from 1990 to the present day the alloy has been of silver and copper (yellow gold).

Proof sets of these coins are listed in the "Proof and Specimen Sets" section. In addition, non-proof coins have been minted, it is believed for each of the four coins for every year. The one ounce £100 Britannia is primarily issued as a bullion coin in the non-proof standard, originally in competition with the South African Krugerrand. Its price is quoted daily on the financial pages of some newspapers.

There were five reverse designs by Philip Nathan:- 1987-1996 Standing Britannia, 1997 Chariot, 1998-2000 Standing Britannia, 2001 Una and the Lion, 2002 Standing Britannia, 2003 Britannia's Helmeted Head, 2004 Standing Britannia, 2005 Britannia seated, 2006 Standing Britannia. For 2007 the design is a Seated Britannia with lion at her feet, by Christopher Le Brun. The 2008 design is of Britannia standing and facing left, by John Bergdahl. The 2009 reverse is similar to that of 1997, Britannia on a chariot, while 2010 has Suzie Zamit's Britannia potrait with a Corinthian style helmet. The 2011 design is by David Mach, and portrays a seated Britannia with trident and shield, replicating the design on a 1937 penny, superimposed on a Union Flag. The rotation of the coin from left to right, or vice-versa, creates an illusion of Britannia moving with the ripple of the flag.

In general the proof coins have reverse features frosted, The proofs with Standing Britannia and Una and the Lion reverses include P NATHAN on the reverse, whereas the equivalent bullion coins include NATHAN. The other three reverses have PN on both proofs and bullion coins.

2012 was the 25th anniversary of the Gold Britannia coin series, and the reverse design chosen was that of the 1987 coins, standing Britannia, by Philip Nathan. This was repeated in 2013, but only for Brilliant Uncirculated "Bullion" coins. A separate new series was introduced for Proof coins, a seated Britannia with an owl was featured, the artist being Robert Hunt. The range of Britannia Proofs was increased from 4 to 6, with the addition of a Five-ounce coin (qv) and a one-twentieth of an ounce, curiously denominated at One Pound and with a diameter of 12mm, just larger than a Maundy One Penny. All 2013 Gold Britannias are minted in 0.999 Au alloy.

2014 and 2015 each saw three Reverse designs. The Nathan outstretched arm of Britannia continued as the bullion coin. The series by new artists of Britannia designs were of a standing Britannia facing left with lion (2014) by Jody Clark, and a "head and shoulders" Britannia holding the trident on her right shoulder, by Antony Dufont, the latter coin included the Clark portrayal of the Queen on the obverse.

The 2016 series Reverse was designed by Suzie Zamit and depicts Britannia as the Warrior Queen. The 2017 series celebrating the 30th anniversary of the gold Britannia used a design by Louis Tamlin which depicts a helmeted outline of Britain.

A further new denomination appeared in 2014, the gold one-fortieth of an ounce, diameter 8mm and face value 50 pence.

OLYMPIC GAMES HIGH VALUES

The issue of the second series of three coins in the Olympic Games gold proof coin was in 2011, with the completion of the 9-coin series in 2012. The obverses all have the 1998 Ian Rank-Broadley portrait of the Queen, but a few 2011 £100 coins were issued without his initials IRB under her portrait. Reverses are summarised below:

DATE	FACE VALUE	FINE GOLD WEIGHT	FEATURED GOD	FEATURED PART OF OLYMPIC MOTTO
2010	£100 £25 £25	1 Troy oz 1/4 Troy oz 1/4 Troy oz	Neptune Diana Mercury	CITIUS
2011	£100 £25 £25	1 Troy oz 1/4 Troy oz 1/4 Troy oz	Jupiter Juno Apollo	ALTIUS
2012	£100 £25 £25	1 Troy oz 1/4 Troy oz 1/4 Troy oz	Mars Vulcan Minerva	FORTIUS

PRECIOUS METAL BULLION AND COLLECTOR COINS (SERIES)

The Shengxiào Collection

The Shengxiào Collection of Lunar Coins by designer Wuon-Gean Ho was begun for the Year of the Horse in 2014 bringing the Royal Mint in line with most other major mints of the world. As the series is growing we are listing them separately here, however, the larger denominatiions have also been listed under their respective headings.

Date	Weight Face value/	Auth. issue qty	Issue price
2014 YEAR OF THE HORSE			
Silver bullion.....................................1 ounce /£2	—	BV
Silver Proof ....1 ounce/£2	8,888	£85
Silver Proof ....5 ounces/£10	1,488	£450
Gold BU .... One-tenth ounce/£10	2,888	£225
Gold bullion....................................1 ounce/£100	—	BV
Gold Proof......................................1 ounce/£100	888	£1,950
2015 YEAR OF THE SHEEP			
Silver bullion.....................................1 ounce /£2	—	BV
Silver Proof ....1 ounce/£2	9,888	£85
Silver Proof with gold plating............1 ounce/£2	4,888	£120
Silver Proof ....5 ounces/£10	1,088	£395
Gold BU .... One-tenth ounce/£10	2,888	£225
Gold bullion....................................1 ounce/£100	—	BV
Gold Proof......................................1 ounce/£100	888	£1,950
Gold Proof...................................5 ounces/£500	38	£7,500
2016 YEAR OF THE MONKEY			
Silver bullion.....................................1 ounce /£2	—	BV
Silver Proof ....1 ounce/£2	8,888	£85
Silver Proof ....5 ounces/£10	588	£395
Silver Proof .... 1 kilo/£500	88	£2,000
Gold BU .... One-tenth ounce/£10	1,888	£175
Gold bullion....................................1 ounce/£100	—	BV
Gold Proof......................................1 ounce/£100	888	£1,495
Gold Proof...................................5 ounces/£500	38	£7,500
Gold Proof................................... 1 kilo/£1,000	8	£42,500
2017 YEAR OF THE ROOSTER			
Silver bullion.....................................1 ounce /£2	—	BV
Silver Proof ....1 ounce/£2	3,888	£85
Silver Proof ....5 ounces/£10	388	£415
Silver Proof .... 1 kilo/£500	88	£2,050
Gold BU .... One-tenth ounce/£10	2,088	£205
Gold bullion....................................1 ounce/£100	—	BV
Gold Proof......................................1 ounce/£100	688	£1,780
Gold Proof...................................5 ounces/£500	38	£8,250
Gold Proof................................... 1 kilo/£1,000	8	£49,995
2018 YEAR OF THE DOG			
Silver bullion.....................................1 ounce /£2	—	BV
Silver Proof ....1 ounce/£2	5,088	£85
Silver Proof ....5 ounces/£10	388	£415
Silver Proof .... 1 kilo/£500	108	£2,050
Gold BU .... One-tenth ounce/£10	1,088	£175
Gold bullion....................................1 ounce/£100	—	BV
Gold Proof......................................1 ounce/£100	888	£1,795

The Queen's Beasts

In 2016 a new series of coins was introduced by the Royal Mint entitled "The Queen's Beasts". These are intended as a homage to Her Majesty becoming Britain's longest reigning monarch and each coin in the the series represents one of the heraldic animals sculpted by James Woodford, RA, for the Coronation ceremony held in Westminster Abbey in 1953. The 6-foot tall sculptures each symbolised the various strands of royal ancestry and were inspired by the King's Beasts of Henry VIII that still line the bridge at Hampton Court .So far four beasts have been chosen as the subjects of the reverse designs of the series: the the Lion, the Griffin, the Dragon and the Unicorn. The coins all carry the effigy of Her Majesty the Queen by Jody Clark on the obverse with the heraldic beasts, by the same designer, appearing on the reverse. The coins have been struck in a variety of metals and in different sizes. To make it simple for collectors to follow the series we list them below rather than under their various denominations.

Date	Weight Face value/	Auth. issue qty	Issue price
THE LION OF ENGLAND			
2016 Silver bullion .... 2 ounces/£5	—	BV
2016 Gold bullion .... 1 ounce/£100	—	BV
2017 Cu-Ni BU £5	—	£13
2017 Silver Proof .... 1 ounce/£2	8,500	£85
2017 Silver Proof .... 5 ounces/£10	2,500	£415
2017 Silver bullion .... 10 ounces/£10	—	BV
2017 Silver Proof ....,.. ......1 kilo/£500	350	£2,050
2017 Gold Proof .... Quarter ounce/£25	2,500	£475
2017 Gold Proof .... 1 ounce/£100	1,000	£1,780
2017 Gold Proof .... 5 ounces/£500	125	£9,25
2017 Gold proof ....,.... .....1 kilo/£1,000	—	£49,995
2017 Platinum bullion,........ .... 1 ounce/£100	—	BV
THE GRIFFIN OF EDWARD III		
2017 Silver bullion .... 2 ounces/£5	—	BV
2017 Gold bullion .... Quarter ounce/£25	—	BV
2017 Gold bullion .... 1 ounce/£100	—	BV
THE DRAGON OF WALES		
2017 Silver bullion .... 2 ounces/£5	—	BV
2017 Gold bullion .... Quarter ounce/£25	—	BV
2017 Gold bullion .... 1 ounce/£100	—	BV
THE UNICORN OF SCOTLAND		
2017 Cu-Ni BU £5	—	£13
2017 Silver Proof ... ., 1 ounce/£2	6,250	£85
2017 Silver Proof .... 5 ounces/£10	750	£415
2017 Silver Proof .... 10 ounces/£10	850	£795
2017 Silver Proof ....1 kilo/£500	225	£2,050
2017 Gold Proof .... Quarter ounce/£25	1,500	£475

This information is correct at the time of going to press (September 2017) but, as the reader can see, there are numerous possibilities for other coins in each series to achieve uniformity, as well, of course, as the remaining six beasts which will be released in eased in due course. To keep up to date on the new releases visit www.royalmint.com and www.royalmintbullion.com or check in COIN NEWS magazine every month.

Commencing in 2017, the Royal Mint will be producing a new Bullion series entitled "Landmarks of Britain". The first issue will feature Big Ben, with a face value of £2. As this is a bullion series, although with a mintage limit of 50,000, it will follow the same principles as the popular Britannia series

With an interesting programme of issues intended to promote coin collecting, the Royal Mint produced a series of coins which were offered to the public at face value. The first issue was made in 2013 and was a £20 coin. The series was extended in 2015 to include a £100. In the same year the £50 silver coin in the Britannia series was offered as part of this programme. The issues are listed below.

HUNDRED POUNDS

Following on from the late 2013 introduction of the Twenty Pounds (see below) a "Hundred Pounds for £100" appeared, again a 0.999 Fine Silver coin, of two ounces weight, in early 2015.

DATE	Mintage	UNC
2015 Big Ben, BU	50,000	£100
2015 Buckingham Palace, BU	50,000	£100
2016 Trafalgar Square	45,000	£100

FIFTY POUNDS

A new denomination introduced in 2015, with the slogan "Fifty Pounds for £50". A double first for Jody Clark, minted in 99.99 silver, diameter 34mm.

DATE	Mintage	UNC
2015 Britannia BU	100,000	£50

TWENTY POUNDS

Another new denomination was added in late 2013. Marketed by the Royal Mint under the slogan "Twenty Pounds for £20", it is a 27mm diameter 0.999 Fine silver coin.

DATE	Mintage	UNC
2013 Pistrucci St George & Dragon BU	250,000	£24
2014 Centenary of the outbreak of the First World War	—	£24
2015 Sir Winston Churchill	—	£20
2015 The Longest Reigning Monarch, New Portrait	—	£20
2016 The 90th Birthday of Her Majesty the Queen	—	£20
2016 The Welsh Dragon	—	£20

PROOF AND SPECIMEN SETS

NOTE: The prices quoted in this guide were set at August 2017 with the price of gold around £1000 per ounce and silver £13 per ounce—market fluctuations will have a marked effect on the values of modern precious metal coins. However, the prices quoted here for the *recently issued* sets are the original Royal Mint retail prices.

The following listings are an attempt to include all officially marketed products from the Royal Mint of two coins or more, but excluding those which included non-UK coins. It is appreciated that not all have been advertised as new to the public, but it is assumed that at some time they have been, or will be, available. In a few cases, therefore, the prices may be conjectural but are, nevertheless, attempts at listing realistic values, in some instances based on an original retail price. In the case of Elizabeth II sets, if no metal is stated in the listing, the coins in the sets are of the same metal as the circulation coin equivalent. In addition to the above we have excluded historical gold coin sets, such as sets of sovereigns from different mints, where the dates of the coins vary from one set to another.

DATE   FDC

GEORGE IV
1826 £5–farthing (11 coins) ....From £45,000

WILLIAM IV
1831 Coronation £2–farthing (14 coins) ....From £35,000

VICTORIA
1839 "Una and the Lion" £5–farthing (15 coins)...From £75,000
1853 Sovereign–quarter farthing, including "Gothic" crown (16 coins) .... From £50,000
1887 Golden Jubilee £5–3d (11 coins) £30,000
1887 Golden Jubilee Crown–3d (7 coins)..£3500
1893 £5–3d (10 coins) £28,000
1893 Crown–3d (6 coins)..£5000

EDWARD VII
1902 Coronation £5–Maundy penny, matt proofs (13 coins) £6500
1902 Coronation Sovereign–Maundy penny, matt proofs (11 coins) £3500

GEORGE V
1911 Coronation £5–Maundy penny (12 coins)..£8000
1911 Sovereign–Maundy penny (10 coins) £3500
1911 Coronation Halfcrown–Maundy penny (8 coins) £1500
1927 New types Crown–3d (6 coins)..£850

GEORGE VI
1937 Coronation £5–half sovereign (4 coins) £6500
1937 Coronation Crown–farthing including Maundy money (15 coins) £550
1950 Mid-century Halfcrown–farthing (9 coins) £200
1951 Festival of Britain, Crown–farthing (10 coins)..£250

ELIZABETH II
1953 Proof Coronation Crown–farthing (10 coins) £125
1953 Currency (plastic) set halfcrown–farthing (9 coins)..£15
1968 Specimen decimal set 10p, 5p and 1971-dated bronze in blue wallet (5 coins)................£3
1970 Proof Last £sd coins (issued from 1972) Halfcrown–halfpenny (8 coins)..........................£20
1971 Proof (issued 1973) 50p–half penny (6 coins) £18
1972 Proof (issued 1976) 50p–half penny (7 coins including Silver Wedding crown) £24
1973 Proof (issued 1976) 50p–half penny (6 coins) £16
1974 Proof (issued 1976) 50p–half penny (6 coins) £18
1975 Proof (issued 1976) 50p–half penny (6 coins)..£18

DATE   FDC

1976 Proof 50p–half penny (6 coins) £18
1977 Proof 50p–penny (7 coins including Silver Jubilee crown) £22
1978 Proof 50p–half penny (6 coins) £16
1979 Proof 50p–half penny (6 coins) £18
1980 Proof gold sovereign series (4 coins) £2500
1980 — 50p–half penny (6 coins) £16
1981 Proof £5, sovereign, Royal Wedding Silver crown, 50p–half penny (9 coins) £800
1981 — 50p–half penny (6 coins) £18
1982 Proof gold sovereign series (4 coins) £2500
1982 — 50p–half penny (7 coins) £20
1982 Uncirculated 50p–half penny (7 coins) £15
1983 Proof gold double-sovereign to half sovereign (3 coins) £1000
1983 — £1–half penny (8 coins) (includes H. J. Heinz sets) £25
1983 Uncirculated £1–half penny (8 coins) (includes Benson & Hedges and Martini sets) £30
1983 — — (8 coins) (only Benson & Hedges and Martini sets) with "2 NEW PENCE" legend ...£1000
1983 — 50p–half penny (7 coins) (H. J. Heinz sets) £16
1983 — — (7 coins) (H. J. Heinz set) with "2 NEW PENCE" legend £1000
1984 Proof gold five pounds, sovereign and half-sovereigns (3 coins) £1000
1984 — £1 (Scottish rev.)–half penny (8 coins) £20
1984 BU £1 (Scottish rev.)–half penny (8 coins) £16
1985 New portrait proof gold sovereign series (4 coins) £1250
1985 Proof £1–1p in de luxe case (7 coins) £25
1985 — in standard case £20
1985 BU £1–1p (7 coins) in folder £15
1986 Proof gold Commonwealth Games £2, sovereign and half sovereign (3 coins) £1000
1986 — Commonwealth Games £2–1p, de luxe case (8 coins) £30
1986 — — in standard case (8 coins) £25
1986 BU £2–1p in folder (8 coins) £20
1987 Proof gold Britannia set (4 coins) £2000
1987 — — £25 and £10 (2 coins) £450
1987 — — double- to half sovereign (3 coins) £1000
1987 — £1–1p in de luxe case (7 coins) £35
1987 — £1–1p in standard case (7 coins) £25
1987 BU £1–1p in folder (7 coins) £20
1988 Proof gold Britannia set (4 coins) £2000
1988 — — £25 and £10 (2 coins) £450
1988 — — double- to half sovereign (3 coins) £1000
1988 — £1–1p in de luxe case (7 coins) £35
1988 — £1–1p in standard case (7 coins) £30
1988 BU £1–1p in folder (7 coins) (includes Bradford & Bingley sets) £18
1989 Proof gold Britannia set (4 coins) £2000
1989 — — £25 and £10 (2 coins) £450
1989 — — 500th anniversary of the sovereign series set (4 coins) £4000
1989 — — — double- to half sovereign (3 coins) £2000
1989 — Silver Bill of Rights £2, Claim of Right £2 (2 coins) £65
1989 — — Piedfort as above (2 coins) £100
1989 BU £2 in folder (2 coins) £25
1989 Proof £2 (both)–1p in de luxe case (9 coins) £35
1989 — in standard case (9 coins) £30
1989 BU £1–1p in folder (7 coins) £25
1990 Proof gold Britannia set (4 coins) £2000
1990 — — sovereign series set (4 coins) £2000
1990— — double- to half sovereign (3 coins) £1000
1990 — silver 5p, 2 sizes (2 coins) £28
1990 — £1–1p in de luxe case (8 coins) £35
1990 — £1–1p standard case (8 coins) £30
1990 BU £1–1p in folder (8 coins) £20
1991 Proof gold Britannia set (4 coins) £2000
1991 — — sovereign series set (4 coins) £2000
1991 — — double- to half sovereign (3 coins) £1000
1991 — £1–1p in de luxe case (7 coins) £35
1991 — £1–1p in standard case (7 coins) £28
1991 BU £1–1p in folder (7 coins) £18

DATE	FDC
1992 Proof gold Britannia set (4 coins)	£2000
1992 — — sovereign series set (4 coins)	£2000
1992 — — double- to half sovereign (3 coins)	£1000
1992 — £1–1p including two each 50p and 10p in de luxe case (9 coins)	£38
1992 — £1–1p as above in standard case (9 coins)	£32
1992 BU £1–1p as above in folder (9 coins)	£16
1992 — with Enhanced Effigy on obverse of 20p	£25
1992 Proof silver 10p, two sizes (2 coins)	£25
1993 Proof gold Britannia set (4 coins)	£2000
1993 — — sovereign series set (4 coins plus silver Pistrucci medal)	£2000
1993 — — double- to half sovereign (3 coins)	£1000
1993 — Coronation anniversary £5–1p in de luxe case (8 coins)	£38
1993 — — in standard case (8 coins)	£35
1993 BU £1–1p including 1992 EU 50p (8 coins)	£15
1994 Proof gold Britannia set (4 coins)	£2000
1994 — — sovereign series set (4 coins)	£2000
1994 — — £2 to half sovereign (3 coins)	£1000
1994 — Bank of England Tercentenary £2–1p in de luxe case (8 coins)	£38
1994 — — in standard case (8 coins)	£35
1994 BU £1–1p in folder (7 coins)	£18
1994 Proof gold 1992 and 1994 50p (2 coins)	£350
1994 — "Family silver" set £2–50p (3 coins)	£65
1995 Proof gold Britannia set (4 coins)	£2000
1995 — — sovereign series (4 coins)	£2000
1995 — — £2 to half sovereign (3 coins)	£850
1995 — 50th Anniversary of WWII £2–1p in de luxe case (8 coins)	£40
1995 — — as above in standard case (8 coins)	£35
1995 BU as above in folder (8 coins)	£16
1995 Proof "Family Silver" set £2 (two) and £1 (3 coins)	£90
1996 Proof gold Britannia set (4 coins)	£2000
1996 — — sovereign series set (4 coins)	£2000
1996 — — double- to half sovereign (3 coins)	£1000
1996 — Royal 70th Birthday £5–1p in de luxe case (9 coins)	£50
1996 — — as above in standard case (9 coins)	£45
1996 BU Football £2–1p in folder (8 coins)	£20
1996 Proof gold Britannia £10 and half-sovereign (2 coins)	£550
1996 — — sovereign and silver £1 (2 coins)	£250
1996 — "Family silver" set £5–£1 (3 coins)	£205
1996 — silver 25th Anniversary of Decimal currency £1–1p (7 coins)	£150
1996 Circulation and BU 25th Anniversary of Decimalisation 2s 6d–halfpenny (misc.) and £1–1p in folder (14 coins)	£25
1997 Proof gold Britannia set (4 coins)	£2000
1997 — — sovereign series set (4 coins)	£2000
1997 — — — £2 to half sovereign (3 coins)	£1000
1997 — — Silver Britannia set (4 coins)	£150
1997 — Golden Wedding £5 1p in red leather case	£45
1997 — — as above in standard case (10 coins)	£36
1997 BU £2 to 1p in folder (9 coins)	£25
1997 Proof silver 50p set, two sizes (2 coins)	£45
1997/1998 Proof silver £2 set, both dates (2 coins)	£70
1998 Proof gold Britannia set (4 coins)	£2000
1998 — — sovereign series set (4 coins)	£2000
1998 — — — double- to half sovereign (3 coins)	£1000
1998 Proof silver Britannia set (4 coins)	£185
1998 — Prince of Wales £5–1p (10 coins) in red leather case	£45
1998 — — as above in standard case (10 coins)	£38
1998 BU £2–1p in folder (9 coins)	£16
1998 Proof silver European/NHS 50p set (2 coins)	£60
1998 BU Britannia/EU 50p set (2 coins)	£8
1999 Proof gold Britannia set (4 coins)	£2000
1999 — — Sovereign series set (4 coins)	£2000
1999 — — — £2 to half sovereign (3 coins)	£1000
1999 — Princess Diana £5–1p in red leather case (9 coins)	£65
1999 — — as above in standard case (9 coins)	£45

DATE	FDC
1999 BU £2–1p (8 coins) in folder	£20
1999 Proof "Family Silver" set. Both £5, £2 and £1 (4 coins)	£150
1999 Britannia Millennium set. Bullion £2 and BU £5 (2 coins)	£30
1999/2000 Reverse frosted proof set, two x £1 (2 coins)	£75
2000 Proof gold Britannia set (4 coins)	£2000
2000 — — Sovereign series set (4 coins)	£2000
2000 — — — double- to half sovereign (3 coins)	£1000
2000 Millennium £5–1p in de luxe case (10 coins)	£50
2000 — — as above in standard case (10 coins)	£45
2000 — Silver set Millennium £5 to 1p plus Maundy (13 coins)	£225
2000 BU £2–1p set in folder (9 coins)	£20
2000 Millennium "Time Capsule" BU £5 to 1p (9 coins)	£30
2001 Proof gold Britannia set (4 coins)	£2000
2001 — — Sovereign series set (4 coins)	£2000
2001 — — — £2–half sovereign (3 coins)	£1000
2001 — Silver Britannia set (4 coins)	£150
2001 — Victoria £5–1p in Executive case (10 coins)	£100
2001 — — as above in red leather case (10 coins)	£75
2001 — — as above in "Gift" case (10 coins)	£48
2001 — — as above in standard case (10 coins)	£40
2001 BU £2–1p in folder (9 coins)	£18
2002 Proof gold Britannia set (4 coins)	£2000
2002 — — Sovereign series set, all Shield rev. (4 coins)	£2000
2002 — — — double- to half sovereign (3 coins)	£1000
2002 — Golden Jubilee set £5–1p plus Maundy (13 coins)	£4500
2002 — Golden Jubilee £5–1p in Executive case (9 coins)	£75
2002 — — as above in red leather de luxe case (9 coins)	£50
2002 — — as above in "Gift" case (9 coins)	£42
2002 — — as above in standard case (9 coins)	£40
2002 BU £2–1p (8 coins) in folder	£16
2002 Proof Gold Commonwealth Games £2 set (4 coins)	£2000
2002 — Silver Piedfort Commonwealth Games £2 set (4 coins)	£250
2002 — Commonwealth Games £2 set (4 coins)	£125
2002 — Commonwealth Games £2 set (4 coins)	£30
2002 BU Commonwealth Games £2 set (4 coins) in folder	£25
2003 Proof gold Britannia set (4 coins)	£2000
2003 — — £50–£10 (3 coins)	£1000
2003 — — — type set, one of each £100 reverse (4 coins)	£2500
2003 — — Sovereign series set (4 coins)	£2000
2003 — — — series £2–half sovereign (3 coins)	£1000
2003 — Silver Britannia set (4 coins)	£45
2003 — — type set (one of each £2 reverse) (4 coins)	£85
2003 — £5 to 1p, two of each £2 and 50p in Executive case (11 coins)	£80
2003 — — as above in red leather case (11 coins)	£55
2003 — — as above in standard case (11 coins)	£48
2003 BU £2 (two)–1p in folder (10 coins)	£22
2003 Proof silver Piedfort set. DNA £2, £1 and Suffragette 50p (3 coins)	£150
2003 Proof "Family Silver" set £5, Britannia and DNA £2, £1 and Suffragette 50p (5 coins)	£175
2003 Circ & BU "God Save the Queen" Coronation anniversary set 5s/0d to farthing (1953) and £5 to 1p (2003) in folder (19 coins)	£55
2003 Circulation or bullion "Royal Sovereign" collection, example of each Elizabeth II date (21 coins)	£3500
2004 Proof gold Britannia set (4 coins)	£2000
2004 — — — £50 to £10 (3 coins)	£1000
2004 — — Sovereign series set (4 coins)	£2000
2004 — — — Series £2-half sovereign (3 coins)	£1000
2004 (Issue date) Royal Portrait gold sovereign set, all proof except the first: Gillick, Machin, Maklouf and Rank-Broadley sovereigns, and the 2nd, 3rd and 4th of above half-sovereigns, various dates (7 coins)	£1500
2004 Proof silver Britannia set (4 coins)	£150
2004 — "Family Silver" set £5, Britannia and Trevithick £2, £1 and Bannister 50p (5 coins)	£165
2004 — Silver Piedfort set, Trevithick £2, £1 and Bannister 50p (3 coins)	£175
2004 — £2 to 1p, two each of £2 and 50p in Executive case (10 coins)	£75

DATE   FDC

2004 — — as above in red leather case (10 coins)..£45
2004 — — as above in standard case (10 coins)...£40
2004 BU £2 to 1p in folder (10 coins)...£22
2004 — "New Coinage" set, Trevithick £2, £1 and Bannister 50p (3 coins) £10
2004 BU "Season's Greetings" £2 to 1p and Royal Mint Christmas medal in folder (8 coins) £18
2005 Proof Gold Britannia set (4 coins)..£2000
2005 — — — £50 to £10 (3 coins)...£1000
2005 — — Sovereign series set (4 coins)..£2000
2005 — — — series, double to half sovereign (3 coins) £1000
2005 — Silver Britannia (4 coins) £135
2005 — Gold Trafalgar and Nelson £5 crowns (2 coins) £2000
2005 — Silver, as above (2 coins) £85
2005 — — Piedfort, as above (2 coins)..£135
2005 — Silver Piedfort set, Gunpowder Plot and World War II £2, £1 and Johnson 50p (4 coins) £200
2005 — £5 to 1p, two of each of £5, £2 and 50p in Executive case (12 coins) £80
2005 — — as above in red leather case (12 coins) £60
2005 — — as above in standard case (12 coins) £45
2005 BU Trafalgar and Nelson £5 crowns in pack (2 coins)...£25
2005 — £2 (two) to 1p in folder (10 coins) £25
2005 — "New Coinage" set, Gunpowder Plot £2, £1 and Johnson 50p (3 coins).................................£10
2005 — "Merry Xmas" £2 to 1p and Royal Mint Christmas medal in folder (8 coins) £20
2006 Proof Gold Britannia set (4 coins)..£2000
2006 — — Sovereign Series set (4 coins)..£2000
2006 — — — series, double to half sovereign (3 coins) £1000
2006 — Silver Britannia (4 coins) £145
2006 — Silver Brunel £2 coin set (2 coins) £75
2006 — — Piedfort Brunel £2 coin set (2 coins)..£125
2006 — Gold Brunel £2 coin set (2 coins) £950
2006 — Silver VC 50p coin set (2 coins) £58
2006 — Silver Piedfort VC 50p coin set (2 coins) £115
2006 — Gold VC 50p coin set (2 coins) £675
2006 — Silver proof set, £5 to 1p plus Maundy coins (13 coins)..£325
2006   Piedfort collection £5, with trumpets enhanced with 23 carat gold, both Brunel £2, £1,
            both VC 50p (6 coins) £350
2006 — — Britannia £2 "Golden Silhouette" collection, five different reverses, all dated 2006 (5 coins) £350
2006 — Britannia £25 Gold "Portrait" collection, five different reverses, all dated 2006 (5 coins) £1550
2006 — £5 to 1p, three of each £2 and 50p in Executive case (13 coins) £80
2006 — as above in red leather case (13 coins) £55
2006 — as above in standard case (13 coins) £45
2006 BU £2 (two), £1, 50p (two) and to 1p in folder (10 coins)...£18
2006 Proof Brunel £2 in folder (2 coins)...£15
2006 — VC 50p in folder (2 coins)..£15
2006   Gold Half Sovereign set dated 2005 Noad and 2006 Pistrucci St George and the Dragon (2 coins) £250
2007 — Gold Britannia set (4 coins)...£2500
2007 — — Sovereign Series set (4 coins)..£2000
2007 — — — series, double to half sovereign (3 coins) £1000
2007 — — Sovereign and half-sovereign (2 coins) £375
2007 — "Family Silver" set, Britannia, £5 crown, Union and Slavery £2, Gateshead £1
            and Scouting 50p (6 coins) £225
2007 Proof Silver Piedfort Collection, as "Family Silver" above but excluding a Britannia (5 coins)......£300
2007 — Silver £1 Bridge series coins, dated 2004 to 2007 (4 coins) £135
2007 — Silver Proof Piedfort £1 Bridge Series, dated 2004 to 2007 (4 coins) £275
2007 — Gold £1 Bridge series coins, dated as above (4 coins) £2000
2007 — £5 to 1p, three £2 and two 50p in Executive case (12 coins) £85
2007 — as above, Deluxe in red leather case (12 coins) £65
2007 — as above, in standard case (12 coins) £50
2007 BU £2 (two) to 1p (9 coins) £18
2007 Proof Silver Britannia (four coins) £145
2007 — Platinum Britannia (4 coins) £5000
2007 Satin Proof Silver Britannia, 20th Anniversary Collection, six different reverses, all dated 2007 (6 coins) £300
2007 50th Anniversary Sovereign set, 1957 circulation standard and 2007 Proof (2 coins) £450
2008 Proof Gold Britannia set (4 coins)...£2000
2008 — Platinum Britannia set (4 coins) £5000

DATE	FDC
2008 — Silver Britannia set (4 coins)	£150
2008 — Gold Sovereign series set (4 coins)	£2000
2008 — — — double to half-sovereign (3 coins)	£1000
2008 — — Sovereign and half-sovereign (2 coins)	£500
2008 — "Family silver" set, 2x £5, Britannia £2, Olympiad £2 and Royal Arms £1 (5 coins)	£200
2008 — Silver Piedfort Collection, 2x £5, Olympiad £2 and Shield of Royal Arms £1 (4 coins)	£285
2008 — 2 x £5, 2 x £2, £1 to 1p in Executive case (11 coins)	£85
2008 — as above, Deluxe in black leather case (11 coins)	£55
2008 — as above, in standard back case (11 coins)	£60
2008 BU 2 x £2, Royal Arms £1 to 1p (9 coins)	£20
2008 — "Emblems of Britain" ("old" Revs) Royal Arms £1 to 1p (7 coins)	£15
2008 — "Royal Shield of Arms" ("new" Revs) Shield of Royal Arms £1 to 1p (7 coins)	£15
2008 — Above two sets housed in one sleeve	£28
2008 Proof Base Metal "Royal Shield of Arms" set, £1 to 1p (7 coins)	£40
2008 — Silver "Emblems of Britain" set, £1 to 1p (7 coins)	£160
2008 — — "Royal Shield of Arms" set, £1 to 1p (7 coins)	£160
2008 — — Above two sets in one black case	£325
2008 — Gold "Emblems of Britain" set, £1 to 1p (7 coins)	£3500
2008 — — "Royal Shield of Arms" set, £1 to 1p (7 coins)	£3500
2008 — — Above two sets in one oak-veneer case	£6750
2008 — Platinum "Emblems of Britain" set, £1 to 1p (7 coins)	£8500
2008 — — "Royal Shield of Arms" set, £1 to 1p (7 coins)	£8500
2008 — — Above two sets in one walnut veneer case	£15,750
2008 — Silver Piedfort "Royal Shield of Arms" set, £1 to 1p (7 coins)	£325
2008 — Gold set of 14 £1 coins, one of each Rev used since 1983, all dated 2008 (25th anniversary) (14 coins)	£9500
2008 — Silver with gold Rev highlighting as above (14 coins)	£500
2008 — 2 x £2, Royal Arms £1 to 1p (9 coins) Christmas Coin Sets, two different outer sleeves, Father Christmas or Three Wise men	£20
2009 Proof Gold Britannia set (4 coins)	£2200
2009 — Platinum Britannia set (4 coins)	£4000
2009 — Silver Britannia set (4 coins)	£150
2009 — Gold Sovereign series set (5 coins)	£2700
2009 — — — double to half-sovereign (3 coins)	£1000
2009 — — sovereign and half-sovereign (2 coins)	£450
2009 — "Family Silver" set, Henry VIII £5, Britannia £2, Darwin and Burns £2, £1 and Kew 50p (6 coins)	£225
2009 — Silver Piedfort collection, Henry VIII £5, Darwin and Burns £2 and Kew Gardens 50p (4 coins)	£275
2009 — Silver Set, £5 to 1p (12 coins)	£275
2009 — Base metal Executive set, £5 to 1p (12 coins)	£80
2009 — — Deluxe set, £5 to 1p (12 coins)	£55
2009 — — Standard set, £5 to 1p (12 coins)	£45
2009 BU Base metal set, £2 to 1p (11 coins)	£22
2009 — — —, £1 to 1p "Royal Shield of Arms" set (7 coins)	£12
2009 — — —, £2 to 1p (8 coins)	£15
2009 Proof set of 50p coins as detailed in FIFTY PENCE section, CuNi (16 coins)	£195
2009 — Silver (16 coins)	£425
2009 — Gold (16 coins)	£8500
2009 — Gold Piedfort (16 coins)	£20,000
2009 "Mind" set of £5 coins, silver (6 coins)	£350
2010 Gold Britannia set (4 coins)	£2750
2010 — — —, £50 to £10 (3 coins)	£1500
2010 — Silver Britannia set (4 coins)	£140
2010 — Gold Olympic Series "Faster", £100 and £25 (2), (3 coins)	£2000
2010 — Sovereign series set (5 coins)	£2750
2010 — — double to half (3 coins)	£1250
2010 — — — sovereign to quarter (3 coins)	£550
2010 — "Silver Celebration" set, Restoration £5, Nightingale £2, London and Belfast £1 and Girlguiding 50p (5 coins)	£185
2010 Silver Piedfort set, coins as in "Silver Celebration" set (5 coins)	£300
2010 — Silver Collection, £5 to 1p (13 coins)	£300
2010 — Base Metal Executive Set, £5 to 1p (13 coins)	£80

DATE	FDC
2010 — — Deluxe set	£50
2010 — — Standard set	£40
2010 BU — Capital Cities £1 (2 coins)	£15
2010 — — Set, £2 to 1p (12 coins)	£35
2010 — — Definitive pack, £2 to 1p (8 coins)	£20
2010 Proof "Body" Collection of £5 coins, silver (6 coins)	£300
2010 Proof "Spirit" Collection of £5 coins, silver (6 coins)	£300
2011 Proof Gold Britannia set (4 coins)	£2750
2011 — Premium set (3 coins)	£1500
2011 — Sovereign set (5 coins)	£3000
2011 — — double to half (3 coins)	£1200
2011 — — sovereign to quarter (3 coins)	£650
2011 — Silver Britannia set (4 coins)	£180
2011 — Olympic gold "Higher" set (3 coins)	£2650
2011 — — — "Faster" (2010) and "Higher" set (6 coins) in 9-coin case	£5300
2011 — Silver Collection, £5 to 1p (14 coins)	£400
2011 — — Celebration set, Duke of Edinburgh £5, Mary Rose and King James bible Cardiff and Edinburgh £1 and WWF 50p (6 coins)	£250
2011 — — — Piedfort, as above (6 coins)	£395
2011 Executive Proof Base metal set (14 coins)	£85
2011 De-luxe Proof Base metal set (14 coins)	£50
2011 Standard Proof Base metal set (14 coins)	£40
2011 BU set including £2, £1 and 50p commemoratives (13 coins)	£26
2011 BU set of Definitives (8 coins)	£25
2012 Proof Gold Britannia Set (4 coins)	£3600
2012 — — — £50 down (3 coins)	£1900
2012 — — — Half-ounce anniversary(9coins)	£9500
2012 — Sovereign set (5 coins)	£4000
2012 — — Double to Half (3 coins)	£1650
2012 — — Sovereign to Quarter (3 coins)	£825
2012 — Silver Britannia set (4 coins)	£195
2012 — Silver Britannia Half-Ounce Anniversary (9 coins)	£500
2012 BU Sovereign set Double to Half (3 coins)	£1550
2012 Proof Olympic gold Stronger set (3 coins)	£3500
2012 — — — 2x £25 (2 coins)	£1200
2010, 2011, 2012 Proof Olympic gold complete set (9 coins)	£10,500
2009, 2010, 2011, 2012 Complete Countdown sets:	
Gold Proof (4 coins)	£11,500
Silver Proof Piedfort (4 coins)	£850
Silver Proof (4 coins)	£325
CuNi BU (4 coins)	£45
2012 Proof Gold set, Diamond Jubilee £5, Dickens & Technology £2, £1 to 1p (10 coins)	£8500
2012 — Silver set, as above with Selective Gold plating on £1 to 1p coins (10 coins)	£490
2012 — set (Premium) (10 coins)	£100
2012 — set (Collector) (10 coins)	£55
2012 BU set, include Diamond Jubilee £5 (10 coins)	£40
2012 — set, Technology £2 to 1p (8 coins)	£21
2012 Proof Gold, Diamond Jubilee £5 and Double Sovereign (2 coins)	£3200
2012 — Olympic and Paralympic £5 (2 coins)	£5500
2012 — Gold Piedfort 50p set, one each of the coins of Olympic sports in which Team GB gained gold medals (11 coins)	£25,000
2013 Proof Gold Britannia set, £100 to £1 (5 coins)	£3100
2013 — — — £50 to £10 (3 coins)	£1375
2013 — — —.£25 to £1 (3 coins)	£675
2013 — Silver Britannia set, £2 to 10p (5 coins)	£195
2013 — — — 20p and 10p (2 coins)	£39
2013 — Sovereign set (5 coins)	£4000
2013 — — Double to Half (3 coins)	£1650
2013 — — One to Quarter (3 coins)	£825
2013 — Gold £5 Portraits set (4 coins)	£9500
2013 — Silver Portraits set (4 coins)	1,465 £400
2013 — Silver Piedfort Portraits set (4 coins)	697 £800
2013 — Gold set, £5 Coronation anniversary to 1p (15 coins)	£12,500

DATE	FDC
2013 — Gold set of both London Underground £2 (2 coins)	£2000
2013 — Silver Piedfort set, as above (2 coins)	£200
2013 — Silver set, as above (2 coins)	£100
2013 BU set, as above (2 coins)	£20
2013 — Gold set, 30th anniversary of the One Pound coin, reverses from 1983 (Sewell), 1988 (Gorringe) and 2013 (Dent). (3 coins)	£3600
2013 — Silver, as above (3 coins)	£150
2013 BU Sovereign set, Double to Half (3 coins), struck June 2, 2013	£1550
2013 Proof Silver annual set, £5 Coronation anniv to 1p (15 coins)	£600
2013 — — Piedfort commemorative set (7 coins)	£650
2013 — "Premium" set (15 coins plus a "Latent Image" item)	£150
2013 — "Collector" set (15 coins)	£110
2013 — Commemorative set (7 coins)	£65
2013 BU annual set (15 coins)	£50
2013 — Definitive Set (8 coins)	£25
2014 Proof Gold Britannia (Clark) set £100 to 50p (6 coins)	£2600
2014 — — — £50 to £10 (3 coins)	£1175
2014 — — — £25 to £1 (3 coins)	£595
2014 — Silver Britannia (Clark) set £2 to 5p (6 coins)	£200
2014 — — 20p to 5p (3 coins)	£45
2014 — Sovereign set (5 coins)	£3300
2014 — — Double to half (3 coins)	£1300
2014 — — One to quarter (3 coins)	£625
2014 — Gold Commemorative set, £5 Queen Anne, 2 x £2, 2 x £1, 50p (6 coins)	£5500
2014 — Silver Piedfort set, as above (6 coins)	£570
2014 — — set as above (6 coins)	£295
2014 — — all major coins of 2014 (14 coins)	£560
2014 — Premium set (14 coins and a premium medal)	£155
2014 — Collector set (14 coins)	£110
2014 — Commemorative set (6 coins)	£65
2014 BU annual set (14 coins)	£50
2014 — definitive set (8 coins)	£25
2014 — Floral £1 set, Scotland and Northern Ireland (2 coins)	£18
2014 Proof Silver Outbreak of First World War set of £5 (6 coins)	£450
2014 — Gold set as above (6 coins)	—
2014 — Silver Portrait of Britain £5 Silver collection (4 coins)	£36
2015 Proof Gold Britannia (Dufort) set £100 to 50p, Clark portrait (6 coins)	£2,600
2015 — — — — £50 to £10 (3 coins)	£1,175
2015 — — — £10 to 50p (3 coins)	£350
2015 — Silver Britannia (Dufort) set £2 to 5p, Clark portrait (6 coins)	£200
2015 — Sovereign set, Rank-Broadley portrait (5 coins)	£2700
2015 — — Double to half, Rank-Broadley portrait (3 coins)	£1300
2015 — — One to quarter, Rank-Broadley portrait (3 coins)	£625
2015 — Gold Commemorative set, 2 x £5, 2 x £2, 2 x £1, 50p, Rank-Broadley portrait (5 coins)	£5500
2015 — Silver Piedfort set, as above (5 coins)	£570
2015 — — set as above (5 coins)	£295
2015 — Base metal set as above (5 coins)	£65
2015 — Platinum definitive set £2 to 1p, Rank-Broadley portrait plus £2 to 1p Clark portrait (16 coins)	£12,500
2015 — Gold ditto	£7,600
2015 — Silver ditto	£480
2015 — Base metal ditto	£120
2015 BU definitive set as per Platinum set above (16 coins)	£50

The above four entries are also available as 8-coin sets with either the Rank-Broadley ("Final Edition") or the Clark ("First Edition" portrait. These are issued at half the prices quoted above.

2015 Proof Silver set of definitive and commemorative coins, Rank-Broadley portrait (13 coins)	£560
2015 — Premium set as above (13 coins and a Premium medal)	£155
2015 BU Collector set as above (13 coins and medal)	£110
2015 Proof Double to half sovereign, Clark portrait (3 coins)	£1,200
2015 — Silver commemorative set, Anniversary of First World War (6 coins)	£450
2015 Portrait of Britain Silver Proof Collection (4x£5 with colour)	£310
2016 Proof Gold Britannia (Zamit) set (6 coins)	£2,895
2016 — — — £50 to £10 (3 coins)	£1,350

2016 — Silver Britannia (Zamit) set (6 coins)..£200
2016 — Sovereign set, Butler Portrait (5 coins) £2,700
2016 — — Double to half, Butler Portrait (3 coins) £1,200
2016— — One to quarter, Butler Portrait (3 coins)..£625
2016 — Gold Commemorative set, £5, 5x £2, £1, 50p (8 coins) £6,100
2016 — Silver Piedfort set, as above (8 coins)...£595
2016 — — set as above (8 coins) £395
2016 — Base metal set as above (8 coins) £95
2016 — silver set, commemoratives and definitives (16 coins) £595
2016 — Base metal set as above, Premium plus Medal (16 coins) £195
2016 — — Collector set (16 coins)..£145
2016 Portrait of Britain Silver Proof Collection (4x£5 with colour) £310
2016 BU Annual set including commemoratives (16 coins)..£55
2016 — Definitive set (8 coins) £30
2016 Proof Silver set of £5 coins, Anniversary of First World War (6 coins) £450
2017 — "Premium" set (13 coins & premium medal) £195
2017 — "Collector" Proof set (13 coins & medal) £145
2017 — Commemorative Proof (5 coins), 2x£5, 2x£2, 50p £95
2017 — Silver Proof Piedfort Commemorative set (coins as above) £595
2017 — Silver Proof Commemorative set (coins as above)..£350
2017 — Silver Proof set (13 coins £5–1p) £625
2017 BU annual set (13 coins as above)..£55
2017 Definitive set (8 coins) £30
2017 — Portrait of Britain Silver Proof Collection (4x£5 with colour)..£310
2017 — Proof Silver Outbreak of First World War set of £5 (6 coins) £450
2017 — Silver Proof Britannia (6 coins £20–5p) by Louis Tamlin...£215
2017 — Gold Proof Britannia set (3 coins £50–£10) by Louis Tamlin £1,425
2017 — Gold Proof Briannia set (6 coins £100–50p) by Louis Tamlin £3,295

In addition to the above the Royal Mint produce the BU sets detailed above in Wedding and in Baby gift packs each year. Also the following patterns have been made available:

1999 (dated 1994) Bi-metal £2, plus three unprocessed or part-processed elements... —
2003 Set of patterns of £1 coins with bridges designs, in gold, hall-marked on edges (4 coins) .... —
2003 — silver £1 as above (4 coins)...£150
2004 — gold £1 featuring heraldic animal heads, hall-marked on edge (4 coins) £1000
2004 — silver £1 featuring heraldic animal heads, hall-marked on edge (4 coins)..£350

IMPORTANT NOTE:

In this section the prices quoted were set at August 2017 with the price of gold at around £1000 per ounce and silver £13 per ounce. As the market for precious metals is notoriously volatile and unpredictable any price fluctuations have a marked effect on the values of modern precious metal coins, therefore it is important to seek professional advice when requiring a valuation for any of the precious metal sets listed. *The prices quoted here are for guidance only whereas the prices quoted for the recently issued sets are the original Royal Mint retail prices.*

SCOTLAND

The coins illustrated are pennies representative of the reign, unless otherwise stated.

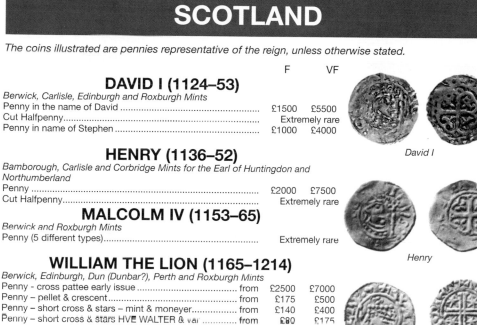

	F	VF
## DAVID I (1124–53)		
Berwick, Carlisle, Edinburgh and Roxburgh Mints		
Penny in the name of David	£1500	£5500
Cut Halfpenny..	Extremely rare	
Penny in name of Stephen	£1000	£4000

David I

HENRY (1136–52)
Bamborough, Carlisle and Corbridge Mints for the Earl of Huntingdon and Northumberland

	F	VF
Penny	£2000	£7500
Cut Halfpenny..	Extremely rare	

MALCOLM IV (1153–65)
Berwick and Roxburgh Mints

Penny (5 different types)..	Extremely rare	

Henry

WILLIAM THE LION (1165–1214)
Berwick, Edinburgh, Dun (Dunbar?), Perth and Roxburgh Mints

	F	VF
Penny - cross pattee early issue .... from	£2500	£7000
Penny – pellet & crescent.. from	£175	£500
Penny – short cross & stars – mint & moneyer.................. from	£140	£400
Penny – short cross & stars HVE WALTER & var .... from	£80	£175

ALEXANDER II (1214–49)
Berwick and Roxburgh Mints

	F	VF
Penny – in the name of William the Lion .... from	£400	£1200
Penny – in own name .... from	£600	£1750

William the Lion

ALEXANDER III (1249–86)

FIRST COINAGE (1250–80)
Pennies struck at the Mints at

	F	VF
Aberdeen .... from	£140	£325
Ayr .... from	£200	£550
Berwick .... from	£75	£175
Dun (Dumfries / Dunfermline? / Dundee?)....................... from	£160	£400
Edinburgh .... from	£140	£325
Forfar... from	£275	£750
Fres (Dumfries) .... from	£275	£650
Glasgow .... from	£275	£650
Inverness .... from	£260	£580
Kinghorn.. from	£275	£750
Lanark.. from	£245	£625
Montrose .... from	£530	£1100
Perth.. from	£100	£265
Roxburgh... from	£110	£285
St Andrews .... from	£260	£575
Stirling .... from	£190	£525

Alexander II

Alexander III First Coinage

SECOND COINAGE (1280–86)

	F	VF
Penny	£65	£145
Halfpenny	£90	£325
Farthing	£275	£825

Alexander III Second Coinage

	F	VF

JOHN BALIOL (1292–1306)

FIRST COINAGE (*Rough Surface issue*)

Penny .... from	£125	£275
Halfpenny .... from	£650	Ex. rare
Penny – St. Andrews .... from	£175	£475
Halfpenny – St. Andrews .... from	£800	Ex. rare

SECOND COINAGE (*Smooth Surface issue*)

Penny .... from	£200	£475
Halfpenny .... from	£150	£425
Farthing	Extremely rare	
Penny – St. Andrews .... from	£350	£950
Halfpenny – St. Andrews	Extremely rare	

John Baliol

ROBERT BRUCE (1306–29)

Berwick Mint

Penny .... from	£600	£1500
Halfpenny .... from	£650	£17500
Farthing .... from	£850	£2250

Robert Bruce

DAVID II (1329–71)

Aberdeen and Edinburgh Mints

Noble	Extremely Rare	
Groat (Edinburgh) .... from	£100	£250
Groat (Aberdeen) .... from	£750	£1750
Halfgroat (Edinburgh) .... from	£95	£260
Halfgroat (Aberdeen) .... from	£525	£1250
Penny 1st Coinage 2nd Issue .... from	£65	£195
Penny 2nd Coinage (Edinburgh) ..... from	£100	£275
Penny 2nd Coinage (Aberdeen) ...... from	£450	£1100
Halfpenny .... from	£250	£725
Farthing .... from	£450	£1250

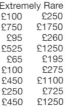

David II

ROBERT II (1371–90)

Dundee, Edinburgh and Perth Mints

Groat .... from	£100	£275
Halfgroat .... from	£135	£395
Penny .... from	£85	£215
Halfpenny .... from	£95	£275

Robert II

ROBERT III (1390–1406)

Aberdeen, Dumbarton, Edinburgh, Perth Mints

Lion or crown .... from	£1750	£5750
Demy lion or halfcrown .... from	£1250	£4500
Groat .... from	£90	£225
Halfgroat .... from	£175	£350
Penny .... from	£250	£725
Halfpenny .... from	£275	£850

JAMES I (1406–37)

Aberdeen, Edinburgh, Inverness, Linlithgow, Perth, Stirling Mints

Demy .... from	£850	£2500
Half demy .... from	£750	£2250
Groat Edinburgh .... from	£175	£395
Groat Other Mints .... from	£300	£850
Penny .... from	£250	£650
Halfpenny	Extremely rare	

Robert III Lion

F   VF

JAMES II (1437–60)

Aberdeen, Edinburgh, Linlithgow, Perth, Roxburgh, Stirling Mints

	F	VF
Demy .... from	£1050	£2950
Lion .... from	£1250	£4500
Half lion	Extremely rare	
Early groats (fleur-de-lis) Edinburgh .... from	£195	£550
Early groats (fleur-de-lis) Other Mints	Extremely rare	
Later groats (crown) Edinburgh .... from	£225	£650
Later groats (crown) Other Mints .... from	£450	£1250
Later Halfgroats (crown) Edinburgh .... from	£600	£1650
Later Halfgroats (crown) Other Mints	Extremely rare	
Penny (billon) .... from	£250	£650

JAMES III (1460–88)

Aberdeen, Berwick and Edinburgh Mints

	F	VF
Rider	£1750	£4500
Half rider	£1750	£4500
Quarter rider	£2500	£7000
Unicorn	£2750	£7500
Groat (facing bust) Edinburgh .... from	£130	£375
Groat (facing bust) Berwick .... from	£500	£1450
Groat (thistle & mullet) Edinburgh	£250	£650
Groat (threequarter bust) Aberdeen .... from	£550	£1650
Halfgroat .... from	£450	£1250
Penny (silver) .... from	£325	£950
Plack (billon) .... from	£175	£450
Half plack) .... from	£195	£525
Penny (billon) .... from	£150	£425
Farthing (copper)	£200	£650
Penny – ecclesiastical issue .... from	£70	£185
Farthing – ecclesiastical issue .... from	£125	£350

James III Groat, Berwick Mint

JAMES IV (1488–1513)

Edinburgh Mint

	F	VF
Unicorn	£1500	£4250
Half unicorn	£1250	£3500
Lion or crown	Extremely rare	
Half lion	Extremely rare	
Groat .... from	£400	£1375
Halfgroat .... from	£700	£2000
Penny (silver) .... from	£150	£400
Plack .... from	£40	£100
Half plack	Extremely rare	
Penny (billon) .... from	£55	£135

James IV Unicorn

JAMES V (1513–42)

Edinburgh Mint

	F	VF
Unicorn	£2050	£5125
Half Unicorn	Extremely rare	
Crown	£1350	£4250
Ducat or Bonnet piece .... from	£1250	£5000
Two-thirds ducat	£2500	£6500
One-third ducat	£3500	£9500
Groat .... from	£160	£450
One-third groat .... from	£275	£775
Plack .... from	£50	£125
Bawbee .... from	£60	£165
Half bawbee .... from	£140	£325
Quarter bawbee	Extremely rare	

James V Ducat or Bonnet Piece

	F	VF

MARY (1542–67)

Edinburgh and Stirling Mints

FIRST PERIOD (1542–58)

	F	VF
Crown	£1500	£4250
Twenty shillings	Extremely rare	
Lion (Forty-four shillings)	£1350	£4000
Half lion (Twenty-two shillings)	£1500	£4250
Ryals (Three pounds	£4000	£11500
Half ryal	£4500	£12500
Portrait testoon	£5000	£14500
Non-portrait testoon .... from	£250	£750
Half testoon .... from	£250	£750
Bawbee .... from	£65	£180
Half bawbee .... from	£125	£325
Bawbee - Stirling	£125	£400
Penny (facing bust) .... from	£325	£900
Penny (no bust) .... from	£225	£650
Lion .... from	£50	£145
Plack .... from	£70	£195

Mary Lion or Forty-Four Shillings

SECOND PERIOD (Francis and Mary, 1558–60)

	F	VF
Ducat (Sixty shillings)	Extremely rare	
Non-portrait testoon .... from	£325	£850
Half testoon .... from	£375	£1000
12 penny groat .... from	£80	£225
Lion .... from	£55	£135

THIRD PERIOD (Widowhood, 1560–65)

	F	VF
Portrait testoon	£3250	£9500
Half testoon.	£3000	£8500

FOURTH PERIOD (Henry and Mary, 1565–67)

	F	VF
Portrait ryal.	£45000	£125000
Non-portrait ryal .... from	£900	£1850
Two-third ryal .... from	£650	£1550
One-third ryal .... from	£850	£2550

FIFTH PERIOD (Second widowhood, 1567)

	F	VF
Non-portrait ryal .... from	£850	£2250
Two thirds ryal .... from	£475	£1350
One-third ryal .... from	£650	£1550

JAMES VI (1567–1603)

(Before accession to the English throne)

FIRST COINAGE (1567–71)

	F	VF
Ryal .... from	£450	£1100
Two-thirds ryal .... from	£350	£900
One-third ryal .... from	£350	£900

SECOND COINAGE (1571–80)

	F	VF
Twenty pounds	£25,000	£75,000
Noble (or half merk) .... from	£125	£300
Half noble (or quarter merk) .... from	£125	£300
Two merks or Thistle dollar .... from	£1500	£3750
Merk .... from	£2500	£7250

*James VI Fourth coinage
Ten Shillings*

THIRD COINAGE (1580–81)

	F	VF
Ducat	£5000	£14500
Sixteen shillings	£2500	£7250
Eight shillings	£1950	£5750

	F	VF
Four shillings	£4000	£9500
Two shillings	Extremely rare	

FOURTH COINAGE (1582–88)

	F	VF
Lion noble	£5500	£15000
Two-third lion noble	£4750	£13500
One-third lion noble	Extremely rare	
Forty shillings	£5000	£14500
Thirty shillings	£800	£2500
Twenty shillings	£425	£1250
Ten shillings	£425	£1250

FIFTH COINAGE (1588)

	F	VF
Thistle noble	£1700	£5250

SIXTH COINAGE (1591–93)

		F	VF
"Hat" piece		£3500	£10000
"Balance" half merk	from	£300	£895
"Balance" quarter merk		£725	£2000

James VI Seventh Coinage Rider

SEVENTH COINAGE (1594–1601)

		F	VF
Rider		£850	£2750
Half rider		£1000	£3500
Ten shillings	from	£150	£425
Five shillings	from	£125	£375
Thirty pence	from	£225	£625
Twelve pence	from	£130	£375

EIGHTH COINAGE (1601–04)

		F	VF
Sword and sceptre piece	from	£550	£1650
Half sword and sceptre piece	from	£425	£1250
Thistle-merk	from	£110	£295
Half thistle-merk	from	£65	£175
Quarter thistle-merk	from	£55	£135
Eighth thistle-merk	trom	£50	£110

BILLON AND COPPER ISSUES

		F	VF
Eightpenny groat	from	£40	£110
Fourpenny groat	from	£350	£1000
Twopenny plack	from	£130	£375
Hardhead	from	£35	£95
Twopence	from	£80	£230
Penny plack	from	£160	£750
Penny	from	£500	£1250

*James VI Seventh Coinage
10 Shillings*

JAMES VI (1603–25)
(After accession to the English throne)

		F	VF
Unit	from	£850	£2350
Double crown	from	£1100	£3250
British crown	from	£550	£1550
Halfcrown	from	£750	£2150
Thistle crown	from	£650	£2050
Sixty shillings	from	£350	£1000
Thirty shillings	from	£150	£425
Twelve shillings	from	£175	£575
Six shillings	from	£500	Ex. rare
Two shillings	from	£35	£100
One shilling	from	£125	£350
Copper twopence	from	£25	£70
Copper penny	from	£85	£250

*James VI after accession thirty
shillings*

297

	F	VF

CHARLES I (1625–49)

FIRST COINAGE (1625–36)

	F	VF
Unit...	£1250	£3500
Double crown	£1000	£3150
British crown..	Extremely rare	
Sixty shillings..	£800	£2500
Thirty shillings...	£150	£425
Twelve shillings...	£150	£425
Six shillings .... from	£350	£1000
Two shillings	£45	£110
One shilling..	£150	£495

SECOND COINAGE (1636)

	F	VF
Half merk	£90	£260
Forty penny piece..	£75	£210
Twenty penny piece.....................................	£70	£200

*Charles I Third Coinage
Sixty Shillings*

THIRD COINAGE (1637–42)

		F	VF
Unit...	from	£1250	£4250
Half unit	from	£950	£2950
British crown................................	from	£600	£1750
British half crown.........................	from	£525	£1500
Sixty shillings..............................		£775	£1850
Thirty shillings.............................	from	£140	£425
Twelve shillings...........................	from	£100	£325
Six shillings.................................	from	£80	£225
Half merk	from	£120	£395
Forty pence	from	£40	£110
Twenty pence	from	£25	£70

FOURTH COINAGE (1642)

	F	VF
Three shillings thistle..................................	£60	£150
Two shillings large II....................................	£40	£110
Two shillings small II...................................	£60	£155
Two shillings no value.................................	£80	£225

*Charles I Fourth Coinage
Two Shillings*

COPPER ISSUES
(1629 Issue)

	F	VF
Twopence (triple thistle..............................	£25	£70
Penny	£175	£500

(1632-39 Issue)

		F	VF
Twopence (Stirling turner.................	from	£25	£70

(1642-50 ISSUE)

	F	VF
Twopence (CR crowned	£20	£55

CHARLES II (1660–85)

FIRST COINAGE
Four merks

		F	VF
1664 Thistle above bust		£1250	£4000
1664 Thistle below bust		£2500	£7250
1665..		Extremely rare	
1670......................................	varieties from	£1550	£6950
1673..		£1550	£6950
1674 F below bust...................	varieties from	£1250	£4000
1675..		£950	£2750

Two merks

	F	VF
1664 Thistle above bust	£1000	£2500
1664 Thistle below bust	£2500	£7250

Charles II two merks

	F	VF
1670	£1200	£3000
1673	£750	£1950
1673 F below bust	£1350	£3250
1674	£1200	£3000
1674 F below bust	£1200	£3000
1675	£750	£1950

Merk

	F	VF
1664 .... varieties from	£250	£715
1665	£275	£780
1666	£325	£850
1668	£325	Ex. rare
1669 .... varieties from	£115	£325
1670	£160	£425
1671	£125	£350
1672 .... varieties from	£115	£325
1673 .... varieties from	£125	£350
1674	£250	£715
1674 F below bust	£225	£650
1675 F below bust	£200	£550
1675	£210	£585

Half merk

	F	VF
1664	£275	£725
1665 .... varieties from	£325	£600
1666 .... varieties from	£300	£750
1667	£325	£600
1668	£150	£400
1669 .... varieties from	£105	£285
1670 .... varieties from	£150	£400
1671 .... varieties from	£105	£285
1672	£150	£400
1673	£175	£475
1675 F below bust	£175	£475
1675	£195	£550

SECOND COINAGE
Dollar

	F	VF
1676	£850	£2225
1679	£750	£1925
1680	£850	£1950
1681	£650	£1625
1682	£575	£1550

Half Dollar

	F	VF
1675	£650	£1500
1676	£750	£1950
1681	£400	£1100

Quarter Dollar

	F	VF
1675	£195	£550
1676 .... varieties from	£100	£275
1677 .... varieties from	£145	£400
1678	£165	£450
1679	£185	£500
1680	£150	£375
1681	£120	£325
1682 .... varieties from	£145	£400

Eighth Dollar

	F	VF
1676 .... varieties from	£85	£210
1677	£125	£300

Charles II Dollar

Charles II Sixteenth Dollar

Charles II Bawbee

	F	VF
1678/7	£195	£495
1679	Extremely rare	
1680 .....varieties from	£150	£345
1682 .....varieties from	£225	£495

Sixteenth Dollar

	F	VF
1677	£85	£210
1678/7 .....varieties from	£120	£320
1679/7	£135	£360
1680 .....varieties from	£135	£360
1681	£85	£210

Copper Issues

	F	VF
Twopence CR crowned .....varieties from	£25	£70
Bawbees 1677-79 .....varieties from	£65	£195
Turners 1677-79 .....varieties from	£45	£125

JAMES VII (1685–89)

Sixty shillings

	F	VF
1688 proof only .....varieties from	—	£3250

Forty shillings

	F	VF
1687 .....varieties from	£400	£950
1688 .....varieties from	£400	£950

Ten shillings

	F	VF
1687	£150	£425
1688 .....varieties from	£250	£700

James VII ten shillings

WILLIAM & MARY (1689–94)

Sixty shillings

	F	VF
1691	£295	£1100
1692	£475	£1750

Forty shillings

	F	VF
1689 .....varieties from	£295	£850
1690 .....varieties from	£185	£525
1691 .....varieties from	£195	£550
1692 .....varieties from	£225	£600
1693 .....varieties from	£195	£550
1694 .....varieties from	£225	£775

Twenty shillings

	F	VF
1693	£450	£1500
1694	Extremely rare	

Ten shillings

	F	VF
1689	Extremely rare	
1690 .....varieties from	£295	£750
1691 .....varieties from	£195	£600
1692 .....varieties from	£195	£600
1694 .....varieties from	£250	£700

Five shillings

	F	VF
1691	£200	£575
1694 .....varieties from	£120	£350

Copper Issues

	F	VF
Bawbees 1691–94 .....varieties from	£100	£275
Bodle (Turners) 1691–94 .....varieties from	£55	£180

William & Mary ten shillings

	F	VF

WILLIAM II (1694–1702)

	F	VF
Pistole	£3000	£7500
Half pistole	£3750	£8500

Forty shillings

		F	VF
1695	varieties from	£175	£550
1696		£200	£525
1697		£250	£550
1698		£200	£495
1699		£325	£650
1700		Extremely rare	

Twenty shillings

		F	VF
1695		£200	£625
1696		£200	£625
1697	varieties from	£250	£700
1698	varieties from	£175	£650
1699		£225	£625

Ten shillings

		F	VF
1695		£150	£375
1696		£150	£375
1697	varieties from	£150	£375
1698	varieties from	£150	£375
1699		£295	£750

Five shillings

		F	VF
1695		£70	£195
1696		£65	£180
1697	varieties from	£75	£225
1699		£95	£275
1700		£85	£230
1701		£125	£350
1702		£125	£350

Copper Issues

		F	VF
Bawbee 1695–97	varieties from	£85	£325
Bodle (Turners) 1695–97	varieties from	£50	£150

William II ten shillings

Anne five shillings

ANNE (1702–14)

Pre-Union 1702 7
Ten shillings

		F	VF
1705		£175	£450
1706	varieties from	£225	£650

Five shillings

		F	VF
1705	varieties from	£85	£225
1706		£85	£225

POST-UNION 1707–14
See listing in English section.

JAMES VIII (The Old Pretender) (1688–1766)

A number of Guineas and Crowns in various metals were struck in 1828 using original dies prepared by Norbert Roettiers, all bearing the date 1716. These coins are extremely rare and are keenly sought after.

Crown

1716	Generally EF+	£2500

Our grateful thanks go to David Stuart of ABC Coins & Tokens who has spent many hours updating the Scottish section for 2017.

ISLE OF MAN

DATE	F	VF	EF	UNC

PENNY (Copper except where stated)

	F	VF	EF	UNC
1709 Cast	£55	£185	£350	—
1709 Silver cast Proof	—	—	—	£2000
1709 Brass	£50	£175	£350	—
1733 "Quocunque"	£40	£75	£275	£450
1733 "Ouocunoue"	£45	£85	£300	£750
1733 Bath metal "Quocunque"	£30	£75	£300	—
1733 Silver Proof	—	—	—	£850
1733 Bronze Proof	—	—	—	£500
1733 Proof	—	—	—	£675
1733 Cap frosted	£35	£75	£300	£500
1733 Brass, cap frosted	£40	£75	£325	£650
1733 Silver Proof cap frosted	—	—	—	£650
1733 Bronze annulets instead of pellets	£50	£100	£400	£500
1758	£30	£50	£250	£450
1758 Proof	—	—	—	£650
1758 Silver Proof	—	—	—	£1000
1786 Engrailed edge	£35	£65	£275	£450
1786 Engrailed edge Proof	—	—	—	£600
1786 Plain edge Proof	—	—	—	£1000
1786 Pellet below bust	£35	£65	£275	£550
1798	£35	£65	£250	£500
1798 Proof	—	—	—	£450
1798 Bronze Proof	—	—	—	£450
1798 Copper-gilt Proof	—	—	—	£2000
1798 Silver Proof	—	—	—	£2500
1813	£40	£75	£300	£500
1813 Proof	—	—	—	£650
1813 Bronze Proof	—	—	—	£650
1813 Copper-gilt Proof	—	—	—	£2500
1839	£35	£75	£200	£450
1839 Proof	—	—	—	£500

HALF PENCE (Copper except where stated)

	F	VF	EF	UNC
1709 Cast	£50	£125	£250	—
1709 Brass	£55	£185	£500	—
1723 Silver	£725	£1250	£3500	—
1723 Copper	£300	£600	£1750	£2500
1733 Copper	£35	£55	£225	£450
1733 Bronze	£35	£55	£225	£450
1733 Silver Proof plain cap	—	—	—	£700
1733 Silver Proof frosted cap	—	—	—	—
1733 Bronze Proof	—	—	—	£500
1733 Bath metal plain cap	£40	£50	£215	—
1733 Bath metal frosted cap	£40	£50	£215	—
1758	£40	£50	£215	£450
1758 Proof	—	—	—	£800
1786 Engrailed edge	£30	£45	£120	£350
1786 Proof engrailed edge	—	—	—	£450
1786 Plain edge	£40	£65	£250	£350
1786 Proof plain edge	—	—	—	£650
1786 Bronze Proof	—	—	—	£450
1798	£35	£45	£150	£350
1798 Proof	—	—	—	£450
1798 Bronze Proof	—	—	—	£400

DATE	F	VF	EF	UNC
1798 Copper-gilt Proof	—	—	—	£1500
1798 Silver Proof	—	—	—	£1500
1813	£30	£45	£150	£300
1813 Proof	—	—	—	£375
1813 Bronze Proof	—	—	—	£350
1813 Copper-gilt Proof	—	—	—	£1250
1839	£30	£45	£150	£300
1839 Bronze Proof	—	—	—	£450

FARTHING

	F	VF	EF	UNC
1839 Copper	£30	£45	£150	£300
1839 Bronze Proof	—	—	—	£450
1839 Copper-gilt Proof	—	—	—	£2500

The last issue of coins made in the Isle of Man had been in 1839 but in 1970 Spink & Son Ltd was commissioned to produce a modern coinage for the Isle of Man Government which was struck at the Royal Mint. From 1973 onwards the Pobjoy Mint took over the contract and became a very prolific producer of definitive and commemorative issues. It is not proposed to give a complete listing of all these coins but the Crown and 25p, which from the collector's point of view are the most interesting in the series, are listed below. However, as the prices for these items vary dramatically according to the source it has been decided not to price them. Additionally a special 50p coin was issued to celebrate Christmas each year. In 2017 the contract to produce the coinage was awarded to the Tower Mint and their initial new designs appear later in the book.

The listings that follow are of the ordinary uncirculated cupro-nickel crown-size coins. Many of these coins were also produced in other metals, including silver, gold and platinum in non proof and proof form and in 1984 some were also issued in silver clad cupro-nickel in proof form.

DATE

1970 Manx Cat
1972 Royal Silver Wedding
1974 Centenary of Churchill's birth£16
1975 Manx Cat
1976 Bi-Centenary of American Independence
1976 Centenary of the Horse Drawn Tram
1977 Silver Jubilee
1977 Silver Jubilee Appeal
1978 25th Anniversary of the Coronation
1979 300th Anniversary of Manx Coinage
1979 Millennium of Tynwald (5 coins)
1980 Winter Olympics
1980 Derby Bicentennial
1980 22nd Olympics (3 coins)
1980 80th Birthday of Queen Mother
1981 Duke of Edinburgh Award Scheme (4 coins)
1981 Year of Disabled (4 coins)
1981 Prince of Wales' Wedding (2 coins)
1982 12th World Cup—Spain (4 coins)
1982 Maritime Heritage (4 coins)
1983 Manned Flight (4 coins)
1984 23rd Olympics (4 coins)
1984 Quincentenary of College of Arms (4 coins)
1984 Commonwealth Parliamentary Conference (4 coins)
1985 Queen Mother (6 coins)
1986 13th World Cup—Mexico (6 coins)
1986 Prince Andrew Wedding (2 coins)
1987 200th Anniversary of the United States Constitution

DATE

1987 America's Cup Races (5 coins)
1988 Bicentenary of Steam Navigation (6 coins)
1988 Australia Bicentennial (6 coins)
1988 Manx Cat
1989 Royal Visit
1989 Bicentenary of the Mutiny on the Bounty (4 coins)
1989 Persian Cat
1989 Bicentenary of Washington's Inauguration (4 coins)
1990 150th Anniversary of the Penny Black
1990 World Cup—Italy (4 coins)
1990 25th Anniversary of Churchill's Death (2 coins)
1990 Alley Cat
1990 Queen Mother's 90th Birthday
1991 Norwegian Forest Cat
1991 Centenary of the American Numismatic Association
1991 1992 America's Cup
1991 10th Anniversary of Prince of Wales' Wedding (2 coins)
1992 Discovery of America (4 coins)
1992 Siamese Cat
1992 1992 America's Cup
1993 Maine Coon Cat
1993 Preserve Planet Earth—Dinosaurs (2 coins)
1994 Preserve Planet Earth—Mammoth
1994 Year of the Dog
1994 World Football Cup (6 coins)
1994 Japanese Bobtail Cat
1994 Normandy Landings (8 coins)
1994 Preserve Planet Earth—Endangered Animals (3 coins)
1995 Man in Flight—Series i (8 coins)
1995 Man in Flight—Series ii (8 coins)
1995 Queen Mother's 95th Birthday
1995 Year of the Pig
1995 Turkish Cat
1995 Preserve Planet Earth—Egret and Otter
1995 America's Cup
1995 Aircraft of World War II (19 coins)
1995 Famous World Inventions—Series i (12 coins)
1996 Year of the Rat
1996 70th Birthday of HM the Queen
1996 The Flower Fairies—Series i (4 coins)
1996 Famous World Inventions—Series ii (6 coins)
1996 Olympic Games (6 coins)
1996 Preserve Planet Earth—Killer Whale and Razorbill
1996 Burmese Cat
1996 Robert Burns (4 coins)
1996 King Arthur & the Knights of the Round Table (5 coins)
1996 European Football Championships (8 coins)
1996 Football Championships Winner
1996 Explorers (2 coins)
1997 Year of the Ox
1997 The Flower Fairies—Series ii (4 coins)
1997 Royal Golden Wedding (2 coins)
1997 Explorers—Eriksson and Nansen (2 coins)
1997 Long-haired Smoke Cat
1997 10th Anniversary of the "Cats on Coins" series (silver only)
1997 90th Anniversary of the TT Races (4 coins)
1998 The Millennium (16 coins issued over 3 years)
1998 Year of the Tiger
1998 FIFA World Cup (4 coins)
1998 Birman Cat
1998 The Flower Fairies—Series iii (4 coins)
1998 18th Winter Olympics, Nagano (4 coins)
1998 Explorers—Vasco da Gama and Marco Polo (2 coins)
1998 125th Anniversary of Steam Railway (8 coins)
1998 International Year of the Oceans (4 coins)
1999 50th Birthday of HRH the Prince of Wales
1999 Year of the Rabbit

DATE

1999 27th Olympics in Sydney (5 coins)
1999 Rugby World Cup (6 coins)
1999 Wedding of HRH Prince Edward and Sophie Rhys-Jones
1999 Queen Mother's 100th Birthday (4 coins)
1999 The Millennium (4 coins)
1999 Titanium Millennium crown
2000 Year of the Dragon
2000 Scottish Fold cat
2000 Millennium—own a piece of time
2000 Explorers, Francisco Piarro and Wilem Brents (2 coins)
2000 Life and times of the Queen Mother (4 coins)
2000 Queen Mother's 100th Birthday
2000 60th Anniversary of the Battle of Britain
2000 BT Global Challenge
2000 18th Birthday of HRH Prince William
2001 Year of the Snake
2001 The Somali cat
2001 Life and times of the Queen Mother (2 coins)
2001 Explorers, Martin Frobisher and Roald Amundsen (2 coins)
2001 75th Birthday of HM the Queen
2001 Joey Dunlop
2001 Harry Potter (6 coins)
2002 Year of the Horse
2002 The XIX Winter Olympiad, Salt Lake City (2 coins)
2002 World Cup 2002 in Japan/Korea (4 coins)
2002 The Bengal Cat
2002 The Queen's Golden Jubilee—i (1 coin)
2002 Introduction of the Euro
2002 The Queen's Golden Jubilee—ii (4 coins)
2002 A Tribute to Diana Princess of Wales—5 years on
2003 Year of the Goat
2003 The Balinese Cat
2003 Anniversary of the "Star of India"
2003 Lord of the Rings (5 coins)
2004 Olympics (4 coins)
2004 100 Years of Powered Flight (2 coins)
2005 Lord of the Rings: The Return of the King
2005 Manx Hero Lt. John Quilliam and the Battle of Trafalgar (2 coins)
2005 The Himalayan Cat with kittens
2005 Bicentenary of the Battle of Trafalgar (6 coins)
2005 60th Anniversary of D-Day (6 coins)
2005 60th Anniversary of Victory in Europe
2005 200th Anniversary of the Battle of Trafalgar
2005 400th Anniversary of the Gun Powder Plot (2 coins)
2005 Bicentenary of the Battle of Trafalgar and Death of Nelson
2005 Italy and the Isle of Man TT races (2 coins)
2005 Harry Potter and the Goblet of Fire (4 coins)
2006 100 Years of Norwegian Independence
2006 80th Birthday of Her Majesty the Queen (4 coins)
2006 The Battles that Changed the World—Part II (6 coins)
2006 150th Anniversary of the Victoria Cross (2 coins)
2006 30th Anniversary of the first Translantic Flight
2007 The Ragdoll Cat
2007 Fairy Tales—Sleeping Beauty, The Three Little Pigs (2 coins)
2007 The Graceful Swan
2007 The Royal Diamond Wedding Anniversary
2007 The Centenary of the TT races
2007 The Centenary of the Scouting
2008 50th Anniversary of Paddington Bear
2008 Prince Charles 60th Birthday
2008 Centenary of the Olympics
2008 Burmilla Cat
2008 Year of Planet Earth
2008 The Adorable Snowman
2008 UEFA European Football Championships
2008 The Return of Tutankhamun

DATE

2008 The Olympic Collection—The Olympics coming to London
2009 Winter Olympics (2 coins)
2009 The Chinchilla Cat
2009 40th Anniversary of the 1st Concorde Test Flight
2009 50 Years of Championship Racing
2009 Fifa World Cup South Africa 2010
2010 50 Years of racing by the Suzuki Racing Team
2010 Abyssinian Cat and her Kitten
2010 Celebrating 15 Years of the Gold Noble
2010 25th Anniversary of the Gold Angel coin
2011 Year of the Rabbit coloured coin
2011 Engagement of HRH Prince William to Catherine Middleton
2011 Royal Wedding of HRH Prince William and Catherine Middleton
2011 Buckingham Palace
2011 A Lifetime of Service—Queen Elizabeth II and Prince Philip
2011 The Turkish Angora Cat
2011 Donatello's famous Chellini Madonna
2011 TT Races
2012 European Football Championships (4 coins)
2012 Manx Cat Coin
2012 Centenary of RMS *Titanic*
2012 Juno Moneta Coin
2012 Petra Coin
2012 River Thames Diamond Jubilee Pageant
2012 Olympics (6 coins).
2013 St. Patrick Commemorative
2013 Kermode Bear
2013 Anniversary of Queen Victoria and Queen Elizabeth II Coronations
2013 Siberian Cat
2013 Winter Olympic (4 coins)
2013 Lifetime of Service—Queen Elizabeth II and Prince Philip
2014 Centenary of WWI
2014 200th Anniversary of Matthew Flinders
2014 Snowshoe Cat
2014 The Snowman & Snowdog Christmas crown (+coloured issue)
2014 70th Anniversary of D-Day (poppies picked out in red)
2015 75th Anniversary of the Battle of Britain (search lights in yellow)
2015 200th Anniversary of the Battle of Waterloo—Napoleon
2015 200th Anniversary of the Battle of Waterloo—Wellington
2015 Sir Winston Churchill
2015 Selkirk Rex Cat
2015 175th Anniversary of the Penny Black Stamp (issued in a pack)
2015 Paddington Bear
2015 Her Majesty the Queen Elizabeth II Longest reigning Monarch
2016 Tobacco Brown Cat

DECIMAL COINAGE—TOWER MINT ISSUES

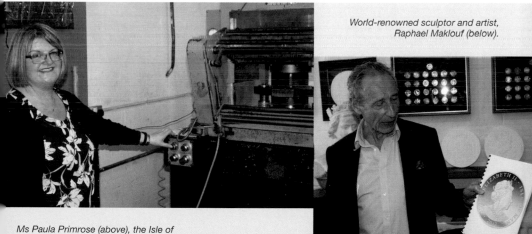

FIVE POUNDS—Triskele symbol ("Alpaca" metal)
TWO POUNDS—Tower of Refuge (Cupro-nickel/Nickel-brass)
ONE POUNDS—Raven and Falcon (Nickel-brass)
FIFTY PENCE—Manx Loughtan Sheep (Cupro-nickel)
TWENTY PENCE—Viking Longship (Cupro-nickel)
TEN PENCE—The Manx Cat(Nickel plated steel)
FIVE PENCE—Manx Shearwater bird (Nickel plated steel)

These designs, introduced in 2017, will replace the existing series. It remains to be seen what other coins will be issued but no doubt these coins will be struck in other metals for collectors in due course. The on-going situation and any commemorative issues that appear will be reported in COIN NEWS.

World-renowned sculptor and artist, Raphael Maklouf (below).

Ms Paula Primrose (above), the Isle of Man's chief Accountant.

GUERNSEY

DATE	F	VF	EF	UNC

TEN SHILLINGS
	F	VF	EF	UNC
1966	—	£5	£10	£15
1966 Proof	—	—	—	£30

THREEPENCE
	F	VF	EF	UNC
1956	£1	£4	£8	£10
1956 Proof	—	—	—	£15
1959	£1	£4	£8	£15
1966 Proof	—	—	—	£15

EIGHT DOUBLES
	F	VF	EF	UNC
1834	£10	£15	£50	£175
1858 5 berries	£6	£10	£50	£150
1858 4 berries	£6	£10	£50	£160
1864 1 stalk	£6	£10	£40	£70
1864 3 stalks	£6	£10	£30	£65
1868	£6	£10	£30	£65
1874	£4	£6	£15	£50
1885H	£4	£6	£15	£45
1889H	£3	£4	£15	£40
1893H small date	£3	£4	£15	£40
1893H large date	£3	£4	£15	£40
1902H	£3	£4	£15	£40
1903H	£3	£4	£15	£40
1910	£3	£4	£15	£40
1911H	£3	£4	£15	£45
1914H	£1	£3	£10	£30
1918H	£1	£3	£8	£25
1920H	£1	£3	£8	£25
1934H	£1	£3	£10	£35
1934H Proof	—	—	—	£200
1938H	£1	£3	£10	£25
1945H	£1	£2	£8	£15
1947H	£1	£2	£8	£15
1949H	—	£2	£9	£15
1956	—	£1	£7	£15
1956	—	£1	£5	£15
1959	—	£1	£5	£15
1966 Proof	—	—	—	£35

FOUR DOUBLES
	F	VF	EF	UNC
1830	£4	£9	£50	£125
1830 Mule with obv. St Helena 1/2d	—	£850	—	—
1858	£6	£12	£50	£135
1864 Single stalk	£2	£6	£20	£60
1864 3 stalks	£2	£6	£25	£65
1868	£3	£7	£22	£75
1874	£2	£6	£22	£75
1885H	£2	£6	£20	£45
1889H	£2	£3	£15	£35
1893H	£2	£3	£15	£35
1902H	£2	£3	£10	£30
1903H	£2	£3	£13	£30
1906H	£2	£3	£10	£25
1908H	£2	£3	£10	£25
1910H	£2	£3	£10	£25
1911H	£2	£3	£8	£25
1914H	£2	£3	£13	£45
1918H	£2	£3	£12	£35
1920H	£2	£3	£10	£35
1945H	£2	£3	£10	£35
1949H	£2	£3	£12	£35
1956	£1	£2	£8	£15
1966 Proof	—	—	—	£20

DATE	F	VF	EF	UNC
TWO DOUBLES				
1858	£6	£10	£50	£200
1868 Single stick	£6	£12	£55	£200
1868 3 stalks	£7	£15	£85	£225
1874	£4	£10	£50	£150
1885H	£3	£6	£20	£35
1889H	£3	£5	£20	£35
1899H	£3	£5	£25	£50
1902H	£3	£5	£20	£35
1903H	£3	£5	£20	£35
1906H	£3	£5	£20	£35
1908H	£3	£5	£20	£35
1911H	£3	£5	£25	£45
1914H	£3	£5	£25	£45
1917H	£7	£20	£85	£225
1918H	£3	£5	£15	£30
1920H	£3	£5	£15	£30
1929H	£2	£3	£12	£20
ONE DOUBLE				
1830	£3	£4	£22	£45
1868	£4	£10	£35	£120
1868/30	£5	£7	£27	£85
1885H	£2	£3	£8	£20
1889H	£1	£2	£6	£20
1893H	£1	£2	£6	£20
1899H	£1	£2	£6	£20
1902	£1	£2	£6	£20
1903H	£1	£2	£6	£20
1911H	£1	£2	£8	£20
1911 (new shield)	£1	£2	£6	£20
1914H	£1	£2	£8	£20
1929H	£1	£2	£6	£20
1933H	£1	£2	£6	£20
1938H	£1	£2	£6	£20

DECIMAL COINAGE

Ordinary circulating coinage from 1986 onwards is usually available in uncirculated condition at a small premium above face value thus it is not listed here. The coins listed are cupro-nickel unless otherwise stated.

	UNC
ONE HUNDRED POUNDS	
1994 50th Anniversary of Normandy Landings. Gold proof	£1500
1995 Anniversary of the Liberation. Gold proof	£1500
FIFTY POUNDS	
1994 50th Anniversary of Normandy Landings. Gold proof	£950
1995 Anniversary of the Liberation. Gold proof	£950
1998 Queen Elizabeth and Queen Mother Gold proof	£1000
1999 Queen Elizabeth and Queen Mother Gold	£900
2004 Anniversary of D-Day. Gold	£1100
2013 70th Anniversary of the Dambuster Raid. Silver proof 10oz	£600
TWENTY-FIVE POUNDS	
1994 50th Anniversary of Normandy Landings. Gold	£ 420
1994 — Gold proof	£ 420
1995 Anniversary of the Liberation. Gold proof	£ 420
1995 Queen Mothers 95th Birthday. Gold	£ 420
1996 European Football Championships. Gold proof	£ 420
1997 Royal Golden Wedding. Gold proof	£ 420
1998 Royal Air Force. Gold proof	£ 420
2000 Queen Mother 100th Birthday. Gold proof	£ 420
2001 Queen Victoria centennial Gold proof	£ 420
2001 Queen Victoria gold proof	£ 420
2001 HM the Queen's 75th Birthday. Gold proof	£425
2002 Princess Diana memorial. Gold proof	£ 420
2002 Duke of Wellington. Gold proof	£ 420

DATE	UNC
2002 Golden Jubilee. Gold proof	£ 420
2002 Queen Mother. Gold proof	£ 420
2003 Golden Jubilee. Gold proof	£ 420
2003 Golden Hind. Gold proof	£ 420
2004 Anniversary of D-Day. Gold proof	£ 420
2004 Age of Steam—Truro. Gold proof	£ 420
2004 Age of Steam—Mallard. Gold proof	£ 420
2004 HMS Invincible. Gold proof	£ 420
2005 HMS Ark Royal. Gold proof	£ 420
2006 FIFA World Cup. Gold proof	£ 420

TEN POUNDS

1994 50th Anniversary of Normandy Landings. Gold proof	£225
1995 Anniversary of the Liberation. Gold proof	£225
2000 Century of Monarchy. Silver proof	£150
2000 Guernsey Gold proof 'Nugget'	£250
2001 19th Century Monarchy. Silver proof	£150
2002 18th Century Monarchy. Silver proof	£150
2004 Anniversary of D-Day. Silver proof	£150
2012 Diamond Jubilee. 5 oz Silver proof	£250
2013 Coronation Jubilee. 5 oz Silver proof	£250
2017 Sapphire Jubilee. 5 oz Silver proof	—

FIVE POUNDS

1995 Queen Mother's 95th birthday	£25
1995 — Silver proof	£55
1995 — Small size gold	£250
1996 HM the Queen's 70th birthday	£18
1996 — Silver proof	£55
1996 European Football Championships	£35
1996 — Silver proof	£55
1997 Royal Golden Wedding	£25
1997 — Silver proof	£55
1997 — Small size gold. BU	£250
1997 Castles of the British Isles—Castle Cornet, Guernsey	£20
1997 — Silver proof	£65
1997 Castles of the British Isles—Caernarfon Castle. Silver proof	£75
1997 Castles of the British Isles—Leeds Castle. Silver proof	£75
1998 Royal Air Force.	£15
1998 Royal Air Force. Silver proof	£70
1999 Millennium. Brass	£25
1999 — Silver proof	£55
1999 Wedding of HRH Prince Edward and Sophie Rhys-Jones	£25
1999 — Silver proof	£55
1999 Queen Mother	£25
1999 — Silver proof	£80
1999 Winston Churchill	£15
1999 — Gold	£1000
2000 Queen Mother's 100th Birthday	£10
2000 — Silver proof	£85
2000 — Small size gold. proof	£200
2000 Centuries of the British Monarchy	£45
2000 — Silver proof	£85
2000 — Small size gold. proof	£200
2001 The Reign of Queen Victoria	£20
2001 — Gold proof	£360
2001 — proof	£60
2001 — Silver proof	£60
2001 HM the Queen's 75th Birthday	£15
2001 — Silver proof	£60
2001 — Small size gold. proof	£200
2001 19th Century Monarchy	£20
2001 — Silver proof	£60
2001 — Small size gold. proof	£200
2002 Golden Jubilee (two types)	£15
2002 — Silver proof	£65
2002 Princess Diana Memorial	£15
2002 — proof	£60

DATE	UNC
2002 — Gold proof	£1000
2002 Century of Monarchy	£15
2002 — Silver proof	£60
2002 — Small size gold. proof	£200
2002 Queen Mother Memoriam	£20
2002 — proof	£25
2002 — Silver proof	£65
2002 — Small size gold proof	£200
2002 — Large size gold proof	£1000
2003 Duke of Wellington	£15
2003 — Silver proof	£50
2003 — Small size gold proof	£200
2003 — Large size gold proof	£1000
2003 Prince William	£20
2003 — Silver proof	£60
2003 — Gold proof	£1000
2003 Golden Hind	£20
2003 17th Century Monarchy	£25
2003 History of the Royal Navy, Nelson	£20
2003 — Nelson with coloured flag. proof	£30
2004 — Invincible. Silver proof	£50
2004 16th Century monarchs	£15
2004 History of the Railways, Mallard	£12
2004 — City of Truro	£15
2004 — The Boat Train	£12
2004 — The Train Spotter	£15
2004 History of the Royal Navy, Henry VIII	£15
2004 — Invincible	£15
2004 Anniversary of D-Day	£12
2004 — Silver proof	£50
2004 Gold proof	£1000
2004 Anniversary of the Crimean War. Plain	£12
2004 — with colour	£15
2004 — Silver proof	£55
2004 — Gold proof with colour	£1250
2005 200th Anniversary of the Battle of Trafalgar	£25
2005 60th Anniversary of the Liberation of the Channel Islands	£25
2005 End of World War II. Silver proof	£55
2005 — Gold proof	£1250
2005 Anniversary of Liberation. Gold proof	£1250
2006 Royal 80th Birthday. Silver proof	£55
2006 FIFA World Cup. Silver proof	£55
2006 Great Britons—Sir Winston Churchill Silver. Issued as part of set.	£60
2006 80th Birthday of Her Majesty the Queen	£25
2007 History of the Royal Navy—Henry VIII, The Golden Hind (2 coins)	£65
2007 Royal Diamond Wedding	£25
2008 90th Anniversary of the RAF (10 different designs in silver proof) ea.	£35
2009 British warships (6 different designs in silver proof) ea.	£35
2009 Anniversary of Apollo Moon landings. Cu-ni	£5
2009 — Silver proof	£35
2010 Charles II Unite. Gold proof	£1500
2010 Florence Nightingale. Gold proof	£1500
2011 350th Anniversary of the Crown Jewels. Silver proof	£95
2011 90th Anniversary of the British Legion (gold-plated copper)	£45
2011 — Silver proof	£95
2011 40th Anniversary of decimalisation, proof	£20
2011 Anniversary of the sinking of the *Titanic*	£20
2011 — Silver proof	£55
2011 30th Birthday of Duke of Cambridge	£20
2011 — Silver proof	£55
2011 Wedding of Prince William and Kate Middleton	£25
2011 — Silver proof	£55
2011 400th Anniversary of the King James Bible	£25
2012 Diamond Jubilee £5	£25
2012 — Gold proof	£1500
2012 The Tribute to the British Army. Gold proof	£2000
2013 70th Anniversary of the Dambuster Raid.	£20
2013 — Silver proof	£65
2013 — Gold proof	£2000

DATE	UNC
2013 Coronation Jubilee	£25
2013 — Silver proof	£55
2013 — Gold proof	£2000
2013 200th Guinea Anniv.	£25
2013 — Silver proof	£55
2013 — Gold proof	£2000
2014 Centenary of the First World War. Silver proof	£85
2014 — 5oz Silver proof	£450
2014 — Gold proof	£2500
2016 Battle of the Somme proof	—
2016 90th Birthday of HM the Queen. Silver proof	—
2017 Sapphire Jubilee. Silver plated	—

TWO POUNDS

1985 40th anniversary of Liberation	£10
1985 — proof	£30
1985 — Silver proof	£55
1986 Commonwealth Games, in plastic case	£12
1986 — in special folder	£12
1986 — .500 Silver	£45
1986 — .925 Silver proof	£55
1987 900th Anniv. of death of William the Conqueror, in folder	£15
1987 — Silver proof	£55
1987 — Gold proof	£1300
1988 William II, in presentation folder	£15
1988 — Silver proof	£55
1989 Henry I, in presentation folder	£15
1989 — Silver proof	£55
1989 Royal Visit	£15
1989 — Silver proof	£55
1990 Queen Mother's 90th birthday	£15
1990 — Silver proof	£55
1991 Henry II, in presentation folder	£15
1991 — Silver proof	£55
1993 40th Anniversary of the Coronation	£15
1993 — Silver proof	£60
1994 Anniversary of the Normandy Landings	£15
1994 — Silver proof	£55
1995 50th Anniversary of Liberation	£154
1995 — Silver proof	£55
1995 — Silver Piedfort proof	£100
1997 Conserving Nature i	£12
1997 — Silver proof	£55
1997 Bimetallic Latent image	£8
1997 — proof	£10
1998 Conserving Nature ii	£10
1998 Bimetallic Latent image	£6
2003 —	£6
2006 —	£8
2011 Prince Philip's 90th Birthday (conjoined portraits)	£6
2011 — Silver proof	£50
2012 "8 Doubles" modern variant	—

ONE POUND

1981	£10
1981 Gold proof	£145
1981 Gold piedfort	£345
1983 New specification, new reverse	£10
1985 New design (in folder)	£10
1995 Queen Mother's 95th Birthday. Silver proof	£50
1996 Queen's 70th Birthday. Silver proof	£55
1997 Royal Golden Wedding. Silver BU	£20
1997 — Silver proof	£55
1997 Castles of the British Isles—Tower of London. Silver proof only	£35
1998 Royal Air Force. Silver proof	£45
1999 Wedding of Prince Edward. Silver proof	£55
1999 Queen Mother. Silver proof	£55
1999 Winston Churchill. Silver proof	£55
2000 Millennium. Silver proof (gold plated)	£65
2000 Queen Mother's 100th Birthday. Silver proof	£45

DATE	UNC
2001	£2
2001 HM the Queen's 75th Birthday. Silver proof	£45
2002 William of Normandy. Silver	£20
2003	£2
2006	£2

FIFTY PENCE

1969	£4
1970	£6
1971 proof	£9
1981	£4
1982	£4
1985 New design	£4
2000 60th Anniversary of the Battle of Britain.	£4
2000 — Silver proof	£55
2000 — Silver piedfort	£55
2000 — Gold proof	£365
2003	£2
2006	£2
2008	£2
2012 The Diamond Jubilee (coloured portrait)	£10
2012 — Cu-Ni Fine Gold-Plated	£5
2013 60th Anniversary of Coronation (two different designs: Queen in State Coach and Queen in White Dress), Gold clad steel	£5 ea.
2013 The RAF 617 Squadron Gold-Plated coin	£25
2013 50th Anniversary of the Flying Scotsman's retirement in 1963	£25
2014 New Queen Elizabeth II	£45
2015 Queen Elizabeth II—Reflections of a Reign, Cu-Ni	£5
2016 90th Birthday of Queen Elizabeth II (two round crown-size coloured coins)	£5 ea.
2017 Sapphire Jubilee, Cu-Ni	£10

TWENTY-FIVE PENCE

1972 Royal Silver Wedding	£12
1972 — Silver proof	£45
1977 Royal Silver Jubilee	£10
1977 — Silver proof	£45
1978 Royal Visit	£10
1978 — Silver proof	£45
1980 Queen Mother's 80th birthday	£10
1980 — Silver proof	£45
1981 Royal Wedding	£10
1981 — Silver proof	£45

Since the introduction of decimal coinage a number of companies have been involved in marketing the coins of the Channel Islands. As a consequence many special limited edition commemorative coins have been issued in a wide variety of sizes, metals and finishes. These are very numerous with some issues being produced in very small numbers and many are omitted from our listings. These issues are generally outside of the scope of this catalogue but we intend to cover them more fully in a future edition.

JERSEY

DATE	F	VF	EF	UNC

FIVE SHILLINGS

	F	VF	EF	UNC
1966	—	£3	£7	£15
1966 Proof	—	£3	£9	£25

ONE QUARTER OF A SHILLING

	F	VF	EF	UNC
1957	—	£2	£5	£10
1960 Proof	—	—	£5	£15
1964	—	—	£4	£10
1966	—	—	£4	£10

ONE TWELFTH OF A SHILLING

	F	VF	EF	UNC
1877H	£2	£3	£18	£60
1877H Proof in nickel	—	—	—	£1275
1877 Proof only	—	—	—	£475
1877 Proof in nickel	—	—	—	£1275
1881	£3	£3	£15	£60
1888	£2	£3	£15	£50
1894	£2	£3	£20	£50
1909	£2	£3	£15	£35
1911	£2	£3	£10	£30
1913	£2	£3	£10	£30
1923 Spade shield	£2	£3	£10	£30
1923 Square shield	£2	£3	£10	£30
1926	£2	£3	£12	£45
1931	£2	£3	£8	£15
1933	£2	£3	£8	£15
1935	£2	£3	£8	£15
1937	£2	£3	£8	£15
1946	£2	£3	£8	£15
1947	—	£3	£8	£15
"1945" GVI	—	—	£2	£10
"1945" QE2	—	—	£2	£8
1957	—	—	£2	£7
1960 1660–1960 300th anniversary	—	—	£2	£7
1960 Mule	—	—	—	£150
1964	—	£2	£3	£10
1966 "1066–1966"	—	—	£1	£8

ONE THIRTEENTH OF A SHILLING

	F	VF	EF	UNC
1841	£4	£8	£40	£200
1844	£4	£9	£40	£200
1851	£5	£12	£60	£250
1858	£4	£9	£45	£200
1861	£5	£13	£60	£175
1865 Proof only	—	—	—	£750
1866 with LCW	£2	£5	£95	£150
1866 without LCW Proof only	—	—	—	£400
1870	£4	£8	£40	£125
1871	£4	£8	£42	£125

ONE TWENTY-FOURTH OF A SHILLING

	F	VF	EF	UNC
1877H	£3	£4	£15	£60
1877 Proof only	—	—	—	£300
1888	£3	£4	£15	£45
1894	£3	£4	£15	£45
1909	£3	£4	£15	£45
1911	£2	£3	£10	£45

DATE	F	VF	EF	UNC
1913	£2	£3	£10	£45
1923 Spade shield	£2	£3	£10	£35
1923 Square shield	£2	£3	£8	£35
1926	£2	£3	£10	£25
1931	£2	£3	£10	£25
1933	£2	£3	£10	£25
1935	£2	£3	£10	£25
1937	£1	£2	£6	£20
1946	£1	£2	£6	£20
1947	£1	£2	£6	£20

ONE TWENTY-SIXTH OF A SHILLING

	F	VF	EF	UNC
1841	£4	£7	£30	£100
1844	£4	£7	£25	£100
1851	£3	£6	£25	£100
1858	£4	£11	£50	£200
1861	£3	£6	£25	£65
1866	£3	£6	£30	£85
1870	£3	£6	£20	£55
1871	£3	£6	£20	£55

ONE FORTY-EIGHTH OF A SHILLING

	F	VF	EF	UNC
1877H	£6	£12	£60	£150
1877 Proof only	—	—	—	£450

ONE FIFTY-SECOND OF A SHILLING

	F	VF	EF	UNC
1841	£9	£25	£60	£200
1861 Proof only	—	—	—	£650

DECIMAL COINAGE

Ordinary circulating coinage from 1986 onwards is usually available in
uncirculated condition at a small premium above face value thus it is not
listed here.

ONE HUNDRED POUNDS

1990 50th Anniversary of the Battle of Britain. Gold Proof. £1000
1995 50th Anniversary of Liberation. Gold proof £1000

FIFTY POUNDS

1972 Silver Wedding. Gold proof £850
1990 50th Anniversary of the Battle of Britain. Gold proof £850
1995 50th Anniversary of Liberation. Gold proof £850
2003 Golden Jubilee. Silver Proof (100mm) £650
2013 RMS Titanic Centenary. 10oz Silver Proof £600

TWENTY-FIVE POUNDS

1972 25th Royal Wedding anniversary Gold £300
1972 — Gold proof £375
1990 50th Anniversary of Battle of Britain. Gold proof £350
1995 50th Anniversary of Liberation. Gold proof £350
2002 Princess Diana memorial. Gold proof £360
2002 Queen Mother. Gold proof £350
2002 Golden Jubilee. Gold proof £350
2002 Duke of Wellington. Gold proof £350
2003 Golden Jubilee. Gold proof £350
2003 History of the Royal Navy. Naval Commanders £350
2003 — Francis Drake £350
2003 — Sovereign of the Seas £350
2004 60th Anniversary of D-Day. Gold proof £350
2004 Charge of the Light Brigade. Gold proof £350
2004 HMS Victory. Gold proof £350
2004 John Fisher 1841–1920 Gold proof £350
2004 The Coronation Scot. Gold proof £350
2004 The Flying Scotsman. Gold proof £350
2004 Golden Arrow. Gold proof £350

DATE	UNC
2004 Rocket and Evening Star. Gold proof	£350
2005 Andrew Cunningham. Gold proof	£350
2005 HMS Conqueror. Gold Proof	£350
2005 200th Anniversary of Nelson. Gold proof	£350
2009 500th Anniversary of Accession. Gold proof	£350

TWENTY POUNDS
1972 Royal Wedding. The Ormer. Gold	£300
1972 — Gold proof	£300

TEN POUNDS
1972 25th Royal Wedding anniversary. Gold	£75
1972 — Gold proof	£180
1990 50th Anniversary of the Battle of Britain. Gold proof	£180
1995 50th Anniversary of Liberation. Gold proof	£140
2003 Coronation Anniversary. Gold/silver proof	£50
2004 Crimea. Silver proof	£20
2205 Trafalgar. Silver proof	£20
2005 — Silver/gold proof	£110
2005 End of World War II. Silver proof	£25
2007 Diamond Wedding. Platinum proof	£280
2008 History of RAF. Silver proof	£25
2008 — Silver/Gold proof	£110
2011 Royal Wedding of HRH Prince William & Catherine Middleton, silver (65mm)	£395
2012 Poppy. 5oz Silver Proof	£350
2013 Flying Scotsman. 5oz Silver Proof	£350

(Enlarged)

(Reduced)

FIVE POUNDS
1972 Gold proof	£65
1990 50th Anniversary of the Battle of Britain. Silver Proof (5 ounces)	£180
1997 Royal Golden Wedding	£10
1997 — Silver proof	£25
2000 Millennium. Silver proof	£35
2002 Princess Diana memorial	£12
2002 — Silver proof	£30
2002 — Gold proof	£800
2002 Royal Golden Jubilee	£25
2003 Golden Jubilee	£20
2003 — Silver proof	£55
2003 — Gold proof	£1000
2003 Prince William 21st Birthday	£15
2003 — Silver Proof	£55
2003 —Gold proof	£1000
2003 Naval Commanders	£15
2003 — Silver proof	£55
2003 — Gold proof	£1000
2003 Francis Drake	£15
2003 — Silver proof	£55
2003 — Gold proof	£1000
2003 Sovereign of the Seas	£15
2003 — Silver proof	£55
2003 — Gold proof	£1000
2004 60th Anniversary of 'D' Day	£15
2004 — Silver proof	£55
2004 — Gold proof	£1000
2004 Charge of the Light Brigade	£15
2004 — Silver proof	£50
2004 — Gold proof	£1000
2004 HMS Victory	£15
2004 — Silver proof	£55
2004 — Gold proof	£1000
2004 John Fisher 1841–1920	£15
2004 — Silver proof	£55

(Enlarged)

DATE	UNC
2004 — Gold proof	£1000
2004 The Coronation Scot	£15
2004 — Silver proof	£55
2004 — Gold proof	£1000
2004 The Flying Scotsman	£15
2004 — Silver proof	£55
2004 — Silver/Gold proof	£500
2004 — Gold proof	£1000
2004 Golden Arrow	£15
2004 — Silver proof	£55
2004 — Gold proof	£1000
2005 Driver and Fireman	£15
2005 — Silver proof	£45
2005 — Gold proof	£1000
2005 Box Tunnel and King Loco	£15
2005 — Silver Proof	£45
2005 — Gold Proof	£1000
2005 Rocket and Evening Star	£15
2005 — Silver proof	£45
2005 — Silver/Gold proof	£500
2005 — Gold proof	£1000
2005 200th Anniversary of the Battle of Trafalgar	£30
2005 Andrew Cunningham	£20
2005 — Silver proof	£65
2005 — Gold proof	£1000
2006 HMS Conqueror	£15
2006 Silver proof	£20
2005 — Gold proof	£1000
2005 Battle of Trafalgar	£15
2005 — Silver proof	£45
2005 — Gold proof (9mm)	£500
2005 — Gold proof (38.6mm)	£1000
2005 Returning Evacuees	£15
2005 — Silver proof	£45
2005 — Gold proof	£1000
2005 Searchlights and Big Ben	£15
2005 — Silver proof	£45
2005 — Gold proof	£1000
2006 60th Anniversary of the Liberation of the Channel Islands	£30
2006 80th Birthday of Her Majesty the Queen (3-coin set)	—
2006 Sir Winston Churchill	£15
2006 — Silver proof	£45
2006 — Gold proof	£1000
2006 Charles Darwin	£15
2006 — Silver proof	£45
2006 — Gold proof	£1000
2006 Bobby Moore	£20
2006 — Silver Proof	£55
2006 — Gold Proof	£1150
2006 Florence Nightingale	£20
2006 — Silver proof	£55
2006 — Gold proof	£1000
2006 Queen Mother	£20
2006 — Silver proof	£55
2006 — Gold proof	£1000
2006 Henry VIII	£15
2006 — Silver proof	£55
2006 — Gold proof	£1000
2006 Princess Diana	£20
2006 — Silver Proof	£60
2006 — Gold Proof	£1250
2006 Sir Christopher Wren	£15
2006 — Silver proof	£55
2006 — Gold proof	£1000
2006 HM the Queen's 80th Birthday—Streamers	£15
2006 — Silver proof	£60

DATE	UNC
2006 — Gold proof	£1000
2006 HM the Queen's 80th Birthday—Trooping colour	£25
2006 — Proof	£60
2006 — Silver proof	£1000
2006 — Silver/Gold proof	£650
2006 — Gold proof	£1150
2006 HM the Queen's 80th Birthday—Wembley Stadium	£20
2006 — Silver proof	£55
2006 — Gold proof	£1150
2006 Guy Gibson	£15
2006 — Silver proof	£55
2006 — Gold proof	£1150
2006 Eric James Nicholson	£15
2006 — Silver proof	£55
2006 — Gold proof	£1150
2006 Hook, Chard and Bromhead	£15
2006 — Silver proof	£55
2006 — Gold proof	£1150
2006 1st Lancs Fusiliers	£15
2006 — Silver proof	£55
2006 — Gold proof	£1150
2006 Noel Chavasse	£15
2006 — Silver proof	£55
2006 — Gold proof	£1150
2006 David Mackay	£15
2006 — Silver proof	£55
2006 — Gold proof	£1150
2006 Coronation Scot. Silver proof	£60
2006 Flying Scotsman. Silver proof	£60
2006 Fireman and Driver. Silver proof	£60
2006 Box Tunnel. Silver proof	£60
2007 Diamond Wedding balcony scene waving	£15
2007 — Silver proof	£60
2007 Diamond Wedding cake	£15
2007 — Silver proof	£60
2007 Diamond Wedding balcony scene waving	£15
2007 —Silver proof	£60
2007 Diamond Wedding HM the Queen and Prince Philip	£20
2007 — Silver proof	£60
2007 Diamond Wedding arrival at Abbey	£20
2007 — Silver proof	£55
2007 — Gold proof	£1150
2008 George & Dragon	£20
2008 Dambusters, Wallis, Chadwick, Gibson	£15
2008 — Silver/Copper proof	£30
2008 — Silver proof	£55
2008 Frank Whittle	£15
2008 — Silver proof	£55
2008 — Gold proof	£1150
2008 R. J. Mitchell	£15
2008 — Silver proof	£55
2008 — Gold proof	£1150
2008 Maj. Gen. Sir Hugh Trenchard	£15
2008 — Silver proof	£55
2008 — Gold proof	£1150
2008 Bomber Command	£15
2008 — Silver proof	£55
2008 — Gold proof	£1150
2008 Coastal Command	£20
2008 — Silver proof	£60
2008 — Gold proof	£1200
2008 Fighter Command	£20
2008 — Silver proof	£60
2008 — Gold proof	£1200
2008 Battle of Britain	£20
2008 — Silver proof	£60
2008 — Gold proof	£1200

DATE	UNC
2008 RBL Poppy	£20
2008 — Silver proof	£60
2008 — Gold proof	£1200
2008 Flying Legends	£15
2008 — Silver proof	£55
2008 — Gold proof	£1150
2009 George & Dragon. Silver proof	£50
2009 Battle of Agincourt. Silver proof	£55
2009 Battle of the Somme. Silver proof	£55
2009 Capt. Cook and *Endeavour*. Silver proof	£55
2009 500th Anniversary of Accession of Henry VIII. Silver proof	£55
2011 Landmark birthdays of HM the Queen & Prince Philip	£15
2011 90th Anniversary of the British Legion (poppy-shaped)	£40
2011 — Silver proof	£95
2011 — 5oz silver	£500
2011 — Gold proof	£2500
2011 30th Birthday of the Duke of Cambridge. Silver proof	£50
2011 Wedding of Prince William and Kate Middleton. Silver proof	£50
2011 — Gold proof	£1500
2011 Spirit of the Nation (4 coins). Silver proof, each	£50
2012 HM the Queen's Diamond Jubilee. Gold proof	£2000
2012 Poppy. Silver Proof	£65
2012 — Gold Proof	£2000
2012 RMS *Titanic* Centenary	£15
2012 — Silver Proof	£65
2013 Coronation Jubilee. Silver proof	£65
2013 — Gold Proof	£2000
2013 The Flying Scotsman. Silver proof	£65
2013 350th Guinea Anniversary. Silver proof	£55
2013 — Gold Proof	£2000
2013 Poppy Coin. Silver proof	£95
2014 70th Anniversary of D-Day. Silver proof	£85
2014 — Gold Proof	£2500
2014 Remembrance Day (two designs), Cu-Ni	—
2014 — Silver	—
2014 The Red Arrows 50th Display Season. Silver proof	£95
2014 William Shakespeare—450th Birthday. Silver proof	£80
2015 Remembrance day "Lest we forget", Cu-Ni	—
2015 50th Anniversary of Winston Churchill's death, Cu-Ni	—
2015 The Longest Reign, Cu-Ni	—
2015 200th Anniversary of the Battle of Waterloo, Cu-Ni	—
2015 Red Arrows, Cu-Ni	—
2016 90th Birthday of Queen Elizabeth II	—
2016 Remembrance Day, Cu-Ni	—

TWO POUNDS FIFTY PENCE

1972 Royal Silver Wedding	£25
1972 — Silver proof	£35

TWO POUNDS

(note all modern Proof coins have frosted relief)

1972 Royal Silver Wedding. Silver	£25
1972 — Silver proof	£35
1981 Royal Wedding, nickel silver (crown size)	£5
1981 — in presentation pack	£8
1981 — Silver proof	£20
1981 — Gold proof	£450
1985 40th Anniversary of Liberation (crown size)	£5
1985 — in presentation pack	£12
1985 — Silver proof	£20
1985 — Gold proof	£1150
1986 Commonwealth Games	£6
1986 — in presentation case	£8
1986 — .500 silver	£12
1986 — .925 silver proof	£20

DATE	UNC
1987 World Wildlife Fund 25th Anniversary	£80
1987 — Silver proof	£25
1989 Royal Visit	£15
1989 — Silver proof	£25
1990 Queen Mother's 90th Birthday	£15
1990 — Silver proof	£25
1990 — Gold proof	£600
1990 50th Anniversary of the Battle of Britain, silver proof	£30
1993 40th Anniversary of the Coronation	£15
1993 — Silver proof	£20
1993— Gold proof	£600
1995 50th Anniversary of Liberation	£15
1995 — Silver Proof	£25
1995 — — Piedfort	£75
1996 HM the Queen's 70th Birthday	£15
1996 — Silver proof	£25
1997 Bi-metal	£5
1997 — Silver proof	£50
1997 — new portrait	£5
1998 —	£5
2003 —	£5
2005 —	£5
2006 —	£5
2007 —	£5
2011 Prince Philip's 90th Birthday	£12
2012 HM the Queen's Diamond Jubilee. Gold proof	£1000

ONE POUND

1972 Royal Silver Wedding	£15
1972 — Silver proof	£20
1981	£15
1981 Silver proof	£15
1981 Gold proof	£350
1983 New designs and specifications on presentation card (St Helier)	£5
1983 — Silver proof	£20
1983 — Gold proof	£350
1984 Presentation wallet (St Saviour)	£20
1984 — Silver proof	£45
1984 — Gold proof	£450
1984 Presentation wallet (St Brelade)	£20
1984 — Silver proof	£45
1984 — Gold proof	£500
1985 Presentation wallet (St Clement)	£25
1985 — Silver proof	£45
1985 — Gold proof	£500
1985 Presentation wallet (St Lawrence)	£25
1985 — Silver proof	£40
1985 — Gold proof	£490
1986 Presentation wallet (St Peter)	£15
1986 — Silver proof	£35
1986 — Gold proof	£500
1986 Presentation wallet (Grouville)	£20
1986 — Silver proof	£40
1986 — Gold proof	£500
1987 Presentation wallet (St Martin)	£20
1987 — Silver proof	£40
1987 — Gold proof	£500
1987 Presentation wallet (St Ouen)	£18
1987 — Silver proof	£40
1987 — Gold proof	£500
1988 Presentation wallet (Trinity)	£20
1988 — Silver proof	£40
1988 — Gold proof	£500

DATE	UNC
1988 Presentation wallet (St John)	£15
1988 — Silver proof	£40
1988 — Gold proof	£450
1989 Presentation wallet (St Mary)	£15
1989 — Silver proof	£40
1989 — Gold proof	£450

1991 Ship Building in Jersey Series

DATE	UNC
1991 "Tickler". Nickel-brass	£5
1991 "Tickler". Silver proof	£25
1991 — Gold proof Piedfort	£500
1991 "Percy Douglas". Nickel-brass	£5
1991 "Percy Douglas". Silver proof	£25
1991 — Gold proof Piedfort	£500
1992 "The Hebe". Nickel-brass	£5
1992 "The Hebe". Silver proof	£25
1992 — Gold proof Piedfort	£500
1992 "Coat of Arms". Nickel-brass	£5
1992 "Coat of Arms". Silver proof	£25
1992 — Gold proof Piedfort	£500
1993 "The Gemini". Nickel-brass	£5
1993 "The Gemini". Silver proof	£25
1993 — Gold proof Piedfort	£500
1993 "The Century". Nickel-brass	£5
1993 "The Century". Silver proof	£25
1993 — Gold proof Piedfort	£500
1994 "Resolute". Nickel-brass	£5
1994 "Resolute". Silver proof	£25
1994 — Gold proof Piedfort	£500
1997 — Nickel-brass	£5
1998 — — Nickel-brass	£5
2003 — — Nickel-brass	£5
2005 — — Nickel-brass	£5
2006 — — Nickel-brass	£5
2007 Diana Commem. Gold Proof	£450
2012 Diamond Jubilee. Gold Proof	£450
2012 Anniversary of the *Titanic*	—
2013 Coronation Jubilee. Gold Proof	£500

FIFTY PENCE

1969	£10
1972 Royal Silver Wedding. Silver	£12
1972 — Silver proof	£12
1980 —	£1
1980 Arms	£2
1980 — Proof	£5
1981 —	£1
1981 —	£5
1981 — Proof	£5
1983 Grosnez Castle	£10
1983 — Silver proof	£12
1984 —	£2
1985 40th Anniversary of Liberation	£3
1986	£5
1986	£5
1987	£5
1988	£5
1989	£5
1990	£5
1992	£5
1994	£5
1997	£5
1997 Smaller size	£4

DATE	UNC
1998 —	£3
2003	£3
2003 Coronation Anniversary (4 types)	£4
2003 — 4 types. Silver proof..	£15
2005	£4
2006..	£4
2009	£5
2011 Diamond Jubilee (full colour reverse, gold-plated)...........................	£15
2013 Coronation Jubilee	£25

TWENTY-FIVE PENCE

1977 Royal Jubilee..	£3
1977 — Silver proof..	£20

TWENTY PENCE

1982 Corbiere Lighthouse (cased)	£8
1982 — Silver proof piedfort...	£35
1983 — Obv. with date, rev. no date on rocks	£5
1983 — — Silver proof..	£15
1984 —	£1
1986 —	£1
1987 —	£1
1989 —	£1
1992 —	£1
1994 —	£1
1996 —	£1
1997 —	£1
1998 —	£1
2002 —	£1
2003 —	£1
2005 —	£1
2006 —	£1
2007 —	£1
2009 —	£1

SOVEREIGN—Gold sovereign size

1999 The Millennium. King William on Throne	£250
1999 — Gold proof...	£300

TEN PENCE

1968 Arms	£1
1975 Arms..	£1
1979 (dated 1975 on thick flan)...	£2
1980 —	£1
1980 — Proof...	£5
1981 -	£1
1981 — Proof	£5
1983 L'Hermitage	£1
1983 — Silver proof..	£5
1984 —	£1
1985 —	£1
1986 —	£1
1987 —	£1
1988 —	£1
1989 —	£1
1990 —	£1
1992 —	£1
1997 —	£1
2002 —	£1
2003 —	£1
2005 —	£1
2006 —	£1
2007 —	£1

DATE	UNC

FIVE PENCE

1968 Arms	£1
1980 —	£1
1981 —	£1
1981 — Proof	£2
1983 Seymour Towers	£1
1983 — Silver proof	£5
1984 —	£1
1985 —	£1
1986 —	£1
1987 —	£2
1988 —	£1
1990 —	£1
1991 —	£1
1992 —	£5
1993 —	£1
1997 —	£4
1998 —	£1
2002 —	£1
2003 —	£1
2005 —	£5
2006 —	£1
2008 —	£1

Other denominations are generally available at face value or a small premium above.

Since the introduction of decimal coinage a number of companies have been involved in marketing the coins of the Channel Islands. As a consequence many special limited edition commemorative coins have been issued in a wide variety of sizes, metals and finishes. These are very numerous with some issues being produced in very small numbers and many are omitted from our listings. These issues are generally outside of the scope of this catalogue but we intend to cover them more fully in a future edition.

ALDERNEY

DATE	UNC

ONE THOUSAND POUNDS
2003 Concorde. Gold proof.. —
2004 D-Day Anniversary. Gold proof.. —
2011 Royal Wedding of Prince William and Catherine Middleton............. —

ONE HUNDRED POUNDS
1994 50th Anniversary of D-Day Landings. Gold proof £285
2003 Prince Wiliam. Gold proof (100mm) .... —
2005 Trafalgar Anniversary. Gold proof (100mm)....................................... —

FIFTY POUNDS
1994 50th Anniversary of D–Day Landing. Gold proof............................. £500
2003 Anniversay of Coronation (4 types). Silver proof ea. (100mm) £500
2003 Prince William. Silver proof (100mm).. £500
2004 Anniversary of D-Day. Silver proof (100mm) £500
2005 200th Anniversary of the Battle of Trafalgar. Silver proof (100mm) ... £500

TWENTY FIVE POUNDS
1993 40th Anniversary of Coronation. Gold proof...................................... £200
1994 50th Anniversary of D-Day Landings. Gold proof £200
1997 Royal Golden Wedding. Gold proof £295
1997 — Silver proof... £40
1999 Winston Churchill. Gold proof £350
2000 Queen Mother. Gold proof.. £325
2000 60th Anniversary of the Battle of Britain. Gold proof £275
2001 Royal Birthday. Gold proof £300
2002 Golden Jubilee. Gold proof £295
2002 Princess Diana. Gold proof £295
2002 Duke of Wellington. Gold proof £300
2003 Prince William. Gold proof £300
2003 HMS Mary Rose. Gold proof £300
2004 D-Day Anniversary. Gold proof... £395
2004 The Rocket. Gold proof £295
2004 Merchant Navy Class Locomotive. Gold proof £295
2005 Battle of Saints Passage. Gold proof £295
2006 World Cup 2006 (4 Coins). Gold ea... £350

TEN POUNDS
1994 50th Anniversary of D–Day Landing. Gold proof.............................. £150
2003 Concorde. Silver proof (65mm) £280
2005 60th Anniversary of the Liberation of the Channel Islands (65mm)... £250
2007 80th Birthday of Her Majesty the Queen (65mm)............................. £180
2008 Concorde. Silver proof £180
2008 90th Anniversary of the end of WWI. Silver Proof £180
2009 50th Anniversary of the Mini—Silver with colour............................... £180
2012 Prince William's 30th Birthday .... —

FIVE POUNDS
1995 Queen Mother £15
1995 — Silver proof... £50
1995 — Silver piedfort... £155
1995 — Gold proof... £900
1996 HM the Queen's 70th Birthday £20
1996 — Silver proof... £60
1996 — Silver piedfort... £150
1996 — Gold proof... £1000
1999 Eclipse of the Sun £25
1999 — Silver proof with colour centre.. £55
1999 Winston Churchill. Gold proof £1000
2000 60th Anniversary of the Battle of Britain... £25
2000 — Silver proof... £55

DATE	UNC
2000 Queen Mother. 100th Birthday. Silver proof	£50
2000 Millennium. Silver proof	£35
2001 HM Queen's 75th Birthday.	£15
2001 — Silver proof.	£45
2002 Golden Jubilee. Silver proof	£50
2002 50 Years of Reign.	£15
2002 — Silver proof.	£50
2002 Diana memorial	£15
2002 — Silver proof.	£45
2002 — Gold proof.	£900
2002 Duke of Wellington	£20
2002 — Silver proof.	£50
2002 — Gold proof.	£900
2003 Prince William	£20
2003 — Silver proof.	£50
2003 — Gold proof.	£900
2003 Mary Rose	£20
2003 — Silver proof.	£120
2003 Alfred the Great. Silver proof	£150
2003 — Gold proof.	£1000
2003 Last Flight of Concorde	£25
2003 — Silver proof.	£150
2003 — Gold proof.	£1000
2004 Anniversary of D-Day	£20
2004 — Silver proof	£75
2004 — Gold proof	£1000
2004 Florence Nightingale	320
2004 — Silver proof.	£45
2004 150th Anniversary of the Crimean War.	£20
2004 — Silver proof.	£45
2004 — Gold proof.	£1000
2004 The Rocket	£20
2004 — Silver proof.	£45
2004 — Gold proof.	£900
2004 Royal Scot	£20
2004 — Silver proof.	£45
2004 Merchant Navy Class Locomotive	£20
2004 — Silver proof.	£45
2005 End of WWII. Silver proof	£45
2005 — Gold proof.	£900
2005 200th Anniversary of the Battle of Trafalgar	£16
2005 — Silver proof.	£50
2005 History of the Royal Navy. John Woodward. Silver proof	£30
2005 Anniversary of Liberation. Gold proof	£1000
2005 Anniversary of the Battle of Saints Passage	£15
2005 — Silver proof.	£45
2005 HMS Revenge 1591	£15
2005 — Silver proof.	£45
2006 80th Birthday of Her Majesty the Queen (3-coin set) ea	£20
2006 Gold plated portraits of Her Majesty the Queen	—
2006 80th Birthday of Her Majesty the Queen (3-coin set) ea	£16
2007 History of the Royal Navy—*Mary Rose* (2 coins) ea	£16
2007 150th Anniversary of the Victoria Cross (18 coin set). Silver proof	£250
2007 Monarchs of England (12 coin set). Gold plated	£150
2008 90th Anniversary of the end of WWI (3 coins). Gold proof	£2500
2008 Classic British Motorcars (18 coin set). Silver proof.	£250
2008 Concorde. Gold proof.	£1000
2009 50th Anniversary of the Mini (4 coins). Silver proof ea.	£50
2011 Royal Engagement gold proof	£1000
2011 — Gold plated silver proof	£150
2011 — Silver proof.	£55
2011 — Cupro Nickel	£15
2011 John Lennon Silver proof	£55
2011 Battle of Britain 70th Anniversary silver proof	£55
2012 RMS *Titanic*	£15
2012 Remembrance Day (Re-issued 2013)	£25
2014 70th Anniversary of D-Day	£15

DATE	UNC
2014 — Silver proof..	£25
2014 — Gold proof...	£1000
2014 Destiny to Dynasty. Silver proof	£25
2014 300th Anniversary of the Coronation of King George I......................	£20
2014 — Silver proof..	£25
2014 — Gold proof...	£1000
2014 Centenary of the birth of poet Dylan Thomas	£15
2014 — Silver proof..	£45
2014 — Gold proof...	£1000
2014 Remembrance Day "Remember the Fallen"	—
2015 Churchill Quotations (4-coin set)	£40
2015 — Silver proof (4-coin)...	£250
2015 70th Anniversary of VE Day..	£15
2015 — Silver proof..	£45
2015 — Silver proof piedfort	£75
2015 150th Anniversary of the Salvation Army	£10
2015 — Silver proof..	£45
2015 Remembrance Day...	—
2015 — Silver	—
2015 — — piedfort..	—
2016 The FIFA World Cup	£15
2016 — Silver proof..	£45
2016 — Gold proof...	£1000
2016 Remembrance Day...	—
2016 — Silver Proof..	—
2016 — — piedfort..	—

TWO POUNDS

1989 Royal Visit	£12
1989 — Silver proof..	£25
1989 — Silver piedfort..	£45
1989 — Gold proof...	£1000
1990 Queen Mother's 90th Birthday	£12
1990 — Silver proof..	£25
1990 — Silver piedfort..	£45
1990 — Gold proof...	£1000
1992 40th Anniversary of Accession..	£15
1992 — Silver proof..	£35
1992 — Silver piedfort..	£50
1992 — Gold proof...	£1000
1993 40th Anniversary of Coronation...	£15
1993 — Silver proof..	£35
1993 — Silver piedfort..	£50
1994 50th Anniversary of D-Day Landings..................................	£15
1994 — Silver proof..	£35
1994 — Silver piedfort..	£50
1995 50th Anniversary of Return of Islanders	£15
1995 — Silver proof..	£35
1995 — Silver piedfort..	£50
1995 — Gold proof	£1000
1997 WWF Puffin..	£18
1997 — Silver proof..	£35
1997 Royal Golden Wedding..	£20
1997 — Silver proof..	£50
1999 Eclipse of the Sun. Silver..	£20
1999 — Silver proof..	£50
1999 — Gold proof...	£1250
2000 Millennium. Silver proof	£50

ONE POUND

1993 40th Anniversary of Coronation Silver proof	£50
1995 50th Anniversary of VE Day Silver proof............................	£45
1995 — Gold proof...	£500
2008 Concorde. Gold proof..	£275
2009 50th Anniversary of the Mini. Gold proof...........................	£375

IRELAND

As in the English hammered section (q.v.) the prices given here are for the most common coins in the series. For a more specialised listing the reader is referred to Coincraft's *Standard Catalogue of Scotland, Ireland, Channel Islands & Isle of Man*, or other specialised publications. Collectors should be aware that with most of the coins of the Irish series there are many varieties struck at different mints. The coins listed are all silver unless mentioned otherwise. Another important factor to consider when collecting early Irish coins is that few examples exist in high grades.

	F	VF

HIBERNO-NORSE ISSUES (995–1155)
Penny, imitating English silver pennies,
many various types £250 £575

JOHN, Lord of Ireland (1185–99)
Halfpenny, profile .... Extremely rare
Halfpenny, facing £100 £375
Farthing £350 £1275

Hiberno-Norse phase II example.

JOHN de COURCY, Lord of Ulster (1177–1205)
Halfpenny .... Extremely rare
Farthing £700 £3200

JOHN as King of England and Lord of Ireland (c. 1199–1216)
Penny £70 £350
Halfpenny £160 £4750
Farthing £650 £2500

John Lord of Ireland penny.

HENRY III (1216–72)
Penny £150 £525

EDWARD I (1272–1307)
Penny £75 £175
Halfpenny £75 £175
Farthing £150 £425

Henry III penny.

No Irish coins were struck for Edward II (1307–27).

EDWARD III (1327–77)
Halfpenny .... Extremely rare

No Irish coins were struck for Richard II (1377–99), Henry IV (1399–1413) or Henry V (1413–22).

HENRY VI (1422–61)
Penny .... Extremely rare

Edward I penny.

	F	VF

EDWARD IV (1461–83)

	F	VF
"Anonymous crown" groat	£650	£13200
— penny	£1200	—
"Titled crown" groat	£1600	—
— halfgroat..................................		Extremely rare
— penny		Extremely rare
Cross on rose/Sun groat	£1850	—
Bust/Rose on sun double groat	£2250	£7200
— groat......................................	£2250	—
— halfgroat..................................		Extremely rare
— penny		Extremely rare
Bust/Cross & pellets groat — First issue	£150	£575
— halfgroat..................................	£600	£1600
— penny	£100	£375
— halfpenny		Extremely rare
— Second (light) issue..........................	£120	£465
— halfgroat..................................	£650	£1700
— penny	£100	
£250 — halfpenny		Extremely rare
Bust/Rose on cross groat.....................	£570	£1500
— penny	£80	£245

Billon/Copper issues

	F	VF
Small crown/Cross farthing (1460–61) ..	£1700	—
— half farthing ("Patrick")....................	£1100	—
Large crown/Cross farthing (1462)........		Extremely rare
Patricius/Salvator farthing (1463–65)	£350	£2000
— half farthing..............................		Extremely rare
Shield/Rose on sun farthing.................	£200	£950

Edward IV groat.
"Anonymous crown" issue.

Edward IV penny struck in Dublin.

RICHARD III (1483–85)

	F	VF
Bust/Rose on cross groat.....................	£1100	£3950
— halfgroat..................................		Unique
— penny		Unique
Bust/Cross and pellets penny	£100	£3200
Shield/Three-crowns groat...................	£650	£2900

HENRY VII (1485–1509)

Early issues (1483–90)

	F	VF
Shield/Three crowns groat	£170	£525
— halfgroat..................................	£250	£565
— penny	£650	£2600
— halfpenny		Extremely rare

Later issues (1488–90)

	F	VF
Shield/Three crowns groat	£100	£385
— halfgroat..................................	£200	£600
— penny	£500	£1350
Facing bust groat (1496–1505).............	£150	£425
— halfgroat..................................	£1100	—
— penny	£950	—

Richard III bust/rose on cross groat.

LAMBERT SIMNEL
(as EDWARD VI, Pretender, 1487)

	F	VF
Shield/Three crowns groat	£1300	£4500

Henry VII groat.

	F	VF

HENRY VIII (1509–47)

"Harp" groat £120 £3750
— halfgroat... £500 £2600

*The "Harp" coins have crowned initials either side of the reverse harp,
e.g. HR (Henricus Rex), HA (Henry and Anne Boleyn), HI (Henry and Jane
Seymour), HK (Henry and Katherine Howard).*

Posthumous (Portrait) issues
Sixpence £175 £575
Threepence £150 £575
Threehalfpence...................................... £500 £1775
Threefarthings £650 £2200

*Henry VIII Posthumous portrait
issues threepence.*

EDWARD VI (1547–53)

Shilling (base silver) 1552 (MDLII).......... £1100 £3600
Brass contemporary copy £100 £375

MARY (1553–54)

Shilling 1553 (MDLIII)........................... £950 £3500
Shilling 1554 (MDLIIII)........................... Extremely rare
Groat... Extremely rare
Halfgroat... Extremely rare
Penny .... Extremely rare

PHILIP & MARY (1554–58)

Shilling.. £350 £1500
Groat... £150 £475
Penny .... Extremely rare

ELIZABETH I (1558–1603)

Base silver portrait coinage
Shilling.. £375 £1600
Groat... £200 £795
Fine silver, portrait coinage (1561)
Shilling.. £300 £1100
Groat... £350 £1200
Third (base silver) shield coinage
Shilling £250 £795
Sixpence... £200 £550
Copper
Threepence.. £275 £750
Penny £60 £220
Halfpenny £100 £325

Philip & Mary shilling

JAMES I (1603–25)

Shilling.. £110 £425
Sixpence... £110 £275

Coins struck under Royal Licence
from 1613

"Harrington" farthing (small size).......... £75 £275
"Harrington" farthing (large size) £75 £225
"Lennox" farthing £75 £225

*Elizabeth I "fine" shilling of
1561.*

CHARLES I (1625–49)

During the reign of Charles I and the Great Rebellion many coins were struck under unusual circumstances, making the series a difficult but fascinating area for study. Many of the "coins" were simply made from odd-shaped pieces of plate struck with the weight or value.

	F	VF
Coins struck under Royal Licence from 1625		
"Richmond" farthing.............................	£55	£220
"Maltravers" farthing	£50	£220
"Rose" farthing....................................	£50	£220
Siege money of the Irish Rebellion, 1642–49		
"Inchiquin" Money (1642)		
Crown..	£2300	£6200
Halfcrown	£2000	£5200
Shilling..		Extremely rare
Ninepence		Extremely rare
Sixpence...		Extremely rare
Groat...		Extremely rare
"Dublin" Money (1643)		
Crown..	£1000	£3600
Halfcrown	£600	£2600
"Ormonde" Money (1643–44)		
Crown..	£575	£1600
Halfcrown	£375	£1100
Shilling..	£150	£475
Sixpence...	£150	£475
Groat...	£120	£375
Threepence..	£120	£320
Twopence..	£500	£1600
"Ormonde" gold coinage (1646)		
Double pistole. 2 known (both in museums)		Extremely rare
Pistole. 10 known (only 1 in private ownership		Extremely rare
"Ormonde" Money (1649)		
Crown		Extremely rare
Halfcrown	£1300	£3950
Dublin Money 1649		
Crown..	£2900	£7950
Halfcrown	£2200	£4850

Charles I "Ormonde" crown.

Issues of the Confederated Catholics

	F	VF
Kilkenny issues (1642–43)		
Halfpenny	£310	£1000
Farthing	£410	£1200
Rebel Money (1643–44)		
Crown..	£2600	£5600
Halfcrown	£3000	£5600
"Blacksmith's" Money (16??)		
Imitation of English Tower halfcrown.....	£750	£3200

A rare Charles I "Rebel" halfcrown.

	F	VF

Local Town issues of "Cities of Refuge"

Bandon
Farthing (copper) .... | | Extremely rare

Cork
Shilling		Extremely rare
Sixpence	£775	£1400
Halfpenny (copper)		Extremely rare
Farthing (copper)	£620	—

Kinsale
| Farthing (copper) .... | £400 | — |

Youghal
| Farthing (copper) .... | £500 | £2200 |

CHARLES II (1660–85)

	Fair	F	VF	EF
"Armstrong" coinage				
Farthing (1660–61)	£75	£250	—	—
"St Patrick's" coinage				
Halfpenny	£235	£475	—	—
Farthing	£85	£200	£500	£1600
Legg's Regal coinage				
Halfpennies				
1680 large lettering	£35	£100	£295	—
1681 large lettering	—	£200	£695	—
1681 small lettering			Extremely rare	
1682 small lettering	—	£200	£675	—
1683 small lettering	£35	£45	£420	
1684 small lettering	£50	£125	£675	

Halfpenny of Charles I.

JAMES II (1685–88)

REGAL COINAGE

Halfpennies

1685	£35	£85	£320	£750
1686	£35	£65	£200	£650
1687			Extremely rare	
1688	£35	£110	£300	£1375

"St Patrick" farthing of Charles II.

Our grateful thanks to Del Parker, specialist in Irish rarities, for supplying the images for this section. An impressive and extensive range of Irish coins can be viewed and purchased at his website at www.irishcoins.com.

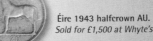

	Fair	F	VF	EF

EMERGENCY COINAGE

GUN MONEY
Most of these coins were struck in gun metal but a few rare specimens are also known struck in gold and in silver

Crowns

1690 (many varieties)......................from	£45	£65	£625	—

Large halfcrowns
Dated July 1689–May 1690

....from	£35	£65	£225	—

Small halfcrowns
Dated April–October1690

....from	£35	£65	£230	—

Large shillings
Dated from July 1689–April 1690

....from	£35	£75	£125	£495

Small shillings
Dated from April–September 1690

....from	£25	£35	£125	£425

Sixpences
Dated from June 1689–October 1690

....from	£35	£60	£295	—

"Gun Money" crown.

PEWTER MONEY (1689–90)

Crown..	£700	£1200	£3200	—
Groat..			Extremely rare	
Penny large bust...................	£200	£675	—	—
— small bust	£165	£485	£1375	—
Halfpenny large bust	£130	£345	£800	—
— small bust	£110	£245	£695	—

LIMERICK MONEY (1690–91)

Halfpenny, reversed N in HIBERNIA......	£35	£75	£275	—
Farthing, reversed N in HIBERNIA.........	£35	£75	£275	—
— normal N	£45	£135	£325	—

WILLIAM & MARY (1689–94)

Halfpennies

1692..	£15	£50	£100	£675
1693..	£15	£50	£85	£675
1694..	£25	£75	£135	£750

William & Mary halfpenny of 1693.

WILLIAM III (1694–1702)

1696 Halfpenny draped bust................	£35	£85	£265	—
1696 — crude undraped bust	£45	£275	£895	—

No Irish coins were struck during the reign of Queen Anne (1706–11).

DATE	F	VF	EF	UNC

GEORGE I (1714–27)

Farthings

	F	VF	EF	UNC
1722 D.G. REX Harp to left (Pattern)	£650	£1550	£2375	—
1723 D.G. REX Harp to right	£120	£225	£525	—
1723 DEI GRATIA REX Harp to right	£35	£65	£265	£625
1723 — Silver Proof	—	—	—	£2600
1724 DEI GRATIA REX Harp to right	£60	£150	£365	£875

Halfpennies

	F	VF	EF	UNC
1722 Holding Harp left	£55	£130	£395	£1100
1722 Holding Harp right	£45	£110	£350	£800
1723/2 Harp right	£50	£150	£350	£800
1723 Harp right	£25	£65	£200	£565
1723 Silver Proof	—	—	—	£3575
1723 Obv. Rs altered from Bs	£35	£100	£295	—
1723 No stop after date	£25	£80	£295	£525
1724 Rev. legend divided	£40	£100	£300	—
1724 Rev. legend continuous	£40	£110	£395	—

GEORGE II (1727–60)

Farthings

	F	VF	EF	UNC
1737	£35	£60	£185	£495
1737 Proof	—	—	—	£525
1737 Silver Proof	—	—	—	£1275
1738	£35	£65	£165	£485
1744	£35	£65	£165	£485
1760	£30	£50	£100	£385

Halfpenny of George II

Halfpennies

	F	VF	EF	UNC
1736	£25	£60	£225	£625
1736 Proof	—	—	—	£675
1736 Silver Proof	—	—	—	£1375
1737	£25	£50	£220	—
1738	£30	£60	£220	—
1741	£30	£60	£220	—
1742	£30	£60	£220	—
1743	£30	£60	£185	—
1744/3	£30	£60	£195	—
1744	£30	£60	£375	—
1746	£30	£60	£250	—
1747	£30	£60	£225	—
1748	£30	£60	£225	—
1749	£30	£60	£225	—
1750	£30	£60	£225	—
1751	£30	£60	£225	—
1752	£30	£60	£225	—
1753	£30	£60	£250	—
1755	£30	£110	£350	—
*1760	£30	£75	£250	—

GEORGE III (1760–1820)

All copper unless otherwise stated

Pennies

	F	VF	EF	UNC
1805	£20	£40	£190	£485
1805 Proof	—	—	—	£595
1805 in Bronze Proof	—	—	—	£595
1805 in Copper Gilt Proof	—	—	—	£585
1805 in Silver Proof (restrike)	—	—	—	£3275

George III proof penny 1805

DATE	F	VF	EF	UNC

Halfpennies

	F	VF	EF	UNC
1766	£30	£55	£165	—
1769	£30	£55	£165	—
1769 Longer bust	£40	£75	£250	£675
1774 Pattern only Proof	—	—	—	£2100
1775	£30	£55	£200	£475
1775 Proof	—	—	—	£675
1776	£55	£140	£400	—
1781	£45	£60	£175	£420
1782	£45	£60	£175	£420
1805	£18	£45	£120	£420
1805 Copper Proof	—	—	—	£420
1805 in Bronze	—	—	—	£300
1805 in Gilt Copper	—	—	—	£475
1805 in Silver (restrike)	—	—	—	£1850

Farthings

	F	VF	EF	UNC
1806	£20	£35	£100	£200
1806 Copper Proof	—	—	—	£375
1806 Bronzed Copper Proof	—	—	—	£265
1806 Copper Gilt Proof	—	—	—	£350
1806 Silver Proof (restrike)	—	—	—	£1150

One of the scarcer dates, a 1776 George III halfpenny.

GEORGE IV (1820–30)

Pennies

	F	VF	EF	UNC
1822	£20	£40	£195	£410
1822 Proof	—	—	—	£595
1823	£12	£25	£150	£410
1823 Proof	—	—	—	£620

DATE	F	VF	EF	UNC
Halfpennies				
1822	£20	£40	£125	£410
1822 Proof	—	—	—	£620
1823	£20	£40	£125	£410
1823 Proof	—	—	—	£675

NB Prooflike Uncirculated Pennies and Halfpennies of 1822/23 are often mis-described as Proofs. The true Proofs are rare. Some are on heavier, thicker flans.

Farthings				
1822 (Pattern) Proof	—	—	—	£1875

TOKEN ISSUES BY THE BANK OF IRELAND

Five Pence in Silver				
1805	£30	£45	£75	£375
1806	£30	£65	£150	£395
1806/5	£60	£145	£450	£1475

Ten Pence in Silver				
1805	£20	£35	£95	£265
1806	£20	£65	£150	£295
1813	£20	£35	£95	£320
1813 Proof	—	—	—	£475

Thirty Pence in Silver				
1808	£45	£100	£250	£675

1804 six shillings.

Six Shillings				
1804 in Silver	£100	£250	£465	£1875
1804 Proof	—	—	—	£1795
1804 in Copper (restrike)	—	—	—	£775
1804 Copper Gilt	—	—	—	£1750
1804 in Gilt Silver	—	—	—	£3100

In this series fully struck specimens, with sharp hair curls, etc., are worth appreciably more than the prices quoted.

IRISH FREE STATE/EIRE

DATE	F	VF	EF	UNC
TEN SHILLINGS				
1966 Easter Rising	—	£12	£18	£45
1966 Cased Proof	—	—	—	£45
1966 special double case	—	—	—	£85

HALF CROWNS
Silver

DATE	F	VF	EF	UNC
1928	£7	£12	£40	£80
1928 Proof	—	—	—	£95
1930	£12	£35	£175	£575
1931	£12	£35	£175	£545
1933	£12	£25	£175	£575
1934	£12	£12	£55	£275
1937	£60	£200	£650	£1900
Modified obverse: Eire				
1938				Unique
1939	£7	£17	£30	£85
1939 Proof	—	—	—	£650
1940	£8	£18	£35	£95
1941	£7	£17	£35	£95
1942	£7	£20	£35	£90
1943	£85	£300	£995	£3450
Cupro-nickel				
1951	£2	£3	£20	£65
1951 Proof	—	—	—	£525
1954	£2	£3	£15	£95
1954 Proof	—	—	—	£525
1955	£2	£3	£15	£45
1955	—	—	—	£600
1959	£2	£3	£12	£50
1961	£2	£3	£25	£60
1961 Obv as 1928, rev. as 1951	£30	£75	£325	£775
1962	£2	£3	£6	£35
1963	£2	£3	£6	£35
1964	£2	£3	£6	£35
1966	£2	£3	£6	£35
1967	£2	£3	£6	£35

FLORINS
Silver

DATE	F	VF	EF	UNC
1928	£3	£6	£25	£65
1928 Proof	—	—	—	£80
1930	£5	£20	£150	£475
1930 Proof				Unique
1931	£5	£20	£175	£475
1933	£5	£18	£140	£475
1934	£15	£125	£275	£775
1934 Proof	—	—	—	£3100
1935	£5	£18	£65	£200
1937	£6	£25	£140	£415
Modified obverse: Eire				
1939	£3	£6	£35	£85
1939 Proof	—	—	—	£685
1940	£5	£6	£30	£85
1941	£5	£6	£35	£80
1941 Proof	—	—	—	£875
1942	£6	£15	£30	£85
1943	£3000	£5500	£10000	£22500

Beware of fake 1943 florins.

DATE	F	VF	EF	UNC

Cupro-nickel

1951..	60p	£2	£15	£50
1951 Proof...	—	—	—	£495
1954..	60p	£2	£10	£45
1954 Proof...	—	—	—	£410
1955..	—	£2	£6	£50
1955 Proof...	—	—	—	£555
1959..	40p	£2	£6	£45
1961..	60p	£3	£15	£55
1962..	40p	£2	£6	£30
1963..	30p	£2	£6	£30
1964..	30p	£2	£6	£30
1965..	30p	£2	£6	£30
1966..	30p	£2	£6	£30
1968..	30p	£2	£6	£30

SHILLINGS
Silver

1928..	£3	£10	£208	£50
1928 Proof...	—	—	—	£75
1930..	£6	£25	£100	£465
1930 Proof...	—	—	—	£865
1931..	£3	£17	£95	£475
1933..	£3	£17	£95	£460
1935..	£3	£13	£50	£160
1937..	£10	£75	£250	£1350
1939..	£3	£6	£25	£75
1939 Proof...	—	—	—	£775
1940..	£3	£6	£17	£60
1941..	£3	£5	£17	£60
1942..	£3	£5	£12	£55

Cupro-nickel

1951..	£1	£2	£6	£25
1951 Proof...	—	—	—	£450
1954..	£1	£2	£6	£25
1954 Proof...	—	—	—	£500
1955..	£1	£2	£6	£25
1959..	£1	£2	£6	£35
1962..	50p	£2	£3	£22
1963..	50p	£2	£3	£15
1964..	50p	£2	£3	£15
1966..	50p	£2	£3	£15
1968..	50p	£2	£3	£15

SIXPENCES
Nickel

1928..	£1	£6	£20	£60
1928 Proof...	—	—	—	£65
1934..	£1	£3	£18	£100
1935..	£1	£3	£25	£130

Modified obverse: Eire

1939..	£1	£2	£10	£65
1939 Proof...	—	—	—	£675
1940..	£1	£2	£6	£65

Cupro-nickel

1942..	£1	£2	£9	£65
1945	£3	£12	£35	£100
1946..	£5	£10	£100	£400
1947..	£2	£2	£25	£90
1948..	£1	£3	£15	£75
1949..	£1	£2	£10	£50
1950..	£2	£3	£25	£100
1952..	£1	£2	£5	£25

DATE	F	VF	EF	UNC
1953	£1	£2	£5	£35
1953 Proof	—	—	—	£125
1955	£1	£2	£4	£30
1956	£1	£2	£3	£30
1956 Proof	—	—	—	£175
1958	£2	£3	£12	£70
1958 Proof	—	—	—	£395
1959	50p	60p	£3	£25
1960	50p	60p	£2	£25
1961	—	£2	£3	£25
1962	£2	£6	£35	£80
1963	£1	£3	£6	£20
1964	£1	£2	£5	£15
1966	£1	£2	£5	£15
1967	£1	£2	£2	£12
1968	£1	£2	£2	£12
1969	£2	£3	£6	£25

THREEPENCES
Nickel

	F	VF	EF	UNC
1928	£2	£3	£10	£45
1928 Proof	—	—	—	£45
1933	£3	£13	£75	£385
1934	£1	£3	£15	£85

Modified obverse: Eire

	F	VF	EF	UNC
1935	£2	£4	£30	£235
1939	£3	£7	£60	£385
1939 Proof	—	—	—	£1100
1940	£2	£3	£13	£75

Cupro-nickel

	F	VF	EF	UNC
1942	—	£2	£6	£55
1942 Proof	—	—	—	£525
1943	£2	£3	£15	£80
1946	£2	£5	£10	£55
1946 Proof	—	—	—	£520
1948	£2	£3	£25	£85
1949	—	£2	£6	£45
1950	—	£2	£6	£35
1950 Proof	—	—	—	£555
1953	—	£2	£4	£20
1956	—	£2	£3	£12
1961	—	60p	£2	£5
1962	—	60p	£2	£10
1963	—	60p	£2	£10
1964	—	60p	£2	£5
1965	—	60p	£2	£5
1966	—	60p	£2	£5
1967	—	60p	£2	£5
1968	—	—	£2	£5

PENNIES

	F	VF	EF	UNC
1928	£2	£3	£12	£55
1928 Proof	—	—	—	£65
1931	£2	£4	£35	£125
1931 Proof	—	—	—	£1100
1933	£2	£5	£50	£275
1935	£1	£2	£25	£85
1937	£1	£2	£35	£135
1937 Proof	—	—	—	£1100

Modified obverse: Eire

	F	VF	EF	UNC
1938		Only two known		
1940	£10	£50	£175	£765
1941	£1	£2	£10	£35
1942	—	£1	£5	£25

DATE	F	VF	EF	UNC
1943	—	£2	£6	£45
1946	—	£2	£4	£20
1948	—	£2	£4	£20
1949	—	£2	£4	£20
1949 Proof	—	—	—	£500
1950	—	£2	£6	£35
1952	—	£2	£4	£12
1962	—	£2	£4	£15
1962 Proof	—	—	—	£200
1963	—	—	£2	£15
1963 Proof	—	—	—	£210
1964	—	—	£2	£10
1964 Proof	—	—	—	£510
1965	—	—	£1	£5
1966	—	—	£1	£5
1967	—	—	£1	£5
1968	—	—	£1	£5
1968 Proof	—	—	—	£300

HALFPENNIES

DATE	F	VF	EF	UNC
1928	£2	£3	£12	£45
1928 Proof	—	—	—	£45
1933	£6	£20	£100	£520
1935	£5	£10	£50	£220
1937	£2	£5	£15	£65

Modified obverse: Eire

DATE	F	VF	EF	UNC
1939	£5	£10	£50	£210
1939 Proof	—	—	—	£885
1940	£2	£4	£50	£195
1941	£1	£2	£6	£25
1942	£1	£2	£6	£25
1943	£1	£2	£8	£35
1946	£2	£5	£20	£100
1949	£1	£2	£6	£25
1953	—	£2	£3	£12
1953 Proof	—	—	—	£500
1964	—	—	£1	£5
1965	—	—	£1	£6
1966	—	—	£1	£4
1967	—	—	£1	£4

FARTHINGS

DATE	F	VF	EF	UNC
1928	£3	£4	£15	£30
1928 Proof	—	—	—	£45
1930	£3	£4	£10	£32
1931	£4	£6	£15	£35
1931 Proof	—	—	—	£875
1932	£4	£6	£18	£45
1933	£3	£4	£12	£32
1935	£4	£6	£18	£35
1936	£4	£6	£18	£35
1937	£3	£4	£12	£32

Modified obverse: Eire

DATE	F	VF	EF	UNC
1939	£3	£4	£10	£18
1939 Proof	—	—	—	£675
1940	£4	£5	£10	£25
1941	£3	£4	£6	£12
1943	£3	£4	£6	£12
1944	£3	£4	£6	£12
1946	£3	£4	£6	£12
1949	£4	£6	£8	£25
1949 Proof	—	—	—	£475
1953	£3	£4	£5	10
1953 Proof	—	—	—	£345
1959	£3	£4	£5	£13
1966	£3	£4	£5	£13

For the 1928–50 copper issues it is worth noting that UNC means UNC with some lustre. BU examples with full lustre are extremely elusive and are worth much more than the quoted prices.

IRISH DECIMAL COINAGE

DATE	MINTAGE	BU

HALF PENCE

1971	100,500,000	£5
1975	10,500,000	£6
1976	5,500,000	£6
1978	20,300,000	£5
1980	20,600,000	£4
1982	9,700,000	£4
1985	2,800,000	Rare
1986. Only issued in the 1986 set	19,750,000	£100

ONE PENNY

1971	100,500,000	£5
1974	10,000,000	£10
1975	10,000,000	£15
1976	38,200,000	£5
1978	25,700,000	£8
1979	21,800,000	£12
1980	86,700,000	£3
1982	54,200,000	£5
1985	19,200,000	£8
1986	36,600,000	£5
1988	56,800,000	£5
1990	65,100,000	£5
1992	25,600,000	£6
1993	10,000,000	£6
1994	45,800,000	£5
1995	70,800,000	£3
1996	190,100,000	£1
1998	40,700,000	£1
2000	Unknown	£1

TWO PENCE

1971	75,500,000	£5
1975	20,000,000	£8
1976	5400,000	£12
1978	12,000,000	£12
1979	32,400,000	£8
1980	59,800,000	£6
1982	30,400,000	£5
1985	14,500,000	£6
1986	23,900,000	£6
1988	35,900,000	£5
1990	34,300,000	£5
1992	10,200,000	£8

DATE	MINTAGE	BU
1995	55,500,000	£5
1996	69,300,000	£2
1998	33,700,000	£2
2000	Unknown	£1

FIVE PENCE

1969 Toned	5,000,000	£5
1970	10,000,000	£5
1971	8,000,000	£8
1974	7,000,000	£10
1975	10,000,000	£10
1976	20,600,000	£5
1978	28,500,000	£5
1980	22,200,000	£5
1982	24,400,000	£4
1985	4,200,000	£8
1986	15,300,000	£5
1990	7,500,000	£5

Size reduced to 18.4mm

1992	74,500,000	£5
1993	89,100,000	£5
1994	31,100,000	£5
1995	12,000,000	£5
1996	14,700,000	£2
1998	158,500,000	£1
2000	Unknown	£1

TEN PENCE

1969	27,000,000	£12
1971	4,000,000	£12
1973	2,500,000	£16
1974	7,500,000	£12
1975	15,000,000	£12
1976	9,400,000	£12
1978	30,900,000	£10
1980	44,600,000	£8
1982	7,400,000	£8
1985	4,100,000	£10
1986. Only issued in the 1986 set	11,280	£285

Size reduced to 22mm

1992	2 known	—
1993	80,100,000	£5
1994	58,500,000	£5

341

DATE	MINTAGE	BU	DATE	MINTAGE	BU

DATE	MINTAGE	BU
1995	16,100,000	£5
1996	18,400,000	£3
1997	10,000,000	£3
1998	10,000,000	£3
1999	24,500,000	£3
2000	Unknown	£3

TWENTY PENCE

DATE	MINTAGE	BU
1985. Only 600 minted and 556 melted down, only 3 known	Extremely rare	
1986	50,400,000	£8
1988	20,700,000	£6
1992	14,800,000	£5
1994	11,100,000	£5
1995	18,200,000	£5
1996	29,300,000	£5
1998	25,000,000	£3
1999	11,000,000	£3
2000	Unknown	£2

FIFTY PENCE

DATE	MINTAGE	BU
1970	9,000,000	£8
1971	650,000	£7
1974	1,000,000	£55
1975	2,000,000	£55
1976	3,000,000	£45
1977	4,800,000	£55
1978	4,500,000	£45
1979	4,000,000	£45
1981	6,000,000	£25
1982	2,000,000	£25
1983	7,000,000	£25
1986. Only issued in the 1986 set	10,000	£320
1988	7,000,000	£5
1988 Dublin Millennium	5,000,000	£5
1988 — Proof	50,000	£25
1996	6,000,000	£7
1997	6,000,000	£7
1998	13,800,000	£5
1999	7,000,000	£4
2000	Unknown	£4

ONE POUND

DATE	MINTAGE	BU
1990	42,300,000	£5
1990 Proof	50,000	£25
1994	14,900,000	£5
1995	9,200,000	£5
1995 UN silver proof in case of issue	2,850	£175
1996	9,200,000	£5
1998	22,960,000	£4
1999	10,000,000	£5
2000	4,000,000	£5

	MINTAGE	BU
2000 Millennium	5,000,000	£5
2000 – Silver Proof Piedfort	90,000	£35

OFFICIAL COIN SETS ISSUED BY THE CENTRAL BANK

1971 Specimen set in green wallet. 6 coins	£20
1975 6 coin set	£55
1978 6 coin set	£55
1978 6 coin set. Black cover, scarce	£75
1982 6 coin set. Black cover	£75
1986 Specimen set in card folder 1/2p to 50p, 7 coins. Very scarce. Most sets have glue problems	£650
1996 7 coin set	£60
1998 7 coin set	£50
2000 Millennium set. Last decimal set	£125
2000 — With 1999 instead of the 2000 £1 coin	£275

Dublin Millennium 50p

OFFICIAL AND SEMI-OFFICIAL COMMEMORATIVE MEDALS

It is probably a strong love of history, rather than the strict disciplines of coin collecting that make collectors turn to commemorative medals. The link between the two is intertwined, and it is to be hoped that collectors will be encouraged to venture into the wider world of medallions, encouraged by this brief guide, originally supplied by Daniel Fearon (author of the *Catalogue of British Commemorative Medals)* and kindly updated again this year by Charles Riley.

DATE	VF	EF

JAMES I

1603 Coronation (possibly by
   C. Anthony), 29mm, Silver £1200   £1800

QUEEN ANNE

1603 Coronation, 29mm, AR............................. £800   £1500

CHARLES I

1626 Coronation (by N. Briot), 30mm, Silver....... £650   £1000
1633 Scottish Coronation (by N. Briot), 28mm,
   Silver.. £450   £795
1649 Memorial (by J. Roettier). Struck after the
   Restoration, 50mm, Bronze............................ £120   £250

CROMWELL

1653 Lord Protector (by T. Simon), 38mm,
   Silver.. £700   £1700
— Cast examples.. £350   £600

CHARLES II

1651 Scottish Coronation, in exile (from design
   by Sir J. Balfour), 32mm, Silver £1300   £2300

CHARLES II

1661 Coronation (by T. Simon), 29mm
— Gold... £1800   £3500
— Silver.. £350   £550
1685 Death (by N. Roettier), 39mm, Bronze........ £150   £325

James I Coronation, 1603

Charles II Coronation, 1661

DATE	VF	EF

JAMES II
1685 Coronation (by J. Roettier), 34mm
— Gold £2000 £3600
— Silver £350 £800

MARY
1685 Coronation (by J. Roettier), 34mm
— Gold £1500 £3000
— Silver £300 £600

WILLIAM & MARY
1689 Coronation (by J. Roettier), 32mm
— Gold £1750 £3000
— Silver £350 £525
1689 Coronation, "Perseus" (by G. Bower),
   38mm, Gold £1750 £3000

MARY
1694 Death (by N. Roettier), 39mm, Bronze........ £95 £245

WILLIAM III
1697 "The State of Britain" (by J. Croker), 69mm,
   Silver £850 £1500

ANNE
1702 Accession, "Entirely English" (by J. Croker), 34mm
— Gold £1500 £2750
— Silver £150 £295
1702 Coronation (by J. Croker), 36mm
— Gold £1800 £3200
— Silver £225 £300
1707 Union with Scotland (by J. Croker, rev. by S. Bull), 34mm
— Gold £1500 £2800
— Silver £200 £300
1713 Peace of Utrecht (by J. Croker—issued in gold to Members
of Parliament), 34mm
— Gold £850 £1500
— Silver £150 £275

Queen Anne, 1702–1713.

GEORGE I
1714 Coronation (by J. Croker), 34mm
— Gold £1250 £1750
— Silver £150 £250
1727 Death (by J. Dassier), 31mm, Silver £150 £275

GEORGE II
1727 Coronation (by J. Croker), 34mm
— Gold £1500 £3200
— Silver £175 £350

QUEEN CAROLINE
1727 Coronation (by J. Croker), 34mm
— Gold £1750 £3000
— Silver £185 £375
1732 The Royal Family (by J. Croker), 70mm
— Silver £1500 £3000
— Bronze.. £400 £700

George I Coronation, 1714.

DATE	VF	EF

GEORGE III
1761 Coronation (by L. Natter), 34mm
— Gold	£2750	£4250
— Silver	£350	£550
— Bronze...	£150	£250

QUEEN CHARLOTTE
1761 Coronation (by L. Natter), 34mm
— Gold	£1850	£3500
— Silver	£375	£600
— Bronze...	£150	£295
1810 Golden Jubilee, "Frogmore", 48mm, Silver	£130	£275
— Bronze...	£95	£175

GEORGE IV
1821 Coronation (by B. Pistrucci), 35mm
— Gold	£900	£1600
— Silver	£200	£325
— Bronze...	£65	£110

George III, Coronation, 1761

WILLIAM IV
1831 Coronation (by W. Wyon; rev.shows
   Queen Adelaide), 33mm
— Gold	£1150	£2250
— Silver	£175	£325
— Bronze...	£65	£100

QUEEN VICTORIA
1838 Coronation (by B. Pistrucci), 37mm
— Gold	£1000	£1500
— Silver	£185	£320
— Bronze...	£45	£95

Queen Victoria Coronation, 1838

Queen Victoria Diamond Jubilee 1897

346

DATE	VF	EF

1887 Golden Jubilee (by J. E. Boehm, rev. by Lord Leighton)

	VF	EF
— Gold, 58mm	£2750	£4250
— Silver, 78mm	£250	£500
— Bronze, 78mm	£95	£180

1897 Diamond Jubilee (by G. de Saulles),

	VF	EF
— Gold, 56mm	£2750	£4250
— Silver, 56mm	£95	£125
— Bronze, 56mm	£35	£60
— Gold, 25mm	£450	£600
— Silver, 25mm	£20	£35

EDWARD VII

1902 Coronation (August 9) (by G. W. de Saulles)

	VF	EF
— Gold, 56mm	£3250	£3750
— Silver, 56mm	£95	£150
— Bronze, 56mm	£30	£55
— Gold, 31mm	£500	£700
— Silver, 31mm	£20	£30

*Some rare examples of the official medal show the date as June 26, the original date set for the Coronation which was postponed because the King developed appendicitis.

GEORGE V

1911 Coronation (by B. Mackennal)

	VF	EF
— Gold, 51mm	£3250	£3750
— Silver, 51mm	£95	£250
— Bronze, 51mm	£30	£65
— Gold, 31mm	£500	£700
— Silver, 31mm	£20	£35

1935 Silver Jubilee (by P. Metcalfe)

	VF	EF
— Gold, 58mm	£3500	£4250
— Silver, 58mm	£100	£150
— Gold, 32mm	£500	£700
— Silver, 32mm	£20	£30

PRINCE EDWARD

1911 Investiture as Prince of Wales (by W. Goscombe John)

	VF	EF
— Gold, 31mm	£1000	£1250
— Silver, 31mm	£50	£85

EDWARD VIII

1936 Abdication (by L. E. Pinches), 35mm

	VF	EF
— Gold	£750	£1200
— Silver	£45	£65
— Bronze...	£20	£35

GEORGE VI

1937 Coronation (by P. Metcalfe)

	VF	EF
— Gold, 58mm	£3500	£4000
— Silver, 58mm	£65	£95
— Gold, 32mm	£650	£750
— Silver, 32mm	£25	£35
— Bronze, 32mm	£12	£15

George V Silver Jubilee, 1935

Edward, Prince of Wales, 1911

Edward VIII, Abdication, 1936.

DATE	VF	EF

ELIZABETH II
1953 Coronation (by Spink & Son)—illustrated
— Gold, 57mm	£3000	£3500
— Silver, 57mm	£65	£125
— Bronze, 57mm	£35	£65
— Gold, 32mm	£450	£550
— Silver, 32mm	£25	£35
— Bronze, 32mm	£12	£15

1977 Silver Jubilee (by A. Machin)
— Silver, 57mm	—	£70
— Silver, 44mm	—	£40

The gold medals are priced for 18ct—they can also be found as 22ct and 9ct, and prices should be adjusted accordingly.

PRINCE CHARLES
1969 Investiture as Prince of Wales (by M. Rizello)
— Silver, 57mm	—	£75
— Bronze gilt, 57mm...	—	£40
— Silver, 45mm	—	£35
— Gold, 32mm	—	£450
— Silver, 32mm	—	£35
— Bronze, 32mm	—	£10

QUEEN ELIZABETH THE QUEEN MOTHER
1980 80th Birthday (by L. Durbin)
— Silver, 57mm	—	£65
— Silver, 38mm	—	£38
— Bronze, 38mm	—	£25

N.B.—Official Medals usually command a premium when still in their original case of issue.

Prince Charles, Prince of Wales 1969.

The Royal Mint Museum contains a charming group of medallic portraits of seven of the children of Queen Victoria and Prince Albert. They appear to have been made in 1850 and therefore do not include the two children who were born after that date. The skilfully-executed portraits are the work of Leonard Wyon, a member of the extremely talented family of engravers whose name is so well known to numismatists. The son of William Wyon, he was actually born in the Royal Mint in 1826. These particular portraits were not commissioned by the Mint and little is known about the circumstances in which they were prepared, but for some reason the dies have survived in the Royal Mint Museum, along with single-sided bronze impressions roughly the size of a half-crown.

Images and information courtesy of Dr Kevin Clancy, The Royal Mint.

DIRECTORY *section*

ON the following pages will be found the most useful names and addresses needed by the coin collector.

At the time of going to press with this edition of the YEARBOOK the information is correct, as far as we have been able to ascertain. However, people move and establishments change, so it is always advisable to make contact with the person or organisation listed before travelling any distance, to ensure that the journey is not wasted.

Should any of the information in this section not be correct we would very much appreciate being advised in good time for the preparation of the next edition of the COIN YEARBOOK.

Dealers who display this symbol are Members of the

British Numismatic Trade Association

Buy in confidence from members of the British Numismatic Trade Association—an association formed to promote the very highest standards of professionalism in all matters involving members of the public in the sale or purchase of numismatic items.

BNTA MEMBERS IN COUNTY ORDER

LONDON AREA

*A.H. Baldwin & Sons Ltd · www.baldwin.co.uk
*ArtAncient Ltd · www.artancient.com
ATS Bullion Ltd · www.atsbullion.com
*Baldwin's of St. James's · info@bsjauctions.com
Beaver Coin Room · www.beaverhotel.co.uk
Jon Blyth · www.jonblyth.com
Bonhams incorporating Glendining's · www.bonhams.com
Arthur Bryant Coins Ltd · www.bryantcoins.com
*Classical Numismatic Group Inc / Seaby Coins
            · www.cngcoins.com
*Philip Cohen Numismatics · www.coinheritage.co.uk
The Coin Cabinet Ltd · www.thecoincabinet.co.uk
Andre de Clermont · www.declermont.com
*Dix Noonan Webb · www.dnw.co.uk

Christopher Eimer · www.christophereimer.co.uk
Harrow Coin & Stamp Centre
*Knightsbridge Coins
C. J. Martin (Coins) Ltd · www.antiquities.co.uk
Nigel Mills · www.nigelmills.net
Morton & Eden Ltd · www.mortonandeden.com
Numismatica Ars Classica · www.arsclassicacoins.com
Physical Gold Ltd · www.physicalgold.co.uk
Roma Numismatics Ltd · www.romanumismatics.com
Simmons Gallery · www.simmonsgallery.co.uk
*Sovereign Rarities Ltd · www.sovr.co.uk
*Spink & Son Ltd · www.spink.com
Surena Ancient Art & Numismatic
The London Coin Company Ltd
            · www.thelondoncoincompany.com

The BNTA is a member of the International Numismatic Commission.

AVON
Saltford Coins · www.saltfordcoins.com

BEDFORDSHIRE
Simon Monks · www.simonmonks.co.uk

BERKSHIRE
*Douglas Saville Numismatic Books
· www.douglassaville.com

BUCKINGHAMSHIRE
Charles Riley · www.charlesriley.co.uk

CAMBRIDGESHIRE
Den of Antiquity International Ltd · www.denofantiquity.co.uk

CHESHIRE
Colin Cooke · www.colincooke.com

CORNWALL
Richard W Jeffery

DEVON
Glenn S Ogden · www.glennogdencoins.com

DORSET
Dorset Coin Co. Ltd · www.dorsetcoincompany.co.uk

ESSEX
Time Line Originals · www.time-lines.co.uk

GLOUCESTERSHIRE
Format of Birmingham
Ilbury Coins Ltd · www.silburycoins.com

HAMPSHIRE
Studio Coins · www.studiocoins.net
Victory Coins
West Essex Coin Investments

HERTFORDSHIRE
DRG Coins and Antiquities · www.drgcoinsantiquities.com
KB Coins · www.kbcoins.com
David Miller
Whitmore Coins, Tokens and Medallions
· john@whitmorectm.com

KENT
London Coins · www.londoncoins.co.uk
Peter Morris · www.petermorris.co.uk

LEICESTERSHIRE
Hall's Hammered Coins · www.hallshammeredcoins.com

MONMOUTHSHIRE
Anthony M. Halse · www.coinsandtokens.com

NORFOLK
BucksCoins · www.buckscoins.com
Roderick Richardson · www.roderickrichardson.com
Chris Rudd · www.celticcoins.com

NOTTINGHAMSHIRE
History in Coins · www.historyincoins.com

OXFORDSHIRE
*Richard Gladdle · Gladdle@plumpudding.org

SHROPSHIRE
M. Veissid · m.veissid@btinternet.com

SUFFOLK
*Lockdale Coins Ltd · www.lockdales.com
Mike R. Vosper Coins · www.vosper4coins.co.uk

SURREY
Daniel Fearon · www.danielfearon.com
M. J. Hughes · www.gbgoldcoins.co.uk
Kingston Coin Company
· www.kingstoncoincompany.co.uk
Mark Rasmussen Numismatist · www.rascoins.com

SUSSEX
John Newman Coins · www.johnnewmancoins.com

TYNE AND WEAR
*Corbitts Ltd · www.corbitts.com

WARWICKSHIRE
*Peter Viola
*Warwick & Warwick Ltd
· www.warwickandwarwick.com

WEST MIDLANDS
*Atkinsons Coins and Bullion
· www.atkinsonsbullion.com
*Birmingham Coins
David Craddock
Paul Davis Birmingham Ltd

YORKSHIRE
Airedale Coins · www.airedalecoins.co.uk
AMR Coins · www.amrcoins.com
Keith Chapman · www.anglosaxoncoins.com
Paul Clayton
Paul Davies
*Paul Dawson York Ltd

WALES
Lloyd Bennett · www.coinsofbritain.com
*North Wales Coins Ltd
Colin Rumney

SCOTLAND
Paul Menzies Ltd · www.paulmenziesltd.com
*Scotmint Ltd · www.scotmint.com

IRELAND
ICE Ltd · iceauctiongalleries@gmail.com
Ormonde Coins · www.ormondecoins.com

(Those members with a retail premises are indicated with an *)

MUSEUMS
& libraries

Listed below are the Museums and Libraries in the UK which have coins or items of numismatic interest on display or available to the general public.

A

• Kings Museum, University of Aberdeen, Old Aberdeen Town House, **Aberdeen**, AB9 1AS. Tel: 01224 274 330.

• Curtis Museum (1855), High Street, **Alton**, Hants, GU34 1BA. Tel: 01420 82802. *General collection of British coins.*

• Ashburton Museum, The Bullring, **Ashburton**, Devon, TQ13 7DT. Tel: 01364 652 539. *Ancient British and Roman antiquities including local coin finds.*

• Ashwell Village Museum (1930), Swan Street, **Ashwell**, Baldock, Herts, SG7 5NY. Tel: 01462 742 956 *Roman coins from local finds, local trade tokens, Anglo-Gallic coins and jetons.*

• Buckinghamshire County Museum (1862), Church Street, **Aylesbury**, Bucks, HP20 2QP. Tel: 01296 331 441. *Roman and medieval English coins found locally, 17th/18th century Buckinghamshire tokens, commemorative medals.*

B

• Banbury Museum, Castle Quay Shopping Center, Spiceball Park Road, **Banbury**, Oxon, OX16 2PQ. Tel: 01295 753 752. *Wrexlin Hoard of Roman coins.*

• Museum of North Devon (1931), The Square, **Barnstaple**, EX32 8LN. Tel: 01271 346 747. *General coin and medal collection, including local finds. Medals of the Royal Devonshire Yeomanry.*

• Roman Baths Museum, Abbey Church Yard, Stall St, **Bath**, Avon, BA1 1LZ. Tel: 01225 477 785. *Comprehensive collection of Roman coins from local finds.*

• Bagshaw Museum and Art Gallery (1911), Wilton Park, **Batley**, West Yorkshire, WF17 0AS. Tel: 01924 324 765. *Roman, Scottish, Irish, English hammered, British and foreign coins, local traders' tokens, political medalets, campaign medals and decorations.*

• The Higgins Art Gallery and Museum (1961), Castle Lane, **Bedford**, MK40 3XD. Tel: 01234 718 618. *Collections of the Bedford Library and Scientific Institute, the Beds Archaeological Society and Bedford Modern School (Pritchard Memorial) Museum.*

• Ulster Museum (1928), Botanic Gardens, **Belfast**, BT9 5AB. Tel: 0845 608 0000. *Irish, English and British coins and commemorative medals.*

• Berwick Museum and Art Gallery (1867), The Clock Block, Berwick Barracks, Parade, **Berwick**, TD15 1DQG. Tel: 01289 309 538. *Roman, Scottish and medieval coins.*

• Treasure House and Art Gallery (1910), Champney Road, **Beverley**, Humberside, HU17 8HE. Tel: 01482 392 780. *Beverley trade tokens, Roman, English, British and foreign coins.*

• Bignor Roman Villa (1811), **Bignor**, nr Pulborough, West Sussex, RH20 1PH. Tel: 01798 869 259. *Roman coins found locally.*

• City Museum and Art Gallery (1861), Chamberlain Square, **Birmingham**, B3 3DH. Tel: 0121 348 8038. *Coins, medals and tokens - special emphasis on the products of the Soho, Heaton, Birmingham and Watt mints.*

• Blackburn Museum, Museum Street, **Blackburn**, Lancs, BB1 7AJ. Tel: 01254 667 130. *Incorporates the Hart (5,000 Greek, Roman and early English) and Hornby (500 English coins) collections, as well as the museum's own collection of British and Commonwealth coins.*

• Bognor Regis Museum, 25 – 27 West Street, **Bognor Regis**, West Sussex, PO21 1XA. Tel: 01243 865 636 *Roman, English and British coins and trade tokens.*

• Bolton Museum and Art Gallery,(1893), Le Mans Crescent, **Bolton**, Lancashire, BL1 1SE. **Temporarily closed. Anticipated re-opening 2018**

• Roman Town and Museum (1949) Main Street, Aldborough, **Boroughbridge**, N. Yorks, YO51 9ES. Tel: 01423 322 768. *Roman coins.*

• The Museum (1929), South Street, **Boston**, Lincs, PE21 6HT. Tel: 01205 365 954. *Small collection of English coins.*

• Natural Science Society Museum (1903), 39 Christchurch Road, **Bournemouth**, Dorset, BH1 3NS. Tel: 01202 553 525. *Greek, Roman and English hammered coins (including the Hengistbury Hoard), local trade tokens.*

• Bolling Hall Museum (1915), Bowling Hall Road, **Bradford**, West Yorkshire, BD4 7LP. Tel: 01274 431 826. *Some 2,000 coins and tokens, mostly 18th–20th centuries.*

• Bridport Museum (1932), 25 South Street, **Bridport**, Dorset DT6 3RJ. Tel: 01308 458 703. *Roman coins, mainly from excavations at Claudian Fort.*

• Bristol Museum and Art Gallery (1820), Queen's Road, **Bristol**, BS8 1RL. Tel: 0117 922 3571. *Ancient British, Roman (mainly from local hoards), English hammered coins, especially from the Bristol mint, and several hundred local trade tokens.*

• Buxton Museum and Art Gallery (1891), Terrace Road, **Buxton**, Derbyshire, SK17 6DA. Tel: 01629 533 540. *English and British coins, tokens and commemorative medals. Numismatic library.*

C

• Segontium Fort Museum (1928), Beddgelert Road, **Caernarfon**, Gwynedd, LL55 2LN. Tel: 01286 675 625. *Roman coins and artifacts excavated from the fort.*

• Fitzwilliam Museum (1816), Trumpington Street, **Cambridge**, CB2 1RB. Tel: 01223 332 900. *Ancient, English, medieval European, oriental coins, medals, plaques, seals and cameos.*

• National Museum & Galleries of Wales, Cathays Park, **Cardiff**, CF10 3NP. Tel: 0300 111 2 333. *Greek, Celtic, Roman and British coins and tokens with the emphasis on Welsh interest. Also military, civilian and comm. medals.*

• Guildhall Museum (1979), 31-33 Fisher Street, **Carlisle**, Cumbria, CA3 8JE. Tel: 01228 618 718. *General collection of coins and medals.*

• Tullie House (1877), Castle Street, **Carlisle**, Cumbria, CA3 8TP. Tel: 01228 618 718. *Roman, medieval and later coins from local finds, including medieval counterfeiter's coin-moulds.*

• Gough's Caves Museum (1934), The Cliffs, **Cheddar**, Somerset, BS27 3QF. Tel: 01934 742 343. *Roman coins.*

• Chelmsford Museum (1835), Oaklands Park, Moulsham Street, **Chelmsford**, Essex, CM2 9AQ. Tel: 0245 605 700. *Ancient British, Roman, medieval and later coins mainly from local finds, local medals.*

• Chepstow Museum, Bridge Street, Chepstow, (1949), **Chepstow**, Gwent, NP15 5EZ. Tel: 01291 625 981. *Local coins and trade tokens.*

• Grosvenor Museum (1886), 27 Grosvenor Street, **Chester**, CH1 2DD. Tel: 01244 972 197. *Roman coins from the fortress site, Anglo-Saxon, English medieval and post-medieval coins of the Chester and Rhuddlan mints, trade tokens, English and British milled coins.*

• Public Library (1879), New Beetwell Street, **Chesterfield**, Derbyshire, S40 1QN. Tel: 01629 533 400. *Roman coins from local finds, Derbyshire trade tokens, medals, seals and railway passes. Numismatic library and publications.*

• Red House Museum (1919), Quay Road, **Christchurch**, Dorset. Tel: 01202 482 860. *Coins of archaeological significance from Hampshire and Dorset, notably the South Hants Hoard, ancient British, Armorican, Gallo-Belgic, Celtic and Roman coins, local trade tokens and medals.*

• Corinium Museum (1856), Park Street, **Cirencester**, Glos. Tel:01285 655 611. *Roman coins.*

• Colchester and Essex Museum (1860), The Castle, **Colchester**, Essex. Tel: 01206 282 939. *Ancient British and Roman coins from local finds, medieval coins (especially the Colchester Hoard), later English coins and Essex trade tokens, commemorative medals.*

D

• Public Library, Museum and Art Gallery (1921), Crown Street, **Darlington**, Co Durham DL1 1ND. Tel: 01325 462 034. *Coins, medals and tokens.*

• Borough Museum (1908), 18 - 20 Market Street, **Dartford**, Kent, DA1 1EU. Tel: 01322 224 739. *Roman, medieval and later English hammered coins, trade tokens and commemorative medals.*

• Dartmouth Museum (1953), The Butterwalk, **Dartmouth**, Devon TQ6 9PZ. Tel: 01803 832 923. *Coins and medals of a historical and maritime nature.*

• Museum and Art Gallery (1878), The Strand, **Derby**, DE1 1BS. Tel:01332 641 901. *Roman coins, English silver and copper regal coins, Derbyshire tradesmen's tokens, British campaign medals and decorations of the Derbyshire Yeomanry and the 9/12 Royal Lancers.*

• Museum and Art Gallery (1909), Chequer Road, **Doncaster**, South Yorkshire, DN1 2AE. Tel: 01302 734 293. *General collection of English and foreign silver and bronze coins, Representative collection of Roman imperial silver and bronze coins, including a number from local hoards. English trade tokens, principally of local issues, medals.*

• Dorset County Museum (1846), High West Street, **Dorchester**, Dorset, DT1 1XA. Tel: 01305 262 735. *British, Roman, medieval and later coins of local interest.*

• Burgh Museum (1835), The Observatory, Rotchell Road, **Dumfries** Tel: 01387 253 374. *Greek, Roman, Anglo-Saxon, medieval English and Scottish coins, especially from local hoards. Numismatic library.*

• The McManus Dundee's Art Galleries and Museums (1873). Albert Square, **Dundee**, DD1 1DA. Tel:01382 307 200. *Coins and medals of local interest.*

• The Cathedral Treasury (995 AD), The College, **Durham**, DH1 3EH. Tel: 0191 386 4266. *Greek and Roman coins bequeathed by Canon Sir George Wheeler (1724), Renaissance to modern medals, medieval English coins, especially those struck at the Durham ecclesiastical mint.*

• Durham Heritage Centre, St Mary le Bow, North Bailey, **Durham**, DH1 3ET. Tel: 0191 384 5589. *Roman, medieval and later coins, mainly from local finds.*

E

• National Museum of Scotland (1781), Chambers Street, **Edinburgh**, EH1 1JF. Tel: 0300 123 6789.

Roman, Anglo-Saxon, Englsh and Scottish coins, trade tokens, commemorative medals and communion tokens. Numismatic library. Publications.

• Royal Albert Memorial Museum (1868), Queen Street, **Exeter**, EX4 3RX. Tel: 01392 265 858. *Roman and medieval. Coins of the Exeter Mint.*

G

• Hunterian Museum (1807), Gilbert Scott Building, University Of Glasgow, University Avenue, **Glasgow**, G12 8QQ. Tel: 0141 330 4221. *Greek, Roman, Byzantine, Scottish, English and Irish coins, Papal and other European medals, Indian and Oriental coins, trade and communion tokens.*

• Kelvingrove Art Gallery and Museum (1888), Argyle Street, **Glasgow.** Tel: 0141 276 9599. *General collection of coins, trade tokens, communion tokens, commemorative and military medals.*

• Riverside Museum (1974), 100 Pointhouse Place **Glasgow**, G3 8RS. Tel: 0141 357 3929. *Transport tokens and passes, commemorative medals, badges and insignia of railway companies and shipping lines.*

• City Museum and Art Gallery (1859), Brunswick Road, **Gloucester.** Tel: 01452 396 131. *Ancient British, Roman, Anglo-Saxon (from local finds), early medieval (from local mints), Gloucestershire trade tokens.*

• Guernsey Museum and Art Gallery, St Peter Port, **Guernsey.** Tel: 01481 726 518. *Armorican, Roman, medieval and later coins, including the coins, medals, tokens and paper money of Guernsey.*

• Guildford Museum (1898), Castle Hill, **Guildford**, Surrey, GU1 3SX. Tel: 01483 444 751. *Roman and medieval coins and later medals.*

H

• Gray Museum and Art Gallery, Church Square, Clarence Road, **Hartlepool**, Cleveland. Tel: 01429 869 706. *General collection, including coins from local finds.*

• Public Museum and Art Gallery (1890), John's Place, Cambridge Road, **Hastings**, East Sussex. Tel: 01424 721 952. *General collection of English coins, collection of Anglo-Saxon coins from Sussex mints.*

• City Museum (1874), Broad Street, **Hereford Temporarily Closed**

• Hertford Museum (1902), 18 Bull Plain, **Hertford.** Tel: 01992 582 686. *British, Roman, medieval and later English coins and medals.*

• Honiton and Allhallows Public Museum (1946), High Street, **Honiton**, Devon. Tel:01404 44966. *Small general collection, including coins from local finds.*

• Museum and Art Gallery (1891), 19 New Church Road, **Hove**. Tel:0300 029 0900. *English coins, Sussex trade tokens and hop tallies, campaign medals, orders and decorations, comm. medals.*

• Tolson Memorial Museum (1920), Ravensknowle Park, **Huddersfield**, West Yorkshire. Tel: 01484 223 240. *Representative collection of British coins and tokens, Roman and medieval coins, mainly from local finds.*

• Hull and East Riding Museum (1928), 36 High Street, **Hull.** Tel: 01482 300 300. *Celtic, Roman and medieval coins and artifacts from local finds. Some later coins including tradesmen's tokens.*

I

• The Manx Museum, Douglas, **Isle of Man.** Tel: 01624 648 000. *Roman, Celtic, Hiberno-Norse, Viking, medieval English and Scottish coins, mainly from local finds, Manx traders' tokens from the 17th to 19th centuries, Manx coins from 1709 to the present day.*

J

• Jersey Museum, Weighbridge, St Helier, **Jersey** Tel: 01534 633 300. *Armorican, Gallo-Belgic, Roman, medieval English and French coins, coins, paper money and tokens of Jersey.*

K

• Cliffe Castle Museum, Spring Gardens Lane, **Keighley** West Yorkshire. Tel: 01535 618 231. *Roman coins found locally.*

• Dick Institute Museum and Art Gallery (1893), Elmbank Avenue, **Kilmarnock**, Ayrshire. Tel: 01563 554 300. *General collection of coins and medals, and the Hunter-Selkirk collection of communion tokens.*

L

• City Museum (1923), Old Town Hall, Market Square, **Lancaster.** Tel: 01524 64637. *Roman, Anglo-Saxon, medieval English coins, provincial trade tokens, medals of the King's Own Royal Lancashire Regiment.*

• City Museum (1820), Municipal Buildings, The Headrow, **Leeds**, West Yorkshire. Tel: 0113 378 5001. *Greek, Roman, Anglo-Saxon, English medieval, Scottish, Irish, British, Commonwealth and foreign coins. Several Roman and Saxon hoards. The Backhouse collection of Yorkshire banknotes, the Thornton collection of Yorkshire tokens, British and foreign commemorative medals.*

• Leicester Museum and Art Gallery (1849), 53 New Walk, **Leicester**. Tel: 0116 225 4900. *Roman, medieval and later coins, mainly from local finds, tokens, commemorative medals, campaign medals and decorations.*

• Pennington Hall Museum and Art Gallery, **Leigh**, Lancashire. *Roman and British coins and medals.*

• City Library, Art Gallery and Museum (1859), The Friary, **Lichfield**, Staffs Tel: 01543 510 700. *Roman, medieval and later English coins, Staffordshire trade tokens and commemorative medals.*

• World Museum(1851), William Brown Street, **Liverpool**, L3 8EN. Tel: 0151 478 4393. *General collection of Roman, medievaland later British coins, tokens.*

• Bank of England Museum, Threadneedle Street, **London**. Tel: 020 7601 5545. *Exhibits relating to gold bullion, coins, tokens and medals, the design and manufacture of banknotes, and a comprehensive collection of bank notes dating from the 17th century to the present day.*

• British Museum(1752), HSBC Coin Gallery, Great Russell Street, **London**, WC1. Tel: 020 7323 8181. *Almost a million coins, medals, tokens and badges of all period from Lydia, 7th century BC to the present time. Extensive library of books and periodicals.*

• British Numismatic Society (1903), Warburg Institute, Woburn Square, **London**, WC1. *Library containing over 5,000 volumes, including sale catalogues, periodicals and pamphlets. Open to members only.*

• Gunnersbury Park Museum (1927), Acton, **London**, W3. **Temporarily closed and will reopen in 2018**

• Horniman Museum and Library (1890), 100 London Road, Forest Hill, **London**, SE23 3PQ Tel: 020 8699 1872. *General collection, primitive currency, some tokens.*

• Imperial War Museum, Lambeth Road, **London**, SE1 6HZ. Tel: 020 7416 5000. *Emergency coinage of two world wars, occupation and invasion money, extensive collection of German Notgeld, commemorative, propaganda and military medals, badges and insignia.*

• Sir John Soane's Museum (1833), 13 Lincoln's Inn Fields, **London**, WC2. Tel: 020 7405 2107. *Napoleonic medals and medallic series of the late 18th and early 19th centuries.*

• National Maritime Museum, Romney Road, Greenwich, **London**, SE10. Tel: 020 8858 4422. *Commemorative medals with a nautical or maritime theme, naval medals and decorations.*

• Victoria and Albert Museum (1852), Cromwell Road, South Kensington, **London**, SW7 2RL. Tel: 020 7942 2000. *Byzantine gold and medieval Hispano-Mauresque coins (Department of Metalwork), large collection of Renaissance and later medals (Department of Architecture and Sculpture). Numismatic books.*

• Ludlow Museum (1833). The Assembly Rooms. Castle Square, **Ludlow**. Tel: 01584 878 697. *Roman and medieval coins from local finds.*

• Luton Museum and Art Gallery (1927), Wardown House, Old Bedford Road, **Luton**, Beds. Tel: 01582 546 722. *Coins, tokens and medals.*

M

• Museum and Art Gallery (1858), St Faiths Street, **Maidstone**, Kent. Tel: 01622 602838. *Ancient British, Roman, Anglo-Saxon and medieval coins found in Kent, modern British coins, Kent trade tokens, banknotes, hop tallies and tokens, primitive currency, collections of Kent Numismatic Society.*

• The Manchester Museum (1868), The University, **Manchester**. Tel: 0161 275 2648. *Very fine collections of Greek and Roman coins, comprehensive collections of English, European and Oriental coins, over 30,000 in all.*

• Margate Museum (1923), Market Place, Margate Old Town, **Margate**, Kent. Tel: 01843 231 213. *Small collection of coins, including Roman from local finds.*

• Montrose Museum and Art Gallery (1836). Panmure Place, **Montrose**, Angus, DD10 8HF. Tel: 01674 662 660). *Scottish and British coins.*

N

• Newark-on-Trent Museum (1912), 14 Appletongate, **Newark**, Notts. Tel 01636 655765. *Siege pieces, trade tokens and coins from local finds and hoards.*

• Newbury District Museum, The Wharf, **Newbury**, Berkshire. Tel: 01635 519562. *Ancient British, Roman and medieval coins and artifacts, later coins and tokens.*

• Great North Museum, Hannock Barras Bridge, **Newcastle-upon-Tyne.** Tel: 0191 208 6765. *Ancient coins.*

O

• Heberden Coin Room, Ashmolean Museum (1683), **Oxford**. Tel: 01865 278000. *Extensive collections of all periods, notably Greek, Roman, English and Oriental coins, Renaissance portrait and later medals, tokens and paper money. Large library. Numerous publications.*

P

• Peterborough Museum (1881), Priestgate, **Peterborough**, Cambs. Tel: 01733 864 663. *Roman (mainly from local hoards and finds), Anglo-Saxon, medieval English, British and modern European coins, English and British commemorative medals and tokens.*

• City Museum and Art Gallery (1897), Drake Circus, **Plymouth**, Devon. Tel: 01752 264878. *General collections of British and Commonwealth coins and tokens, Devon trade tokens and Plymouth tradesmen's checks, Ancient British and Roman coins from local sites.*

• Waterfront Museum, 4 High Street, **Poole**, BH15 1DW. Tel:01202 262 600. *General collection of British and foreign coins, medals and tokens (view by appointment).*

• Portsmouth Museum (1972), Museum Road, Old **Portsmouth**, PO1 2LJ. Tel: 023 9283 4779. *Roman, medieval and later coins mainly from local finds and archaeological excavation, British coins, trade tokens of Hampshire, commemorative medals.*

• Harris Museum and Art Gallery (1893), Market Square, **Preston**, PR1 2PP. Tel: 01772 258 248. *English and British coins, tokens and medals.*

R

• The Museum of Reading (1883), Blagrave Street, **Reading**, RG1 1QH. Tel: 0118 937 3400. *British, Roman and medieval English coins, many from local finds, tradesmen's tokens and commemorative medals.*

• Rochdale Pioneers Museum (1905), 31 Toad Lane, **Rochdale**, OL12 ONU. Tel: 01706 524 920. *Roman and medieval coins from local finds, Rochdale trade tokens, miscellaneous British and foreign coins and medals.*

• Clifton Park Museum (1893), Clifton Park, **Rotherham**, S65 2AA. Tel: 01709 336 633. *Collection includes Roman coins from Templeborough Forts, medieval English coins from local hoards and a general collection of British coins.*

S

• Saffron Walden Museum (1832) (1939), Museum Street, **Saffron** Walden, CB10 1JL. Tel: 01799 510 333. *Ancient British, Roman, medieval and later coins, mainly from local finds and archaeological excavation, trade tokens and commemorative medals.*

• Verulamium Museum, St Michael's, **St Albans**, Herts . Tel: 01727 751 810. *Coins and artifacts excavated from the Roman town.*

• Salisbury and South Wiltshire Museum (1861), The Kings House 65 The Close, **Salisbury**, Wilts. Tel: 01722 332 151. *Collection of coins minted or found locally, including finds of Iron Age, Roman, Saxon and medieval coins, as well as 18th and 19th century tradesmen's tokens.*

• Richborough Castle Museum (1930), **Sandwich**, Kent. Tel: 0304 612013. *Roman coins of 1st–5th centuries from excavations of the Richborough site.*

• Rotunda Museum (1829), Vernon Road, **Scarborough**, YO11 2PS. Tel: 01723 353 665. *Collection of over 4,000 Roman coins, 1,500 English and 600 coins from local finds, siege pieces and trade.*

• Gold Hill Museum (1946), Gold Hill, **Shaftesbury**, Dorset, SP7 8JW. Tel: 01747 852 157. *Hoard of Saxon coins.*

• City Museum (1875), Weston Park, **Sheffield.** Tel: 0114 278 2600. *Over 5,000 coins of all periods, but mainly English and modern British. European coins, imperial Roman (including three hoards of about 500 coins each), Yorkshire trade tokens, British historical medals, campaign medals. Library.*

• Shrewsbury Museum and Art Gallery, The Square, **Shrewsbury**. Tel: 01743 361 196. *Coins minted at Shrewsbury 925-1180, Civil War coinage of 1642, Shropshire tradesmen's tokens, English coins and medals.*

• Atkinson Art Gallery (1878), Lord Street, **Southport,** Lancs. Tel: 01704 533 133. *Roman coins.*

• Southwold Museum (1933), 9-11 Victoria Street, **Southwold**, IP18 6HZ. Tel: 01502 726 097. *General collection of coins, specialised Suffolk trade tokens.*

• Stockport Museum (1860), 30-31 Market Place, **Stockport**, Cheshire SK1 1ES. Tel: 0161 474 4444 *Miscellaneous collection of coins, tokens and medals.*

• Museum in the Park (1899), Stratford Park, Stratford Road, **Stroud**, Glos GL5 4AF. Tel: 01453 7633 394. *Ancient British, Roman, Saxon, Norman, later medieval English, British coins and Gloucestershire trade tokens.*

• Sunderland Museum and Winter Gardens (1846), Burdon Road, **Sunderland**, Tyne & Wear SR1 1PP. Tel: 0191 553 2323. *Roman imperial, medieval and later English, including examples of the pennies minted at Durham, modern British and foreign coins, 17th-19th century tradesmen's tokens and local medallions.*

• Swansea Museum (1835), Victoria Road, **Swansea**, W. Glamorgan, SA1 1SN. Tel: 01792 653 763. *Coins and medals of local interest.*

T

• Tamworth Castle and Museum (1899), The Holloway, **Tamworth**, Staffs. Tel: 01827 709 626. *Anglo-Saxon coins, medieval English including coins of the Tamworth mint, later English and British coins, tokens, commemorative medallions and medals.*

• The Museum of Somerset, Taunton Castle, Castle Green, **Taunton**, Somerset TA1 4AA. Tel: 01823 255 510/320 200. *Celtic, Roman, Anglo-Saxon, early Medieval, tokens, medallions and banknotes. Strong emphasis on locally-found items.*

• Thurrock Museum and Heritage Srvice (1956), Second Floor, Thameside Complex, Orsett Road, Grays, Essex, RM17 5DX. Tel: 01375 413 965. *Roman coins.*

• Royal Cornwall Museum (1818), River Street, **Truro**, Cornwall TR1 2SJ. Tel: 01872 272 205. *Coins, tokens and medals pertaining principally to the county of Cornwall.*

W

• Wakefield Museum (1919), Burton Street, **Wakefield,** West Yorkshire WF1 2EB. Tel: 01924 295 351. *Roman and medieval English silver and copper coins.*

• Epping Forest District Museum, 39/41 Sun Street, **Waltham Abbey**, Essex, EN 9. *Ancient British, Roman and medieval coins, Essex tradesmen's tokensof local interest.*

• Warrington Museum and Art Gallery (1848). Bold Street, **Warrington**, Cheshire, WA1 1JG. Tel: 01925 30550. *Coins, medals and tokens.*

• Worcester City Museum (1833), Foregate Street, **Worcester.** Tel: 01905 25371. *Roman, medieval and later coins and tokens. Coins of the Worcester mint.*

• Wells Museum (18903), 8 Cathedral Green, **Wells,** Somerset. Tel: 01749 3477. *Ancient and modern British and world coins, local trade tokens and medals.*

• Municipal Museum and Art Gallery (1878), Station Road, **Wigan**, Lancashire. *British, Commonwealth and foreign coins from about 1660 to the present. Roman coins from local sites, commemorative medals.*

• City Museum (1851), The Square, **Winchester**, Hants. Tel: 01962 848 269. *Roman and medieval coins chiefly from local hoards and finds. Hampshire tradesmen's tokens and commemorative medals. Small reference library.*

• Wisbech and Fenland Museum (1835), Museum Square, **Wisbech,** Cambridgeshire. Tel: 01945 583 817, *British Roman, medieval and later coins, medals and tokens.*

Y

• York Castle Museum (1938), Eye of York, **York**, YO1 9RY. Tel: 01904 687 687. *English and British coins, campaign medals, orders and decorations, comemorative medals.*

• Jorvik Viking Centre (1984), Coppergate, **York.** Tel: 01904 615 505. *Coins and artefacts pertaining to the Viking occupation of York.*

• The Yorkshire Museum (1823), Museum Gardens, **York** YO1 7FR. Tel: 01904 687 687. *Roman imperial, medieval English and later coins, about 12,000 in all.*

CLUB *directory*

Details given here are the names of Numismatic Clubs and Societies, their date of foundation, and their usual venues, days and times of meetings. Meetings are monthly unless otherwise stated. Finally, the telephone number of the club secretary is given; the names and addresses of club secretaries are withheld for security reasons, but full details may be obtained by writing to the Secretary of the British Association of Numismatic Societies, Chris Comber, numis@hotmail.co.uk or visiting the website at www.coinclubs.org.uk.

Ayeshire Coin Club 1st Thurs, Oct to April, 19.30. Call for Venue, Tel: 07527 240 016

Banknote Society of Scotland (1994) Meetings are held in Edinburgh. Email for dates and venue, bnss2006@ntlworld.com

Bath & Bristol Numismatic Society (1950). Fry's Club, Keynsham, Bristol. 2nd Thu, 19.30. Email: jagmartin553@gmail.

Bedfordshire Numismatic Society (1966). 2nd Thu. Email for venue details: nigel.lutt2@virginmedia.com

Bexley Coin Club (1968). St Martin's Church Hall, Erith Road, Barnehurst, Bexleyheath, Kent. 1st Mon ,(exc Jan, Aug & Sept), 19.30. Tel: 020 8303 0510.

Birmingham Numismatic Society (1964). Friend's Meeting House, Bull Street. Email: bhamns@hotmail.co.uk

Matthew Boulton Lunar Society (1994). The Old School House, Chapel Lane, Birmingham, B47 6JX Tel: 01564 821 582.

British Banking History Society. 22 Delamere Road, Gatley, Cheadle, SK8 4PH.

British Numismatic Society (1903). Warburg Institute, Woburn Square, London WC1H 0AB. Email: secretary@britnumsoc.org

Cambridgeshire Numismatic Society (1946). Friends' Meeting House, 12 Jesus Lane Cambridge, CB5 8BA. 4th Mon, (Sept–June), 19.30. Tel: 01223 332 918

Chester & North Wales Coin & Banknote Society (1996). Liver Hotel, 110 Brook Street, Chester. 4th Tue, 20.00. Tel: 01829 260 897

Crewe & District Coin and Medal Society. Memorial Hall, Church Lane, Wistaston, Crewe, CW2 8ER. 2nd Tue, (exc Jan & July), 19.30 Tel: 07828 602 611

Derbyshire Numismatic Society The Friends Meeting House, St Helen's Street, Derby Tel: 01283 223 893

Devon & Exeter Numismatic Society, Courtenay Room, The St James Centre, Stadium Way, Exeter. 3rd Wed. Tel: 01395 568 830

Essex Numismatic Society (1966). Chelmsford Museum, Moulsham Street, Chelmsford, Essex. 4th Fri (exc Dec), 20.00. Tel: 01277 656 627.

Glasgow & West of Scotland Numismatic Society (1947). Ibrox Parish Church Halls, Clifford Street, Glasgow, G51 1QH. 2nd Thu, Oct-April, 19.30. Tel: 0141 641 2382

Harrow Coin Club (1968). The Scout Building, off Walton Road, Wealdstone, Harrow, HA1 4UX. 2nd Mon, 19.30. Tel: 0208 368 3087.

Havering Numismatic Society (1967). Fairkytes Arts Centre, Billet Lane, Hornchurch, Essex, RM11 1AX 1st Tue, 19.30. Email: mail@havering-ns.org.uk

Huddersfield Numismatic Society (1947). The County Hotel, 4 Princess Street, Huddersfield, HD1 2TT. Call for meeting dates. Tel: 01484 866 814.

International Bank Note Society (London Branch) (1961). Spink, 69 Southampton Row, Bloomsbury, London, WC1B 4ET. Last Thu (exc Sept & Dec), 18.30.

International Bank Note Society (East Midlands Branch), Highfields Community Fire Station, Hassocks Lane, Beeston, Nottingham, NG9 2 GQ. Last Saturday of every odd month. Tel: 0115 928 9720.

Ireland, Numismatic Society of (Northern Branch). For dates and venues visit: www. numsocirelandnb.com

Ireland, Numismatic Society of, Ely House, 8 Ely Place, Dublin 2. For dates and venues visit: www. numismaticsocietyofireland.com

Ipswich Numismatic Society, The Golden Hind, 470 Nacton Road, Ipswich, IP3 9NF. 3rd Weds. Email: administrator@ipnumsoc.org.uk.

Lancashire & Cheshire Numismatic Society (1933). Manchester Museum, Oxford Road, Manchester, M13 9PL. 3rd Sat, 14.00. Tel: 01204 849 469

London Numismatic Club (1947). Room 11 Mary Ward Center, 42 Queens Street, London, WC1N 3AQ. 1st Tues (except Jan, Aug and Sept). Email: g.buddle@btopenworld.com.

Loughborough Coin & Search Society (1964). Rosebery Medical Center, Rosebery Street, Loughborough, Leics, LE11 5DX 1st Thu, 19.30. www.lcss.org.uk

Northampton Numismatic Society (1969). Old Scouts RFC, Rushmere Road, Northampton, NN1 5RY. 1st Fri, 10.30

Norwich Coin & Medal Society, The White Horse Inn, Trowse, Norwich, NR14 8ST. 3rd Mon. Tel: 07894 437 847.

Numismatic Society of Nottinghamshire (1948). Lecture Theatre, Lakeside Arts Center and Museu, University of Nottingham, University Park, Nottingham, NG7 2RD. 2nd Tue (Sep-Apr). Tel: 0115 925 7674.

Orders & Medals Research Society (1942). Spink, 69 Southampton Row, Bloomsbury, London, WC1B 4ET. Last Monday of the month (that is not a Bank Holiday) of the odd numbered months plus April and October. 18.00.

Ormskirk & West Lancashire Numismatic Society (1970). The Eagle & Child, Maltkiln Lane, Bispham Green L40 1SN. 1st Thu, 20.15. Tel: 01704 531 266)

Peterborough & District Numismatic Society (1967). Belsize Community Centre, Celta Road Peterborough, Cambs. 4th Tue (exc June, July & Aug), 19.30. Tel: 01733 567 763.

Reading Coin Club (1964). Abbey Baptist Church, Abbey Square, Reading, RG1 3BE 1st Mon, 19.00. Tel: 01344 774 155.

Royal Numismatic Society (1836). Warburg Institute, Woburn Square, London, WC1H 0AB. (some meetings held at Spink, 69 Southampton Row, Bloomsbury Road, London WC1B 4ET). 3rd Tues 18.00. Email: info@numismatics.org.uk. Tel: 0207 323 8541.

St Albans & Hertfordshire Numismatic Society (1948). Call for venue and dates Tel: 01727 824 434.

Southampton and District Numismatic Society (1953). Central Baptist Church, Devonshire Road, Polygon, Southampton SO15 2GY. Email: sue717@btinternet.com.

South Wales & Monmouthshire Numismatic Society (1958). 1st Mon (except Bank Holidays when 2nd Mon), 19.30. For venue call Tel: 029 20561564.

Thurrock Numismatic Society (1970). Stanley Lazell Hall, Dell Road, Grays, Essex, RM17 5JZ 3rd Wed, 19.30. Tel: 01375 413 964.

Tyneside Numismatic Society (1954). The Plough Inn, 369 Old Durham Road, Gateshead, NE9 5LA. 2nd Weds, 19.30. Tel: 0161 825 824.

Wessex Numismatic Society (1948). Edward Wright Room, Beaufort Community Centre, Southbourne, Bournemouth, Dorset. 1st Tues (exc Aug), 20.00. Tel: 01425 507446

Wiltshire Numismatic Society (1965). The Raven Inn, Poulshot, Nr. Devizes, Wiltshire. 3rd Weds, (March–Dec), 20.00. Tel: 01225 703 143.

Worthing & District Numismatic Society (1967). The Chatsworth Hotel, Worthing, BN11 3DU. 3rd Thu, 20.00. Tel: 01243 697434.

Yorkshire Numismatic Society (1909). See website for venues and dates. www.yorkshirenumismatic. blogspot.co.uk

Important Notice to Club Secretaries:

If your details as listed are incorrect please let us know in time for the next edition of the **COIN YEARBOOK.** Amendments can be sent via post to: 40, Southernhay East, Exeter, Devon EX1 1PE or via email to: jayne@tokenpublishing.com

IMPORTANT ORGANISATIONS

ADA
The Antiquities Dealers Association
Secretary: Susan Hadida, Duke's Court, 32 Duke Street, London SW1Y 6DU

ANA
The American Numismatic Association
818 North Cascade Avenue, Colorado Springs, CO 80903, USA

BNTA
The British Numismatic Trade Association
Secretary: Christel Swan 3 Unwin Mansions, Queens Club Gardens, London, W14 9TH

IAPN
International Association of Professional Numismatists
Secretary: Jean-Luc Van der Schueren, 14 Rue de la Bourse, B–1000, Brussels.

IBNS
International Bank Note Society
Membership Secretary: John Vanden Bossche Email: uksecretary@ibns.biz

RNS
Royal Numismatic Society
Dept of Coins & Medals, British Museum, London WC1B 3DG.

BAMS
British Art Medal Society
Philip Attwood, Dept of Coins & Medals, British Museum, London WC1B 3DG.

BNS
British Numismatic Society
Secretary: Peter Preston-Morley.
Email: secretary@britnumsoc.0rg

**Society activities are featured every month in the "Diary Section" of COIN NEWS magazine—available from all good newsagents or on subscription.
Telephone 01404 46972 for more details or log onto
www.tokenpublishing.com**

Society meetings are a great place to meet like-minded collectors. In February 2017, the Norwich Coin and Medal Society celebrated 50 years.

DIRECTORY *of auctioneers*

Listed here are the major auction houses which handle coins, medals, banknotes and other items of numismatic interest. Many of them hold regular public auctions, whilst others handle numismatic material infrequently. A number of coin companies also hold regular Postal Auctions—these are marked with a Ⓟ

Auction World Company Ltd
1-15-5 Hamamatsucho,Minato-ku,
Tokyo, 105-0013 Japan. www.auction-world.co

Baldwin's of St James
10 Charles II Street, London, SW1Y 4AA.
Tel: 020 7930 7888, fax 0207 930 8214,
Email: info@bsjauctions.com, www.bsjauctions.com.

Biddle & Webb
Icknield Square, Birmingham, B16 0PP.
Tel: 0121 455 8042, www.biddleandwebb.com

Blyth & Co
Arkenstall Center, Haddenham, Cambs, CB6 3XD. Tel: 01353 930 094, www.blyths.com

Bonhams (incorporating Glendinings)
Montpelier Street, Knightsbridge, London,
SW7 1HH. Tel: 020 7393 3914, www.bonhams.com.

BSA Auctions
Units 1/2, Cantilupe Court, Cantilupe Road, Ross on Wye, Herefordshire, HR9 7AN . Tel: 01989 769 529, www.the-saleroom.com

cgb.fr
36, Rue Vivienne, 75002, Paris, France.
Email: contact@cgb.fr, www.cgb.fr.

Chilcotts Auctioneers
Silver Street, Honiton, EX14 1QN. Tel: 01404 47783,
email: info@chilcottsauctioneers.co.uk

Christies
8 King Street, St James's, London SW1Y 6QT.
Tel: 020 7839 9060.

Classical Numismatic Group Inc (Seaby Coins)
20 Bloomsbury Street, London, WC1B 3QA.
Tel: 020 7495 1888 ,fax 020 7499 5916,
Email: cng@cngcoins.com,
www.historicalcoins.com. Ⓟ

The Coin Cabinet
Tel 0800 088 5350
www.thecoincabinet.co.uk.

Corbitts
5 Moseley Sreet, Newcastle upon Tyne NE1 1YE.
Tel: 0191 232 7268, fax 0191 261 4130.
www.corbitts.com

Croydon Coin Auctions
PO Box 201, Croydon, CR9 7AQ. Tel: 020 8656 4583, www.croydoncoinauctions.co.uk.

Davissons Ltd.
PO Box 323, Cold Spring, MN 56320 USA.
Tel: 001 320 685 3835, info@davcoin.com,
www.davcoin.com.

Dix Noonan Webb (IAPN)
16 Bolton Street, Piccadilly, London, W1J 8BQ
Tel: 020 7016 1700, auctions@dnw.co.uk,
www.dnw.co.uk.

Duke's
Brewery Square, Dorchester, Dorset DT1 1GA.
Tel: 01305 265 080, enquiries@dukesauctions.
com www.dukes-auctions.com

English Coin Auctions
3 Elders Street, Scarborough, YO11 1DZ
Tel: 01723 364 760, wwwenglishcoinauctionscom

Jean Elsen & ses Fils s.a.
Avenue de Tervueren 65, B–1040, Brussels.
Tel: 0032 2 734 6356, Email: numismatique@e
lsen.eu www.elsen.eu.

Fellows & Sons
Augusta House, 19 Augusta Street, Hockley,
Birmingham, B18 6JA. Tel: 0121 212 2131,
www.fellows.co.uk.

B. Frank & Son
3 South Avenue, Ryton, Tyne & Wear NE40 3LD.
Tel: 0191 413 8749, Email: bfrankandson@aol.com.
www.bfrankandson.com.

Gadoury
57, rue Grimaldi, 98000 MONACO.
Tel: 0 377 93 25 12 96, Email: contact@gadoury.com,
www.gadoury.com.

Goldberg Coins & Collectibles
11400 W. Olympic Blvd, Suite 800, Los Angeles,
Hills CA 90064. Tel: 001 310.551 2646, info@
goldbergcoins.com, www.goldbergcoins.com.

Heritage World Coin Auctions
3500 Maple Avenue, 17th Floor, Dallas, Texas
75219, USA. Tel: 001 214 528 3500, Bid@HA.com
www.ha.com).

International Coin Exchange
Charter House, 5 Pembroke Row, Dublin 2. Tel:
00353 8684 93355, email: iceauctiongalleries@
gmail.com, www.ice-auction.com.

Kleeford Coin Auctions
Tel: 01773 528 743, email: kleeford@btinternet.
com ℗

Fritz Rudolf Künker
Nobbenburger, Strasse 4A, 49076, Osnabrüeck,
Germany. Tel: 0049 5419 62020, fax: 0049 541 96 20
222, email: service@kuenker.de, www.kuenker.de

Lawrence Fine Art Auctioneers
The Linen Yard, South Street, Crewkerne, Somer
set TA18 8AB. Tel: 01460 73041, email: enquir
ies@lawrences.co.uk, www.lawrences.co.uk.

Lockdale Coins
52 Barrack Square, Martlesham Heath, Ipswich,
Suffolk, IP5 3RF. Tel: 01473 627 110, sales@
lockdales.com, www.lockdales.com.

London Coins
Tel: 01474 871464, email: info@londoncoins.
co.uk, www.londoncoins.co.uk.

Mavin International
20 Kramat Lane, #01-04/05 United House,
Singapore 228773. Tel: 65 6238 7177,
mail@mavininternational.com.

Morton & Eden Ltd
Nash House, St Georges Street, London W1S
2FQ. Tel: 020 7493 5344, fax 020 7495 6325,
info@mortonandeden.com,
www.mortonandeden.com.

Mowbray Collectables
Email: paul@mowbrays.co.nz, www.mowbraycol
lectables.co.nz

Noble Numismatics
169 Macquire Street, Sydney, NSW 2000
Australia. Tel: 0061 2922 34578, fax: 0061 29233
6009, Email: info@noble.com.au,
www.noble.com.au.

Numismatica Ars Classica NAC AG
Suite 1, Claridge House, 32 Davies Street,
London W1K 4ND. Tel: 020 7839 7270,
email: info@arsclassicacoins.com.

Numis-Or
4, Rue des Barques 1207, Geneva Switzerland
Tel: 0041 2273 59255, email: info@numisor.ch,
www.numisor.ch

Pacific Rim Online Auction
P O Box 847, North Sydney, NSW 2060, Australia. Tel
0061 29588 7111,
www.pacificrimonlineauctions.com
Online coin auction.

Penrith, Farmers' & Kidds PLC
Skirsgill Saleroom, Penrith, Cumbria, CA11 0DN.
Tel: 01768 890 781, email: info@pfkauctions.
co.uk,www.pfkauctions.co.uk

Chris A. Rudd (IAPN, BNTA)
PO Box 222, Aylsham, Norfolk, NR11 6TY.
Tel: 01263 735 007, email: liz@celticcoins.com,
www.celticcoins.com

Simmons Gallery
PO Box 104, Leytonstone, London. Tel: 020 8989
8097. www.simmonsgallery.co.uk ℗

Smiths of Newent
The Old Chapel, Culver Street, Newent, GL18 1DB.
Tel: 01531 821 776, email: enquiries@smithsauction-
room.co.uk, www.smithsnewentauctions.co.uk.

Spink & Son Ltd
69 Southampton Row, Bloomsbury, London
WC1B 4ET. Tel: 020 7563 4000, fax 020 7563
4066, email: concierge@spink.com,
www.spink.com.

Stacks, Bowers and Ponterio
1231 East Dyer Road, Suite 100, Santa Ana,
California, 92705, USA. Tel: 001 800 458 4646,
email: info@StacksBowers.com,
www.stacksbowers.com

Tennants Auctioneers
The Auction Centre, Leyburn, North Yorkshire,
DL8 5SG. Tel: 01969 623 780, email: enquiry@
tennants-ltd.co.uk, www.tennants.co.uk.

The-saleroom.com
The Harlequin Building, 65 Southwark Street,
London, SE1 0HR. Tel: 0203 725 555, email: sup
port@auctiontechnologygroup.com,
www.the-saleroom.com.

Thomson Roddick Auctioneers
The Auction Centre, Marconi Road, Carlisle,
CA2 7NA. Tel: 01228 528 939, email: carlisle@
thomsonroddick.com. Also at The Auction Centre,
118 Carnethie Street, Rosewell, Edinburgh, EH24
www.thomsonroddck.com.

Timeline Auctions
The Court House, 363 Main Road, Harwich,
Essex CO12 4DN Tel: 01277 815 121, email:
enquiries@timelineauctions.com
www.timelineauctions.com.

Trevanion and Dean
The Joyce Building, Station Road, Whitchurch, SY13
1ND. Tel: 01948 800 202, email: info@trevanionand
dean.co.uk

Warwick & Warwick
Chalon House, Scarbank, Millers Road, Warwick
CV34 5DB. Tel: 01926 499 031 fax 01926 491 906,
richard.beale@warwickandwarwick.com,
www.warwickandwarwick.com.

Whyte's Auctions
38 Molesworth Street, Dublin 2, Ireland.
Tel: +00 3531 676 2888, www.whytes.com.

Woolley & Wallis
51-61 Castle Street, Salisbury, Wiltshire SP1 3SU.
Tel: 01722 424500, www.woolleyandwallis.co.uk

DIRECTORY *of fairs*

Listed below are the names of the fair organisers, their venue details where known along with contact telephone numbers. Please call the organisers direct for information on dates etc.

Aberdeen
Doubletree by Hilton Hotel Aberdeen TreeTops, Springfield Road, Aderdeen, AB15 7AQ.
Alba Fairs Tel: 07767 020343.

Berlin. World Money Fair 2018
Estrel Convention Center, Sonnenalle, 12057 Berlin, Germany. Tel: +41(0)61 3825504

Birmingham
National Motor Cycle Museum, Bickenhill, Birmingham. *Midland Stamp & Coin Fair Tel: 01694 731 781, www.coinfairs.co.uk.*

Britannia Medal Fair
Carisbrooke Hall, The Victory Services Club, 63/79 Seymour Street, London W2 2HF.
Mark Carter Tel: 01753 534 777
City Hall, Cathays Park, Cardiff, CF10 3ND.
M. J. Promotions. Tel: 01792 415293.

Cheltenham
The Regency Hotel, Gloucester Road, GL51 0SS
St Andrews United Reform Church, Montpellier, GL50 1SP
Mark Grimsley Tel: 0117 962 3203.

Dublin
Serpentine Hall, RDS, Ballsbridge, Dublin 4.
Mike Kelly Tel: 00353 86 8714 880.

East Grinstead
Chequer Mead Arts Center, De La Warr Road, East Grinstead, RH19 3BS.
Malcolm Green Tel: 01342 327 554

Exeter
The America Hall, De La Rue Way, Pinhoe, EX4 8PX.
Michael Hale Collectors Fairs Tel: 01749 677669.

Frankfurt 2017
Ludwig-Erhard-Anlage1, 60327 Frankfurt, Hesse,
Numismata International Tel: +49 (0) 89 268 359.

Harrogate
Old Swan Hotel, Swan Road, HG1 2SR.
Simon Monks Tel: 01234 270 260.

Inverness
Kingsmills Hotel, Culcabock Road, Inverness, IV2 3LP.
Alba Fairs Tel: 07767 020343.

London
Holiday Inn, Coram Street, Bloomsbury, WC1 1HT.
London Coin Fair, *Lu Vessid Tel: 01694 731 781*

London
Bloomsbury Hotel, 16-22 Great Russell Street, WC1 3NN.
Bloomsbury Fairs Tel: 01242 898 107.

London IBNS
Venue as above.
IBNS Web: www.theibns.org

Maastricht
Maastricht Exhibiton and Convention Center, Forum 100, 6229 GV Maastricht, The Netherlands.
mif events Tel: +32 (0) 89 46 09 33.

Munich 2018
MOC Veranstaltungscenter, Lilienthalallee 40, 80939 Munich, Bavaria, Germany
Numismata International Tel: +49 (0) 89 268 359.

New York International Numismatic Convention 2018
Grand Hyatt Hotel, 109 East 42nd Street, New York 10022, USA.
www.nyinc.info/

Philadelphia. World's Fair of Money 2018
Pennsylvania Convention Center, 1101 Arch Street Philadelphia, PA 19107 USA.
American Numismatic Association 001 800 514 2646

Plymouth
The Guildhall, Armada Way, PL1 2ER
Peter Jones Tel: 01489 582673.

Wakefield
Cedar Court Hotel, Denby Dale Road, Calder Grove, Wakefield, WF4 3QZ.
Eddie Smith Tel: 01552 684 681.

Weston-super-Mare
Victoria Methodist Church Hall, Station Road, BS23 1XU.
Michael Hale Tel: 01749 677 669

York
The Grandstand, York Race Course, YO23 1EX
York Coin Fair, Tel: 01793 513 431 (Chris Rainey), 020 8946 4489 (Kate Puleston).

Information correct at time of going to press

Important annual events — The B.N.T.A. (Coinex), Tel: 07799 662181 for details
The I.B.N.S. (World Paper Money Fair), Email: enquiries@wpmf.info for details

DEALERS *directory*

The dealers listed below have comprehensive stocks of coins and medals, unless otherwise stated. Specialities, where known, are noted. Many of those listed are postal dealers only, so to avoid disappointment always make contact by telephone or mail in the first instance, particularly before travelling any distance.

Abbreviations:
ADA— — Antiquities Dealers Association
ANA — American Numismatic Association
BADA — British Antique Dealers Association
BNTA — British Numismatic Trade Association
IAPN — International Association of Professional Numismatists
IBNS — International Bank Note Society
P — — Postal only
L — — Publishes regular lists

ABC Coins & Tokens
PO Box 52, Alnwick, Northumberland, NE66 1YE. Tel: 01665 603 851, email: d–stuart@d–stuart. demon.co.uk, www.abccoinsandtokens.com.
A. Ackroyd (IBNS)
62 Albert Road, Parkstone, Poole, Dorset BH12 2DB. Tel/fax: 01202 739 039, www.AAnotes.com.
P L *Banknotes and Cheques*
Joan Allen Electronics Ltd
5 & 6 The Courtyard, Market Square, Westerham, Kent TN16 1AZ. Tel: 01959 571 255. *Metal Detectors.*
Allgold Coins
P.O Box 260, Wallington, SM5 4H. Tel: 0844 544 7952, email: sales@allgoldcoins.co.uk, wwwallgoldcoins.co.uk. *Quality Sovereigns.*
A. J. W. Coins
Tel: 08456 807 087, email: andrewwide@ajw-coins. co.uk, www.ajw-coins.com. **P** *Sovereigns and CGS-UK specialist.*
Dave Allen Collectables
St Neots Antiques Emporium, 13 Fishers Yard, St Neots, PE19 2AG. Tel: 07541 461 021. Email: coinsandmedals@outlook.com, www.daveallencollectables.co.uk. *Coins, Medals, Banknotes, Bullion and Jewellery.*
AMR COINS
PO Box 352, Leeds, LS19 9GG. Tel: 07527 569 308, www.amrcoins.com. *Quality English Coins specialising in rare hammered and milled coins of exceptional quality.*
Ancient & Gothic
PO Box 5390, Bournemouth, BH7 6XR. Tel: 01202 431 721 **P L** *Greek, Roman, Celtic and Biblical coins. English Hammered Coins & Antiquities.*

Argentum Coins
PO Box 130, Peterlee, Co Durham SR8 9BE Tel: 07720 769 005, email: john.stephenson815@sky. com, www.argentumandcoins.co.uk. *British milled coins from 1662 to date.*
Arghans
Unit 9, Callington Business Park, Tinners Way Moss side, Callington, PL17 7SH. Tel: 01579 382 405, email: keithp44@waitrose.com. *British Banknotes.*
ARL Collectables
P O Box 380, Reigate, Surrey, RH2 2BU. Tel: 01737 242 975, www.litherlandcollectables.com. Coins, Banknotes, Medallions and Paper Emphemera.
SP Asimi
The Emporium, 112 High Street, Hungerford, RG17 0 NB. Tel: 01488 686959. *British Milled Coins*
Athens Numismatic Gallery
Akadimias 39, Athens 10672, Greece. Tel: 0030 210 364 8386, www.athensnumismaticgallery.com. *Rare & Common Sovereigns. British & World Coins.*
Atlas Numismatics
Tel: 001 718643 4383, email, info@atlasnumismatics. com, www.atlasnumismatics.com *Ancient, World and US Coinage*
ATS Bullion (BNTA)
2, Savoy Court, Strand. London, WC2R 0EZ. Tel: 020 7240 4040, email: sales@atsbullion.com, www.atsbullion.com. *Bullion and Modern Coins.*
A. H. Baldwin & Sons Ltd (ANA, BADA, BNTA, IAPN)
399 The Strand, London WC2R 0LX. Tel: 020 7930 6879, fax 020 7930 9450, email: coins@baldwin.co.uk *Coins, Tokens, Numismatic Books.*
B & G Coins
PO Box 1219, Spalding, PE11 9FY. Email: info@ bandgcoins.co.uk. *Coins, Banknotes and Medals*
Baird & Co
20 - 21 Gemini Business Park, Hornet Way, London, E6 7FF. Tel: 020 7474 1000, www.goldline.co.uk. *Bullion Merchants*
Bath Stamp and Coin Shop
12 -13 Pulteney Bridge, Bath, Avon BA2 4AY. Tel: 01225 431 918, *Vinyage Coins and Banknotes.*
Michael Beaumont
PO Box 8, Carlton, Notts NG4 4QZ. Tel: 0115 9878361. **P** *Gold & Silver English/Foreign Coins.*

Beaver Coin Room (BNTA)
57 Philbeach Gardens, London SW5 9ED.
Tel: 020 7373 4553. **P** *European coins and medals.*
R. P. & P. J. Beckett
Maes y Derw, Capel Dewi, Llandyssul, Dyfed
SA44 4PJ. Tel: 01559 395 276, email:
beckett@xin.co.uk. **P** *Coin Sets and Banknotes.*
Lloyd Bennett (BNTA)
PO Box 2, Monmouth, Gwent NP25 3YR. Tel:
07714 284 939, email: Lloydbennett@Coinofbritain.
biz, www.coinsofbritain.com *English Hammered and
Milled Coins.*
Berkshire Coin Center
35 Castle Street, Reading, RG1 7SB. Tel: 0118 957
5593. *British and World Coins. Militaria.*
Stephen J. Betts
49-63 Spencer Street, Hockley, Birmingham B18
6DE. Tel: 0121 233 2413 **P L**,
*Medieval and Modern Coins, Counters, Jetons,
Tokens and Countermarks.*
Bigbury Mint
Unit 1 River Park, Ermington, Devon, PL21 9NT. Tel:
01548 830717. *Specialists in reproduction
Hammered Coins*
Jon Blyth
Office 63, 2 Lansdowne Row, Mayfair, London
W1J 6HL. Tel:07919 307 645, jonblyth@hotmail.com,
www.jonblyth.com. *Specialists in quality British Coins*
Bonhams (incorporating Glendinings)
Montpelier Street, Knightsbridge, London,
SW7 1HH. Tel: 0207 393 3914, www.bonhams.com.
Barry Boswell and Kate Bouvier
24 Townsend Lane, Upper Boddington, Daventry,
Northants, NN11 6DR. Tel: 01327 261 877, email:
kate@thebanknotestore.com. *British and World
Banknotes.*
James & Chester Brett
jc.brett@btinternet.com **P L** *British and World
Coins.*
J. Bridgeman Coins
129a Blackburn Road, Accrington, Lancs
Tel: 01254 384757. *British & World Coins.*
Britaly Coins Ltd
Victoria Court, 91 Huddersfield Road, Holmfirth,HD9
3JA. Tel: 07479 862 432, email: info@britalycoins.
co.uk, www.britalycoins.co.uk. *British and World
Coins.*
Arthur Bryant Coins
PO Box 67499, London, NW3 3SN, Tel: 07768 645
686, email: abcoins@live.co.uk,
www.bryantcoins.com. *British Coins and Medals.*
BRM Coins
3 Minshull Street, Knutsford,Cheshire, WA16 6HG.
Tel: 01565 651 480. *British Coins.*
Bucks Coins
St Mary's House, Duke Street, Norwich NR3 1QA
Callers by appointment only. Tel: 01603 927 020.
English Milled Coins, Celtic and Roman.
Iain Burn
2 Compton Gardens, 53 Park Road, Camberley,
Surrey GU15 2SP. Tel: 01276 23304.
Bank of England & Treasury Notes.
Cambridgeshire Coins
12 Signet Court, Swanns Road Cambridge,
CB5 8LA. Tel: 01223 503 073, email: info
cambridgeshirecoins.com,
wwwcambridgeshirecoins.com. *Coins, Banknotes
and Accessories.*
Cambridge Stamp Center Ltd
9 Sussex Street, Cambridge, CB4 4HU. Tel: 01223
63980. *British Coins*

Castle Galleries
81 Castle Street, Salisbury, Wiltshire SP1 3SP.
Tel: 01722 333 734. *British Coins, Medals and Tokens.*
Cathedral Coins
23 Kirkgate, Rippon, North Yorkshire, HG4 1PB.
Tel: 01765 701 400
Cathedral Court Medals
First Floor Office, 30A Market Place, West Ripon,
North Yorks HG4 1BN. Tel: 01765 601 400. *Coin and
Medal Sales. Medal Mounting and Framing.*
Central Bank of Ireland
PO Box 559, Dublin 1. Tel: +353 (0) 1248 3605,
Ireland. *Issuer of new Coin and Banknote issues of
Ireland. Commemorative Coins and Coin Sets*
Lance Chaplin
17 Wanstead Lane, Ilford, Essex IG1 3SB.
Tel: 020 8554 7154. www.shaftesburycoins.com.
P L*Roman, Greek, Celtic, Hammered Coins and
Antiquities.*
Chard (BNTA)
32-36 Harrowside, Blackpool, FY4 1RJ. Tel: 01253
343081, www.chards.co.uk, *British and World Coins.*
Jeremy Cheek Coins Ltd
Tel: 01923 450385/07773 872686, email:
jeremycoins@aol.com. *Advice, valuation and
representation at auctions.*
Simon Chester Coins
196, High Road, London, Farnham, N22 8HH
Tel: 07774 886688, email:
simosimonchestercoins.com
British Milled Coins
Nigel A. Clark
28 Ulundi Road, Blackheath, London SE3 7UG.
Tel: 020 8858 4020, email: nigel.a.clark@btinternet.
com. **P L** *17th & 19th century Tokens. Farthings.*
Classical Numismatic Group (IAPN)
20 Bloomsbury Street, London, WC1B 3QA.
Tel: 020 7495 1888, email cng@cngcoins.com,
www.cngcoins.com. **P** *Ancient and world coins.
Publishers of the Classical Numismatic Review.
Regular High Quality Auctions of Ancient Coins.*
Paul Clayton (BNTA)
PO Box 21, Wetherby, West Yorkshire LS22 5JY.
Tel: 01937 582 693. *Modern Gold Coins.*
André de Clermont (BNTA)
10 Charles II Street, London, SW1Y 4AA. Tel: 020
7584 7200. *World Coins, especially Islamic.*
M. Coeshaw
PO Box 115, Leicester LE3 8JJ. Tel: 0116 287 3808.
P *Coins, Banknotes, Coin Albums and Cases.*
Philip Cohen Numismatics (ANA, BNTA)
20 Cecil Court, Charing Cross Road, London,
WC2N 4HE. Tel: 020 7379 0615, www.coinheritage.
co.uk
Coin & Collectors Centre
PO Box 22, Pontefract, West Yorkshire WF8
1YT. Tel: 01977 704 112, email sales@coincentre.
co.uk, www.coincentre.co.uk. **P***British Coins.*
Coinage of England
11, 1 Sloane Court East, Chelsea, SW3 4TQ. Tel:
020 3686 3593, *Fine and Rare English Coins.*
Coincraft (ANA, IBNS)
45 Great Russell Street, London, WC1B 3JL.
Tel: 020 7636 1188 or 020 7637 8785, fax 020
7323 2860, email: info@coincraft.com. **L**
(newspaper format). *Coins and Banknotes.*
Coinote
74 Elwick Road, Hartlepool TS26 9AP. Tel: 01429 890
894. www.coinnote.co.uk. *Coins, Medals, Banknotes
and Accessories.*

Coinswap.co.uk
Swap, Sell or Trade Coins.

Coins of Canterbury
PO Box 47, Faversham, Kent,, ME13 7HX. Tel: 01795 531 980. ℗ *English Coins.*

Collectors' World (Mark Ray)
188 Wollaton Road, Wollaton, Nottingham NG8 1HJ. Tel: 01159 280 347. *Coins, Banknotes, Accessories.*

Constania CB
15 Church Road, Northwood, Middlesex, HA6 1AR. ℗ *Roman and Medieval Hammered Coins.*

Colin Cooke
P.O. Box 602, Altrincham, WA14 5UN. Tel: 0161 927 9524, fax 0161 927 9540, email coins@colin cooke.com, www.colincooke.com. Ⓛ*British Coins.*

Colonial Coins & Medals
218 Adelaide Street, Brisbane, QLD 4001. Email:coinshop@bigpond.net.au. *Auctions of World Coins.*

Copperbark Ltd
Suite 35, 37, St Andrew's Street, Norwich, NR2 4TP. Tel: 07834 434 780, email: copperbark.ltd@gmail. com, www.copperbark.com. *English, Russian and 17th Century Tokens.*

Corbitts (BNTA)
5 Mosley Street, Newcastle Upon Tyne NE1 1YE. Tel: 0191 232 7268, fax: 0191 261 4130. *Dealers and Auctioneers of all Coins and Medals.*

David Craddock
PO Box 3785, Camp Hill, Birmingham, B11 2NF. Tel: 0121 733 2259 Ⓛ*Crown to Farthings. Copper and Bronze Specialist. Some foreign.*

Roy Cudworth
8 Park Avenue, Clayton West, Huddersfield HD8 9PT. *British and World Coins.*

Paul Dawson
47 The Shambles, York, YO1 7XL. Tel: 01904 654 769, email: pauldawsonyork@hotmail.com, www. pauldawsonyork.co.uk. *Ancient and British coins.*

Mark Davidson
PO Box 197, South Croydon, Surrey, CR3 0ZD. Tel: 020 8651 3890. *Ancient, Hammered & milled Coinage.*

Paul Davis
PO Box 418, Birmingham, B17 0RZ. Tel: 0121 427 7179. *British and World Coins.*

R. Davis
Tel: 01332 862 755 days / 740828 evenings, email: robdaviscc@gmail.com. *Maker of Traditional Coin Cabinets.*

Paul Davies Ltd (ANA, BNTA, IAPN)
PO Box 17, Ilkley, West Yorkshire LS29 8TZ. Tel: 01943 603 116, fax 01943 816 326, paul@ pauldaviesltd.co.uk. ℗ *World Coins.*

Ian Davison
PO Box 256, Durham DH1 2GW. Tel 0191 3750 808. Ⓛ *English Hammered and Milled Coins 1066–1910.*

Dei Gratia
PO Box 3568, Buckingham MK18 4ZS Tel: 01280 848 000.℗Ⓛ *Pre–Roman to Modern Coins. Antiquities, Banknotes.*

Den of Antiquity
PO Box 1114, Cambridge, CB25 9WJ. Tel: 01223 863 002, www.denofantiquity.co.uk.) *Ancient and Medieval Coins.*

Clive Dennett (BNTA)
66 St Benedicts Street, Norwich, Norfolk, NR2 4AR. Tel: 01603 624 315, Ⓛ *Specialising in paper money.*

C. J. Denton (ANA, BNTA, FRNS)
PO Box 25, Orpington, Kent BR6 8PU. Tel: 01689 873 690.℗ *Irish Coins.*

Detecnicks
3 Orchard Crescent, Arundel Road, Fontwell. West Sussex BN18 0SA. Tel: 01243 545 060. *Retail shop. Wide range of Detectors.*

Michael Dickinson (ANA, BNTA)
Ramsay House, 825 High Road Finchley, London N12 8UB. Tel: 0181 441 7175.℗ *British and World Coins.*

Douglassaville.com
Tel: 0118 918 7628, www.douglassaville.com. *Out of Print, Second-Hand and Rare Coin and Medal Books.*

Drake Sterling Numismatics Pty Ltd
GPO Box 2913, Sydney 2001, Australia. UK callers Tel: 020 7097 1781, www.drakesterling.co.uk. *British and British Colonial Gold Coins*

Eagle Coins
Winterhaven, Mourneabbey, Mallow, Co. Cork, Ireland. Tel: 010 35322 29385.℗Ⓛ *Irish Coins.*

East of England Coins
Leprosy Mission Orton Goldhay, Peterborough, Cambridgeshire, PE2 5GZ. Tel: 01733235277 *Coins, Tokens and Banknotes*

Educational Coin Company
Box 892, Highland, New York 12528, USA. Tel:001 845 691 6100. *World Banknotes.*

Christopher Eimer (ANA, BNTA, IAPN)
PO Box 352 London NW11 7RF. Tel: 020 8458 9933, email: art@christophereimer.co.uk ℗ *Commemorative Medals.*

Malcolm Ellis Coins
Petworth Road, Witley, Surrey, GU8 5LX. Tel: 01428 685 566, www.malcolmelliscoins.co.uk). *Collectors and Dealers of British and Foreign Coins*

Elm Hill Collectables
41-43 Elm Hill, Norwich, Norfolk NR3 1HG. Tel: 01603 627 413. *Coins & Banknotes .*

Europa Numismatics (ANA, BNTA)
PO Box 119, High Wycombe, Bucks HP11 1QL. Tel: 01494 437 307 ℗ *European Coins.*

Evesham Stamp & Coin Centre
Magpie Antiques, Manchester House,1 High Street, Evesham, Worcs WR11 4DA. Tel: 01386 41631. *British Coins.*

Michael E. Ewins
Meyrick Heights, 20 Meyrick Park Crescent, Bournemouth, Dorset BH3 7AQ. Tel: 01202 290 674. ℗ *World Coins.*

Robin Finnegan Stamp Shop
83 Skinnergate, Darlington, Co Durham DL3 7LX. Tel: 01325 489 820/357 674. *World coins.*

David Fletcher (Mint Coins) (ANA,)
PO Box 64, Coventry, Warwickshire CV1 5YR. Tel; 02476 696 300. ℗ *World New Issues.*

Format of Birmingham Ltd (ANA, BNTA, IAPN, IBNS)
PO Box 1276, Cheltenham, Gloucestershire, GL50 9ZW. Tel: 01242 518 495. Ⓛ *Coins, Tokens and Medals.*

B. Frank & Son
3 South Avenue, Ryton, Tyne & Wear NE40 3LD. Tel: 0191 413 8749, Email: bfrankandson@aol. com, www.bfrankandson.com. *Coins, Banknotes and Cheques*

Galata Coins Ltd (ANA)
The Old White Lion, Market Street, Llanfylin, Powys SY22 5BX. Tel: 01691 648 765.℗*British and World Coins.*

G. Gant
Glazenwood, 37 Augustus Way, Witham, Essex CM8 1HH. ℗*British and Commonwealth Coins.*

A. & S. Gillis
59 Roy Kilner Way, Wombwell, Barnsley, South Yorkshire S73 3DY. Tel: 01226 750 371, www.gilliscoins.com. *Ancient Coins and Antiquities.*

Richard Gladdle – Northamptonshire
Suite 80, 29/30 Horse Fair, Banbury, Oxfordshire, OX16 0BW. Tel: 01327 858 511, email: gladdle@ plumpudding.org. *Tokens.* **P** **L**

Glance Back Books
17 Upper Street, Chepstow, Gwent, NP6 5EX. Tel: 001291 626562. *Coins and Banknotes*

GM Coins
Tel: 01242 627 344, email: info@gmcoinsco. uk, www.gmcoins.co.uk. *Hammered and Milled Coins.*

Adrian Gorka Bond
Tel: 07500 772 080, email: sales@ 1stsovereign. co.uk, www.1stsovereign.co.uk. *Coins bought and sold.*

Goulborn
4 Sussex Street, Rhyl LL18 1SG. Tel: 01745 338 112. *English Coins and Medallions.*

Ian Gradon
PO Box 359, Durham DH7 6WZ. Tel 0191 3719 700, email: rarebanknote@gmail.com, www.worldnotes. co.uk. **L** *World Banknotes.*

Eric Green—Agent in UK for Ronald J. Gillio Inc
1013 State Street, Santa Barbara, California, USA 93101. Tel: 020 8907 0015, Mobile 0468 454948. *Gold Coins, Medals and Paper Money of the World.*

Philip Green
Suite 207, 792 Wilmslow Road, Didsbury, Manchester M20 6UG. Tel: 0161 440 0685. *Gold Coins.*

Gurnhills of Leicester
8 Nothampton Street, Leicester, LE1 1PA.Tel: 07434 010 925. *British and World Coins and Banknotes.*

Hallmark Coins Ltd
PO Box 69991, I Canada Square, Canary Warf, London. Tel: 0800 612 7327 email: Info@ hallmarkcoins.co.uk, www.hallmarkcoins.co.uk. *British Coins.*

Anthony Halse
PO Box 1056, Newport, Gwent NP18 2WA. Tel: 01633 413 238.**P** **L***English and Foreign Coins and Tokens.*

A. D. Hamilton & Co (ANA)
7 St Vincent Place, Glasgow, G1 2DW. Tel: 0141 221 5423, email: jefffineman@hotmail.com, www. adhamilton.co.uk.*British and World Coins.*

Hammered British Coins
PO Box 2330, Salisbury, SP2 2LN. Tel: 07825 226 435, www.hammeredbritishcoins.com. *British Coins.*

Peter Hancock
40–41 West Street, Chichester, West Sussex, PO19 1RP. Tel: 01243 786 173. *World Coins, Medals and Banknotes.*

Hanocks
52–53 Burlington Arcade, London W1V 9AE. Tel: 020 7493 8904. *World Gold Coins.*

Munthandel G. Henzen
PO Box 42, NL – 3958ZT, Amerognen, Netherlands. Tel: 0031 343 430564 fax 0031 343 430542, email: info@henzen.org, www.henzen.org. **L***Ancients, Dutch and Foreign Coins.*

History In Coins
Tel: 07944 374600, email:andrewhowitt@hotmail.com, www.historyincoins.com. *World Coins.*

Craig Holmes
6 Marlborough Drive, Bangor, Co Down BT19 1HB. **P** **L***Low cost Banknotes of the World.*

R. G. Holmes
11 Cross Park, Ilfracombe, Devon EX34 8BJ. Tel: 01271 864 474. **P** **L**
Coins, World Crowns and Banknotes.

HTSM Coins
26 Dosk Avenue, Glasgow G13 4LQ. Tel: 0141 562 9530, email: htsm@ntlworld.com**P** **L**
British and foreign coins and Banknotes.

M. J. Hughes Coins
27 Market Street, Alton, Hampshire, GU34 1HA. Tel: 01420 768 161, email: info@mjhughes.co.uk *World Coins and Bullion.*

T. A. Hull
15 Tangmere Crescent, Hornchurch, Essex RM12 5PL.**P** **L** *British Coins, Farthings, Tokens.*

J. Hume
107 Halsbury Road East, Northolt, Middlesex UB5 4PY. Tel: 020 8864 1731.**P** **L** *Chinese Coins.*

D. A. Hunter
Email: coins@dahunter.co.uk, www.dahunter.co.uk/ coins. **P** **L** *Uk and World Coins*

D. D. & A. Ingle
380 Carlton Hill, Nottingham, NG4 1JA. Tel: 0115 987 3325. *World Coins.*

R. Ingram Coins
206 Honeysuckle Road, Bassett, Southampton, SO16 3BU. Tel: 023 8032 4258, email: info@ ringramcoins.com, www.ringramcoins.com.**P** **L**
Dealers in UK Coins.

F. J. Jeffery & Son Ltd
Haines Croft, Corsham Road, Whitley, Melksham, Wilts, SN12 8QF. Tel: 01225 703 143.**P** **L**, *British, Commonwealth and Foreign Coins.*

Richard W. Jeffery
Tel: 01736 871 263. **P** *British and World Coins, Banknotes.*

JN Coins
PO Box 1030, Ipswich, OP1 9XL. Tel: 07916 145 038, info@jncoins.co.uk(www.jncoins.co.uk). *British Coins from Celtic to Modern.*

Kates Paper Money (IBNS)
Kate Gibson, PO Box 819, Camberley, Surrey, GU16 6ZU. Email: kate@katespapermoney.co.uk, www.katespapermoney.com. *Banknotes.*

KB Coins (BNTA)
PO BOX 499, Stevenage, Herts, SG1 9JT. Tel: 01438 312 661, fax 01438 311 990. www.kbcoins. com **L** *Mainly British Coins.*

Kleeford Coins
Tel: 07484 272 837, kleeford@btinternet.com www.kleefordcoins.webs.com, . **P** *Monthly Auctions of Coins, Banknotes, Tokens & Medals.*

K&M Coins
PO Box 3662, Wolverhampton WV10 6ZW. Tel: 0771 238 1880, email: M_Bagguley@hotmail. com. *English Milled Coins.*

Knightsbridge Coins (ANA, BNTA, IAPN, PNG)
43 Duke Street, St James's, London, SW1Y 6DD. Tel: 020 7930 8215/7597, info@knightsbridgecoins. com. *Quality Coins of the World.*

Lancashire Coin and Medal Co
31 Adelaide Street, Fleetwood, Lancs, FY7 6AD. Tel: 01253 779308. **P** *British Coins and Medals.*

Liberty Coins and Bullion
17g Vyse Street, Birmingham, B18 6LE. Tel: 0121 554 4432, www.libertycoinsbullion.co.uk. *Coins and Precious Metals*

Lighthouse Publications (Duncannon Partnership)
4 Beaufort Road, Reigate, Surrey RH2 9DJ Tel: 01737 244 222 www.duncannon.co.uk. **L** *Coin Albums, Cabinets and Numismatic Accessories.*

Lindner Publications Ltd
3a Hayle Industrial Park, Hayle, Cornwall TR27 5JR.
Tel: 01736 751 910, email: prinzpublications@gmail.
com. ⓛ *Manufacturers of Coin Albums, Cabinets and Accessories.*

Jan Lis (BNTA)
Beaver Coin Room, 57 Philbeach Gardens, London
SW5 9ED. Tel: 020 7373 4553 fax 020 7373 4555.
By appointment only. *European Coins.*

Keith Lloyd
1 Dashwood Close, Pinewood, Ipswich, Suffolk
IP8 3SR. Tel: 01473 403 506.ⓟ ⓛ *Ancient Coins.*

Lockdale Coins (BNTA)
52 Barrack Square, Martlesham Heath, Ipswich,
Suffolk, IP5 3RF. Tel: 01473 627 110, www.lockdales.
com.ⓛ *World Coins, Medals and Banknotes*

Stephen Lockett (BNTA)
4–6 Upper Street, New Ash Green, Kent, DA3 8JJ.
Tel: 01474 871464. *British and World Coins.*

The London Coin Company
PO Box 495, Stanmore, Greater London, HA7 9HS
Tel: 0800 085 2933, 020 8343 2231,
www.thelondoncoincomany.com).
Modern Gold and Silver Coins.

Mike Longfield Detectors
83 Station Road, Balsall Common, nr Coventry,
Warwickshire CV7 7FN. Tel: 01676 533 274.
. *Metal Detectors.*

MA Shops
www.mashops.com. On-line coin mall. *Coins, Medals, Banknotes and Accessories.*

Mannin Collections Ltd
5 Castle Street, Peel, Isle of Man, IM5 1AN. Tel:
01624 843 897, email: manncoll@advsys.co.uk, *IOM Coins, Tokens, etc.*

Manston Coins of Bath
8 Bartletts St. Antique Centre, Bath. Tel: 01225
487 888. *Coins, Tokens and Medals.*

I. Markovits
1–3 Cobbold Mews, London W12 9LB.
Tel: 020 8749 3000. *Enamelled Coins.*

C. J. Martin Coins (BNTA)
The Gallery, Trent Park Equestrian Centre, Bramley
Road, London, N14 4UW. Tel: 020 8364 4565,
www.ancientart.co.uk.ⓟ ⓛBi– monthly catalogue.
Greek, Roman & English Hammered Coins.

Maverick Numismatics
07403 111843, www.mavericknumismatics.com).
Coin and Currency Design.

M. G. Coins & Antiquities
12 Mansfield, High Wych, Herts CM21 0JT. Tel 01279
721 719. ⓛ*Ancient and Hammered Coins, Antiquities.*

M&H Coins
PO Box 10985, Brentwood, CM14 9JB. Tel: 07504
804 019, www.mhcoins.co.uk. ⓛ *British Hammered and Milled Coins.*

Michael Coins
PO Box 3100 Reading RG1 9ZL. *World Coins and Banknotes.*

David Miller Coins & Antiquities (ANA, BNTA)
PO Box 711, Hemel Hempstead, HP2 4UH. Tel/fax
01442 251 492. *Ancient Hammered English Coins.*

Timothy Millett
PO Box 20851, London SE22 0YN. Tel: 0208 693
1111, www.historicmedals.com. ⓛ *Historical Medals.*

Nigelmills.net
PO Box 53126, London, E18 1YR. Email: nigelmills@
onetel.com,
www.nigelmills.net *Coins and Antiquities.*

Graeme & Linda Monk (ANA, BNTA)
PO Box 201, Croydon, Surrey, CR9 7AQ.
Tel: 020 8656 4583 fax 020 8656 4583. ⓟ .

Monetary Research Institute
PO Box 3174, Houston, TX 77253-3174, Tel: 001
713 827 1796, email: info@mriguide.com. *Bankers Guide to Foreign Currency*

Moore Antiquities
Unit 12, Ford Lane Industrial Estate, Ford, nr.
Arundel, West Sussex BN18 0AA. Tel: 01243 824
232, email moore.antiquities@virgin.net.
Coins and Artefacts up to the 18th Century.

Mike Morey
19 Elmtrees, Long Crendon, Bucks HP18 9DG.ⓟ ⓛ
British Coins, Halfcrowns to Farthings.

Peter Morris (BNTA, IBNS)
1 Station Concourse, Bromley North Station,
Bromley, BR1 1NN or PO Box 223, Bromley,
BR1 4EQ. Tel: 020 8313 3410, email: info@
petermorris.co.uk, www.petermorris.co.uk
co.uk). ⓛ *British and World Coins, Proof Sets and Numismatic Books.*

N3 Coins—London
Email: mail@n3coins.com,
www.n3coins.com. *Roman and Ancient Coins.*

Colin Narbeth & Son Ltd (ANA, IBNS)
20 Cecil Court, Leicester Square, London,WC2N.
4HE .Tel: 020 7379 6975, www.colin–narbeth.com
World Banknotes.

Newcastle Coin Dealers
7 Nile Street, North Shields, NE29 0BD. Tel: 07939
999 286, email: newcastlecoin@outlook.com, www.
newcastlecoindealers.co.uk. *Modern British and World Coins/Banknotes*

John Newman Coins
P O Box 4890, Worthing, BN119WS. Tel**:** 01903
239 867, email: john@newmancoins.co.uk,
www.johnnewmancoins.co.uk**.** *English hammered coins, British Milled Coins and British Tokens.*

Peter Nichols Cabinet Makers
The Workshop, 383a High Road,
Chilwell,Nottingham, NG9 5EA. Tel: 0115 922 4149,
email: orders@coincabinets.com,
www.coincabinets.com. *Manufacturers of Bespoke Mahogany Coin and Medal Cabinets.*

Wayne Nicholls
PO Box 44, Bilston, West Midlands. Tel: 01543
45476. ⓛ *Choice English Coins.*

North Wales Coins Ltd (BNTA)
1b Penrhyn Road, Colwyn Bay, Clwyd. Tel: 01492
533 023. *British Coins.*

NP Collectables
9 Main Street, Gedney Dyke, Spalding, Lincs PE12
0AJ. Tel: 01406 365 211ⓟ ⓛ. *English Hammered and Milled Coins.*

Notability Notes (IBNS)
PO Box 3530, Swindon, SN2 9FZ. Tel: 07545
572 721, email: info@notability-banknotes.com,
www.notability-banknotes.com). *British/World Notes.*

Oddysey Antiquities
PO Box 61, Southport PR9 0PZ.Tel: 01704 232 494.
Classical Antiquities, Ancient and Hammered Coins.

Glenn S. Ogden
Tel: 01626 859 350 or 07971 709 427, email:
glennogdencoins@hotmail.com,
www. glennogdencoins.com, ⓟ ⓛ *English Milled Coinage.*

John Ogden Coins
Hodge Clough Cottage, Moorside, Oldham OL1
4JW. Tel: 0161 678 0709ⓟ ⓛ*Ancient and Hammered.*

Don Oliver Gold Coins
Stanford House, 23 Market Street, Stourbridge,
West Midlands DY8 1AB. Tel: 01384 877 901.
British Gold Coins.
Roger Outing
36 Church Lane, Huddersfield, HD8 9LY. Tel: 01484
860 415, email: rogerandlizbanknotes4u.co.uk,
www.chequemate4collectors.co.uk). *World
Banknotes.*
P&D Medallions
PO Box 269, Berkhampstead, Herts HP4 3FT.
Tel: 01442 865 127, www.pdmedallions.co.uk.
(P) *Historical and Commemorative Medals.*
Del Parker
PO Box 12670, Dallas, TX 75209, USA.
Tel: + 1 214 352 1475, Email: info@delparker.com
www.irishcoins.com. *Irish, American Coins. Irish Art
Medals and Banknotes.* (L)
Pavlos S. Pavlou
58 Davies Streer, Mayfair, London W1K 5JF. Tel: 020
7629 9449, email: pspavlou@hotmail.com. *Ancient to
Modern*
PCGS
Tel:+33 (0) 949 833 0600, email:info@pcgs.com,
www.pcgs.com. *Coin Grading and Authentication
Service.*
www.pennycrowncoins.co.uk
PO Box 831, Amersham, HP6 9GF. Tel: 01494
776141. *Specialising in British Milled Coins 1662–
1970.*
Penrith Coin & Stamp Centre
37 King Street, Penrith, Cumbria CA11 7AY. Tel:
01768 864 185.*World Coins.*
Pentland Coins (IBNS)
Pentland House, 92 High Street, Wick, Caithness
KW14 L5. (P) *British and World Coins and Banknotes.*
B. C. Pickard
1 Treeside, Christchurch, Dorset BH23 4PF. Tel:
01425 275763, email: bcpickard@fsmail.net). (P)
Stone Age, Greek, Roman Items (inc. coins) for sale.
Pobjoy Mint Ltd (ANA)
Millennium House, Kingswood Park, Bonsor
Drive, Kingswood, Surrey KT20 6AY. Tel: 01737
818 182 fax 01737 818199. Europe's largest private
mint. *New issues.*
David Pratchett
UCCE, PO Box 57648, Mill Hill, London NW7
0FE. Tel: 07831 662594, fax 020 7930 1152, email:
uccedcp@aol.com, www.coinsonline.co.uk). Mon–
Fri 10.00–7.30. *Gold and Silver World Coins.*
George Rankin Coin Co Ltd (ANA)
325 Bethnal Green Road, London E2 6AH. Tel: 020
7739 1940. *World Coins.*
Mark Rasmussen (BNTA, IAPN)
PO Box 42, Betchworth, Surrey, RH3 7YR. Tel: 01306
884 880, email: mark.rasmussen@rascoins.com,
www.rascoins.com. (L) *Quality Hammered, Milled
Coins.*
Mark T. Ray (see Collectors World)
Rhyl Coin Shop
12 Sussex Street, Rhyl, Clwyd. Tel: 01745 338 112.
World Coins and Banknotes.
Chris Rigby
PO Box 181, Worcester WR1 1YE. Tel: 01905 28028.
(P) (L)*Modern British Coins.*
Roderick Richardson (BNTA)
The Old Granary Antiques Centre, King's Staithe
Lane, King's Lynn, PE30 1LZ. Tel: 01553 670
833, www.roderickrichardson.com. (L) *English,
Hammered and Early Milled Coins. High quality lists
issued.*

Charles Riley (BNTA)
PO Box 733, Aylesbury HP22 9AX. Tel: 01296
747 598, charlesrileycoins@gmail.com.
www.charlesriley.co.uk. *Coins and Medallions.*
Robin–on–Acle Coins
193 Main Road Essex CO12 3PH. Tel: 01255
554 440, email: enquiries@robin–on–acle–coins.
co.uk. *Ancient to Modern Coins and Paper Money.*
Roma Numismatics
20 Fitzroy Square, London, W1T 6EJ
Tel: 020 7121 6518, www.romanumismatics.com.
Dealers and Auctioneers of Fine Ancient Coins.
Royal Australian Mint
(www.ramint.gov.au). *New Coin Issues.*
Royal Gold
PO Box 123, Saxonwold, 2132, South Africa,
Tel: +27 11 483 0161, email: royalg@iafrica.com,
www.royalgold.co.za. *Gold Coins.*
Colin de Rouffignac (BNTA)
57, Wigan Lane, Wigan, Lancs WN1 2LF. Tel: 01942
237 927. *P. English and Scottish Hammered.*
R. P. Coins
PO Box 367, Prestwich, Manchester, M25 9ZH.
Tel: 07802 713 444, www.rpcoins.co.uk.
Coins, Books, Catalogues and Accessories.
Chris A. Rudd (IAPN, BNTA)
PO Box 222, Aylsham, Norfolk, NR11 6TY.
Tel: 01263 735 007 fax 01263 731 777,
www.celticcoins.com.(P)(L) *Celtic Coins.*
Colin Rumney (BNTA)
PO Box 34, Denbighshire, North Wales, LL16 4YQ.
Tel: 01745 890 621. *All world including ancients.*
R & J Coins
21b Alexandra Street, Southend-on-Sea, Essex, SS1
1DA. Tel: 01702 345 995. *World Coins.*
Safe Albums (UK) Ltd
16 Falcon Business Park, 38 Ivanhoe Road,
Finchampstead, Berkshire RG40 4QQ. Tel: 0118 932
8976 fax 0118 032 0612. *Accessories.*
Saltford Coins
Harcourt, Bath Road, Saltford, Bristol, Avon
BS31 3DQ. Tel: 01225 873 512, email: info@
saltfordcoins.com, www.saltfordcoins.com
(P) *British, Commonwealth, World Coins and
medallions.*
Satin Coins
PO Box 63, Stockport, Cheshire SK4 5BU.
Tel: 07940 393 583 answer machine.
Scotmint Ltd
68 Sandgate, Ayr, Scotland KA7 1BX
Tel: 01292 268 244, email: rob@scotmint.com,
www.scotmint.com. *Coins, Medals and Banknotes.
Retail shop.*
David Seaman
PO Box 449, Waltham Cross, EN9 3WZ. Tel: 01992
719 723, email: davidseamancoins@outlook.com.
(P)(L) *Hammered, Milled, Maundy.*
Patrick Semmens
3 Hospital Road, Half Key, Malvern, Worcs WR14
1UZ. Tel: 0886 33123. (P) *European and British coins.*
Mark Senior
553 Falmer Road, Woodingdean, Brighton, Sussex
Tel: 01273 309 359. By appointment only.
(P)(L)*Saxon, Norman and English hammered.*
S. E. Sewell
Cronin, Westhorpe Road, Finningham, Stowmarket,
Suffolk, IP14 4TN. Tel: 01449 782 185 or 07739
071 822,
email: sewellmedals@hotmail.com,
www.sewellmedals.co.uk). *Mainly British Milled.*

Sharps Pixley
54, St James's Street, London SW1A 1JT Tel: 020 7871 0532, www.sharpspixley.com. *Safe deposit boxes in St James's, buying and selling Gold Bullion.*

Silbury Coins
PO Box 281, Cirencester, Gloucs GL7 9ET. Tel: 01242 898 107, email: info@silburycoins.com, www.silburycoins.com. *Iron Age, Roman, Saxon, Viking, Medieval Coins and later.*

Simmons Gallery (ANA, BNTA, IBNS)
PO Box 104, Leytonstone, London E11 1ND Tel:020 898 98097, www.simmonsgallery.co.uk. **L** *Coins, Tokens and Medals.*

E. Smith (ANA, IBNS)
PO Box 348, Lincoln LN6 0TX Tel: 01522 684 681 fax 01522 689 528. Organiser of the Wakefield (formally known as Leeds) monthly coin fair. **P** *World Coins and Paper Money.*

Neil Smith
PO Box 774, Lincoln LN4 2WX. Tel: 01522 522 772 fax 01522 689 528. *GB and World Gold Coins 1816 to date, including Modern Proof Issues.*

Jim Smythe
PO Box 6970, Birmingham B23 7WD. Email: Jimdens@aol.com.**P L***19th/20th Century British and World Coins.*

Sovereign Rarities Ltd (BNTA)
32, St George Street, London W1S 2EA Tel: 0203 019 1185, www.sovereignrrrities.com. *Quality British and World Coins.*

Spink & Son Ltd (ANA, BNTA, IAPN, IBNS)
69 Southampton Row, Bloomsbury, London. WC1B 4ET. Tel: 020 7563 4000, fax 020 7563 4066, email: info@spinkandson.com, www.spink.com. *Ancient to Modern World Coins. Medals, Banknotes.*

Stamford Coins
65–67 Stamford Street, Bradford, West Yorkshire, BD4 8SD. Tel: 07791 873 595, email: stamfordcoins@hotmail.co.uk.

Stamp & Collectors Centre
404 York Town Road, College Town, Camberley, Surrey GU15 4PR. Tel:01276 32587 fax 01276 32505. *World Coins and Medals.*

St Edmunds Coins & Banknotes
PO Box 118, Bury St Edmunds IP33 2NE. Tel: 01284 761 894.

Sterling Coins & Medals
2 Somerset Road, Boscombe, Bournemouth, Dorset BH7 6JH. Tel: 01202 423 881. *World Coins and Medals.*

Studio Coins (ANA, BNTA)
Studio 111, 80 High Street, Winchester, Hants SO23 9AT. Tel: 01962 853 156 email: stephenmitchell13@bttconnect.com. **P** *English Coins.*

The Coin House
Tel: 01935 824 878, email: thecoinhouse@btinternet.com. *Quality Investment Coins and Silver Bars.*

The East India Company
Tel: 0203 205 3394, email, service@theeastindiacompany.com. *Gold and Silver Coins*

The Royal Mint
Llantrisant, Pontyclun, CF72 8YT. Tel: 01443 222111. *Coins*

Time Line Originals
PO Box 193, Upminster, RM14 3WH. Tel: 01708 222 384/07775 651 218, email: sales@time–lines.co.uk.

Stuart J. Timmins
Smallwood Lodge Bookshop, Newport, Salop. Tel: 01952 813 232. *Numismatic Literature.*

R. Tims
39 Villiers Road, Watford, Herts WD1 4AL.**P L** *Uncirculated World Banknotes.*

Token Publishing Ltd
40, Southernhay East, Exeter, Devon EX1 1PE, Tel: 01404 46972, email info@tokenpublishing.com, www.tokenpublishing.com
Publishers of COIN NEWS, COIN YEARBOOK, MEDAL YEARBOOK, BANKOTE YEARBOOK and suppliers of Numismatic Titles, Krause catalogues and Coin Accessories..

Michael Trenerry
PO Box 55, Truro, TR1 2YQ. Tel: 01872 277 977, email: veryfinecoins@aol.com. By appointment only. **L** *Roman, Celtic and English Hammered Coins and Tokens.*

Vera Trinder Ltd
Unit 3a, Hayle Ind Park, Hayle, Cornwall TR27 5JR. Tel:01736 751 910, email: richardvtrinder@aol.com www.veratrinder.co.uk. **L** *Coin Accessories.*

Robert Tye
7–9 Clifford Street, York, YO1 9RA. Tel: 0845 4 900 724, email: orders@earlyworlscoins.com. **P***European and Oriental Hammered Coins.*

Universal Currency Coin Exhange
PO Box 57648, Mill Hill, London, NW7 0FE. Tel: 07831 662 594, email: uccedcp@aol.com. *German, Canadian and American Coins. Accumulations.*

Vale
Tel: 01322 405 911, email: valecoins@ntlworld.com *British Coins and Medals.*

Van der Schueren, John-Luc (IAPN)
14 Rue de la Borse, 1,000 Bussels, Belgium. Email: iapnsecret@compuserve.com, www.coins.be. . *Coins and Tokens of the World and of the Low Countries.*

Tony Vaughan Collectables
PO Box 364, Wolverhampton, WV3 9PW. Tel: 01902 27351. **P L** *World Coins and Medals.*

Victory Coins (BNTA)
PO Box 948, Southsea, Hampshire, PO1 9LZ. Tel: 023 92 751908. *British and World Coins.*

Mark J. Vincenzi (BNTA)
Rylands, Earls Colne, Essex CO6 2LE. Tel: 01787 222 555. **P** *Greek, Roman, Hammered.*

Mike Vosper
PO Box 32, Hockwold, Brandon IP26 4HX. Tel: 01842 828 292, email: mikevosper@vosper4coins.co.uk, www.vosper4coins.co.uk). *Roman, Hammered.*

Weighton Coin Wonders
50 Market Place, Market Weighton, York, Y043 3AL, Tel: 01430 879 740, www.weightoncoin.co.uk. *Modern Gold, Silver Proofs and Sets.*

John Welsh
PO Box 150, Burton–on–Trent, Staffs DE13 7LB. Tel: 01543 473 073 fax 0543 473 234. **P L***British Coins.*

Wessex Coins
PO Box 482, Southampton, SO30 9FB. Tel: 02380 972 059, email: info@wessexcoins.co.uk, www.wessexcoins.co.uk. *Ancient Greek, Roman, English Hammered Coins and Antiquities, also Shipwreck Treasure.*

Pam West (IBNS, BNTA)
PO Box 257, Sutton, Surrey, SM3 9WW. Tel: 020 8641 3224, email: pam@britishnotes.co.uk, www.britishnotes.co.uk.**P L** *English Banknotes*

West Essex Coin Investments (BNTA, IBNS)
Croft Cottage, Station Road, Alderholt, Fordingbridge, Hants SP6 3AZ. Tel: 01425 656 459. *British and World Coins and Paper Money.*

West Wales Coins
PO Box 60 Clynderwen SA67 9AS. Email: westwalescoins@gmail.com, wwwwestwalescoins. com. *Coins and Banknotes*

West Wicklow Coins
Blessington, Co Wicklow, Ireland. Tel: 00353 45 858 767, email: westwicklowcoins@hotmail.com. Irish and *World Coins.*

Trevor Wilkin
PO Box 182 Cammeray, NSW 2602, Australia. Tel: 0061 9438 5040, email trevorsnotes@bigpond.com. *World Banknotes*

Simon Willis Coins
43a St Marys Road, Market Harborough, LE16 7DS. Tel:07908 240 978, swcoins@simonwilliscoins.com, www.simonwilliscoins.com. *Quality Hammered and Early Milled British Coins.*

Worldwide Coins (IBNS)
PO Box 11, Wavertree, Liverpool L15 0FG. Tel: 0845 634 1809, email: sales@worldwidecoins.co.uk, www.worldwidecoins.co.uk. *World Coins and Paper Money.*

World Treasure Books
PO Box 5, Newport, Isle of Wight PO30 5QE. Tel: 01983 740 712. **L** *Coins, Books, Metal Detectors.*

Barry Wright
54 Dooley Drive, Bootle, Merseyside. L3O 8RT.**P L** *World Banknotes.*

I. S. Wright (Australia Numismatic Co)
64 Parramatta Road, Forest Lodge NSW, 2037, Australia. Tel:0061 3 9264 7555, email: ausnumis@ netconnect.comau. **P** *Coins, Banknotes, Medallions, Tokens.*

D. Yapp
PO Box 4718, Shrewsbury Mail Centre SY1 9EA. Tel: 01743 232 557, www.david-yapp.com.**L** *World and British Banknotes.*

York Coins
PO Box 160, Red Hook, New York 12571. Tel: 001 718 544 0120 email: antony@yorkcoins.com. *Ancient Coins.*

York Coin and Stamp Centre
Cavendish Antique & Collectors Centre, 44 Stone gate, York, YO1 8AS.
Retail Shop. Coins and Medals.

Information included in this Directory is correct at the time of going to press. An extensive range of dealers can also be found on our website at www.tokenpublishing.com

TREASURE *and the Law*

Until the introduction of the new Treasure Act, the legal position regarding articles of gold, silver or bullion, found long after they were hidden or abandoned, was not as simple and straightforward as it might be supposed. Furthermore, this was a case where the law in England and Wales differed fundamentally from that in Scotland.

Treasure Trove was one of the most ancient rights of the Crown, deriving from the age-old right of the monarch to gold, silver or bullion treasure whose owner was not known. In England and Wales, the law applied only to objects made of, or containing, gold or silver, whether in the form of coin, jewellery, plate or bullion. Moreover, the object had to be shown to have been deliberately hidden with intent to retrieve and the owner could not be readily found. The English law therefore excluded precious stones and jewels set in base metals or alloys such as bronze or pewter. It also took no account of artifacts in pottery, stone, bone, wood or glass which might be of immense antiquarian value.

In recent years, as a result of the rise in metal-detecting as a hobby, the archaeological lobby brought pressure to bear on Parliament to change the law and bring it into line with Scotland where the rules on Treasure Trove were far more rigorously interpreted. In Scotland the Crown is entitled to *all* abandoned property, even if it has not been hidden and is of little value. This applies even to objects dumped in skips on the pavement. Strictly speaking you would be committing a criminal offence if you removed an old chair from a skip without the owner's permission, although in practice such helping oneself rarely proceeds to a prosecution. In 1958 an archaeological expedition from Aberdeen University found several valuable

In October 2016, a Civil War hoard was found in Lincolnshire. The hoard, which comprised of over 1,000 silver coins, was found by Steven Ingram with his metal detector in a ploughed field near the village of Ewerby. (For the full report, see COIN NEWS, January 2017)

artifacts on St Ninian's Isle, Shetland. These included silver vessels and ornaments, as well as a porpoise bone which had incised decoration on it. The archaeologists challenged the rights of the Crown to this treasure, arguing that the Crown would have to prove that the articles had been deliberately hidden, and that a porpoise bone was in any case not valuable enough to count as treasure. The High Court, however, decided that as long as the property had been abandoned, it belonged automatically to the Crown. Its value, intrinsic or otherwise, or whether or not it was hidden, did not make any difference. Since then, as a result of this decision in case law, the criteria for Treasure Trove have been very strictly applied in Scotland. It would have only required a similar test case in England or Wales to result in a similar tightening of the rules. This has been resisted, mainly by the detectorist lobby, but inevitably the government considered legislation to control the use of metal detectors, if not to ban them altogether.

In England and Wales a find of gold or silver coins, artifacts or ornaments, or objects which contain some of these metals, which appears to have been concealed by the original owner, was deemed to be Treasure Trove. It was not even necessary for the articles to be buried in the ground; objects concealed in thatched roofs or under the floorboards of buildings have been judged to be Treasure Trove. Such finds had to be notified immediately to the police who then informed the district coroner. He then convened an inquest which decided whether all or part of the find was Treasure Trove. Establishing the gold or silver content was straightforward, but the coroner's inquest had to decide whether the material was hidden deliberately and not just lost or abandoned, and that the owner could not be located. A gold coin found on or near a country footpath might reasonably have been dropped by the original possessor through a hole in pocket or purse and in such cases it was very unlikely that it would be deemed Treasure Trove, even if the coin turned out to be very rare. In this instance the coroner would then have had to determine who was the lawful owner of the find: the actual finder, the owner of the land where it was found or even the tenant of the land. As a rule, however, it was left to the finder and landowner to decide between them who the owner of the coin should be, and in some cases the matter could only be resolved by referring to a civil court. For this reason it was vital that metal detectorists should secure permission *in writing* from landowners before going on to their land, defining rights and obligations on both sides, in order to determine the disposal or share-out of any finds or proceeds from the sale of finds, *beforehand*.

If the coroner decided that the articles were deliberately concealed, and declared them to be Treasure Trove, the find automatically reverted to the Crown. In practice the find was considered by the Treasure Trove Reviewing Committee of the Treasury. They might decide that although the articles, *invariably coins,* were gold or silver, they were so common that they were not required by the British Museum or one of the other great national collections, and would return them to the finder to dispose of at their discretion. If some or

Another Lincolnshire find is this silver coin, Esuprasu Aota Cosn, unearthed by a detectorist near Spilisby. The coin was eventually auctioned in the May Chris Rudd List 152 Auction for £900 (pre-sale estimate £750).

all of the coins were deemed vital for inclusion in a national collection the finder was recompensed with the full market value of the material. On the other hand, if someone found gold or silver which might be Treasure Trove and failed to declare it at the time, that person was liable to prosecution under the Theft Act 1968 should the find subsequently come to light. Not only could they face a heavy fine but the articles would be forfeit to the Crown, and of course no reward or recompense was then payable either.

The anomalies and inconsistencies of existing law on Treasure Trove were eliminated and the position considerably tightened up by the passage, on July 5, 1996, of the Treasure Act.

Announcing that the Treasure Act had received the Royal Assent, Lord Inglewood, National Heritage Minister, said, "This represents the first legislation on Treasure Trove to be passed in England and Wales and will replace Common Law precedents and practices dating back to the Middle Ages. The Act, which offers a clearer definition of treasure and simplified procedures for dealing with finds, will come into force after a code of practice has been drawn up and agreed by both Houses of Parliament". The Act came into force in England, Wales and Northern Ireland on September 24, 1997, replacing the Common Law of Treasure Trove.

The act was introduced as a Private Member's Bill by Sir Anthony Grant, after the failure of an earlier attempt by Lord Perth. For the first time, it would be a criminal offence to fail to report within 14 days the discovery of an item which could be declared Treasure Trove. Finders will continue to be rewarded for reporting their discoveries promptly, while landowners and occupiers will also be eligible for rewards for the first time.

The Treasure Act covers man-made objects and defines treasure as objects other than coins which are at least 300 years old and contain at least 10 per cent by weight of gold or silver; coins more than 300 years old which are found in hoards (a minimum of two coins if the precious metal content is more than 10 per cent, and a minimum of 10 coins if the precious metal content is below 10 per cent). The act also embraces all objects found in clear archaeological association with items which are treasure under the above definitions. It also covers any object which would have been Treasure Trove under the previous definitions (e.g. hoards of 19th century gold or silver coins).

An extension to The Act from January 1992 provides that groups of prehistoric bronze implements are also deemed to be Treasure.

The maximum penalty for failing to report the discovery of treasure within 14 days will be a fine of £5,000 or three months imprisonment, or both.

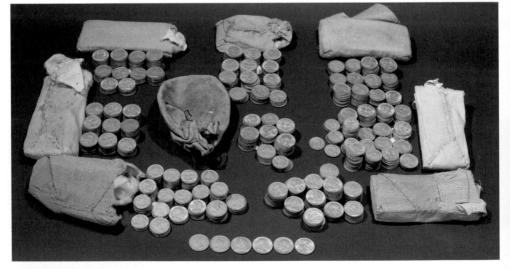

A "hoard" can turn up in the most unexpected places. In November 2016, a piano tuner discovered seven, draw-string bags of sovereigns and half sovereigns secreted in an 80 year old piano. The stash comprises of 633 sovereigns and 280 half sovereigns with the earliest dated 1847 and the latest 1915. Current market value puts the value of the find at over half a million pounds (full story published COIN NEWS, June 2017).

In Scotland the police pass the goods on to the procurator fiscal who acts as the local representative of the Queen's and Lord Treasurer's Remembrancer. If the articles are of little value, historically or intrinsically, the finder will usually be allowed to keep them. If they are retained for the appropriate national collection then a reward equal to the market value is payable.

A favourite haunt of metal-detectorists these days is the beach, and many hobbyists make quite a lucrative living by sweeping the beaches especially just after a Bank Holiday. It's surprising how much loose change gets lost from pockets and handbags over a holiday weekend. Technically the coins recovered from the beach are lost property, in which case they ought to be surrendered to the police, otherwise the finder may be guilty of theft. In practice, however, the law turns a blind eye to coins, on the sensible grounds that it would be impossible to prove ownership. On the other hand, banknotes are treated as lost property since someone could in theory at least identify a note as his by citing the serial number.

In the case of other objects, such as watches and jewellery, of course the law governing lost property is enforced, and the old adage of "finders keepers" does not apply. Any object of value, identifiable as belonging to someone, that is washed up on the foreshore or found in territorial waters is known technically as "wreck". This includes not just a wrecked ship, but any cargo that was being carried by a ship.

If wreck is not claimed by its owner, it falls to the Crown. In this case it is not necessary to prove deliberate concealment, as in the case of Treasure Trove. This law has a specific numismatic application in the case of the gold and silver coins washed up after storms around our shores, from Shetland to the Scillies. Such coins, emanating from wrecks of Spanish treasure ships and Dutch East Indiamen in particular, are well documented, and any such finds ought to be reported immediately to the police.

Stray finds of coins, as well as other objects of value, on public places, such as the street, a public park or a sports ground, are also subject to law. In this case the finder must take all reasonable steps to locate the owner. Anyone who keeps a coin without making reasonable effort to find the owner could be prosecuted for theft. As with the beach, however, such "reasonable effort" would clearly be impractical. Finding coins on private premises is another matter. In this case large bodies, such as the Post Office, British Rail, the British Airports Authority, bus companies, municipal authorities, hospitals, the owners of department stores, theatre and cinema proprietors and the like, may have bye-laws, rules and regulations for dealing with lost property found within their precincts, or in their vehicles. If you found a purse or wallet on a bus or train, or in a telephone kiosk or a shop, common sense (and your conscience) would tell you to hand it over to the driver, conductor, shopkeeper or official in charge.

As a rule, unclaimed lost property reverts eventually to the finder, but not always; British Rail and some other organisations have a rule that in such cases the property reverts to the organisation. In any event, failure to disclose the find immediately might render you liable to prosecution for stealing by finding.

ADVERTISERS *Directory*

See our website at tokenpublishing.com for up-to-date dealer entries, with hyperlinks taking you directly to their websites.